INTERNATIONAL ECONOMICS

INTERNATIONAL ECONOMICS

Miltiades Chacholiades

Professor of Economics
Georgia State University

McGRAW-HILL PUBLISHING COMPANY

New York St. Louis San Francisco Auckland Bogotá Caracas
Hamburg Lisbon London Madrid Mexico Milan Montreal New Delhi
Oklahoma City Paris San Juan São Paulo Singapore Sydney Tokyo Toronto

INTERNATIONAL ECONOMICS

2 3 4 5 6 7 8 9 0 DOC DOC 9 4 3 2 1 0

ISBN 0-07-010358-5

This book was set in Meridien by the College Composition Unit
in cooperation with Monotype Composition Company.
The editors were Scott D. Stratford, Ira C. Roberts, Michael Morales,
Eileen Gualberto, and Cynthia Phelps;
the production supervisor was Louise Karam.
The cover was designed by Lea Chacholiades.
New drawings were done by Hadel Studio.
R. R. Donnelley & Sons Company was printer and binder.

Library of Congress Cataloging-in-Publication-Data

Chacholiades, Miltiades.
International economics/Miltiades Chacholiades
p. cm—(McGraw-Hill international series in business and economics)
Rev. ed. of: Principles of international economics. © 1981.
Includes bibliographies and indexes.
ISBN 0-07-010358-5
1. International economic relations. 2. Commercial policy. 3. International trade.
I. Chacholiades, Miltiades. Principles of international economics. II. Title. III. Series.
HF1411.C412 1990
337—dc19 89-2669

To Lea and Clifford

CONTENTS

PART TWO INTERNATIONAL FINANCE

LIST OF APPLICATIONS

CASES

TABLES

FIGURES

PREFACE

During the last two decades the world economy has undergone major structural changes, such as the introduction of flexible exchange rates, the rise and fall of OPEC, and the success of newly industrialized countries in penetrating the markets of developed economies with their manufactures. At the same time, international economists have been busy developing new approaches and refining older ideas in an attempt to provide better answers to such perennial questions as the merits of free trade relative to protection and the nature of the balance-of-payments adjustment mechanism. The 1990s promise to present formidable challenges to policymakers, ranging from the need to deal with the world debt crisis to the reform of the international monetary system.

Despite the plethora of textbooks, there is still a need for a book that would incorporate all these developments and provide a sensible balance among theory, institutions, and empirical evidence, so that students will be well prepared to face the future complexities of the world economy. I hope this gap is now filled by *International Economics.*

This book provides an up-to-date and balanced approach to world economic relations; integrates theory and empirical evidence; and presents in a logical, intuitive fashion the basic principles of our discipline at a level appropriate for undergraduate students whose only background is an introductory course in economics and a desire to learn.

COMPETITIVE ADVANTAGES

Perhaps the most important feature of this book is the inclusion of empirical applications which bring the theory closer to the real world. Examples include the free-trade agreement between Canada and the United States, countertrade, the trade deficit of the United States, and the policy mix of the first Reagan Administration.

The latest developments in the theory of international trade and finance, such as monopolistic competition and international trade, the efficiency of the foreign exchange market, exchange-rate overshooting, and target zones have been incorporated. Because of the widespread interest in the new monetary approach a whole chapter has been devoted to it. This chapter also proposes a new common-sense reconciliation between the monetary and traditional approaches to the balance of payments. The LDC debt is singled out as a major problem facing the world economy today. Because of its complexity and possible repercussions to the prosperity of developed and developing countries alike, the world debt crisis is studied in a separate chapter.

The text has been designed to be as "self-teaching" as possible. Difficult material (such as the derivation of the Marshall-Lerner condition, the optimal tariff rate, and the foreign-trade multipliers) has been relegated to brief appendixes at the end of the book. All appendixes are optional and can be omitted without interrupting the continuity of the book. They are, however, carefully keyed into the main text to allow easy integration for those who choose to use them.

ORGANIZATION

The book is divided into two parts. Part One (Chapters 2–10) deals with international trade. Part Two (Chapters 11–20) focuses on international finance. Ideally the book can serve the needs of a two-semester course, with international trade covered in the first semester and international finance covered in the second semester. However, the book is quite flexible and can be used in several different ways. For instance, a course in international finance could cover Part Two only (plus perhaps Chapter 2, depending on the tastes of the instructor), without prior knowledge of Part One. Similarly, a one-semester course in international economics could cover Chapters 2–4, 7, 11, 12, 14, 15, and 17–19.

For the benefit of the reader, each chapter concludes with a brief summary, problems, and a list of suggested additional readings. Some of the more difficult problems are marked by an asterisk.

OTHER IMPORTANT FEATURES

International Economics is in a sense the second edition of the *Principles of International Economics,* which was published in 1981. However, the revision was so extensive and the introduction of new material was so overwhelming that a new title was considered appropriate. Some instance are:

- The old chapters on opportunity cost, community indifference, and international equilibrium were combined into a single chapter.
- The chapter on the Hechscher-Ohlin model now contains in one place a simplified discussion of the four main propositions: the Hechscher-Ohlin theorem, the factor-price equalization theorem, the Stolper-Samuelson theorem, and the Rybczynski theorem.

• The old chapters on money and the balance of payments, and fiscal and monetay policy for internal and external balance were fused together to form Chapter 17.

All of these changes made room for the empirical applications, new theoretical developments, and the two new chapters on the world debt crisis and on the monetary approach. In my judgment, the result is a treatment of international economics that is systematic, intuitive, up-to-date, and relevant.

An *Instructor's Manual* is available to accompany this text. Each chapter in the manual begins with a brief summary of the contents of the corresponding textbook chapter; it provides a list of key concepts and terms for review; it gives answers to almost all problems that appear at the end of each chapter; and it finally concludes with a set of additional questions.

ACKNOWLEDGMENTS

I wish to thank Saul Z. Barr, University of Tennessee; Clayton K.S. Chun, United States Air Force Academy; Richard McIntyre, University of Rhode Island; Terry Monson, Michigan Technological University; Farhad Rassekh, University of Hartford; Roy Ruffin, Houston University; Garry B. Stone, Northeastern University; and Abdul M. Turay, Mississippi State University, who reviewed the manuscript, and also my colleagues Loraine Donaldson and John Klein, who read parts of the manuscript and made helpful comments. My thanks are also due to Robert Baldwin, John P. Angelides, Steven Skeet Chang, Ben L. Kyer, Samanta Thapa, and the Canadian Consul General in Atlanta, Geoffrey Elliot. Needless to say, any remaining deficiences are all mine.

My editors, Scott Stratford, Ira Roberts, Eileen Gualberto, Michael Morales and Cynthia Phelps, have been very understanding, cooperative, and supportive at all phases of the manuscript. My research assistants, Kwoh-Cheung Chan, Eungmin Kang, Jon Mansfield, Chairin Weerastavanee, and Zheng-Yu Zhu, have also been very helpful throughout the writing of this book. Amy Gaffney worked cheerfully and competently with the word processor. Ann I. Sprague and Marilyn H. King also helped. Above all, I wish to thank my wife and daughters (Lea, Marina, and Linda) for their understanding and encouragement during the time I spent preparing this text.

Miltiades Chacholiades

INTERNATIONAL ECONOMICS

CHAPTER 1

INTRODUCTION

1-1 THE RELEVANCE OF INTERNATIONAL ECONOMICS

Until the early 1970s, the relationship between the United States and the world economy was asymmetrical. To most Americans, the U.S. economy appeared to be self-sufficient and closed. For instance, in the 1960s U.S. exports and imports were less than 5 percent of gross national product (GNP), and the U.S. economy was thought to be immune to economic events that occurred in faraway places, such as Frankfurt, Riyadh, Seoul, Taipei, and Tokyo. In contrast, foreign countries were greatly influenced by events that took place in the United States, because of the sheer size of its economy. For example, in 1986 the share of U.S. imports in total world imports was almost 19 percent. A U.S. recession spelled gloom for the rest of the world. According to a popular saying, when America sneezed, Japan and Europe used to catch cold.

But as the Greek philosopher Heraclitus noted a long time ago, nothing stays the same. America's exports and imports have grown substantially over the years. From 1970 to 1980 the share of both U.S. exports and imports in GNP doubled. This is shown in Figure 1-1. Of course, adjustment is never easy. With the opening up of the U.S. economy, many traditionally important industries (such as steel and autos) came under severe attack by foreign competition. As Toyotas flooded the U.S. market, producers in the United States faced a hard choice: to either trim their budgets or close their doors. Many workers lost their jobs, and louder and louder calls for "protection from ruinous foreign competition" were heard. As a result, the country that championed free trade in the world economy had second thoughts about the benefits of free trade and felt morally obligated to defend its honest workers from the influx of foreign products.

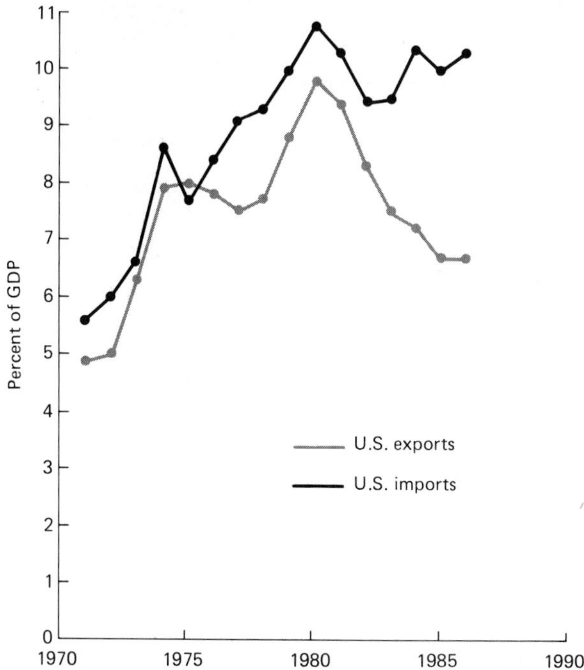

FIGURE 1-1 **U.S. exports and imports of goods and nonfactor services as percent of gross domestic product, 1971–1986.**

Is free trade a friend or a foe? Since the time of Adam Smith, economists have vigorously supported the idea of free trade. It is one of the prime objectives of this book to clarify this fundamental issue. We should bear in mind, however, that when things go sour, special-interest groups, politicians, and editorial writers arouse the patriotic feelings of the citizens, who are led to believe that buying a foreign product is a sacrilegious act. The stakes are high. There has never been a better time than now to study international economics.

Although international economics has become important to the United States only recently, other foreign countries have long been aware of the relevance of international trade to welfare, prosperity, and growth. Figure 1-2 shows the 1986 shares of exports and imports in gross domestic product (GDP) for a small sample of countries. All of these countries participate in world trade to a greater degree than the United States.

1-2 THE SCOPE OF INTERNATIONAL ECONOMICS

What is international economics about? International economics studies how a number of distinct economies interact with one another in the process of allocating scarce resources to satisfy human wants. Whereas general economic theory deals with the problems of a single closed economy, international economics focuses on the problems of two or more economies; it examines the same problems as general economic theory, but discusses them in their international setting. Clearly, international economics is more general than the economics of a closed economy, the latter being a special case of international economics in which the number of trading countries is reduced from many to one. The study of general economic theory as it deals with the problems of a closed economy is only a first (but necessary) step toward the study of the behavior of a real economy. Surely, there is no closed economy in the real world except the world economy.

Parallel to the breakdown of economic theory into microeconomics and macroeconomics is the division of international economics into two major branches: (1) **international trade** and (2) **international finance.** The former is a long-run static-equilibrium theory of barter in which the short-run monetary-adjustment process is assumed completed, with money assuming its true classical role as a veil. The approach of international trade theory is basically microeconomic in nature. International finance theory is centered upon the monetary aspects of international monetary relations. Its approach is mainly macroeconomic in nature, and it deals particularly with the short-run problems of balance-of-payments disequilibrium and adjustment.

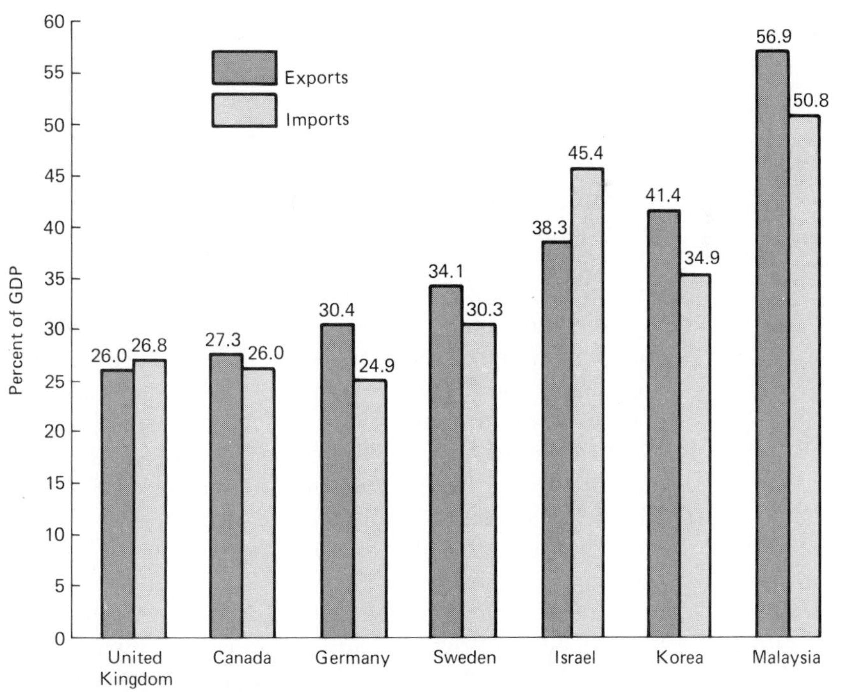

FIGURE 1-2 **Exports and imports of goods and nonfactor services as percent of gross domestic product, 1986.**

1-3 THE ROLE OF TRADE

Even in the most primitive societies, people cooperate in the use of their scarce resources. The reason is obvious: Through such cooperation more goods are produced. The high degree of specialization that exists in our society reflects the fact that specialization increases the standard of living by making more goods and services available for consumption.

The importance of trade springs from the extensive degree of specialization that exists in twentieth century societies. *Specialization necessarily implies trade and cannot occur without it.* This follows from the fact that people usually want to have a "balanced diet." Specialized producers use only a small part—maybe none—of their output for their personal consumption and exchange the surplus for the goods and services of other specialized producers. For instance, a shoemaker does not, and cannot, consume only shoes; shoemakers need, in addition, many other goods and services, such as food, clothing, shelter, entertainment, and transportation. To obtain these other goods and services, shoemakers exchange their surplus production of shoes (which, for practical purposes, may be identified with the total output of shoes) for the specialized outputs of farmers, auto producers, physicians, tailors, builders, and the like. Such an exchange of goods and services among specialized producers is exactly what is meant by trade.

The exchange of goods and services among residents of the same country is usually called **domestic trade.** This book is concerned with **international trade,** that is, the exchange of goods and services among residents of different countries. For simplicity, in this book we shall speak of countries as economic units. It is important to remember, however, that it is the individual residents who carry out the transactions.

Countries cannot live alone any more effectively than individuals can. Each country tends to specialize in the production of those commodities it can produce more cheaply than other countries, and then exchanges its surplus for the surpluses of other countries. This process brings about an international division of labor that makes it possible for all nations to consume more of all goods and services than in the absence of such specialization.

The commodities a country imports can be divided into two categories: (1) those commodities that other countries produce more cheaply than the importing country and (2) those commodities that the importing country cannot produce at all. For instance, the United States may import textiles from Taiwan because Taiwan produces textiles more cheaply than the United States, not because the United States cannot produce textiles domestically. In contrast, Japan imports oil from Saudi Arabia simply because Japan does not have any oil fields.

In the same way that the division of labor (specialization) within a single closed economy increases the standard of living of all its residents, the international division of labor (specialization among nations) increases the standard of living of all countries. And just as specialization within a single closed economy necessarily implies the existence of domestic trade and cannot occur without it, international specialization necessarily implies the existence of international trade and cannot occur without it either.

Given the preceding discussion on the mutual gains from trade, one would expect the flow of commodity trade across national frontiers to be free from government interference. Yet for hundreds of years the nations of the world have impeded the free flow of international trade by means of tariffs, quotas, technical or administrative rules and procedures, and exchange control. In general, these policies are influenced by political, sociological, and economic considerations, and they reduce world efficiency and welfare. In this book, we shall explore in detail the nature and economic effects of such barriers to free trade as well as the motives behind them.

Being aware of the existence and importance of the gains from trade, nations often move to liberalize international trade. Basically, there are two approaches to international trade liberalization: the international approach and the regional approach. The former involves international conferences under the aegis of the General Agreement on Tariffs and Trade (GATT), such as the Kennedy Round and the Tokyo Round of multilateral trade negotiations, whose purpose is to reduce tariffs and nontariff barriers to international trade. The regional approach involves agreements among small numbers of nations whose purpose is to promote free trade among themselves while maintaining barriers to trade with the rest of the world. Examples of such regional agreements are provided by the European Community and the recent Free Trade Agreement between the United States and Canada.

1-4 THE ROLE OF INTERNATIONAL MONETARY RELATIONS

Although in the long run money is a mere veil, its short-run significance is unquestionable. Indeed, economies, including the world economy, live only in the short run. The long run is an ideal that is almost never attained.

International finance deals with the foreign exchange market and the balance of payments. In particular, it studies the short-run adjustment processes and the difficulties that the world economy faces in attaining international equilibrium. In addition, international finance is concerned with the economic policies that may be necessary for the achievement of international equilibrium when the automatic processes are too slow or are not working properly.

The importance of a smoothly functioning international monetary system cannot be underestimated. The main function of the international monetary system is to enable the fundamental economic processes of production and distribution to operate as smoothly and efficiently as possible, to maximize, so to speak, the gains from trade by permitting the fullest use of efficient division of labor among the nations of the world.

Adam Smith called the international monetary system the "great wheel." When the wheel turns effortlessly, international specialization produces a maximum flow of goods and services that go to satisfy human wants in every corner of the globe. But when the wheel turns badly, the international flow of goods and services is interrupted, with serious consequences to the economic welfare of nations. As it turns out, when the short-run processes work smoothly and the wheel turns effortlessly, international monetary relations do not make the headlines. Rather, they become inconspicuous and are taken for granted. People become aware of the significance of international monetary relations during international monetary crises (that is, when the wheel turns badly).

When the short-run processes do not work smoothly, those countries suffering from serious balance-of-payments problems (particularly deficits) often attempt to solve their problems by imposing trade restrictions. Unfortunately, such restrictions on international trade reverse the beneficial division of labor among countries and deny the world the potential gains from international specialization and exchange.

1-5 THE PLAN OF THE BOOK

This book deals with both branches of international economics, namely, international trade and international finance. Its main concern is not only with the basic theoretical principles of international economics, but also with the available empirical evidence and the question of international economic policy. Numerous empirical applications throughout the book illustrate the relevance of theoretical principles to the international economic affairs of open economies. The book is divided into two parts: international trade (Part One) and international finance (Part Two).

International Trade

Chapters 2 through 6 deal with the causes and effects of trade. In particular, Chapter 2 examines the classical law of comparative advantage in the context of the simple labor theory of value and generalizes the results by introducing the concept of opportunity cost. Although simple and straightforward, this is an important chapter, and the student must study it carefully before proceeding to the rest of the book. The discussion of Chapter 2 is limited to two commodities and two countries. Appendix 1 extends the results to many commodities and many countries.

The important topic of international equilibrium is examined in Chapter 3, which in a sense generalizes the results of Chapter 2. Chapter 3 introduces three new concepts: (1) increasing opportunity costs, (2) social indifference curves, and (3) offer curves. Supporting technical material is summarized for the interested student in five appendixes: 2 (Some Special Cases of Social Indifference Curves), 3 (The Neoclassical Theory of Production: Review), 4 (Allocation of Factors between Industries and Production Possibilities), 5 (Meade's Geometric Technique), and 6 (Production, Income, and Substitution Effects).

Chapter 4 presents the Heckscher-Ohlin model, the gist of which can be summarized by two propositions: (1) The *cause* of international trade is to be found largely in differences between the factor endowments of different countries (**Heckscher-Ohlin theorem**), and (2) the *effect* of international trade is to tend to equalize factor prices between countries and thus serve to some extent as a substitute for factor mobility (**factor-price equalization theorem**).

The Heckscher-Ohlin model is important not only to international economics but to other fields as well (such as the theory of growth and the theory of distribution). The analysis of Chapter 4 is cast in rather simple terms so that students can easily understand it.

Alternative trade theories and the empirical verification of international trade models are the subject matter of Chapter 5. In particular, this chapter deals with the empirical testing of the Ricardian model of Chapter 2 and the Heckscher-Ohlin model of Chapter 4 (Leontief paradox). The rest of the chapter deals with the specific-factors model, intraindustry trade, increasing returns, monopolistic competition, Linder's thesis, and the product cycle. Appendix 7 discusses the phenomenon of factor intensity reversals.

Chapter 7 deals with the comparative statics analysis of the effects of factor endowment growth and technical progress on the growing open economy's production, consumption, terms of trade, and social welfare. Even though the subject matter of this chapter is important, it may be omitted, especially in a one-semester course.

Chapters 7 through 10 deal with commercial policy. In particular, Chapter 7 examines the effects of the most common instrument of commercial policy, the tariff on an imported good. Technical material is conveniently summarized for the interested reader in two appendixes: 8 (Metzler's Paradox) and 9 (The Theory of Effective Protection). Chapter 8 considers the optimal tariff, the theory of domestic distortions, the infant-industry argument for protection, and several other arguments for protection. Appendix 10 shows how to determine the optimal tariff rate. Appendix 11 illustrates the paradoxical phenomenon of "immiserizing" growth—growth that leaves a country worse off due to distortions.

The effects of other nontariff barriers to international trade are studied in Chapter 9. After a brief discussion of export taxes and export subsidies, this chapter examines the effects of quantitative restrictions (or quotas), international cartels, dumping, and other nontariff barriers. It also provides some highlights of U.S. tariff history and some discussion of the trade negotiations that have taken place during the postwar era under the aegis of GATT. Technical material is reserved for two appendixes: 12 (A Formula for the Cartel Markup) and 13 (The Theory of Persistent Dumping).

Finally, Chapter 10 deals exclusively with the regional approach to international trade liberalization. Specifically, this chapter examines the partial equilibrium approach to preferential trading.

International Finance

The foreign exchange market and the balance of payments are examined in Chapters 11 and 12, respectively. These concepts are indispensable for preparing to deal with the great issues of international finance. In particular, Chapter 11 examines the nature, organization, and functions of the foreign exchange market; the forward market and its relationship to the spot market; and finally the Eurodollar market. Appendix 14 provides a brief algebraic formulation of the theory of covered interest arbitrage. Chapter 12 deals with the basic principles of balance-of-payments accounting and the concept of balance-of-payments equilibrium, including some discussion of various well-known accounting balances, such as the merchandise balance, the balance on goods and services, the current account balance, and the official settlements balance.

Chapter 13 draws on concepts developed in the first part of the book (especially Chapters 2 and 3) to develop a rather simplified model that illustrates well most issues of international finance. In this sense, this chapter serves as a general introduction to the rest of the book.

Chapters 14 and 15 study two important adjustment mechanisms: the price-adjustment mechanism (Chapter 14) and the income-adjustment mechanism (Chapter 15). In particular, Chapter 15 develops the partial equilibrium model and studies the effects of exchange-rate adjustments on the balance of payments (and the terms of trade). In addition, it considers the special problems of nontraded goods and the price-specie-flow mechanism. Appendix 15 develops the Marshall-Lerner condition.

Chapter 15 examines the national income multiplier theory and the balance-of-trade multiplier theory. It also considers the problem of attaining internal and external balance simultaneously through the application of fiscal policy and exchange-rate adjustments. It concludes with a brief discussion of direct controls. Appendix 16 extends the discussion to include foreign repercussions.

Chapter 16 discusses the dimensions, causes, and consequences of the world debt crisis, which has dominated the news during the 1980s.

Chapter 17 develops the Mundellian approach to internal and external balance (that is, the appropriate use of fiscal and monetary policy), the assignment problem, and the drawbacks of the fiscal-monetary mix. Appendix 17 derives the *IS* and *LM* curves as well as the external balance schedule; it also provides two illustrations of Mundell's assignment rule.

The economics of the flexible-exchange-rate system are examined in Chapter 18. In particular, this chapter deals with the theory of employment under flexible exchange rates and the question of insulation, the difficulties of stabilization policy, the problem of whether fixed or flexible exchange rates better shield the open economy against the vagaries of economic disturbances, and some important arguments in the continuing debate over fixed and flexible exchange rates.

The monetary approach under fixed and flexible exchange rates is reviewed in Chapter 19, which also offers a reconciliation between the monetary approach and the traditional theories. The purchasing-power-parity theory is also discussed in this chapter.

The book concludes with Chapter 20, which considers the special problems that arise in connection with the international monetary system. In particular, Chapter 20 examines the characteristics of a good international monetary system; the important concepts of adjustment, liquidity, and confidence; and the actual systems that have existed over the last century or so, such as the gold standard, the interwar attempts to restore the gold standard, the Bretton Woods system, the present system of managed flexibility, and the new European Monetary System.

INTERNATIONAL TRADE

CHAPTER 2

THE LAW OF COMPARATIVE ADVANTAGE

Without doubt, development of the **law of comparative advantage,** or **comparative cost,** must be singled out as one of the greatest achievements of the classical school of economic thought. The message of this fundamental law is very simple: All countries of the world can benefit from international specialization and free trade. Equally simple is the model used to obtain this important result. In addition to being aesthetically pleasing, the closely reasoned doctrine of comparative advantage is so powerful that it quickly exposes the many fallacies that are contained in the propaganda for protection. Any interference with free trade can be shown to be harmful to the welfare of the world.

This chapter deals primarily with the often misunderstood law of comparative advantage. To appreciate the contributions of the classical economists, we begin with a brief discussion of **mercantilism**—the economic doctrine that prevailed during the seventeenth and eighteenth centuries up until the publication in 1776 of *The Wealth of Nations* by Adam Smith. Next we present the **theory of absolute advantage** formulated by Adam Smith. We then continue with the **theory of comparative advantage,** which is probably due to Robert Torrens but is generally associated with David Ricardo. Both the theory of absolute advantage and the theory of comparative advantage suffer from a severe drawback: they both depend on the labor theory of value. In the 1930s, Gottfried Haberler developed his theory of opportunity costs, which actually freed the classical theory of international trade from the restrictive assumption of the labor theory of value.

We conclude this chapter with a discussion of the theory of opportunity costs.

2-1 THE MERCANTILIST THESIS ON TRADE

The mercantilists were preoccupied with the accumulation of large quantities of monetary metals (gold and silver). Since the supply of gold was relatively fixed, the mercantilists believed that a nation (especially one which did not have any gold mines of its own) could augment its stock of gold at the expense of other nations. They argued that exports are a blessing because they lead to an inflow of precious metals. Imports, they thought, are a burden because they lead to an outflow of bullion. Hence the mercantilists advocated a national policy of **protectionism:** They encouraged exports (by means of subsidies) and discouraged imports (by means of tariffs).

What was the rationale for the pursuit of the mercantilist objective? No doubt the mercantilists, who at least in England were largely merchants themselves, were motivated by their self-interest. More gold meant more money in circulation and greater business activity, leading to larger profits.

Adam Smith proposed that the mercantilists failed to draw a distinction between **wealth** (that is, the stock of consumable and durable goods plus the stock of natural resources and human skills) and **treasure.** Indeed by identifying wealth with treasure, the mercantilists concluded that a nation could become powerful only if it accumulated large quantities of precious metals. The notion of accumulating treasures was not necessarily absurd, because large amounts of monetary metals were necessary to finance large armies and navies and their activities in war and peace. (It may be recalled that the mercantilist period was characterized by continuous friction and frequent wars between aggressive powers.)

Finally, we cannot overlook the fact that a balance-of-trade surplus (that is, an excess of exports relative to imports) stimulates national output and employment. (We return to this idea in Chapter 15.) The link between the balance of trade and national income explains why nations suffering from high unemployment seek to restrict imports in an effort to stimulate domestic production and employment. In the 1980s the "protectionist" sentiment in the U.S. Congress has become very strong in view of the large deficits in the U.S. balance of trade. The persistence of these deficits has heightened the fear of losing jobs and incomes to import competition.

2-2 THREE BASIC QUESTIONS

The trouble with mercantilism was that it failed to address the relevant issues about foreign trade. The pertinent issues were finally raised by Adam Smith and the rest of the classical economists. In particular, the **classical theory of international trade** (associated with Adam Smith, David Ricardo, Robert Torrens, and John Stuart Mill) is concerned with the following three important questions:

1 What are the **gains from trade?** In other words, do countries benefit from international trade? Where do the gains from trade come from, and how are they divided among the trading countries? To put it differently, what are the *costs of protection?* How high is the cost of complete *self-sufficiency?*

2 What is the **structure** (or **direction** or **pattern**) **of trade?** In other words, which goods are exported, and which are imported, by each trading country? What are the fundamental laws that govern the international allocation of resources and the flow of trade?

3 What are the **terms of trade?** In other words, at what prices are the exported and imported goods exchanged?

The above questions are basic to the theory of international trade and form the foundation for most of the discussion of Part One of this book.

2-3 ABSOLUTE ADVANTAGE

Adam Smith (1937) emphasized the importance of free trade in increasing the wealth of all trading nations. According to Adam Smith mutually beneficial trade is based on the principle of **absolute advantage.** He declared that "it is the maxim of every prudent master of a family, never to attempt to make at home what it will cost him more to make than to buy." He later stated (pp. 424–426):

> What is prudence in the conduct of every private family, can scarce be folly in that of a great kingdom. If a foreign country can supply us with a commodity cheaper than we ourselves make it, better buy it of them with some part of the produce of our own industry, employed in a way in which we have some advantage.... By means of glasses, hotbeds, and hotwalls, very good grapes can be raised in Scotland, and very good wine too can be made of them at about thirty times the expense for which at least equally good can be bought from foreign countries. Would it be a reasonable law to prohibit the importation of all foreign wines, merely to encourage the making of claret and burgundy in Scotland?...As long as the one country has those advantages, and the other wants them, it will always be more advantageous for the latter, rather to buy of the former than to make.

Absolute Advantage and the Gains from Trade

What Adam Smith asserted is this. A country may be more efficient in the production of some commodities and less efficient in the production of other commodities relative to another nation. Irrespective of the cause of the difference in efficiency, both countries can benefit if each specializes in the production of what it can do more efficiently than the other country. For instance, the United States is more efficient than Brazil in the production of computers, whereas Brazil is more efficient than the United States in the production of coffee. The United States should specialize in computers and Brazil in coffee. Then the United States can export to Brazil its surplus production of computers in exchange for Brazil's surplus production of coffee. This pattern of **international specialization and exchange** (or **international division of labor**) is efficient and leads to increased output of both computers and coffee. Herein lies the essence of the gains from trade: *With increased outputs of both commodities both countries can enjoy higher standards of living.*

Whereas the mercantilists believed that one nation could benefit only at the expense of another nation and advocated a national policy of protectionism, Adam Smith argued correctly that *all* countries would benefit from free trade and championed a policy of **laissez-faire** (that is, absence of governmental interference in economic affairs). With free trade, the resources of the world would be allocated efficiently, generating gains for each and every trading nation. Any interference with the free flow of trade would impede the efficient allocation of resources worldwide and would deny to the world community the opportunity to enjoy the potential gains from trade.

The Labor Theory of Value

The classical theory of international trade is based on the **labor theory of value,** which asserts that labor is the only factor of production and that in a **closed economy** (that is, an economy that exports and imports nothing) goods exchange for one another according to the relative amounts of labor they embody. Adam Smith (1937, p. 47) explains this proposition by means of the following well-known example of hunting:

> If among a nation of hunters, for example, it usually costs twice the labor to kill a beaver which it does to kill a deer, one beaver should naturally exchange for or be worth two deer.

The labor theory of value is an oversimplification of reality for several reasons. First, labor is not homogeneous. For example, the services provided by an auto mechanic and the services offered by a physician are not the same. Second, labor is not the sole factor of production. Usually goods are produced by various combinations of labor skills, capital goods, and natural resources. Finally, the cost of a commodity depends not only on the amount of labor used in its production, but also on the length of time during which that labor is embodied (or invested) in production, as in the aging of wine.

Despite the obvious shortcomings of the labor theory of value, we adopt it as our point of departure for two reasons. First, it enables us, with relatively little effort, to bring out quite sharply the nature of the problem of international specialization and the gains from trade. Second, even after we dispense with the simplified world of the labor theory of value, the results obtained from it continue to be valid.

Illustration of Absolute Advantage

Adam Smith's principle of **absolute advantage** can be easily clarified by means of a simple illustration. Consider two countries, America and Britain, endowed with homogeneous labor and producing two commodities, food and clothing. Suppose that one day of labor can produce either 2 units of food or 4 units of clothing in America, and either 1 unit of food or 6 units of clothing in Britain. All this information is summarized in Table 2-1.

Evidently, America is more efficient than Britain in the production of food, because with the same amount of labor America produces more food than Britain ($2 > 1$). Similarly, Britain is more efficient than America in the production of clothing ($6 > 4$). We express this state of affairs by saying that *America*

TABLE 2-1 ABSOLUTE ADVANTAGE
(Output per Unit of Labor)

	America	Britain
Food	2	1
Clothing	4	6

has an absolute advantage in the production of food, and Britain has an absolute advantage in the production of clothing. In the absence of international trade, 1 unit of food will exchange for 2 units of clothing in America and for 6 units of clothing in Britain.

Is free trade between America and Britain mutually beneficial? Adam Smith would answer yes. We can illustrate Adam Smith's proposition as follows: Let America export to Britain 2 units of food ($2F$) in exchange for 6 units of British clothing ($6C$). America gains $2C$ (or saves the amount of labor needed to produce $2C$, that is, one-half day of labor), because domestically America can exchange $2F$ for only $4C$. Similarly, Britain gains $1F$ (or saves 1 day of labor), because domestically in Britain $6C$ can exchange for only $1F$.

Are there any economic forces that can be counted on to induce America to specialize in food, and Britain in clothing? This is an important question and we shall return to it in Section 2-6. For the moment, we simply want to note that before trade takes place, food is cheap in America (where $1F = 2C$) and expensive in Britain (where $1F = 6C$). By the same token, clothing is expensive in America (where $1C = \frac{1}{2}F$) and cheap in Britain (where $1C = \frac{1}{6}F$). Now the golden rule for profitable business is to buy cheap and sell dear. Thus business people would have a strong incentive to buy food in America where it is cheap and sell it in Britain where it is expensive. Similarly, a strong incentive exists to purchase clothing in Britain where it is cheap and sell it in America where it is expensive.

The alert reader will think of the analogy between international trade and technical progress. In the same way that technical progress makes possible the production of commodities using fewer resources, international trade enables countries to obtain commodities at lower prices. The indirect acquisition of commodities through international trade is tantamount to the discovery of more efficient production techniques. For instance, assuming that the terms of trade are $1F{:}3C$, as before, we could say that trade acts like a new technique, whereby 1 unit of food can be transformed into 3 units of clothing and vice versa.

Absolute Advantage Is Not Needed for Profitable Trade

What is the fundamental reason for the existence of the gains from trade? "Absolute advantage," Adam Smith would respond. Even today many people fall into the trap of believing that exporters must have an absolute advantage over their foreign rivals. This explains, for instance, why many people have felt recently that perhaps one day Japan will be able to undersell the United States in every line of production, such as automobiles, television sets, tractors, steel, and everything else under the sun. Such a view is totally absurd, of course.

Common sense dictates that every country must be able to produce something. Otherwise, how will a nonproductive nation pay for its imports? The truth of the matter is that absolute advantage can explain only a small portion of world trade. As it turns out, *mutually beneficial trade does not necessarily require exporters to have an absolute advantage over their foreign rivals.* At the beginning of the nineteenth century (just four decades after Adam Smith), David Ricardo (and Robert Torrens) demonstrated that mutually beneficial trade is possible when only comparative advantage exists—a far weaker condition than absolute advantage. Indeed, absolute advantage is only a special case of the general principle of comparative advantage.

2-4 COMPARATIVE ADVANTAGE

David Ricardo considered as typical the case in which one country is more efficient than another in every line of production. For instance, this may be the case of trade between an advanced country (such as the United States) and a developing nation (such as India). Even under these circumstances, Ricardo (as well as Robert Torrens) showed that free trade can still benefit both countries. Obviously, Adam Smith's principle of absolute advantage can no longer offer any guidance for international specialization. Ricardo had to develop a new concept: the principle of **comparative advantage.** This important law, which has remained unchallenged for almost two centuries, finds many practical applications outside the domain of international economics. This section clarifies the Ricardian contribution.

Illustration of Comparative Advantage

To gain further insight into Ricardo's world of comparative advantage, return to Table 2-1 and assume that America experiences a rapid pace of technical progress that doubles the productivity of American labor. Specifically, assume that now 1 unit (or day) of American labor can produce either 4 units of food or 8 units of clothing, as shown in Table 2-2. Note again that in the absence of

TABLE 2-2 COMPARATIVE ADVANTAGE
(Output per Unit of Labor)

	America	Britain
Food	4	1
Clothing	8	6

international trade, $1F$ will exchange for $2C$ in America, as was the case in Table 2-1. In Britain $1F$ will continue to exchange for $6C$, of course, because the productivity of British labor remains the same by assumption.

In the new illustration of Table 2-2, America has an absolute advantage in the production of both commodities. Surely if America and Britain were two regions of the same country, all workers would migrate to the more efficient region, America. Eventually all commodities would end up being produced in America, where costs are lower in an absolute sense. Nevertheless, Ricardo emphasized that the main distinguishing feature of international trade is the international immobility of labor coupled with its perfect mobility within countries. What happens in the presence of labor immobility between America and Britain? Is international trade still mutually beneficial?

Fallacious Arguments against Free Trade

It is interesting at this point to note some of the arguments against free trade that could be advanced in both America and Britain.

On the one hand, in Britain some politicians and editorial writers might argue that America's efficiency is so great that its producers would undersell British producers in every line of production. How could the British producers, who are technologically inferior to their American counterparts, compete? To protect Britain's "honest" workers from ruinous foreign competition, import tariffs are needed. It is often suggested that a "scientific" tariff that "equalizes costs of production" be imposed. (The notion of the "scientific" tariff was actually embodied in the Tariff Act of 1922 and was retained in the Smoot-Hawley Act of 1930.)

On the other hand, American politicians and editorial writers might argue that because the British wage rate is so much lower than the American wage rate, the American real wage rate will be drastically reduced if American workers are subjected to the competition of British cheap labor. Accordingly, tariffs are needed to protect the American standard of living from the cheap foreign labor.

The greatest contribution of Ricardo and Torrens was to show that both of the preceding arguments are wrong. They are pseudo arguments that do not stand up to scientific scrutiny. Indeed, Ricardo and Torrens showed that the workers of both America and Britain can benefit from free international trade.

Definition of Comparative Advantage

An advanced country may be more efficient than a developing nation in every line of production, but the former's degree of superiority may be different from one commodity to another. According to Ricardo, the advanced country is said to have a **comparative advantage** in the commodity in which that nation's degree of superiority is higher, and a **comparative disadvantage** in the commodity in which its degree of superiority is lower, relative to the developing country. For instance, in the example of Table 2-2, America's degree of superiority in food (given by the ratio $4F \div 1F$) is greater than its degree of superiority in clothing (given by the ratio $8C \div 6C$). Accordingly, America has a comparative advantage in the production of food and a comparative disadvantage in the production of clothing (because $4F \div 1F > 8C \div 6C$). Note how America's absolute advantage in clothing is converted into a comparative *dis*advantage.

Similarly, the developing nation is said to have a comparative advantage in the commodity in which its degree of inferiority is lower, and a comparative disadvantage in the commodity in which its inferiority is higher, relative to the advanced country. For instance, in the example of Table 2-2 Britain has a comparative advantage in clothing and a comparative disadvantage in food (because $6C \div 8C > 1F \div 4F$). Note again how Britain's absolute *dis*advantage in clothing is converted into a comparative advantage.

Comparative advantage, as opposed to absolute advantage, is a relative term. In a two-country, two-commodity model, after we determine that one country has a comparative advantage in one commodity, then automatically we can conclude that the other country has a comparative advantage in the other commodity. That this should be so follows from the fact that essentially the same inequality is used to determine each country's comparative advantage. Thus the inequality $4F \div 1F > 8C \div 6C$ is equivalent to the inequality $6C \div 8C > 1F \div 4F$.

The Law of Comparative Advantage

Can free trade be mutually beneficial even when one country has an absolute advantage in the production of every commodity? Ricardo and Torrens would shout yes. This great classical achievement is summarized by the law of comparative advantage.

Law of Comparative Advantage: **When each country specializes in the production of that commodity in which the nation has a comparative advantage, the total world output of every commodity necessarily increases (potentially) with the result that all countries become better off (save the limiting case of a "large" country).**

How can we prove the law of comparative advantage? Return to Table 2-2 and let America export to Britain 4 units of food ($4F$) in exchange for 12 units of British clothing ($12C$). Evidently America gains $4C$ (or saves one-half day of labor) because domestically America can exchange $4F$ for only $8C$. Is America's gain Britain's loss? No, it is not. Britain actually gains $2F$ (or saves 2 days of labor) because domestically in Britain $12C$ exchange for only $2F$.

Are there any economic forces to induce America to specialize in food, and Britain in clothing? As in the example of absolute advantage, note again that before trade takes place, food is cheaper in America (where $1F = 2C$) than in Britain (where $1F = 6C$); and by the same token, clothing is cheaper in Britain than in America. (Indeed, as we demonstrate later, in Section 2-7, the difference in the autarkic relative commodity prices of America and Britain is the only crucial consideration in the existence of gains from trade.) Consequently, businesspeople would have a strong incentive to buy food in America (where it is cheap) and sell the food in Britain (where it is expensive). Businesspeople would also have a strong incentive to buy cloth in Britain and sell it in America.

Some socialist economists (most notably Argyri Emmanuel) focus on the **unequal exchange** of American labor for British labor and argue that America (the advanced country) exploits Britain (the developing nation). For instance, in the earlier example, America uses only 1 unit of labor to produce $4F$, whereas Britain employs 2 units of labor to produce $12C$. (Incidentally, economists use the term **double factoral terms of trade**—a monstrous piece of jargon—to refer to the exchange ratio of America's labor for British labor.) Thus, America, they claim, exploits Britain because 1 unit of American labor exchanges for 2 units of British labor. The exchange is unequal and unfair! Our analysis shows clearly that such a conclusion is absurd. We have shown already that both countries do benefit from this exchange. The important consideration is that free trade enables Britain to obtain $4F$ not at a total cost of 4 units of labor (which would be the case if Britain produced $4F$ at home), but at a total cost of only 2 units of labor (which is the quantity of British labor necessary for the production of $12C$ exported to America). Surely, the quantity of American labor embodied in $4F$ (exported to Britain) is irrelevant to the issue of the British gains from trade.

Large Country versus Small Country

It is often thought that a large country, because of its sheer size and economic power, can reap all the gains from trade by taking advantage of a small and powerless nation. This irrational feeling is incorrect. In the arena of world trade the rules of the game are not the same as those that prevail in a wrestling arena, where a big guy can push around a weak wrestler. Indeed, in international trade the opposite is true. When two trading countries are of unequal size, all the gains from trade may accrue to the *small* nation, with the large country gaining nothing. This is the importance of being unimportant!

For instance, suppose that the world consists of the United States and the island of Cyprus only. Assume also that Cyprus has a comparative advantage in wine. Because of the tremendous difference in size, it would be impossible for Cyprus to satisfy the huge U.S. market for wine. Accordingly, the United States also would have to produce some wine, and world prices would have to reflect U.S. costs. That is, the *terms of trade will coincide with America's autarkic relative prices.* But without any difference between the equilibrium terms of trade and America's autarkic relative prices, America can gain nothing. (In terms of the example of Table 2-2, it is as if America is "forced" to exchange $4F$ for $8C$.) Under these circumstances, all the gains from trade will accrue to Cyprus (the small country). The large country, America, will merely reshuffle its resources in order to make it possible for the small country, Cyprus, to specialize in the production of wine and reap all the benefits. Such is the work of the "invisible hand" of Adam Smith.

"Equal" Advantage

Free trade is mutually beneficial if and only if a comparative advantage exists. If not, then there is no basis for trade. For instance, if America's degree of superiority relative to Britain is the same in food as it is in clothing, then there is no basis for mutually beneficial trade. Return to Table 2-2 and assume that in Britain 1 unit of labor can produce either $1F$ or $2C$ (instead of $6C$). In this case, there is no basis for mutually profitable trade because America's relative superiority is the same in food as it is in clothing ($4F \div 1F = 8C \div 2C$). This is the special case of **equal advantage** in which neither country has a comparative advantage in any commodity.

General Validity of the Law of Comparative Advantage

The law of comparative advantage has general validity. For instance, it applies to the division of labor between individual persons. Examples are not difficult to find. A physician, though a great bookkeeper himself, employs somebody else to do his bookkeeping because his comparative advantage lies in medicine. The same is true of a business manager who employs a secretary to do his typing, a lawyer who hires a gardener, and a teacher who has an assistant to grade the students' papers.

2-5 THE CASE OF GREEK BANANAS

As Adam Smith did before him, Ricardo ridiculed the foolishness of the English in using hothouses and other extraordinary means to produce costly grapes to brew their own wine at home. One might think that following Ricardo's demonstration such foolishness would be completely eradicated. How sad, then, it is to learn that the Ricardian lesson is not fully absorbed even today.

A good case in point is the peculiar one of Greek bananas, as Berry Newman, a staff reporter with *The Wall Street Journal,* explained humorously in a recent article. In 1971 the Greek dictatorship outlawed the trade in foreign bananas. Colonel Stelios Pattakos gave the order. Apparently, Pattakos was friendly with some farmers in Crete, where he was born. His order to halt banana imports was intended to provide support to these Cretans. When the dictatorship collapsed, in 1974, Colonel Pattakos was sentenced to life imprisonment "for non-banana-related offenses." Democracy returned but bananas did not. Bureaucrats, Newman notes, determined that a banana avalanche would hurt the apple business. Evidently, Newman argues, they were afraid that "everybody would suddenly stop eating apples and start eating bananas." As a result, consumers cannot buy the bananas they yearn for at reasonable prices, even though smuggling cannot be stopped. The few Greek banana farmers are making big money; and, Newman continues, there is even an attempt to grow bananas in Greek greenhouses! "So Pattakos got life, and the Greek people got life without bananas."

Note: All quotations are extracted from Newman (1985).

2-6 COMPARATIVE COSTS EXPRESSED IN MONEY

In all but the most primitive cultures, people do not directly exchange one commodity for another. Rather, they sell one commodity for money, and then use money to purchase the commodities they wish. In their calculations, people use money prices, not the exchange relations (or terms of trade) between commodities. The flow of world trade is determined directly not by comparative differences in labor cost, but by absolute differences in money prices. It is therefore important to explain how comparative labor-cost differences are transformed into money-price differences.

Return again to the example of Table 2-2. We saw earlier that Britain has a comparative advantage in clothing. But how is it possible for Britain, the less efficient country, to export anything at all to America, the more efficient country? How is it possible for the money cost of clothing to be lower in Britain than in America? That becomes possible when British wages are sufficiently lower than American wages! Let us see how this works.

Suppose that America's money-wage rate is \$48 per day. Given the data summarized in Table 2-2, the average cost of production per unit of food in America is \$12, because one day of American labor produces 4 units of food (that is, \$48 ÷ 4 = \$12); and the average cost of production per unit of clothing in America is \$6 (that is, \$48 ÷ 8 = \$6). Similarly, assume that Britain's money-wage rate is £12 per day (where the symbol £ stands for pounds, the British currency). Again the average cost of production in Britain is £12 per unit of food (that is, £12 ÷ 1 = £12), and £2 per unit of clothing (that is, £12 ÷ 6 = £2). These costs are shown in columns (1) and (3) of Table 2-3.

Is food cheaper in America or Britain? Is clothing cheaper in America or Britain? We do not know yet. To answer these questions, we must express all prices in terms of the same currency. To do so, we must have an exchange rate between the two currencies. How many dollars exchange for 1 pound? At the moment, we cannot determine precisely what this **rate of exchange** is, although, as we shall see, we can specify certain limits for it. To illustrate how the rate of exchange presently works, assume for the moment that £1 = \$2, that is, 1 pound is equivalent to 2 dollars.

Column (2) of Table 2-3 gives the American cost of food and clothing in pounds on the assumption that £1 = \$2. Similarly, column (4) of Table 2-3 gives the British cost of food and clothing in dollars, again on the assumption

TABLE 2-3 MONEY PRICES OF FOOD AND CLOTHING
(Assumption: £1 = \$2)

	America		Britain	
	Dollars (1)	**Pounds (2)**	**Pounds (3)**	**Dollars (4)**
Food	12	6	12	24
Clothing	6	3	2	4

that £1 = $2. Whether we compare prices in dollars or pounds, it is evident from Table 2-3 that food is cheaper in America ($12 < $24, or £6 < £12) but clothing is cheaper in Britain (£2 < £3, or $4 < $6). Therefore, America will stop the production of clothing and specialize in the production of food and Britain will stop the production of food and specialize in the production of clothing. In addition, both in dollars and pounds, the price of food in the international market is three times as high as the price of clothing (that is, $12 = 3 × $4 and £6 = 3 × £2). This means that 1 unit of food exchanges for 3 units of clothing, which is consistent with the assumption we made for our discussion of the gains from trade. Accordingly, our earlier conclusions concerning the gains from trade are now confirmed.

Given that the money-wage rates in America and Britain are $48 and £12, respectively, the preceding pattern of specialization will come about as long as £1 exchanges for something between $1 and $3. The reader is urged to try various rates of exchange between $1 and $3 and to show that for all those rates Britain's cost of clothing is lower than America's.

When £1 exchanges for more than $3, both commodities are cheaper in America. For instance, at £1 = $4, Britain's costs of food and clothing are, respectively, $48 and $8, which are higher than America's corresponding costs of $12 and $6. Similarly, when £1 exchanges for less than $1, both commodities are cheaper in Britain. For instance, at £1 = $0.50, the British costs of food and clothing become, respectively, $6 and $1, which are now lower than America's corresponding costs. Thus, unless £1 exchanges for something between $1 and $3, one country will undersell the other in every line of production. How, then, can we be absolutely sure that international specialization will actually proceed according to the law of comparative advantage?

While it is possible for the rate of exchange to lie outside the admissible range of between $1 and $3, such a state of affairs cannot last for long. It is a short-run disequilibrium situation that will be corrected in one of two ways, depending on the institutional arrangement of the **foreign exchange market.** Thus, either the forces of supply and demand in the foreign exchange market will cause the rate of exchange to change until it is made to lie between $1 and $3, or the money-wage rates of America and Britain will be forced to change in such a way as to shift the admissible range of the rate of exchange to accommodate the current rate. There is no need to pursue the short-run adjustment mechanism any further at this moment. We return to it in Part Two of the book. (See especially the discussion in Chapter 13.) The purpose of our present discussion is merely to show that our earlier conclusions based on barter economies are not inconsistent with the functioning of economies using money.

There is one fundamental difference between absolute advantage and comparative advantage. In the presence of absolute advantage, there can be no presumption as to which country's wage rate may be higher than the other's. This is not the case with comparative advantage, because we can show that *the more efficient country (America) must have a higher wage rate than the less efficient country (Britain).* This is indeed verified in our example. Thus, while the American wage rate is \$48, the upper limit for the British wage rate is only \$36 (that is, 12×3, where £12 is the British wage rate and £1 = \$3 the most favorable rate of exchange from Britain's point of view). This is an important conclusion: *Wages are high where labor productivity is high.*

It must be clear by now why the argument that America cannot compete with Britain because of the cheap British labor is fallacious. The higher American wage rate stands on the firm foundation of higher American labor productivity, and the lower British wage rate is no threat to the American standard of living.

The other argument, that Britain must protect its "honest" workers from American competition because America is so technologically advanced that it will undersell Britain in every line of production, is equally fallacious. We have seen that *every country has, by definition, a comparative advantage.* Erecting tariff walls, whether "scientific" or otherwise, and interfering with the free flow of international trade, prevents the world from maximizing the fruits of the international division of labor. In particular, a "scientific" tariff to "equalize costs of production" tends to eliminate all trade among nations and with it all those gains that could be achieved.

2-7 OPPORTUNITY COST

So far, it has been demonstrated that international trade does not require offsetting absolute advantages but is possible, and indeed profitable, to both trading countries whenever a comparative advantage exists. However, our conclusion seems to depend on the restrictive assumption of the labor theory of value. As noted earlier, the labor theory of value is not valid and must eventually be replaced by a more general theory of production. What happens to the law of comparative advantage after the labor theory of value is discarded? Should this classical law be discarded also? Fortunately, this is not the case. In the 1930s Gottfried Haberler came to the rescue of the law of comparative advantage with his **theory of opportunity costs.** As Haberler (1936, p. 126) put it, we can dispense with the labor theory of value "without having to discard the results obtained from it: these will remain, just as a building remains after the scaffolding, having served its purpose, is removed."

An Overview of the Theory of Opportunity Costs

What is the opportunity cost of a commodity (such as food)? It is the amount of some other commodity (such as clothing) that must be sacrificed in order to release just enough resources to produce one extra unit of food. Cost is *forsaken opportunity*—not the amount of some input (such as labor). For instance, if America must give up 2 units of clothing ($2C$) to free sufficient labor (or resources in general) to produce one additional unit of food, then the opportunity cost of food is $2C$. Return to Tables 2-1 and 2-2 and confirm that in both cases the opportunity cost of food is $2C$ in America and $6C$ in Britain.

Haberler showed that comparative advantage can be recast in terms of opportunity cost: *The low-cost producer of a commodity has a comparative advantage in that commodity.* But never forget that the significant concept of cost that must be used in the present context is opportunity cost—*not* labor cost. For instance, America (the low-cost producer of food) has a comparative advantage in food (because $2C < 6C$).

The crucial point to remember is that once comparative advantage is defined in terms of opportunity cost, which reflects forgone production of other commodities, *it makes no difference whether commodities are actually produced by labor alone or by any number of factors of production*. This accounts for the superiority of the theory of opportunity costs, which, like the deus ex machina, saves the classical conclusions. As Haberler repeatedly emphasized, the sole purpose of the labor theory of value is to determine the opportunity cost of one commodity in terms of another in each of two countries.

Note that the opportunity cost of clothing in terms of food is the reciprocal of the opportunity cost of food in terms of clothing. For instance, in the examples of Tables 2-1 and 2-2 the opportunity cost of clothing is $\frac{1}{2}F$ in America and $\frac{1}{6}F$ in Britain. Thus, Britain (the low-cost producer of clothing) has a comparative advantage in clothing.

It is also true that, in general, the autarkic relative prices in America and Britain are equal to their respective opportunity costs. For instance, in America the opportunity cost of food is 2 units of clothing and from Table 2-3 it is apparent that the price of food relative to the price of clothing is also 2: $\$12 \div \$6 = 2$. Although, later in the book, we shall consider cases in which opportunity costs differ from relative market prices, we shall treat all those cases as exceptional and assume from now on that opportunity costs are in general equal to relative prices. Any anomalous cases will be noted separately. With this convention, we can define comparative advantage in terms of autarkic relative prices. For instance, in our earlier example, America has a comparative advantage in the production of food because before trade, food is relatively cheaper in America than in Britain.

Production-Possibilities Frontiers

We now introduce the concept of the **production-possibilities frontier** (or **transformation curve**) in an effort to restate the preceding analysis graphically. This step is essential for two reasons. First, it will help us sharpen our understanding of the earlier analysis. Second, it will prepare the ground for the neoclassical and modern theories.

Drawn in commodity space, a country's production-possibilities frontier exhibits the menu of maximal combinations of commodities that the economy can produce given (1) its resources (or factor endowment) and (2) its technical know-how (or technology).

Return to the information in Table 2-2 and assume that America is endowed with 125 units of labor, while Britain is endowed with 200 units of labor. By arbitrarily allocating labor between food and clothing, we can discover all alternative combinations of food and clothing that can be produced in each of the two countries, as shown in Table 2-4.

Consider initially the first four columns of Table 2-4. The entries in columns (1) and (3) show, respectively, the amounts of American labor allocated to food and clothing. Since America is endowed with 125 units of labor, in each of these allocations, that is, G, H, I, J, K, and M—the letter *L* is not used in this sequence in order to avoid confusion with the factor "labor"—the sum of labor allocated to food and labor allocated to clothing must always equal 125. Thus, when 100 units of labor are allocated to food, 25 units of labor are allocated to clothing; when 75 units of labor are allocated to food, 50 units of labor are allocated to clothing; and so on. Given the allocations of labor in columns (1) and (3), we easily compute the resultant amount of output from our knowledge that in America 1 unit of labor can produce either 4 units of food or 8 units of clothing (recall Table 2-2). For instance, when 100*L* are allocated to food and 25*L* to clothing, America produces 400 units of food (that is, 100×4) and 200 units of clothing (that is, 25×8). In the same way, we determined all entries in columns (2) and (4).

The entries in columns (5)–(8), giving Britain's production possibilities, were similarly derived. Keep in mind that Britain is endowed with 200 units of labor and that 1 unit of British labor can produce either 1 unit of food or 6 units of clothing. To illustrate: When 160 units of labor are allocated to food, and thus 40 units of labor are allocated to clothing, 160 units of food (that is, 160×1) and 240 units of clothing (that is, 40×6), are produced.

The production information contained in columns (2), (4), (6), and (8) is used to draw the graphs in Figure 2-1. The left panel shows America's production-possibilities frontier and the right panel, Britain's. The letters *M* through *G* and *M** through *G** have been placed on the left and right panel, respectively, to facilitate the association between points on the frontiers and the entries in Table 2-4. Note that both production-possibilities frontiers are linear. This is an important feature of the classical model and is primarily due to two assumptions: (1) There is only one factor (labor) and (2) labor productivity remains constant irrespective of the scale of operations in either industry.

TABLE 2-4 ALTERNATIVE COMBINATIONS OF FOOD AND CLOTHING

	America					Britain			
	Food		Clothing			Food		Clothing	
	Labor (1)	Output (2)	Labor (3)	Output (4)		Labor (5)	Output (6)	Labor (7)	Output (8)
G	125	500	0	0	G*	200	200	0	0
H	100	400	25	200	H*	160	160	40	240
I	75	300	50	400	I*	120	120	80	480
J	50	200	75	600	J*	80	80	120	720
K	25	100	100	800	K*	40	40	160	960
M	0	0	125	1,000	M*	0	0	200	1,200

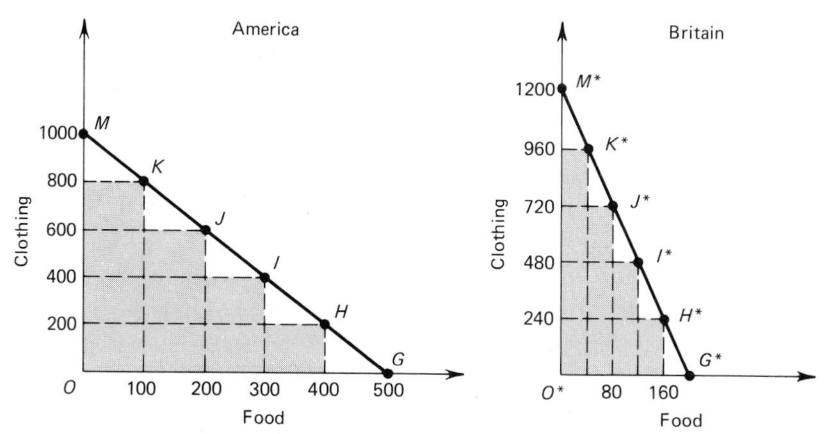

FIGURE 2-1 **Production-possibilities frontiers of America and Britain.** The points on America's production frontier correspond to the entries in columns (2) and (4) of Table 2-4. Similarly, the points on Britain's production frontier correspond to the entries in columns (6) and (8) of Table 2-4. (Note that both panels are drawn to the same scale.)

The absolute slope of America's production-possibilities frontier (that is, $1000 \div 500 = 2$) gives America's opportunity cost of food in terms of clothing. Similarly, the absolute slope of Britain's production-possibilities frontier (that is, $1200 \div 200 = 6$) gives Britain's opportunity cost of food in terms of clothing. Britain's frontier, which is drawn on the same scale as America's, is much steeper than America's. This confirms graphically our earlier conclusion that America has a comparative advantage in food and Britain one in clothing.

The Gains from Trade Again

The concept of the production-possibilities frontier is a constant reminder of the **law of scarcity,** that is, the empirical observation that no country has ever been able to *produce* as much as it desired of all commodities. A country just can never produce outside its production-possibilities frontier. Yet international specialization and free trade can enable countries to *consume* beyond their production-possibilities frontiers.

This is shown in Figure 2-2, which utilizes the production-possibilities frontiers of Figure 2-1. Figure 2-2 is based on the assumption that America specializes completely in the production of food and Britain, in clothing. The total world production is 500 units of food and 1,200 units of clothing, as shown by the sides of rectangle *GORO**. Rectangle *GORO** is obtained by rotating Britain's production-possibilities frontier by 180° and placing point *M** on point *G*.

Before trade, America can consume only what it can produce. The same goes for Britain. Therefore, before international specialization and trade, both America and Britain consume along their respective production-possibilities frontiers. Measuring American consumption of food and clothing with respect to origin *O*, we see that America can consume only combinations that lie along line *GM*. Similarly, measuring British consumption of food and clothing with respect to origin *O**, Britain can consume, before trade, only combinations along line *GG**.

Evidently *international specialization according to comparative advantage enhances the consumption possibilities of the two countries by the shaded area GMRG**. This shaded area is indeed the source of the gains from trade. When the divergence between the slopes of the two production-possibilities frontiers is large, the shaded area and the gains from trade become large also. In the limiting case of "equal" advantage, in which the two frontiers have equal slope, the shaded area shrinks to zero and the gains from trade disappear. This confirms our earlier conclusion that in the "equal"-advantage case there is no basis for trade.

How are the gains from trade distributed between America and Britain? That depends on the equilibrium terms of trade. We shall study this problem in Chapter 3. For the moment note that when the terms of trade lie between the autarkic price ratios of the two countries, both countries benefit. For instance, assume that one unit of food exchanges for three units of clothing. This is shown in Figure 2-2 by terms-of-trade line *GN*. The slope of *GN* gives the assumed terms of trade. America could, for instance, export to Britain 200 units of food in exchange for 600 units of clothing. This exchange would enable both countries to consume at point *E*, which lies beyond both production-possibilities frontiers, as do all points in the shaded area *GMRG**.

Terms-of-trade line *GN* can be viewed as a blade cutting the gains-from-trade area into two parts: *GMRN* and *GNG**. Portion *GMRN* goes to America, while portion *GNG** goes to Britain. Obviously, the closer the terms-of-trade line lies to a country's production-possibilities frontier, the smaller becomes that

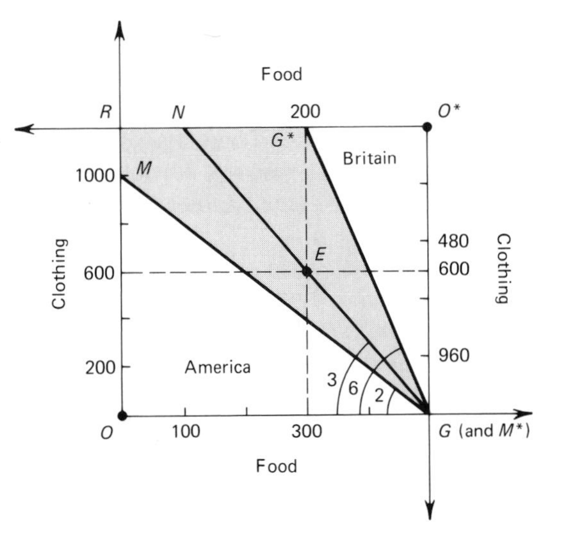

FIGURE 2-2 **The gains from trade.** America specializes in food, and Britain in clothing. The sides of rectangle *GORO** show the total world production of food and clothing. Rectangle *GORO** is obtained by rotating Britain's production-possibilities frontier by 180° and placing point *M** on point *G*. The shaded area, *GMRG,** shows the gains from trade. Like a blade, the terms-of-trade line, *GN*, divides the gains from trade into two parts: *GMRN* (America's share) and *GNG** (Britain's share).

country's share of the gains. In the limiting case, where the terms-of-trade line coincides with, say, America's frontier, America gains nothing and all the gains go to Britain.

2-8 SUMMARY

1 Preoccupied with the accumulation of precious metals, the mercantilists advocated a national policy of protectionism in order to achieve a balance-of-trade surplus and thus a gold inflow.

2 The classical theory of international trade is mainly concerned with (a) the gains from trade, (b) the structure of trade, and (c) the terms of trade.

3 Although it is generally recognized that the labor theory of value is not valid, its use can elucidate the problem of international specialization and the gains from trade. The major results obtained in this fashion continue to hold even after the labor theory of value is discarded.

4 Absolute advantage is not necessary for profitable international trade. Indeed, a basis for profitable trade exists even when one country is more efficient than another in every line of production, assuming only that the first country's degree of superiority differs from industry to industry. In this case, the "advanced" country should (and will) specialize in the production of those commodities in which its absolute advantage is highest, and import those commodities in which its absolute advantage is lowest.

5 The equilibrium terms of trade necessarily lie between the autarkic price ratios of the trading countries. The division of the gains from trade between countries depends crucially on the equilibrium terms of trade.

6 Comparative differences in cost can be easily converted into absolute differences in money prices.

7 Comparative advantage can be cast in terms of opportunity cost, which reflects forgone production of other commodities. Thus, a country should produce (and export) those goods in which its opportunity cost is lowest, and import those goods in which its opportunity cost is highest. This approach actually frees the classical theory from the restrictive assumption of the labor theory of value.

8 Opportunity costs are given graphically by the absolute slope of the production-possibilities frontier (or transformation curve).

PROBLEMS[1]

1 In Argentina one unit of labor produces either 1 bicycle or 10 bushels of wheat. In Brazil eight units of labor produce either 2 bicycles or 8 bushels of wheat.

a Determine the opportunity cost of bicycles in terms of wheat in Argentina and Brazil.

b In which commodity does Brazil have a comparative advantage? Argentina?

[1]Problems that appear with asterisks are more difficult.

c Assume that the wage rate in Brazil is $1. Find the possible range of Argentina's money-wage rate (in terms of dollars) under free trade.

2 Portugal is endowed with 100 units of labor and produces two commodities, wine and cloth. Each unit of labor produces either 4 bottles of wine or 1 yard of cloth. The world relative price of wine in terms of cloth is 2.

a Can Portugal gain from free trade? How?

b Draw Portugal's production-possibilities frontier. Then indicate the point on the production frontier at which Portugal will produce under free trade. Finally, show the combinations of wine and cloth available for consumption in Portugal under free trade.

***3** America and Britain use labor to produce three commodities: X, Y, and Z. The quantity of each commodity produced by one unit of labor in America and Britain is given in the following table:

	Commodities		
	X	Y	Z
America	6	4	2
Britain	1	1	1

a Arrange the three commodities in the order of comparative advantage for America.

b Assume that under free-trade conditions commodity Y is produced by both countries. Determine *all* relative prices and explain which commodities are exported by America and which by Britain.

c Return to the equilibrium configuration described in **b.** If Britain's money wage rate is £1 and £1 = $2, what is America's money-wage rate (in dollars)?

4 In Canada one unit of labor produces either 2 boxes of shingles or 1 bushel of corn. The money-wage rate in the production of corn is $5, but because of a strong labor movement, the wage rate in the production of shingles is $20.

a What is the opportunity cost of corn in terms of shingles in Canada?

b What are the prices of shingles and corn (in dollars) in Canada?

c What is the relative price of corn in terms of shingles in Canada?

***d** Suppose that Canada is given the opportunity to trade shingles and corn in the world market, in which 1 box of shingles exchanges for 1 bushel of corn. Which commodity will Canada export? Will Canada benefit from free trade? Why or why not?

SUGGESTED READING

Cairnes, J. E. (1874). *Some Leading Principles of Political Economy.* Macmillan and Company, London.

Chacholiades, M. (1978). *International Trade Theory and Policy.* McGraw-Hill Book Company, New York, chaps. 2–3.

Chipman, J. S. (1965). "A Survey of the Theory of International Trade." *Econometrica,* vol. 33, pp. 477–519.

Haberler, G. (1936). *The Theory of International Trade.* W. Hodge and Company, London, chaps. 9–11.

Mill, J. S. (1902). *Principles of Political Economy.* Appleton, New York, chaps. 17, 18, and 25.

Newman, B. (1985). "The Greeks Have a Word for Bananas But Lack Bananas." *The Wall Street Journal,* July 28, p. 1, col. 4.

Ricardo, D. (1821). *The Principles of Political Economy and Taxation.* J. Murray, London, chap. 7.

Smith, A. (1937). *An Inquiry into the Nature and Causes of the Wealth of Nations.* The Modern Library, New York.

Torrens, R. (1808). *The Economists Refuted.* S. A. and H. Oddy, London. Reprinted in R. Torrens, *The Principles and Practical Operation of Sir Robert Peel's Act of 1844 Explained and Defended,* 3d ed., Longmans, London, 1858.

———(1815). *An Essay on the External Corn Trade.* J. Hatchard, London.

Viner, J. (1937). *Studies in the Theory of International Trade.* Harper and Brothers, New York, chap. 7.

CHAPTER 3

INTERNATIONAL EQUILIBRIUM WITH INCREASING COSTS

This chapter does three things: (1) It extends the classical model of trade (presented in Chapter 2) to the more general case of increasing opportunity costs, (2) it introduces demand by means of social indifference curves, and (3) it studies systematically the important topic of international equilibrium by developing the useful concept of offer curves.

3-1 INCREASING OPPORTUNITY COSTS

Linear production-possibilities frontiers (such as those developed in Section 2-7 on the basis of the labor theory of value) imply that opportunity costs are *constant*—that the opportunity cost of a commodity does not change as the output of the commodity increases from zero to its maximum. Recall that America's opportunity cost of food in terms of clothing was given by the absolute slope of America's production-possibilities frontier and that since the production-possibilities frontier was linear with a unique slope, America's opportunity costs were constant.

Neoclassical economists raised serious objections to the Ricardian assumption of constant opportunity costs. To begin with, constant opportunity costs contradict the empirical observation that many industries operate under conditions of increasing costs. What is even worse, constant opportunity costs lead to *complete specialization*. Return to Figure 2-2, and observe that both America and Britain specialize completely: America produces only food, and Britain only clothing. But complete specialization is not consistent with the facts, either. For instance, the United States continues to produce domestically most of the commodities (such as TV sets, automobiles, and textiles) it imports. Finally, as is shown in Appendix 4, there are strong theoretical reasons for rejecting constant opportunity costs and replacing them with **increasing opportunity costs.**

Graphical Illustration of Increasing Opportunity Costs

Increasing opportunity costs means that, as the production of one commodity (say, food) continues to increase by one unit at a time, *increasing* amounts of another commodity (say, clothing) must be sacrificed in order to release the necessary resources. Graphically, increasing opportunity costs are illustrated by a production-possibilities frontier that is concave to (or bowed out from) the origin, as shown in Figure 3-1.

For instance, suppose that the economy currently produces 2 units of food and 58 units of clothing, as shown by point *E*. As the economy moves gradually to point *J* by raising the output of food by one unit at a time, the output of clothing falls by *increasing* amounts—3, 5, 10, and 26—as indicated by the vertical sides (*EK, GM, HN,* and *IR*) of the unshaded "triangles." Because the production-possibilities frontier is concave, the successive "steps" of the unshaded "ladder" *EJ* tend to become deeper and deeper, indicating increasing opportunity costs.

When the successive increases in the output of food become very small (or "infinitesimal"), then the opportunity cost of food in terms of clothing is actually given by the absolute slope of the production-possibilities frontier at the current production point. Again it is clear that as the economy moves from *E* to *J*, the tangent to the production-possibilities frontier becomes progressively steeper, implying increasing opportunity costs.

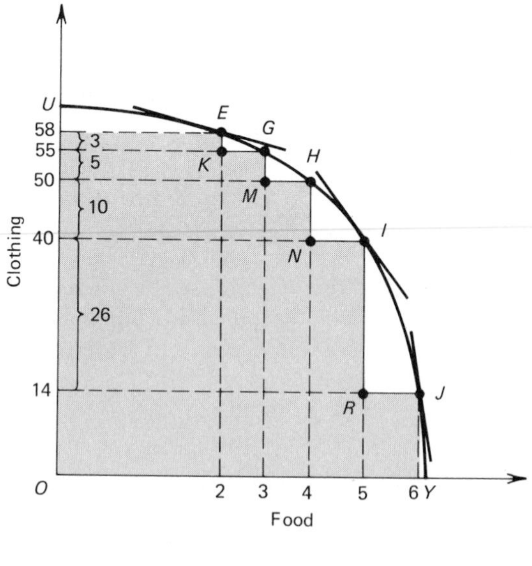

FIGURE 3-1 **Increasing opportunity costs.** Starting at *E* and raising the output of food by one unit at a time causes the output of clothing to fall by increasing amounts (3, 5, 10, and 26 units), as shown by the lengths of the vertical sides (*EK, GM, HN,* and *IR*) of the unshaded "triangles." The slope of the production-possibilities frontier becomes progressively steeper and steeper.

Finally note that a concave production-possibilities frontier implies that *both* industries experience increasing opportunity costs. This is a mathematical necessity. Recall that the opportunity cost of clothing in terms of food is merely the reciprocal of the opportunity cost of food in terms of clothing. As the economy moves from *J* to *E* (that is, as the output of clothing expands at the expense of food) the opportunity cost of foods falls (as has been shown); and by mathematical necessity, the opportunity cost of clothing rises.

Causes of Increasing Opportunity Costs

What lies behind the phenomenon of increasing opportunity costs? There are two alternative explanations for this phenomenon. The first explanation rests on the idea that factors of production are **product specific,** that is, specialized in the production of certain commodities and of relatively less use in the production of other commodities. The second explanation starts with the premise that all factors are homogeneous (in the sense that all workers and all acres of land have the same productivity in the production of both food and clothing) and attributes the phenomenon of increasing opportunity costs to the fact that different industries use factors in different proportions. We pursue the first explanation below and the second in Appendix 4.

Examples of product-specific factors are not hard to find. For instance, while highly skilled labor may be required for the production of clothing, such skills may be totally useless in the production of food. Similarly, the fertility of land differs from acre to acre and from industry to industry: While a piece of land may be good for growing grapes, it may be of much less use, or of no use at all, for raising cattle. Likewise, minerals can only be produced from certain ore-bearing types of land. And so on.

How does the product specificity of factors explain the phenomenon of increasing opportunity costs? Suppose that currently all resources are employed in the production of clothing. Imagine now that the economy continually transfers resources from the production of clothing to the production of food. At the beginning, resources that are highly efficient in the production of food (for example, the best grade of fertile land) will be transferred from clothing to food. Thus, while the output of food will be rising fast, the output of clothing will be falling slowly; that is, the opportunity cost of food will be very low. As the production of food continues to increase, it becomes necessary to employ less-fertile land and workers who are highly skilled in the production of clothing. Thus, the opportunity cost of food will rise and the production-possibilities frontier will become concave to the origin.

The degree of specificity of a factor may be a function of time. With the passage of time, new skills may be acquired, and one type of machinery may be converted into something else through depreciation and reinvestment. In the very short run, some factors may be totally specific to the production of food and useless to the production of clothing and the rest of the factors may be specific to the production of clothing and useless to the production of food. This extreme situation is best illustrated by the case of already produced outputs, for example, already harvested crops. The production-possibilities frontier reduces, in this case, to a rectangle.

The Marginal Rate of Transformation and Marginal Cost

The opportunity cost of food in terms of clothing, also known as the **marginal rate of transformation** (MRT), is equal to the ratio of the *monetary* marginal costs of food and clothing. We can illustrate this important proposition by means of a numerical example.

Suppose that at the current levels of output (indicated by some point on the production-possibilities frontier), the marginal cost of food (MC_f) is \$20 and the marginal cost of clothing (MC_c) is \$10. How much clothing will the economy have to sacrifice for 1 extra unit of food? (That is, what is the opportunity cost of food in terms of clothing, or the MRT?) To increase the output of food by 1 unit, the economy must transfer \$20 worth of resources from the clothing industry to the food industry, because $MC_f = \$20$. But by withdrawing \$20 worth of resources from the clothing industry, the economy will lose 2 units of clothing, because $MC_c = \$10$. Thus $MRT = MC_f \div MC_c = \$20 \div \$10 = 2$.

3-2 COMMUNITY INDIFFERENCE

Ricardo was unable to determine the equilibrium terms of trade because his model of comparative advantage dealt only with supply. To determine equilibrium prices we must also introduce demand, as John Stuart Mill emphasized. The purpose of this part is to introduce demand. First, we review briefly the properties of **indifference curves** and the concept of **consumer equilibrium;** and second, we discuss the useful concept of **social indifference curves,** which summarize the tastes of a society as opposed to the tastes of an individual consumer.

Indifference Curves

Economists usually represent the tastes of a consumer by means of indifference curves. An indifference curve is the locus of all alternative combinations of, say, food and clothing that enable the consumer to attain a given level of **satisfaction** or **utility.** (Recall that utility cannot be measured cardinally, as output is—utility is an ordinal concept.) The collection of all indifference curves forms the **indifference map.**

Indifference curves are illustrated in Figure 3-2. Their general properties are:

1 One (and only one) indifference curve passes through each point in commodity space.

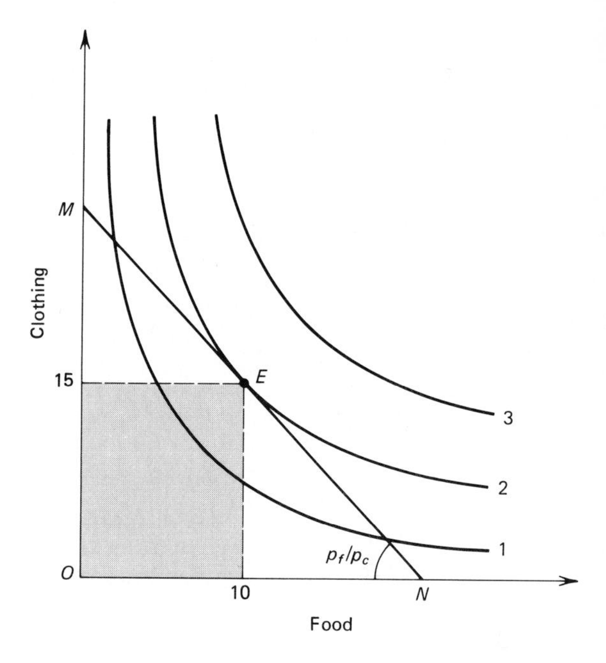

FIGURE 3-2 **The indifference map and consumer equilibrium.** The consumer maximizes utility at the point at which the budget line (*MN*) becomes tangent to the highest indifference curve (2), as illustrated by point *E*.

2 They slope downward.

3 They never intersect each other.

4 They represent levels of satisfaction or utility; specifically, a movement from a lower to a higher indifference curve (such as from curve 1 to curve 2) implies an increase in the utility enjoyed by the consumer.

5 They are convex to the origin.

The **marginal rate of substitution** of food for clothing shows the number of units of clothing that the consumer could give up for an extra unit of food and still continue to enjoy the same level of satisfaction or utility, that is, continue to consume along the same indifference curve. This marginal rate of substitution is given graphically by the absolute slope of the indifference curve at a specified consumption point. The assumed convexity of indifference curves implies that the marginal rate of substitution is diminishing. That is, as the substitution of one commodity for another proceeds, that substitution becomes progressively more difficult.

The object of the consumer is to reach the highest possible indifference curve, that is, attain the highest level of satisfaction given a fixed money income and fixed commodity prices. This is accomplished at the point (*E*) where the consumer's **budget line** (*MN*) becomes just tangent to the highest indifference curve (curve 2), as shown in Figure 3-2. At consumer equilibrium point *E*, the marginal rate of substitution of food for clothing (MRS_{FC}) equals the relative price of food (p_f/p_c). The equality $MRS_{FC} = p_f/p_c$ is a necessary condition for utility maximization.

Two Simplifying Assumptions

The **neoclassical theory of international trade** makes two simplifying assumptions: (1) The tastes of a society—as opposed to the tastes of the individual consumer—can be conveniently summarized by a social indifference map, which is qualitatively similar to the indifference map of an individual consumer; and (2) society behaves as if it were trying to attain the highest possible social indifference curve. These simplifications, which we shall adopt in this book, raise several questions. For instance, what meaning should be attached to a social indifference curve? Do social indifference curves having the same properties as the indifference curves of an individual consumer exist? If they do exist, how can they be derived? We discuss these questions below.

The Uses of Social Indifference Curves

Why do we need social indifference curves? For the same reasons we need indifference curves for the individual consumer: (1) to describe **positive behavior** and (2) to show how **welfare** changes when a change in consumption occurs.

For instance, given the budget line of the consumer (which depends only on the consumer's income and on commodity prices), we can determine, as in Figure 3-2, how much food and how much clothing the consumer will buy. Now suppose that the price of food falls while the price of clothing and the income of the consumer stay the same. The consumer will shift to a new equilibrium by determining the point of tangency between the *new* budget line and the highest possible indifference curve. The consumer's purchases of food and clothing will change in a certain way. This is what we mean by "positive behavior."

Is the consumer better off or worse off as a result of the reduction in the price of food? This is a **normative** question. It can be shown that the consumer is better off (that is, the consumer experiences an increase in economic welfare, or well-being) since the reduction in the price of food enables consumption on a higher indifference curve. (As we saw earlier, one of the properties of indifference curves is that movement from a lower to a higher indifference curve implies an increase in the satisfaction or utility enjoyed by the consumer.)

Similarly, we need social indifference curves to determine the aggregate consumption levels of food and clothing, given the budget line of society. Further, as that budget line shifts (following a change in prices or national income), we need social indifference curves to determine how the aggregate consumption levels of food and clothing will change. In addition, we like to be able to say whether social welfare increases or decreases following a structural change (brought about by a government policy, a change in world markets, an invention, or some other factor).

Definition and Difficulties

An individual consumer's indifference curve gives all combinations of food and clothing that yield the same amount of utility to the consumer. In principle, indifference curves can be derived by asking consumers to reveal their preferences. For instance, given any two combinations of food and clothing, say, A and B, we could ask the consumer whether A is preferred to B, or B to A, or whether the consumer is indifferent between them. If the consumer is indifferent, then we know that A and B lie on the same indifference curve. By giving the consumer more options, we can discover the entire indifference map.

How are we to define a social indifference curve? One might be tempted to say that a social indifference curve is the locus of all combinations of food and clothing that yield the same amount of **social welfare.** But what is social welfare, and how can it be measured? Further, how can we determine all those combinations that yield the same amount of social welfare? We cannot subject society to the kind of questioning to which we subjected the individual consumer because society is composed of many individuals with divergent views. A majority vote will not do.

Economists today agree that social welfare is a function of the welfare of each and every citizen. Nevertheless, unlike earlier generations of economists, modern economists stop short of suggesting that social welfare is the sum of all individual satisfactions enjoyed by all consumers. For one thing, the utility enjoyed by each consumer is an ordinal concept and cannot be measured cardinally. For another, **interpersonal comparisons of utility** are ruled out as unscientific. For instance, suppose that one individual becomes better off, and at the same time another individual becomes worse off. We cannot say what happens to social welfare unless we find a way to compare the gain of the first individual with the loss of the second individual. Such a comparison, though, requires a judgment of a purely ethical nature and cannot be made objectively. Different ethical observers will pass different judgments.

Modern economists accept the **Paretian ethic** that when one individual becomes better off without anyone else becoming worse off, social welfare increases. However, when some individuals become better off and others worse off, we are still unable to say whether social welfare increases or decreases, although some progress has been made by means of the **compensation principle.** According to this principle, social welfare is said to improve *potentially* when the gainers can use part of their gains to compensate the losers so that everybody *could* become better off. The main drawback of the compensation principle is that no actual compensation takes place.

It must be clear now why, in general, it is not possible to draw a social indifference curve and pretend it is the locus of all combinations of food and clothing that yield the same amount of social welfare. Points along a social indifference curve represent *aggregate* amounts of food and clothing—they give absolutely no information regarding the *distribution* of these aggregates among the individual consumers. Hence, even if we were to accept someone's ethical belief of how one individual's welfare is to be added to another's, a given combination of food and clothing (say, 100 units of food and 80 units of clothing) would represent not one level of social welfare but many, each level depending on how the 100 units of food and the 80 units of clothing were distributed among the members of the society. Also, if the supplies of food and clothing were to increase to, say, 120 and 110, respectively (a change which would normally imply a shift to a higher indifference curve and higher welfare), we could not assert that social welfare would increase, because we would have no information on the distribution of income. In general social indifference curves do not exist.

An important justification for the continued use of social indifference curves is, besides their simplicity, the fact that they give rise to results that are qualitatively similar to those derived more laboriously by the use of a totally disaggregated model. This is indeed the reason why we use them in this book.

3-3 GENERAL EQUILIBRIUM IN A SINGLE ECONOMY

In this section we demonstrate how the basic tools we studied in Sections 3-1 and 3-2 (that is, the production-possibilities frontier and the social indifference map) can be used to portray general equilibrium in a single economy.

Equilibrium in a Closed Economy

In the absence of trade, the economy acts like a huge consumer whose budget line is given by the production-possibilities frontier and whose tastes are given by the social indifference map. General equilibrium occurs at the point at which the production-possibilities frontier is tangent to the highest possible social indifference curve. This remarkable result is not brought about by the deliberate actions of any central authority. This is the outcome of one of the most complex social processes, in which millions of individuals play an important role, acting as individual consumers and producers in the pursuit of their own self-interests. These divergent interests are guided and coordinated by the forces of competition (Adam Smith's invisible hand) until a general equilibrium is reached. All this is shown in Figure 3-3.

The common absolute slope of the production-possibilities frontier UP_0V and social indifference curve 1 at the general equilibrium point P_0 gives the equilibrium relative price of food in terms of clothing, that is, p_f/p_c. *Therefore, in general equilibrium, the commodity price ratio is equal to both the opportunity cost of food in terms of clothing (also known as the marginal rate of transformation) and the marginal rate of substitution in consumption.*

Note, however, the basic difference between the cases of constant cost and increasing opportunity cost. In the former (constant cost), the equilibrium price

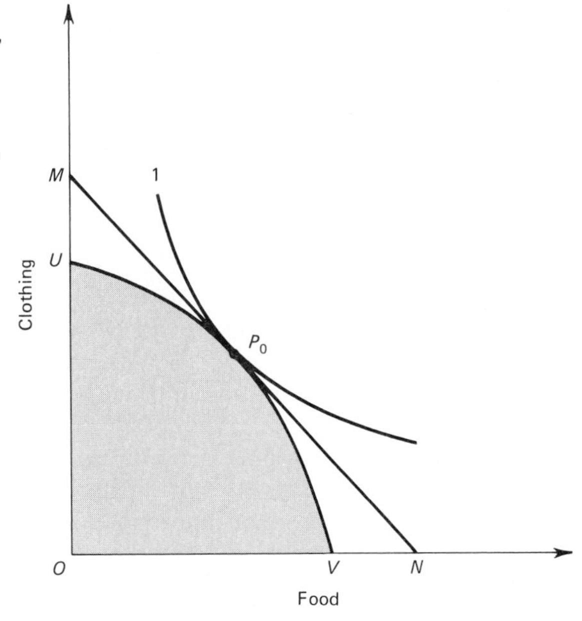

FIGURE 3-3 **General equilibrium in a closed economy.** In the absence of trade, general equilibrium occurs at P_0, where the production-possibilities frontier touches the highest possible social indifference curve. The absolute slope of the common tangent *MN* at P_0 gives the equilibrium relative price of food in terms of clothing, that is, p_f/p_c.

ratio can be inferred from the *unique* slope of the production-possibilities frontier without any information about demand—assuming only that both commodities are produced and consumed in equilibrium. Under increasing opportunity costs, the equilibrium price ratio cannot be inferred from the production-possibilities frontier alone: Full information about demand is also necessary. To use Marshall's metaphor, it is both blades of the scissors that do the cutting.

Equilibrium in a Small Open Economy

Assume now that as a result of some exogenous event, such as a huge reduction of transportation costs or the elimination of prohibitive tariffs, our closed economy is granted the opportunity to trade food and clothing in the international market. For the moment, we assume that the country in our example is so small that its sales and purchases (exports and imports) in the world markets do not have any appreciable effect on world prices. In short, our economy is a **price taker** in international trade. How does our country reach general equilibrium now that trade with the rest of the world is possible?

An important implication of international trade is that *the decision to produce is divorced from the decision to consume.* Unlike a closed economy, which produces that basket of commodities its citizens want to consume, an open economy uses international trade to cut the Gordian knot between production and consumption. The decision about what commodities to produce rests on the profit-maximizing activities of firms; and the decision about what commodities to consume rests on the utility-maximizing activities of individual consumers. Any divergence between domestic production and consumption is made good through international trade. Let us see how this is done.

Consider Figure 3-4, where autarkic equilibrium occurs at P_0 (as in Figure 3-3). After the introduction of free trade, perfect competition forces our domestic price ratio to be the same as the international price ratio. Our producers adjust their production plans so that their marginal costs become equal to the given international prices, and our consumers adjust their consumption plans so that their marginal rates of substitution are equal to the given international price ratio. In Figure 3-4, we assume that the international price ratio is given by the absolute slope of line *ST.* Thus food is cheaper in the international market because line *ST* is flatter than the tangent (not drawn) to the production-possibilities frontier at P_0. As our domestic price ratio falls to *ST,* the food producers find the price of food to be lower than their marginal cost. The motive of profit maximization forces them to cut output and release factors until the marginal cost of food becomes equal to the new, lower price of food. Similarly, the clothing producers find the increased price of clothing to be higher than their marginal cost. They realize that more profits can be reaped by expanding their output. Indeed, to maximize their profits, the clothing producers must continue to increase their output until their marginal cost becomes equal to the new, higher price of clothing. They accomplish this by employing the resources released by the food industry.

As the production of food falls and the production of clothing rises, the economy moves along the production-possibilities frontier from P_0 toward *U.* In par-

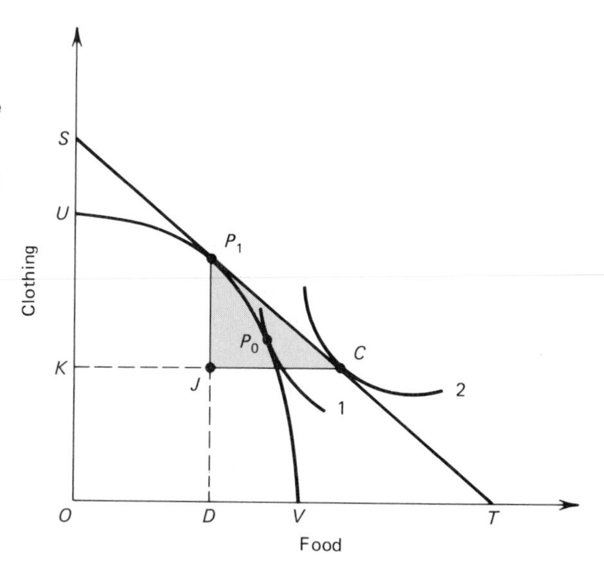

FIGURE 3-4 **General equilibrium in a small open economy.** Autarkic equilibrium occurs at P_0. As free trade becomes possible at relative prices indicated by the absolute slope of line *ST*, production shifts to P_1 and consumption to *C*. Thus the economy exports P_1J units of clothing and imports *JC* units of food.

ticular, the economy moves to P_1, where the ratio of marginal costs (slope of the production-possibilities frontier) equals the international price ratio (slope of ST). Accordingly, at P_1 prices are indeed equal to marginal costs, and all producers maximize their profits. Because of increasing opportunity costs our open economy continues to produce both commodities even after international trade is introduced. Thus unlike the Ricardian case of constant opportunity costs, in the present case of increasing opportunity costs the introduction of free trade does not lead to complete specialization.

It is important to note that national income (that is, the value of output produced) is *maximized* at P_1. This is a fundamental result of perfect competition. For instance, if the society insisted on producing at P_0 (that is, at the autarkic equilibrium point), or at any point other than P_1, its "community budget line" would be inferior to ST. (This proposition is confirmed by the fact that any line that intersects the production-possibilities frontier and is parallel to ST necessarily lies closer to the origin than ST.) Accordingly, national income is maximized at P_1, where the marginal rate of transformation is equal to the international price ratio.

Because of its great significance, community budget line ST is called the **consumption-possibilities frontier.** This means that by producing at P_1, our economy can actually consume any combination of food and clothing along line ST. This is accomplished, of course, by trading appropriate amounts of food and clothing in the international market.

What is the relationship between production-possibilities frontier UV and consumption-possibilities frontier ST? They have only one point in common: optimum production point P_1. Everywhere else, the consumption-possibilities frontier lies beyond the production-possibilities frontier. This is a remarkable result. It shows that while our country is always constrained by its production-possibilities frontier as far as production is concerned, *free international trade makes it possible for the country to consume beyond the boundaries of the production frontier.* Herein lies the essence of the gains from trade.

Where does our economy consume after it is opened up to international trade? At point C, where the consumption-possibilities frontier touches the highest possible social indifference curve (curve 2). Note that our economy would not have been able to reach social indifference curve 2 had it remained closed—the production-possibilities frontier does not reach social indifference curve 2.

What are our country's exports and imports at the free-trade equilibrium? These are determined as the differences between the amounts produced and the amounts consumed. Graphically, they are given by the perpendicular sides of **trade triangle** P_1JC. Thus, our economy exports P_1J units of clothing and imports JC units of food. Observe that $P_1J = P_1D - JD$; that is, the exports of clothing are given by the difference between the domestic production and consumption of clothing. Similarly, $JC = KC - KJ$; that is, the imports of food are equal to the domestic consumption of food minus the domestic production of food.

In summary, the opportunity to trade enables our small economy to divorce the production decision (or bundle) from the consumption decision (or bundle). In particular, the economy produces at P_1 (where the marginal rate of transformation is equal to the international price ratio) and consumes at *C* (where consumption-possibilities frontier *ST* is tangent to social indifference curve 2). Point *C* lies outside of the production frontier. Consumption is reconciled with production through trade. Any production surplus is exported, and any excess consumption over domestic production is accommodated by means of imports.

The Gains from Trade

It is often thought that gains from trade accrue only to advanced countries that have the capacity to shift resources easily between sectors. This is not true. Free trade is beneficial to every country, even to a backward country that lacks the capacity to transform its autarkic production mix. To clarify this point, economists divide the total gain from trade into the following two components:

1 The **consumption gain** (or the **gain from international exchange**), which accrues to the economy when the same bundle of commodities is produced under free trade as under autarky.

2 The **production gain** (or the **gain from specialization**), which accrues to the economy in addition to the consumption gain as a result of the shift of the production point from its autarkic equilibrium location to its free-trade position.

The above decomposition of the total gain is illustrated in Figure 3-5. Autarkic equilibrium occurs at *R*, where the economy attains social indifference curve 1. When free trade is introduced at relative prices indicated by the *absolute* slope of consumption-possibilities frontier *SN*, the economy produces at *Q* and consumes at *T*, attaining social indifference curve 3. The *total* gain from trade, represented by the movement from *R* to *T*, is decomposed into two parts: (1) a movement from *R* to *E*, which is obtained by freezing the production point at *R*, plus (2) a movement from *E* to *T*, which results from the movement of the production point from *R* to *Q*. The movement from *R* to *E* is the consumption gain, and the movement from *E* to *T* is the production gain.

If this were a backward economy that lacked the capacity to transform its autarkic output mix, its production-possibilities frontier would be given by rectangle *OGRH*. With free trade, this backward country would continue to produce at *R* (and thus its production gain would be zero) but would shift its consumption to *E*. The movement from *R* to *E* would be a positive consumption gain.

3-4 A NEOCLASSICAL DEMONSTRATION OF COMPARATIVE ADVANTAGE

The present section reconsiders the theory of comparative advantage but within the neoclassical world of increasing opportunity costs. Not only does this step

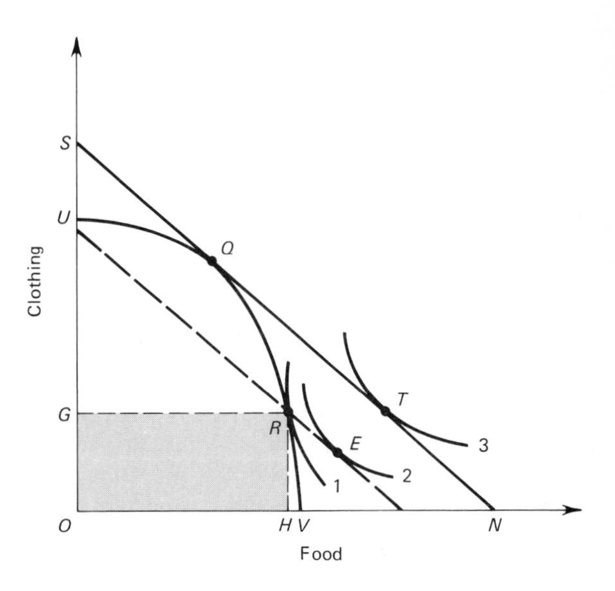

FIGURE 3-5 **Decomposition of the total gain into a consumption gain plus a production gain.** With free trade, production shifts from *R* (autarkic equilibrium) to *Q*, and consumption to *T*. The total gain from trade (shown by the movement from *R* to *T*) is decomposed into a consumption gain (movement from *R* to *E*) plus a production gain (movement from *E* to *T*).

prepare the ground for future investigations, it also enables us to keep in touch with the basic questions raised in Chapter 2.

The Setting

Assume two countries, America and Britain. Each country produces two commodities, food and clothing, under increasing opportunity costs. The autarkic equilibrium positions of America and Britain are illustrated in Figure 3-6. In the first panel, America produces and consumes at *E*, at which America's production-possibilities frontier *MN* is tangent to social indifference curve 1. America's pretrade relative price of food p (given by the absolute slope of the production frontier *MN* at *E*) is by assumption equal to 2. Similarly, in the second panel, Britain produces and consumes at E^*, at which Britain's production frontier M^*N^* is tangent to social indifference curve 1*. Britain's pretrade relative price of food p^* (given by the absolute slope of M^*N^* at E^*) is by assumption equal to 6. Accordingly, in the initial autarkic equilibrium states, food is cheaper in America than in Britain ($2 < 6$).

Is trade between America and Britain possible? Is it mutually beneficial? Which commodity should each country export? At what terms of trade will food and clothing be traded under a regime of free trade? These are fundamental questions, and our analysis has progressed sufficiently to permit us to venture at least some tentative answers.

Comparative Advantage and the Gains from Trade

We learned in Chapter 2 that in the Ricardian world of constant opportunity costs, a country should specialize in the production of that commodity which, under autarky, it produces relatively more cheaply than the other country. This fundamental principle continues to hold in the neoclassical world of increasing opportunity costs. Thus America should specialize in the production of food, and Britain in clothing. The proof of this proposition is very simple.

Recall that America's autarkic relative price of food is 2 and Britain's 6. Since prices are equal to opportunity costs, this means that to increase its production of food by 1 unit, America must sacrifice only 2 units of clothing. But for each unit of food Britain gives up, the nation can increase its output of clothing by 6 units. The final outcome of such a reorganization of production is, of course, a net amount of 4 units of clothing (that is, $6 - 2$). Such gains can continue to be reaped by further adjustments in production as long as the opportunity cost of food is lower in America than in Britain.

As America specializes in the production of food by transferring resources from the clothing industry to the food industry, the nation moves downward along its production frontier from autarkic equilibrium point *E* toward *N*. During this process, America's opportunity cost of food (in terms of clothing) in-

FIGURE 3-6 **Specialization based on comparative advantage, and the resulting gains from trade.** In autarky, America produces and consumes at *E*, and Britain at *E**. With trade, America shifts production from *E* to *Q* and consumes at *S* by exporting *VQ* units of food to Britain in exchange for *VS* units of British clothing. America is better off with trade because *S* lies on a higher indifference curve than *E*. Indeed, in our illustration, America consumes more food and more clothing at *S* than at *E*. Britain shifts production from *E** to *Q**, and consumption from *E** to *S**. Britain's welfare increases also. Trade triangles *SVQ* and *Q*V*S** are identical.

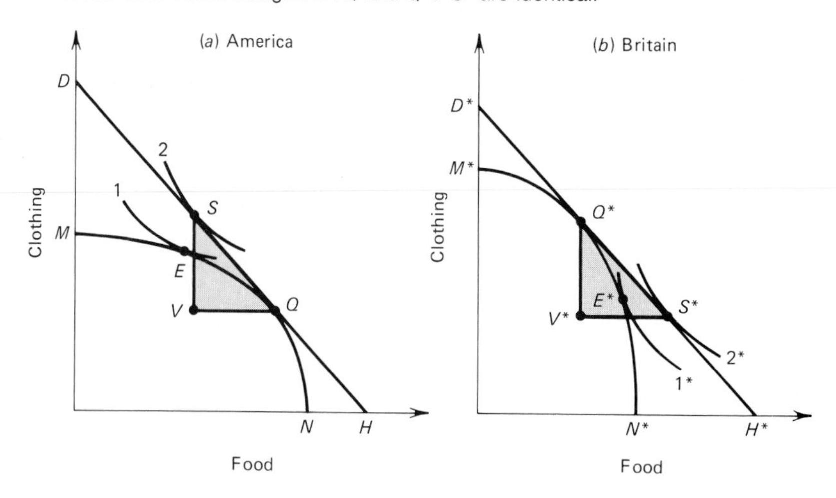

creases steadily as implied by the gradual rise in the (absolute) slope of its production frontier. Britain does the opposite, because it specializes in the production of clothing. As Britain transfers resources from the food industry to the clothing industry, the nation moves upward along its production frontier (from E^* toward M^*). Britain's opportunity cost of food (in terms of clothing) *decreases* steadily, as evidenced by the gradual decline in the (absolute) slope of its production frontier. This process of international specialization continues until two conditions are met: (1) the opportunity cost of food is the same in both countries, and (2) trade is *balanced,* that is, each country is willing to export what the other country is willing to import. When these two conditions are satisfied, we know that no further gains from trade can be achieved and that international equilibrium is attained.

Figure 3-6 also illustrates the final outcome of the preceding process of international specialization according to comparative advantage. This result is obtained through trial and error. The equilibrium relative price of food is assumed to be 5. It coincides with the common absolute slope of America's and Britain's consumption-possibilities frontiers, that is, DH and D^*H^*, respectively. America shifts its production point from E to Q as Britain shifts its production point from E^* to Q^*. America consumes at S by exporting VQ units of food to Britain in exchange for VS units of British clothing. America's equilibrium exports and imports are given by the perpendicular sides of trade triangle SVQ. Britain consumes at S^* by exporting V^*Q^* units of clothing to America in exchange for V^*S^* units of American food. Note that the British trade triangle $Q^*V^*S^*$ and the American trade triangle SVQ are identical. Thus, $VS = V^*Q^*$ and $VQ = V^*S^*$.

Several comments are now in order.

1 The equilibrium terms of trade lie *between* the autarkic price ratios of America and Britain.

2 At the equilibrium terms of trade, world supply equals world demand in both the food market and the clothing market.

3 Specialization and free trade enable both countries to become better off. America improves her welfare by moving to social indifference curve 2 and Britain benefits by moving to social indifference curve 2.* Free trade enables both countries to consume outside their respective production frontiers.

4 In the free-trade equilibrium position neither America nor Britain specializes completely. Each country continues to produce both commodities.

5 Even though comparative advantage is decided by opportunity-cost differences, we must never forget that it is the pretrade (or autarkic) differences that are relevant. With trade, there cannot be any difference in opportunity costs, because free trade equalizes opportunity costs across countries. Yet pretrade opportunity costs are not observable in the real world.

3-5 DIFFERENCES IN TASTES AS A BASIS FOR TRADE

Two countries may produce two commodities equally well but because their tastes are different, there may be a basis for mutually beneficial trade. This is shown in Figure 3-7. We assume that America and Britain share the *same* production-possibilities frontier (MN). However, America has a strong preference for clothing whereas Britain has a strong preference for food.

In the absence of trade, a commodity is more expensive in the country that has the stronger preference for it. In our example, this means that in autarky food is more expensive in Britain and clothing is more expensive in America, as illustrated in Figure 3-7. Thus, in the absence of trade, America produces and consumes at A (where the production frontier MN is tangent to America's social indifference curve 1); and Britain, at B (where MN is tangent to Britain's social indifference curve 1*). America has a comparative advantage in food, and Britain in clothing.

The opening of trade equalizes relative commodity prices in America and Britain. Unlike the more usual case of Section 3-4 (as well as the Ricardian case), in which free trade causes the production patterns of the two countries to become more *dis*similar, in the present case trade permits each country to spe-

FIGURE 3-7 **Trade based on different tastes.** America and Britain share the same production frontier *MN*. In autarky, America produces and consumes at *A*, and Britain at *B*. With free trade, both countries produce at *Q*, but America consumes at *A′*, and Britain at *B′*. Trade triangles *A′VQ* and *QSB′* are identical.

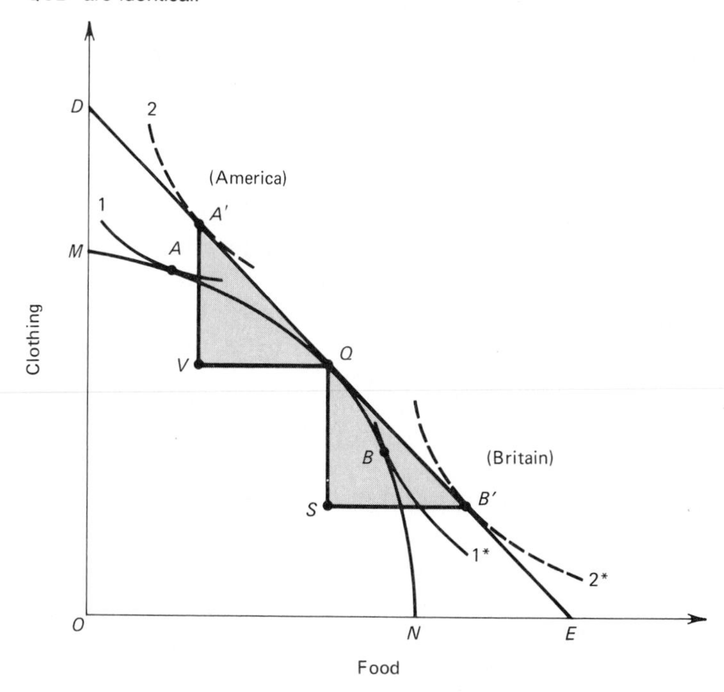

cialize less in production. Apparently, prior to trade, America had used for the production of clothing (its favored commodity) some resources best suited for the production of food; and Britain had used for the production of food (Britain's favored commodity) some resources more suited for clothing. With free trade possible, both countries reverse their autarkic allocation of resources: America transfers resources from the clothing industry back to the food industry where they are more efficient, and Britain does the opposite. Indeed because trade equalizes relative commodity prices, both countries produce at the same point, Q, that is, *their production patterns become identical.* The clothing-preferring country, America, caters to its preference for clothing by exporting VQ units of food in exchange for VA' units of British clothing. As a result, America reaches the higher indifference curve 2 at point A'. The food-preferring country, Britain, also caters to its greater taste for food by consuming at point B', which lies on higher indifference curve 2*. Note again that the two shaded trade triangles, $A'VQ$ and QSB' are identical.

3-6 OFFER CURVES

We have already portrayed international equilibrium in Figure 3-6. Unfortunately, Figure 3-6 does not give us a general method of determining international equilibrium. Such a diagram can only be constructed through trial and error. To determine international equilibrium systematically, Alfred Marshall introduced an alternative device, the **offer curve.** The nature of Marshall's ingenious device, how it is derived, and how it is used in international economics is studied in this section. It is also studied further in Appendix 5.

Definition of Offers and Offer Curves

An offer curve merely shows the **offers** of a country at alternative terms of trade. An offer is represented by two numbers: the amount of, say, food, that the country is willing to export and the amount of clothing that the country is willing to import. The locus of all offers of the country is the nation's offer curve.

Even though an offer explicitly gives the quantities of exports and imports, it involves three elements: exports, imports, and the terms of trade. Because of the long-run equality between the value of exports and the value of imports of a country, there exists a strict relationship among exports, imports, and the terms of trade, which is summarized by the formula

$$\text{Relative price of food} = \frac{\text{imports of clothing}}{\text{exports of food}}$$

For instance, suppose that the price of food is \$2 and the price of clothing \$5 and that America is willing to export 500 units of food and import 200 units of clothing. Obviously, the value of exports ($\$2 \times 500 = \$1000$) is equal to the value of imports ($\$5 \times 200 = \$1000$). But we also have: $\$2 \div \$5 = 200 \div 500$.

The above equality holds for all offers. Accordingly, when two of the three elements of an offer are given, the third element is easily inferred. Typically, an offer curve explicitly gives only the amounts that a country is willing to export and import. The country's terms of trade are then determined by the ratio of imports to exports.

A Methodological Point

When we speak of exports and imports in the present context, we do not mean the quantities of food and clothing that are actually shipped by one country to another. Rather, we mean those quantities of food and clothing that a country is willing to export or import, as the case may be. It is evident that the amount of food actually shipped by America to Britain must be precisely equal to the amount of food actually imported by Britain whether the market for food is in equilibrium or not. There can be no difference in the quantities actually traded between the two countries. For a market to be in equilibrium, however, it is necessary for all buyers to be able to buy all they want at current prices and for all sellers to be able to sell all they wish at current prices. Only in the absence of any frustrated buyers or sellers do we have equilibrium. It is for this reason that in the present context, the term **exports** means the quantity that a country is willing to export at the current terms of trade. Similarly, the term **imports** means the quantity that a country is willing to import at the current terms of trade. Hence, America's exports of food and Britain's imports of food are equal only in equilibrium.

Determination of Offers

How are offers determined? We already know the answer to this question. Return to Figure 3-6, and observe that at terms-of-trade *DH* America produces at *Q* and consumes at *S*. Therefore, America's offer is *VQ* units of exports of food and VS units of imports of clothing. As was said earlier, this offer is determined by the perpendicular sides of trade triangle *SVQ*. To determine other offers at other terms of trade, we follow the same procedure, that is, we draw other price lines, determine tangencies, and complete the corresponding trade triangles.

Derivation of Offer Curves

Each offer determines a point on the offer curve. To derive the entire offer curve, we first determine several offers, or points. We then connect all these points by means of a continuous line, as shown in Figures 3-8 (for America) and 3-9 (for Britain). To keep both diagrams simple, we assume that America has a comparative advantage in food, and Britain in clothing.

Panel (*a*) of Figure 3-8 is similar to panel (*a*) of Figure 3-6: it shows the production and consumption decisions of America together with the relevant trade triangles. Panel (*b*) gives the various offers of America at alternative terms of trade as well as America's offer curve. For instance, at the autarkic relative price of food (which is assumed to be equal to 2), America produces and consumes at *E* in panel (*a*). Since America's offer is zero units of food and zero units of clothing, the offer is represented in panel (*b*) by the origin of the diagram. As the relative price of food increases to 3 (shown by price line *DH*), America shifts its production to point *Q*, and its consumption to point *S*, generating trade triangle *SVQ*. The implied American offer is shown in panel (*b*) by point *S*. (For easy reference, we use the same symbol to denote both the consumption point and the corresponding offer.) Observe that triangle *SJO* in panel (*b*) is identical to trade triangle *SVQ* in panel (*a*). The only insignificant difference lies in the fact that triangle *SJO* is the mirror image of trade triangle *SVQ*. It is as if a page in the "triangular book" *SVQ* has been flipped over to the left. For this reason, the absolute slope of **terms-of-trade line** TOT_2 in panel (*b*) is equal to the absolute slope of consumption-possibilities frontier *DH* in panel (*a*).

Similarly, at terms of trade equal to $p = 4$, America produces at *R* and consumes at *K*, generating trade triangle *KGR*. The implied offer is shown in panel (*b*) by point *K*. Again triangles *KGR* and *KLO* are identical, and the absolute slope of terms-of-trade line TOT_3 is equal to the absolute slope of consumption-possibilities frontier *GT*.

FIGURE 3-8 **Derivation of America's offer curve.** At the autarkic relative price of food (*p*), assumed to be equal to 2, America produces and consumes at *E* in panel (a) and trades at the origin of panel (*b*). At $p = 3$, America shifts production to *Q* and consumption to *S* in panel (a) and trades at *S* in panel (b). Similarly, at $p = 4$, America produces at *R* and consumes at K in panel (a) and trades at *K* in panel (b). Trade triangles *SVQ* and *KGR* are identical to triangles *SJO* and *KLO*, respectively. The locus of all trade points (such as *S* and *K*) in panel (b) is America's offer curve.

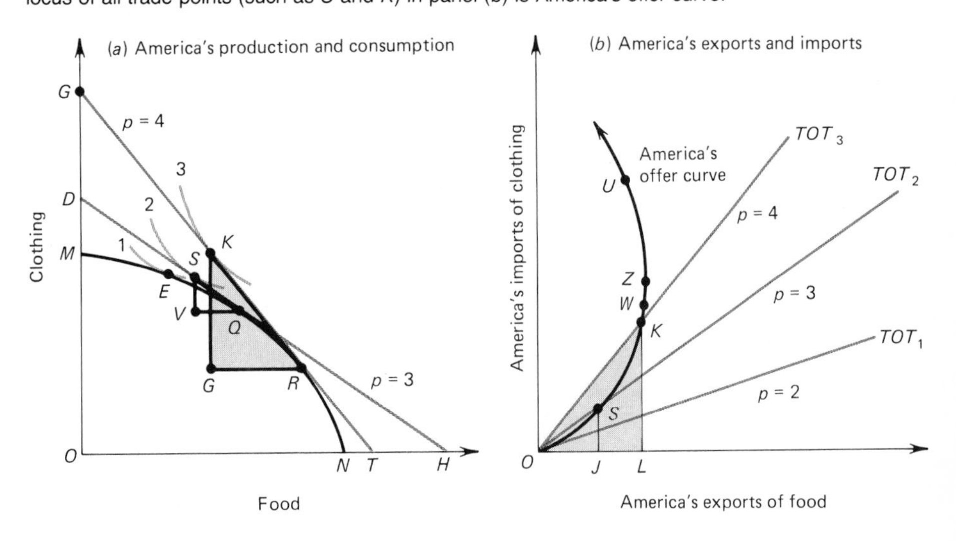

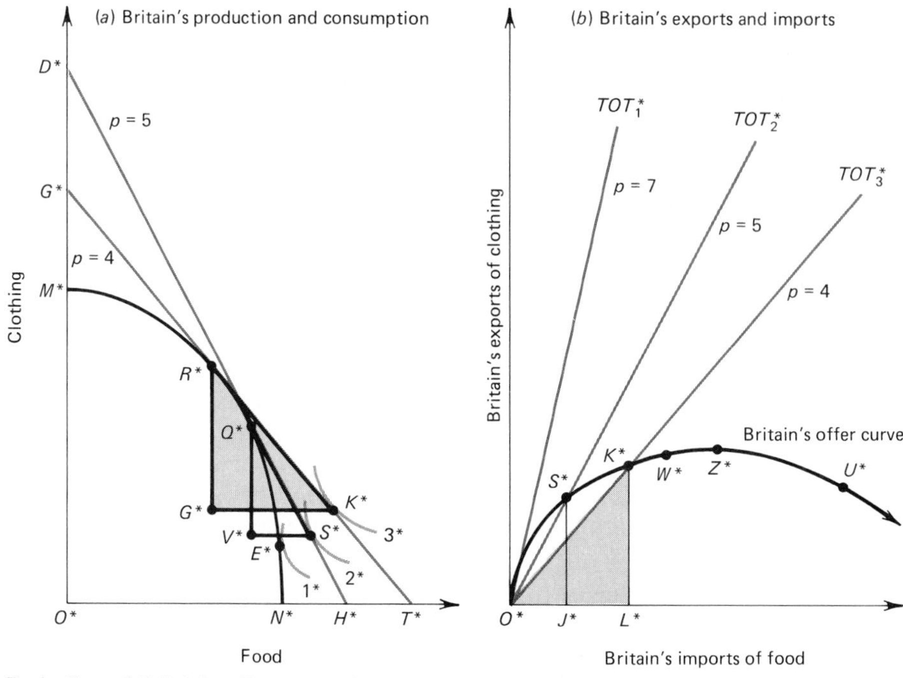

FIGURE 3-9 **Derivation of Britain's offer curve.** Autarkic equilibrium point E^* in panel (a) corresponds to the origin (O^*) in panel (b). At $p = 5$, Britain produces at Q^* and consumes at S^* in panel (a), generating trade point S^* in panel (b). At $p = 4$, Britain produces at R^* and consumes at K^* in panel (a), generating trade point K^* in panel (b). The locus of all trade points (such as S^* and K^*) in panel (b) is Britain's offer curve.

America's offer curve is the locus of all offers such as O, S, and K, as illustrated in panel (b). Note that terms-of-trade line TOT_1, whose absolute slope corresponds to the autarkic relative price of food in America ($p = 2$), meets the offer curve at the origin only. Indeed, terms-of-trade line TOT_1 is *tangent* to the offer curve at the origin. America's offer curve lies above and to the left of TOT_2. Finally, for mnemonic purposes, note that America's offer curve faces the axis measuring American imports like an "empty bowl" standing ready to "receive" imports.

Figure 3-9, which is analogous to Figure 3-8, shows how to derive the offer curve of Britain—a country having a comparative advantage in clothing. Autarkic equilibrium occurs at E^*, at which the relative price of food (p) is 7. Since at $p = 7$ Britain's offer is zero, it is represented in panel (b) by the origin of the diagram. At $p = 5$, Britain produces at Q^* and consumes at S^*, and the corresponding offer is shown by point S^* in panel (b). Trade triangle $Q^*V^*S^*$ is identical to triangle $S^*J^*O^*$. Similarly at $p = 4$, Britain produces at R^* and consumes at K^*. Britain's corresponding offer is given by point K^* in panel (b). Trade triangle $R^*G^*K^*$ is identical to triangle $K^*L^*O^*$. Britain's offer curve lies below and to the right of TOT_1^*, which is merely tangent to it at the origin. Again Britain's offer curve faces the axis of British imports like an "empty bowl." Britain's offer curve has a curvature which is opposite to that of America's offer curve because British imports of food are measured along the horizontal axis.

The Nature of Offer Curves

An offer curve represents a very complex relationship that we must always keep in mind. Edgeworth (1905, p. 70) summarized the complexity of this relationship in the following well-known statement:

> There is more than meets the eye in Professor Marshall's foreign trade curves. As it has been said by one who used this sort of curve, a movement along a supply-and-demand curve of international trade should be considered as attended with rearrangements of internal trade; as the movement of the hand of a clock corresponds to considerable unseen movements of the machinery.

Edgeworth was actually quoting himself (Edgeworth, 1894, pp. 424–425).

An offer curve is neither a demand curve nor a supply curve but a combination of elements of both. What is more, as Edgeworth so beautifully described, any movement along an offer curve usually implies a movement along the production-possibilities frontier. As shown in Appendix 4, a movement along the production frontier actually involves the following: a shift of resources from one industry to the other, a change in the methods of production, and a change in factor prices and the distribution of income. On top of all these changes that occur in the production sector of the economy, we must add the changes that occur in consumption as a result of the price and income changes. Accordingly, even a small movement along the offer curve implies a total reorganization of the economy, just "as the movement of the hand of a clock corresponds to considerable unseen movements of the machinery."

For our present purposes, we shall be content merely with the use of offer curves in the determination of international equilibrium. Nevertheless, the reader should always keep in mind the considerable unseen movements of the economic machinery. As economists, we must be profoundly concerned with what goes on behind the offer curves. Future chapters will illuminate this complex economic process as much as possible.

The Elasticity of Demand for Imports and the Offer Curve

When the price of a commodity falls, the quantity demanded increases. The **elasticity of demand** is merely the ratio of the percentage change in the quantity demanded to the percentage change in the price. When these percentage changes are equal (in absolute terms), the elasticity of demand is *unity*.

When the quantity demanded changes faster than the price, the elasticity of demand is higher than unity, and we say that demand is **elastic.** Finally, when the quantity demanded changes more slowly than the price, the elasticity of demand is lower than unity, and we say that demand is **inelastic.**

There is an important relationship between the elasticity of demand and the total expenditure (price × quantity) on the commodity under consideration. Suppose that the price falls by 1 percent. If the quantity demanded increases by more than 1 percent (that is, if demand is elastic), then the total expenditure on the commodity will increase. If the quantity demanded increases by less than 1 percent (that is, if demand is inelastic), then total expenditure will fall. In the limiting case of unit elastic demand, total expenditure remains the same.

The above ideas are directly applicable to the demand for imports. For instance, the **elasticity of demand for imports** of food is given by the ratio of the percentage change in the quantity of food imported to the percentage change in the relative price of food. The same relationship that exists between the ordinary elasticity of demand and changes in total expenditure also exists between the elasticity of demand for imports and total expenditure on imports. This observation is very important, because we can use it to predict from the mere shape of the offer curve whether the demand for imports is elastic or inelastic at a certain point.

Return to Figure 3-9. What is the total expenditure on the imports of food at point K^*? By definition, we have:

$$\begin{aligned}\text{Total expenditure on imports of food} &= \text{relative price of food} \times \text{imports of food}\\ &= \text{exports of clothing}\end{aligned}$$

Accordingly, the total expenditure on imports of food equals the amount of clothing that the country must export to pay for the imports of food. Remember that a country pays for its imports by means of its exports. For instance, at K^* the total expenditure for the imports of O^*L^* units of food is represented by the amount of L^*K^* units of clothing.

Suppose now that the relative price of food is given by the slope of terms-of-trade line TOT_3^* and the economy trades at K^*. Is the demand for imports elastic or inelastic at K^*? Consider a very small reduction in the relative price of food. This price reduction can be represented by a small clockwise rotation of line TOT_3^* as implied by line OW^* (not drawn). At this lower price, the economy will be willing to trade at W^*. What has happened to the total expenditure on imports? Note that point K^* happens to be on an upward-sloping region of the offer curve. Accordingly, as food becomes cheaper and the country moves from K^* to W^*, the total exports of clothing (that is, total expenditure on imports) increase. From this, we immediately infer that the demand for imports is elastic at K^*.

Following this analysis, we conclude that Britain's demand for imports is elastic at all points (such as S^* and K^*) which lie in upward-sloping region OZ^* of the offer curve; it is inelastic at all points (such as U^*) which lie in downward-sloping region Z^*U^*; and it is unit elastic at point Z^*, at which Britain's offer curve is momentarily horizontal.

Referring to Figure 3-8, we can also conclude that America's demand for imports (of clothing) is elastic over upward-sloping region OZ of the offer curve; it is inelastic over backward-bending region ZU; and it is unit elastic at point Z (where America's offer curve is vertical).

3-7 INTERNATIONAL EQUILIBRIUM

International equilibrium occurs when the terms of trade are such that trade is balanced. At that point world supply equals world demand in each and every market. All producers sell all they wish to sell, and all consumers buy all they wish to buy. All are satisfied, and they have no incentive to change their behavior. How is international equilibrium attained? How do we bring world supply and demand together to determine the equilibrium terms of trade? We can use our new tools, the offer curves, to provide a systematic answer to this important problem.

International equilibrium occurs at the intersection of the two offer curves. Only at the terms of trade implied by that intersection will the desired trade flows of the two nations be balanced. This is shown in Figure 3-10, which brings together the offer curves of America and Britain derived in Figures 3-8 and 3-9. The equilibrium terms of trade ($p = 4$) are given by terms-of-trade line

FIGURE 3-10 **International equilibrium.** International equilibrium occurs at K, where the offer curves intersect. America exports OL units of food to Britain and imports OL^* units of clothing from Britain. The slope of terms-of-trade line TOT_3 gives equilibrium terms of trade OL^*/OL.

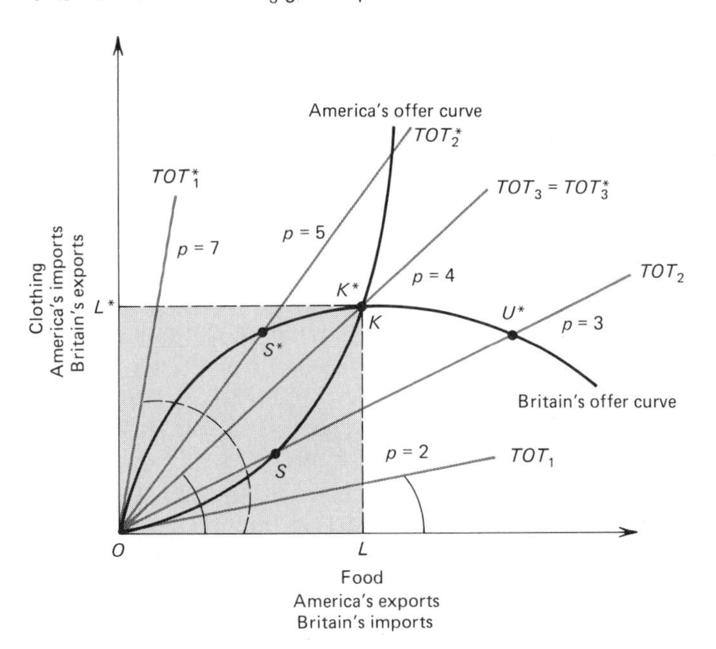

TOT_3, which now coincides with TOT_3^*. At $p = 4$, America exports OL units of food to Britain in exchange for OL^* units of British clothing, as shown by point K on America's offer curve. Britain's offer, given by K^*, matches America's offer, as evidenced by the fact that points K and K^* coincide. Thus, at the equilibrium terms of trade ($p = 4$), all markets clear and international equilibrium prevails.

The equilibrium terms of trade (that is, the relative price of food) lie between the autarkic prices of America and Britain. This is illustrated by the fact that terms-of-trade line $TOT_3 = TOT_3^*$ lies between terms-of-trade lines TOT_1 (giving America's autarkic price ratio) and TOT_1^* (giving Britain's autarkic price ratio).

The intersection of the two offer curves (point K or K^*) is the only point at which each country's desired imports are exactly matched by the other country's desired exports. For instance, at terms of trade $p = 3$, indicated by terms-of-trade line TOT_2, America's offer (S) is much smaller than Britain's offer (U^*). In this case, there will be an excess demand for food (because America is not willing to export as much food as Britain is willing to import), putting an upward pressure on the price of food. At the same time, there will be an excess supply of clothing (because America is not willing to import as much clothing as Britain is willing to export), putting a downward pressure on the price of clothing. Both of these pressures will cause the relative price of food to rise until international equilibrium is attained at K.

3-8 THE TERMS OF TRADE

The preceding analysis sheds much light on the significance of the concept of terms of trade in international equilibrium. The domestic employment of factors; the techniques of production; the distribution of income; the production, consumption, exporting, and importing of commodities—all depend on the terms of trade. No wonder, then, that economists as well as statisticians, policymakers, and politicians pay so much attention to this concept.

So far we have used the phrase "terms of trade" to mean the relative price of the exported commodity. For instance, in our earlier discussion, in which America imported clothing and exported food, America's terms of trade were defined as the relative price of food—that is, the ratio of the price of food to the price of clothing. As we have seen, the relative price of food (or America's terms of trade) shows the number of units of clothing that exchange in the international market for one unit of food. These terms of trade are often referred to as **commodity terms of trade** or **net barter terms of trade.**

In practice, each country exports and imports many commodities, not just one. For this reason, the price of exports is calculated as an index number of export prices. Similarly, the price of imports is calculated as an index number of import prices. Such export price and import price indices are regularly reported by the International Monetary Fund in its monthly *International Financial Statistics.* The net barter terms of trade are then equal to the ratio of the two indices:

$$\text{Terms of trade} = \frac{\text{index of export prices}}{\text{index of import prices}}$$

Table 3-1 presents data on the terms of trade of various countries for the years 1982–1985.

A rise in the statistical measure of the terms of trade of, say, America, is usually referred to as an "improvement" (or "favorable" movement) in its terms of trade. Similarly, a fall in America's terms of trade is referred to as a "deterioration" (or "unfavorable" movement) in its terms of trade. The idea, of course, is that America's terms of trade represent the number of units of imports that the nation can obtain per unit of exports. A rise in America's terms of trade, then, means that the nation can obtain more units of imports per unit of exports, and for this reason it is thought that America is better off. Similarly, a fall in America's terms of trade means that the nation gets fewer imports per unit of exports, and its welfare allegedly deteriorates. Such feelings are usually reinforced by a diagram, such as Figure 3-4, in which a terms-of-trade improvement apparently results in an increase in social welfare, and a terms-of-trade

TABLE 3-1 TERMS OF TRADE, 1982–1985
(1980 = 100)

	1982	1983	1984	1985
Argentina	89	96	97	88
Australia	98	97	95	90
Belgium	95	95	94	95
Brazil	95	87	103	87
Canada	95	97	94	92
France	97	99	100	103
Germany, Federal Republic of	97	99	96	98
Ghana	84	88	99	91
Greece	95	96	97	91
Hong Kong	110	109	109	110
India	104	111	107	115
Israel	93	94	84	95
Italy	95	98	96	97
Ivory Coast	91	92	101	94
Japan	103	106	109	113
Korea, Republic of	100	101	100	105
Malaysia	85	88	93	85
Mexico	110	98	100	98
Netherlands	102	101	102	104
Philippines	89	99	101	96
South Africa	87	86	86	85
Turkey	88	94	90	92
United Kingdom	100	100	99	100
United States	106	112	112	114

Source: The World Bank, *World Development Report 1986,* Oxford University Press, New York, 1986; ibid., *1987,* 1987.

deterioration gives rise to a reduction in social welfare. Unfortunately, the terms-of-trade measure is not a good index of social welfare. Any statements made on the basis of historical changes in a country's terms of trade, if not rejected offhand, must be scrutinized thoroughly before they are actually accepted.

A change in a country's terms of trade may reflect a change in either domestic or foreign economic behavior. When the terms of trade change as a result of foreign behavior (that is, a change in foreign tastes, technology, or factor endowments), then we must conclude on the basis of our earlier analysis (Section 3-3) that an improvement in the terms of trade is equivalent to an increase in American welfare and that a deterioration is equivalent to a reduction in social welfare.

Suppose, however, that the change in America's terms of trade is the result of a change in American economic conditions. In particular, suppose that as a result of tremendous advances in American technology, America can produce large amounts of food very cheaply. As a result, the American production-possibilities frontier shifts outward. Suppose further that this overabundance of food forces a reduction in the relative price of food in world markets. Such a reduction in the relative price of food is not unreasonable but should be expected from the normal operation of the **law of supply and demand.** Nevertheless, the reduction in the relative price of food will be registered by statisticians as an "unfavorable" change in America's terms of trade. Is America worse off because of the mere deterioration of its terms of trade? Such a hasty conclusion is not warranted. The outward shift in the American production-possibilities frontier must also be taken into consideration before a conclusion is reached. The outcome could go either way, as our analysis in Chapter 6 will show.

Conversely, suppose that a hard frost destroys a substantial percentage of the Brazilian coffee crop, as indeed was the case in 1963, 1969, 1972, and especially in 1975, when about half of the 1976 Brazilian coffee crop was destroyed. Because Brazil produces approximately one-third of the world's output, such crop destruction may lead to a substantial increase in the price of coffee. For instance, the 1975 frost led to a quadrupling of the price of coffee within a short period of time. Such an increase in the price of coffee will be registered by statisticians as a "favorable" change in Brazilian terms of trade. But whether Brazilian welfare improves or deteriorates depends not only on the rise of the terms of trade but also on the destruction of the Brazilian crop. Again the outcome could go either way.

3-9 EAST-WEST TRADE

It is generally agreed that international trade between the market-oriented economies of the West and the centrally planned economies of the Soviet bloc is mutually beneficial because such trade bargains are entered into voluntarily on both sides. Yet East-West trade faces many political and economic obstacles. In this section we discuss the difficulties that surround East-West trade; we also give a brief account of the recent Soviet-U.S. wheat deals.

Political Obstacles to East-West Trade

On balance, the East exports raw materials to the West in exchange for new technology and manufactured goods (such as machinery, consumer goods, chemical and building materials, and food). Relative to total world trade, however, East-West trade is much more important to the East than it is to the West.

The political obstacles to East-West trade are deeply rooted in the ideological differences between the two blocs and fluctuate with the general state of international relations. After long, unsuccessful efforts at détente (interrupted by the escalation of the Vietnam war), the visits of President Nixon to China and the USSR in 1972 generated an atmosphere of hope and optimism for improved trade relations between the East and the West. Subsequent developments, however, showed how elusive is the goal of peaceful cooperation between the two superpowers of the world. Concern about Soviet policy toward Jewish emigration, and about human rights generally, has led to U.S. restrictions (such as the 1978 cancellation of a computer sale, which the Soviets eventually replaced by a French one) and the continued denial of most-favored-nation status to the USSR and other East European countries. Soviet-U.S. relations worsened further following the Soviet invasion of Afghanistan, which prompted the American embargo on exports of grain and high-technology goods.

Some political observers are fearful of any serious dependence on, say, Soviet trade. They point to the USSR's sudden cutting of purchases of Icelandic fish in 1948 and of sales of oil to Israel in 1956. (Note, however, that the United States also abruptly reduced the Cuban sugar quota in 1960.)

In addition, many observers on both sides feel that any transaction benefiting the other side, the Enemy, is harmful to their side. Their recommendation is to further restrict East-West trade even if such trade brings direct economic benefits to their own side.

The political obstacles are formidable, but the potential mutual benefits of East-West trade are also high. One wonders if the world will ever be smart enough to throw away the guns and concentrate on peaceful cooperation and free international trade in the pursuit of economic welfare. Surely, the hope to abolish poverty and disease lies in peaceful cooperation, not in mistrust, treachery, hostility, and guns. The 1987 pact banning intermediate-range missiles is a hopeful sign of Soviet-U.S. cooperation as opposed to confrontation. Not unexpectedly, the Soviets are asking for the lifting of the U.S. ban on imports of Russian furs in exchange for U.S. exports of machinery to the Soviet Union.

Economic Obstacles to East-West Trade

We now turn to the economic obstacles to East-West trade, which are no less formidable than the political obstacles. In centrally planned economies, prices—the basis on which one shops—are primarily accounting devices. Unlike the prices that exist in market economies, the prices in the eastern bloc do not reflect opportunity costs; and only to a very limited extent do they serve as signaling devices in the allocation of resources. The latter is instead integrated with the planning mechanism, which seeks to achieve material balances.

For instance, for their own internal purposes, the USSR and other eastern-bloc countries have kept the prices of consumer goods artificially high and the prices of capital goods artificially low. As a result, foreigners are not allowed to trade freely on the basis of such artificial prices, nor can domestic residents buy and sell freely abroad. If such trade were allowed, it would be inefficient; it would also frustrate the main goals of the planners. For this reason, eastern-bloc countries conduct their international trade through foreign-trade organizations. Nevertheless, the function of these organizations is greatly hampered, among other things, by the fact that they cannot compare foreign prices to domestic prices, because the latter are not equal to opportunity costs.

Because of their emphasis on central planning, the leaders of eastern-bloc countries view foreign trade as an economic disturbance that interferes with the planning process. Thus their tendency is to leave no room for international trade in the long run. The foreign-trade organizations are apparently used as emergency devices by means of which the planners expect to correct through imports any deficiencies that may arise in some sectors, or to get rid of any occasional surpluses through exports. However, the full benefits of international trade can be attained only if it is allowed to become an integral part of planning instead of being used as a residuum.

The planning procedures of eastern-bloc countries render their currencies **inconvertible.** This means that foreigners cannot legally hold, for example, rubles and hence are not allowed to spend rubles freely; and similarly, Soviets are not free to use their rubles to buy foreign currencies. Such currency restrictions rule out **multilateral trade,** at least among eastern-bloc countries (East-East trade). For instance, if Czechoslovakia sells tractors to the USSR, it cannot use the rubles it receives to pay for imports from Romania. Instead, the Czechs must use their rubles to purchase whatever commodities the Soviet foreign-trade organization has to sell. The restriction of multilateral trade reduces the scope of potential benefits from East-East trade. However, multilateral exchanges are still possible in East-West trade because the latter can be conducted with convertible western currencies. For instance, the USSR may export natural gas to France in exchange for French francs, and later use the francs to purchase machinery from West Germany.

Another obstacle to East-West trade is the difficulty the East European economies face in expanding their exports fast enough to keep pace with their import needs. This problem is primarily due to the low quality of Eastern exports, particularly consumer goods.

The Soviet-U.S. Wheat Deals

The USSR is the world's largest wheat producer. For instance, in 1980 the USSR produced about 98 million metric tons of wheat, while the United States produced a little over 64 million metric tons. Historically, the USSR has been a major exporter of wheat, but since the early 1970s, the country has turned into a net grain importer due to increased domestic consumption.

Soviet grain imports are particularly heavy whenever the weather causes the Soviet crop to be bad. This was the case in 1972 when the Soviets purchased about one-fourth of the U.S. wheat crop. This unprecedented Soviet-U.S. wheat deal disrupted the U.S. economy, and it was later suspected that the Soviets had taken advantage of their monopoly of information about Soviet crop conditions. The feeling was that the Soviets, knowing that their own harvest would be very poor, quietly purchased large amounts of grain at low prices. This charge was not justified, however, because the Soviet purchases actually unfolded over several months and their intended magnitude was known to the U.S. Department of Agriculture and major grain dealers when most contracts were negotiated.

What actually permitted the Soviets to enjoy a continuing bargain on U.S. grain was the perverse and obsolete U.S. policy. To support farm incomes, U.S. agricultural policy restricted the number of acres of land that farmers could use to plant wheat, and this **acreage control** was allowed to continue even after it became known to be no longer necessary. In addition, the U.S. Department of Agriculture failed to remove its obsolete subsidy on the export of "surplus" grain even when a surplus no longer existed. As a result, U.S. taxpayers' money was used to assist the Soviets to purchase U.S. grain at prices that were much lower than those paid by U.S. consumers.

A few years later, the United States and the USSR negotiated a five-year bilateral grain trade agreement (1977–1981) according to which the USSR was to purchase at least 6 million metric tons of wheat and corn each year and the United States was to permit purchases of up to 8 million metric tons a year, with larger purchases requiring new negotiations.

Following the invasion of Afghanistan, however, the United States on January 5, 1980, imposed an embargo on exports of grain and high technology to the USSR. In addition, the United States tried to persuade other friendly nations to avoid supplying the Soviets with the needed grain. But the Soviets were able after all to find grain from other sources, such as Argentina, Canada, and France. U.S. farmers also recouped part of their lost Soviet sales by exporting wheat to those countries that had increased their sales to the USSR. Indeed, there is evidence that some U.S. grain was shipped to third-party countries and re-exported to the USSR. So the U.S. embargo did not really work. President Ronald Reagan lifted the embargo in 1981 and renewed the five-year grain trade agreement in 1983.

3-10 SUMMARY

1 The fundamental concepts of opportunity cost and social indifference form the basis for the neoclassical theory of international values.

2 Linear production-possibilities frontiers imply *constant* opportunity costs. *Increasing* opportunity costs, illustrated by production-possibilities frontiers that are concave to the origin, offer a better description of reality. In addition to the fact that many industries operate under increasing (not constant) costs, increasing opportunity costs do not lead to the unrealistic situation of complete specialization (whereas constant opportunity costs do).

3 Increasing opportunity costs can be explained in one of two ways: (a) by invoking the product specificity of factors or (b) by observing that technology is such that different commodities use homogeneous factors in different proportions.

4 The production-possibilities frontier shows the maximal combinations of outputs that the economy can produce. It depends on two fundamental data: (a) factor supplies (or endowments) and (b) technology (or production functions).

5 The neoclassical theory of international trade makes two simplifying assumptions: (a) that society's tastes can be summarized by a well-behaved social indifference map and (b) that society tries to reach the highest social indifference curve.

6 There are only a few special cases in which the use of social indifference curves can be made rigorous. In general, social indifference curves do not exist, and their continued use is justified only by the fact that they give rise to results that are qualitatively similar to those derived by more rigorous methods.

7 In a closed economy, general equilibrium occurs at the point where the production-possibilities frontier becomes tangent to the highest possible social indifference curve. The equilibrium commodity price ratio is equal to both the marginal rate of transformation (that is, the slope of the production frontier) and the marginal rate of substitution in consumption (that is, the slope of the social indifference curve) at the equilibrium point.

8 As in the Ricardian model, comparative advantage is decided on the basis of the opportunity costs that prevail in each trading country before trade. However, with increasing opportunity costs, pretrade costs cannot be inferred from the production-possibilities frontier without full information about demand.

9 The opportunity to trade enables an open economy to separate its domestic consumption from its domestic production. In particular, an open economy (a) maximizes its national income by producing at the point where its marginal rate of transformation equals the international price ratio and (b) maximizes its welfare by consuming at the point of tangency between its consumption-possibilities frontier (that is, the community budget line passing through the optimal production point) and the highest social indifference curve, a point that normally lies beyond the production frontier.

10 The total gain from trade is divided into a consumption gain (or gain from international exchange), which is normally positive, and a production gain (or gain from specialization), which could be zero (but never negative) in a backward economy that lacks the capacity to transform its autarkic production bundle into a more profitable bundle.

11 The offer curve is an ingenious device (developed by Alfred Marshall) that summarizes the offers of a country at alternative terms of trade. When the offer curve slopes upward, the country's demand for imports is elastic; when it slopes downward (or bends backward, as happens when imports are measured along the vertical axis), the demand for imports is inelastic. The slope of the offer curve at the origin gives the country's autarkic price ratio.

12 International equilibrium occurs when world supply equals world demand in every market, or alternatively when each country's desired imports match exactly the other country's desired exports (balanced trade). Graphically, international equilibrium occurs at the intersection of the offer curves of the trading countries, with the slope of the terms-of-trade line (which connects the origin with the equilibrium point) giving the equilibrium terms of trade.

13 Because countries export and import many commodities, economists and statisticians measure a country's terms of trade by the ratio of an index of the country's export prices to an index of the country's import prices.

14 An improvement (deterioration) in a country's terms of trade is unambiguously equivalent to an increase (decrease) in that country's welfare only when the change in the terms of trade is due to a change in foreign behavior (such as a change in foreign tastes or technology). When the change in the terms of trade is due to a change in domestic conditions, its effect on domestic welfare cannot always be inferred from the direction of change in the terms of trade.

PROBLEMS[1]

1 The production possibilities of America are summarized in the following table:

	Output combinations				
	A	B	C	D	E
Commodity X	0	20	40	60	80
Commodity Y	100	90	70	40	0

a Draw the production-possibilities frontier of America. (Note: Plot points *A* through *E* and connect them by means of straight-line segments. The implicit assumption is that opportunity costs remain constant between any pair of adjacent points.)

b Determine America's optimum production point for each of the following world price ratios (p_x/p_y): 0.2, 0.8, 1.1, 1.75, and 30.

c Suppose that America consumes commodities in the fixed proportion $1X{:}1Y$ irrespective of prices. If the world price ratio (p_x/p_y) is 0.6, what will America produce, consume, export, and import? Give precise quantities.

2 Germany and France produce wine and cloth under increasing opportunity costs. At their respective autarkic equilibriums, the marginal costs of production are given in the following table:

	Germany	France
Wine	2 marks	4 francs
Cloth	6 marks	24 francs

a Which country has a comparative advantage in the production of wine? In the production of cloth?

b Under free-trade equilibrium, Germany exports 100 units of cloth in exchange for 500 units of French wine. Assuming that the marginal cost of German cloth rises to 7.5 marks and that 1 mark exchanges for 3 francs, determine the equilibrium prices of wine and cloth in France (in francs).

3 Canada and Italy produce typewriters and wheat under increasing opportunity costs. Both countries share the same production-possibilities frontier. However, Italy consumes more bushels of wheat per typewriter than Canada at all conceivable price ratios.

a In which country are typewriters relatively cheaper under autarky?

b Under free trade, what is the relationship between Italy's and Canada's structure of production?

c Which country exports wheat?

d Illustrate your conclusions graphically.

[1]Problems that appear with asterisks are more difficult.

***4** Korea and Taiwan trade two commodities (X and Y). Their offer curves are given by the following equations:

$$Y = 10X^2 + 5X \qquad \text{(Korea's offer curve)}$$

$$Y = -5X^2 + 20X \qquad \text{(Taiwan's offer curve)}$$

a Determine the equilibrium terms of trade and each country's exports and imports.
b Determine the autarkic price ratios of Korea and Taiwan. Then show that the equilibrium terms of trade lie between the autarkic price ratios of the two countries.
c Illustrate your results graphically.

SUGGESTED READING

Chacholiades, M. (1978). *International Trade Theory and Policy.* McGraw-Hill Book Company, New York, chaps. 4–7.

———(1986). *Microeconomics.* Macmillan Publishing Company, New York.

Edgeworth, F. Y. (1894). "The Theory of International Values." *Economic Journal,* vol. 4, pp. 35–50, 424–443, and 606–638. Reprinted in F. Y. Edgeworth, *Papers Relating to Political Economy,* Macmillan and Company, London, 1925.

———(1905). "Review of Henry Cunynghame's *A Geometrical Political Economy.*" *Economic Journal,* vol. 15, pp. 62–71.

Haberler, G. (1936). *The Theory of International Trade.* W. Hodge and Company, London, chap. 12.

Leontief, W. W. (1933). "The Use of Indifference Curves in the Analysis of Foreign Trade." *Quarterly Journal of Economics,* vol. 47, pp. 493–501. Reprinted in H. S. Ellis and L. A. Metzler (eds.), American Economic Association *Readings in the Theory of International Trade,* Richard D. Irwin, Inc., Homewood, Ill., 1950.

Lerner, A. P. (1932). "The Diagrammatic Representation of Cost Conditions in International Trade." *Economica,* vol. 12, pp. 346–356. Reprinted in A. P. Lerner, *Essays in Economic Analysis,* Macmillan and Company, London, 1953.

———(1934). "The Diagrammatic Representation of Demand Conditions in International Trade." *Economica,* N.S. 1, pp. 319–334. Reprinted in A. P. Lerner, *Essays in Economic Analysis,* Macmillan and Company, London, 1953.

Marshall, A. (1879). *The Pure Theory of Foreign Trade.* (Printed for private circulation in 1879; reprinted in 1930.) London School of Economics and Political Science, London.

———(1923). *Money, Credit, and Commerce.* Macmillan and Company, London.

Meade, J. E. (1952). *A Geometry of International Trade.* George Allen and Unwin, London, chaps. 1–4.

Samuelson, P. A. (1956). "Social Indifference Curves." *Quarterly Journal of Economics,* vol. 70, pp. 1–22.

Viner, J. (1937). *Studies in the Theory of International Trade.* Harper and Brothers, New York, chaps. 7 and 9.

CHAPTER 4

THE HECKSCHER-OHLIN MODEL

What are the ultimate determinants of comparative advantage? Neither Ricardo nor Torrens bothered to answer this question. In their theory, comparative advantage depended on comparative differences in labor productivity (that is, differences in technology), but they did not explain the basis for these differences. In Ricardo's analysis the implicit reason was climatic differences.

About a century after the Ricardo-Torrens contribution, the Swedish economists Eli Heckscher (1879–1952) and Bertil Ohlin (1899–1979) offered an exegesis that has become, since the 1930s, the orthodox explanation of the ultimate cause of international trade. Their basic idea rests on two premises: **(1) Commodities differ in their factor requirements. (2) Countries differ in their factor endowments.** According to Heckscher and Ohlin, **a country has a comparative advantage in those commodities that use its abundant factors intensively.** This is why labor-abundant countries, such as India, Korea, and Taiwan, export footwear, rugs, textiles, and other labor-intensive commodities; and land-abundant countries, such as Argentina, Australia, and Canada, export meat, wheat, wool, and other land-intensive commodities.

This chapter discusses the standard **Heckscher-Ohlin model,** also known as the **factor endowment theory.** It elucidates the new concepts of **factor intensity** and **factor abundance,** and explains the main propositions (or theorems) of the model.

4-1 THE BASIC ASSUMPTIONS OF THE HECKSCHER-OHLIN MODEL

Like all theories, the standard Heckscher-Ohlin model rests on several simplifying assumptions that are conveniently summarized in this section for easy reference. (Not all of these assumptions are necessary for every proposition of the Heckscher-Ohlin model.) A brief explanation also follows each assumption.

1 *Number of Countries, Factors, and Commodities:* *There are two countries (America and Britain); each country is endowed with two homogeneous factors of production (labor and capital) and produces two commodities (cloth and steel).*

Because of this assumption, the standard Heckscher-Ohlin model is often referred to as the 2 × 2 × 2 model. This is the smallest "even" model in which the numbers of countries, factors, and commodities are equal. Extending the model to more complicated cases is not easy. In general, the results obtained from larger models do not have the clear, commonsense interpretation that distinguishes the standard model.

2 *Technology:* *Technology is the same in both countries.*

This assumption means that the production function of cloth is the same in Britain as in America. If factor prices were the same in both countries, the British producers of cloth would use exactly the same quantities of labor and capital for each yard of cloth as their American counterparts. The same holds true for the production function of steel.

Ohlin appears to have taken it for granted that production functions are the same everywhere. He based his assumption on the empirical observation that the *laws of physics* are everywhere the same. [In the words of Ohlin (1933, p. 14), "the physical conditions of production... are everywhere the same."] But the laws of physics do not coincide with the economically relevant production functions. The latter incorporate only the *known* efficient techniques. At any one time, the technical know-how cannot be expected to be the same in all countries, especially in a period of incessant invention.

Because the theory of international trade is a long-run, comparative-statics theory, there are those who argue that the only proper assumption to make is that knowledge available to one country is available also to another—sooner or later new inventions in one country are disseminated throughout the rest of the world. This is a powerful argument. The only trouble is that when technical progress is continuous and systematically concentrated in only a small number of countries, the rest of the world appears to be always technologically backward—the other countries never have the time to catch up. To argue that in the long run technical knowledge must be the same in all countries is to ignore an interesting and most important aspect of international economic life. Whether or not production functions are identical between countries is, at bottom, an empirical question.

In the next chapter, we explore the consequences of dropping this assumption.

3 *Constant Returns to Scale:* *Each commodity is produced under constant returns to scale.*

The meaning of the assumption of constant returns to scale is clarified in Appendix 3. Briefly, the meaning of the assumption is that a proportionate change in all inputs causes output to change by the same percentage as all inputs. Constant returns to scale make more sense for an industry than for a single firm.

4 *Strong Factor Intensity:* *One commodity, say, cloth, is always labor intensive relative to the second commodity (steel).*

This assumption means that at the same factor prices, cloth uses more units of labor per unit of capital than steel; or steel uses more capital per worker than cloth. Thus, commodities can be ranked by factor intensity. The meaning of this assumption is clarified further in the following section.

5 *Incomplete Specialization:* *Neither country specializes completely in the production of only one commodity.*

This assumption means that after the introduction of free trade, neither America nor Britain specializes completely in any one commodity (cloth or steel). In a deeper sense, this assumption suggests that the two nations are of approximately the same size, or that neither nation is too small relative to the other.

6 *Perfect Competition:* *Perfect competition rules in all commodity and factor markets.*

The assumption of perfect competition rules out monopolistic and oligopolistic market structures as well as wage and price rigidities. In a perfectly competitive market, all buyers and sellers (of a commodity or factor) are price takers; that is, each one of them is too small to exert individually any appreciable influence on the price. Perfect competitors are also completely informed about the prices that prevail in all parts of the market with the result that the same price holds everywhere (**law of one price**). In addition, prices are determined by supply and demand; and in the long run, commodity prices are equal to their respective costs of production.

7 *Factor Mobility:* *Factors are perfectly mobile within each country but perfectly immobile between countries.*

Like Ricardo, Heckscher and Ohlin draw a sharp distinction between internal and external factor mobility. While they permit the maximum degree of factor mobility between industries within the same country (**internal factor mobility**), they assume that institutional arrangements in the world economy are such that neither labor nor capital can migrate from one nation to the other (**external factor immobility**).

Internal factor mobility ensures that the same wage rate and return to capital obtain in each sector of the nation—factors move quickly and costlessly from a sector where earnings are low to another sector where earnings are high until earnings are everywhere the same. External factor immobility, however, rules out the possibility of eliminating international differences in factor earnings by means of factor migration. For instance, Mexico's workers are not allowed to work in the United States even though Mexican wages are only a fraction of U.S. wages. Because of external factor immobility, such international differences in earnings can persist indefinitely.

8 *Similarity of Tastes:* *Tastes are largely similar (but not necessarily identical) between countries.*

This assumption means that if America and Britain have the same income and face the same commodity prices, then both nations would consume approximately the same basket of commodities. Empirical studies do suggest that there is considerable similarity in demand functions among countries. Whether such similarity is the result of trade itself and the strong **demonstration effect** that easy communication between countries gives rise to is a question that need not concern us at the moment. For our purpose, we shall assume that the tastes of both nations are given by the *same* **social indifference map.**

9 ***Free Trade:*** *World trade is free from any impediments, such as tariffs, quotas, and exchange control.*

10 ***Transportation Costs:*** *Transportation costs are zero.*

The implication of the last two assumptions (free trade and zero transportation costs) is that commodity trade equalizes commodity prices between nations. The relative commodity prices that prevail in America must prevail in Britain also.

We conclude this section with a word of caution. Students are often bothered by seemingly unrealistic assumptions. But *all theory is an abstraction of reality.* We just cannot criticize the simplifying assumptions of a theory only on the grounds that they are not exact replicas of reality. We must always remember that mere observations of real-world phenomena are not enough to explain why and how these phenomena occurred, just as watching a television show does not explain how the hidden mechanism of the television set works. Explanation is provided only by theory. Without theory, we cannot understand or explain how events are linked together. But theory is based, of necessity, on simplifying assumptions.

4-2 THE MEANING OF FACTOR INTENSITY

For its logical validity, the standard Heckscher-Ohlin model requires that one commodity (cloth) be labor intensive relative to the other commodity (steel). What does the term "labor intensive" mean?

Fixed Coefficients of Production

Consider the simple case of **fixed coefficients of production.** Suppose that it takes 6 units of labor and 2 units of capital to produce 1 yard of cloth and 8 units of labor and 4 units of capital to produce 1 ton of steel. All this information is summarized in Table 4-1. Assume that these are the only techniques known. Which is the labor-intensive commodity?

TABLE 4-1 FACTOR INTENSITY

	Inputs per unit of output	
	Labor	**Capital**
Cloth	6	2
Steel	8	4

Do not fall into the trap of arguing that steel is labor intensive relative to cloth because each ton of steel requires more units of labor than each yard of cloth (that is, 8 > 6). Such a comparison is meaningless because the units of measurement (yards and tons) are arbitrary. For instance, suppose that cloth is sold in packages of 10 yards, and we take "a package" to be our new unit of measuring cloth. Then it would take 60 units of labor and 20 units of capital to produce 1 package of cloth; and the absolute amount of labor embodied in 1 package of cloth (60) would now exceed the absolute amount of labor embodied in 1 ton of steel (8). Evidently, the absolute factor quantities embodied in each unit of output (that is, the absolute coefficients of production) are just as arbitrary as the units of measurement. Thus the absolute coefficients of production *cannot* be used to rank commodities. What is important is the *proportion* in which labor and capital are used, not their absolute quantities.

Cloth is labor intensive relative to steel because, *per unit of capital,* the production of cloth requires more units of labor than the production of steel; that is, the **labor-capital ratio** is higher in cloth than in steel ($6 \div 2 > 8 \div 4$). Note that the labor-capital ratio is independent of the units of measurement. For instance, whether we measure cloth in yards or in packages of 10 yards the labor-capital ratio will continue to be the same: $6 \div 2 = 60 \div 20 = 3$.

Factor intensity, like comparative advantage, is a relative term. When cloth is found to be labor intensive relative to steel, it automatically follows that steel is capital intensive relative to cloth; that is, steel must use more units of capital per worker than cloth, or the **capital-labor ratio** must be higher in steel than in cloth. For instance, in terms of the example of Table 4-1, steel is capital intensive relative to cloth because $4 \div 8 > 2 \div 6$.

Variable Coefficients of Production

Suppose now that there are many known techniques for producing cloth and steel. How do we define labor intensity or capital intensity, and how do we decide which is the labor-intensive commodity? Even though there may be many techniques for each commodity, we can rest assured that perfect competition will always force all producers in each industry to choose only one technique: the *optimal* technique (that is, the technique that minimizes cost). It is these optimal techniques that we must compare. Once a pair of optimal techniques is chosen, we can construct a table similar to Table 4-1 and then proceed to rank cloth and steel in terms of labor intensity as before.

How are the optimal techniques selected? We already know the answer from elementary microeconomics. It is also summarized in Appendix 3. For any given wage-rent ratio (w/r), a commodity's optimal coefficients of production are given by the point on the unit isoquant at which the marginal rate of technical substitution of labor for capital is equal to the given wage-rent ratio (w/r), as illustrated in Figure 4-1. Curve SS' is the unit isoquant of the steel industry. When the wage-rent ratio is equal to 2 (as shown by isocost line MN), the optimal coefficients of production for steel are 3 units of labor and 6 units of cap-

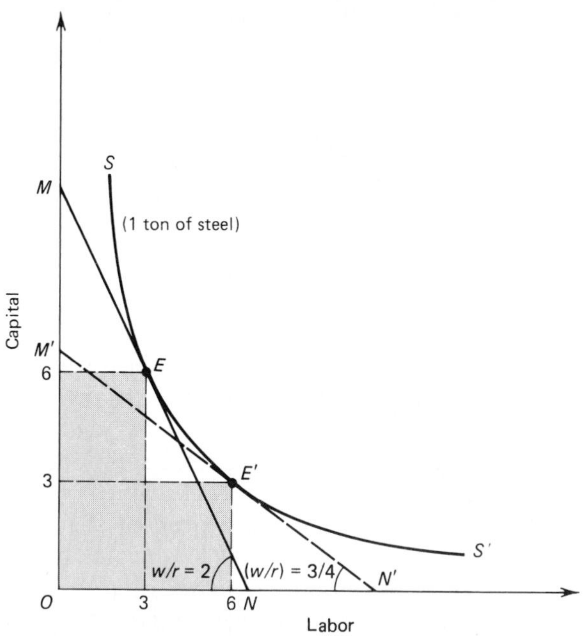

FIGURE 4-1 **The choice of optimal techniques.** The optimal coefficients coincide with the coordinates of that point on the unit isoquant at which the marginal rate of technical substitution of labor for capital equals the given wage-rent ratio, as illustrated by points E and E'.

ital (as shown by point E). Thus the labor-capital ratio is $3 \div 6 = 0.5$. In a similar fashion, we can determine the labor-capital ratio for cloth. Then we can compare the two labor-capital ratios to decide which is the labor-intensive commodity. Note that in determining the optimal techniques, we must use the *same* wage-rent ratio for both industries.

There remains one final problem. *A commodity (say, cloth) may be labor intensive at some wage-rent ratios but capital intensive at others.* Return to Figure 4-1. When the wage-rent ratio falls from 2 to ¾ (as shown by dashed isocost line $M'N'$), the optimal technique shifts from E to E' and steel's labor intensity rises from 0.5 (that is, $3 \div 6$) to 2 (that is, $6 \div 3$), as steel producers substitute labor for capital. Suppose, however, that factor substitutability is much more difficult in the production of cloth than in steel. As the wage-rent ratio falls from 2 to ¾, assume that cloth's labor intensity rises from, say, 1.2 to 1.8 (not shown). In this example, factor intensities are reversed: Cloth is labor intensive relative to steel at $w/r = 2$ (because $1.2 > 0.5$) but capital intensive at $w/r = 3/4$ (because $1.8 < 2$). Such **factor intensity reversals** can potentially ruin the Heckscher-Ohlin model. The **strong factor intensity assumption** (assumption 4 in Section 4-1) rules out the possibility of factor intensity reversals.

Concluding Remarks

We can unequivocally classify cloth as labor intensive relative to steel only when the labor-capital ratio is higher in cloth than in steel at *all* wage-rent ratios. *There is no a priori reason that this should be so.* It is only an assumption (the strong factor intensity assumption). In Chapter 5 and Appendix 7 we shall explore the implications of dropping the strong factor intensity assumption. In the meantime, we shall assume that cloth is labor intensive relative to steel at all wage-rent ratios.

4-3 FACTOR ABUNDANCE

Another concept that needs further clarification is factor abundance. On what basis do we classify countries as labor abundant or capital abundant? Basically, two criteria can be used for this purpose: **physical abundance** and **economic abundance.**

The physical criterion determines factor abundance on the basis of the physical quantities of labor and capital available in various countries. According to the physical criterion, Britain is said to be labor abundant relative to America if Britain is endowed with more units of labor (or workers) *per unit of capital.* The important consideration is not whether Britain's labor force is absolutely larger than America's, but whether Britain's overall *labor-capital ratio* is greater than America's.

The economic criterion classifies countries as labor abundant or capital abundant on the basis of their autarkic equilibrium wage-rent ratios. According to the economic criterion, Britain is labor abundant relative to America if in their isolated autarkic equilibrium states, labor is relatively cheaper in Britain than in America (that is, if Britain's wage-rent ratio is lower than America's).

What is the major difference between the two criteria of factor abundance? The physical criterion is based solely on supply, ignoring completely the influence on demand. The economic criterion, however, uses both supply and demand influences—equilibrium factor prices, like commodity prices, are determined by both supply and demand. In general, demand conditions could outweigh supply conditions with the result that the two criteria might give rise to contradictory classifications. For instance, suppose that Britain's labor-capital ratio is greater than America's, but British consumers have a much stronger bias than American consumers toward the consumption of labor-intensive commodities. Britain's strong consumption bias toward labor-intensive commodities leads to a strong **derived demand** for British labor. It is not inconceivable, then, for British labor to be relatively more expensive in autarky than American labor even though Britain is by assumption labor abundant according to the physical criterion.

In the standard Heckscher-Ohlin model, the assumption that tastes are largely similar between countries eliminates the possibility of contradiction between the two criteria. Any difference in the autarkic wage-rent ratios of America and Britain can be attributed only to differences in factor endowments.

Thus, in the standard Heckscher-Ohlin model we can judge factor abundance on the basis of either criterion.

Finally, observe that factor abundance also is a relative concept. When Britain is found to be labor abundant relative to America (on the basis of either criterion), it must be true that America is capital abundant relative to Britain.

4-4 THE MAIN PROPOSITIONS OF THE HECKSCHER-OHLIN MODEL

The gist of the standard Heckscher-Ohlin model can be summarized in four theorems: the **Heckscher-Ohlin theorem,** the **factor-price equalization theorem,** the **Stolper-Samuelson theorem,** and the **Rybczynski theorem.** This section formulates each of these theorems accurately. The rest of the chapter explains the meaning and implications of the theorems, explores their validity, and provides further insights into the internal structure and functioning of the Heckscher-Ohlin model.

Heckscher-Ohlin Theorem: **A country has a comparative advantage in the commodity which uses intensively the country's abundant factor.** For instance, Britain (a labor-abundant country) will have a comparative advantage in—and will export—cloth (a labor-intensive commodity). Similarly, America (a capital-abundant country) will have a comparative advantage in—and will export—steel (a capital-intensive commodity).

Factor-Price Equalization Theorem: **Free trade equalizes factor rewards (real rentals) between countries and thus serves as a substitute for external factor mobility.** The factor-price equalization theorem is indeed a remarkable result. It asserts that even in the absence of factor migration between countries, free commodity trade leads to an international equilibrium state in which workers earn the same real wage rate and capital earns the same real rental rate in both America and Britain.

Stolper-Samuelson Theorem: **An increase in the relative price of a commodity raises, in terms of both commodities, the real reward of the factor used intensively in production of the commodity and reduces, in terms of both commodities, the real reward of the other factor.** For instance, an increase in the relative price of cloth (a labor-intensive commodity) raises the real wage rate in terms of cloth and steel and lowers the real rental rate for capital services in terms of cloth and steel.

Rybczynski Theorem: **When the coefficients of production are given and factor supplies are fully employed, an expansion in the endowment of one factor of production raises the output of the commodity that uses the expanded factor intensively and reduces the output of the other commodity.** For instance, given the labor and capital requirements for cloth and steel, an expansion in the supply of labor will raise the output of cloth (a labor-intensive commodity) and will lower the output of steel (a capital-intensive commodity).

4-5 THE RYBCZYNSKI THEOREM

We begin with the Rybczynski theorem because it is basic to the functioning of the Heckscher-Ohlin model. In this chapter we need the Rybczynski theorem for illustrating the influence of factor endowments on the shape of the production-possibilities frontier—a result which is fundamental in proving the Heckscher-Ohlin theorem. We use it again in Chapter 6 to show how labor growth and capital accumulation affect the terms of trade. The proof of the Rybczynski theorem is rather simple because it involves a single economy.

Factor Endowments and the Production-Possibilities Frontier

Suppose that 1 yard of cloth requires 4 units of labor plus 1 unit of capital and 1 ton of steel requires 2 units of labor and 3 units of capital, as summarized in Table 4-2. Thus cloth is labor intensive relative to steel because $4 \div 1 > 2 \div 3$. Assume further that the economy is endowed with 900 units of labor and 600 units of capital. Given these labor and capital requirements as well as the supplies of labor and capital, we can derive the economy's production-possibilities frontier, as shown in Figure 4-2.

If the economy had an unlimited supply of capital, it would be able to produce along **labor constraint** *JG*, which is similar to a Ricardian production-possibilities frontier. Thus, employing all its labor ($900L$) in the production of cloth, it would produce 225 yards (that is, $900 \div 4$). Employing all its labor in the production of steel, it could produce 450 tons (that is, $900 \div 2$). By allocating some labor to cloth and some to steel, it would produce output combinations lying on *JG*.

If the economy had an unlimited supply of labor, it would be able to produce along **capital constraint** *MH*, which is similar to the labor constraint except that the roles of labor and capital are reversed. For instance, by using all its capital ($600K$) to make steel, the economy could produce 200 tons; by using all its capital to make cloth, it could produce 600 yards; and by dividing its capital between steel and cloth, it could produce output combinations lying on *MH*.

When the supplies of labor and capital are limited, then both constraints become *binding* and the production-possibilities frontier coincides with the heavy kinked line *JEH*. The economy cannot produce beyond *JE* because of a shortage of labor, and it cannot produce beyond *EH* because of a shortage of capital. But

TABLE 4-2 TECHNOLOGY

	Inputs per unit of output	
	Labor	**Capital**
Cloth	4	1
Steel	2	3

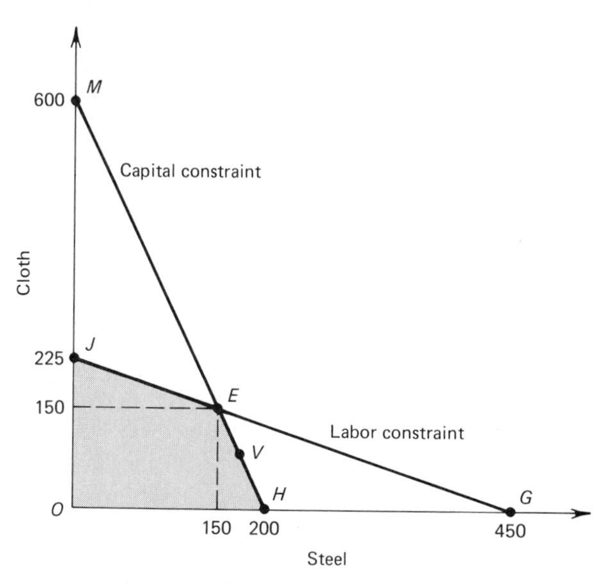

FIGURE 4-2 **Derivation of the production-possibilities frontier.** If the economy had an unlimited supply of capital (labor), it would be able to produce along the labor constraint *JG* (capital constraint *MH*). When the supplies of both factors are limited, both constraints become binding and the production frontier coincides with the heavy kinked line *JEH.* Because steel is capital intensive relative to cloth, the capital constraint is steeper than the labor frontier.

along *JE* some capital remains idle (and the return to capital necessarily drops to zero). Along *EH* some workers remain unemployed (and the wage rate drops to zero). The only point at which both factors are fully employed (with positive rewards) is the intersection, *E,* of the two constraints.

In Figure 4-2, the capital constraint is steeper than the labor constraint. This is no accident. Rather, it is a reflection of the fact that steel (the commodity measured horizontally) is capital intensive relative to cloth. To understand why this is so, assume that the economy is currently at full-employment point *E,* and let the economy increase the output of steel by moving to a point such as *V.* Capital will remain fully employed (because *V* lies *on* the capital constraint), but some workers will become unemployed (because *V* lies inside the labor constraint). The increase in steel has absorbed all the capital, but *not* all the workers, released by the decrease in cloth production. This means that steel uses more capital per worker than cloth; that is, steel is capital intensive relative to cloth.

Illustration of the Rybczynski Theorem

We are now ready to illustrate the Rybczynski theorem. Consider Figure 4-3, which is similar to Figure 4-2. Start at point *E,* at which both factors are fully employed. Suppose that labor grows from $900L$ to $1{,}200L$. How do the full-employment outputs of cloth and steel change? The answer is simple. The labor constraint shifts outward in a parallel fashion from JG to $J'G'$, and the production-possibilities frontier becomes $J'E'H$. The full-employment point moves from E to E'. The output of cloth (the labor-intensive commodity) rises from 150 to 240 yards, while the output of steel (the capital-intensive commodity) *falls* from 150 to 120 tons. Thus the prediction of the Rybczynski theorem is borne out.

Note that as labor grows, the output of the labor-intensive commodity must expand to absorb the extra supply of labor. Because labor must be combined with capital and the supply of capital remains fixed by assumption, the output of the capital-intensive commodity must decrease absolutely in order to release the necessary amount of capital.

Observe also that as labor grows, the production-possibilities frontier bulges out in the direction of the labor-intensive commodity. This point becomes important in the next section.

4-6 THE HECKSCHER-OHLIN THEOREM

In this section, we discuss the Heckscher-Ohlin theorem; namely, the proposition that a country exports the commodity that intensively uses its abundant

FIGURE 4-3 **The Rybczynski theorem.** As labor increases from $900L$ to $1{,}200L$, the labor constraint shifts from JG to $J'G'$, displacing the production frontier from JEH to $J'E'H$. The full-employment point moves from E to E', the output of cloth (labor-intensive commodity) rises from 150 to 240 yards, and the output of steel falls from 150 to 120 tons.

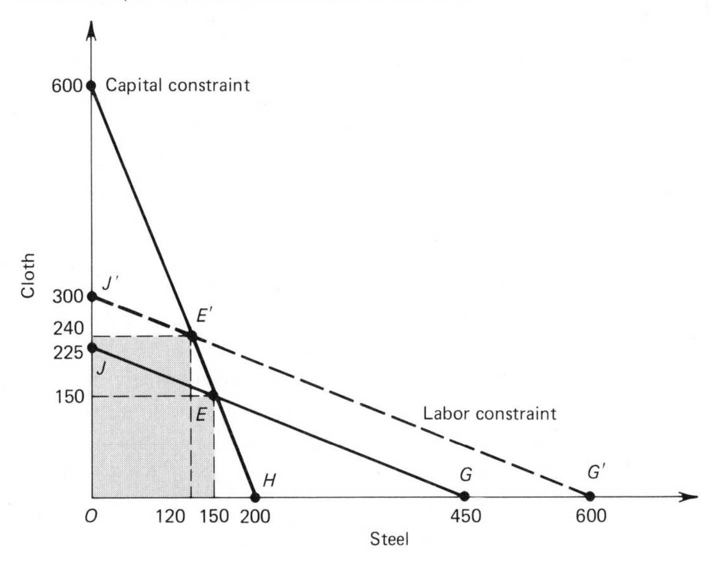

factor. We begin with some brief introductory remarks on the causes of international trade. Then we use the production model of the previous section (where the labor and capital requirements are given) to illustrate the Heckscher-Ohlin theorem. Finally, we generalize our results by allowing many production techniques for each commodity.

The Cause of International Trade

In Chapters 2 and 3 we learned that the immediate cause of trade is the difference between the pretrade price ratios of America and Britain. We also learned that the pretrade prices depend on the production-possibilities frontiers and social indifference maps (or tastes) of the trading countries. Since the production-possibilities frontiers depend, in turn, on technology (production functions) and factor endowments, the ultimate determinants of the structure of trade can be traced back to differences in the three fundamental sets of data of the countries involved: **factor endowments, technology,** and **tastes.** The Heckscher-Ohlin theory assumes that technology and tastes are similar between countries and attributes comparative advantage to differences in factor endowments.

A Single Production Technique

The Heckscher-Ohlin theorem is illustrated in Figure 4-4. America and Britain have identical demand conditions, represented by social indifference curves 1, 2, and 3. They also share the same technology. As in Section 4-5, we assume that there is a single technique for producing cloth and a single technique for producing steel. (It may be convenient, but not necessary, to utilize the technology summarized in Table 4-2.) The two countries differ only in their factor endowments. America has a larger stock of capital than Britain, and Britain has a larger labor force than America. As a result of the assumed divergence in their factor endowments, America's production-possibilities frontier, JQH, is skewed along the horizontal axis because steel is the capital-intensive commodity; and Britain's production-possibilities frontier, $J^*Q^*H^*$, is skewed along the vertical axis because cloth is the labor-intensive commodity. [Note: Given America's production-possibilities frontier JQH, we can obtain Britain's frontier by means of two successive applications of the Rybczynski theorem: (1) Increase the labor force, causing the labor constraint to shift from JQ to J^*Q^*; and (2) decrease the stock of capital, displacing the capital constraint from QH to Q^*H^*.]

In autarky, America attains equilibrium at R, where its production-possibilities frontier touches social indifference curve 1. Britain produces and consumes at Q^*, where its production-possibilities frontier touches social indifference curve 1 also. (For simplicity, we assume that before trade both countries attain the same social indifference curve.) In America the relative price of steel is given by the slope of social indifference curve 1 at R, and in Britain by the slope of the same indifference curve at Q^*. Thus, the relative price of steel (the

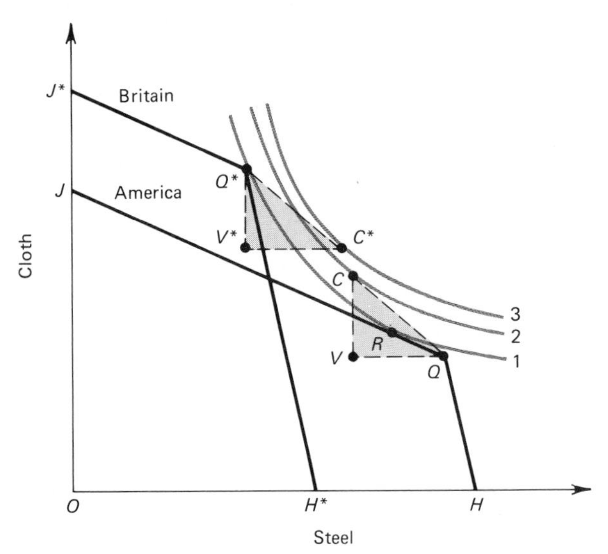

FIGURE 4-4 **The Heckscher-Ohlin theorem with a single technique.** The production frontiers *JQH* and *J*Q*H** reflect the fact that America is endowed with more capital than Britain, while Britain is endowed with more labor than America. Before trade, America produces and consumes at *R*, and Britain at *Q**. With free trade, America shifts production to *Q* and consumption to *C*. Britain maintains production at *Q** but shifts consumption to *C**. Trade triangles *CQV* and *Q*C*V** are identical. America exports steel, and Britain cloth.

capital-intensive commodity) is lower in America (the capital-abundant country), because indifference curve 1 is flatter at *R* than at *Q**. Capital-abundant America has a comparative advantage in capital-intensive steel, and labor-abundant Britain has a comparative advantage in labor-intensive cloth.

With free trade, the relative price of steel rises in America and falls in Britain until the price becomes the same in both countries. The equilibrium relative price of steel is given by the common slope of (parallel) lines *CQ* and *Q*C**, which are the hypotenuses of trade triangles *CQV* and *Q*C*V**, respectively. Britain maintains production at full-employment point *Q** but shifts consumption to *C** on social indifference curve 3, enjoying a pure consumption gain. America shifts production to full-employment point *Q* and consumes at *C* on social indifference curve 2, enjoying both a production gain and a consumption gain. America exports *VQ* (or *V*C**) of steel in exchange for *VC* (or *V*Q**) of British cloth.

In summary, the capital-abundant country exports the capital-intensive commodity, and the labor-abundant country exports the labor-intensive commodity.

Many Production Techniques

With many production techniques, the analysis remains essentially the same. The only significant difference is that the production-possibilities frontiers of the two countries become smoothly continuous (without kinks), as shown in Figure 4-5. As in Figure 4-4, America's production-possibilities frontier *JH* is skewed along the horizontal axis; and Britain's frontier J^*H^* is skewed along the vertical axis. (The derivation of the production-possibilities frontier with many production techniques is reviewed in Appendix 4.)

Before trade, America produces and consumes at *R*, where the nation's production-possibilities frontier is tangent to social indifference curve 1. Britain's autarkic equilibrium occurs at R^*. (For convenience, we continue to assume that, in autarky, both countries attain the same social indifference curve. This assumption can be dropped without serious consequences.) In America, the relative price of steel is given by the slope of social indifference curve 1 at *R*; and in Britain, by the slope at R^*. As before, steel (the capital-

FIGURE 4-5 **The Heckscher-Ohlin theorem with many techniques.** The production frontier *JH* of America (the capital-abundant country) is skewed along the axis for steel (the capital-intensive commodity); and the production frontier J^*H^* of Britain (the labor-abundant country) is skewed along the axis for cloth (the labor-intensive commodity). Before trade, America produces and consumes at *R*, and Britain at R^*. With free trade, America produces at *Q* and consumes at *C*, and Britain at Q^* and C^*, respectively. Trade triangles *CQV* and $Q^*C^*V^*$ are identical. America exports steel, and Britain cloth.

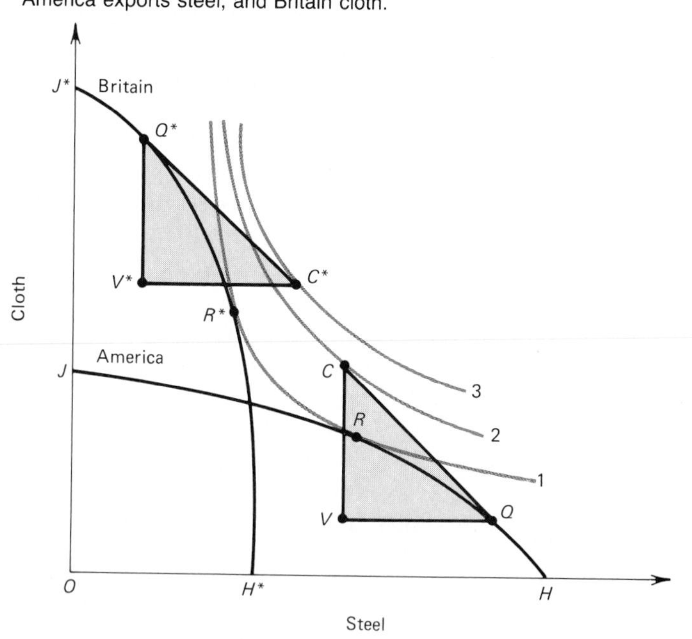

intensive commodity) is cheaper in America (the capital-abundant country), because social indifference curve 1 is flatter at R than at R^*.

With free trade, the relative price of steel rises in America and falls in Britain until it becomes the same in both countries. The equilibrium terms of trade are given by the common slope of (parallel) lines CQ and Q^*C^*, which connect the countries' production points (Q and Q^*) to their consumption points (C and C^*) and form trade triangles CQV and $Q^*C^*V^*$. America exports VQ (or V^*C^*) of steel in exchange for VC (or V^*Q^*) of British cloth. Again capital-abundant America exports capital-intensive steel, and labor-abundant Britain exports labor-intensive cloth. The proof of the Heckscher-Ohlin theorem is complete.

4-7 THE STOLPER-SAMUELSON THEOREM

The classical school demonstrated that free trade enables a country to consume beyond its production-possibilities frontier and thus raise the standard of living of its citizens. For over a century after the Ricardo-Torrens contribution, economists had taken it for granted that free trade would benefit every citizen and that protection would hurt everyone. Stolper and Samuelson (1941) disagreed. They showed that, in general, those who supply the factor used intensively by the import-competing industry can become better off through protection, even though the economy as a whole loses. For example, in the United States unskilled labor has an incentive to seek protection against imports of commodities that are relatively intensive in unskilled labor. This section studies the Stolper-Samuelson theorem, which provides some support for the "cheap foreign labor" argument for protection.

Consider Figure 4-6, which presents the production-possibilities frontier of a "small" open economy, America. Under free-trade conditions, America produces at Q and exports steel in exchange for cloth. (To keep the diagram simple, America's trade triangle is *not* shown.) To protect its import-competing industry (cloth), America imposes a tariff on imports of cloth, which raises the domestic relative price of cloth or lowers the relative price of steel. The first impact of the change in relative prices is reflected in the profitability of the two industries. The producers of cloth will enjoy positive profits, but the producers of steel will sustain losses. In turn, the profits will induce the producers of cloth to expand their output, and the losses will force the steel producers to curtail theirs. Suppose that America eventually moves from Q to Q'.

Even a small movement along the production-possibilities frontier implies a total reorganization of the structure of production. Not only do resources shift from one industry to the other, but also the optimal methods of production, the optimal factor proportions (capital-labor ratios), and the marginal productivities of both factors in both industries—and thus the internal distribution of income—all change with the tariff. The essence of this complex reorganization is captured by the Stolper-Samuelson theorem.

Suppose that the optimal techniques of production employed at Q are those summarized earlier in Table 4-2. The steel industry releases $2L$ and $3K$ per unit

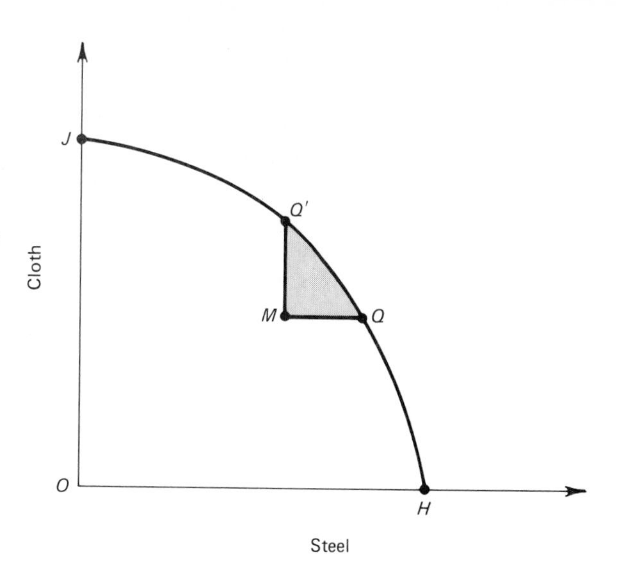

FIGURE 4-6 **The Stolper-Samuelson theorem.** Under free-trade conditions, America (a small, open economy) produces at Q and exports steel in exchange for cloth. A tariff on imports raises the domestic relative price of cloth, causing production to shift from Q to Q' (as resources are transferred from steel to cloth). Such a movement along the production frontier makes both industries more capital intensive, raises the marginal physical product of labor in both industries, and lowers the marginal physical product of capital in both industries.

reduction of steel output, but the cloth industry can employ $4L$ and $1K$ per additional yard of cloth output. Thus the steel industry releases fewer workers per unit of capital (or more capital per worker) than the cloth industry is willing to absorb. For instance, if the output of steel is reduced by 1 ton and the output of cloth is increased by 1 yard, there will emerge an excess demand for labor equal to $2L$ (that is, $4L - 2L$) and an excess supply of capital equal to $2K$ (that is, $3K - 1K$). The excess demand for labor will cause the wage rate to rise, and the excess supply of capital will cause the rental rate of capital to fall. Does it follow then that the *real* wage rate will rise and the *real* rental rate for capital services will fall? Be careful, because in addition to the changes in the nominal factor rentals, the price of cloth rises and the price of steel falls. As it turns out, the wage rate rises more sharply than the price of cloth, and the capital rental rate falls more precipitously than the price of steel—a phenomenon that has become known as the **magnification effect.** Thus, we can unequivocally say that after the imposition of the tariff, workers become better off and capitalists become worse off.

As labor becomes more expensive relative to capital, both industries substitute the cheaper factor (capital) for the more expensive factor (labor); that is, *both industries become more capital intensive* (or less labor intensive). Consequently, the marginal physical product of capital falls in both industries, and the marginal physical product of labor rises in both industries, because of the **law of diminishing returns.** The real factor rentals coincide, of course, with the respective marginal productivities of factors.

It may seem paradoxical that both industries can become more capital intensive at the same time, while the overall factor supplies remain fixed. How is it possible for the capital-labor ratio to remain fixed in the two industries taken together and yet rise in each one of them? To understand this puzzle, which is due to the subtleties of weighted averages, consider a more familiar example based on college life. Suppose that the international economics course attracts a lot of students and so they are divided into two sections. The students in the first section are very intelligent and receive mostly A's and a few B's. In the second section, the students are not so intelligent and receive mostly C's and a few D's. While the overall average grade for the entire course (that is, both sections grouped together) is fixed (say, B), the average grade of *each* individual section will *rise* if the weakest student of the first section is transferred to the second section! The average grade of the first section will rise because it will be losing its weakest student. The average grade of the second section will also rise because it will be gaining a student who is stronger than anybody else in that section. To apply this example to the original puzzle, merely substitute "capital-labor ratio" for "average grade," "steel industry" for the "first section," and "cloth industry" for the "second section."

The proof of the Stolper-Samuelson theorem does *not* depend on the validity of the Heckscher-Ohlin theorem or the factor-price equalization theorem because *the Stolper-Samuelson theorem does not involve any comparison between countries.* The theorem will continue to be correct even in the presence of factor intensity reversals and drastic differences in production functions and tastes between countries.

4-8 THE FACTOR-PRICE EQUALIZATION THEOREM

The factor-price equalization theorem has attracted the attention of many distinguished economists. Heckscher (1919) stated that free trade equalizes factor rewards completely. Ohlin (1933), however, cited several reasons why full factor-price equalization cannot occur in practice, and asserted that free trade brings about a tendency (but only a tendency) toward factor-price equalization. The *partial*-equalization argument was later made rigorous by Stolper and Samuelson (1941). The case for *complete* equalization was finally established by Samuelson (1948, 1949, 1953).

The Meaning of Factor Prices

In the present context, the term "factor prices" does not mean "asset prices of the factors of production." That is, the term "factor prices" does not mean the price of a piece of machinery or the price of a "slave." Rather it means the *rentals* for the services of these factors, such as the *wage rate* for the services of one worker per unit of time (week, month, or year) and the *rental rate* (or *rent*) for the services of capital.

The Effect of International Trade

As noted earlier, the factor-price equalization theorem asserts that even in the absence of factor migration between countries, free commodity trade leads to the equalization of real factor rewards between countries. With free commodity trade, workers can earn the same real wage rate, and capital the same real rental rate, in both America and Britain. This is the *effect* of free commodity trade.

In essence, the Heckscher-Ohlin model points to an indirect exchange of factors between countries. By exporting labor-intensive commodities in exchange for capital-intensive commodities, the labor-abundant country indirectly exports a *net* amount of labor in exchange for a *net* amount of capital; and the capital-abundant country does the opposite. This indirect exchange of factors raises the real wage rate in the labor-abundant country and lowers the rate in the capital-abundant country and also lowers the real rental rate in the labor-abundant country and raises it in the capital-abundant country. Thus the Heckscher-Ohlin model implies that factors do indeed migrate between countries not directly but indirectly through the exports and imports of commodities. If Mohammed cannot go to the mountain, the mountain goes to Mohammed.

Factor Prices and Commodity Prices

The production functions of the cloth and steel industries imply a definite relationship between the wage-rent ratio and the relative costs of production (or relative prices). This relationship is summarized by the following important proposition.

***Proposition:* As labor becomes cheaper relative to capital (that is, as the wage-rent ratio falls), the labor-intensive commodity (cloth) becomes cheaper relative to the capital-intensive commodity (steel).**

The preceding proposition is crucial, and we should always keep it in mind. It is also implicit in the discussion of the Stolper-Samuelson theorem in Section 4-7. There it was argued that an increase in the relative price of cloth (brought about presumably by the imposition of a tariff) causes the wage rate to rise and the rental rate to fall as both industries become more capital intensive. Thus the wage-rent ratio moves in the same direction as the relative price of the labor-intensive commodity (cloth).

Perhaps a numerical illustration can be helpful. Suppose that by a judicious choice of the units of measurement of cloth and steel, the price of cloth is equal to the price of steel, the common price being $100. Thus, initially, the relative price of cloth is by assumption equal to 1 (that is, $100/$100). Because cloth is labor intensive relative to steel, wages are a larger cost element in cloth than in steel. For instance, we may suppose that the per-unit cost of cloth is made up of $80 of wages plus $20 of rents and that the per-unit cost of steel is decomposed into $30 of wages plus $70 of rents. Suppose now that the wage rate falls by 10 percent while the rent for capital services remains constant. How will the relative price of cloth be affected by the decrease in the wage rate? The price will fall! The wage bill will fall by 10 percent in both industries, but the savings per unit of output must be larger for cloth ($0.10 \times \$80 = \$8$) than for steel ($0.10 \times \$30 = \$3$). Thus the relative price of cloth will fall to $\$92 \div \$97 < 1$.

The preceding example may be objectionable because it does not allow any factor substitutability—it might be thought that the result could be reversed if we allowed industries to substitute the cheaper factor (labor) for the more expensive factor (capital). What if the steel industry were able to substitute labor for capital much more easily than the cloth industry? Is it not possible then that steel (the capital-intensive commodity) may become cheaper relative to cloth as the wage rate falls? The answer is no!

Consider Figure 4-7, which shows the unit isoquants for cloth and steel for the carefully selected units of measurement. At the initial factor rentals, represented by isocost line *MN*, the steel industry uses factor combination *S* and the cloth industry uses factor combination *C* per unit of output. After the wage rate drops, the isocost lines become flatter, as shown by the dashed lines through *S′* and *C′*. At the new wage-rent ratio, the steel industry will choose *S′* and the cloth industry will choose *C′*. Note that *C′* lies on a lower isocost line than *S′*; that is, at the lower wage-rent ratio cloth becomes relatively cheaper than steel. Thus as the wage rate falls, the relative price of cloth falls also. This result remains valid as long as cloth is labor intensive relative to steel.

FIGURE 4-7 **Factor prices and commodity prices.** At the initial factor rentals, represented by isocost line *MN*, the steel sector uses factor combination *S* per ton of steel, and the cloth sector uses factor combination *C* per yard of cloth. Unit costs of each product are equal to $100. When the wage rate drops, as shown by the dashed isocost lines, the steel sector chooses factor combination *S′*, and the cloth sector *C′*. Cloth becomes cheaper relative to steel because *C′* lies on a lower isocost line than *S′*.

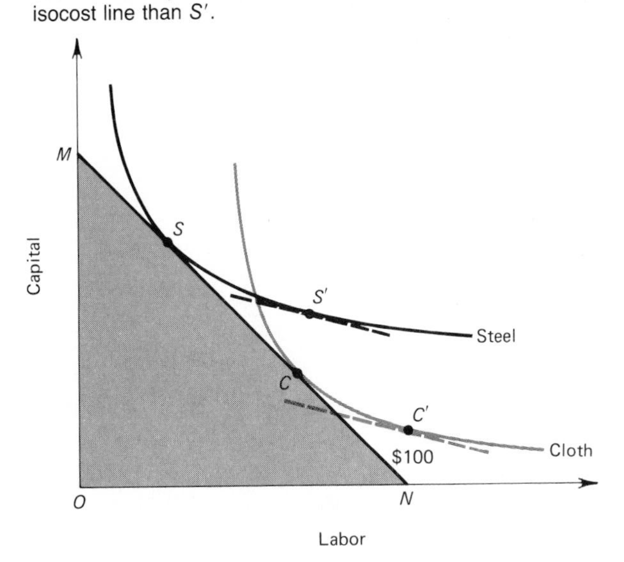

Proof of the Factor-Price Equalization Theorem

In Figure 4-8, upward-sloping curve *PW* summarizes the basic relationship which exists between the wage-rent ratio and the relative price of the labor-intensive commodity (cloth). As the wage-rent ratio falls, cloth becomes cheaper relative to steel. This fundamental relationship, which is based on the existing technology, must be the same in both countries because, by assumption, the production functions of America are identical to the corresponding production functions of Britain. What, then, is the difference, if any, between America and Britain? Factor endowments. The overall capital-labor ratio is higher in America than Britain.

Before trade, different factor endowments force America and Britain to operate at different points along curve *PW,* as illustrated by points *A* and *B,* respectively. Thus, in autarky, the relative price of cloth is given by *OS* in America and by *OD* in Britain, while the wage-rent ratio is given by *OF* in America and by *OR* in Britain. Britain is labor abundant relative to America not only on the basis of the physical criterion, but also on the basis of the economic criterion ($OR < OF$); and cloth (the labor-intensive commodity) is cheaper in Britain

FIGURE 4-8 **Factor-price equalization.** Upward-sloping curve *PW* illustrates the fundamental relationship between factor prices and commodity prices: As the wage-rent ratio falls from, say, *OF* to *OM*, the relative price of cloth (the labor-intensive commodity) declines from *OS* to *ON*. Before trade, America operates at *A*, and Britain at *B*. With free trade, America exports steel, and Britain cloth. At the equilibrium relative price of cloth, *ON*, the same wage-rent ratio, *OM*, prevails in both countries. The marginal physical productivities of labor and capital are also equalized between countries.

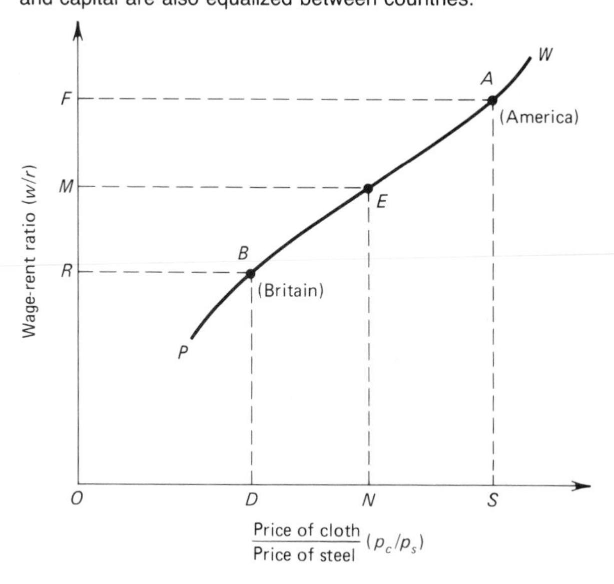

than in America ($OD < OS$). Britain has a comparative advantage in cloth and America has a comparative advantage in steel—just as the Heckscher-Ohlin theorem predicts.

When free commodity trade is allowed between the two countries, America will export steel to Britain in exchange for cloth. The relative price of steel will rise in America and will fall in Britain until a common commodity-price ratio, say, *ON*, is established in both countries. What does this commodity price equalization (which is brought about by free commodity trade) imply for the factor prices in America and Britain?

For any commodity price ratio at which a country produces positive amounts of both steel and cloth, the corresponding wage-rent ratio is always read off curve *PW* of Figure 4-8, which is common to both countries by assumption. In the absence of complete specialization in either country, both America and Britain operate, after trade, at a common point, say, *E*. Accordingly, the same wage-rent ratio, *OM*, will prevail in both countries. Does the equalization of the wage-rent ratio between countries imply the equalization of the real wage rate and the real rental rate also? It most certainly does! The real factor rentals are, of course, given by the marginal physical productivities of the factors. As explained in Appendix 3, these marginal productivities depend only on the proportion in which labor and capital are used in the production of steel and cloth—not on the absolute quantities of labor and capital employed by each industry. This follows from the assumption of constant returns to scale. Further, each industry's capital-labor ratio is perfectly determined when the wage-rent ratio is given. Since the production functions are by assumption identical between countries, the equalization of the wage-rent ratio between America and Britain necessarily equalizes America's marginal physical productivities of labor and capital to the corresponding marginal productivities of Britain.

The Relevance of the Factor-Price Equalization Theorem

The significance of the factor-price equalization theorem is based on the fact that the equalization of real factor rewards between countries is an important Pareto-optimality condition for the efficient allocation of resources worldwide. In the same way that efficient resource allocation within a closed economy requires that identical units of the same homogeneous factor earn the same rewards, efficient resource allocation in the world economy requires complete factor-price equalization. After all, the world economy is the only closed economy we know of.

A casual look at the real world can convince us quickly that factor prices are not actually equalized among nations. Domestic servants, bricklayers, shoemakers, barbers, and so on do not earn the same wages in India and Pakistan as they do in the United States and West Germany. No doubt, some of these differences reflect disparities in skills (or human capital). But not all factor-price differentials between countries can be explained away in this fashion. It appears, therefore, that freer factor movements can enable the world economy to enjoy large gains in potential welfare—in addition to the gains from free trade in commodities.

The factor-price equalization theorem emphasizes that free commodity trade is a substitute, albeit imperfect, for factor movements between countries; and it directs our attention toward the examination of the relevant variables that determine the impact of free commodity trade on factor prices. This important theorem can also tell us how far we can hope to go toward world efficiency (while maintaining barriers to factor movements) through free commodity trade plus technical assistance plus, possibly, capital movements (the latter two being "foreign aid").

4-9 SUMMARY

1 The standard Heckscher-Ohlin model (also known as the $2 \times 2 \times 2$ model) assumes that each of two countries is endowed with two homogeneous factors (labor and capital) and produces two commodities (cloth and steel) under constant returns to scale.

It is also assumed that the two countries share the same technology, have the same tastes, and neither country specializes completely in the production of only one commodity.

The factors are perfectly mobile within each country but perfectly immobile between countries.

One commodity (cloth) is labor intensive relative to the other commodity (steel) at all factor prices (strong factor intensity).

Perfect competition rules in all markets.

Trade is free from any impediments.

Transportation costs are zero.

2 Although Ohlin took it for granted that production functions are identical between countries, the issue cannot be settled by a priori arguments—it is an empirical problem.

3 The labor-intensive commodity is the one that uses the greater number of units of labor per unit of capital at all wage-rent ratios. Like comparative advantage, factor intensity is a relative concept.

4 According to the physical criterion, a country is labor abundant when its overall labor-capital ratio exceeds that of a second country. According to the economic criterion, a country is labor abundant when its pretrade wage-rent ratio is lower than the corresponding wage-rent ratio of the second country. When tastes are similar between countries, the two criteria lead to the same ranking of countries.

5 The gist of the Heckscher-Ohlin model (also known as the factor endowment theory) can be summarized in four theorems: the Heckscher-Ohlin theorem, the factor-price equalization theorem, the Stolper-Samuelson theorem, and the Rybczynski theorem.

6 The Heckscher-Ohlin theorem states that a country has a comparative advantage in the production of the commodity that more intensively uses the country's more abundant factor.

7 The factor-price equalization theorem states that free international trade equalizes factor prices between countries, relatively and absolutely, and thus serves as a substitute for international factor mobility.

8 The Stolper-Samuelson theorem states that an increase in the relative price of a commodity raises the real wage of the factor used intensively in the commodity's production, and reduces the real wage of the other factor.

9 The Rybczynski theorem states that when only one factor increases, the output of the commodity that intensively uses the increased factor expands, while the output of the other commodity contracts, assuming that the coefficients of production are given.

10 The production frontier of the labor-abundant country (capital-abundant country) is skewed along the axis measuring the labor-intensive commodity (capital-intensive commodity).

11 When the wage-rent ratio rises, both industries become more capital intensive (or less labor intensive).

12 The production functions imply a fundamental relationship between factor prices and commodity prices (or costs): *As the wage-rent ratio falls, the labor-intensive commodity becomes cheaper relative to the capital-intensive commodity.* This fundamental relationship (which is common to both countries because they share the same technology) lies at the very heart of both the factor-price equalization theorem and the Heckscher-Ohlin theorem.

13 Because of the fundamental relationship between factor prices and commodity prices, the labor-intensive commodity is necessarily cheaper before trade in the country with the lowest wage-rent ratio (that is, the labor-abundant country). In other words, the labor-abundant country necessarily has a comparative advantage in the labor-intensive commodity.

14 When free trade leads to (a) commodity-price equalization between countries and (b) incomplete specialization in each country, factor prices are necessarily equalized, both relatively and absolutely. This must be so because of the existence of a one-to-one correspondence between commodity prices and factor prices.

PROBLEMS[1]

1 Spain is a small, open economy that trades commodities X and Y in the world market at the fixed terms of trade $1X{:}2Y$. Spain is endowed with 37,200 units of labor and 18,000 units of capital. At the current equilibrium, the optimal coefficients of production are as follows:

[1]Problems that appear with asterisks are more difficult.

	Labor	Capital
X	4	3
Y	5	1

Assume also that Spain consumes commodities in the fixed proportion $1X{:}1Y$ at all conceivable prices.

a Determine Spain's labor and capital constraints.
b Determine Spain's outputs of X and Y.
c Determine Spain's consumption of X and Y.
d Determine Spain's exports and imports of X and Y.
e Suppose that through capital accumulation Spain's supply of capital increases to 18,440 units. How does this capital accumulation affect Spain's production, consumption, exports, and imports of X and Y?
f Illustrate your conclusions graphically.

2 Consider the standard Heckscher-Ohlin model, but suppose that the production function of steel is identical to the production function of cloth. All other assumptions of the Heckscher-Ohlin model remain valid.

a What does the identity of production functions between steel and cloth imply about the *shape* of the production-possibilities frontiers of America and Britain?
b Is there a basis for trade between America and Britain?
c Explain the implications of the identity of production functions between steel and cloth (*not just between countries*) for the following theorems: Heckscher-Ohlin, factor-price equalization, Rybczynski, and Stolper-Samuelson.

3 Germany and Japan share the same Leontief-type, fixed-coefficient technology in which one unit of commodity X requires $5L$ and $1K$, and one unit of commodity Y requires $3L$ and $2K$. Germany is endowed with $2{,}900L$ and $1{,}000K$; and Britain is endowed with $3{,}550L$ and $1{,}200K$.

a Which is the labor-intensive commodity?
b Which is the labor-abundant country?
***c** Assume that tastes in both Germany and Japan are given by the same utility function, $U = XY$. Determine each country's autarkic price-ratio and the equilibrium terms of trade under free-trade conditions.

4 Greece and Italy produce under constant returns to scale two commodities, food (F) and clothing (C). Greece is labor abundant relative to Italy (on both the physical criterion and the economic criterion), and clothing is labor-intensive relative to food at all wage-rent ratios. An initial international equilibrium is disturbed by a shift in demand in favor of clothing. What long-run effects can you predict on the following variables?

a The equilibrium terms of trade.
b The outputs of food and clothing in Greece and Italy.
c The marginal physical products of labor and capital in each industry.

SUGGESTED READING

Bhagwati, J. N. (1964). "The Pure Theory of International Trade: A Survey," *Economic Journal,* vol. 74, pp. 1–84.

Chacholiades, M. (1978). *International Trade Theory and Policy.* McGraw-Hill Book Company, New York, chaps. 8–10.

——— (1987). "Some Fundamental Propositions in the Theory of International Trade." In G. C. Bitros and C. A. Davos (eds.), *Essays in Memory of Pindaros Christodoulopoulos,* Papazisis Publishers, Athens, 1987.

Chipman, J. S. (1966). "A Survey of the Theory of International Trade: Part 3, The Modern Theory." *Econometrica,* vol. 34, pp. 18–76.

Heckscher, E. (1919). "The Effect of Foreign Trade on the Distribution of Income." *Ekonomisk Tidskrift,* vol. 21, pp. 1–32. Reprinted in H. S. Ellis and L. A. Metzler (eds.), American Economic Association *Readings in the Theory of International Trade,* Richard D. Irwin, Inc., Homewood, Ill., 1950.

Johnson, H. G. (1957). "Factor Endowments, International Trade and Factor Prices." *Manchester School of Economics and Social Studies,* vol. 25 (September), pp. 270–283. Reprinted in H. G. Johnson, *International Trade and Economic Growth,* George Allen and Unwin, London, 1958.

Jones, R. W. (1956). "Factor Proportions and the Heckscher-Ohlin Theorem." *Review of Economic Studies,* vol. 24, pp. 1–10.

Jones, R. W., and J. P. Neary (1984). "The Positive Theory of International Trade." In R. W. Jones and P. B. Kenen (eds.), *Handbook of International Economics,* vol. I, North-Holland Publishing Company, Amsterdam, 1984.

Lerner, A. P. (1953). *Essays in Economic Analysis.* Macmillan and Company, London.

Ohlin, B. (1933). *Interregional and International Trade.* Harvard University Press, Cambridge, Mass.

Rybczynski, T. M. (1955). "Factor Endowment and Relative Commodity Prices." *Economica,* vol. 22, pp. 336–341.

Samuelson, P. A. (1948). "International Trade and the Equalization of Factor Prices." *Economic Journal,* vol. 58, pp. 165–184.

——— (1949). "International Factor Price Equalization Once Again." *Economic Journal,* vol. 59, pp. 181–197. Reprinted in R. E. Caves and H. G. Johnson (eds.), American Economic Association *Readings in International Economics,* Richard D. Irwin, Inc., Homewood, Ill., 1968.

——— (1953). "Prices of Factors and Goods in General Equilibrium." *Review of Economic Studies,* vol. 21, pp. 1–20.

Stolper, W. F., and P. A. Samuelson (1941). "Protection and Real Wages." *Review of Economic Studies,* vol. 9, pp. 58–73. Reprinted in H. S. Ellis and L. A. Metzler (eds.), American Economic Association *Readings in the Theory of International Trade,* Richard D. Irwin, Inc., Homewood, Ill., 1950.

CHAPTER 5

ALTERNATIVE TRADE THEORIES AND EMPIRICAL TESTING

In the preceding chapters, we discussed two serious theories of the ultimate determinants of comparative advantage: the Ricardian theory and the Heckscher-Ohlin theory. For Ricardo, comparative advantage depended on comparative differences in labor productivity. For Heckscher and Ohlin, the cause of trade was based on differences in factor endowments.

In this chapter, we begin with the empirical testing of the Ricardian and Heckscher-Ohlin theories. Then we discuss several alternative trade theories that seem to explain a significant portion of world trade not accounted for by the standard Heckscher-Ohlin model.

5-1 EMPIRICAL TESTING OF THE RICARDIAN THEORY

The first serious attempt to test empirically the predictive capacity of the classical theory was made by MacDougall (1951). Similar studies supporting MacDougall's initial empirical findings were made by Balassa (1963) and Stern (1962). All three studies were carried out on the basis of data for the United States and the United Kingdom for the years 1937 (MacDougall), 1950 (Balassa), and 1950 and 1959 (Stern).

MacDougall found that in 1937 wages in the United States were about twice as high as wages in the United Kingdom. He argued that in all those industries in which output per worker was more than twice as high in the United States as in the United Kingdom, U.S. money costs of production would be lower than the corresponding U.K. money costs. In these industries the United States would have a cost advantage over the United Kingdom, and U.S. producers would undersell British producers. In all those industries in which output per worker was about twice as high in the United States as in the United Kingdom, neither country would enjoy a significant cost advantage. In the rest of the industries (in which output per U.S. worker was less than twice the output per U.K. worker), the United Kingdom would have a cost advantage over the United States, and U.K. producers would undersell their U.S. counterparts.

To test his hypothesis, MacDougall calculated the following two ratios for some 25 industry groups: (1) the **export ratio** (that is, the ratio of U.S. exports to U.K. exports) and (2) the **productivity ratio** (that is, the ratio of output per U.S. worker to output per U.K. worker). In calculating the export ratio, MacDougall excluded the mutual trade between the United States and the United Kingdom for two reasons. First, more than 95 percent of U.S. and British exports in 1937 went to third countries because of the high U.S. and British tariffs. Second, U.S. and British tariffs varied from industry to industry and tended to offset differences in labor productivity, while at the same time both U.S. and U.K. exporters faced the same tariff walls in the rest of the world.

MacDougall found that 20 out of his 25 industry groups obeyed this general rule: *When the productivity ratio was higher than 2, the United States had a larger share of the export market; and when the productivity ratio was lower than 2, Britain had the larger share.* MacDougall and other economists took these findings as support for the classical theory.

Figure 5-1 (drawn on a double logarithmic scale) summarizes MacDougall's results and brings out another striking fact: The observed points lie fairly close to a positively sloped straight line (*KL*). This shows that there is a tendency for

FIGURE 5-1 **MacDougall's findings (1937).** *(After MacDougall, 1951.)*

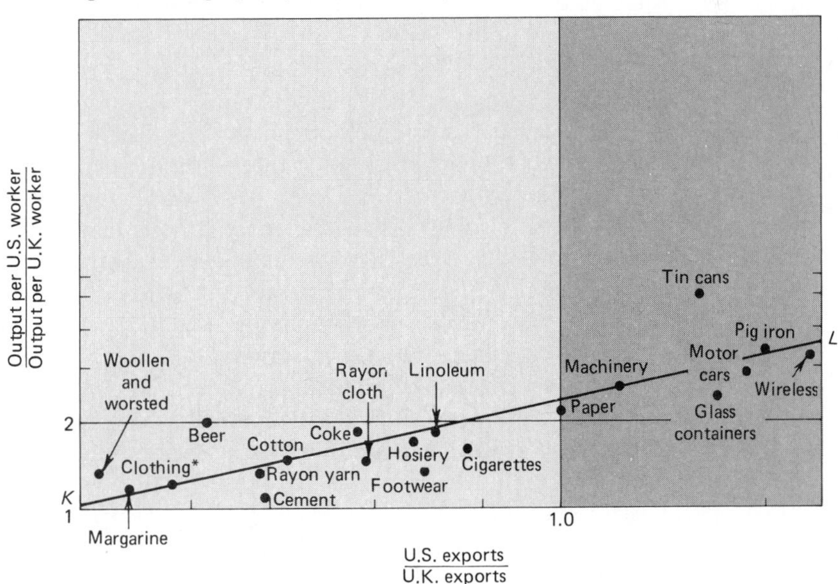

each country to capture an ever-increasing share of the export market as its comparative advantage grows.

The classical theory, of course, does not imply such a relationship. Indeed, the classical theory suggests that when the productivity ratio exceeds 2, the United States will capture the entire export market and when the productivity ratio is lower than 2, the United Kingdom will capture the entire export market. Only when the productivity ratio is exactly 2 will the two countries share the export market (although in this case, in which neither country has a cost advantage, the classical theory predicts nothing about the sharing of an export market).

Why does the country that has the cost advantage not capture the whole export market, as the classical theory would lead us to believe? MacDougall attributes this phenomenon to the existence of imperfect markets (monopolistic and oligopolistic), nonhomogeneous products, transport costs, and the like. For instance, each of the 25 industry groups studied by MacDougall is an aggregate of related but nevertheless different products. Even though the United Kingdom may have an overall advantage in a certain industry group, such as footwear, the United States may still have a cost advantage in the production of certain kinds of shoes. Or if foreign buyers perceive British cars to be different from American cars in some crucial respects, some buyers may prefer to buy British cars even though the United States has a cost advantage.

Until future research refutes the important findings of MacDougall (which were confirmed by Balassa and Stern), we must conclude that they provide strong evidence that the classical theory really works. However, the greatest defect of the classical theory continues to be that it does not shed any light on what determines comparative advantage and on how comparative advantage may be expected to change in the future.

5-2 THE LEONTIEF PARADOX

For two decades after its reformulation by Bertil Ohlin, the Heckscher-Ohlin theorem (that is, the proposition that a country exports those commodities that use its abundant factor more intensively) was generally accepted on the basis of casual empiricism. The first and most famous empirical study of the theorem was conducted by Wassily W. Leontief (1954) using U.S. data for the year 1947. Leontief expected to show that the United States, the most capital-abundant country in the world by any criterion, exported capital-intensive commodities and imported labor-intensive commodities. Instead, Leontief concluded that U.S. import-competing production required 30 percent *more* capital per worker than U.S. export production. This finding, which was just the opposite of what the Heckscher-Ohlin model predicted, became known as the **Leontief paradox.**

To perform his test, Leontief used the 1947 **input-output table** of the U.S. economy. He aggregated the industries into 50 sectors (38 of which traded their products directly on the international market). He also grouped all factors into two categories—labor and capital. Then he estimated the capital and labor requirements for the production of a representative bundle of $1 million of U.S. exports and a representative bundle of $1 million of U.S. import-competing commodities. The results of Leontief's calculations are shown in column (1) of Table 5-1. The capital-labor ratio was about $14,000 per worker-year in export production and about $18,100 per worker-year in import-competing production.

Because foreign data on labor and capital requirements of actual U.S. imports were not available, Leontief was practically forced to calculate the input requirements of U.S. import-competing commodities rather than the factor requirements of actual imports. For instance, instead of estimating the amounts of foreign labor and capital embodied, say, in a Toyota, Leontief's procedure amounted to calculating the quantities of U.S. labor and capital used to produce a Ford (the import-competing commodity). For this reason, he also had to ignore noncompetitive imports, that is, products not produced in the United States, mainly coffee, tea, and jute.

Some economists complained that 1947 was not a typical year, mainly because the postwar reconstruction of the world economy had not been corrected by that time. To quiet his critics, Leontief (1956) repeated the test using the average composition of U.S. exports and imports that prevailed in 1951. In this later study, he retained the 1947 U.S. production structure but disaggregated it into 192 sectors of commodity groups. He again found that U.S. import replacements were more capital intensive relative to U.S. exports even though their capital intensity over U.S. exports was reduced to only 6 percent. Leontief's 1956 findings are summarized in columns (2) and (3) of Table 5-1.

TABLE 5-1 FACTOR CONTENT OF U.S. TRADE

	Leontief (1954)	Leontief (1956)		Baldwin (1971)		Stern & Maskus (1981)	
	All industries (1)	All industries (2)	Excl. N.R. (3)	All industries (4)	Excl. N.R. (5)	All industries (6)	Excl. N.R. (7)
Year of trade data	**1947**	**1951**	**1951**	**1962**	**1962**	**1972**	**1972**
Year of input data	**1947**	**1947**	**1947**	**1958**	**1958**	**1972**	**1972**
Capital ($ thousands)							
Imports	3,091	2,303	2,093	2,132	1,259	1,368	497
Exports	2,551	2,257	2,577	1,876	1,223	1,478	455
Labor (worker-years)							
Imports	170	168	207	119	106	96	29
Exports	182	174	224	131	107	99	24
Capital-labor ratio ($ thousands per worker-year)							
Imports	18.1	13.7	10.1	18.0	11.9	14.2	17.3
Exports	14.0	13.0	11.5	14.2	11.5	15.0	18.7
Import-export ratio	1.30	1.06	0.88	1.27	1.04	0.95	0.93

N.R. = natural resource industries.

Several economists have reapplied the basic methodology of Leontief to more recent years. In the last four columns of Table 5-1, we summarize the findings of Baldwin (1971), and Stern and Maskus (1981). In general, the new studies have reaffirmed the Leontief paradox for the early years but detected that the paradox may have disappeared by the early 1970s. For instance, Baldwin ascertained that in 1962 U.S. import substitutes were about 27 percent more capital intensive than U.S. exports—a result which is not much different from Leontief's original estimate. Stern and Maskus, however, demonstrated that in 1972 the paradox was reversed—the capital-labor ratio was higher in U.S. export production (about $18,700 per worker-year) than in U.S. import-competing production (about $17,300 per worker-year).

Recently, Leamer (1980) took an important step toward resolving the Leontief paradox. Noting that the United States was a net exporter of both capital and labor services, Leamer argued (by counterexample) that one should compare the capital-labor ratios of U.S. production and U.S. consumption, not the capital-labor ratios of exports and imports. He found that in 1947 the capital-labor ratio was indeed greater in U.S. production than in U.S. consumption—a result that was also confirmed by Stern and Maskus, using 1972 data. The presumed Leamer resolution of the Leontief paradox was disputed, however, by Brecher and Choudhri (1982). The latter argued that a country can be a net exporter of labor services only if the expenditure per worker is lower in that country than in the rest of the world, but this was clearly not the case for the United States. So the paradox continues.

The Leontief paradox has stimulated an enormous amount of empirical and theoretical research. These efforts have enabled us to understand the strengths and weaknesses of the Heckscher-Ohlin model.

5-3 EXPLANATIONS OF THE LEONTIEF PARADOX

The empirical evidence that has accumulated so far does not dispel the Leontief paradox. How then can we reconcile the empirical findings with the Heckscher-Ohlin theorem? Many attempts have been made to explain the paradox, some successful, others unsuccessful. Some economists have sought a reconciliation within the Heckscher-Ohlin model itself. Others have tried to go beyond the Heckscher-Ohlin model and provide new theories that are basically dynamic in character and that deal with technical progress and the product cycle. Here we review some of the principal explanations of the Leontief paradox.

Effectiveness of U.S. Labor

The first unsuccessful attempt to explain Leontief's paradox was made by Leontief himself. He asserted that the apparent higher abundance of capital per worker in the United States relative to that of other countries is actually an illusion. The United States, Leontief argued, is instead a labor-abundant country, because U.S. workers are much more productive than foreign workers. In particular, he suggested that one worker-year of U.S. labor is equivalent to three worker-years of foreign labor—the number of U.S. workers must be multiplied by 3. Leontief attributed the higher productivity of U.S. labor not to the employment of a larger amount of capital per worker but rather to the presence in the United States of entrepreneurship, superior organization, and a favorable environment.

Unfortunately, it is very difficult to accept Leontief's explanation. Entrepreneurship, superior organization, and a favorable environment may indeed raise the productivity of U.S. labor. Nevertheless, these qualities also raise the productivity of U.S. capital. Leontief's argument may be admissible only to the extent that these factors raise the productivity of U.S. labor much more than they raise the productivity of U.S. capital—for if they raise the productivity of U.S. capital by the same amount by which they raise the productivity of U.S. labor, then the greater abundance of capital in the United States relative to other countries remains intact.

To test Leontief's conjecture empirically, Kreinin (1965) conducted a survey of managers and engineers familiar with production conditions in the United States and abroad. The results of the survey confirmed that U.S. labor is indeed superior to its foreign counterpart, although such superiority amounts perhaps to 20 or 25 percent (not 300 percent, as Leontief claimed) and is not sufficient to convert the United States into a labor-abundant country.

Consumption Bias

Suppose that the United States has more capital per worker than the rest of the world, but that U.S. tastes are more strongly biased toward the consumption of capital-intensive commodities. In the absence of international trade, the relative price of labor might be lower in the United States than in the rest of the world, and the United States would export labor-intensive commodities. (This possibility was discussed in Section 4-3.)

Nevertheless, no economist has argued strongly that consumption bias is the major explanation of the Leontief paradox. For one thing, empirical studies suggest that there is considerable similarity in demand functions among countries. For another, as per capita incomes rise, people tend to spend more on labor-intensive commodities (such as services) than on capital-intensive commodities. Hence, if there is indeed a consumption bias in the United States, the bias must be toward labor-intensive rather than capital-intensive commodities—that is, the opposite of what is actually needed to explain Leontief's paradox.

Factor Intensity Reversals

One of the fundamental assumptions of the Heckscher-Ohlin model is that one commodity (steel) is capital intensive relative to the other commodity (cloth) at all wage-rent ratios. As noted in Section 4-2, there is no a priori reason for this strong factor intensity assumption to be valid in practice. For instance, steel may be capital intensive (relative to cloth) at low wage-rent ratios, but labor intensive at high wage-rent ratios. If factor endowments are such that steel is capital intensive in Britain (where the wage-rent ratio is low), but labor intensive in America (where the wage-rent ratio is high), then one of the two countries *must* exhibit a Leontief paradox: If labor-abundant Britain exports cloth, then capital-abundant America must export steel (America's labor-intensive commodity) and thus exhibit a Leontief paradox. If America exports cloth, then Britain must export steel (Britain's capital-intensive commodity) and thus exhibit a Leontief paradox. Hence, in this example, the country that exports steel manifests a Leontief paradox.

Economists have tried to determine empirically whether factor intensity reversals occur extensively in the real world and whether they are responsible for the Leontief paradox. So far the empirical findings are inconclusive. Factor intensity reversals do occur, of course, in the real world. For instance, agriculture is capital intensive in the United States (where little labor is combined with elaborate mechanical equipment) but labor intensive in other countries (where much manual labor is combined with rudimentary tools). Yet most economists believe that factor intensity reversals are not so prevalent in the real world as to account for the Leontief paradox.

Because of its inherent complexity, the phenomenon of factor intensity reversals, along with its theoretical implications for the Heckscher-Ohlin model, is studied separately in Appendix 7.

Tariffs and Other Distortions

Virtually all nations interfere with the free flow of their international trade by means of tariff and nontariff barriers (see Chapters 7–10). Travis (1964) has argued that these tariff and nontariff barriers may have been responsible for the Leontief paradox. The U.S. tariff most heavily protects import-competing industries that use large quantities of labor, especially unskilled labor. Because of this bias in the U.S. tariff, the structure of U.S. imports is biased toward more-capital-intensive commodities, which in turn raises the average capital-labor ratio of U.S. import-competing production.

Baldwin (1971) showed that there is a grain of truth in the Travis thesis in the sense that tariff and nontariff barriers operate in the direction of, but are not responsible for, the Leontief paradox. According to Baldwin, if all tariff and nontariff barriers were removed, the capital-labor ratio of U.S. imports would fall by only 5 percent, and that is not enough to explain the Leontief paradox.

In connection with market imperfections, Diab (1956, pp. 53–56) made the interesting suggestion that perhaps production abroad by U.S. corporations or their subsidiaries (aided by U.S. capital, technology, and labor and managerial skills) should be considered an extension of the U.S. economy. Diab argued that once these "American economic colonies" are structurally incorporated into the "mother economy of the United States," their (highly capital-intensive) shipments to the United States would be regarded as part of U.S. internal trade rather than as U.S. imports. In turn, such a procedure may reverse the capital intensity of U.S. trade with the rest of the world, and thus explain the Leontief paradox.

Natural Resources

Jaroslav Vanek (1963) articulated a plausible explanation of the Leontief paradox by focusing on a third factor: natural resources. The United States is no longer abundant in natural resources relative to the rest of the world as it once was. We are now importing large amounts of a variety of metals and minerals that we used to export, such as bauxite, copper, iron, lead, magnesium, uranium, zinc, and especially oil. Typically, the production of such natural resource products requires large quantities of physical capital. By importing natural resource products (because of their scarcity), the United States necessarily imports large quantities of capital as well (because of the strong complementarity of capital to natural resources). Thus when we concentrate on just two factors (labor and capital), the United States appears to be importing capital-intensive commodities.

A number of economists recalculated the factor content of U.S. trade after excluding the natural resource industries. Three such calculations are shown in Table 5-1, columns (3), (5), and (7). (Note that the definition of natural resource industries is arbitrary and differs slightly from study to study.) As is evident from column (3), Leontief (1956) succeeded in reversing the paradox. He showed that when natural resource products are excluded, the capital intensity of U.S. exports exceeds that of U.S. import substitutes. Baldwin (1971), however, found no such thing. His results, in column (5), show that when natural resource products are excluded, the capital intensity of U.S. import substitutes drops substantially but does *not* go below the capital intensity of U.S. exports. Thus the paradox continues. The calculations of Stern and Maskus, in column (7), refer to a year (1972) in which the Leontief paradox seems to have disappeared. Surprisingly, they show that the exclusion of natural resource products *raises* the capital intensity of both U.S. exports and import substitutes. Surely the last word is not in yet.

Labor Skills and Human Capital

Is labor a single factor of production? Was Leontief justified in grouping all labor together? Many economists said no. The services of a tomato picker are not the same thing as the services of an ophthalmologist. Picking tomatoes requires no particular skills or training—just "raw" labor. Operating on a person's eyes, however, requires a lot of knowledge and skills that are acquired by spending many years in medical school and in postgraduate training. Economists use the fancy term **human capital** to refer to the education, training, and skills of workers. Human capital is created by "investing" in education.

Society can improve its productive capacity by using part of its resources either to increase its stock of, say, durable machines (investment in physical capital) or to enhance the skills of its labor force (investment in human capital). In both cases, the outcome is a durable asset that provides services for a long time. This should be clear enough, but the distinction between labor and capital is blurred. The services of an ophthalmologist are mostly human capital services; and most of the ophthalmologist's earnings are a return to the human capital invested in the person. It is inappropriate to combine the services of a tomato picker with the services of an ophthalmologist and call the sum "labor."

There are two alternative ways in which the concept of human capital may be used to explain the Leontief paradox. One approach, followed by Donald Keesing (1966), is to argue that the United States is a skill-abundant country and has a comparative advantage in skill-intensive commodities. There is plenty of empirical evidence supporting this view. Relative to foreign countries, the United States has a labor force that is highly trained and richly endowed with skills. At the same time, the U.S. export industries employ more skilled labor than U.S. import-competing industries. Indirect proof of this phenomenon was provided by Kravis (1956a), who observed that wages in U.S. export industries tend to be higher than wages in U.S. import-competing industries—a tendency that seems to exist in most countries. Baldwin (1971) clinched the thesis by showing that the proportion of engineers and scientists is much higher in U.S. export industries than in U.S. import-competing industries.

Alternatively, we can argue that the capital intensity of U.S. exports and import substitutes should be computed after the value of human capital is added to the physical capital. But how do we determine the value of human capital? That would be easy if we had market prices for human capital. In a free society, however, there is no market for skilled workers—that would amount to slavery. Thus some indirect method must be used to evaluate human capital. Kenen (1965), on the one hand, estimated the value of human capital involved in U.S. exports and import substitutes by *capitalizing the excess income of skilled over unskilled workers.* He then added his estimates of human capital to Leontief's estimates of physical capital and found that the Leontief paradox was reversed (but only for rates of discount less than 12.7 percent). Baldwin (1971), on the other hand, used the *costs of education plus forgone earnings* to obtain a crude measure of the human capital involved in U.S. export and import-competing production. He concluded that the addition of such a measure of human capital to the estimates of physical capital was not sufficient to reverse the Leontief paradox, except when the natural resource products were excluded.

Some critics object to the procedure of adding human capital to physical capital. They argue that such an addition makes sense only if the two types of capital are perfect substitutes, and that seems implausible. In the short run, this objection is valid; but then the same objection can be raised for adding together buildings, machinery, airplanes, and all kinds of durable capital goods. In long-run equilibrium, however, which is the proper context for discussing the Heckscher-Ohlin theorem, the objection does not seem valid. Society has a certain "productive capacity" that can be converted into different types of capital goods, including human capital. It is this "malleable" productive capacity that is captured by the sum of physical capital plus human capital. The degree of substitutability between physical capital and human capital is irrelevant.

5-4 THE SPECIFIC-FACTORS MODEL

In this section, we study the specific-factors model, whose origins go back to Bastable and Cairnes. During the period between World War I and World War II, the model was endorsed by Haberler and other economists before it was overshadowed by the Heckscher-Ohlin model.

The New Scenario

The **specific-factors model** differs only slightly from the Heckscher-Ohlin model. Consider again two countries, America and Britain, producing two commodities, corn and steel. Unlike the Heckscher-Ohlin model, assume that each country is endowed with *three* distinct factors: labor, capital, and land. Labor is used in the production of both corn and steel, and it is perfectly mobile between the two sectors. Capital and land are **specific factors:** Capital is used only in the production of steel, and land is used only in the production of corn. As with the Heckscher-Ohlin model, assume constant returns to scale in the production of both commodities, identical technology across countries, perfect competition in all markets, similarity of tastes, free trade, and zero transportation costs.

The questions we want to explore in the rest of this section are similar to those we raised in relation to the Heckscher-Ohlin model. What determines the structure of trade? What is the effect of trade on factor prices? How does a change in relative commodity prices affect the domestic distribution of income? What are the effects of an increase in the supply of a factor of production, assuming that relative commodity prices remain constant?

Many economists think of the specific-factors model as the short-run version of the Heckscher-Ohlin model. Instead of using "land" and "capital" as the two specific factors, they allow each sector to have its own supply of capital equipment which in the short run is specific to that sector. But with the passage of time, such capital can be transferred from one sector to another via depreciation and replacement.

Specific Factors and Increasing Opportunity Costs

The specific-factors model leads to *increasing* opportunity costs because of the **law of diminishing returns** (that is, the proposition that as more units of the variable factor are added to the fixed factor, the marginal physical product of the variable factor diminishes after a point).

First, observe that the opportunity cost of steel in terms of corn coincides with the ratio of the marginal physical product of labor in the production of corn (MPP_{LC}) to the marginal physical product of labor in the production of steel (MPP_{LS}). Suppose that America transfers $1L$ from corn to steel. The output of corn will fall by MPP_{LC} or, say, 10 bushels. The output of steel will increase by MPP_{LS} or, say, 5 tons. For each additional ton of steel, America will give up 2 bushels of corn, that is, the opportunity cost of steel in terms of corn is $MPP_{LC} \div MPP_{LS} = 10 \div 5 = 2$.

As more and more labor is transferred from the production of corn to the production of steel, the law of diminishing returns comes into play: MPP_{LS} *decreases* because *more* units of labor (variable factor) are combined with capital (fixed factor), and MPP_{LC} *increases* because *fewer* units of labor are used with land (fixed factor). Hence, the ratio $MPP_{LC} \div MPP_{LS}$ (that is, the opportunity cost of steel in terms of corn) increases.

The Structure of Trade

The specific-factors model leads to an important proposition: **The structure of trade is determined by the relative abundance of the specific factors.** To illustrate this proposition, we adopt the following assumptions:

1 The two countries have the *same* supplies of the variable factor, labor.
2 America has more capital (fixed factor) than Britain.
3 Britain has more land (fixed factor) than America.
4 America and Britain have identical tastes, which are represented by the same social indifference map.

Given the preceding assumptions, we can show that America has a comparative advantage in steel, which requires the specific factor capital (America's abundant factor). Similarly, Britain has a comparative advantage in corn, which uses the specific factor land (Britain's abundant factor). This result is in agreement with the Heckscher-Ohlin theorem; it is illustrated in Figure 5-2, which is similar to Figure 4-5.

First, note that America's production frontier is skewed along the horizontal axis, and Britain's along the vertical axis. This is no accident. America's production frontier *JH* must intersect the steel (horizontal) axis at a higher level of output than Britain's frontier J^*H^*—by assumption, America is endowed with more capital than Britain. Similarly, Britain's production frontier must intersect the corn (vertical) axis at a higher output than America's frontier because Britain is endowed with more land than America. Hence, the two frontiers must be skewed in the manner shown in Figure 5-2.

Before trade is opened between the two countries, America produces and consumes at point *A* (where America's production frontier *JH* is tangent to social indifference curve 1). Britain produces and consumes at point *B*. Thus the relative price of steel is lower in America than in Britain because indifference curve 1 is flatter at *A* than at *B*. America will export steel, and Britain corn.

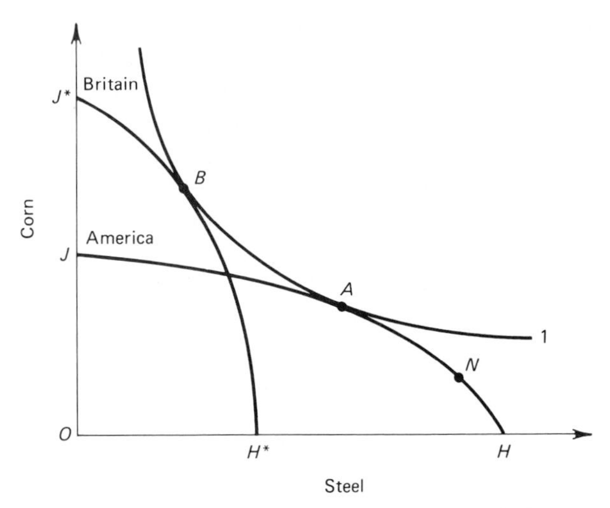

FIGURE 5-2 **Specific factors and the structure of trade.** America's production frontier, JH, is skewed along the steel (horizontal) axis because steel uses the specific factor capital (America's abundant factor). Britain's frontier, J^*H^*, is skewed along the corn (vertical) axis because corn uses land (Britain's abundant factor). America has a comparative advantage in steel and Britain in corn because steel is cheaper at A (America's autarkic equilibrium) than at B (Britain's autarkic equilibrium).

Free Trade and Income Distribution

How does the introduction of trade affect factor rewards? Return to Figure 5-2 and consider the case of America. With free trade, the relative price of steel rises, displacing American production from point A to, say, point N. This is accomplished by transferring labor from the corn sector to the steel sector. We cannot say whether the American workers will become better off or worse off. The preceding discussion has shown that the marginal physical product of labor falls in the steel sector and rises in the corn sector. Those workers who have a strong bias in the consumption of corn will welcome the change, but those who have a bias in steel will become worse off. The effects on owners of capital and land are, however, unambiguous.

Consider the owners of capital first. With more workers employed per unit of capital in the steel sector, the marginal physical product of capital in the production of steel (or the real return to capital expressed in terms of steel) rises. Since trade also makes corn cheaper in America, the real return to capital rises in terms of corn as well. Thus the American owners of capital become better off unambiguously regardless of their tastes.

The landowners are worse off. After trade is opened up, fewer workers are employed per acre of land in the production of corn; hence the marginal physical product of land in the production of corn, or the real return to land expressed in terms of corn, diminishes. Because trade also makes steel more expensive, the real return to land falls in terms of steel as well. Thus the American landowners are unambiguously worse off.

The opposite effects must occur in Britain because free trade causes the British relative price of steel to fall. Thus British landowners gain and British owners of capital lose. British workers may become better off or worse off depending on their tastes—their real wage rate rises in terms of steel but falls in terms of corn.

The preceding effects of free trade on the real earnings of the specific factors (but not the variable factor) are similar to those predicted by the Stolper-Samuelson theorem studied in Section 4-7.

The Effects of Factor Growth in a Small Open Economy

Suppose that America is a small open economy that is a price taker in world markets. Let America's supply of capital (a specific factor) expand. What effects should we expect on the outputs of corn and steel and the real earnings of the factors of production? Suppose for the moment that America maintains the pregrowth allocation of labor (the mobile factor) between the two sectors. How would the increase in the supply of capital affect the opportunity cost of steel in terms of corn? Since the capital-labor ratio in the steel industry will rise, the marginal physical product of labor (MPP_{LS}) will also rise, causing the opportunity cost of steel in terms of corn (that is, the ratio $MPP_{LC} \div MPP_{LS}$) to *fall.* To restore equilibrium, America will have to transfer labor from the corn sector to the steel sector. The output of corn will fall and the output of steel will rise even further. Note that these output effects of an increase in the supply of capital (a specific factor) are analogous to those predicted by the Rybczynski theorem in the context of the Heckscher-Ohlin model. However, in the latter case the output effects were the only effects of factor growth. In the present case, there are additional effects on real factor earnings.

The real wage rate rises both in terms of corn and in terms of steel. It rises in terms of corn because the marginal physical product of labor rises in the corn sector as labor is transferred from the production of corn to the production of steel. It must also rise in terms of steel because the relative price of steel remains the same. [An alternative proof of the latter proposition is to argue as follows: (1) The ratio of the marginal physical products of labor must remain the same. (2) The marginal physical product of labor in the corn sector rises. (3) Hence, the marginal physical product of labor in the steel sector must rise as well.]

When the mobile factor (labor) expands, *both* sectors will expand their outputs in order to absorb the extra labor. The marginal physical product of labor will *fall* by the same percentage in *both* sectors in order to keep the value of the ratio $MPP_{LC} \div MPP_{LS}$ constant. Even though workers become worse off, the owners of both specific factors become better off as their real earnings rise in terms of both commodities.

5-5 EMPIRICAL CHALLENGES TO TRADITIONAL THEORIES

Many economists believe that the traditional trade theories (that is, the Ricardian theory and the Heckscher-Ohlin model) fail to provide a complete explanation of the structure of world trade. This assessment goes beyond the fact (noted earlier in this chapter) that empirical studies seem to provide only limited support for the traditional theories. Many authors emphasize, in addition, that the world trade data contain several **empirical regularities** (or **stylized facts**) that appear to be inconsistent with the traditional theories. As a result, a variety of alternative theories have been suggested in recent years as possible explanations of the empirical puzzles. The purpose of this section is to discuss briefly the empirical challenges to the traditional theories. The rest of this chapter explores alternative trade theories, which are usually offered as a supplement (not a substitute) to the traditional models.

Three Stylized Facts

The following empirical regularities of the pattern of world trade present formidable challenges to the traditional trade theories.

1 Trade among Similar Economies

Today more than half the world trade takes place among industrialized countries, which share relatively *similar* factor endowments. In addition, throughout the post-World War II period the proportion of world trade among industrialized countries has grown steadily, while at the same time their per capita incomes have moved closer to one another, presumably reflecting greater similarity in factor endowments. This "stylized fact" (that is, expanding trade among similar economies) contradicts the Heckscher-Ohlin model, which attributes comparative advantage to *differences* in factor endowments.

2 Intraindustry Trade

A large and growing portion of world trade, especially among industrialized countries, involves exchanges of very similar products, or **intraindustry trade.** For instance, Japan exports Toyotas to the United States while at the same time the United States exports Cadillacs to Japan. There is still disagreement about the empirical relevance of intraindustry trade. Some economists point out that perhaps the empirical measures of intraindustry trade are far too large because of aggregation. They argue that much of the apparent intraindustry trade disappears when finer levels of disaggregation are used in measuring it. This argument has, of course, some merit but cannot provide any justification for the phenomenal growth of intraindustry trade during the postwar period.

The Heckscher-Ohlin theory is inconsistent with the phenomenon of intraindustry trade. According to the Heckscher-Ohlin model, a country's exported commodities are intensive in its abundant factor while the imported commodities are intensive in the scarce factor; that is, the exported and imported commodities *differ* in their factor content. Intraindustry trade, however, involves commodities of similar factor intensity—a phenomenon that is hard to explain within the context of the Heckscher-Ohlin model.

3 Trade Liberalization
During the postwar period trade has been liberalized considerably. The formation of the European Community and other free trade areas plus successive rounds of multilateral tariff reductions by the industrialized nations have led to substantial growth in the volume of world trade. The traditional theory of international trade would lead one to expect that such trade liberalization would be accompanied by enormous reallocation of resources and social conflict. For instance, the Stolper-Samuelson theorem predicts that trade liberalization reduces the real income of one of the factors of production, and it is reasonable to assume that the injured factor would bitterly resist the liberalization of trade. None of these predictions came true, however. The record shows that little resource reallocation took place. Instead trade appears to have increased the productivity of all factors of production, leaving everyone better off.

5-6 INCREASING RETURNS

Both the Heckscher-Ohlin model and the Ricardian model are built on the assumption of constant returns to scale. Yet in many countries of the world, such as the United States, Britain, Japan, and Germany, one observes a large number of manufacturing industries that appear to be subject to **increasing returns to scale** (or **economies of scale**). Increasing returns have long been regarded as a separate reason for trade as well as a determinant of the pattern of trade. The renewed interest in increasing returns lies in the fact that they help explain the empirical puzzles discussed in the previous section.

Reasons for Increasing Returns to Scale

A factory could always be duplicated; thus, doubling all inputs (such as plant, raw materials, and workers) must double the output. This line of thought leads to a presumption that returns to scale are constant. However, there are important reasons for the existence of increasing returns to scale. We can summarize them as follows:

1 Indivisibilities
It may be easy to duplicate a plant or a process, but it may not be possible to halve them. If a person operates a computer, we could find a second person with roughly the same skills to operate a second computer, but we cannot devise a "half-computer" operated by a "half-person." As a result, at a small scale of operations a producer may be forced to employ less efficient inputs because the more efficient inputs may become available only at a larger scale. Such **indivisibilities** give rise to increasing returns.

2 Division of Labor

Adam Smith emphasized the importance of the economies generated by the **division of labor.** In his famous example of the pin factory, Smith calculated that division of labor made it possible for 10 workers to produce 48,000 pins per day, so that each worker produced the equivalent of 4,800 pins. Without division of labor, he explained, a worker might not make even one pin in a day. As the scale of operations expands, labor becomes more productive because of increased specialization. Division of labor enhances the dexterity of each worker and saves time by making it unnecessary for workers to shift from one task to another. In short, division of labor gives rise to increasing returns.

3 Geometrical Relations

Doubling the walls of a warehouse *quadruples* warehouse space. Similarly, doubling the radius of a pipe (used, say, to transport oil), doubles the quantity of metal needed for its construction but *quadruples* its capacity. These examples show that the laws of physics often conspire to generate increasing returns.

4 Inventories

Typically, the optimal level of inventories increases less than in proportion to the firm's output (or sales). For instance, as output increases by 50 percent, inventories (input) may have to increase by only 30 percent, implying increasing returns.

5 Once-and-for-all Inputs

Some inputs (such as the designing of an automobile or the proofreading of a book) need not increase at all as output expands. Hence output increases proportionately more than inputs, implying increasing returns.

Increasing Returns and Market Structure

As we have just seen, increasing returns are attributable to certain "economies"—economies that are reflected in cost reductions. These economies may be internal or external to the firm. **Internal economies** (such as division of labor) are within the control of the firm and account for the downward-sloping portion of the firm's average-cost curve. **External economies** are cost reductions that reveal themselves as *downward shifts* of the average-cost curve of the individual firm as the industry's output expands.

Unlimited increasing returns due to internal economies are incompatible with perfect competition. For when the internal economies of a firm continue indefinitely, and thus the average-cost curve slopes downward throughout, the firm will find it profitable to increase output beyond all bounds (provided that its average-cost curve dips below the average-revenue curve after a certain point). Eventually the firm will capture the entire market; that is, the firm will become a **monopoly** (single seller of a commodity that has no close substitutes). Alternatively, increasing returns may be such as to permit only a few firms into the industry; that is, increasing returns may lead to **oligopoly.**

Historically, increasing returns have been incorporated into the trade model on the assumption that scale economies are external to the firm—an assumption that, as Alfred Marshall showed, preserves perfect competition. Recently, however, some theorists have developed trade models that attribute increasing returns to internal economies.

To avoid the complications of an oligopolistic market structure in the presence of internal scale economies, we may invoke the newly developed theory of **contestable markets.** A market is contestable when there are potential competitors who can enter and exit rapidly from the market. Established firms have no advantage over these potential competitors. For our purposes, the main implication of contestable markets is that *the threat of entry forces firms to price the commodities at average cost* even though some of the commodities are produced by monopolistic or oligopolistic firms.

Decreasing Opportunity Costs and International Trade

Increasing returns to scale are usually portrayed by means of a production frontier that is totally *convex* to the origin (although other shapes cannot be excluded). A convex production frontier implies *decreasing* opportunity costs, which enable even totally similar economies to engage in mutually beneficial trade. This is illustrated in Figure 5-3.

FIGURE 5-3 **Decreasing opportunity costs and the gains from trade.** Before trade, both America and Britain produce and consume at *E* on their common production frontier, *UV*, which is convex to the origin. After trade, America produces at *V* and consumes at *A*; and Britain produces at *U* and consumes at *B*. Both countries benefit, even though the equilibrium terms of trade (given by the slope of *AV* or *UB*) are not different from the common autarkic relative price ratio (given by the slope of *ST*).

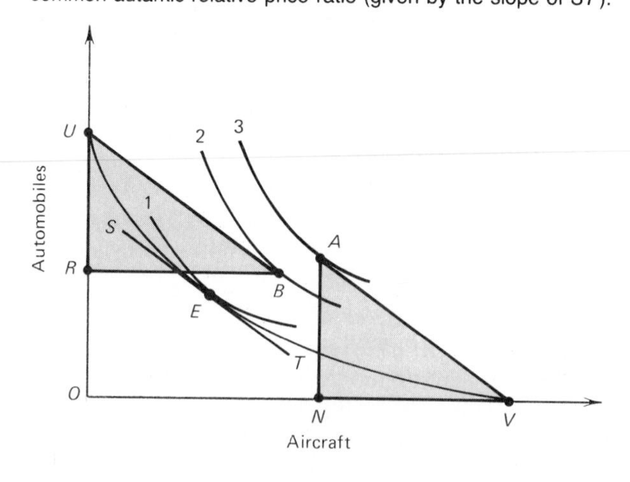

We assume that two nations, America and Britain, are identical in every respect. They use their resources to produce two commodities, automobiles and aircraft, under increasing returns to scale. Because they are identical, America and Britain share the same production frontier, *UV* (which is convex to the origin) and the same social indifference map (illustrated by curves 1, 2, and 3).

To simplify our exposition, we assume that relative prices are always equal to opportunity costs. This equality may be the result of an appropriate system of taxes and subsidies on the production of commodities as well as the use of factors of production. Alternatively, the equality between opportunity costs and relative prices may prevail because markets are contestable. In any case, the reason for the equality is not important.

With identical production frontiers and social indifference maps, the autarkic equilibria of America and Britain are also the same. Thus in autarky both countries produce and consume at *E* (where production frontier *UV* is tangent to social indifference curve 1). The pretrade prices of America and Britain are also equal, as shown by the common price line, *ST*.

Does the equality of their autarkic prices prevent America and Britain from engaging in mutually beneficial trade? Not at all. With trade, one nation (say, America) could specialize completely in aircraft, as shown by point *V*. Similarly, the other country (Britain) could specialize completely in automobiles, as shown by point *U*. America could then consume at *A*, and Britain at *B*. Thus America could export *NV* (or *RB*) aircraft to Britain in exchange for *NA* (or *RU*) British automobiles. Again trade triangles *ANV* and *URB* are identical. Note that both countries specialize completely, as in the Ricardian world of constant costs.

The fact that America benefits more than Britain (because America attains a higher social indifference curve than Britain) is not as significant as the fact that two similar economies gain significantly from free trade. Note also that these gains from trade exist despite the fact that the autarkic relative prices of the two countries are the same and the equilibrium terms of trade are not different from the common autarkic relative prices—by construction, lines *ST*, *AV*, and *UB* are all parallel.

The European Community offers an important historical application of the present analysis. Before its formation, European plants were very small and inefficient because they catered mostly to a small domestic market. With the formation of the European Community tariffs were eliminated, the market expanded considerably, and trade grew rapidly. As plant size increased substantially, the costs of production fell sharply and everybody became better off. That was a cause for celebration, not social conflict. Adam Smith was right when he observed that *the division of labor is limited by the extent of the market.*

5-7 MONOPOLISTIC COMPETITION AND INTERNATIONAL TRADE

In an effort to explain the widespread phenomenon of intraindustry trade, economists have recently incorporated **monopolistic competition** into the basic trade models. The model of monopolistic competition was developed by Edward H. Chamberlin (1933). It rests on the empirical observation that a large number of industries are composed of many small firms that produce **differentiated products,** that is, products that satisfy the same basic need but are not perfect substitutes. Some examples of differentiated products are automobiles (a Toyota is not identical to a Taurus), typewriters (a Smith-Corona is not identical to a Brother), toothpastes (Colgate is not identical to Crest), aspirin (Anacin is not identical to Bayer), and soft drinks (a Coca-Cola Classic is not identical to a Pepsi).

Product differentiation combined with increasing returns to scale can easily explain intraindustry trade. Assume that increasing returns are exhausted at a fairly low level of output, so that each industry can accommodate many producers, with each producer producing a different brand. In addition, assume that each nation has a **taste for variety.** Thus consumers may like variety as such. For example, consumers do not like to wear the same color of suit or dress always; sometimes they may like to wear white, sometimes black, and sometimes red. Alternatively, each individual may have a most preferred variety (such as a hair style), but different consumers may prefer different varieties, so that in the aggregate there may exist a taste for variety. Under these circumstances, each country will specialize in different varieties of the product and engage in intraindustry trade (in addition to the traditional form of interindustry trade) in order to satisfy its citizens' taste for variety.

Intraindustry trade in differentiated products has two important implications for the gains from trade. First, through foreign trade, consumers gain access to greater variety as more brands become available. Second, unit costs and prices decline because of the underlying increasing returns. For both of these reasons, the gains from trade are larger under monopolistic competition. Indeed, it is possible for all factors to benefit from intraindustry trade. Perhaps this last observation may explain the absence of any social conflict or resistance by special-interest groups after the formation of the European Community, which prompted a phenomenal increase in intraindustry trade.

5-8 LINDER'S THESIS

The Swedish economist and politician Staffan Burenstam Linder (1961) advanced the hypothesis that a country exports those manufactured products for which there is a broad local market. He asserted that manufacturers initiate the production of a new product in order to serve the domestic market, which is more familiar to them. In the process, they develop the skills for making the product cheaply. Eventually, they export the product to other countries with similar tastes and income levels.

Linder's thesis is known as the **spillover theory,** in which exports grow out of domestic production. It applies only to manufactures, not to primary products. Trade in primary products is determined by factor endowments (especially natural resources), as in the Heckscher-Ohlin model. One important implication of Linder's thesis is that trade in manufactures is high between countries of similar per capita income. This conclusion contradicts, of course, the Heckscher-Ohlin model.

Empirical studies have not provided much support for Linder's hypothesis. Exceptions to Linder's thesis are not difficult to find. For instance, artificial Christmas trees and ornaments are exported by non-Christian countries, such as Japan and Korea, which lack a domestic market for them.

5-9 TECHNOLOGICAL GAP AND PRODUCT CYCLE

The Heckscher-Ohlin theory is static. Several distinguished economists have argued recently that perhaps the composition of trade depends on dynamic factors, such as technical change. In particular, it has been argued that what allows the United States to compete successfully in world markets is its ability to supply a steady flow of new products.

The **technological-gap theory,** proposed by Posner (1961), makes use of the sequence of innovation and imitation particularly as it affects exports. As a new product is developed and becomes profitable in the domestic markets, the innovating firm, which enjoys a temporary monopoly, initially has an easy access to foreign markets. At first, the country's exports grow. Later on, however, the profits of the innovating firm prompt imitation in other countries, which may actually prove to have a comparative advantage in the production of the new product after the innovation is disseminated. But as the innovating country loses, through imitation, its absolute advantage in one product, a new cycle of innovation-imitation begins in another product. Thus, the innovating country may continue to develop new products and may continue to have a temporary absolute advantage in products that are eventually produced more efficiently in other countries. Note that catering for the domestic market first, before expanding into foreign markets, is an idea which was stressed originally by Linder (1961).

Kravis (1956b) argued that a country's exports are determined by *availability.* He did not give a precise definition to the term "availability." He used it in the sense that the domestic supply of exports is "elastic" (perhaps relative to the corresponding foreign supply). Kravis claimed that availability is a reflection of a country's relative abundance of natural resources and temporary superiority in technology that innovation confers upon the country.

The technological-gap theory fails to explain why the gap is what it is and why it is not larger or smaller. Vernon (1966) generalized the theory into the **product cycle,** which stresses the standardization of products. In particular, Vernon suggested three stages: **new product**, **maturing product**, and **standardized product**. He also suggested that input requirements change over the life cycle of a new product. For instance, at the new-product stage, production requires much highly skilled labor for the development and improvement of the product. As the product matures, marketing and capital costs become dominant. Finally, at the standardized product stage, the technology stabilizes and the product enjoys general consumer acceptance. This leads to mass production, which largely requires raw materials, capital, and unskilled labor. Accordingly, as the product matures and becomes standardized, comparative advantage may shift from a country relatively abundant in skilled labor to a country abundant in unskilled labor.

Keesing (1967), Gruber, Mehta, and Vernon (1967), and others have taken research and development (R&D) expenditures as a proxy for temporary, comparative cost advantages created by the development of new products. They have found a strong correlation between the intensity of R&D activity and export performance. Such evidence tends to support both the technological-gap theory and the product-cycle theory.

Why does the United States have a comparative advantage based on technology and innovation? Several factors are usually cited for this phenomenon. First, the United States has a per capita income that is high by international standards—a fact that creates unique consumption patterns and a favorable market for new or improved products. Second, the development of new or improved products requires much skilled labor, which is relatively abundant in the United States. Third, because of the high U.S. labor costs and the alleged tendency of innovations to be labor saving, there is a greater incentive to innovate in the United States. Finally, the development and marketing of new or improved products may be associated with economies of scale, which tend to be realizable in large, high-income markets like those of the United States. This last point is, of course, closely related to the first.

5-10 SUMMARY

1 Empirical studies by MacDougall and other economists provide strong support for the classical theory of comparative advantage.

2 Leontief tested the hypothesis that U.S. exports are capital intensive relative to U.S. imports. However, he reached the paradoxical conclusion that the United States actually exports labor-intensive commodities and imports capital-intensive commodities.

3 Two unacceptable explanations of the Leontief paradox are as follows: (a) U.S. labor is so much more superior to foreign labor that the United States is actually a labor-abundant country. (b) Perhaps the United States has a strong consumption bias toward capital-intensive goods.

4 More serious explanations of the Leontief paradox are as follows: (a) Factor-intensity reversals separate the United States from the rest of the world and invalidate the Heckscher-Ohlin theorem. (b) By protecting U.S. industries that are relatively intensive in unskilled labor, U.S. tariff and nontariff barriers to international trade tend to exclude labor-intensive imports. (c) Natural resources are relatively scarce in the United States. As a result, the United States imports natural resource products, which are highly capital intensive. (d) U.S. export industries intensively use skilled labor, which is relatively abundant in America. (e) A large portion of wages paid to skilled labor is actually a return to human capital. When the human capital element of skilled labor is properly accounted for, the Leontief paradox is reversed.

5 According to the specific-factors model (which many economists view as a short-run version of the Heckscher-Ohlin model) comparative advantage is determined by the relative abundance of the specific factors. With the introduction of trade, the specific factor used in the production of the commodity whose price rises becomes better off, and the other specific factor becomes worse off. The effect of trade on the real income of the mobile factor is ambiguous.

6 When a specific factor expands in a small, open economy, the output of the commodity using the expanded factor rises and the output of the other commodity falls. This result is analogous to the Rybczynski theorem.

7 When the mobile factor grows, the outputs of both commodities expand, the mobile factor becomes worse off, and the specific factors become better off.

8 Trade among similar economies, intraindustry trade, and ease of adjustment of trade liberalization pose formidable challenges to the traditional theories of trade. Long regarded as a separate reason for trade, increasing returns can help explain these empirical puzzles.

9 With decreasing opportunity costs, countries are likely to specialize completely, as in the Ricardian model of constant costs. Further, countries can benefit from trade considerably even in the absence of any changes in relative prices. All factors can become better off with trade.

10 Intraindustry trade in differentiated products has two important implications for the gains from trade: (a) Consumers gain access to greater variety, and (b) unit costs and prices decline because of the underlying increasing returns.

11 Linder asserted that a country exports those manufactured products for which there is a broad local market. Empirical studies have not provided much support for Linder's thesis.

12 The technological-gap theory is based on the sequence of innovation and imitation (particularly as they affect exports). The argument is that the United States has a comparative advantage in research and development and tends to export technologically advanced manufactured goods.

13 The product-cycle theory suggests three product stages (new product, maturing product, and standardized product). It then explains the speed of dissemination of innovation on the basis of both the changing input requirements over the life cycle of a new product and the factor endowments of countries.

PROBLEMS

1 France is endowed with 4,000 workers and 2,000 acres of land. Germany is endowed with 6,000 workers and 30,000 acres of land. Both countries share the same technology in the production of two commodities, X and Y. At the final international equilibrium, the optimal unit coefficients of production are as follows:

	France		Germany	
	Labor	Land	Labor	Land
Commodity X	6	2	1	8
Commodity Y	4	3	2	6

a Determine the precise amounts of X and Y produced by each country.
b Assuming that tastes are the same in France and Germany, which commodity is exported by France? Which commodity is exported by Germany?
c Which country exhibits a Leontief paradox?
d Does free trade equalize factor prices in this example? Why or why not?

2 Mexico and Brazil are endowed with fixed quantities of three factors of production: labor, capital, and land. They use labor (mobile factor) and capital (specific factor) to produce cars, and they use labor and land (specific factor) to produce wheat.
a At their respective autarkic equilibria, the marginal productivity of labor (mobile factor) is 200 bushels of wheat or 2 cars in Mexico, and 80 bushels of wheat or 4 cars in Brazil. Which country has a comparative advantage in the production of wheat? Cars?
b When free trade is introduced between Mexico and Brazil, the equilibrium terms of trade settle at 50 bushels of wheat per car. If a statistical estimate shows that the marginal physical product of labor in the production of cars is 3 in both countries, what is the marginal physical product of labor in the production of wheat in Mexico? In Brazil?

3 America and Britain share the same production-possibilities frontier. The following table gives data on five points (A, B, C, D, and E) of the common frontier:

	A	B	C	D	E
Commodity X	0	10	30	60	100
Commodity Y	200	150	100	50	0

In autarky, America produces combination C, and Britain combination D.
a Plot points *A* through *E* on graph paper and connect them with straight-line segments.
b Determine the opportunity cost of X in terms of Y as production shifts from point *A* to point *B;* from point *B* to point *C;* from point *C* to point *D;* and from point *D* to point *E.*
c Can both countries benefit if America specializes completely in the production of X and Britain in Y?
d Can both countries benefit if America specializes completely in Y and Britain in X?

4 a What empirical regularities (or stylized facts) are revealed by world trade data?
b How do the observed empirical regularities contradict the Heckscher-Ohlin model?
c How does product differentiation combined with increasing returns explain intraindustry trade?
d How does the theory of the product cycle explain the observed pattern of trade?

SUGGESTED READING

Balassa, B. (1963). "An Empirical Demonstration of Comparative Cost." *Review of Economics and Statistics,* vol. 45, pp. 231–238.

——— (1966). "Tariff Reductions and Trade in Manufactures Among the Industrial Countries." *American Economic Review,* vol. 56 (June), pp. 466–473.

Baldwin, R. E. (1971). "Determinants of the Commodity Structure of U.S. Trade." *American Economic Review,* vol. 61, no. 1 (March), pp. 126–146.

Brecher, R. A., and E. U. Choudhri (1982). "The Leontief Paradox, Continued." *Journal of Political Economy,* vol. 90 (August), pp. 820–823.

Chacholiades, M. (1970). "Increasing Returns and the Theory of Comparative Advantage." *Southern Economic Journal,* vol. 37, pp. 157–162.

Chamberlin, E. H. (1933). *The Theory of Monopolistic Competition.* Harvard University Press, Cambridge, Mass.

Diab, M. A. (1956). *The United States Capital Position and the Structure of Its Foreign Trade.* North-Holland Publishing Company, Amsterdam.

Ellsworth, P. T. (1954). "The Structure of American Foreign Trade: A New View Examined." *Review of Economics and Statistics,* vol. 36 (August), pp. 279–285.

Grubel, H. G., and P. J. Lloyd (1975). *Intra-Industry Trade: The Theory and Measurement of International Trade in Differentiated Products.* John Wiley & Sons, New York.

Gruber, W., D. Mehta, and R. Vernon (1967). "The R&D Factor in International Trade and Investment of United States Industries." *Journal of Political Economy,* vol. 75 (February), pp. 20–37. Reprinted (with footnotes and references omitted) in R. E. Baldwin and J. D. Richardson (eds.), *International Trade and Finance,* Little, Brown and Company, Boston, 1974.

Jones, R. W. (1971). "A Three-Factor Model in Theory, Trade, and History." In J. N. Bhagwati et al. (eds.), *Trade, Balance of Payments, and Growth: Essays in Honor of Charles P. Kindleberger,* North-Holland Publishing Company, Amsterdam, 1971.

Keesing, D. B. (1966). "Labor Skills and Comparative Advantage." *American Economic Review,* vol. 56 (May), pp. 249–258.

——— (1967). "The Impact of Research and Development on United States Trade." *Journal of Political Economy,* vol. 75, no. 1, pp. 38–48. Reprinted in P. B. Kenen and R. Lawrence (eds.), *The Open Economy,* Columbia University Press, New York, 1968.

Kenen, P. B. (1965). "Nature, Capital and Trade." *Journal of Political Economy,* vol. 73 (October), pp. 437–460.

Kravis, I. B. (1956a). "Wages and Foreign Trade." *Review of Economics and Statistics,* vol. 38 (February), pp. 14–30.

——— (1956b). "Availability and Other Influences on the Commodity Composition of Trade." *Journal of Political Economy,* vol. 64 (April), pp. 143–155.

Kreinin, M. E. (1965). "Comparative Labor Effectiveness and the Leontief Scarce Factor Paradox." *American Economic Review,* vol. 55 (March), pp. 131–140.

Leamer, E. E. (1980). "The Leontief Paradox, Reconsidered." *Journal of Political Economy,* vol. 88 (June), pp. 495–503.

Leontief, W. W. (1954). "Domestic Production and Foreign Trade: the American Capital Position Re-examined." *Economia Internazionale,* vol. 7 (February), pp. 3–32. Reprinted in R. E. Caves and H. G. Johnson (eds.), American Economics Association *Readings in International Economics,* Richard D. Irwin, Inc., Homewood, Ill., 1968.

——— (1956). "Factor Proportions and the Structure of American Trade: Further Theoretical and Empirical Analysis." *Review of Economics and Statistics,* vol. 38 (November), pp. 386–407.

Linder, S. B. (1961). *An Essay on Trade and Transformation.* Almqvist and Wiksell, Stockholm.

MacDougall, G. D. A. (1951). "British and American Exports: A Study Suggested by the Theory of Comparative Costs, Part I." *Economic Journal,* vol. 61, pp. 697–724. Reprinted in R. E. Caves and H. G. Johnson (eds.), *Readings in International Economics,* Richard D. Irwin, Inc., Homewood, Ill., 1968.

Matthews, R. C. O. (1950). "Reciprocal Demand and Increasing Returns." *Review of Economic Studies,* vol. 17, pp. 149–158.

Posner, M. V. (1961). "International Trade and Technical Change." *Oxford Economic Papers,* vol. 13, pp. 323–341.

Samuelson, P. A. (1971). "Ohlin Was Right." *Swedish Journal of Economics,* vol. 73, pp. 365–384.

Stern, R. M. (1962). "British and American Productivity and Comparative Costs in International Trade." *Oxford Economic Papers,* vol. 14, pp. 275–296.

Stern, R. M., and K. E. Maskus (1981). "Determinants of the Structure of U.S. Foreign Trade, 1958–76." *Journal of International Economics,* vol. 11 (May), pp. 207–224.

Travis, W. P. (1964). *The Theory of Trade and Protection.* Harvard University Press, Cambridge, Mass.

Vanek, J. (1959). "The Natural Resource Content of Foreign Trade, 1870–1955, and the Relative Abundance of Natural Resources in the United States." *Review of Economics and Statistics,* vol. 41 (May), pp. 146–153.

——— (1963). *The Natural Resource Content of United States Foreign Trade, 1870–1955.* The MIT Press, Cambridge, Mass.

Vernon, R. (1966). "International Investment and International Trade in the Product Cycle." *Quarterly Journal of Economics,* vol. 80 (May), pp. 190–207.

———, ed. (1970). *The Technology Factor in International Trade.* Columbia University Press, New York.

CHAPTER **6**

GROWTH AND TRADE

The preceding chapters are hampered by the assumption that factor endowments and technology, the fundamental data that delimit the production-possibilities frontier or transformation curve, are given. But in our constantly changing world neither factor endowments nor technology remain static. With the passage of time, factor endowments grow, and new and more efficient methods of production replace older, less efficient ones. Factor-endowment growth and technical progress give rise to some interesting problems. The study of these problems is known as the **theory of the effects of economic growth on trade.**

Many economists have emphasized the importance of international trade during the growth process. Trade unleashes several dynamic forces that are conducive to economic growth. As markets expand, competition becomes less personal and producers tend to encroach upon each other's markets. This increased competition improves economic efficiency, often through technical progress, and leads to increased investment, which is necessary in order to take advantage of the newly created opportunities. It is generally agreed that for many countries in North America and western Europe that developed during the nineteenth century, international trade did serve as an **engine of growth.**

This chapter deals with the **comparative statics analysis** of the effects of **factor endowment growth** and **technical progress** on the growing economy's production, consumption, terms of trade, and social welfare. The discussion is divided into three parts. Part A deals with the nature of the growth process and the peculiarities of each of the three basic sources of economic growth (labor growth, capital accumulation, and technical progress). Parts B and C deal with the effects of growth on "small" and "large" countries, respectively.

PART A

The Nature of the Growth Process

6-1 THE SOURCES OF ECONOMIC GROWTH

The three main sources of economic growth are **labor growth, capital accumulation,** and **technical progress.** Their common characteristic is that **they all cause the growing economy's transformation curve to shift outward over time.** The following discussion deals briefly with some of the peculiarities of each of these three sources of economic growth.

Labor Growth

The reader is no doubt aware of the unprecedented population explosion the world has experienced during the last two centuries. During this time more than 3 billion people have been added to the world's population (which currently stands at about 5 billion). Population continues to grow in most countries. It grows faster in the developing countries of Africa, Asia, and Latin America (such as Brazil, China, India, Indonesia, Kenya, Mexico, Pakistan, and Zambia) than in the advanced countries of North America and western Europe (such as France, Italy, the United Kingdom, the United States, and West Germany).

Population growth leads, of course, to labor growth, and the expansion of the supply of labor causes the production-possibilities frontier to shift outward. Nevertheless, it would be a mistake to conclude, on the basis of the outward shift of the transformation curve alone, that a country with a growing population will become better off.

An important yardstick of welfare is provided by the economy's per capita income. Because of the **law of diminishing returns,** labor growth in itself tends to lower per capita income and the standard of living. It was particularly for this reason that Malthus, a contemporary of Ricardo, painted a rather gloomy picture of the world—namely, that labor growth would drive wages down to the minimum subsistence level. While wages are above the subsistence level, Malthus argued, population will continue to grow; and when wages fall below the subsistence level, population will die off either through an increase in the death rate (because of disease, famine, and war) or perhaps through a reduction in the birthrate (as a result of birth control). Only at the subsistence level can there be long-run equilibrium. It is no wonder, then, that Thomas Carlyle called economics the "dismal science" after he read Malthus.

Capital Accumulation

One of the basic facts of economic history in western Europe, North America, Japan, and Australia is that the stock of capital increased much faster than population. Economists refer to this phenomenon as **capital deepening.** Like labor growth, capital accumulation causes the transformation curve to shift outward over time. However, unlike labor growth, capital accumulation leads to a higher per capita income and standard of living.

The term *capital* should be understood to mean "produced means of production"—for example, machines. How does capital come into existence? Through **saving and investment.** By abstaining from current consumption (saving), the economy frees factors from the production of consumption goods and diverts the factors toward the formation of new capital goods (investment).

Unlike the growth of the labor force, which modern economists consider exogenous (determined by demographic factors), the growth of the capital stock is endogenous. That is, the capital stock is determined by the behavior of the economic system itself: The acts of saving and investment form an integral part of the economic process. This view of capital accumulation leads directly to the construction of a dynamic model of economic growth in which today's production affects tomorrow's capital stock and production. However, this is the domain of the **modern theory of economic growth,** which lies beyond the scope of this book.

Our approach is rather modest. We wish to discuss the effects of labor growth, capital accumulation, and technical progress within a *comparative statics* framework. In other words, we shall ask questions such as this: How does a *once-and-for-all* increase in our home country's labor force or stock of capital affect our economy's production, consumption, terms of trade, and social welfare? In this discussion, we shall make no attempt to explain where the factor increases come from. We shall only study their long-run, comparative statics effects.

Technical Progress

Technical progress is an important factor of economic growth. It occurs when increased output can be obtained over time from given resources of capital and labor. Graphically, technical progress can be viewed as an **inward shift of all isoquants** of an industry undergoing technical progress. The importance of technical progress was overlooked by Malthus.

Even a casual glance at the data reveals that the United States must have experienced remarkable technical progress during the twentieth century. While the capital-output ratio of the United States has remained fairly close to 3 (years),[1] the stock of capital has increased much faster than the supply of labor (that is, capital deepening has been taking place), and the real rate of interest has shown no long-run trend. It appears, then, that technical progress did occur and actually offset the diminishing returns to capital. Several empirical studies by Abramovitz, Fabricant, Kendrick, Solow, and others seem to confirm this

[1]Since capital is a stock (measured at a particular time) and income is a flow (measured over a period of time, such as a year), the capital-output ratio has the same dimensionality as income, that is, time (or years).

important conclusion. These studies show that by far the larger part of the observed increase in per capita income is the result of technical progress rather than capital deepening.

6-2 CLASSIFICATION OF TECHNICAL PROGRESS

Technical progress is usually classified as **neutral, labor saving,** or **capital saving.** Unfortunately, there exist several distinct sets of definitions for these three classifications. In general, the different definitions give rise to different classifications of otherwise similar phenomena. The most appropriate for our purposes are the definitions formulated by Sir John Hicks, usually referred to as the **Hicksian definitions.** These are the only definitions discussed below.

We will assume that constant returns to scale prevail before and after the occurrence of technical progress and that technical progress occurs in a once-and-for-all fashion.

Neutral Technical Progress

Graphically, this type of technical progress amounts to a mere renumbering of the isoquants of the industry undergoing change. After the technical change, each isoquant bears a larger number of units of output. It is as if the productivity of all factors of production increased at a uniform rate with the mere passage of time. This is the simplest type of technical progress. Most of our discussion in this chapter will be restricted to the effects of neutral technical progress.

More formally, neutral technical progress occurs in an industry when (1) increased output is obtained from given quantities of labor and capital and (2) the same capital-labor ratio is optimal before and after the change for each and every value of the wage-rent ratio. In other words, the isoquants of the industry undergoing neutral technical progress shift inward, and in addition the marginal rate of technical substitution of labor for capital is the same before and after the technical change for all possible capital-labor ratios.

Labor-saving Technical Progress

Labor-saving technical progress occurs in an industry when (1) increased output is obtained from given quantities of labor and capital and (2) for any wage-rent ratio, fewer units of labor per unit of capital (that is, a larger capital-labor ratio) are optimally employed after the change than before. Thus, *labor is being saved per unit of capital employed.* This does not mean that only labor is saved while capital is not. Whatever combination of labor and capital was originally used to produce a specified amount of output, there is at least one new combination of fewer units of labor and fewer units of capital that yields the same amount of output after the change. Remember that *for all types of technical progress each isoquant shifts totally inward.* The case of labor-saving technical progress is illustrated in Figure 6-1.

Many economists, such as Sir John Hicks and William Fellner, have argued that there exists an inherent bias in our capitalistic system toward labor-saving technical progress. They attribute this bias to the continuous rise in real wage rates, which allegedly induces businesses to invent labor-saving techniques. This bias toward labor-saving inventions is usually offered as an explanation for the observed failure of capital deepening to bring down the rate of return to capital. Karl Marx employed a similar reasoning and argued that labor-saving technical progress enables capitalists to maintain a "reserve army of the unemployed" and keep wages at the minimum subsistence level, that is, perpetuate the "misery of the proletariat."

Capital-saving Technical Progress

Capital-saving technical progress occurs in an industry when (1) increased output is obtained from given quantities of labor and capital and (2) for any wage-rent ratio, fewer units of capital per unit of labor (that is, a smaller capital-labor ratio) are optimally employed after the change than before. Therefore, *capital is*

FIGURE 6-1 **Labor-saving technical progress.** The unit isoquant is given by curve *bb* before the change and by curve *aa* after the change. Note that new unit isoquant *aa* lies totally inside old unit isoquant *bb*. In addition, at the wage-rent ratio depicted by the slope of *bb* at *B*, the capital-labor ratio after the change (shown by the slope of ray *OA*) is higher than the capital-labor ratio before the change (shown by the slope of ray *OB*).

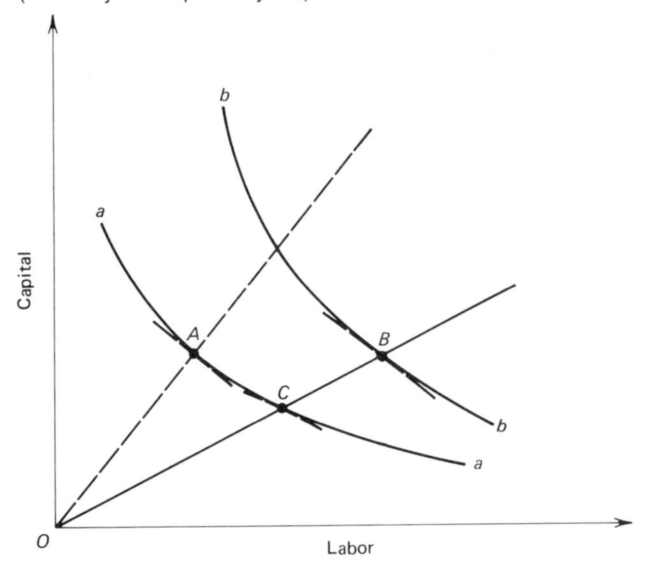

being saved per unit of labor employed. Again, this does not mean that only capital is saved while labor is not. The case of capital-saving technical progress is illustrated in Figure 6-2.

PART B

The Effects of Growth on Small Countries

This part will discuss the effects of economic growth on a small country that is a price taker in the international market. Not only does this analysis shed light on those economies which in the real world are actually small in the sense that their exports and imports have no influence on their terms of trade, but it also serves as an important building block in the investigation into the effects of economic growth on large countries (Part C), whose exports and imports do affect their terms of trade.

FIGURE 6-2 **Capital-saving technical progress.** Curves *bb* and *aa* are the unit isoquants before and after the change, respectively. New isoquant *aa* lies totally inside old isoquant *bb*. In addition, at the wage-rent ratio depicted by the slope of *bb* at *B*, the optimal capital-labor ratio falls from the slope of *OB* (before the change) to the slope of *OA* (after the change).

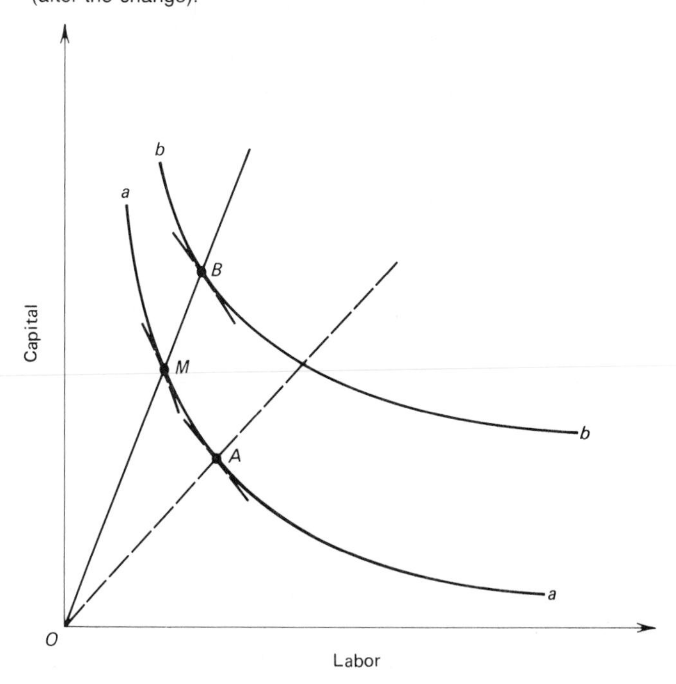

6-3 THE SCENARIO

Assume that Austria is endowed with fixed quantities of two homogeneous factors, labor and capital, and produces two commodities, steel and cloth, under constant returns to scale. Assume further that cloth is labor intensive relative to steel at all factor-price ratios. Austria is a ''small'' country and trades steel and cloth in a huge international market at fixed prices.

In the rest of this part, we will let Austria experience various types of growth. Our objective is to study how each type of growth affects Austria's production, consumption, exports, and imports of food and cloth. In addition, we are concerned with the effect of growth on Austria's social welfare.

To avoid any confusion and muddled thinking insofar as growth's effect on social welfare is concerned, we assume that Austria is inhabited by a number of citizens who have identical tastes and factor endowments. Accordingly, we can deduce the effect of growth on Austria's social welfare from the effect of growth on Austria's **representative citizen:** If growth makes one representative citizen better off, it makes all better off and social welfare improves; and if growth makes one representative citizen worse off, it makes all worse off and social welfare deteriorates.

When all citizens are identical with respect to tastes and factor endowments, the production-possibilities frontier can be scaled down in proportion to the representative citizen. (All this is made possible by the assumption of constant returns to scale.) With constant terms of trade, growth makes the representative citizen better off (worse off) if it shifts the scaled down production-possibilities frontier outward (inward).

Figure 6-3 illustrates Austria's pregrowth equilibrium position. Curve *UEV* is Austria's pregrowth production-possibilities frontier. The given international price ratio is depicted by the slope of the production-possibilities frontier at *E*. Before growth, Austria produces at point *E*.

6-4 FACTOR ACCUMULATION

Any increase in Austria's factor endowments necessarily causes its production-possibilities frontier to shift outward. The precise shift of the production-possibilities frontier and the concomitant output changes depend only on how Austria's factor endowments grow. As it turns out, any arbitrary increase in factor endowments can always be broken down into a combination of two simple cases: balanced factor growth and single-factor growth.

Balanced Factor Growth

Suppose that Austria's labor and capital grow at the *same* rate (say, 5 percent) so that the overall capital-labor ratio remains constant. How is Austria's production-possibilities frontier affected? How do the outputs of steel and cloth change? Intuitively, balanced growth means that the number of the economy's representative citizens increases (by, say, 5 percent). Since each representative

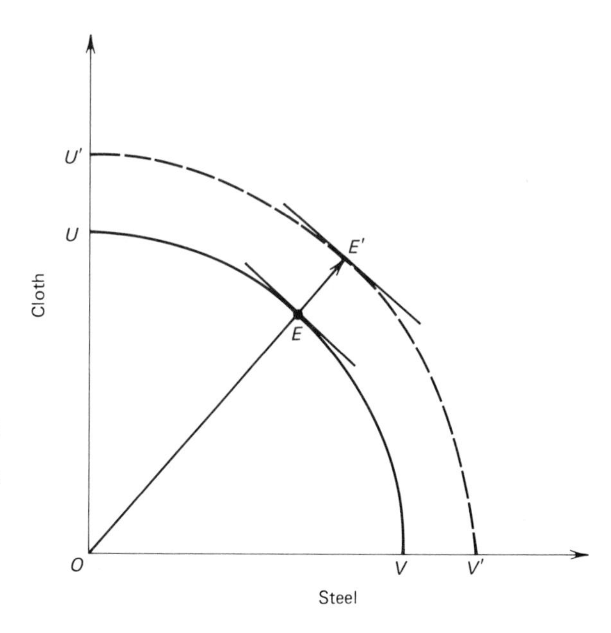

FIGURE 6-3 **Balanced growth.** When labor and capital increase at the same rate, production-possibilities frontier *UV* shifts out evenly in all directions, as illustrated by dashed curve *U'V'*. The optimum production point shifts from *E* to *E'*, and steel and cloth grow at the same rate as labor and capital. The slopes at *E* and *E'* are the same.

citizen does as all others do, it follows that the outputs of steel and cloth must increase at the same rate (that is, 5 percent). As a result, the production frontier shifts outward evenly in all directions, as shown in Figure 6-3 by dashed curve *U'E'V'*. This is the case of **balanced growth.** It is also known as **neutral production effect,** since no production bias is revealed toward either steel or cloth—both expand at the same rate.

How does balanced growth affect Austria's social welfare? Be careful. Because Austria's production-possibilities frontier shifts outward and apparently Austria can move to a "higher" social indifference curve, one might assume that Austria's social welfare increases. This is illusory, however. The only significant effect of balanced factor growth is the increase in the number of representative citizens. Each citizen is producing and consuming exactly the same amounts of steel and cloth before and after growth. Accordingly, each citizen's status quo is maintained, with the citizen becoming neither better off nor worse off. Unless we pass the ethical judgment that society is better off with more citizens (presumably because the nation can offer a stronger defense against an external enemy), we must conclude that balanced growth leaves Austria's social welfare intact.

One final note: Since the number of representative citizens increases by, say, 5 percent, *aggregate* production, consumption, exports, and imports of steel and cloth all increase at the same rate (that is, 5 percent). The fact that Austria's *volume of trade necessarily increases* (at the balanced growth rate) assumes significance in the next part of this chapter.

Single-Factor Growth

Suppose that only one factor grows, that is, either labor or capital but not both. How do the outputs of steel and cloth change? We already know the answer from our discussion of the **Rybczynski theorem** in Chapter 4. Thus when the endowment of only one factor of production increases, *the output of the commodity that intensively uses the increased factor expands, and the output of the other commodity contracts absolutely.* Note that *because Austria's terms of trade remain constant by assumption,* the wage-rent ratio as well as the optimal coefficients of production of steel and cloth must also remain constant. (This follows from the one-to-one correspondence that necessarily exists between relative commodity prices and factor prices. See Section 4-8.)

The cases of sheer labor and sheer capital growth are illustrated in Figures 6-4 and 6-5, respectively. In each case, the production-possibilities frontier shifts outward from *UV* to *U'V'*, and the optimum production point from *E* to *E'*. Note the production bias in favor of the commodity that uses the expanded factor intensively.

How does single-factor growth affect Austria's social welfare? We must again look at the representative citizen. With sheer labor growth, the representative citizen necessarily becomes *worse off.* The fixed amount of capital is spread more thinly over the expanded population. Therefore, each representative citizen has less capital to work with, and everyone's *individual* production-possibilities frontier shifts *inward.* With sheer labor growth, Austria experiences *negative*

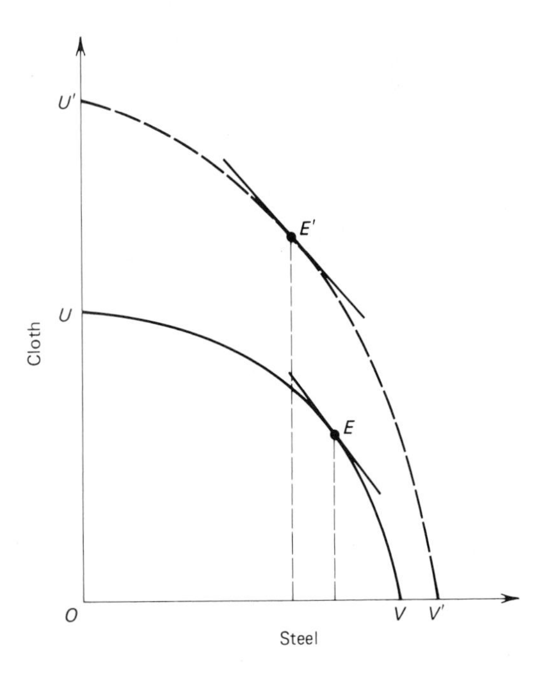

FIGURE 6-4 **Sheer labor growth.** When only labor increases, production-possibilities frontier *UV* shifts outward but with a marked bias in favor of the labor-intensive commodity (cloth), as shown by dashed curve *U'V'*. The optimum production point shifts from *E* to *E'*, at which the output of steel is absolutely smaller. The slopes at *E* and *E'* are the same.

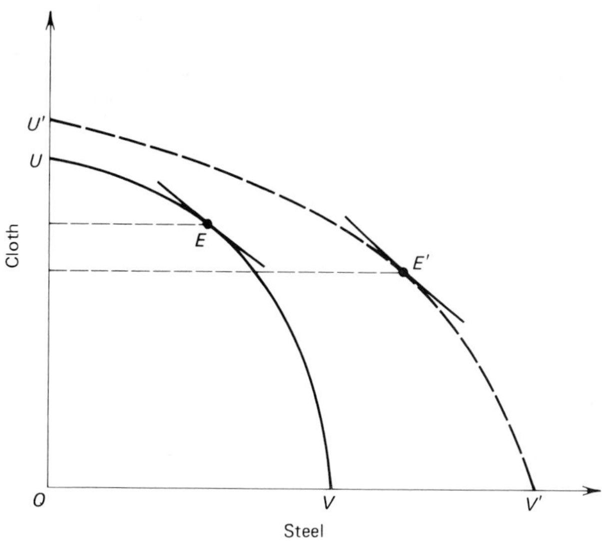

FIGURE 6-5 **Sheer capital growth.** When only capital increases, production-possibilities frontier *UV* shifts outward, but with a marked bias in favor of the capital-intensive commodity (steel), as shown by dashed curve *U′V′*. The optimum production point shifts from *E* to *E′*, at which the output of cloth is absolutely smaller. The slopes at *E* and *E′* are the same.

capital deepening, and its social welfare *falls, even though its overall production-possibilities frontier shifts outward.*

With sheer capital growth Austria experiences *positive* capital deepening. Now its representative citizen has more capital to work with, and thus everyone's *individual* production-possibilities frontier shifts *outward.* The representative citizen becomes better off, and social welfare improves.

How does sheer labor growth affect Austria's volume of trade? That depends on the nation's structure of trade. If Austria *exports* the *capital-intensive commodity,* steel, whose output *falls,* Austria's volume of trade will *fall,* since its consumption of steel can be expected to increase. (For simplicity, we exclude inferiority in the consumption of either commodity throughout this chapter.) If Austria *imports* the capital-intensive commodity, the nation's volume of trade will tend to rise.

With sheer capital growth, Austria's volume of trade will expand when it *exports* the capital-intensive commodity (steel); and trade will contract when Austria exports the labor-intensive commodity (cloth).

Other Cases of Factor Accumulation

Any arbitrary increase in the endowments of labor and capital can be broken down into a case of balanced growth plus a case of sheer labor (or capital) growth. However, more definitive results can be obtained if the following case is kept in mind also: *When the additional amounts of labor and capital happen to be in the proportion in which the two factors are employed by one of the two industries, say, the steel industry, then the output of that industry (steel) increases while the output of the other industry remains the same.*

6-5 TECHNICAL PROGRESS

Like factor accumulation, technical progress causes the growing economy's (Austria's) production-possibilities frontier to shift outward. But unlike factor accumulation, technical progress also causes the scaled down production-possibilities frontier of the representative citizen *always* to shift outward. (Recall that the production-possibilities frontier of the representative citizen shifts *outward* when capital deepening is *positive* and *inward* when it is *negative.*) Accordingly, insofar as the effect of technical progress on the social welfare of a *small* country is concerned, the answer must be very clear: **Technical progress always increases the social welfare of small countries.** This remarkable result is true for all types of technical progress.

Unfortunately, the analysis of the outward shift of the production-possibilities frontier is not as easy in the case of technical progress as it is in the case of factor accumulation. Two reasons account for this:

1 There are three types of technical progress (neutral, labor saving, and capital saving), and they can occur in one or both industries and at different rates. Accordingly, the approach must be taxonomic, which is very cumbersome.

2 In general, technical progress alters the basic relationship between factor prices and commodity prices (as illustrated by curve *PW* in Figure 4-8).

The rest of this section clarifies the effect of technical progress on the basic relationship between factor prices and commodity prices and then studies in some detail some cases that illustrate the special problems to which technical progress gives rise.

Technical Progress and the Relationship between Factor Prices and Commodity Prices

Suppose that technical progress occurs in the cloth industry only. Then, for any *given* factor prices, the relative price of cloth must be lower after the change than before, irrespective of the type of technical progress. This must be so because the unit isoquant for cloth necessarily shifts inward with technical progress, and thus a *lower* isocost line is tangent to it after the change than before. Accordingly, the average cost of cloth, which is equal to the price of cloth, is necessarily lower after the change *for any given factor prices.* Since the price of steel remains the same by assumption, the *relative* price of cloth necessarily falls. This can be illustrated in Figure 4-8 by *shifting* curve *PW* to the left.

When both industries experience technical progress, the analysis becomes more complicated. In general, the effect on relative commodity prices depends not only on the rates but also the types of technical progress experienced by the two industries. For instance, if both industries undergo neutral technical progress at precisely the same rate (for example, if the outputs of steel and cloth increase by 20 percent at all factor combinations), then the relative price of cloth remains the same at all factor prices. But if neutral technical progress is more rapid in the steel industry than in the cloth industry (for example, if the output of steel increases by 30 percent and the output of cloth by 10 percent at all factor combinations), then the relative price of cloth must be higher after the change at all factor prices, that is, curve *PW* of Figure 4-8 must shift to the right.

Balanced Growth with Neutral Technical Progress

Suppose that Austria's steel and cloth industries undergo *neutral* technical progress at the *same* rate, say, 25 percent. How does Austria's production-possibilities frontier shift? What happens to Austria's production of steel and cloth as well as the nation's volume of trade at the given international terms of trade?

This case is very similar to the case of balanced factor accumulation that we studied in the preceding section. Austria's production-possibilities frontier again shifts out evenly in all directions, and all initial combinations of steel and cloth increase by 25 percent, as shown in Figure 6-3. At every commodity price ratio, Austria continues, after technical progress has taken place, to produce steel and cloth in the same proportion as before the change. This type of balanced growth gives rise to a neutral production effect in the sense that both steel and cloth expand at the same rate—no bias is revealed in either direction.

Unlike balanced factor accumulation, balanced neutral technical progress necessarily improves the welfare of Austria's representative citizen. Now the scaled down production-possibilities frontier of the representative citizen also shifts out evenly in all directions like the aggregate production frontier. Austria's social welfare improves.

How does balanced neutral technical progress affect Austria's volume of trade at the given terms of trade? That depends on how Austria's consumption behaves. If the consumption of steel and cloth increases at the same rate as production (for example, 25 percent), then the volume of trade must increase at the same rate also. Otherwise, Austria's volume of trade may either increase or decrease depending on whether Austria's consumers have a bias toward the imported or the exported commodity, as the reader should be able to show.

Neutral Technical Progress in the Export Industry

Small-country Austria currently exports steel and imports cloth at constant terms of trade. Suppose that *neutral* technical progress occurs in the export industry (steel) only. How does Austria's production-possibilities frontier shift? How do Austria's outputs of steel and cloth change at the given terms of trade?

Consider Figure 6-6. Austria's initial production frontier is given by curve *UV*. After technical progress, the output of steel rises by 25 percent for each output of cloth, as illustrated by dashed curve *UV'*. For instance, point *E* shifts to *E'* as the output of steel increases from 300 to 375 tons (that is, by 25 percent). Similarly, all other points on initial frontier *UV* shift to the right by 25 percent.

How does neutral technical progress in the steel industry affect Austria's production of steel and cloth at the given terms of trade? Suppose that before technical progress, Austria produces at point *E* on initial production frontier *UV*. If Austria maintained its output of cloth at 200 yards, the nation would be able to increase its output of steel to 375 tons, as shown by point *E'*. However, the opportunity cost of steel is lower at *E'* than at *E*—the tangent to dashed frontier *UV'* at *E'* (not shown) is flatter than the tangent to *UV* at *E*. This reflects the fact that the cost of steel falls after the steel industry experiences technical progress. Thus at the pregrowth commodity prices indicated by the slope at *E*, Austria must be producing somewhere in region *E'V'*, as illustrated by point *P*.

In summary, **the output of the industry experiencing neutral technical progress (steel) increases, while the output of the other industry (cloth) decreases.**

PART C

The Effects of Growth on Large Countries

Our analysis so far has been carried out under the simplifying assumption that the growing country is "small" in the sense that it is a price taker in the international market. The time has now come to drop this simplifying assumption

FIGURE 6-6 **Neutral technical progress in the steel industry.** Production-possibilities frontier *UV* shifts outward in the direction of steel, as illustrated by dashed curve *UV'*. For instance, point *E* shifts to *E'*. The production point, however, shifts from *E* to *P* because technical progress tends to make steel relatively cheaper. The slopes at *E* and *P* are the same.

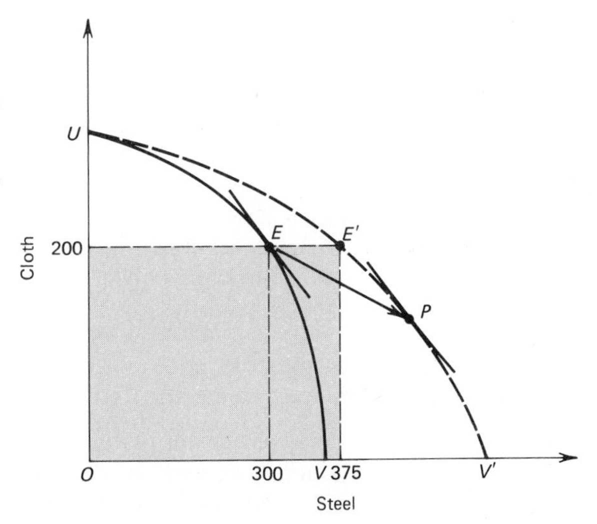

and consider the effects of economic growth on the "large" country, whose exports and imports do affect the terms of trade. As we mentioned earlier, the analysis of the small country serves as an important building block in our new investigation.

6-6 THE TERMS-OF-TRADE EFFECT

How does growth affect the terms of trade of the growing country? That depends on what happens to the desired volume of trade of the growing country at the pregrowth terms of trade. *If the desired volume of trade expands, the terms of trade deteriorate; and if the desired volume of trade contracts, the terms of trade improve.* This section elucidates this important proposition, which reflects the workings of the **law of supply and demand.**

The New Scenario

Consider again two countries, America and Britain. Each country is endowed with two factors, labor and capital, and produces two commodities, steel and cloth, under constant returns to scale. We assume throughout that steel is capital intensive relative to cloth at all factor prices both before and after technical progress. Each country is inhabited by individuals who have identical tastes and factor endowments. America's representative citizen is distinctly different from Britain's because America, the capital-abundant country, is endowed with more units of capital per worker than Britain. Thus, America's representative citizen has more capital to work with than Britain's representative citizen.

The pregrowth international equilibrium position can be shown in terms of the familiar offer curves, as illustrated in Figure 6-7. Equilibrium occurs initially at the intersection of the pregrowth offer curves, that is, at point *E*. America exports *OS* tons of steel to Britain in exchange for *OC* yards of cloth. This pattern of trade is in line with the Heckscher-Ohlin theorem. The slope of terms-of-trade line *TOT* (that is, *OC*/*OS*) gives the relative price of steel in terms of cloth, which is America's terms of trade.

When a country grows, its offer curve necessarily shifts, giving rise to a new international equilibrium. In general, the growing country's terms of trade may either improve or deteriorate during this process depending on just how its offer curve shifts.

In what follows, we assume that only America grows. Thus, only America's offer curve shifts through time. Britain's offer curve remains the same. The equilibrium point travels along Britain's offer curve as America's offer curve shifts.

The Effect of Growth on the Volume and Terms of Trade

Consider again Figure 6-7. Assume that at the pregrowth terms of trade America's growth is such that the nation's desired volume of trade *expands* from *OE* to *OJ*. This means that at the pregrowth terms of trade America's demand

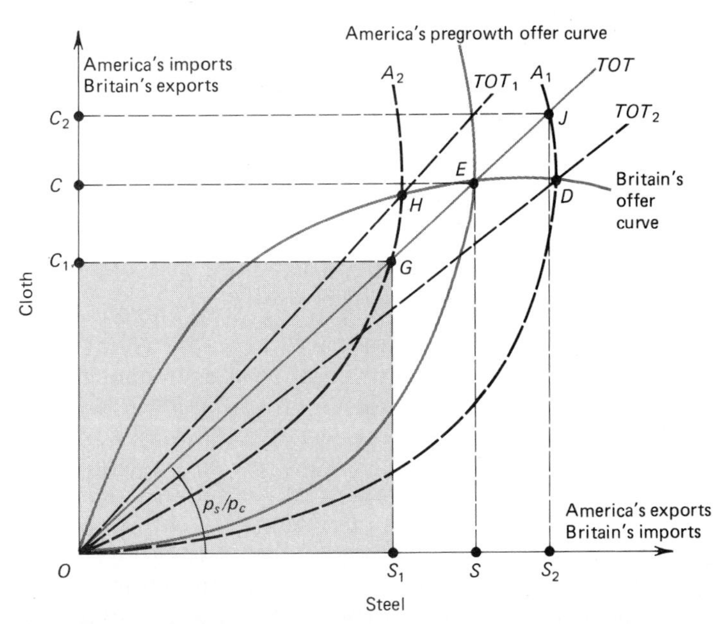

FIGURE 6-7 **The effect of growth on the terms of trade.** Equilibrium occurs initially at E, where America exports steel and Britain cloth. When America's volume of trade expands with growth, as illustrated by dashed curve $ODJA_1$, the nation's terms of trade deteriorate. Thus, steel is cheaper at postgrowth equilibrium point D than at the initial point, E. When America's volume of trade contracts with growth, the nation's terms of trade improve. This is illustrated by the shift of America's offer curve to $OGHA_2$, with postgrowth equilibrium occurring at H.

for imports of cloth increases by CC_2. Also, America's supply of exports of steel increases by SS_2. (Compare points E and J.) Since Britain's (that is, the rest of the world's) demand for imports of steel and supply of exports of cloth remain the same (by assumption), it follows that at the pregrowth terms of trade there emerges a surplus of steel (SS_2) and a shortage of cloth (CC_2). As a result, the price of steel tends to fall relative to the price of cloth; that is, *America's terms of trade tend to deteriorate.* This is illustrated by the shift of America's offer curve to $ODJA_1$, giving rise to a new international equilibrium at D. America's terms of trade after growth are given by the slope of terms-of-trade line TOT_2, which is smaller than the slope of TOT.

When America's volume of trade tends to *contract* at constant prices, its terms of trade tend to *improve.* This proposition is also illustrated in Figure 6-7. Assume that growth causes America's offer curve to shift to the left, as shown by dashed curve $OGHA_2$. At pregrowth prices, America's desired volume of trade contracts from OE to OG. America's supply of exports of steel decreases by S_1S, while its demand for imports of cloth decreases by C_1C. Accordingly, there emerges a shortage of steel (S_1S) as well as a surplus of cloth (C_1C). As a result, the relative price of steel tends to rise, as illustrated by the slope of terms-of-trade line TOT_1 at new equilibrium point H. Hence we reach the following important conclusion:

When America's volume of trade tends to expand at constant prices, America's terms of trade tend to deteriorate; and when the desired volume of trade tends to contract, the terms of trade tend to improve.

Types of Growth and Terms-of-Trade Effect

The effect of growth on America's desired volume of trade at pregrowth prices, and thus the terms-of-trade effect, depends on the particular type of growth experienced by America. This must be clear from our earlier discussion in Part B. The following general propositions summarize the effect of growth on the desired volume of trade and terms of trade (note that both propositions disregard inferiority in consumption. The consumption of an inferior good falls when income rises):

Proposition 1: **Other things being equal, any type of growth that expands America's output of exportables more than it expands America's output of importables causes America's volume of trade (at constant prices) to expand and its terms of trade to worsen.** For instance, this is the case when America's abundant factor increases or when neutral technical progress occurs in the export industry.

Proposition 2: **Other things being equal, any type of growth that expands America's output of importables and contracts its output of exportables causes America's volume of trade (at constant prices) to decline and her terms of trade to improve.** For instance, this is the case when America's scarce factor increases, or when neutral technical progress occurs in the import-competing industry.

Note that **balanced growth** tends to expand America's volume of trade at the balanced growth rate, assuming only that tastes are **homothetic** (which in essence means that the percentages of income spent on different commodities, such as 60 percent on food and 40 percent on cloth, remain constant at all income levels), so that each commodity's consumption expands at the common rate. This is taken by some economists to mean that growth has a built-in bias toward terms-of-trade deterioration because balanced growth implies *neutrality* all around. This is, of course, true, but on the assumption that only one country grows. If both America and Britain experience balanced growth at the same rate, the volumes of trade of the two countries will be growing *pari passu,* and there will be no tendency for the terms of trade of either country to deteriorate. Accordingly, we must conclude that, in general, there are no a priori reasons to believe that on balance growth will worsen the terms of trade of a country.

6-7 THE EFFECT OF GROWTH ON SOCIAL WELFARE

How does America's growth affect the nation's social welfare? This is an important question, and our analysis has progressed sufficiently to venture an answer.

As before, we assume that America is inhabited by identical individuals with respect to tastes and factor endowments both before and after growth. Accordingly, we can infer the effect of growth on America's social welfare from the effect of growth on America's representative citizen.

The Two Effects on Welfare

In general, we can distinguish between two effects: a **wealth effect** and a **terms-of-trade effect.** The wealth effect corresponds to the shift of the production-possibilities frontier of America's representative citizen, and it may be either positive or negative. Similarly, the terms-of-trade effect corresponds to the change in the relative price of America's exportables, and this too can be either positive or negative.

The total effect on the welfare of America's representative citizen is the sum of the wealth effect plus the terms-of-trade effect. When neither is unfavorable, America's representative citizen definitely becomes better off with growth; and when neither is favorable, the citizen definitely becomes worse off. But when one effect is favorable and the other unfavorable, the total effect is indeterminate: the outcome depends on which of the two effects outweighs the other.

Factor Accumulation versus Technical Progress

Technical progress always gives rise to a favorable wealth effect. Thus, technical progress of whatever type and in whichever industry causes America's production-possibilities frontier to shift outward; and because the *number* of representative citizens remains the same, the scaled down production frontier of America's representative citizen shifts outward also. Thus, **the wealth effect of technical progress is always positive.**

However, **the wealth effect of factor accumulation may be positive, negative, or zero.** When capital increases faster than labor (that is, when America experiences capital deepening), the overall capital-labor ratio rises, each citizen has more capital to work with, and the production frontier of the representative citizen shifts *outward* (positive wealth effect). When labor increases faster than capital (negative capital deepening), each citizen has less capital to work with, and the production frontier of the representative citizen shifts *inward* (negative wealth effect). Finally, when labor and capital increase at the same rate (balanced growth), the production frontier of the representative citizen remains the same (zero wealth effect).

Other things being equal, when growth is the result of technical progress that occurs predominantly in the import-competing sector rather than the export sector, then America's terms of trade will tend to *improve.* Therefore, America's representative citizen will tend to become better off, enjoying both a favorable wealth effect plus a favorable terms-of-trade effect. When technical progress occurs predominantly in the export sector instead, America's terms of trade will tend to deteriorate, and the representative citizen may become either worse off or better off.

Immiserizing Growth

The paradox that a growing country may become worse off with growth was first noted by Edgeworth (1894, pp. 40–42). Bhagwati (1958) rediscovered this phenomenon, which he named **immiserizing growth.**

Economists have been aware of the detrimental effects on welfare of rapid labor growth relative to capital since the beginning of economic science. What is surprising here is that even technical progress may reduce social welfare.

Immiserizing growth is very similar to the problem of agriculture. Increased agricultural output is often anathema to the farmer because prices fall sharply as a result of the low elasticity of demand for agricultural products. Increased agricultural output often means lower income for the farmer! The story of agriculture can be easily extended to international trade. Think of Malaya or Ghana exporting their entire output of rubber or cocoa in exchange for food. Assume further that the foreign demand for imports of rubber or cocoa is inelastic. An expansion of domestic production and hence exports (since by assumption all domestic output is exported) would result in a smaller volume of food imported and lower social welfare. The actors of the agricultural drama are indeed the same as those of immiserizing growth—only they wear a different costume.

The possibility of immiserizing growth is illustrated in Figure 6-8. Before growth America produces at P_0 and consumes at C_0. As a result of technical progress, which is concentrated predominantly in the export sector (steel industry), America's production frontier shifts outward from UV to $U'V'$. Because America's volume of trade expands at the pregrowth terms of trade (given by the slope of MN), America's terms of trade fall to the level indicated by the slope of SP_1T. America's production shifts from P_0 to P_1 and consumption from C_0 to C_1. Thus, economic growth reduces America's welfare, since social indifference curve 1 lies below social indifference curve 2.

Note that Figure 6-8 illustrates what happens to America's representative citizen as well. For this purpose, curves UV and $U'V'$ must be interpreted as the scaled down production frontiers of the representative citizen before and after growth, respectively; curves 1 and 2 as the indifference curves; and, finally, curves MN and ST as the budget lines before and after growth, respectively.

What conditions are necessary for the occurrence of immiserizing growth? At least six seem crucial:

1 *America's growth must cause the nation's desired volume of trade to increase substantially at constant prices.* This condition ensures that America's supply of exports increases enormously with growth and causes its terms of trade to deteriorate. Although not strictly necessary, export-biased growth (that is, growth which is heavily biased toward the export sector) certainly satisfies this condition.

2 *Britain's (that is, the rest-of-the world's) import demand elasticity for America's exportables (steel) must be very low.* This condition implies that America's terms of trade must fall sharply to restore international equilibrium.

3 *America must be heavily dependent on foreign trade.* In other words, America's exports of steel must be a very high percentage of America's domestic produc-

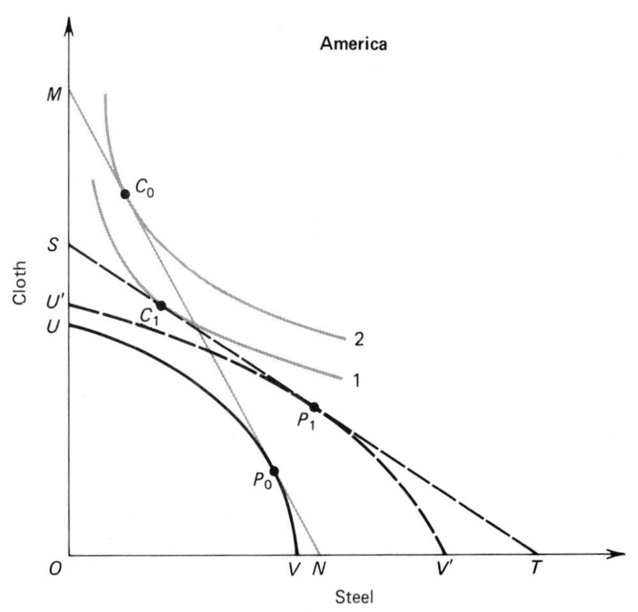

FIGURE 6-8 **Immiserizing growth.** Before growth, America produces at P_0 and consumes at C_0. Technical progress (concentrated predominantly in the export sector) causes America's production-possibilities frontier, *UV*, to shift outward, as illustrated by dashed curve *U′V′*. America's terms of trade fall to the level indicated by the slope at P_1. America's production shifts from P_0 to P_1 while the nation's consumption shifts from C_0 to C_1. Since C_1 lies on social indifference curve 1, which is lower than curve 2, America becomes worse off with growth.

tion of steel. This condition ensures that the terms-of-trade deterioration will be great enough to offset the favorable wealth effect.

4 *America's technical progress must be relatively small.* This condition is most crucial. If technical progress is very large in the sense that it pushes the production-possibilities frontier so far out that the curve at least touches the social indifference curve attained by America before growth, then technical progress will improve America's welfare irrespective of what happens to the terms of trade.

5 *America must be a "large" country.* Under free-trade conditions, immiserizing growth can occur only if the growing country is important enough in world markets to affect its terms of trade. If the growing country is small, that is, a price taker, its terms of trade will remain unaltered, and its social welfare will improve because of the favorable wealth effect. This condition is apparently related to condition 2.[2]

[2]A "small" country can also experience immiserizing growth, but only if it is providing tariff protection for its import-competing industry or is suffering from some other distortion. This possibility, which was first noticed by Johnson (1967), is considered in Appendix 11.

6 *America must not pursue an optimal-tariff policy.* The significance of this condition will become clearer in Chapter 8. For the moment, we may note that if America pursues an optimal-tariff policy, then technical progress always improves America's social welfare. Put differently, the phenomenon of immiserizing growth occurs in the presence of a *foreign distortion:* Either a growing large country does not impose the optimal tariff or a growing small country (whose optimal tariff is zero) provides tariff protection for its import-competing industry. *Domestic distortions* may also give rise to immiserizing growth.

Some economists believe that Brazil may have satisfied the conditions for immiserizing growth before the 1930s, when coffee constituted over 70 percent of the Brazilian value of exports and Brazil's share of the world market for coffee was more than 50 percent.

6-8 GROWTH IN THE WORLD ECONOMY

In this section, we present some empirical evidence on the growth of world production, trade, and per capita income during the last couple of decades.

Table 6-1 gives the population and gross national product (GNP) per capita for three groups of countries: developing countries, high-income oil exporters, and industrial countries. Even though considerable diversity exists within each individual group of countries, the data are very informative.

In 1985 the world population stood at about 4.8 billion. Out of this total, nearly 360 million people were living in such countries as the USSR, Albania, Angola, Bulgaria, Cuba, Czechoslovakia, East Germany, North Korea, and Mongolia, which are not included in the data presented here. Approximately 3.5 billion people lived in developing countries; their per capita income in 1980 was roughly $670. Most of these people still live under conditions of extreme poverty, and their future does not look very bright. Close to one-sixth of the world population lived in industrial countries and enjoyed a per capita income of over $10,000 annually.

Table 6-2 displays the annual growth rates of per capita GNP, exports, and gross domestic product (GDP). (GDP is the value of final goods produced within a country, while GNP measures the total domestic and foreign output claimed by the residents of a country. For instance, the income of an American citizen working in France is not part of U.S. GDP because it is not earned in the United States, but it is part of U.S. GNP.)

TABLE 6-1 POPULATION AND GNP PER CAPITA

	Developing countries	High-income oil exporters	Industrial countries
Population (millions)			
1980	3,123	16	716
1985	3,451	19	737
1980 GNP (billions of dollars)	2,078	223	7,613
1980 GNP per capita (dollars)	670	14,400	10,630

Source: Adapted from The World Bank, *World Development Report 1987,* Oxford University Press, New York, 1987, Tables A.1 and A.2 (p. 171).

TABLE 6-2 ANNUAL GROWTH RATES OF GDP, PER CAPITA GNP, AND EXPORTS, 1965–1985

	1965–1973	1973–1980	1982	1983	1984	1985
Developing countries						
GDP	6.5	5.4	2.1	2.1	5.1	4.8
GNP per capita	4.0	3.1	−0.7	0.1	3.1	2.7
Export volume	4.9	4.7	0.2	5.1	11.5	1.4
High-income oil exporters						
GDP	8.3	7.9	−0.5	−6.9	1.2	−3.8
GNP per capita	3.9	5.7	−6.7	−14.3	−2.4	−8.6
Export volume	12.8	−0.6	−21.3	−23.5	−7.0	−11.6
Industrial countries						
GDP	4.7	2.8	−0.5	2.2	4.6	2.8
GNP per capita	3.7	2.1	−1.3	1.6	4.1	2.4
Export volume	9.4	5.4	−1.8	1.9	10.2	5.3
World export volume	8.8	4.4	−3.2	0.7	9.5	3.5
Manufactures	10.7	6.1	−2.7	4.2	12.6	5.2
Food	5.0	6.6	0.1	−5.1	6.8	0.7
Nonfood	3.1	1.0	−3.0	−0.5	7.3	7.8
Metals and minerals	6.8	8.7	−0.6	−1.5	7.7	3.9
Fuels	8.6	0.0	−7.0	−6.5	1.2	−2.3

Source: Adapted from The World Bank, *World Development Report 1987,* Oxford University Press, New York, 1987, Tables A.2, A.3, and A.8 (pp. 171, 172, and 175).

During the period 1965–1985, GDP was rising faster in developing countries than in industrial countries. Because population was rising faster in the developing nations, however, the growth rate of GNP per capita was approximately the same for the two groups. Given this performance, the gap between the per capita incomes of developing and industrial countries continued to widen.

The world export volume grew at the healthy rate of 8.8 per year during the period 1965–1973. It was higher for manufactures than for food and nonfood items. Also, the export volume of industrial countries grew twice as fast as that of developing countries but only during the period 1965–1973. Since 1973 the great disparity between the export performance of the two groups has more or less disappeared. Comparing the growth rates of the export volume and GNP per capita, it becomes obvious that the industrial countries experienced *protrade-biased growth* (that is, their export volume increased faster than their GDP), while the developing countries experienced *neutral growth* (that is, their export volume grew roughly at about the same rate as their GDP).

Three conclusions seem clear from Table 6-3: (1) In developing nations, the industrial and service sectors expanded at the expense of agriculture. (2) In industrial countries, the service sector expanded at the expense of both agriculture and industry. (3) The share of exports of manufactures increased at the expense of exports of primary products in both groups of countries, even though the share of exports of primary products continues to be much higher in developing nations than in industrial nations.

6-9 THE PREBISCH-SINGER THESIS

In the 1950s several economists, such as Rául Prebisch, Hans Singer, and Gunnar Myrdal, argued that primary exporting countries, particularly those of the third world, had

TABLE 6-3 STRUCTURE OF PRODUCTION AND MERCHANDISE EXPORTS

	1965	1985
Distribution of GDP		
Agriculture		
Developing countries	29%	20%
Industrial countries	5	3
Industry		
Developing countries	29	34
Industrial countries	40	36
Services		
Developing countries	42	47
Industrial countries	55	61
Share of merchandise exports		
Primary commodities		
Developing countries	80	60
Industrial countries	30	24
Manufactures		
Developing countries	20	41
Industrial countries	69	77

Source: Adapted from The World Bank, *World Development Report 1987,* Oxford University Press, New York, 1987, Tables 3 and 11 (pp. 206–207 and 222–223).

been experiencing a systematic deterioration in their (net barter) terms of trade. The implication was that the developing nations had to export increasing amounts of their primary products in exchange for imports of manufactures from the industrially advanced countries.

Theoretical Foundations of the Prebisch-Singer Thesis

The **Prebisch-Singer thesis** rests on two theoretically unconvincing arguments. These are:

1 Demand Bias

The demand for manufactures tends to grow much faster than the demand for primary products. This is attributed partly to the hypothesis (derived from **Engel's Law**) that the income elasticity of demand is much higher for manufactures than for primary products, and partly to the presumption that technical progress saves raw materials. Other things equal, such demand bias causes the terms of trade of primary-product exporters to deteriorate over time.

There are three objections to the demand-bias argument. First, the terms "primary-product exporters" and "developing nations" are not synonymous. For instance, the United States, Canada, and Australia are major exporters of food, while countries like South Korea and Taiwan export manufactured products, such as transistor radios and automobiles. Second, the supply of manufactures has experienced phenomenal growth in the advanced countries; hence we cannot argue on the basis of the demand bias alone that the primary products have been getting cheaper relative to manufactures, because prices are determined by demand *and* supply. Third, technical progress constantly gives rise to new products and processes that make up for any reduced use of raw materials in the production of other products. It is commonly recognized now that the often cited dramatic fall in the price of natural rubber due to the development of low-cost synthetic rubber is a rather unique phenomenon.

2 Market Imperfections

In developed nations, technical progress does not lead to lower prices. Rather, any productivity gains are either kept by the manufacturers in the form of higher profits (because of the oligopolistic nature of their markets) or are passed on to the workers in the form of higher wages (because of the power of the labor unions). In developing nations where there is labor surplus, technical progress results in lower prices as factor returns hold steady. Thus developed countries benefit both from their own productivity gains and those of developing nations. As a result the terms of trade of developing nations tend to deteriorate over time.

There is a grain of truth in the imperfections argument; but it explains the *level* of the terms of trade (and thus the division of the gains from trade between the industrialized North and the developing South), not their tendency to fall over time.

Empirical Foundations of the Prebisch-Singer Thesis

Because price indices were not available for many developing countries, Prebisch (1950) in his original empirical work used the terms of trade for the United Kingdom from 1870 to 1938. He found that British terms of trade improved substantially during this period, rising from 100 in 1870 to 170 in 1938. He took this finding to mean that the terms of trade of developing nations (which exported food and raw materials to the United Kingdom in exchange for British manufactured products) deteriorated significantly during the same period.

Prebisch's empirical finding was criticized on several statistical grounds, such as the treatment of transportation costs and new products, the sensitivity of the results to the selection of the beginning and end of the period, and the inability to account for the improved quality of manufactures. For instance, the automobile of the 1980s is not the same as that of the 1920s. Hence the reported terms-of-trade deterioration is overstated, particularly because the quality of primary products tends to remain constant over time. Thus the higher prices received by the United Kingdom reflected to a great extent the improved quality of British products.

The criticism of Prebisch's work prompted further empirical studies, but no clear trend could be established for the terms of trade of developing nations. This does not mean, of course, that the developing countries never experience deteriorating terms of trade or that such occasional phenomena do not disrupt their development process. It only means that we must reject the notion that the Prebisch-Singer thesis is an ineluctable phenomenon that must be accepted as an economic law. In short, there is no evidence that economic forces conspire in some way to make the rich richer and the poor poorer.

Table 6-4 presents some recent data on the change in export prices and in terms of trade for three country groups: developing countries, high-income oil exporters, and industrial countries. The terms of trade of developing countries improved steadily during the 15-year period 1965–1980, they worsened slightly for the next two years (1981 and 1982), then resumed their mild improvement for another two years (1983 and 1984), and finally experienced a modest deterioration for 1985 and 1986. Excluding the more violent terms-of-trade fluctuations for the oil exporters, it appears that the changes in the terms of trade of both developing and industrial countries during the period 1965–1986 have been relatively small.

Note that the present discussion does *not* address the issue of whether or not the *level* of the terms of trade of developing nations is satisfactory. For further discussion of the latter issue, which is basically an ethical (or moral) problem, see Donaldson (1984, chap. 10).

The Income and Single Factoral Terms of Trade

It is now recognized that the net barter terms of trade are not a good indicator of the effect of changes in world trade conditions on the income or welfare of developing nations. A far better measure of the effect of price changes on income is provided by the **income terms of trade,** which are equal to the net barter terms of trade multiplied by the volume of exports. In effect, the income terms of trade measure the purchasing power of exports in terms of imports, or the nation's capacity to import based on export revenue. For instance, assume that the foreign demand for Zambian copper is elastic and Zambia increases its copper exports. Zambia's barter terms of trade would deteriorate as the price of copper fell in world markets, but the income terms of trade would improve as copper revenue rose. If we further assume that the opportunity cost of the resources shifted into copper production is zero (that is, if these resources could not have produced goods and services of equal value in other sectors), then the improvement in the income terms of trade would make Zambia better off.

When the increase in exports is due to higher productivity (technical progress), it becomes necessary to use an alternative concept, the **single factoral terms of trade,** which are equal to the net barter terms of trade multiplied by a productivity index of all factors engaged in the nation's export sector. In effect, the single factoral terms of trade

TABLE 6-4 CHANGE IN EXPORT PRICES AND IN TERMS OF TRADE, 1965–1986
(Average Annual Percentage Change)

	Change in export prices			Change in terms of trade		
	Developing countries	High-income oil exporters	Industrial countries	Developing countries	High-income oil exporters	Industrial countries
1965–1973	6.4	7.6	4.8	0.7	0.3	−1.0
1973–1980	14.0	26.9	10.4	1.6	13.4	−3.0
1981	0.5	12.0	−4.9	−0.9	19.5	−1.8
1982	−6.7	−9.2	−3.4	−1.8	−5.4	3.0
1983	−2.4	−8.8	−3.0	0.0	−6.6	0.1
1984	−1.0	−3.1	−3.1	0.7	1.3	0.3
1985*	−3.1	−3.1	−1.6	−0.8	−1.3	1.0
1986†	−1.2	−49.5	15.3	−4.3	−56.2	8.3

*Estimated.
†Projected.
Source: Adapted from The World Bank, *World Development Report 1987,* Oxford University Press, New York, 1987, Table A-9 (p. 176).

measure the quantity of imports per unit of domestic inputs embodied in exports. For instance, suppose that the productivity of Zambian labor employed in the production of copper doubles. If the net barter terms of trade remained constant, the single factoral terms of trade (and thus Zambian income in terms of imports) would also double. Indeed the single factoral terms of trade would rise even if the net barter terms of trade fell by anything less than 50 percent.

6-10 SUMMARY

1 The three main sources of economic growth are labor growth, capital accumulation, and technical progress. Their common characteristic is that they all cause the growing economy's production-possibilities frontier to shift outward over time.

2 When a country grows, its offer curve necessarily shifts, giving rise to a new international equilibrium.

3 When a growing country's volume of trade expands at pregrowth prices, its terms of trade deteriorate. This occurs for any type of growth (such as growth of the abundant factor and neutral technical progress in the export industry) that expands the output of exportables more than it expands the output of importables.

4 When a growing country's volume of trade contracts at pregrowth prices, its terms of trade improve. This occurs for any type of growth (such as growth of the scarce factor or neutral technical progress in the import-competing industry) that expands the output of importables and contracts the output of exportables.

5 In judging the effect of growth on social welfare, it is useful to assume that the growing country is made up of "representative citizens" (that is, citizens who have identical tastes and factor endowments). If growth makes one representative citizen better off (worse off), it makes all better off (worse off), and social welfare improves (deteriorates).

6 Because of constant returns to scale, the growing economy's production-possibilities frontier can be scaled down in proportion to the representative citizen.

7 Growth has two effects on the welfare of the representative citizen: (a) a wealth effect and (b) a terms-of-trade effect. When both effects are positive (negative), the representative citizen becomes better off (worse off). When one effect is positive and the other negative, the total effect is indeterminate.

8 The wealth effect of factor accumulation will be (a) positive, when capital grows faster than labor, with the result that the representative citizen has more capital to work with and thus the citizen's individual production-possibilities frontier shifts outward; (b) negative, when labor grows faster than capital and the representative citizen has less capital to work with; or (c) zero, when labor and capital grow at the same rate (balanced growth).

9 When there is balanced factor growth (that is, when the number of representative citizens increases), the capital-labor ratio remains constant; the economy's production-possibilities frontier shifts out evenly in all directions, even though the production-possibilities frontier of the representative citizen stays the same; and at the pregrowth terms of trade, the economy's aggregate production and consumption of all goods as well as its volume of trade increase at the balanced growth rate.

10 The Rybczynski theorem states that when only one factor increases and the terms of trade are fixed, the output of the commodity that intensively uses the increased factor expands, while the output of the other commodity contracts.

11 At fixed terms of trade, the output of the industry that happens to use the two factors in the proportion in which the additional amounts of labor and capital become available expands, while the output of the other industry remains the same.

12 Technical progress occurs when increased output can be obtained over time from given amounts of capital and labor. It is usually classified into neutral, labor saving, and capital saving. Graphically, technical progress can be viewed as an inward shift of all isoquants of the industry undergoing change. In particular, neutral technical progress amounts to a mere renumbering of the isoquants.

13 Technical progress always gives rise to a positive (favorable) wealth effect. Accordingly, with fixed terms of trade, technical progress always improves social welfare.

14 The commodity of the industry that experiences technical progress becomes cheaper relative to the second commodity at all factor prices. When both industries experience technical progress, the effect on relative prices depends on circumstances.

15 When the terms of trade are fixed, the output of the industry that experiences neutral technical progress increases, while the output of the other industry decreases.

16 When both industries undergo neutral technical progress at the same rate, the production-possibilities frontier shifts out evenly in all directions, as in the case of balanced factor growth. At fixed terms of trade, production and consumption of each commodity as well as the volume of trade increase at the same rate (assuming homothetic tastes).

17 When technical progress occurs predominantly in the export sector, a large country that is heavily dependent on foreign trade and does not pursue an optimal tariff policy may experience immiserizing growth. This occurs when a strong negative terms-of-trade effect (due to a low elasticity of demand for imports by the rest of the world) outweighs a weak wealth effect of a relatively small technical change in the export sector.

PROBLEMS

1 A small open economy, Finland, is currently endowed with 1,000 units of labor (L) and 2,000 units of capital (K) and produces two commodities, X and Y, under con-

stant returns to scale. At the prevailing terms of trade, $3Y{:}1X$, Finland's optimal coefficients of production are as follows:

	Labor (*L*)	Capital (*K*)
Commodity X	4	2
Commodity Y	1	8

Answer the following questions to the extent that the given information is sufficient. If the information is insufficient, state what additional information is needed.

a Determine Finland's outputs of X and Y.

b Suppose that Finland's endowment increases to $1{,}100L$ and $2{,}200K$. Determine the effects on Finland's outputs of X and Y, exports, imports, and social welfare.

2 Consider the standard Heckscher-Ohlin model of Chapter 4. At the current international equilibrium, the capital-abundant country, America, exports 100 units of the capital-intensive commodity (steel) to Britain in exchange for 500 units of the labor-intensive commodity (cloth). Factor prices are equalized between countries. Suppose that 1,000 British workers are allowed to emigrate to America, but they are forced to leave the capital they own in Britain. The emigrant workers continue, however, to receive the income earned by the capital they leave behind. Determine the qualitative effects of such emigration on the outputs of X and Y, exports, imports, the terms of trade, the real factor rewards, and social welfare in each of the two countries. (Note: In answering this question you may assume that all citizens have the same tastes. In addition, before emigration of the workers, each country's capital is distributed evenly among that country's citizens.)

3 Suppose that Australia specializes completely in the production of wheat, which the nation produces with labor alone. Australia is endowed with 1,000 workers, and each worker produces 5 bushels of wheat. At the current international equilibrium, 1 bushel of wheat exchanges for 4 yards of cloth.

a Because of a technical innovation in the production of wheat, each Australian worker now produces 8 bushels of wheat. The relative abundance of wheat causes the terms of trade to fall to 2 yards of cloth per bushel of wheat. Can you predict what happens to the welfare of each individual Australian citizen?

b Assume that the terms of trade remain constant at their new, lower level. How far should the productivity of Australian labor rise before we can be absolutely sure (without knowing each citizen's indifference map) that the technical innovation in the production of wheat causes social welfare to rise?

c Alternatively, assume that the productivity of Australian labor remains at 8 bushels of wheat. How far can Australia's terms of trade deteriorate before social welfare may begin to fall?

d Illustrate your conclusions graphically.

4 Greece is a small open economy endowed with fixed quantities of labor (L) and capital (K). The nation produces two commodities, wine (W) and cloth (C), under constant returns to scale. Wine is capital intensive relative to cloth. The initial international equilibrium at which Greece exports wine and imports cloth is disturbed by neutral technical progress in the production of wine.

a Determine the qualitative effects of the technical progress on Greece's outputs and consumption of wine and cloth and the volumes of exports and imports at the initial terms of trade. (Note: Assume that tastes are homothetic.)

b Is Greece's representative citizen made better off as a result of the technical progress?

c How would you amend your answer to part b if Greece were a large country capable of influencing prices on the world markets?

SUGGESTED READING

Behrman, J. R. (1978). *Development, the International Economic Order, and Commodity Agreements.* Addison-Wesley Publishing Company, Reading, Mass.

Bhagwati, J. (1958). "Immiserizing Growth: A Geometrical Note." *Review of Economic Studies,* vol. 25, pp. 201–205. Reprinted in R. E. Caves and H. G. Johnson (eds.), American Economic Association *Readings in International Economics,* Richard D. Irwin, Inc., Homewood, Ill., 1968.

Chacholiades, M. (1978). *International Trade Theory and Policy.* McGraw-Hill Book Company, New York, chaps. 12 and 13.

Donaldson, L. (1984). *Economic Development: Analysis and Policy.* West Publishing Company, St. Paul, Minn., chap. 10.

Edgeworth, F. Y. (1894). "The Theory of International Values." *Economic Journal,* vol. 4, pp. 35–50.

Findlay, R., and H. Grubert (1959). "Factor Intensities, Technological Progress, and the Terms of Trade." *Oxford Economic Papers,* vol. 11, pp. 111–121.

Hicks, J. R. (1932). *The Theory of Wages.* Macmillan and Company, London, chap. 6.

Johnson, H. G. (1962). *Money, Trade and Economic Growth.* Harvard University Press, Cambridge, Mass., chap. 4. Reprinted in R. E. Caves and H. G. Johnson (eds.), American Economic Association *Readings in International Economics,* Richard D. Irwin, Inc., Homewood, Ill., 1968.

——— (1967). "The Possibility of Income Losses from Increased Efficiency or Factor Accumulation in the Presence of Tariffs." *Economic Journal,* vol. 77, pp. 151–154. Reprinted in H. G. Johnson, *Aspects of the Theory of Tariffs,* Harvard University Press, Cambridge, Mass., 1972.

Prebisch, R. (1950). "The Economic Development of Latin America and Its Principal Problems." *Economic Bulletin for Latin America,* United Nations, Commission for Latin America, New York, 1950.

Rybczynski, T. M. (1955). "Factor Endowment and Relative Commodity Prices." *Economica,* vol. 22, pp. 336–341. Reprinted in R. E. Caves and H. G. Johnson (eds.), American Economic Association *Readings in International Economics,* Richard D. Irwin, Inc. Homewood, Ill., 1968.

Singer, H. W. (1950). "The Distribution of Gains between Investing and Borrowing Countries." *American Economic Review,* vol. 40, pp. 473–485. Reprinted in R. E. Caves and H. G. Johnson (eds.), American Economic Association *Readings in International Economics,* Richard D. Irwin, Inc., Homewood, Ill., 1968.

CHAPTER 7

THE THEORY OF TARIFFS

So far in this book we have demonstrated that free trade benefits all trading countries. This thesis has never been refuted, even though most arguments for protection are asserted with great conviction. Given the mutual gains from free trade, one would expect the flow of commodity trade across national borders to be free from government interference. Yet for hundreds of years the nations of the world have impeded the free flow of international trade by means of several devices, such as tariffs, quotas, technical or administrative rules and procedures, and exchange control. Such policies, which are designed to affect a country's trade relations with the rest of the world, are usually known as **commercial policies.** In general, these policies are influenced by political, sociological, and economic considerations. Chapters 7–10 explore the nature and economic effects of such barriers to free trade as well as the motives behind them. This chapter deals primarily with the effects of the most common instrument of commercial policy, the tariff on an imported good. (Similar effects are generated by other forms of trade restriction, as shown in Chapter 9.)

7-1 TYPES OF TARIFF

The tariff is a tax, or duty, levied on a commodity when it crosses a national boundary. The most common tariff is the **import duty,** that is, the tax imposed on an imported commodity. A less common tariff is the **export duty,** that is, the tax levied on an exported commodity. Export duties are often levied by primary-product exporting countries either to raise revenue or to create scarcity in world markets and thus raise world prices. For example, rice exports have been taxed by Thailand and Burma; cocoa exports, by Ghana; and coffee exports, by Brazil. The Constitution of the United States prohibits the imposition of export taxes. Accordingly, the U.S. government resorts to other forms of export restriction (such as export quotas) whenever conditions justify such trade intervention.

Ad Valorem, Specific, and Compound Tariffs

In general, taxes (whether on imports or exports) can be imposed in any one of three forms, as follows:

1 The **ad valorem duty.** This tax, or duty, is legally specified as a fixed percentage of the value of the commodity imported or exported, inclusive or exclusive of transport costs. For instance, suppose that an ad valorem import duty of 10 percent is imposed on the value of imports, exclusive of transport costs. An importer of commodities that are valued at \$100 must pay a \$10 import duty to the government, that is, $0.10 \times \$100 = \$10$.

2 The **specific duty.** This tax is legally specified as a fixed sum of money per physical unit imported or exported. For instance, a U.S. importer of a Japanese car may be required to pay a \$1,000 import duty to the U.S. government irrespective of the price paid for the car.

3 The **compound duty.** This is a combination of an ad valorem tax *and* a specific tax. For instance, the U.S. importer of a foreign car may be required to pay \$1,000 plus 1 percent of the value of the car.

The United States uses both ad valorem and specific duties (approximately in the same frequency), but European countries use primarily ad valorem taxes.

Differences between Ad Valorem and Specific Rates

Given the price of the commodity (exported or imported) there exists a one-to-one correspondence between ad valorem rates and specific rates. For instance, the import duty on an imported car whose price is \$10,000 may be specified as either \$1,000 (specific duty) or 10 percent of the price of the car (ad valorem duty). Is it, then, immaterial whether a country specifies its taxes on the specific or the ad valorem basis? No. Such a conclusion is not warranted because there are some important differences between the two, as follows:

1 *For a commodity that comes in many varieties, some cheaper than others, the ad valorem tax is more equitable than the specific tax.* For instance, suppose that a flat specific tax rate of \$1,000 is imposed on every car imported into the United States. The **ad valorem incidence** (that is, the equivalent ad valorem tax), which is the best measure of the degree of protection, is 10 percent for a \$10,000 Toyota, but only 2 percent for a \$50,000 Mercedes-Benz. Evidently, the specific tax is **regressive** in the sense that it imposes a heavier burden on the cheaper qualities.

2 *The level of protection provided by a specific tariff varies inversely with the general level of prices, but the ad valorem tariff always provides the same level of protection.* As noted earlier, the degree of protection provided by a tariff is best measured by its ad valorem incidence. The ad valorem incidence of a specific tax falls during periods of **inflation** (rising prices) and rises during periods of **deflation** (falling prices). Since the tendency of prices is to rise through time, producers of products subject to specific duties often complain about erosion in the level of their protection because of inflation. For instance, if the price of, say, a Toyota doubles from $5,000 to $10,000, the ad valorem incidence (and thus the degree of protection) provided by a $1,000 specific import tax is halved (from 20 to 10 percent).

3 *Administratively, the specific duty is very easy to apply whereas an ad valorem duty can be calculated only after the value of the commodity is determined.*

The calculation of a commodity value for tariff purposes is not always straightforward. It is necessary to decide first what must be included in the commodity value. In general, a country may use either the f.o.b. ("free on board") price or the c.i.f. ("cost, insurance, freight") price. The **f.o.b. price** coincides with the cost of the commodity on board ship at the port of embarkation. A variant of the f.o.b. price is the **f.a.s.** ("free along side") **price,** which is lower than the f.o.b. price by the amount of the ship-loading costs. The **c.i.f. price** coincides with the cost of the commodity at the port of entry. Thus, the c.i.f. price is higher than the f.o.b. price by the amount of the transport costs, that is, ocean freight, insurance, etc.

7-2 THE PARTIAL EQUILIBRIUM ANALYSIS OF THE TARIFF

A tariff on imports raises the domestic price of importables. As a result, the domestic output of the import-competing industry expands while the domestic consumption of importables contracts. Imports fall because the gap between domestic consumption and domestic production shrinks. Tariff revenue is collected by the government, and income is redistributed from consumers to producers. In this section, we study all these effects within the context of partial equilibrium analysis, which prepares the ground for the general equilibrium analysis presented in the rest of the chapter. Throughout this section we assume that the tariff-imposing country is *small,* that is, a price taker in world markets.

The effects of a tariff are illustrated in Figure 7-1. Downward-sloping line D_d is the domestic demand schedule for cloth. Upward-sloping line S_d is the domestic supply schedule for cloth. In autarky, equilibrium occurs at E, at which the price of cloth is $25 per yard. Assume that the world price of cloth is $10 per yard, as shown by infinitely elastic supply curve S_w. Under free-trade conditions, the domestic price of cloth is driven down to the world price of $10 per yard, domestic consumption rises to 150 million yards per year (point C), and domestic production falls to 30 million yards per year (point K). Imports are equal to 120 million yards per year (that is, 150 − 30), as shown by horizontal distance KC.

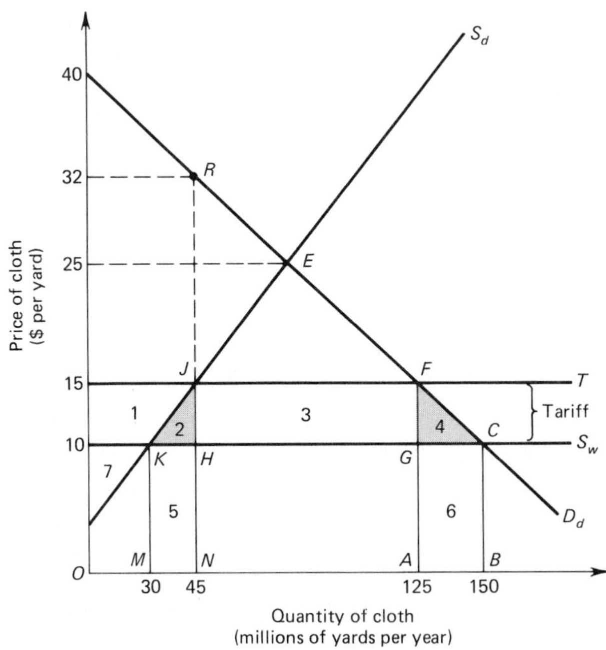

FIGURE 7-1 **The Effects of an Import Tariff.** In autarky, equilibrium occurs at the intersection (point *E*) of domestic demand schedule D_d and domestic supply schedule S_d. At the free-trade price of $10, consumption increases to 150 million yards (point *C*), of which 30 million yards are produced domestically and 120 million yards are imported. With a 50 percent tariff, the domestic price rises to $15, domestic consumption falls to 125 million yards (point *F*), domestic production expands to 45 million yards (point *J*), and imports shrink to 80 million yards (or *JF*). Consumer surplus is reduced by the sum of areas 1, 2, 3, and 4, of which area 3 accrues to the government in the form of tariff revenue, and area 1 goes to domestic producers as additional producer surplus. Shaded triangular areas 2 and 4 illustrate the deadweight loss of the tariff.

Suppose now that a tariff of $5, or 50 percent, raises the domestic price of imported cloth to $15 per yard. This is illustrated by shifting the world supply curve, S_w, upward by the amount of the tariff, as shown by horizontal line *T*. As long as domestic cloth is a perfect substitute for foreign cloth, domestic cloth producers are also able to charge $15 per yard. Thus the domestic price rises to $15 for both foreign and domestic cloth. This price increase has the following effects:

1 Consumption Effect The domestic consumers reduce their consumption of cloth to 125 million yards per year (point *F*). The reduction of 25 million yards, indicated by horizontal distance *GC*, is known as the **consumption effect** of the tariff.

2 Production Effect The higher price of cloth makes it profitable for domestic producers of cloth to increase their output to 45 million yards per year (point *J*). Thus the tariff attracts resources into the *protected* cloth industry from other sectors of the economy. The increase of 15 million yards, illustrated by horizontal distance *KH*, is known as the **protective effect** (or **production effect**) of the tariff.

3 Trade Effect The tariff causes imports to fall to 80 million yards per year, as indicated by horizontal distance *JF*. The reduction in imports (from 120 million to 80 million yards per year) equals the increase in domestic production (15 million yards) plus the decrease in domestic consumption (25 million yards) and is known as the **trade effect** of the tariff.

When the tariff rate is at least as high as the difference between the autarkic price ($25) and the world price ($10), the volume of imports drops to zero; that is, the tariff becomes *prohibitive*. A **prohibitive tariff** forces the country to return to autarky and is equivalent to a total ban on the imports of cloth.

4 Revenue Effect After the imposition of the tariff, the government collects $400 million per year (that is, $5 × 80 million), as illustrated by area 3 (or *JHGF*). This is known as the **revenue effect** of the tariff. Note that the revenue effect of a prohibitive tariff is zero.

5 Redistribution Effect The tariff redistributes income from consumers to producers. The net loss to consumers is given by the sum of areas 1, 2, 3, and 4, which represents the reduction in **consumer surplus.** Area 1 is transferred to producers as additional **producer surplus,** and area 3 corresponds to the tariff revenue collected by the government. The two shaded triangular areas (2 and 4) are unaccounted for; they depict the **deadweight loss** of the tariff.

It may be recalled from **microeconomics** that the area under the demand curve and above the current price is the consumer surplus. To understand why this is a surplus (or net benefit) think as follows: Each point on the demand curve shows the marginal valuation placed by consumers on the last unit, and the difference between the marginal valuation and the actual price is a net benefit to consumers. For instance, at *R* the last unit is worth $32 to consumers; otherwise they would not be willing to buy it. But under free-trade conditions they pay only $10, thus enjoying a net benefit of $22 (that is, $32 − $10). The triangular area under the demand curve, D_d, and above the world supply curve, S_w, represents the consumer surplus, that is, the total net benefit enjoyed by consumers for each of the 150 million yards of cloth they purchase at the world price of $10 per yard. When the tariff raises the price to $15, consumption shifts to point *F*, and the consumer surplus diminishes by the sum of areas 1, 2, 3, and 4.

Similarly, the triangular area above the supply curve and below the current price represents a net benefit to producers. This area is known as the producer surplus. The rationale for this interpretation is simple. Each point on the supply curve represents the marginal cost of the last unit, and the difference between the actual price and the marginal cost is a net benefit to producers. The total producer surplus corresponds to triangular area 7 under free-trade conditions, but expands to the sum of areas 1 and 7 after the imposition of the tariff.

The deadweight loss of the tariff has two components: shaded area 2 (related to the increase in the domestic output of cloth, *KH*) and shaded area 4 (related to the reduction in the domestic consumption of cloth, *GC*). Shaded area 2 represents the additional cost that society incurs by replacing *KH* imports (that is, 15 million yards) with domestic production. The amount *KH* was formerly imported from abroad at the total cost given by area 5. This same amount (*KH*) is now produced at home at the total cost given by the sum of areas 2 and 5. Obviously, the country incurs an additional cost, which is equal to area 2.

Similarly, shaded area 4 represents a net loss in consumer surplus. The quantity *GC* (or 25 million yards) was formerly imported from abroad at the total cost equal to area 6. The same quantity had the total consumer value given by the sum of areas 4 and 6, and thus generated the consumer surplus equal to area 4. Because of the tariff, consumers are denied the opportunity to enjoy this portion of consumer surplus.

7-3 THE GENERAL EQUILIBRIUM ANALYSIS OF THE TARIFF: THE SMALL-COUNTRY CASE

The partial equilibrium approach focuses only on the protected industry. But protection has effects that reverberate beyond the sector in which the tariff is originally imposed. To capture all effects of the tariff, we must adopt a general equilibrium approach. This section deals with the general equilibrium effects of a tariff imposed by a small country, that is, a price taker in world markets.

Free-Trade Equilibrium

Assume that a small country, Austria, is endowed with labor and capital and produces steel and cloth under constant returns to scale. To fix ideas, we suppose that Austria exports steel and imports cloth at current world prices: $p_s = \$10$ and $p_c = \$50$, respectively. Under free-trade conditions, the prices that rule in world markets prevail in Austria also. Thus the relative price of cloth is everywhere 5 (that is, \$50/\$10). In an effort to protect its domestic cloth industry, Austria imposes a 20 percent tariff on imports of cloth. How does the tariff affect Austria's economy?

The Effect on Domestic Prices

The most obvious and direct effect of the tariff is on domestic prices. A tariff is a discriminatory tax in the sense that it is applied only to commodities imported from the rest of the world—it is not applied to commodities produced domestically. As a result, the tariff drives a wedge between domestic prices and world prices. In our case, the domestic price of cloth rises to 1.20 × \$50 = \$60. That is, the domestic buyers of cloth must now pay a tariff of 20 percent of \$50, or \$10, in addition to the world price of \$50. The domestic producers receive the domestic price of \$60—not the world price of \$50. Accordingly, while in the world markets the relative price of cloth remains at 5 (that is, \$50/\$10), in Austria it rises to 6 (that is, \$60/\$10). This change in the domestic relative price of cloth has profound effects on the domestic organization of the economy of the small country.

The Effect on Domestic Production

As we have just seen, the relative price of the imported commodity (cloth) rises by the full extent of the tariff. As a result, resources shift from the production of steel (export industry) to the production of cloth (import-competing industry), as illustrated in Figure 7-2. Before Austria imposes the tariff, production occurs at P_0, where the opportunity cost of steel in terms of cloth (given by the absolute slope of production-possibilities frontier *UV* at P_0) is equal to the given relative price of steel in the world markets (shown by the slope of consumption-possibilities frontier *MN*). After the imposition of the tariff, the relative price of cloth increases (or the relative price of steel decreases) in Austria, as shown by the slope of line *DF*, causing production to shift from P_0 to P_1. Thus the tariff causes resources to shift from the steel industry to the *protected* cloth industry. This is the **protective effect** of the tariff.

The Effect on the Value of Production and Welfare

An important effect of a tariff is *the reduction in the value of output produced at world prices.* Thus, in Figure 7-2 the value of production at world prices is necessarily lower at P_1 than at the free-trade, optimal production point P_0. This is illustrated by the fact that dashed line SP_1T, which is parallel to *MN*, lies inside free-trade consumption-possibilities frontier *MN*. This should not come as a surprise. The value of production at world prices is *maximized* at free-trade production point P_0. Hence, production at any other point gives rise to a lower real income.

The reduction in the value of production (at world prices) works to the detriment of the welfare of the tariff-imposing country. For instance, once the production point shifts to P_1, the small country can consume only along dashed line SP_1T. Social welfare necessarily declines as Austria shifts to a lower social indifference curve.

The Effect on Domestic Consumption

As we have seen, once production shifts to P_1 the economy will consume along dashed line SP_1T. But where exactly on SP_1T will the economy consume? Cer-

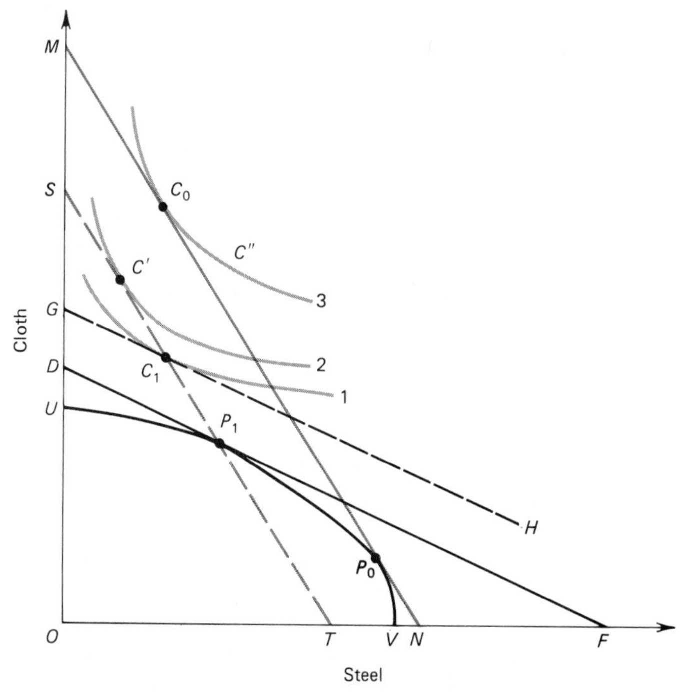

FIGURE 7-2 **The effects of a tariff on domestic production, consumption, and real income.** Production occurs initially at P_0, where the domestic opportunity cost of steel (shown by the slope of production-possibilities frontier *UV* at P_0) is equal to the relative price of steel in world markets (shown by the slope of consumption-possibilities frontier *MN*). A tariff on imports of cloth raises the domestic relative price of cloth, as shown by line *DF*. Resources are transferred from the steel industry to the protected cloth industry, as production shifts from P_0 to P_1. Once production shifts to P_1, the country can consume only along dashed line SP_1T. Thus, the economy's real income and welfare fall with the tariff as the consumption point shifts from C_0 to C_1.

tainly *not* at C′, that is, the point of tangency of line SP_1T to the highest social indifference curve. Recall that the slope of line SP_1T gives the *world* relative prices. The domestic consumers, however, trade at *domestic* relative prices, as indicated by the slope of *DF*. Accordingly, consumption occurs along line SP_1T at the point where the marginal rate of substitution in consumption is equal to the domestic price ratio. This is illustrated by point C_1.

The Tariff Revenue

Return to Figure 7-2 and observe that the value of output produced is *lower* than the value of output consumed *at domestic prices*. Thus, line *DF*, which indicates the value of output produced at domestic prices (that is, what is known in national income accounting as **national income at factor cost**) lies inside line *GH*, which shows the value of consumption at domestic prices (that is, what is known in national income accounting as **aggregate expenditure**). What generates the discrepancy between these two aggregates?

The discrepancy between the value of production and the value of consumption (at domestic prices) is due to the tariff revenue collected by the government. Thus, in the presence of a tariff, aggregate expenditure on steel and cloth must be higher than the income that accrues directly to the factors of production by the precise amount of the tariff revenue. This proposition must be true whether the government spends the tariff revenue directly on steel and cloth for public consumption or redistributes it to private consumers in the form of either lump-sum transfers or a general income tax reduction. In Figure 7-2 the tariff revenue expressed in terms of cloth is given by vertical distance *DG*.

In this book, we shall always assume that the government redistributes the tariff revenue to private consumers. We do this for two reasons. First, in today's international economy the role of the tariff as a source of revenue is insignificant. Accordingly, in a study of the effects of a tariff it is more appropriate to assume that the government has a budget that is already financed by other means and that the government returns the tariff revenue to consumers in one way or another. Second, by assuming that the government returns the tariff revenue to consumers, we do not have to introduce an arbitrary assumption about the use of the tariff revenue—the social indifference map can be used for this purpose also.

Note that the discrepancy between the value of production and the value of consumption arises only when both aggregates are evaluated at domestic prices. When world prices are used, the two aggregates are necessarily equal, as illustrated by the fact that in Figure 7-2 both the production point (P_1) and the consumption point (C_1) lie on dashed line *ST*. This reflects the fact that irrespective of any taxes or subsidies imposed by the small economy, *the value of exports of the rest of the world must be equal to the value of imports of the rest of the world when both aggregates are evaluated at international prices.*

The Effect on the Volume of Trade

When the government redistributes the tariff revenue to private consumers, the tariff causes the volume of trade of the small country to shrink. This is an important effect of the tariff, and it deserves careful consideration.

Since world prices are assumed constant, we can find out what happens to the volume of trade of the small country by concentrating on either the volume of exports of steel or the volume of imports of cloth. We choose the latter.

The volume of imports of cloth is given by the difference between the domestic consumption and production of cloth. As we have seen, the tariff affects both of these variables. Thus the tariff causes the domestic production of cloth (importables) to increase (protective effect). Other things being equal, the increase in the domestic production of cloth reduces the volume of imports because it leaves a smaller gap between domestic consumption and domestic production to be filled with imports.

The change in the domestic consumption of cloth can be broken down into a **substitution effect** plus an **income effect.** Thus, the imposition of the tariff makes cloth relatively more expensive, causing consumers to substitute steel for cloth, as illustrated in Figure 7-2 by the movement from C_0 to C'' along indifference curve 3. In addition to the change in relative prices, the tariff causes the real income of the small country to fall, as illustrated by the movement from indifference curve 3 (point C'') to indifference curve 1 (point C_1). For our purposes, we assume that cloth is a normal commodity (that is, its consumption declines as income falls). Thus the income effect reinforces the substitution effect, and the domestic consumption of cloth clearly diminishes. Accordingly, the tariff causes the volume of imports (and thus the volume of trade) to fall as domestic consumption decreases and domestic production rises. (It can be shown that the volume of trade falls even when the imported commodity is inferior.)

The Prohibitive Tariff

As we have just seen, the tariff causes the volume of trade to shrink. It can also be shown that as the small economy raises the ad valorem tariff rate, the volume of trade shrinks further. When the ad valorem tariff rate is raised too high, the volume of trade drops to zero, that is, the tariff becomes *prohibitive.* A prohibitive tariff forces the country to return to autarky.

The prohibitive tariff is illustrated in Figure 7-3. Curve UV is the production-possibilities frontier, while curves 1 and 2 are two social indifference curves. The world relative price ratio is given by the slope of line MN. Initially the economy produces at P_0 and consumes at C_0. The country imposes a tariff that reduces the domestic price ratio to the slope of DF. Apparently, all trade ceases completely as the economy produces and consumes at autarkic equilibrium point P_1. The tariff is prohibitive.

Figure 7-3 illustrates the *minimum* ad valorem rate at which the tariff becomes prohibitive. Obviously, raising the tariff above this minimum level changes nothing—the tariff continues to be prohibitive.

The Effect on the Internal Distribution of Income

We saw in Chapter 2 that one commonly used argument against free trade is the "cheap foreign labor" argument for protection. This argument is based on the empirical observation that real wages are much higher in industrial nations, such as the United States, than in developing countries, such as India. If American workers, the argument goes, are subjected to the competition of cheap foreign labor, the American real wage rate will be drastically reduced. Thus, tariffs are needed to protect the American standard of living from the cheap foreign labor.

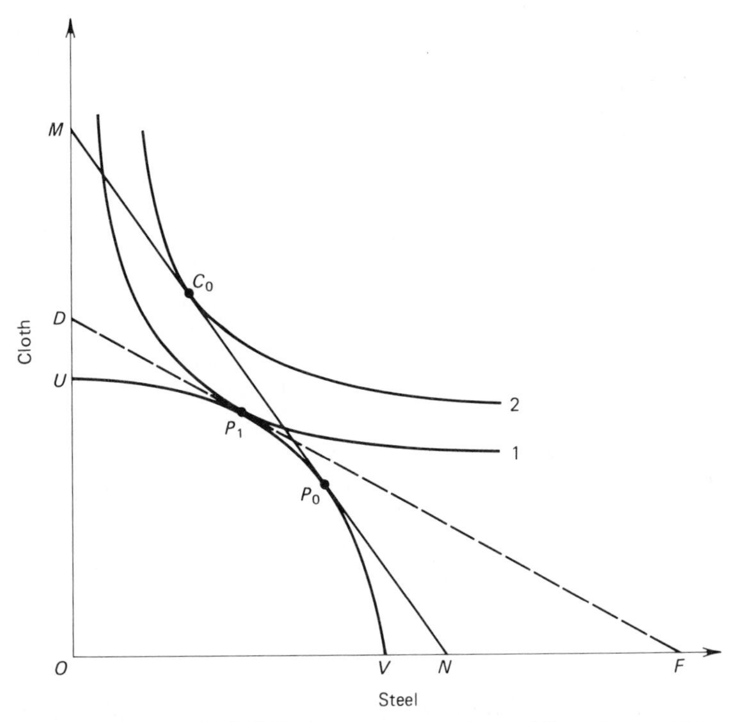

FIGURE 7-3 **The prohibitive tariff.** Initially the economy produces at P_0 and consumes at C_0. A tariff that causes the domestic price ratio to fall from the slope of *MN* (world price ratio) to the slope of *DF* is prohibitive because then the economy produces and consumes at autarkic equilibrium point P_1.

As we pointed out in Chapter 2, the cheap foreign labor argument for protection is a pseudo argument that does not stand up to scientific scrutiny. The higher American wage rate stands on the firm foundation of higher American labor productivity—American workers have better skills and operate with much larger amounts of capital. Cheap foreign labor is no threat to the American standard of living.

Yet there is a grain of truth in the cheap foreign labor argument. As we have seen, a tariff imposed by a small country raises the relative price of the imported commodity (cloth) and shifts resources from the export industry (steel) to the import-competing industry (cloth). The tariff forces a drastic reorganization of the small country's structure of production. Not only do resources shift from one industry to the other, but also the optimal methods of production, the optimal factor proportions, and the marginal productivities of both factors in both industries—and thus the internal distribution of income—all change with the tariff. The essence of this complex reorganization is captured by the following important theorem:

***Stolper-Samuelson theorem:* An increase (decrease) in the relative price of a commodity raises (lowers) the real wage of the factor used intensively in its production.**

As the price of cloth rises with the tariff, resources shift from the steel industry to the cloth industry. Because cloth is labor intensive relative to steel, the steel industry releases more units of capital per unit of labor (or, alternatively, fewer units of labor per unit of capital) than the cloth industry is willing to absorb. As a result, there emerges an excess demand for labor and/or an excess supply of capital, causing the wage rate to rise and rent to fall. As labor becomes more expensive relative to capital, both industries substitute the cheaper factor, capital, for the more expensive factor, labor, that is, both industries become less labor intensive or more capital intensive. Consequently, the marginal physical product of labor *rises* in *both* industries. Similarly, the marginal physical product of capital *falls* in *both* industries. Thus as the tariff causes cloth to become more expensive relative to steel, the real wage rate for labor (that is, the factor used intensively in cloth) rises and the real rent for capital (that is, the factor used intensively in steel) falls.

The implication of the Stolper-Samuelson theorem is that even though the small country as a whole loses from the imposition of the tariff, *the factor used intensively by the import-competing industry becomes better off.* In our example, a worker can buy more steel and more cloth after the tariff. Hence, it is to the advantage of the factor used intensively by the import-competing industry to demand tariff protection, even though the rest of the country will be worse off.

Redistribution of the Tariff Revenue

The Stolper-Samuelson theorem ignores the redistribution of the tariff revenue. Suppose that the government actually redistributes all tariff revenue to the factor whose income is reduced by protection. Is it possible for this factor also to become better off after the tariff? Unfortunately, when the tariff-levying country is small, the answer is no. The reason is simple. As we have seen, the tariff reduces the value of output produced at world prices. Since the real income of the factor used intensively by the import-competing industry increases while the real income of the economy as a whole decreases, it follows that a small country will never be able to compensate (by means of tariff-revenue redistribution) the factor whose income has been reduced by protection.

7-4 THE EFFECTS OF THE TARIFF ON A LARGE COUNTRY

The preceding analysis rests on the assumption that the tariff-levying country is small, that is, a price taker in world markets. Yet that analysis is essential in understanding the effects of a tariff levied by a large country.

When the tariff-levying country is large, its commercial policy necessarily disturbs world markets and brings about a change in the terms of trade. In general, the tariff tends to improve the large country's terms of trade.

This section explores the nature and implications of the terms-of-trade effect of the tariff within the standard two-country, two-commodity model developed in Chapter 4.

The Terms-of-Trade Effect

Assume again two countries, America (home country) and Britain (foreign country). Either country's actions are substantial enough to influence international prices. The initial free-trade equilibrium position can be shown in terms of the familiar offer curves, as illustrated in Figure 7-4. Free-trade equilibrium occurs at the intersection E_0 of the free-trade offer curves. America exports OS_0 tons of steel to Britain in exchange for OC_0 yards of cloth. The slope of terms-of-trade line TOT_0 (that is, OC_0/OS_0) gives the relative price of steel in terms of cloth, which is America's free-trade terms of trade. How does a tariff levied by America affect the initial free-trade equilibrium?

When a country levies a tariff, the country's offer curve shifts, giving rise to a new equilibrium. In particular, when the government redistributes the tariff revenue to the private sector (an assumption that we maintain throughout our

FIGURE 7-4 **The effect of a tariff on the terms of trade.** The initial free-trade equilibrium at E_0 is disturbed by an American tariff. America's offer curve shifts toward the origin, as shown by the nation's dashed tariff-distorted offer curve. Thus, equilibrium shifts to E_1. America's terms of trade improve, as shown by the fact that line TOT_1 is steeper than line TOT_0.

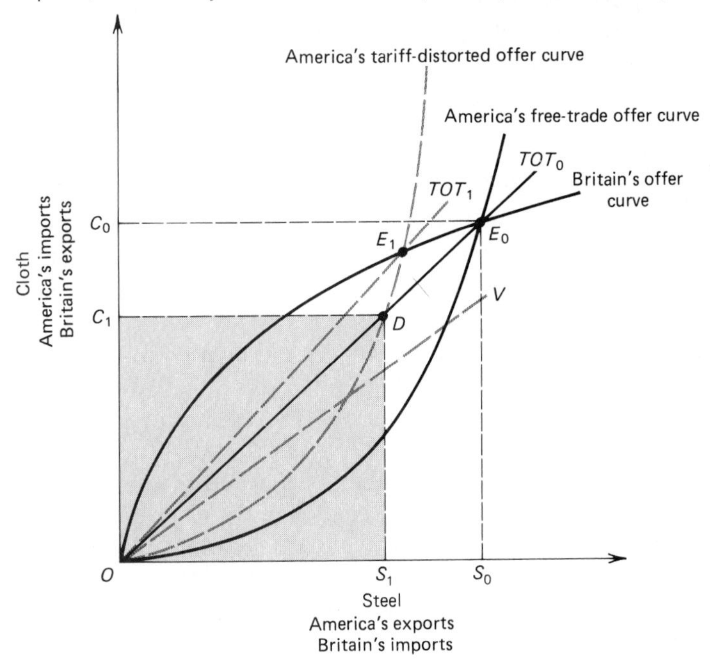

discussion), the offer curve shifts toward the origin, as illustrated in Figure 7-4 by America's **tariff-distorted offer curve.** This result follows from the analysis of Section 7-3. There we saw that a small country's tariff causes the country's desired volume of trade to shrink. For instance, if America were a small country and TOT_0 were the foreign offer curve, a tariff levied by America would cause its free-trade volume of trade, OE_0, to shrink to, say, OD. But this must be true for any given linear foreign offer curve. Accordingly, the tariff-distorted offer curve must lie closer to the origin than the free-trade offer curve, as illustrated in Figure 7-4.

After the tariff, international equilibrium shifts to point E_1, at which America's tariff-distorted offer curve intersects Britain's offer curve. Observe carefully that *America's terms of trade improve:* terms-of-trade line TOT_1 is steeper than terms-of-trade line TOT_0. This is a necessary result.

The large country (America) is able to improve its terms of trade by levying a tariff because the country exploits its **monopoly-monopsony power** in world markets. Recall that at the initial free-trade prices (OC_0/OS_0), America's desired volume of trade contracts (from OE_0 to OD). In particular, America's supply of exports of steel decreases by S_1S_0, while its demand for imports of cloth decreases by C_1C_0. In the market for steel, America acts like a monopolist who restricts supply in order to raise the price; and in the market for cloth, America acts like a monopsonist who restricts demand in order to buy the product at a lower price. As a result of the shortage of steel as well as the surplus of cloth in the world market, the relative price of steel (America's exportables) tends to rise, as illustrated by the fact that terms-of-trade line TOT_1 is steeper than line TOT_0.

Note that a small country lacks any monopoly-monopsony power in world markets. Therefore, the small country is in the same position as a perfect competitor, who cannot affect market prices. This is the fundamental reason why a small country cannot affect its terms of trade while a large country can.

The Effect of a Tariff on Domestic Prices

For problems of domestic resource allocation and income distribution, what is important is the effect of the tariff on the *domestic* price ratio, not the terms-of-trade effect. Does the imported commodity become more expensive, after the imposition of the tariff, in the tariff-levying country? In other words, does the tariff actually protect the import-competing industry?

When the tariff-levying country is small (and thus its terms of trade are fixed), the tariff causes the price of the imported commodity to rise in the domestic market proportionally to the tariff. When the tariff-levying country is large, there is a second influence that must be considered before we can decide what happens to the domestic relative price of the imported commodity: *the resultant reduction in the relative price of the imported commodity in world markets* (that is, the terms-of-trade improvement we studied in the previous subsection). Is it possible for the price of the imported commodity to fall in the world market by more than the tariff? If it does, then the imported commodity actually becomes cheaper not only in world markets but also in the domestic economy. In general, anything is possible. Normally the tariff protects the domestic import-competing industry. That is, normally the imported commodity becomes more expensive in the tariff-levying country while it becomes cheaper in world markets.

Metzler (1949) discovered the paradoxical case in which the tariff makes the imported commodity cheaper all around (that is, both in world markets and domestically). Known as **Metzler's paradox** (or as the **Metzler case**), this curious possibility arises when (1) the foreign demand for imports is inelastic and (2) the tariff-levying country's marginal propensity to import is very low. Under these circumstances, the price of the imported commodity in the world market may fall by more than the amount of the tariff. As a result, the imported commodity may become cheaper in the tariff-levying country also.

The important implication of Metzler's case is, of course, the *negative* protection provided by the tariff to the import-competing industry. Thus, the domestic production of the imported commodity *falls* in the tariff-levying country after the tariff—resources shift out of the import-competing industry and into the export industry. This is indeed a paradoxical phenomenon because tariffs are usually advocated by politicians who want to protect the import-competing industries. It seems ironic that when a country is very successful in improving its terms of trade through commercial policy, the import-competing industry suffers from the effects of negative protection. Metzler's paradox is pursued further in Appendix 8.

7-5 TARIFFS AND WORLD WELFARE

Free-trade advocates always emphasize the deleterious effects of tariffs on world welfare. In particular, a tariff creates a wedge between foreign and domestic prices and interferes with the maximization of the welfare of the world in the following fundamental ways:

1 The tariff reduces the world output of commodities by reversing the process of international division of labor, which is dictated by the law of comparative advantage.

2 The tariff forces a suboptimal allocation of commodities among consumers.

The purpose of this section is to clarify these inefficiencies of tariffs.

Tariffs and World Output

The first inefficiency of tariffs is founded on the law of comparative advantage: When each country specializes in the production of that commodity in which the country has a comparative advantage, the world output of every commodity increases (potentially). Tariffs, in general, prevent the world from maximizing these production gains.

Maximization of world output occurs when the marginal rates of transformation (that is, opportunity costs) are equalized between countries. What is the commonsense meaning of this condition? We can discover its meaning and significance by considering a situation in which it is *not* satisfied.

Suppose that the opportunity cost of steel is 3 yards of cloth in America and 5 yards of cloth in Britain. If America increases its production of steel by 1 ton while Britain decreases its production of steel by 1 ton, the total world production of steel remains constant. What happens to the world output of cloth? Since America's opportunity cost of steel is 3 yards of cloth, America's output of cloth falls by 3 yards. Similarly, Britain's output of cloth increases by 5 yards because Britain's opportunity cost of steel is 5 yards of cloth. Accordingly, the world output of cloth increases by $5 - 3 = 2$ yards, which is the difference between America's and Britain's opportunity cost of steel.

We therefore reach an important conclusion:

When the marginal rates of transformation (that is, opportunity costs) are different between countries, the world can always increase the output of one commodity without reducing the output of any other commodity. Alternatively, when America's and Britain's opportunity costs are equal, the world cannot achieve further production gains; that is, the world output is already at its maximum.

Free trade equalizes commodity prices between countries. Given that commodity prices are equal to opportunity costs, it follows that free trade leads to equalization of opportunity costs between countries. Accordingly, free trade maximizes world output. In other words, under free-trade conditions it is impossible to increase the world output of one commodity without reducing world output of another commodity.

It must be clear by now why tariffs reduce world output. As we have seen, a tariff creates a wedge (or divergence) between foreign and domestic commodity prices. Because commodity prices are equal to opportunity costs, it follows that a tariff creates a divergence between the opportunity costs (or marginal rates of transformation) of countries. A tariff prevents the world from maximizing world output (or from capturing *all* the potential gains from trade). This is the first inefficiency of tariffs.

Tariffs and Consumption

In addition to preventing the world from maximizing world output, a tariff interferes with the optimal allocation of commodities among consumers. How does this second inefficiency of tariffs come about?

A fixed bundle of commodities (for example, 1,000 tons of steel and 2,000 yards of cloth) is optimally allocated between two consumers (or countries) when it is no longer possible to make, with the same bundle of commodities, one consumer (or country) better off without making the other worse off. Optimality is attained when the marginal rates of substitution in consumption are equal between consumers (or countries). Again, we can discover the significance of this condition by considering situations that violate it.

Assume that America's marginal rate of substitution of steel for cloth is 3 and Britain's is 5. We can make Britain better off without reducing America's welfare merely by transferring 1 ton of steel from America to Britain and 3 yards of cloth from Britain to America. America's welfare remains constant because America is willing to exchange 1 ton of steel for 3 yards of cloth—America's marginal rate of substitution of steel for cloth is 3. Britain, however, becomes better off. While Britain is willing to give up 5 yards of cloth for the extra ton of steel—Britain's marginal rate of substitution of steel for cloth is 5—the nation actually exports only 3 yards of cloth to America. Accordingly, Britain is made better off while America's welfare remains constant.

Alternatively, we could transfer 5 yards of cloth from Britain to America (as we also transfer 1 ton of steel from America to Britain) and thus make America better off as we keep Britain's welfare the same. Finally, if we transfer 4 yards of cloth from Britain to America, then both countries become better off. We therefore reach the following important conclusion:

When the marginal rates of substitution are different between countries, it is always possible to reallocate commodities and make one country better off without making the other country worse off. When these marginal rates of substitution are equalized, the allocation of commodities becomes optimal and no further welfare gains are possible.

Free trade makes it possible for countries to equalize their marginal rates of substitution in consumption. Thus each country consumes at the point where its marginal rate of substitution of steel for cloth is equal to the relative price of steel. Free trade equalizes commodity prices between countries. Therefore, free trade equalizes the marginal rates of substitution between countries and leads to optimality. In short, under free trade it is not possible to reallocate a fixed bundle of commodities and make one country better off without making the other country worse off.

A tariff, however, creates a wedge between foreign and domestic prices. Because commodity prices are equal to marginal rates of substitution, it follows that a tariff creates a divergence between the marginal rates of substitution of countries. Therefore, a tariff prevents the world from allocating commodities optimally between countries. This is the second inefficiency introduced by tariffs and reinforces the loss of world output that we studied in the preceding subsection.

7-6 THE TARIFF AS A PRODUCTION SUBSIDY PLUS A CONSUMPTION TAX

A tariff is equivalent to a consumption tax plus a production subsidy on importables. For instance, suppose that Austria imports cloth at the world price of $10 per yard. A 50 percent tariff raises the domestic price of cloth to $15 for both domestic producers and domestic consumers. Alternatively, the same result could be achieved by imposing a 50 percent tax on the domestic consumption of cloth plus a 50 percent subsidy on the domestic production of cloth. A 50 percent consumption tax alone would raise the price paid by consumers to $15, of which $10 would accrue to producers (domestic and foreign) and $5 would go to the government as tax revenue. By adding a 50 percent subsidy to domestic production, the revenue per yard received by domestic producers also rises to $15. Thus the consumption tax raises the price paid by domestic consumers, and the production subsidy raises the price received by domestic producers. The final outcome is the same as with the tariff.

It is less costly to protect the import-competing industry with a production subsidy than with a tariff because the tariff imposes an additional consumption cost. The decomposition of the tariff into a consumption tax plus a production subsidy explains why this is so. The production-subsidy element of the tariff interferes with the optimization of production and involves a production cost (illustrated by area 2 in Figure 7-1 and by the shifting of production from P_0 to P_1 in Figure 7-2). The consumption-tax element of the tariff interferes with the optimization of consumption and involves a consumption cost (illustrated by area 4 in Figure 7-1 and by the movement of consumption from C' to C_1 in Figure 7-2). Thus a production subsidy is more efficient than a tariff because it avoids the unnecessary consumption cost.

In practice, however, governments more often than not use tariffs instead of production subsidies for two reasons: (1) While tariffs generate government revenue, production subsidies require governments to raise revenue. (2) The cost of protection is not as visible with a tariff as it is with a production subsidy; hence consumers are likely to complain less with a tariff than with a production subsidy—just imagine the outrage of taxpayers if they read in the headlines of the daily press that the U.S. government would be providing a subsidy of over $1 billion per year to U.S. textile producers.

7-7 MEASURING THE COSTS OF PROTECTION

During the last three decades, many economists have used the partial equilibrium approach to estimate the deadweight loss of protection. Generally, these estimates have been low—less than 1 percent of gross domestic product (GDP). Such low estimates often give the impression that the deadweight loss is trivial, even though it is an annually recurring cost that lasts for as long as protection is in force. However, such estimates do not include the losses that are usually associated with **X inefficiency** (when protection leads to domestic monopoly, which does not feel any pressure to undertake the necessary effort to minimize costs); nor do they incorporate the losses due to *directly unproductive profit-seeking activities* (such as lobbying efforts that yield income but do not produce any output), or the effects on income and employment beyond the industry under consideration. When *all* the repercussions of protection are taken into account by means of general equilibrium methods, the estimates of the cost of protection increase significantly. For instance, recent studies show that the cost of quotas alone in Turkey in 1978 was as much as 5.4 percent of GDP, while the cost of tariffs, quotas, and export taxes in the Philippines in 1978 was as much as 5.2 percent of GNP.

Empirical studies show that the costs to consumers in the United States amount to many billions of dollars for protecting textiles and clothing as well as standard grades of steel, and to over $1 billion for protecting cars. In the European Community (EC), the cost of protecting videocassette recorders is estimated at almost half a billion dollars.

Note that the *net* social cost of protection is much less than the consumer cost because the higher prices paid by consumers go partly to domestic producers (who expand production to replace imports) and partly to the government (as tariff revenue). Even so, the net social cost of protecting textiles and clothing ranges from $1.4 billion to $6.6 billion in the European Community and the United States. The estimate for protecting steel in the United States is about $2 billion.

Source: Based on The World Bank, *World Development Report 1987*, Oxford University Press, New York, 1987, chaps. 5 and 8.

7-8 EFFECTIVE PROTECTION

Nominal tariff rates (published in the country's tariff schedule) often fail to measure the degree of protection actually received by domestic producers. This is because protection depends not only on the nominal rates imposed on the final product itself, but also on any taxes or subsidies placed on inputs. When an import-competing industry utilizes intermediate products imported from the rest of the world, the precise degree of protection is captured by the **effective rate of protection** accorded to **value added** in production, not the nominal rate imposed on the finished product.

Intermediate Products in International Trade

In the real world, commodities are not usually produced by the direct application of the primary factors labor and land alone. Actual production processes frequently require *intermediate products* as well, that is, goods produced for the purpose of being used as inputs in the production of other goods. For instance, steel is used in the production of automobiles, coal is used in the production of steel, oil is used in the production of electricity, flour is used in the production of bread, leather is used in the production of shoes, and so on.

Intermediate products also play a significant role in international trade—a very large proportion of world trade is in intermediate products. The introduction of intermediate products gives rise to many interesting problems in the theory of international trade. These problems are, however, beyond the scope of this book, and the interested reader is referred to Chacholiades (1979). This section deals only with the concept of the effective rate of protection.

Nominal versus Effective Tariff Rates

When a protected import-competing industry utilizes imported inputs that are themselves subject to duty, the nominal tariff rate does not convey the true level of protection that is provided to the domestic producers and that, in the final analysis, affects resource allocation. The basic reason for this anomaly is the fact that nominal rates apply to the *total* value of imports, while the true level of protection (which is relevant to domestic producers and resource allocation) applies only to the "value added" by domestic producers. **Value added** is the difference between the total value of goods produced and the value of imported inputs and represents the amount of money paid to the domestic factors of production: labor, land, and capital.

The **effective rate of protection** (ERP) is defined as the difference between the value added (per unit of output) at domestic prices (that is, inclusive of tariffs on the finished product and intermediate inputs) and the value added at world prices (that is, prices prevailing under free trade), expressed as a percentage of the latter. In symbols,

$$ERP = \frac{v' - v}{v}$$

where v' stands for value added at domestic prices, and v represents value added at world prices. The effective rate is usually, but not necessarily, much higher than the nominal rate. Indeed, the effective rate is often negative because v' is less than v. (In some extreme cases in which domestic production is so inefficient as to actually destroy value, v itself could be negative.) Two examples should clarify the issue.[1]

Example 1 Suppose that the price of shoes on world markets is $40 a pair and that to produce one pair of shoes, America (home country) must import $30 worth of leather from abroad. Accordingly, America's shoe industry creates $10 worth of value added, that is, price of shoes ($40) less value of imported leather ($30). Assume now that America imposes a 25 percent "nominal" tariff on imported shoes, raising their domestic price to $50, that is, foreign price ($40) plus tariff per pair ($10). What is the effective rate of protection provided to the domestic producers of shoes? The 25 percent nominal tariff rate raises the value added from the original level of $10 to the higher level of $20 (that is, $50 − $30). Thus, *the value added increases by 100 percent, and this is the effective rate of protection that America provides to its shoe-manufacturing activity.*

Example 2 Assume now that in addition to the 25 percent nominal tariff rate on imported shoes, America imposes a 10 percent tariff on imports of leather. What happens to the effective rate of protection of America's shoe-manufacturing activity? Again we must determine the percentage change in the value added of America's shoe industry. We already know that the initial value added is $10. The tariff on shoes raises their price to $50, that is, $40 + 0.25 × $40. However, the tariff on leather raises the cost of leather per pair of shoes from $30 to $33. Accordingly, the value added increases to $17 (that is, $50 − $33). Thus, the value added increases by 70 percent, that is, 100 × ($17 − $10)/$10. This effective rate of 70 percent is certainly lower than the rate of 100 percent that ruled before the imported leather was taxed. Note carefully the inverse effect that the tariff on imported inputs (leather) exerts on the effective rate of protection accorded to final products (shoes). This example is illustrated graphically in Figure 7-5.

[1]For a mathematical formulation of the theory of effective protection, see Appendix 9.

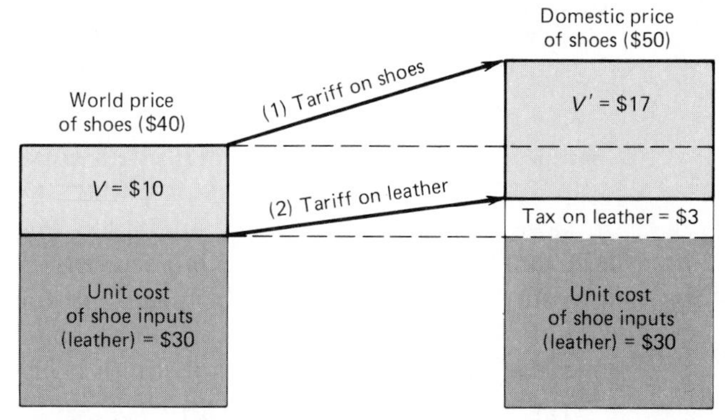

FIGURE 7-5 **Calculation of the effective rate of protection.** The world price of shoes ($40) consists of the unit cost of leather ($30) plus the value added ($10), as shown on the left. The nominal tariff on shoes raises their domestic price to $50 and pulls the top of the value-added rectangle upward, as shown by arrow (1). The nominal tariff on leather adds $3 to its cost per pair of shoes and pushes the bottom of the value-added rectangle upward, as shown by arrow (2). Thus arrow (1) expands value added from the top, but arrow (2) compresses it from the bottom. The net result is an effective rate of protection of 70 percent.

7-9 EMPIRICAL EVIDENCE ON EFFECTIVE PROTECTION

The theory of effective protection has received much attention during the last three decades. As was natural, many researchers provided empirical estimates of effective rates for many industries and countries. A highly selective sample of these empirical findings (based on post-Kennedy Round data) is presented in Tables 7-1 and 7-2.

It is evident from Table 7-1 that the effective tariff rates bear little resemblance to the corresponding nominal tariff rates. Some effective rates are as much as 10 to 13 times higher than the corresponding nominal rates, while other effective rates are actually negative. Granted that the effective rates give a more accurate picture of the true level of protection afforded any given industry, it becomes evident that the nominal rates cannot be trusted as indicators of protection. Before we can pass a judgment as to how high a country's tariff wall is, we must convert the nominal tariff rates into effective rates.

The median effective tariff rates (see the last line of Table 7-1) seem to suggest that effective protection is much higher in Japan and the European Community than in the United States.

Table 7-2 suggests that both the nominal and the effective rates tend to increase with each stage of processing. Developing countries often complain about this bias in the tariff structure of developed nations. They claim that this bias encourages the flow of raw materials and semifinished products to the advanced countries and thus inhibits industrialization in developing countries.

7-10 SUMMARY

1 Nations impede the free flow of trade by means of several devices—such as tariffs and quotas—known as commercial policies.

TABLE 7-1 NOMINAL AND EFFECTIVE TARIFF RATES AFTER THE KENNEDY ROUND

	Tariff rate (percent)						
	EC		Japan		United States		
Commodity group	Nominal	Effective	Nominal	Effective	Nominal	Effective	Free-trade share of value added
Foods and feeds							
Meat and meat products	19.5	36.6	17.9	69.1	5.9	10.3	0.250
Preserved seafoods	21.5	52.6	13.6	34.7	6.0	15.6	0.300
Preserved fruits and vegetables	20.5	44.9	18.5	49.3	14.8	36.8	0.270
Milk, cheese, and butter	22.0	59.9	37.3	248.8	10.8	36.9	0.143
Manufactured and processed foods*	14.6	17.7	24.0	59.3	5.0	1.0	0.228
Flour, cereal, and bakery products	16.1	24.9	22.4	46.4	6.9	15.6	0.320
Cocoa products and chocolate	12.8	34.6	22.8	80.7	4.2	16.2	0.210
Soft drinks	14.9	−19.8	35.0	41.0	1.0	−9.5	0.400
Mill products and prepared feeds	11.4	31.6	13.8	32.2	23.4	111.0	0.270
Wood, paper, and rubber products							
Wood products	8.2	9.5	12.4	22.0	10.4	18.3	0.445
Paper products and wood pulp	7.4	20.1	6.6	12.1	2.7	5.5	0.415
Rubber products	8.3	19.0	9.3	20.2	6.1	12.5	0.360
Yarn, fabrics, and clothing							
Yarns and threads	6.2	19.4	9.9	24.2	19.5	37.1	0.280
Fabrics and clothing	14.3	29.1	13.0	22.0	27.3	40.4	0.340
Jute sacks, bags, and woven fabrics	18.2	42.9	27.1	65.0	1.4	3.2	0.330
Vegetable and animal oils							
Plant and vegetable oils†	11.1	138.0	10.1	64.9	9.4	17.7	0.055
Cottonseed oil	11.0	79.0	25.8	200.3	59.6	465.9	0.120
Rapeseed oil	9.0	57.2	15.1	22.3	20.8	60.9	0.150
Soyabean oil	11.0	148.1	25.4	286.3	22.5	252.9	0.070
Animal and marine fats and oils	5.2	−26.8	5.1	−1.9	4.2	10.7	0.200
Leather, tobacco, and soap							
Leather and leather products	7.8	14.6	14.8	22.6	7.0	12.8	0.397
Cigars and cigarettes	87.1	147.3	339.5	405.6	68.0	113.2	0.530
Soaps and detergents	7.5	14.4	16.6	44.4	7.9	19.3	0.230
Median tariff rate‡	12.2	33.1	16.5	45.4	8.6	18.0	

*Includes roasted coffee.
†Consists of both crude and refined palm kernel oil, groundnut oil, and coconut oil.
‡Median rates for the 123 individual products on product groupings.
Source: A. J. Yeats (1974), "Effective Tariff Protection in the United States, the European Economic Community, and Japan," *Quarterly Review of Economics and Business,* vol. 14 (Summer), p. 45. [Note that the European Economic Community (EEC) is now the European Community (EC).]

2 The tariff is a tax (or duty) levied on a commodity when it crosses a national boundary. The most common instrument of commercial policy is the tariff on an imported commodity. A less common tariff is the export duty.

3 In general, taxes (whether on imports or exports) can be imposed as (a) ad valorem rates, (b) specific rates, or (c) compound rates.

4 There are some important differences between specific and ad valorem rates. Administratively, specific rates are easier to apply since they do not require knowledge of the commodity value, as the ad valorem rates do. However,

TABLE 7-2 ESCALATION OF TARIFF RATE PROTECTION IN THE ECONOMIC COMMUNITY (EC), JAPAN, AND THE UNITED STATES
(Percent)

	EC		Japan		United States	
Production process	**Nominal**	**Effective**	**Nominal**	**Effective**	**Nominal**	**Effective**
Groundnut oil						
Groundnuts, green	0.0	...	0.0	...	18.2	...
Groundnut oil, crude and cake	7.5	92.9	7.6	93.7	18.4	24.6
Groundnut oil, refined	15.0	186.4	10.1	324.8	22.0	64.9
Paper and paper products						
Logs, rough	0.0	...	0.0	...	0.0	...
Wood pulp	1.6	2.5	5.0	10.7	0.0	−0.5
Paper and paper articles	13.1	30.2	5.9	17.6	5.3	12.8
Wood products						
Logs, rough	0.0	...	0.0	...	0.0	...
Sawn wood	1.9	4.9	0.7	2.0	0.0	0.0
Wood manufactures	7.4	10.7	9.8	15.3	7.4	8.4
Dairy products						
Fresh milk and cream	16.0	...	0.0	...	6.5	...
Condensed and evaporated milk	21.3	44.3	31.7	154.8	10.7	30.1
Cheese	23.0	58.8	35.3	175.6	11.5	34.5
Butter	21.0	76.6	45.0	418.5	10.3	46.7
Wool fabrics						
Raw wool	0.0	...	0.0	...	21.1	...
Wool yarn	5.4	16.0	5.0	9.3	30.7	62.2
Wool fabrics	14.0	32.9	14.7	35.1	46.9	90.8
Cotton fabrics						
Raw cotton	0.0	...	0.0	...	6.1	...
Cotton yarn	7.0	22.8	8.1	25.8	8.3	12.0
Cotton fabrics	13.6	29.7	7.2	34.9	15.6	30.7
Leather products						
Bovine hides	0.0	...	0.0	...	0.0	...
Leather	7.0	21.4	6.2	20.2	17.8	57.4
Leather goods excluding shoes	7.1	10.3	10.5	15.8	22.4	32.5
Jute products						
Raw jute	0.0	...	0.0	...	0.1	...
Jute fabrics	21.1	57.8	20.0	54.8	0.0	−0.9
Jute sacks and bags	15.3	9.8	34.3	75.2	2.8	7.3
Palm kernel oil						
Palm nuts, kernels	0.0	...	0.0	...	0.0	...
Palm kernel oil, crude and cake	7.0	87.1	6.4	79.1	4.2	52.3
Palm kernel oil, refined	14.0	195.9	8.0	79.2	3.4	6.1
Chocolate						
Cocoa beans	5.4	...	0.0	...	0.0	...
Cocoa powder and butter	13.6	76.0	15.0	125.0	2.6	22.0
Chocolate products	12.0	−6.8	30.6	36.3	5.7	10.3

Source: A. J. Yeats (1974), "Effective Tariff Protection in the United States, the European Economic Community, and Japan," *Quarterly Review of Economics and Business*, vol. 14 (Summer), p. 47. [Note that the European Economic Community (EEC) is now the European Community (EC).]

the ad valorem incidence of a specific tax tends to fall (rise) with inflation (deflation). In addition, for a commodity with many varieties, a flat ad valorem rate is more equitable than a specific rate—a flat specific rate falls more heavily on the cheaper qualities.

5 According to the partial equilibrium approach, a tariff raises the domestic price of importables, causing their domestic output to expand and their consumption to contract. Imports fall, and consumer surplus is reduced. The producer surplus rises, and the government collects tariff revenue, but society as a whole is penalized by a consumption cost and a production cost.

6 A convenient assumption (followed throughout this book) is that the government returns the tariff revenue to its private citizens (in the form of either lump-sum transfers or a general income tax reduction).

7 A tariff imposed by a small country has the following general equilibrium effects: (a) It raises the domestic price of the imported commodity by the full extent of the tariff, (b) it causes resources to shift from the export industry into the import-competing industry, (c) it reduces the value of output produced at world prices (because the value of output produced is maximized at the free-trade production point), (d) it causes welfare to decline, and (e) it causes the volume of trade to shrink (whether the imported commodity is "normal" or "inferior").

8 At domestic prices, the value of consumption (aggregate expenditure) is higher than the value of production (national income at factor cost) by the amount of the tariff revenue. However, the two aggregates become equal when they are evaluated at world prices.

9 The tariff that reduces the volume of trade to zero is called prohibitive.

10 The Stolper-Samuelson theorem states that an increase (decrease) in the relative price of a commodity raises (lowers) the real wage of the factor used intensively in its production. When tariff protection raises the price of importables, the factor used intensively by the import-competing industry becomes better off and the second factor becomes worse off, even if the government were to redistribute all tariff revenue to this second factor.

11 When a country levies a tariff, its offer curve shifts toward the origin, that is, its volume of trade falls at all terms of trade. When the tariff-levying country is "large" (that is, it has monopoly-monopsony power in international trade), the tariff causes the imported commodity to become relatively cheaper in the rest of the world (that is, the country's terms of trade improve).

12 There is a paradoxical case (the Metzler case) in which the tariff causes the price of the imported commodity to fall in the world market by more than the tariff, with the result that the imported commodity becomes cheaper in the tariff-levying country also. This paradox arises when (a) the foreign demand for imports is inelastic and (b) the tariff-levying country's marginal propensity to import is very low. The implication of Metzler's case is that the "protection" provided to the import-competing industry is *negative* (or perverse).

13 A tariff creates a wedge between foreign and domestic prices and interferes with the maximization of world welfare in two ways: (a) It reduces the world output of commodities by reversing the process of international specialization dictated by the law of comparative advantage (because the tariff creates a divergence between the marginal rates of transformation of countries) and (b) the tariff forces a suboptimal allocation of commodities among consumers (because it creates a divergence between the marginal rates of substitution of countries).

14 A tariff is equivalent to a production subsidy plus a consumption tax on importables.

15 The effective rate of protection is defined as the difference between value added (per unit of output) at domestic prices and value added at world prices, expressed as a percentage of the latter.

PROBLEMS

1 Canada's domestic demand and supply functions for footwear are as follows:

$$Q_d = 500 - 5p \qquad \text{(demand function)}$$

$$7Q_s = -300 + 60p \qquad \text{(supply function)}$$

where Q_d = quantity demanded, Q_s = quantity supplied, and p = price (in dollars). The world price of footwear is $20.

a Determine the autarkic equilibrium price and quantity of footwear in Canada.

b Determine the free-trade equilibrium price, and Canada's quantity demanded, quantity supplied, and imports of footwear.

c Determine the increase in consumer surplus and the decrease in producer surplus resulting from free trade relative to autarky.

d How does a tariff of $5 per unit of imported footwear affect the domestic price, quantity produced, quantity consumed, and imports?

e Determine the tariff revenue and the deadweight loss of the tariff.

f At what minimum ad valorem rate would the tariff on footwear become prohibitive?

g Illustrate your answers graphically.

2 Consider two countries, America and Japan, producing steel (S) and cloth (C) with labor and capital under constant returns to scale. Production functions are identical between countries, cloth is labor intensive relative to steel, and America is capital abundant relative to Japan. At the free-trade equilibrium, America exports steel to Japan in exchange for cloth.

a If America's 25 percent ad valorem tariff rate on the imports of cloth causes the relative price of cloth in America to rise to $5C{:}1S$, what is the corresponding relative price of cloth in Japan?

b Under what circumstances would America's tariff *increase* the volume of imports of cloth from Japan?

c How does an American tariff affect the welfare of each worker in America? In Japan?

d How would you modify your answer to the question in part c if all capital in America is owned equally by all workers? (Note: You may assume that all tariff revenue is redistributed to the American workers.)

3 At the existing international equilibrium, America exports personal computers to Europe in exchange for European wine. Because of tariffs on imports by both America and Europe, the current prices (in dollars) of computers and wine are as follows:

	America	Europe
Computers (per unit)	$2,000	$3,000
Wine (per bottle)	10	5

a What is the opportunity cost of personal computers in terms of wine in America? In Europe?
b What is the marginal rate of substitution of computers for wine in America? In Europe?
c Suppose that an American consumer exchanges 1 personal computer for 300 bottles of wine with a European consumer. Show that the exchange makes both consumers better off.
d Suppose that America transfers resources from the production of wine to the production of personal computers and increases its output of computers by 1 unit. Europe does the opposite, as its output of personal computers falls by 1. Determine the changes in the output of wine in America and Europe. How does this reorganization of production affect the *world* output of personal computers and wine?
e If America and Europe eliminated their tariffs, would it still be possible to increase world output as in preceding question (part d)? Why or why not?

4 Mexico uses $200 worth of imported parts and $100 worth of imported wood to produce a television set whose world price is $600.
a What is the value added of the Mexican television industry?
b Suppose that Mexico imposes a 20 percent ad valorem tariff on imports of television sets. What happens to the value added of the Mexican television industry? What is the effective rate of protection provided to the Mexican producers of television sets?
c Suppose that in addition to the tariff on imports of television sets, Mexico imposes tariffs of 8 and 14 percent on imports of parts and wood, respectively. Calculate the new effective rate of protection.
d Recalculate the effective rate of protection, assuming that the nominal tariff rates on parts and wood are 50 and 35 percent, respectively.

SUGGESTED READING

Balassa, B. (1965). "Tariff Protection in Industrial Countries: An Evaluation." *Journal of Political Economy*, vol. 73 (December), pp. 573–594.

Black, J. (1959). "Arguments for Tariffs." *Oxford Economic Papers* (N.S.), vol. 11, pp. 191–208.

Chacholiades, M. (1978). *International Trade Theory and Policy*. McGraw-Hill Book Company, New York, chaps. 17–19.

———(1979). "Intermediate Products in the Theory of International Trade." *Economic Perspectives*, vol. 1, pp. 151–172.

Corden, W. M. (1966). "The Structure of a Tariff System and the Effective Protective Rate." *Journal of Political Economy*, vol. LXXIV (June), pp. 221–237.

———(1971). *The Theory of Protection*. Oxford University Press, London.

Johnson, H. G. (1972). *Aspects of the Theory of Tariffs*. Harvard University Press, Cambridge, Mass.

Metzler, L. A. (1949). "Tariffs, the Terms of Trade, and the Distribution of National

Income." *Journal of Political Economy,* vol. 57, pp. 1–29. Reprinted in R. E. Caves and H. G. Johnson (eds.), American Economic Association *Readings in International Economics,* Richard D. Irwin, Inc., Homewood, Ill., 1968.

Stolper, W. F., and P. A. Samuelson (1941). "Protection and Real Wages." *Review of Economic Studies,* vol. 9, pp. 50–73. Reprinted in H. S. Ellis and L. A. Metzler (eds.), American Economic Association *Readings in the Theory of International Trade,* Richard D. Irwin, Inc., Homewood, Ill., 1950.

Yeats, A. J. (1974). "Effective Tariff Protection in the United States, the European Economic Community, and Japan." *Quarterly Review of Economics and Business,* vol. 14 (Summer), pp. 41–50.

CHAPTER **8**

ARGUMENTS FOR PROTECTION

The standard theory of tariffs that we discussed in Chapter 7 shows that, in general, tariffs reduce world efficiency and welfare. Yet, as we pointed out earlier, the flow of international trade has been impeded for hundreds of years by several kinds of trade barriers, such as tariffs, quotas, and exchange control. This chapter deals with the most common arguments for trade intervention and attempts to identify the conditions under which a tariff may be preferable to either laissez-faire (that is, doing nothing) or some other policy.

8-1 THE OPTIMAL TARIFF

A tariff gives rise to two conflicting effects on the welfare of a large country: (1) The terms of trade improve, which increases welfare (because the foreigner pays the duty, or some considerable part of it); and (2) the volume of trade falls, which reduces welfare (because of the unfavorable production and consumption costs). Welfare is maximized when the tariff rate is such that the marginal terms-of-trade benefit just balances the marginal volume-of-trade cost. This section deals with the theory of the optimal tariff, which provides an argument for protection.

Monopoly-Monopsony Power in International Trade

Small countries are price takers in world markets; they lack the ability to influence their terms of trade because they do not control a large enough share of world markets. For these small countries, the foreign offer curve coincides with that terms-of-trade line whose slope shows the existing terms of trade in the world market. For small countries, free trade is Pareto optimal.

Large countries possess **monopoly-monopsony power in international trade.** These large countries control a significant share of the world market for some commodity or commodities, such as Brazil in coffee, Japan in automobiles, and the United States in computers. For large countries, free trade is *not* Pareto optimal.

Note that it is not necessary for any individual producer in a large country to possess monopoly power. For instance, each coffee producer in Brazil may be a perfect competitor because he supplies only a negligible fraction of the total world consumption of coffee. Yet Brazil as a nation possesses monopoly power because it produces approximately one-third of the world output of coffee. Similarly, there is no need for any individual buyer of an imported commodity in a large country to possess monopsony power. Thus the individual U.S. citizens who purchase small Japanese cars, such as Toyotas and Hondas, are certainly price takers. Yet the United States as a nation has monopsony power.

A large country can improve its terms of trade by restricting its volume of trade by means of commercial policy. In its export markets, a large country acts like a monopolist, who restricts output and raises price in the pursuit of maximum profit. In its import markets, a large country acts like a monopsonist, who restricts purchases in order to buy the commodity at a lower price.

Marginal versus Average Terms of Trade

To understand the theory of the optimal tariff, we must draw a distinction between the **average terms of trade** and the **marginal terms of trade.** The average terms of trade correspond to the net barter terms of trade we have been using all along: They show the number of units of imports that, *on the average,* a country obtains per unit of exports. The marginal terms of trade show the number of additional units of imports that the country obtains by increasing exports, *at the margin,* by 1 unit. The average and marginal terms of trade are read off the *foreign* country's offer curve, as illustrated in Figure 8-1.

Suppose that America (home country) exports 50 tons of steel to Britain in exchange for 200 yards of cloth, as shown by point *D* on Britain's offer curve. On the average, America imports 4 yards of cloth per ton of exports of steel (that is, 200 ÷ 50), as indicated by the slope of vector *OD.* These are America's average terms of trade.

Imagine now that America increases its exports of steel by 1 ton. Will America be able to increase its imports of cloth by 4 yards? Not at all; Britain is willing to exchange only 2 yards of cloth for the additional ton of steel, as demonstrated by point *G.* Thus America's marginal terms of trade are only 2 yards of cloth.

Note that for small (infinitesimal) changes in exports, the marginal terms of trade coincide with the *slope* of the foreign offer curve. Furthermore, for a *small* country the average and marginal terms of trade are equal, coinciding with the slope of the terms-of-trade line that takes the place of the foreign offer curve.

While the average terms of trade are always positive, the marginal terms of trade are positive in the region *OH,* where the foreign offer curve is upward

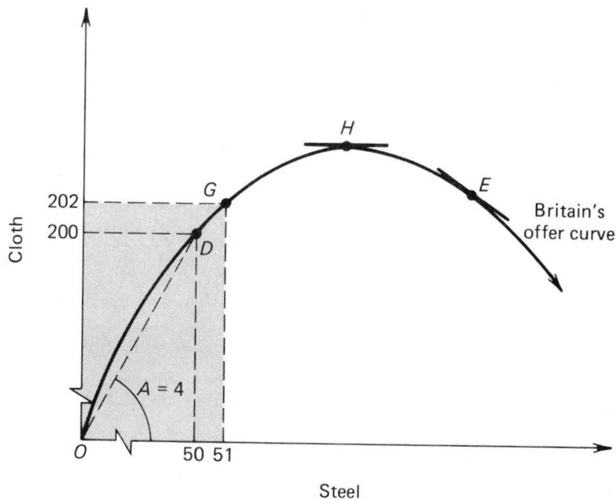

FIGURE 8-1 **Average and marginal terms of trade.** When America (home country) exports 50 tons of steel, Britain returns 200 yards of cloth, as shown by point *D*. Hence, America's average terms of trade (*A*) are equal to 4, as shown by the slope of vector *OD*. If America were to increase its exports of steel by 1 ton, Britain would be willing to increase its exports of cloth by 2 yards (marginal terms of trade), as shown by the movement from *D* to *G*. America's marginal terms of trade are positive in the upward-sloping region, *OH*, of Britain's offer curve; the marginal terms of trade are zero at *H* and become negative in the downward-sloping region, as shown by point *E*.

sloping; they are zero at point *H*, where the tangent to the foreign offer curve is horizontal; and they turn negative thereafter, as the foreign offer curve becomes downward sloping. Note that the marginal terms of trade are positive, negative, or zero according to whether the foreign demand for imports is elastic, inelastic, or unit elastic, respectively. These are the same relationships that exist among "average revenue," "marginal revenue," and "elasticity of demand," provided we interpret Britain's offer curve as a "total revenue curve" emanating from Britain's "ordinary demand for imports" of steel. In that case, "total revenue" would coincide with the volume of cloth exported by Britain to pay for the imports of steel.

The Optimal Volume of Trade

What is the optimal volume of trade for a large country? That is, what volume of trade maximizes the national welfare of a large country? We can discover the answer by applying the logic of the law of comparative advantage.

When the marginal terms of trade exceed the domestic opportunity cost, it is to the benefit of the large country to expand trade. For instance, if America's opportunity cost of steel is 2 yards of cloth while the marginal terms of trade are 5 yards of cloth, America can gain 3 yards of cloth by expanding exports by 1 ton of steel: 5 yards (extra imports) minus 2 yards (opportunity cost of extra ton of steel exported). Conversely, if the domestic opportunity cost exceeds the marginal terms of trade, the large country can benefit by restricting trade. For example, if America's opportunity cost of steel is 4 yards of cloth while the marginal terms of trade are only 3 yards, America can gain 1 yard of cloth by reducing exports of steel by 1 ton: 4 yards (cost saving by not producing the last ton of steel) minus 3 yards (imports given up). When the marginal terms of trade are equal to the domestic opportunity cost, no further gains can be achieved—the volume of trade is optimal. Thus we reach the following important proposition:

When the marginal terms of trade are equal to the domestic opportunity cost of exportables, the volume of trade is optimal from the point of view of the large country (but not of the world).

The principle that welfare is maximized at the point at which the value of the last unit of imports is equal to its marginal cost is reminiscent of the principle that monopoly profits are maximized at the point at which marginal revenue equals marginal cost.

The Need for an Optimal Tariff

In Section 7-5 we argued that free trade is optimal from a global point of view. Is free trade optimal from a national point of view also? Only when the trading country is small.

Free trade causes the domestic price ratio (and thus the domestic opportunity cost of exportables) to equal the *average* terms of trade, but welfare maximization requires the domestic price ratio to be made equal to the *marginal* terms of trade. For a small country, the average and marginal terms of trade are equal; thus free trade maximizes national welfare.

For a large country, the marginal terms of trade are lower than the average terms (just as marginal revenue is less than average revenue); thus laissez-faire pushes the volume of trade beyond its optimal point. An optimal tariff is needed to restrict the volume of trade to its optimal level and thereby maximize the large country's welfare. Appendix 10 presents a geometric derivation of the optimal tariff rate.

Retaliation

Today the optimal-tariff motive for protection does not seem very relevant to the formulation of commercial policy in industrial countries. A major reason is the fear of *retaliation*.

The theory of the optimal tariff rests on the assumption that the foreign country passively continues to maintain a free-trade policy. However, both countries can play the game. Indeed, retaliatory measures by the foreign country can be expected if only because the home country's optimal tariff reduces foreign welfare. Unfortunately, when the foreign country retaliates, it is no longer clear that the home country (which initiated the tariff war) can benefit. Many outcomes are possible. Either of the two countries may benefit while the other loses, or both countries may lose. What is *not* possible is for both countries to benefit because, as we showed in Section 7-5, tariffs reduce the global income pie. Obviously when both countries lose, they can improve their respective levels of social welfare through bilateral trade liberalization.

8-2 TARIFF WARS IN THE 1930s

A historical episode may clarify the implications of tariff retaliation. The U.S. Smoot-Hawley tariff was signed into law on June 17, 1930, over a strong protest by the economics profession. The measure raised the effective rate of tariffs in the United States by almost 50 percent. Not unexpectedly, the new high duties triggered widespread retaliation, which contributed to the worldwide depression.

For instance, in response to tariffs on grapes, oranges, cork, and onions, Spain retaliated with the Wais tariff. Because of new tariffs on watches, embroideries, and shoes, Switzerland boycotted U.S. exports. Against tariffs on hats and olive oil, Italy retaliated with high tariffs on U.S. and French automobiles. In reaction to high duties on many food products, logs, and timber, Canada tripled its tariffs. Australia, Cuba, France, Mexico, and New Zealand also joined in the tariff war.

These beggar-thy-neighbor policies were responsible for the dwindling volume of world trade and the high unemployment and low prices that ensued in all countries. It is estimated that total world imports in 1933 stood at about one-third their 1929 level. Incidentally, the tremendous decline in the U.S. exports of agricultural products (about 66 percent from 1929 to 1932) more than offset the meager increase in domestic demand due to the high U.S. tariff. As a result, farm prices fell precipitously and contributed to rural bank failures.

8-3 THE THEORY OF DOMESTIC DISTORTIONS

The desire to accelerate the pace of economic development of the developing countries and raise their standards of living (through increased capital formation, industrialization, and a larger share of the gains from international trade) gave rise to a renewed interest in the **economic arguments for protection** in the postwar economic writings. The traditional **infant-industry argument** for protection was restated and expanded to include the whole industrial sector, and many new arguments for protection were advanced by several distinguished economists, most notably Lewis (1954), Myrdal (1956), Hagen (1958), and Prebisch (1959). For the most part, these arguments rest on the existence of **external economies** and **factor-price differentials,** which in turn give rise to "domestic distortions" (that is, divergences between market prices and opportunity costs).

The theory of **domestic distortions** is a direct outgrowth of this activity in the area of economic development and deals primarily with (1) the various distortions that prevent the market mechanism from achieving Pareto optimality and (2) the policy recommendations for neutralizing the domestic distortions and restoring Pareto optimality. As it turns out, the theory of domestic distortions is *not* an argument for protection. Trade intervention should not be adopted as a means of correcting domestic distortions. The main proposition of the theory of domestic distortions is that *policy intervention must take place at the exact point at which the distortion occurs.*

Domestic distortions are usually classified into "endogenous distortions" and "policy-induced distortions." **Endogenous distortions** are those distortions that are primarily due to market imperfections, such as external economies and monopolistic or oligopolistic market structures. **Policy-induced distortions** are those distortions that are the result of economic policies, such as tariffs, production subsidies, and consumption taxes. Domestic distortions violate Pareto optimality, but trade intervention is not the remedy. The optimal policy to correct a policy-induced distortion is merely the elimination of the policy that caused the distortion in the first place.

In general, there are four points of intervention through taxes and subsidies: (1) international trade (through export and import taxes and subsidies), (2) domestic production (through production taxes and subsidies), (3) domestic consumption (through consumption taxes and subsidies), and (4) factor employment (through taxes and subsidies on factor use).

Intervention is optimal when it restores Pareto optimality by completely offsetting the existing distortion without giving rise to a new distortion in the process. This is accomplished by adhering to the following rule:

Rule for Optimal Intervention: **Policy intervention restores Pareto optimality when it takes place at the exact point at which the underlying market imperfection occurs and is equal to the degree of distortion, thus offsetting the distortion completely.**

To illustrate the application of this rule, consider the case of high-technology industries (such as the aerospace, computer, and electronics industries), which devote a significant portion of their resources to improving technology. As it turns out, the pioneering firms in these industries cannot capture all the benefits of their investment because the improved technology soon spills over to other firms. Without some kind of support, these industries cannot innovate enough. Should high-technology industries, then, be protected with high tariffs? No, because only a domestic distortion is involved. One possible solution, following from the rule for optimal intervention, is to adopt an industrial policy by means of which resources can be channeled into the high-technology industries. Thus those activities that generate the externalities must be subsidized instead.

This scheme sounds simple enough; yet in practice, there are several complications. First, it may be difficult to identify precisely those activities that generate the externalities. How do we know when Boeing and IBM are engaged in creating new knowledge or new products? Not every activity generates externalities. Second, it may be even more difficult to determine the appropriate level of the optimal subsidy. Is it 20, 50, or 100 percent? Nobody really knows for sure. Third, the spillover benefits may accrue to the foreign firms. To the extent that Japanese or European firms are the recipients of the new knowledge created by U.S. firms, the case for a subsidy by the U.S. government becomes very weak.

Note that the theory of the optimal tariff rests on the existence of a **foreign distortion** (that is, a distortion in international markets), which makes trade intervention optimal from the national viewpoint.

8-4 THE INFANT-INDUSTRY ARGUMENT

The infant-industry argument is an argument for *temporary* protection to correct a distortion that disappears gradually with the passage of time. This argument, which has always had great appeal to young and developing nations, is said to have been formulated in 1791 by Alexander Hamilton, George Washington's secretary of the treasury; developed further by H. C. Carey and others; and later transplanted to Germany by Friedrich List. However, Viner (1965, pp. 71–72) provides evidence to the effect that this argument is of much earlier origin.

The Formulation of the Infant-Industry Argument by John Stuart Mill

Perhaps the clearest formulation of the infant-industry argument is provided by John Stuart Mill (1904, pp. 403–404). Since Mill's exposition is very concise indeed, it is quoted in full:

> The only case in which, on mere principles of political economy, protecting duties can be defensible, is when they are imposed temporarily (especially in a young and rising nation) in hopes of naturalizing a foreign industry, in itself perfectly suitable to the circumstances of the country. The superiority of one country over another in a branch of production often arises only from having begun it sooner. There may be no inherent advantage on one part, or disadvantage on the other, but only a present superiority of acquired skill and experience. A country which has this skill and experience yet to acquire, may in other respects be better adapted to the production than those which were earlier in the field...But it cannot be expected that individuals should, at their own risk, or rather to their certain loss, introduce a new manufacture, and bear the burden of carrying it on, until the producers have been educated up to the level of those with whom the processes are traditional. A protecting duty, continued for a reasonable time, will sometimes be the least inconvenient mode in which the nation can tax itself for the support of such an experiment. But the protection should be confined to cases in which there is good ground of assurance that the industry which it fosters will after a time be able to dispense with it; nor should the domestic producers ever be allowed to expect that it will be continued to them beyond the time necessary for a fair trial of what they are capable of accomplishing.

Thus, the **Mill test for infant-industry protection is whether the infant will eventually overcome its historical handicap and grow up to compete effectively and without protection against earlier starters.**

Further Refinements by Bastable and Johnson

Bastable (1903, p. 140; 1923, pp. 140–143) objected to Mill's formulation of the infant-industry argument. He asserted that the Mill test, though necessary, was not sufficient, and claimed that, in addition, the infant industry must eventually be able to generate sufficient savings in costs to compensate the economy for the losses (due to higher costs to the consumers) it suffers during the learning period when protection is necessary. Bastable correctly considered the incurring of costs during the learning period as a type of *investment* whose returns, it is hoped, would accrue to the economy in the form of future cost reductions (relative to the costs that would have to be incurred in the absence of the development of the domestic industry). The **Bastable test,** then, *requires that the present discounted value of the future benefits be at least as high as the initial cost incurred to help the infant grow.*

Johnson (1965, p. 27) notes that even when the Bastable test is met, the infant-industry argument reduces essentially to the assertion that free competition produces a socially inefficient allocation of investment resources. For the validity of the argument, Johnson continues, it must be demonstrated that because of some domestic distortion, the private sector is prevented from investing sufficient funds in new industries. For instance, in the presence of externalities the private rate of return may be much lower than the social rate of return, and private entrepreneurs may consider an otherwise socially desirable investment unprofitable. Alternatively, the cost of financing investment in new industries may be too high presumably because the capital market is imperfect. In any case, the optimal policy is *not* tariff protection but rather some sort of subsidy to the infant industry, since a domestic, not foreign, distortion is involved.

Economies of the Learning Process and Optimal Policy

Central to the infant-industry argument is the notion that practice makes perfect; during the initial stages of development, the "infants" are assumed to learn both from their own experiences and from each other. This learning process, which generally (but not necessarily) involves external economies, is *irreversible.* This important feature of the infant-industry argument distinguishes it from the case of static external economies. The latter form a *permanent* characteristic of the economy's technology and call for *permanent* government intervention. The infant-industry argument is based on the assumption that the infant industry undergoes a dynamic learning process that generates external economies over a certain period of time and thus calls for only *temporary* government intervention.

When the economies generated during the learning period are *internal* to the firm (for example, economies of scale), Adam Smith's invisible hand can, in general, be counted on to produce a socially efficient allocation of investment resources, and there is no need for government intervention to protect any "infants." There are, of course, exceptions—the capital market may be imperfect, and as a result the cost of financing investment in new industries may be excessively high; or there may be a difference between social and private time preference, assessment of risk, availability of information, foresight, and so on. But even in these exceptional cases, tariff protection is not the answer. In fact, tariff protection is a second-best policy and may even reduce welfare. The first-best policy follows from the general rule for optimal intervention: *The government should intervene at the precise point at which the distortion occurs.* For instance, when an imperfect capital market makes the cost of financing investment in new industries excessively high, the optimal policy is to subsidize the provision of capital to industries.

Two major varieties of the externality argument are usually found in the literature. First, it is claimed that because of the absence of the necessary labor skills, the pioneering entrepreneur of a particular industry must train the labor force. However, the argument goes, the return from the improvement of labor skills cannot be appropriated by the entrepreneur but is, rather, imputed to the labor force, since the workers, after gaining the necessary skills, might be lured away by other entrepreneurs who enter the field late and are willing and able to pay a higher wage. Accordingly, the private rate of return to pioneering entrepreneurs (who cannot be certain of appropriating all the fruits of their investments) is necessarily lower than the social rate of return. Obviously, the optimal policy in the present case is not tariff protection but rather a subsidy to the training of the labor force.

The second externality argument deals with the acquisition of knowledge of production technique. The acquisition of such knowledge necessarily involves the incurring of costs in the present in the hope of reaping profits in the future. But once created, such knowledge cannot be effectively guarded by the pioneering entrepreneur. Others who enter the field subsequently can certainly make use of it. Once again, pioneering entrepreneurs cannot appropriate all the fruits of their investment, and therefore the private rate of return is necessarily lower than the social rate of return. Tariff protection is again a second-best policy and could hurt the country instead of benefiting it. The optimal policy is a direct subsidy to the learning process itself.

Writers in the field of economic development have extended the infant-industry argument to the whole industrial sector. They claim that the external economies generated by firms in one industry are not confined to that particular industry but instead are spread over the whole "infant manufacturing sector." Thus, they think in terms of "infant-economy protection" rather then "infant-industry protection."

Graphical Illustration

The infant-industry argument is illustrated in Figure 8-2. The initial production-possibilities frontier is given by curve UV and the international price ratio (which remains constant throughout by assumption) by the absolute slope of lines L_1P_1, L_2P_2, and L_3P_3. Under laissez-faire, the economy produces at P_1 and

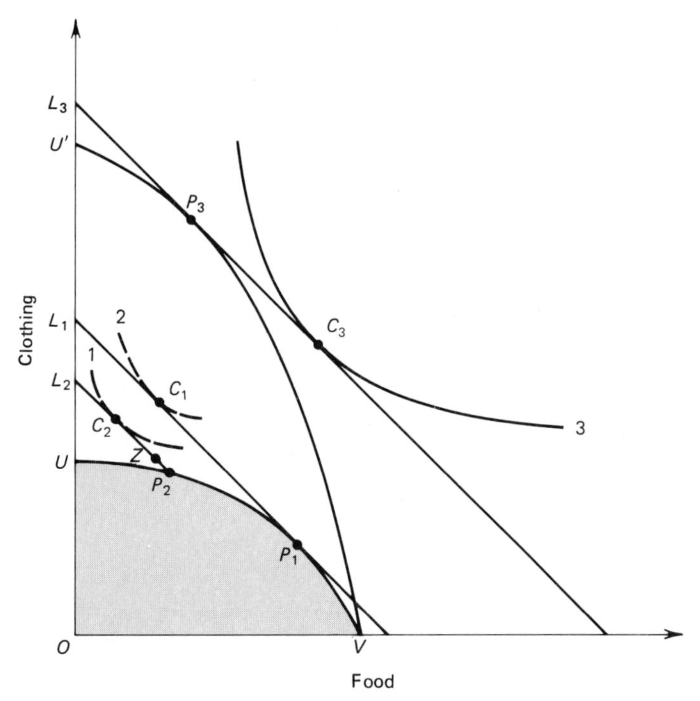

FIGURE 8-2 **The infant-industry argument.** The initial production-possibilities frontier is given by curve UV, and the fixed world price ratio by the slope of L_1P_1. Under laissez-faire, the economy produces at P_1 and consumes at C_1. Immediately after the production subsidy to the clothing industry, production shifts to P_2 and consumption to C_2. Eventually, the production frontier shifts to $U'V$, production to P_3, and consumption to C_3.

consumes at C_1. After a production subsidy is given to the infant clothing industry, however, the production-possibilities frontier shifts outward gradually as a result of the continuous improvement in skills and production techniques, until it eventually attains the position shown by curve $U'V$. Figure 8-2 illustrates the most favorable case, in which the infant industry (clothing) grows to become a net exporter. Thus, the economy eventually produces at P_3 and consumes at C_3.

Note that a temporary production subsidy to the infant clothing industry is more efficient than tariff protection. With a production subsidy, there is no consumption loss—the domestic consumers continue to trade at world prices. Immediately after the production subsidy goes into effect, consumption shifts to C_2, where line L_2P_2 is tangent to the highest possible social indifference curve (curve 1), as shown. With an equivalent tariff instead, consumption would move to a point such as Z (as explained in Chapter 7), where the marginal rate of substitution is equal to the lower domestic price ratio (not shown).

Infant-Industry Protection in Practice: Some Examples

Cases of successful infant-industry protection are difficult to prove or disprove. According to popular beliefs, the Japanese government played a key role in the development of such industries as steel, automobiles, electronics, fertilizers, and synthetic fibers. Other alleged examples of successful infant industries are steel, automobiles, and cement in Korea, and automobiles in Brazil. In a recent study, however, Krueger and Tuncer (1982) demonstrated that for the period 1963–1976 protected industries in Turkey did not experience larger productivity gains than other nonprotected (or less-protected) industries.

8-5 OTHER ECONOMIC ARGUMENTS FOR PROTECTION

Arguments for protection are usually advanced by groups who see their special interests damaged by imports. In this section, we look critically at several economic arguments for protection. Some of these arguments are totally fallacious; others may have a grain of truth.

Tariffs for Revenue

Any nonprohibitive tariff raises revenue for the government. Perhaps tariffs originated as a convenient source of government revenue rather than as a device to limit imports. Usually economists suspect the revenue motive when tariffs are imposed on imported commodities that are not produced at home (as illustrated by tariffs levied by some European countries on coffee and other tropical products), or when imported commodities are taxed at the same rates as domestically produced import substitutes (as illustrated by tariffs on imported wine and tobacco products).

As shown in Table 8-1, many developing nations continue to use the tariff as a main source of revenue. A major reason is that developing nations find it easier to raise revenue by taxing foreign trade at a few ports, using a handful of customs officials, than by adopting the more sophisticated and costly tax systems of industrial countries.

The industrial countries, however, impose tariffs mainly to protect their domestic industries from foreign competition. As shown in Table 8-1, tariff revenue is a negligible percentage of total government revenue for Canada, France, Germany, the United Kingdom, and the United States. Since the end of the nineteenth century, customs receipts in the United States have dwindled from over 50 percent of the total federal revenue to about 1 percent. Like other advanced countries, the United States now relies more heavily on the income tax than on tariffs as a source of revenue.

Cheap Foreign Labor

The "cheap-foreign-labor" argument for protection has always been very popular in the United States. According to this argument, tariffs are needed to protect domestic workers from cheap foreign labor. For instance, wages in India

TABLE 8-1 TARIFF REVENUE AS A PERCENTAGE OF TOTAL GOVERNMENT REVENUE

Country	Percentage
Argentina	13.31
Australia	5.19
Brazil	4.22
Canada	5.26
Colombia	11.58
France	0.03
Germany	0.02*
Ghana	40.90
India	24.07*
Italy	0.21
Ivory Coast	40.73
Korea	14.01
Malaysia	28.23
Mexico	2.73
Pakistan	30.94
United Kingdom	0.01
United States	1.56
Venezuela	18.00

*Provisional, preliminary, or projected.
Source: International Monetary Fund (IMF), *Government Finance Statistics Yearbook,* vol. X, IMF, Washington, D.C., 1986, pp. 32–33.

and Taiwan are only a fraction of U.S. wages. If we freely imported textiles produced by cheap Indian and Taiwanese labor (so the argument goes), then the higher standard of living of U.S. workers would be jeopardized.

The fallacy of this argument should be obvious from our discussion of the law of comparative advantage in Chapter 2. Mutually beneficial trade is possible even when one country has an absolute advantage in the production of every commodity relative to other countries. The higher U.S. standard of living is the result of high efficiency *and* free trade, not tariff protection.

An extreme version of the cheap-foreign-labor argument is the **scientific tariff,** which was actually embodied in the Tariff Act of 1922 and was retained in the Smoot-Hawley Act of 1930. According to this principle, the tariff rate on each imported commodity should be equal to the excess of the domestic production cost over the foreign cost, that is, the tariff should equalize the cost of production. A scientific tariff would eliminate all trade among nations and the potential gains from the international division of labor.

There is no doubt, of course, that some workers may be hurt by imports. The distress and agony noticed in the faces of many textile workers in small Georgia towns is not an illusion—it is real. Are these American citizens totally forgotten? Should their standard of living be compromised so that the rest of us can enjoy cheaper textiles? Has free trade gone awry? The argument that "the benefits to the United States far exceed the injury done to the textile workers" does not sound very convincing, especially if you happen to be a textile worker.

Should we, then, impose much higher tariffs on the imports of textiles? No. The plight of textile workers should not be used as an excuse to erect tariff walls. Remember that free trade is similar to technical progress, and it generates adjustment problems that are just as difficult as those created by technical progress. Yet nobody is arguing that the U.S. government should pass a law to ban all innovation! What can be done then?

A portion of the free-trade benefits that accrue to the rest of society should be used to assist displaced textile workers to acquire new skills so that they can be gainfully employed in other sectors in which the United States has a comparative advantage. In this way, free trade can make everybody better off, including the textile workers. Unfortunately, both in the United States and other countries, adjustment assistance has not worked well, although the United States still favors the principle. The danger is obvious: As the policy options narrow for ameliorating domestic adjustment problems of free trade, the cries for protection are heard louder and governments become more willing to embrace protectionism.

Tariffs to Maintain Employment

It is often argued that tariffs should be imposed in order to maintain the employment of labor in an industry that has been injured by a rise in imports. The fallacy of this argument is that it focuses too narrowly on the directly affected industry and ignores the high costs of preserving jobs by means of protection. For instance, if the protected commodity is used as an input in the production of other commodities, the tariff will raise costs and lead to reduced employment in the industries that use the protected commodity. Moreover, the tariff may cause the exchange rate to appreciate and thus reduce profits and employment in all other export and import-competing industries. Finally, each job saved in the protected industry may end up costing consumers more than the worker's salary. For instance, according to the World Bank's *World Development Report 1987* (Oxford University Press, New York, 1987, p. 152), each job preserved in the U.S. automobile industry cost American consumers between $40,000 and $108,500 a year, or the equivalent of the wages of as many as six ordinary industrial workers.

Industrial Policy

Because of increased competition from foreigners, U.S. attention has focused recently on a host of foreign "unfair trade practices" ranging from export promotional tactics and import restrictions to broad **industrial policies** and **industrial targeting.** The main culprit is thought to be Japan, although these practices have been widespread in both industrial and developing nations, particularly the newly industrialized countries such as Korea and Brazil. Perhaps foreign success rather than the practices themselves are responsible for the U.S. concern and the call for retaliation or even emulation. It is now recognized that support for particular industries (such as steel, automobiles, textiles, and electronics) should be given either when there are strong and demonstrable externalities or when there are legitimate noneconomic grounds, such as national security. (See also the comments made earlier in Section 8-3 in relation to high-technology industries.)

Imperfect Competition and Strategic Trade Policy

Recently James Brander and Barbara Spencer (1983, 1985) have argued that trade policy can be used to tilt the terms of oligopolistic competition in favor of domestic firms in the hope of shifting considerable monopoly profits from foreigners to us. The Brander-Spencer argument, which has become known as **strategic trade policy,** can be illustrated by means of a simple example.

Suppose that because of sufficiently large economies of scale, there is room for either an American or a European producer of a new aircraft. If both firms were to enter the industry, they would incur losses. But if only one of the two firms were to establish itself as the sole manufacturer of the new aircraft, then that firm would earn abnormal profits. Surely it would be to the national interest of a country (for example, America) to encourage the domestic firm to become the sole producer of the new aircraft. America could accomplish this goal by means of, say, a production subsidy that would create a *strategic* advantage for the domestic firm. Thus the subsidy could be such that the American firm would make a profit even if the European firm were to become an active producer as well.

Critics point out that the strategic trade policy argument suffers from severe flaws. First, the effects of trade policy often depend crucially on the oligopoly model used. Because we do not understand how oligopolies behave, we have a variety of oligopoly models. For instance, we may assume that firms compete by setting outputs (**Cournot model**) or prices (**Bertrand model**). Second, the market may be large enough to support several firms, not just two; and free entry may eliminate monopoly profits. Hence, instead of generating excess returns for domestic producers, a subsidy may be passed on to foreign consumers in the form of lower prices. Third, for the correct formulation of trade policy, a government should consider the effects of the policy not only on the targeted industry, but also on the rest of the economy. As the targeted industry attracts resources away from other sectors, firms in those other sectors are placed at a strategic disadvantage. The expected excess returns in the targeted industry may be offset to a considerable extent by losses generated elsewhere in the economy. A related point is that the government does not even know which industry or industries to target; and subsidizing all of them is, paradoxically, equivalent to subsidizing none. In addition, subsidizing the wrong industry may involve the economy in huge losses. Finally, strategic trade policy is a **beggar-thy-neighbor policy** that tends to increase our own income and welfare at the expense of others. Hence, like the optimal tariff, strategic trade policy is likely to provoke retaliation.

8-6 NONECONOMIC ARGUMENTS FOR PROTECTION

So far in this book, we have pretended that the only objective of a nation is to maximize its economic welfare. However, economic welfare is not the sole goal of life. Political, cultural, and sociological objectives are also important. Such noneconomic objectives may make it desirable to pursue activities that are not economically efficient. Even Adam Smith himself stated in a famous passage that national defense matters more than national opulence.

This section deals with the desirability of tariffs and alternative policy measures for the achievement of four specific objectives: (1) a certain level of *production* (perhaps for military reasons); (2) a certain level of *consumption* (usually to restrict the consumption of luxury goods on social grounds); (3) a certain level of *self-sufficiency* (to reduce the dependency on imports for political or military reasons); and (4) a certain level of *employment of a factor of production*, such as labor (to preserve the national character and the traditional way of life). These objectives are called noneconomic because they essentially originate outside the economic model. We need not concern ourselves with either the nature or the rationality of these noneconomic objectives.

The attainment of a noneconomic objective has an economic cost (in the form of a welfare loss), since it generally involves the violation of one or more Pareto-optimality conditions. The object of our investigation, then, is to determine the policy that achieves the noneconomic objective at the least welfare loss, that is, the optimal policy.

We have seen in this chapter that the optimal policy for correcting a distortion is to intervene at the exact point of the distortion. For instance, to remove a distortion in domestic production, the government must intervene with a production tax or subsidy. This optimal rule is also the key to the present case of noneconomic objectives.

When the government pursues a certain policy for achieving a noneconomic objective, a (policy-induced) distortion is necessarily introduced into the economy. The resultant welfare loss is minimized when the government actually intervenes at the exact point at which the noneconomic objective lies. This principle is summarized by the following rule:

If the *production* of a commodity must be encouraged for, say, military reasons, the optimal policy is a *production* subsidy—not a tariff. If the *consumption* of a commodity must be restricted, the optimal policy is a *consumption* tax. Similarly, when the noneconomic objective is to reduce the volume of *imports*, the optimal policy is an appropriate *tariff* on imports; and when the noneconomic objective is to raise the *employment* of some factor, such as labor, in certain activities, the optimal policy is a direct subsidy of the use of labor in those activities.

The case of oil production illustrates the point well. The United States is presently heavily dependent on foreign oil that is still controlled to a great extent by the Organization of Petroleum Exporting Countries (OPEC). For political reasons, the oil-producing nations may discontinue supplying oil to the United

States in the future. It is common knowledge that in 1973 OPEC imposed an oil embargo and that when the embargo was finally lifted, OPEC quadrupled the dollar price of crude oil (from $2.59 to $11.65 a barrel), shaking the economic stability of the world economy. To guard against such a contingency, it may be argued that tariff protection is needed to increase the domestic production of oil (since the capacity to produce oil cannot be increased overnight). This is a powerful argument. However, tariff protection is not the optimal policy. The correct policy depends on what the objective really is. If the main objective is to raise the domestic production of oil, the optimal policy is a production subsidy. But if the true objective is to guard against emergencies (such as another oil embargo), stockpiling may be a cheaper alternative. Indeed, stockpiling has been the policy of the United States for years. In 1988 the nation's strategic petroleum reserve contained more than half a billion barrels of crude oil, or enough to replace all crude oil imports for more than two months.

The real challenge facing the political process is not finding the correct economic policy to achieve a certain objective, but determining whether the chosen objective is legitimate. It is not clear why a country should have its own aircraft industry, computer industry, or automobile industry if the country can buy these commodities more cheaply from foreign nations. Moreover, the excuse of a noneconomic objective may be offered even when the true intention is to provide protection for some special-interest group. For instance, according to the *World Development Report 1987* (p. 144), one industrial country has argued that its *clothing industry is essential for defense because the industry produces uniforms for the army!*

8-7 CANDLEMAKERS VERSUS THE SUN

In the early part of the nineteenth century, Frédéric Bastiat used his pleasant wit to expose the fallacy in the pseudo arguments for protection against cheap foreign imports. Ever since, his satire has been the delight of many. In the following well-known plea of candlemakers and associated industries for protection against the unfair competition of the sun—an imaginary petition to the French Chamber of Deputies—Bastiat (1922) entertains the crowds by ridiculing the usual arguments for protection.

PETITION OF THE MANUFACTURERS OF CANDLES, WAX-LIGHTS, LAMPS, CANDLESTICKS, STREET LAMPS, SNUFFERS, EXTINGUISHERS, AND OF THE PRODUCERS OF OIL, TALLOW, RESIN, ALCOHOL, AND, GENERALLY, OF EVERYTHING CONNECTED WITH LIGHTING: *To Messieurs the Members of the Chamber of Deputies.* GENTLEMEN,—You are on the right road. You reject abstract theories, and have little consideration for cheapness and plenty. Your chief care is the interest of the producer. You desire to protect him from foreign competition, and reserve the *national market* for *national industry.*

We are about to offer you an admirable opportunity of applying your—what shall we call it?—your theory? No; nothing is more deceptive than theory—your doctrine? your system? your principle? But you dislike doctrines, you abhor systems, and as for principles you deny that there are any in social economy. We shall say, then, your practice—your practice without theory and without principle.

We are suffering from the intolerable competition of a foreign rival, placed, it would seem, in a condition so far superior to ours for the production of light that he absolutely *inundates* our *national* market with it at a price fabulously reduced. The moment he shows himself our trade leaves us—all consumers apply to him; and a branch of native industry, having countless ramifications, is all at once rendered completely stagnant. This rival, who is no other than the sun, wages war to the knife against us, and we suspect that he has been raised up by *perfidious Albion* (good policy as times go); inasmuch as he displays towards that haughty island a circumspection with which he dispenses in our case.

What we pray for is, that it may please you to pass a law ordering the shutting up of all windows, skylights, dormer-windows, outside and inside shutters, curtains, blinds, bull's-eyes; in a word, of all openings, holes, chinks, clefts, and fissures, by or through which the light of the sun has been in use to enter houses, to the prejudice of the meritorious manufactures with which we flatter ourselves we have accommodated our country—a country which, in gratitude, ought not to abandon us now to a strife so unequal.

We trust, Gentlemen, that you will not regard this our request as a satire, or refuse it without at least previously hearing the reasons which we have to urge in its support.

And, first, if you shut up as much as possible all access to natural light, and create a demand for artificial light, which of our French manufactures will not be encouraged by it?

If more tallow is consumed, then there must be more oxen and sheep; and, consequently, we shall behold the multiplication of meadows, meat, wool, hides, and, above all, manure, which is the basis and foundation of all agricultural wealth.

If more oil is consumed, then we shall have an extended cultivation of the poppy, of the olive, and of rape. These rich and exhausting plants will come at the right time to enable us to avail ourselves of the increased fertility which the rearing of additional cattle will impart to our lands.

Our heaths will be covered with resinous trees. Numerous swarms of bees will, on the mountains, gather perfumed treasures, now wasting their fragrance on the desert air, like the flowers from which they emanate. No branch of agriculture but will then exhibit a cheering development.

The same remark applies to navigation. Thousands of vessels will proceed to the whale fishery; and, in a short time, we shall possess a navy capable of maintaining the honour of France, and gratifying the patriotic aspirations of your petitioners, the undersigned candlemakers and others.

But what shall we say of the manufacture of *articles de Paris?* Henceforth you will behold gildings, bronzes, crystals, in candlesticks, in lamps, in lustres, in candelabra, shining forth, in spacious warerooms, compared with which those of the present day can be regarded but as mere shops.

No poor *resinier* from his heights on the seacoast, no coalminer from the depth of his sable gallery, but will rejoice in higher wages and increased prosperity.

Only have the goodness to reflect, Gentlemen, and you will be convinced that there is, perhaps, no Frenchman, from the wealthy coalmaster to the humblest vendor of lucifer matches, whose lot will not be ameliorated by the success of this our petition.

We foresee your objections, Gentlemen, but we know that you can oppose to us none but such as you have picked up from the effete works of the partisans of Free Trade. We defy you to utter a single word against us which will not instantly rebound against yourselves and your entire policy.

You will tell us that, if we gain by the protection which we seek, the country will lose by it, because the consumer must bear the loss.

We answer:

You have ceased to have any right to invoke the interest of the consumer; for, whenever his interest is found opposed to that of the producer, you sacrifice the former. You have done so for the purpose of *encouraging labour and increasing employment.* For the same reason you should do so again.

You have yourselves obviated this objection. When you are told that the consumer is interested in the free importation of iron, coal, corn, textile fabrics—yes, you reply, but the producer is interested in their exclusion. Well, be it so; if consumers are interested in the free admission of natural light, the producers of artificial light are equally interested in its prohibition.

But, again, you may say that the producer and consumer are identical. If the manufacturer gain by protection, he will make the agriculturist also a gainer; and if agriculture prosper, it will open a vent to manufactures. Very well; if you confer upon us the monopoly of furnishing light during the day, first of all we shall purchase quantities of tallow, coals, oils, resinous substances, wax, alcohol—besides silver, iron, bronze, crystal—to carry on our manufactures; and then we, and those who furnish us with such commodities, having become rich will consume a great deal, and impart prosperity to all the other branches of our national industry.

If you urge that the light of the sun is a gratuitous gift of nature, and that to reject such gifts is to reject wealth itself under pretence of encouraging the means of acquiring it, we would caution you against giving a death-blow to your own policy. Remember that hitherto you have always repelled foreign products, *because* they approximate more nearly than home products to the character of gratuitous gifts. To comply with the exactions of other monopolists, you have only *half a motive;* and to repulse us simply because we stand on a stronger vantage-ground than others would be to adopt the equation $+ \times + = -$; in other words, it would be to heap *absurdity* upon *absurdity.*

Nature and human labour co-operate in various proportions (depending on countries and climates) in the production of commodities. The part which nature executes is always gratuitous; it is the part executed by human labour which constitutes value, and is paid for.

If a Lisbon orange sells for half the price of a Paris orange, it is because natural, and consequently gratuitous, heat does for the one what artificial, and therefore expensive, heat must do for the other.

When an orange comes to us from Portugal, we may conclude that it is furnished in part gratuitously, in part for an onerous consideration; in other words, it comes to us at *half-price* as compared with those of Paris.

Now, it is precisely the *gratuitous half* (pardon the word) which we contend should be excluded. You say, How can national labour sustain competition with foreign labour, when the former has all the work to do, and the latter only does one-half, the sun supplying the remainder? But if this *half,* being *gratuitous,* determines you to exclude competition, how should the *whole,* being *gratuitous,* induce you to admit competition? If you were consistent, you would, while excluding as hurtful to native industry what is half gratuitous, exclude *a fortiori* and with double zeal, that which is altogether gratuitous.

Once more, when products such as coal, iron, corn, or textile fabrics are sent us from abroad, and we can acquire them with less labour than if we made them ourselves, the difference is a free gift conferred upon us. The gift is more or less considerable in proportion as the difference is more or less great. It amounts to a quarter, a half, or three-quarters of the value of the product, when the foreigner only asks us for three-fourths, a half, or a quarter of the price we should otherwise pay. It is as perfect and complete as it can be, when the donor (like the sun in furnishing us with light) asks us for nothing. The question, and we ask it formally, is this: Do you desire for our country the benefit of gratuitous consumption, or the pretended advantages of onerous production? Make your choice, but be logical; for as long as you exclude, as you do, coal, iron, corn, foreign fabrics, *in proportion* as their price approximates to *zero,* what inconsistency it would be to admit the light of the sun, the price of which is already at *zero* during the entire day!

8-8 SUMMARY

1 The volume of trade is optimal from the national point of view when the marginal terms of trade are equal to the domestic opportunity cost of exportables.

2 Free trade equalizes the domestic price ratio (and thus the domestic opportunity cost of exportables) to the average, not the marginal, terms of trade. For a small country, free trade is optimal because the average and marginal terms of trade are equal.

3 For a large country, laissez-faire pushes the volume of trade beyond the optimal point because the marginal terms of trade are lower than the average;

hence, an optimal tariff is needed to restrict the volume of trade and maximize the large country's welfare.

4 When foreign countries retaliate, the country that initiates the tariff war (by imposing an optimal tariff first) may become worse off.

5 Domestic distortions prevent the market mechanism from achieving Pareto optimality.

6 Endogenous domestic distortions are due to market imperfections. They may occur in production, consumption, or factor employment.

7 Policy-induced distortions are the result of economic policies, such as tariffs and other taxes or subsidies.

8 To restore Pareto optimality, policy intervention (equal to the degree of distortion) must occur at the exact point at which the underlying market imperfection prevails. This is the general rule for optimal intervention.

9 To correct a policy-induced distortion, the optimal policy is to eliminate the policy that caused the distortion in the first place.

10 The theory of the optimal tariff rests on the existence of a foreign distortion (from the national viewpoint). The optimal tariff itself may be viewed as the optimal policy to correct the foreign distortion.

11 Static externalities form a permanent characteristic of technology and call for permanent intervention. The infant-industry argument, however, rests on a dynamic and irreversible learning process that generally generates external economies only over a specific period of time and thus calls for only *temporary* government intervention.

12 The Mill test for infant-industry protection is whether the "infant" will eventually grow sufficiently to compete without protection against earlier starters. The Bastable test requires further that the present discounted value of the future benefits be at least as high as the initial cost incurred to help the infant grow. Johnson argues that, in addition, it must be demonstrated that because of some domestic distortion, the private sector is prevented from investing sufficient funds in new industries.

13 Because an infant industry involves a domestic (not foreign) distortion, the optimal policy is *not* tariff protection but rather some sort of subsidy to the infant industry.

14 Many developing countries continue to use tariffs as a main source of revenue. Industrial countries rely on the income tax instead, imposing tariffs mainly to protect domestic industries.

15 The cheap foreign labor argument for protection (and its extreme variant, the scientific tariff) is fallacious—it ignores the fundamental principle of comparative advantage. The argument for the use of tariffs to maintain employment in some industries is also fallacious.

16 Support for particular industries should be given either when there are strong and demonstrable externalities or when there are legitimate noneconomic grounds, such as national security.

17 The strategic trade policy proposed by Brander and Spencer suffers from severe flaws: (a) Its effects depend crucially on the oligopoly model used; (b) when the market is large enough to support several firms (not just two), free entry may eliminate excess monopoly profits (or rents); (c) it places other nonsupported sectors at a strategic disadvantage; and (d) it is a beggar-thy-neighbor policy that is likely to provoke retaliation.

18 Any policy to achieve a noneconomic objective introduces a distortion and results in a welfare loss. To minimize the welfare loss, intervention must occur at the exact point at which the noneconomic objective lies. Thus, to achieve a production (consumption) goal, the optimal policy is a production (consumption) subsidy or tax; to reduce the volume of imports, the optimal policy is a tariff; and to raise the employment of a factor in certain activities, the optimal policy is a direct subsidy to the use of that factor in those activities.

PROBLEMS

1 Explain the meaning of each of the following statements:

a Free trade is the best policy because tariffs introduce inefficiencies and reduce welfare.

b Free trade is better than autarky, but restricted trade is better than free trade.

c Tariff protection can raise the real wage and standard of living of some American workers, such as textile workers. Indeed a scientific tariff can maximize the benefits of these workers.

There seems to be a contradiction between statements a and b, a and c, and b and c. In each case, state the apparent contradiction and then resolve it.

2 America exports steel to Britain in exchange for British cloth. Britain's offers are summarized in the following table:

Yards of cloth	0	450	800	1,050	1,200	1,250	1,200	1,050
Tons of steel	0	5	10	15	20	25	30	35

a At each British offer determine America's average and marginal terms of trade.

b At what offers is Britain's demand for imports of steel elastic? Inelastic? Unit elastic?

c Suppose that at the free-trade equilibrium, America exports 35 tons of steel in exchange for 1,050 yards of British cloth. Show that it will be to the benefit of America to restrict its exports of steel to 25 tons. Does this restriction cause Britain to lose as much as America gains?

d Suppose that America's optimum volume of exports is 15 tons of steel. Determine a possible range of values for America's optimum tariff rate.

3 Greece is currently importing automobiles at $12,000 each. The government believes that Greek manufacturers could produce similar autos for only $9,000, but only after a five-year learning period during which the domestic cost of autos would fall by $2,000 annually, from $19,000 in the first year to $9,000 in the sixth year.

a Explain why individual manufacturers may not find it profitable to initiate automobile production in Greece.

b Explain how infant-industry protection can help domestic producers overcome their reluctance to develop an auto industry in Greece.

c If the government decides to assist the domestic producers, what form should infant-industry protection take over the initial five-year period?

4 A small country, Belgium, uses labor (mobile factor) plus capital (specific factor) to produce steel, and labor plus land (specific factor) to produce corn. The marginal physical product of labor in the corn industry remains constant at 10 bushels of corn irrespective of how much labor is allocated to the production of corn. The marginal physical product of labor in the steel industry (MPP_{LS}) is given by the equation

$$MPP_{LS} = 100 - 2L_S$$

where L_S = quantity of labor employed in the production of steel. Belgium is endowed with 40 units of labor. The world prices of corn and steel are $P_C = \$4$ and $P_S = \$1$, respectively.

a How much labor does Belgium employ in the production of corn? In the production of steel? What is the money wage rate (in dollars) in Belgium? What are the outputs of steel and corn? What is Belgium's GNP (that is, the value of corn plus the value of steel produced)?

b Suppose that the steel workers organize themselves into a strong labor union that raises their wage to \$80. What is Belgium's new allocation of labor between steel and corn? What are the new outputs of the two industries? What is the value of GNP now? What is the cost of the labor movement in the steel industry?

SUGGESTED READING

Bastable, C. F. (1903). *The Theory of International Trade.* 4th ed. Macmillan and Company, London.

———(1923). *The Commerce of Nations.* 9th ed. (rev.). Methuen & Company, London.

Bastiat, F. (1922). *Economic Sophisms.* G. P. Putnum's Sons, New York, Chapter VII.

Bhagwati, J., and V. K. Ramaswami (1963). "Domestic Distortions, Tariffs, and the Theory of Optimum Subsidy." *Journal of Political Economy,* vol. 71, no. 1 (February), pp. 44–50. Reprinted in R. E. Caves and H. G. Johnson (eds.), American Economic Association *Readings in International Economics,* Richard D. Irwin, Inc., Homewood, Ill., 1968.

Black, J. (1959). "Arguments for Tariffs." *Oxford Economic Papers* (N.S.), vol. 11, pp. 191–220.

Brander, J. A., and B. J. Spencer (1983). "International R&D Rivalry and Industrial Strategy." *Review of Economic Studies,* vol. 50, pp. 707–722.

———(1985). "Export Subsidies and International Market Share Rivalry." *Journal of International Economics,* vol. 18, pp. 83–100.

Corden, W. M. (1957). "Tariffs, Subsidies and the Terms of Trade." *Economica* (N.S.), vol. 24 (August), pp. 235–242.

———(1974). *Trade Policy and Economic Welfare.* Oxford University Press, London.

Hagen, E. (1958). "An Economic Justification of Protectionism." *Quarterly Journal of Economics,* vol. 72 (November), pp. 496–514.

Johnson, H. G. (1965). "Optimal Trade Intervention in the Presence of Domestic Disortions." In R. E. Baldwin et al. (eds.), *Trade, Growth and the Balance of Payments: Essays in Honor of Gottfried Haberler,* Rand McNally & Company, Chicago.

———(1967). "The Possibility of Income Losses from Increased Efficiency or Factor Accumulation in the Presence of Tariffs." *Economic Journal,* vol. 77, no. 305 (March), pp. 151–154. Reprinted in H. G. Johnson, *Aspects of the Theory of Tariffs,* Harvard University Press, Cambridge, Mass., 1972.

Krueger, A. O., and B. Tuncer (1982). "An Empirical Test of the Infant Industry Argument." *American Economic Review,* vol. 72 (December), pp. 1142–1152.

Krugman, P. R., ed. (1986). *Strategic Trade Policy and the New International Economics.* The MIT Press, Cambridge, Mass.

———(1987). "Is Free Trade Passé?" *The Journal of Economic Perspectives,* vol. 1 (Fall), pp. 131–144.

Lewis, A. (1954). "Economic Development with Unlimited Supplies of Labour." *Manchester School* (May), pp. 139–191. Reprinted in A. N. Agarwala and S. P. Singh (eds.), *The Economics of Underdevelopment,* Oxford University Press, London, 1958.

Mill, J. S. (1904). *Principles of Political Economy,* vol. II. J. A. Hill and Company, New York. The first edition of *Principles* appeared in 1848.

Myint, H. (1963). "Infant Industry Arguments for Assistance to Industries in the Setting of Dynamic Trade Theory." In R. Harrod (ed.), *International Trade Theory in a Developing World,* St. Martin's Press, New York.

Myrdal, G. (1956). *An International Economy.* Harper and Row, Publishers, New York.

Prebisch, R. (1959). "Commercial Policy in Underdeveloped Countries." *American Economic Review,* Proceedings, vol. 49 (May), pp. 251–273.

Viner, J. (1965). *Studies in the Theory of International Trade.* Augustus M. Kelley, Publishers, New York.

CHAPTER 9

INSTRUMENTS OF COMMERCIAL POLICY

The tariff is the most common instrument of protection, but it is not the only one. Nations may restrict their foreign trade in many other ways. Indeed, as the tariff walls continue to come down as a result of multilateral trade negotiations, the significance of the nontariff barriers to international trade grows. After a brief discussion of export taxes and subsidies, this chapter examines the effects of various nontariff trade barriers and highlights the commercial policy of the United States.

9-1 EXPORT TAXES

Export taxes are prohibited by the Constitution of the United States and are extremely rare phenomena in other industrial nations. But export taxes are not uncommon in developing nations. For instance, many countries of Africa, South America, and Southeast Asia often tax their exports of raw materials and foodstuffs, such as cocoa (Ghana), coffee (Brazil and Colombia), jute (Pakistan), rice (Burma and Thailand), timber (Ivory Coast and Liberia), tea (Sri Lanka), and tin (Malaysia). Developing nations tax their exports for various reasons, such as (1) to raise revenue, (2) to improve their terms of trade, and (3) to increase the domestic processing of raw materials. This section deals with the effects of export taxes.

Partial Equilibrium Analysis of Export Taxes

Figure 9-1 depicts the hypothetical schedules of domestic demand (DD') and supply (SS') of rice in, say, Thailand. The autarkic equilibrium price of rice is $20

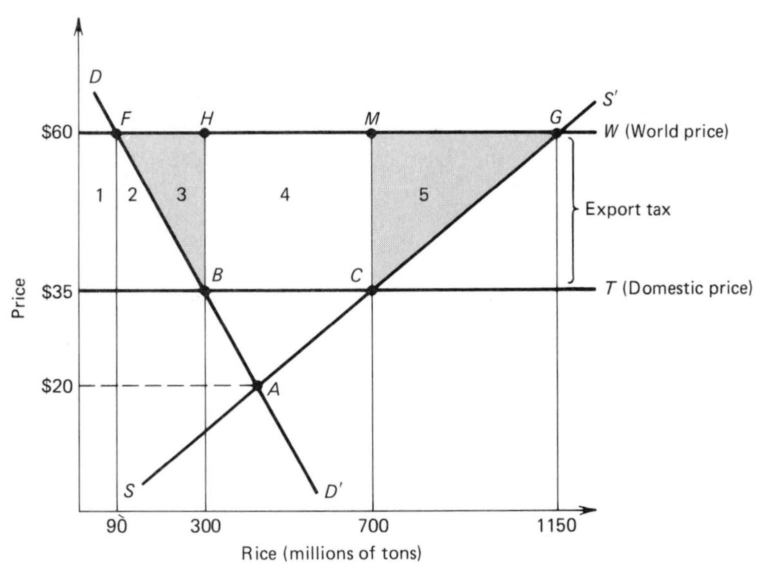

FIGURE 9-1 **The effects of export taxes.** At the world price of $60, domestic production is 1,150 million tons (point *G*), of which 90 million tons (point *F*) are consumed domestically and 1,060 million tons (*FG*) are exported. An export tax of $25 lowers the domestic price to $35. Domestic production decreases to 700 million tons (point *C*), and domestic consumption increases to 300 million tons (point *B*). Exports fall to 400 million tons (*BC*). The producer surplus is reduced by the sum of areas 1, 2, 3, 4, and 5. Area 4 is tax revenue, and the sum of areas 1 and 2 is additional consumer surplus. Shaded area 3 is the loss due to domestic overconsumption, and shaded area 5 is the loss due to domestic underproduction.

per ton, as shown by point *A*. For simplicity, assume that the world price of rice is $60 per ton, as shown by infinitely elastic world demand schedule *W*. In the absence of any trade restrictions, the domestic price of rice must rise to $60 per ton also: At any lower price, exporters would be willing to purchase unlimited quantities of domestic rice and resell it on the world market. At the world price of $60, Thailand produces 1,150 million tons of rice, of which 90 million tons are consumed domestically and 1,060 million tons (*FG*) are exported.

An export tax lowers the price to domestic producers and consumers and generates revenue for the government. Suppose that Thailand imposes an export tax of $25 per ton. The exporters' net revenue falls to $35 per ton ($60 world price less $25 tax to the government). Thus the domestic price must *fall* to $35, as shown by horizontal line *T*, because exporting becomes unprofitable at higher domestic prices. At the lower price of $35, domestic production decreases to 700 million tons (point *C*), domestic consumption rises to 300 million tons (point *B*), and exports fall to 400 million tons (*BC*). In addition, income is redistributed from rice producers to domestic consumers and the government.

Thus, the **producer surplus** is reduced by the sum of areas 1, 2, 3, 4, and 5, of which area 4 is tax revenue collected by the government and the sum of areas 1 and 2 represents additional consumer surplus. The sum of the two shaded triangular areas, 3 and 5, illustrates the deadweight loss of the export tax. Area 3 indicates the deadweight loss due to the domestic overconsumption of rice induced by the export tax, and area 5 shows the loss due to the domestic underproduction of rice induced by the tax. All this is analogous to the case of an import tariff.

Large countries with a significant share of an export market can use an export tax to improve their terms of trade. The export tax creates scarcity in world markets and raises the world prices of the exported commodities. Indeed, export taxes are often imposed in the belief that they are paid by the foreigners. But attempts to tax foreigners may easily turn into excessive taxation of domestic producers, as illustrated in Section 9-2 with Ghana's export tax on cocoa.

General Equilibrium Analysis of Export Taxes

The general equilibrium effects of export taxes on the allocation of resources are symmetrical to the corresponding effects of import taxes. The essence of this proposition is captured by the following remarkable theorem formulated by Lerner (1936):

Lerner's Symmetry theorem: **In a long-run, static-equilibrium model (ignoring possible transitional difficulties, such as unemployment and balance-of-payments disequilibria) a general export tax has the same effects as a general import tax of the same ad valorem percentage.**

Lerner's symmetry theorem is valid within the context of long-run equilibrium only. In the short run an import tax tends to operate in an expansionary, stimulating fashion (and, in general, tends to improve the balance of payments as well), while an export tax tends to operate in an anti-inflationary, depressive manner (and, in general, tends to worsen the balance of payments).

We can demonstrate the symmetry between export and import taxes by showing that their effects on domestic relative prices are identical. For this purpose, assume that the home country is small and is, hence, a price taker in world markets. The country exports food and imports clothing at current world prices: $p_f = \$10$ and $p_c = \$50$, respectively. Under free-trade conditions, world prices prevail in our small economy as well. Thus, 1 unit of clothing exchanges for 5 units of food ($50/$10 = 5).

Assume, first, that our small economy imposes a 20 percent tax on imports of clothing. The domestic price of clothing rises to 1.20 × $50 = $60. This is the price that must be paid by domestic consumers and received by domestic producers. While in world markets 1 unit of clothing continues to exchange for 5 units of food (that is, $50/$10), in our small country 1 unit of clothing now exchanges for 6 units of food (that is, $60/$10).

Alternatively, assume that the small economy imposes a 20 percent tax on exports of food. Evidently, the small economy can continue exporting food if the domestic price of food falls sufficiently so that the cost of food to foreign importers, inclusive of the export tax, continues to be $10. In particular, the domestic price of food must drop to $10/1.20 = $8.33. What is the relative price of clothing after the imposition of the export tax? It is again $50/$8.33 = 6 units of food.

Because the effect on the all-important *relative* price of clothing is the same for the export tax on food as it is for the import tax on clothing, the general microeconomic effects of the export tax must be identical to the corresponding effects of the import tax. It must be clear that this important conclusion remains valid when the tax-levying country is "large." Thus the theory of the optimal tariff is fully applicable to export taxes also.

The symmetry of export taxes and import tariffs leads to an important conclusion: *If export promotion is a goal of policy, then the most direct instrument of achieving it is import liberalization!*

9-2 GHANA'S EXPORT TAXES ON COCOA

Ghana is a tropical country in western Africa. Its area is 239,000 square kilometers—about the size of Oregon. In 1985, its population stood at 12.7 million. Portuguese explorers landed in Ghana in 1471; they called it the Gold Coast because of the ample gold they found there. In the late 1800s, the Gold Coast became a British colony; in 1957, it gained its independence and took the name Ghana.

In the 1950s, Ghana mainly exported one commodity: cocoa. At that time, cocoa accounted for about one-fifth of gross domestic product and earned 60 percent of export revenues, and Ghana was probably the richest country in black Africa. Unfortunately, Ghana embarked on an unsuccessful import-substituting plan, turning sharply away from its export base. The results were disastrous. By 1985, Ghana's per capita income had dropped to $380, which was lower than that of Liberia, Zambia, and the neighboring Ivory Coast. While many things went wrong with Ghana's plan, the failure of export policy was crucial.

The Cocoa Marketing Board used its monopoly power to raise significant tax revenue from foreign sales at the same time that the government kept the external value of the currency very high. From the late 1960s to the late 1970s, the combined effect was to raise the effective export duty by almost 65 percent (from 54.3 to 88.9 percent). As a result, Ghana's share of export markets shrank from 40 percent in 1961–1963 to only 18 percent in 1980–1982, while the market share of the Ivory Coast rose from 9 to 29 percent during the same period.

Incidentally, the tremendous increase in the effective export duty caused Ghana's domestic price of cocoa to fall far below the levels in competing West African countries, such as the Ivory Coast. For instance, in 1965 the domestic price of cocoa was about the same in Ghana as in the Ivory Coast, but by 1980 Ghana's domestic price had fallen to about 18 percent of the corresponding price in the Ivory Coast. This large price discrepancy was responsible for extensive smuggling of cocoa from Ghana to the Ivory Coast.

Source: Adapted from The World Bank, *World Development Report 1986,* Oxford University Press, New York, 1986, p. 76.

9-3 EXPORT SUBSIDIES

An export subsidy is a *negative* export tax. For this reason, a detailed analysis of export subsidies is redundant. In general, the microeconomic effects of export subsidies are the opposite of the corresponding effects of export taxes. The primary purpose of an export subsidy is to increase exports by switching foreign spending to domestic products. This is accomplished, of course, by effectively reducing the prices that foreigners have to pay for the subsidized exported commodities. Accordingly, the terms-of-trade effect of export subsidies is, in general, unfavorable.

Export subsidies may be overt or covert. An overt export subsidy involves a direct payment by the government to the exporter of the subsidized commodity in direct proportion to either the volume or the value of the exports. Covert export subsidies are schemes that provide financial assistance to the exporter indirectly. Such indirect financial assistance is often provided, for instance, through subsidization of credit conditions and of export shipping services by ships of the national flag. For example, the U.S. Export-Import Bank, founded in the 1930s, provides easy credit to U.S. exporters and their foreign customers.

Export subsidies violate international agreements. The General Agreement on Tariffs and Trade (GATT) views export subsidies as "unfair competition" and allows importing countries to retaliate with "countervailing duties." A countervailing duty is levied by the importing country to offset the exporter's subsidy and cannot exceed the amount of the subsidy. The use of countervailing duties is limited to cases in which imports cause, or threaten to cause, injury to a domestic industry.

When foreign countries retaliate with countervailing duties, the country that initiates the export subsidy program actually becomes worse off because the export subsidy program amounts then to a direct income transfer by the export-subsidizing country to the rest of the world.

An important case in which an export subsidy may be granted occurs when the export industry uses imported inputs that are subject to import duties. In this case, which is frequently observed in developing countries, the export industry is granted an export subsidy that is, in effect, a rebate of the tariff paid by the same industry on imported inputs. This type of export subsidy is indeed very sensible. Otherwise, the export industry would be at a disadvantage in world markets.

9-4 QUANTITATIVE RESTRICTIONS

Nations may also restrict their foreign trade by directly limiting the physical volume (or value) of either their imports (**import quota**) or their exports (**export quota**). Frequently governments use quantitative restrictions to protect domestic industries from foreign competition. The microeconomic effects of these quantitative restrictions are very similar to the effects of import and export taxes. But there are also some important differences between quantitative restrictions and trade taxes. Indeed, it is because of these differences that quantitative restrictions are often preferred to trade taxes.

Types of Import Quotas

A quantitative restriction on the imports of a particular commodity may be administered either through an **open quota** (also known as a **global quota**) or through import licenses. A global quota allows a specified amount of imports per year but does not specify where the product may come from or who is entitled to import it. As soon as the specified amount is actually imported, further imports into the country are prohibited for the rest of the time period.

The disadvantages of a global quota are obvious. Merchants (domestic importers and foreign exporters) rush to get their shipments into the country before the limit is reached. Those who are lucky enough to receive their goods in time enjoy abnormal profits—after the quota is filled, domestic prices rise because of the increased scarcity. Those who are late suffer losses—storage costs and even reshipment to the country of origin may be involved. Goods originating in distant places are discriminated against because of the longer transport time involved and the higher loss (the result of higher transport costs) in the event they arrive late. Also, large importing firms that are able to order sizable quantities on short notice (because of trade connections and good credit) have a distinct advantage over small importers. Finally, the rush to get commodities into the quota country as soon as possible may result in greater price fluctuation over the year, especially in the case of perishable goods.

To avoid the chaos of a global quota, governments usually issue import licenses, which they either sell to the importers at a competitive price (or simply for a fee) or just give away on a first-come, first-served basis. The licenses may or may not specify the source from which the commodity is to be procured. Unfortunately, *real* resources are used up as people compete for import licenses.

Equivalence between Import Taxes and Import Quotas

For every import quota there is an **equivalent import tax.** We can understand the various microeconomic effects of import quotas by exploiting this equivalence. Consider Figure 9-2, which illustrates the market for an imported commodity, such as steel. Under free-trade conditions, equilibrium occurs at E, where the domestic demand-for-imports schedule DD' intersects the foreign supply-of-exports schedule SS'; and the home economy imports 50,000 units (per month) at $12 per unit.

Suppose now that the authorities impose an import quota equal to 40,000 units (per month), as shown by vertical line Q. This quota is *effective* because it is lower than the free-trade flow of imports (that is, 50,000 units). The price in the home market rises to $13 (point F) while the price in the rest of the world *falls* to $10 (point H). Like an import tax, an import quota creates a wedge between the domestic and foreign prices.

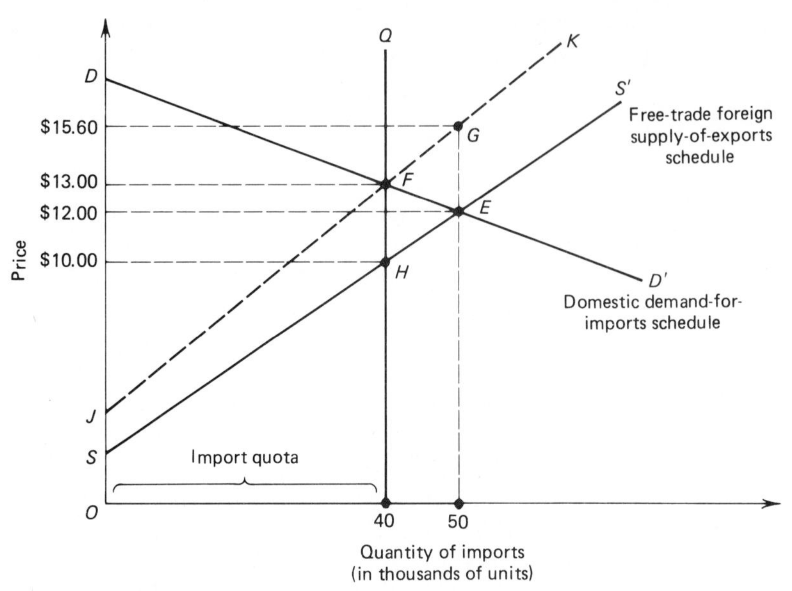

FIGURE 9-2 **Equivalence between an import quota and an import tax.** Under free-trade conditions, equilibrium occurs at *E*, where the domestic demand-for-imports schedule intersects the foreign supply-of-exports schedule. Thus, the country imports 50,000 units at $12 per unit. A quota equal to 40,000 units, represented by vertical line *Q*, raises the domestic price to $13 (point *F*) and lowers the foreign price to $10 (point *H*). A 30 percent import tax achieves the same results as the 40,000-unit import quota by causing the foreign supply-of-exports schedule to shift upward by 30 percent, as shown by dashed line *JK*.

Evidently, the authorities can achieve the same results by imposing a 30 percent import tax. This causes the foreign supply-of-exports schedule to shift upward by 30 percent, as shown by dashed line *JK*. Observe that the vertical distance *EG* (that is, $3.60) is 30 percent of the price at *E* (that is, $12), and the vertical distance *HF* (that is, $3) is 30 percent of the price at *H* (that is, $10). The same relationship holds, of course, for all points along the two schedules. After the imposition of the import tax, the volume of imports falls to 40,000 units, the domestic price rises to $13, and the foreign price falls to $10—exactly as in the case of the import quota. Thus the microeconomic effects of an import quota (on domestic and foreign production, consumption, imports, exports, terms of trade, factor prices, and so on) are exactly the same as those of an equivalent import tax.

Differences between Import Quotas and Import Taxes

We now turn to some important differences between quotas and tariffs.

The Revenue Effect One considerable difference lies with the **revenue effect.** In the case of the tariff, the government in the foregoing example will collect $3 per unit of imports (that is, $3 × 40,000 = $120,000). In the case of the import quota, the outcome is not so certain. In the same example, *if* the license fee per unit of imports is actually determined (by competition or otherwise) to be $3, the import quota will bring into the government treasury the same amount of revenue as the equivalent tariff (that is, $120,000). In this case, the economic effects of the import quota are identical to those of the equivalent tariff, except for the insignificant difference that under an import quota the government revenue is called "license fees" and under an import tax "tariff revenue."

However, depending on how the licensing system actually works, the amount of $120,000 may accrue to the domestic importers, to consumers, to government officials (who may have to be bribed before they will issue the necessary licenses), or to the foreign exporters or even the foreign governments. For instance, if the domestic importers obtain the necessary licenses free of any fees and then organize themselves into a monopoly while the foreign exporters remain unorganized, the domestic importers are likely to get the profit. It is, of course, conceivable that the domestic government, through effective price control measures, may prevent the importers from raising the price of imports to consumers; in that case all the profit may accrue to the consumers. But if the foreign exporters are organized while the domestic importers are not, the profit may accrue to the foreign exporters. Finally, foreign governments may impose an equivalent export tax and collect all the revenue. When the revenue (or profit) actually accrues to the foreigners, the home economy becomes worse off because then the "home" quota is equivalent to a "foreign" export tax.

Certainty Kindleberger (1975, pp. 8–9) emphasizes another important difference between an import quota and a tariff. Even though for every import quota there is always an equivalent tariff, the practical estimation of the equivalent tariff rate is not easy because the supply and demand curves are not known in advance. Thus, an import quota appears to be a more *certain* measure than a tariff.

Moreover, under specific conditions a tariff may not work at all. For instance, when the goal of the government is to raise the domestic price of imports in order to protect the domestic producers, and in addition the foreign supply-of-exports schedule is perfectly inelastic (or very inelastic), the government must impose an import quota—no tariff can do the job. Return to Figure 9-2 and imagine that the foreign supply-of-exports schedule is given by the vertical dashed line through *E*. Further, suppose that the government wishes to raise the domestic price from $12 to $13. To accomplish its goal, the government must impose an import quota equal to 40,000 units per period of time. Under the postulated circumstances, no tariff can affect the initial equilibrium at *E*. To be sure, a tariff will cause the vertical foreign supply schedule to shift upward. Since it is vertical, however, the shift will change nothing, and the foreigners will merely absorb the import tax.

Kindleberger illustrates his point with a historical example. When the increase in the U.S. tariff diverted the 1929–1930 bumper Australian wheat crop to Europe, the French, who wanted higher wheat prices for French peasants, had to impose an import quota—no simple tariff could keep the Australian wheat out because of the inelastic supply of wheat from Australia to Europe once wheat was excluded from America.

Potential Monopoly An import quota may convert a potential into an actual monopoly, while a tariff cannot. In the presence of a tariff, even a monopolist cannot charge more than the world price plus the tariff. In the presence of a quota, however, most of the foreign competitive pressure is removed and the potential monopolist may become an actual monopolist by raising the price well above the world price plus the equivalent tariff.

Consider Figure 9-3, in which the domestic industry of some imported com-

FIGURE 9-3 **Potential monopoly converted to actual monopoly under import quota.** The foreign supply of exports is infinitely elastic at price OP_w. With free trade, domestic consumers purchase a total of $P_w H$ units. The domestic monopolist produces only $P_w G$ units (see point G, at which the monopolist's marginal cost equals the world price), and the country imports the additional amount, GH, from abroad. With the imposition of a specific import tax equal to $P_w P_t$, the equilibrium price rises to OP_t, consumption falls to $P_t K$, imports fall to UK, and domestic production expands to $P_t U$. When the import tax is converted into a quota allowing only UK units of imports, the domestic monopolist reduces production to $P_1 Z$ (see point E, at which the monopolist's marginal cost curve intersects dashed marginal revenue curve MR), and raises the price to OP_1.

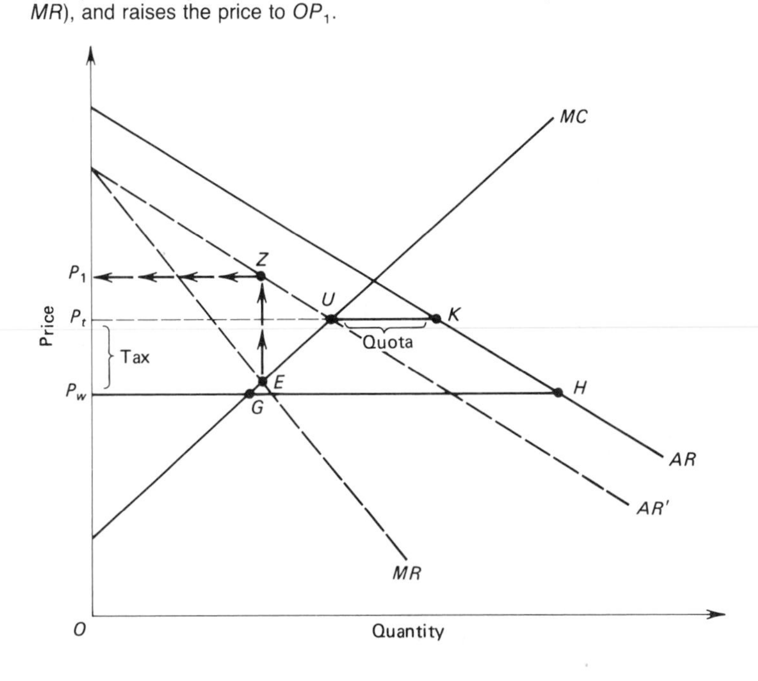

modity is a potential monopoly. The solid *MC* curve is the domestic monopolist's **marginal cost curve.** Similarly, the solid *AR* curve is the domestic demand schedule. The world price of this imported commodity is OP_w, as shown by the infinitely elastic foreign supply-of-exports schedule $P_w H$. Before the domestic government interferes with either tariffs or quotas, the domestic price coincides with world price OP_w. Thus, the domestic consumers buy $P_w H$, of which $P_w G$ is produced by the domestic potential monopolist and *GH* is imported from the rest of the world. When the government imposes a specific import tax of $P_w P_t$, the world price *inclusive of the import tax* becomes equal to OP_t and the domestic price rises to OP_t. At this higher price, the domestic consumers reduce their consumption to $P_t K$, while the potential monopolist raises production to $P_t U$. As a result, imports fall to *UK*.

Suppose now that the government converts the tariff into an import quota, allowing only *UK* units to be imported from the rest of the world. Displace demand schedule *AR* to the left by the amount of the import quota, as shown by dashed curve *AR*′. This curve is now the relevant demand schedule for the domestic monopolist—at least for prices higher than the world prices. To determine the profit-maximizing output of the monopolist, draw the marginal revenue curve, as shown by dashed line *MR*. Profit maximization occurs at *E*, where the monopolist's marginal cost curve intersects the marginal revenue curve. To determine the monopoly price, move upward to curve *AR*′, as shown by the arrows from *E* to *Z*. Thus, the monopolist reduces output to $P_1 Z$ and raises the price to OP_1. In this case the conversion of the tariff into a quota transforms the potential monopolist into an actual monopolist.

Other Differences There are several other, perhaps less important, differences between import quotas and import taxes. First, the equivalent ad valorem tariff rate of a quota tends to change with every shift in the foreign supply-of-exports schedule and the domestic demand-for-imports schedule. An ad valorem import tax, however, always remains constant (unless, of course, it is changed by the government). Similarly, when a tariff is imposed, the quantity of imports tends to change with every shift in the foreign supply-of-exports schedule and the domestic demand-for-imports schedule. Second, when a quota is imposed on an imported raw material (such as steel), the quota raises the costs of production of other final commodities (in whose production it is used as an input) and reduces their profitability on world markets, pretty much like a tariff on raw materials. But while the import taxes on raw materials are often returned to the producers of final goods in the form of export subsidies, no such subsidies are given in the case of quotas. Third, while the cost of a high tariff is quite visible to the consumers, the cost of a quota is not so visible because the equivalent tariff rate is not easily calculated. Thus, while consumers may complain about tariffs, they may ignore quotas. Finally, quotas are much more difficult to administer than tariffs; quotas tend to suspend the workings of the market mechanism and often carry the seeds of corruption and fraud. The valuable import licenses are arbitrarily allocated among importers who may even be willing to bribe eager government officials.

Export Quotas

A nation may also exploit its monopoly power in foreign trade by directly controlling the volume (or value) of its exports. The government may decree that only a given quantity (export quota) may be exported per unit of time. For this purpose, the government may issue export licenses, which it either sells to the country's exporters or simply gives away on a first-come, first-served basis.

Like an export tax, an export quota causes the price of the restricted commodity to rise in the foreign markets and fall in the domestic market. The margin between the domestic and foreign prices may accrue to the government of the restricting country in the form of export license fees; or it may accrue to domestic producers, to intermediaries, to foreign consumers, or even to the government officials who issue the licenses.

Note that for every export quota there is an equivalent export tax. Because of their equivalence and the symmetry between export taxes and import taxes, there exists also a symmetry between export and import quotas.

Voluntary Export Restraints

Voluntary export restraints (VER) are closely related to export and import quotas: The importing country (or countries) uses the threat of import taxes or import quotas to persuade foreign countries to "voluntarily" curtail their exports. This paradoxical situation usually combines elements of protectionist lobbying pressures with a desire on the part of the government of the importing country to conceal its protectionist intentions. For instance, since the 1950s the U.S. government has solicited the cooperation of foreign countries, particularly Japan, to voluntarily curb their exports to the United States of textiles, steel, automobiles, and other commodities. Apparently, the U.S. government, which was under heavy lobbying pressure to protect domestic producers, ruled out the usual protectionist devices of import taxes and import quotas and instead sought voluntary export restraints because of its role as the champion of free trade.

The effect of voluntary export restraints on the importing country's welfare is quite unfavorable. When implemented successfully, voluntary export restraints have all the economic effects of import quotas except that the "tariff equivalent revenue" usually accrues to the foreigners—the foreign suppliers are likely to collude and charge a monopoly price instead of charging the competitive price that exists in world markets.

Voluntary export restraints do not always work. The exporting nations often find ingenious ways of penetrating them. Three examples of VER penetration are as follows:

1 *Switching to unrestricted product categories.* For instance, the Republic of Korea voluntarily agreed to restrain its exports of nonrubber footwear to the United States during the period 1977–1981. By switching to rubber-soled shoes instead, Korea was actually able to *increase* the volume of footwear exports to the United States by 115 percent during the first year of restrictions. In addition, during the same period, footwear exporters from unrestricted countries increased their share of the U.S. market from 4 to 15 percent.

2 *Upgrading quality to increase the profit per unit exported.* This is illustrated by the sales of Japanese cars in the United States and Britain and the exports of clothing and footwear by developing nations.

3 *Setting up factories overseas in unrestricted countries.* For instance, as export restrictions on clothes made in Hong Kong diverted would-be buyers to producers in Bangladesh, Malaysia, and Thailand, Hong Kong firms set up factories overseas in order to evade the restrictions on their exports.

9-5 INTERNATIONAL CARTELS

So far we have studied cases in which a single country restricts its foreign trade unilaterally in one way or another. Yet nations may also restrict their trade multilaterally. Governments, or even private corporations located in various countries, may form an **international cartel,** that is, agree to effectively restrict competition among themselves in an effort to exploit their joint monopoly power. The world economy has a long history of international cartels in many goods and services, such as bauxite, coffee, diamonds, tobacco, and airline and railway services. The majority of cartels tend to disintegrate rapidly. The most notable exception is the Organization of Petroleum Exporting Countries (OPEC). This section deals briefly with the economic principles that govern such international monopolies.

Maximization of Monopoly Profits

The formation of an international cartel is in the first instance an attempt to reap greater profits. How can the cartel members maximize their aggregate profits? Merely by acting as a single profit-maximizing monopolist.

Figure 9-4 illustrates maximization of a cartel's profits. Schedule SS' shows the willingness of the cartel members as a group to supply (or export) to the rest of the world alternative quantities of the cartelized commodity (such as oil) at alternative prices. As the reader may recall from a course in microeconomics, this supply schedule is the horizontal summation of the marginal cost curves of the cartel members.

Demand schedule DD' shows the willingness of the rest of the world to import alternative quantities from the cartel at alternative prices. Thus, demand schedule DD' shows, at each price, the excess of the total domestic consumption over the total domestic production (of the cartelized commodity) of all nonmember countries as a group.

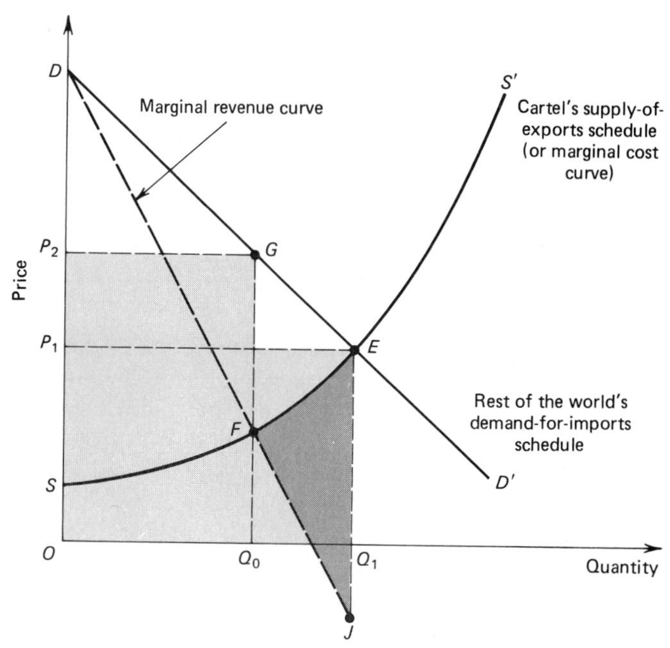

FIGURE 9-4 **Maximization of the cartel's profits.** Perfect competition leads to equilibrium at E, where the cartel's supply-of-exports schedule intersects the rest of the world's demand-for-imports schedule. To maximize profits, the cartel reduces exports from Q_1 to Q_0 and raises its price from P_1 to P_2. In particular, the cartel determines its monopoly exports at the intersection (*F*) of its marginal cost curve (which coincides with the supply-of-exports schedule) and marginal revenue curve (*DJ*). The total profits of the cartel increase by shaded triangular area *FEJ*.

Apparently, under perfect competition, international equilibrium occurs at point *E*, where demand schedule *DD'* intersects supply schedule *SS'*. Accordingly, under perfectly competitive conditions the cartel members as a group export amount Q_1 at equilibrium price P_1 to the rest of the world.

Suppose now that the cartel acts like a single monopolist. Draw the *marginal revenue curve,* as shown by dashed line *DJ,* and let it intersect the cartel's *marginal cost curve* at *F*. To maximize profits, the cartel must curtail its exports to Q_0 and raise its price to P_2. (Monopoly output is determined by the intersection of the marginal cost curve and the marginal revenue curve, that is, point *F;* and the monopoly price is determined from the demand curve at the monopoly output, that is, point *G*).

Shaded triangular area *FEJ* shows the *increase* in the total profits of the cartel members as a group. Thus, at competitive equilibrium point *E*, the cartel's marginal cost (Q_1E) is much higher than the marginal revenue. (Actually, in Figure 9-4 the marginal revenue is negative at the point of perfectly competitive exports, Q_1.) In fact, marginal cost is higher than marginal revenue for all units between Q_1 and Q_0. By curtailing its exports, the cartel "saves" each unit's marginal cost but "loses" the marginal revenue. Since between Q_1 and Q_0 each unit's marginal cost is higher than its marginal revenue, the cartel's profits continue to increase by the difference between marginal cost and marginal revenue until the cartel reduces its output to Q_0. Shaded triangular area *FEJ* merely shows the total increase in profits that results from the reduction in exports from Q_1 to Q_0.

Monopoly pricing by an international cartel interferes with the objective of maximizing world efficiency and potential welfare. Monopoly pricing violates an important Pareto-optimality condition, namely, the equality between marginal cost and price. Under monopoly pricing, the price is always higher than marginal cost, and this results in a suboptimal allocation of resources.

Note that the loss to the world is necessarily much bigger than the increase in the cartel's profits, that is, area *FEJ*. Resources would continue to be misallocated even if the cartel were to give back to the rest of the world the additional profits. Put differently, the rest of the world would be better off by making a direct income transfer to the cartel equal to area *FEJ* with the understanding that the cartel would return to the competitive equilibrium at *E*.

Conditions Necessary for a Successful Cartel

Economic theory identifies two conditions that are necessary for the success of an international cartel. They are the following:

1 The elasticity of demand for imports by the rest of the world must be low in the relevant price range.

2 The cartel members must adhere to the official set of policies (with respect to price and output) voted by the cartel members.

As shown in Appendix 12, the monopoly markup is equal to the reciprocal of the elasticity of demand for imports by the rest of the world at the monopoly price. To be able to achieve a substantial markup, the cartel must face a low elasticity of demand. This condition is actually a combination of the following three conditions:

- The elasticity of demand for total consumption (*not* imports) by the rest of the world must be low.
- The elasticity of supply of the cartelized commodity by the rest of the world (that is, nonmembers of the cartel) must also be low.
- The cartel must control a very large share of the world market for the cartelized commodity.

Turn now to condition 2. An international cartel can maintain a high monopoly price if individual cartel members do not selfishly attempt to capture more profits for themselves by behaving competitively. Each cartel member *does* face such a temptation. The reason is simple: At the monopoly equilibrium, the marginal cost (which presumably is the same for all cartel members) is much lower than the price. Hence, each individual cartel member has the illusion that it can increase its own profits by raising its *own* output—an illusion based on the naive assumption that other cartel members will not attempt to cheat in the same manner. When greedy cartel members behave in this manner, it becomes obvious that the cartel will not be able to effectively restrict output and raise the price. Experience shows that this is a most important reason for the eventual collapse of a cartel.

The behavior of greedy cartel members reminds one of a fable of Aesop. A dog had stolen a piece of meat and was crossing a river on his way home when he saw his own shadow reflected in the stream below. Thinking that it was another dog with a larger piece of meat, he snapped at the supposed treasure. In the process, he dropped the bit he was carrying, and so lost all.

9-6 OPEC

In 1960 the major oil exporters formed the Organization of Petroleum Exporting Countries (OPEC) in order to stabilize the price of oil. Initially, cartel membership was limited to five countries: Iran, Iraq, Kuwait, Saudi Arabia, and Venezuela. By 1973 eight additional countries (Algeria, Ecuador, Gabon, Indonesia, Libya, Nigeria, and the United Arab Emirates) had joined the cartel, and thus OPEC accounted for about two-thirds of world oil reserves and over 85 percent of total world crude oil exports—a remarkable concentration of power.

Initially, OPEC functioned quietly. But the serenity of the world oil markets was shattered in 1973 by the Arab-Israeli "Yom Kippur war." To pressure the West to restrain Israel, the Arab members of OPEC temporarily embargoed oil exports to the United States and other pro-Israeli countries. When the Arab oil embargo was lifted in 1974, OPEC took advantage of the temporary supply shortage to quadruple the price of crude oil within three months, from $2.59 to $11.65 a barrel. OPEC had finally learned how to exploit its enormous market power.

In 1978, because of the Iranian revolution, Iranian oil exports (about a fifth of all OPEC exports) almost disappeared completely, and the price of oil took another upward bound. The upward trend was further enhanced by the Iran-Iraq war, which caused yet another reduction in oil exports. By 1981 the price of Saudi Arabian light crude oil had climbed to $32 a barrel.

In the 1970s OPEC maintained the most lucrative monopoly in the history of the world. Many billions of dollars have been transferred from the oil-importing countries to the oil exporters. What accounted for the success of OPEC? The most important economic reason was the low elasticity of demand for imports of oil by the rest of the world, which reflected the influence of three factors: (1) The elasticity of demand for oil was very low because there were no good substitutes for oil (especially in the short run); (2) the elasticity of supply of oil by non-OPEC countries was also very low because oil exploration and production is a very time-consuming process; and (3) OPEC controlled most of the proven oil reserves and exports of the world. In addition, cheating by cartel members was unimportant—Saudi Arabia (the dominant cartel member) was always willing to adjust its own output to compensate for any occasional overproduction by other cartel members.

In the 1980s, OPEC ran into problems. Declining world demand (due to energy conservation measures) and rising output of non-OPEC countries (due to oil discoveries in the North Sea and Mexico and the completion of the Alaskan pipeline) caused OPEC's market share to shrink to about one-third, down from one-half in 1977. At the same time, most OPEC members developed enormous domestic needs for additional funds and Saudi Arabia stopped playing the role of the Good Samaritan. By 1988 the price of oil had been driven down to about $16 a barrel, and charges of cheating were heard louder than ever before. Nobody knows for sure how long the current oil glut will last.

9-7 THE VOLUNTARY EXPORT RESTRAINT ON JAPANESE AUTOS

Despite the relative success of Volkswagen in the late 1950s, the U.S. auto industry continued to be largely insulated in the 1960s from foreign competition, mainly because of the preference of American consumers for big cars. But the sharp oil price increases of the 1970s changed all that. Most American consumers reconsidered their love affair with the large gas-guzzling automobiles and decided to switch to smaller, more efficient cars. With the second oil shock of 1978–1979, fuel-efficient foreign cars, mostly Japanese, became more popular than ever, capturing almost 30 percent of the U.S. market. In 1980, the U.S. auto industry lost $4 billion on sales of 6.3 million cars. This performance, which was the worst in the industry's history, reflected the combined effect of a number of factors, such as regulation (ranging from seat belts to tougher emission standards), deteriorating product quality of U.S. automobiles relative to that of Japanese imports, and the higher wages of American auto workers relative to their Japanese counterparts. Like a wounded giant, the U.S. auto industry began to appeal for temporary protection from Japanese imports.

In 1981, President Ronald Reagan announced that the Japanese had agreed to "voluntarily" limit their automobile exports to the United States to 1.68 million units per year. The purpose of this voluntary export restraint was to buy the U.S. automobile industry and its workers time to adjust to the new rigors of world competition. By 1983, the industry generated more than $6 billion in after-tax profits; and on the surface, at least, the operation appeared to be successful. Yet there were hidden costs.

It has been estimated that the voluntary export restraint increased the earnings of the Japanese auto producers by $2 billion per year. Surely, an equivalent tariff instead would have been preferable to American taxpayers. In addition, employment creation was very expensive: The cost per job saved was nearly $160,000 per year!

In 1984–1985, the original quota was revised upward to 1.85 million units. When the agreement was finally allowed to expire in 1985, the Japanese government signified its intention to continue its export restriction, but at the higher ceiling of 2.3 million cars. Ironically, because of the rising value of the yen, Japanese auto exports to the United States declined 6.1 percent in 1987 to 2.2 million autos, and Japanese automakers will not be able to even fill their 1988 allotment. As a result, some Japanese officials argued that 1988 was a good time to scrap the restraints. However, the Japanese Ministry of International Trade and Industry (MITI) announced in January 1988 that the restrictions will continue because of rising protectionist sentiments in the U.S. Congress.

9-8 DUMPING

This section deals with the various forms of dumping and the economic policy problems that dumping raises.

Dumping is **international price discrimination.** It occurs when a monopolist (or imperfect competitor) charges a lower price to foreign buyers than to domestic customers for the same (or a comparable) commodity. (**Reverse dumping** occurs when foreign buyers pay a higher price than domestic buyers.) Successful price discrimination requires that the *different markets be separated from one another.* It should not be possible for traders to purchase from the monopolist commodities sold in the cheaper market and then resell them in the dearer market. Similarly, customers in the dearer market should not be able to transfer themselves into the cheaper market in order to benefit from the lower price. This condition is usually satisfied in international trade, as the domestic and foreign markets are separated from each other geographically and by tariff walls or other barriers to trade. The cost of transferring goods from the cheap, foreign market to the dearer, domestic market is usually prohibitive.

Types of Dumping

Economists usually distinguish among three different types of dumping: *persistent dumping, predatory dumping,* and *sporadic dumping.*

Persistent dumping arises from the pursuit of maximum profits by a monopolist who realizes that the domestic and foreign markets are disconnected by transportation costs, tariffs, and other trade barriers. Because the elasticity of demand for a commodity is usually higher in the world market than in the domestic market (mainly because of the greater availability of substitutes in the world market relative to the domestic market), the monopolist maximizes profits by charging a higher price to domestic customers (where the demand elasticity is low) than to foreign buyers (where the demand elasticity is high). This proposition is explained in Appendix 13.

Predatory dumping is usually classified as an "unfair method of competition" and the most harmful form of dumping. It occurs when a producer, in an effort to eliminate competitors and gain control of the foreign market, deliberately sells abroad at a reduced price for a short period of time. Assuming that this policy is successful and that all competitors go out of business, the producer later exploits the newly acquired monopoly power by substantially raising the price. Thus, predatory dumping is only *temporary* price discrimination; the main objective of the producer is to maximize long-run profits by increasing its monopoly power, even though this may involve short-run losses.

Sporadic dumping is occasional price discrimination by a producer who happens to have an occasional surplus due to overproduction (presumably because of excess capacity or unanticipated changes in market conditions or just bad production planning). To avoid spoiling the domestic market, the producer sells the occasional surplus to foreign buyers at reduced prices. Thus, sporadic dumping is very similar to "going out of business" sales by domestic retailers.

Note that export subsidies may be considered a form of (official) dumping because they effectively lower the prices charged to foreign buyers. For this reason, GATT prohibits export subsidies with respect to manufactures, except when the subsidies happen to be rebates of indirect taxes, such as sales taxes or import taxes on raw materials.

Because of the special status of agriculture, governments frequently practice dumping in order to dispose of accumulated surpluses of agricultural products. Thus, in an effort to support the domestic farmers, a government may institute a **price floor** well above the equilibrium price and purchase from the farmers, at the stipulated price floor, any quantity they cannot sell. Surely the government cannot sell any accumulated surplus to the domestic buyers, who buy all they want at the price floor from the farmers. The only viable option for the government is to sell the surplus to foreign buyers at reduced prices.

Economic Policy toward Dumping

Dumping, in all its forms, violates fundamental Pareto-optimality conditions, and for this reason is harmful to world welfare. On the one hand, a producer practicing dumping raises prices above the marginal cost (which is the basic evil of monopoly) and, on the other, charges different prices to different consumers.

Of course, sporadic dumping is only a temporary phenomenon, and economists tend to regard its (possible) effects on economic welfare as an insignificant nuisance. In fact, from the point of view of the importing country, sporadic dumping is not all that bad, since it provides benefits to the consumers (who temporarily pay lower prices) without causing any serious damage to the domestic industry.

Predatory dumping may have serious consequences on the welfare of the importing country by driving domestic producers out of business and penalizing consumers (in the long run) with much higher prices. Indeed, predatory dumping is the most harmful form of dumping.

Persistent dumping lies between the extremes of sporadic dumping and predatory dumping insofar as its effects on the welfare of the world in general and on the welfare of the importing country in particular are concerned.

Unfortunately, in practice it is extremely difficult to distinguish among the three types of dumping. As a result, economic policy is usually directed toward all dumping.

At least in the short run, any kind of dumping benefits the consumers of the importing country. Indeed, excluding the case of predatory dumping, one could argue that dumping raises the potential welfare of the importing country. Yet importing countries typically retaliate against dumping either by imposing antidumping, or countervailing, duties to offset the price differential or by threatening to do so. The main justification for this is the immense pressure put on the governments of the importing countries by their domestic producers, who seek protection against the unfair foreign competition.

In the United States, antidumping legislation dates back to the Anti-Dumping Act of 1921. The 1974 Trade Act provides that the U.S. government may impose countervailing duties or other restrictions under two conditions: (1) The U.S. Treasury Department must first determine that an imported commodity is being sold in the United States at a price that is lower than the price prevailing in the exporting country, and (2) the International Trade Commission must testify on the basis of an extensive investigation that U.S. industry "is being or is likely to be *injured* or is prevented from being established" by reason of such imports (italics added).

Dumping in Action: Some Recent Cases

During the turbulent 1970s, the United States experienced many cases of dumping. Japan was accused of dumping steel and television sets, and European automobile manufacturers were accused of dumping cars. Most of these dumpers eventually raised their prices in order to avoid countervailing duties. Nevertheless, countervailing duties were applied against several commodities, such as Brazilian handbags and Italian glass.

More recently, the United States retaliated against dumping of semiconductor chips by Japanese manufacturers. In the spring of 1987, punitive tariffs were imposed on $300 million of annual imports of a variety of Japanese products, such as computers, color television sets, and power tools. Most of these punitive tariffs were lifted in November 1987 after the Reagan administration became convinced that the Japanese were no longer setting unfairly low prices for their goods in foreign markets.

Another recent case of dumping involved South Korean automobiles. In November 1987 Canada's revenue department ruled that Hyundai cars had been dumped on the Canadian market and imposed stiff provisional import duties on the South Korean vehicles. These provisional duties were supposed to offset the **margin of dumping,** which the revenue department estimated at 37.3 percent for Hyundai's Pony car, 36.6 percent for the Stellar car, and 35 percent for the Exel model. However, in March 1988, the Canadian Import Tribunal determined that the dumping of Hyundai cars "has not caused, is not causing and is not likely to cause material injury" to Canadian production. As a result, the antidumping duties have been removed.

9-9 OTHER NONTARIFF BARRIERS

Nations may interfere with the free flow of trade in several other ways. These additional nontariff barriers include exchange control (used extensively by developing countries), technical and administrative protection, and government procurement policies. We discuss exchange control in Part Two. In this section, we restrict our comments to technical and administrative protection and government procurement policies.

Technical, Administrative, and Other Regulations

There are countless government rules and regulations that either intentionally or unintentionally impede the free flow of trade. Such technical and administrative rules include formalities of customs clearance, safety regulations (such as safety specifications for automobiles, tractors, and electrical equipment), health regulations (such as laws that provide for the production of food under hygienic conditions), labeling requirements (such as mark of origin), and technical standards. While many of these regulations serve legitimate objectives, they are frequently offered as an excuse for restricting trade.

Government Procurement Policies

Governments buy huge amounts of goods and services, and their procurement policies have a substantial effect on the free flow of trade. All governments tend to buy domestic products. This tendency was intensified in the 1930s under the slogans "Buy American," "Buy British," and "Buy French."

Under our Buy American Act of 1933, the U.S. government is required to favor domestic suppliers unless their prices are unreasonably high. But what is an "unreasonably high" price? Initially, a domestic price was considered unreasonable if it was higher than a corresponding foreign price by more than 6 percent. Since 1962 the price differential has been raised to 50 percent, at least for defense contracts. However, in December 1979 the United States (and other nations) formally signed the Tokyo Round trade liberalization agreement, which repealed "Buy American" laws.

Besides the desire to protect domestic producers, there are several reasons a government may want to do its shopping at home. First, the government pays no tariffs; hence a small price advantage given to domestic suppliers merely restores the degree of protection implied for them in the nation's tariff schedule. Second, for political and military reasons a government may just refuse to buy military equipment from a foe. Finally, for reasons of national prestige a government may prefer to use domestically produced commodities, such as automobiles and airplanes. In doing so, however, the government pays a higher price, which is economically inefficient.

9-10 THE POITIERS PLAN

In 1981 France was importing more than 64,000 videocassette recorders (VCRs) per month, mostly from Japan. To stem this huge influx of VCRs, the French devised a diabolic plan. In October 1982, the French government decreed that all imports of VCRs would have to pass through the small town of Poitiers, which is located hundreds of miles inland from France's northern ports. But the inconvenience of transporting a shipment of VCRs to Poitiers was only the beginning. Poitiers had a tiny customs crew, who insisted on strictly enforcing a myriad of customs regulations. For instance, all documents of each shipment were checked for accuracy, many VCRs were taken out of their boxes for inspection of their serial numbers, and some VCRs were dismantled to make sure they were actually built in their reported country of origin.

The monstrous "Poitiers plan" became a nightmare for VCR importers. It took two to three months to clear a truckload of VCRs, compared to one day before the introduction of the new policy. The effect on VCR imports was immediate. After the plan was inaugurated, less than 10,000 VCRs cleared the Poitiers customs each month, while the rest of the supply waited in bonded warehouses throughout the town.

Japan filed a complaint with GATT and then suspended or curbed VCR shipments to France. Denmark, Germany, and the Netherlands, which also export VCRs to France, complained to the executive committee of the European Community (EC), which in turn brought charges against France at the European Court of Justice for breach of EC free-trade rules.

Source: The World Bank, *World Development Report 1987*, Oxford University Press, New York, 1987, p. 141.

9-11 HIGHLIGHTS OF U.S. TARIFF HISTORY AND TRADE LIBERALIZATION

Since the Great Depression of the 1930s, the nations of the world have made tremendous progress toward trade liberalization. This progress is fundamentally due to two factors: (1) the liberal mood of the United States embodied in the Reciprocal Trade Agreements Act of 1934 and later legislation and (2) the development, after World War II, of international organizations, such as the General Agreement on Tariffs and Trade (GATT), which have provided the institutional framework for multilateral negotiations. In this section, we briefly review some of these developments.

The Trade Agreements Act of 1934

During the early 1930s, U.S. exports fell sharply. There were two reasons for this. First, the total volume of world trade declined significantly because of the Great Depression. Second, the Smoot-Hawley Tariff Act of 1930 raised the average duty on imports to an all-time high (53 percent) and provoked foreign retaliation, which in turn caused a further reduction in U.S. exports. The U.S. relative share of world trade decreased in the face of a dwindling absolute volume of world trade. Against this background, and in an effort to boost sagging U.S. exports, the U.S. Congress in 1934 passed the Trade Agreements Act, which basically reflected the change in U.S. attitudes toward free trade. The principles embodied in the Trade Agreements Act have remained the basis of U.S. commercial policy in all subsequent legislation.

The Trade Agreements Act of 1934 removed the formulation of U.S. commercial policy from the political atmosphere of the Congress and transferred it to the President. Further, the bill authorized the President to negotiate agreements with foreign nations to lower tariff rates as much as 50 percent of the rates set under the Smoot-Hawley Act. The Trade Agreements Act was founded on two important principles: First, any tariff reductions should be mutual; and second, the bilaterally agreed-upon tariff cuts should be extended to all trading partners—a provision that became known as the **most-favored-nation principle.** The Trade Agreements Act was repeatedly renewed (a total of 11 times) until it was finally replaced by the Trade Expansion Act of 1962. Under the authority of the Trade Agreements Act and its renewals, the United States achieved significant tariff reductions. By 1940 the United States had signed bilateral trade agreements with 20 foreign nations, and by 1947 the tariff rates that prevailed in 1934 had been cut in half.

Despite the apparent success of the Trade Agreements Act, it soon became evident that the trade liberalization process suffered from a severe drawback: Because of both the **bilateral approach** to tariff reductions and the most-favored-nation principle, there were in general too many third countries that benefited from the bilateral trade agreements between the United States and its partners. These free-rider countries benefited from the lower tariff rates negotiated between the United States and its partners without having to make any reciprocal concessions of their own. To avoid this drawback, the United States and its partners restricted their tariff concessions to commodities that typically dominated bilateral trade so that only minor suppliers could benefit from the most-favored-nation rule. This severe constraint imposed by the bilateral approach was eventually removed as countries adopted the **multilateral approach** to tariff bargaining.

The General Agreement on Tariffs and Trade (GATT)

After World War II and against the background of the international upheaval of the 1930s, the trading nations of the world proposed (at the 1947–1948 U.N. Conference on Trade and Employment in Havana) the creation of an International Trade Organization (ITO) to promote international cooperation in trade, to settle disputes over commercial policy, and to move toward freer trade. The U.S. Congress, however, refused to ratify this proposal, and the International Trade Organization never became fact. As a substitute for the stillborn ITO, the trading nations successfully negotiated the formation of another organization, known as the General Agreement on Tariffs and Trade (GATT). This new organization (which is headquartered in Geneva, Switzerland) was created by an executive intergovernmental agreement that did not require congressional approval, as its authority emanated from the Trade Agreements Act of 1934 and later legislation.

Although GATT is not a comprehensive commercial policy code, it rests on three fundamental principles:

1 The **principle of nondiscrimination** that is embodied in the unconditional most-favored-nation clause. This principle is the cornerstone of GATT. Its significance is due to two factors: First, discrimination interferes with the efficient allocation of resources and the maximization of world welfare; and second, discrimination provokes retaliation. However, there are some important exceptions to most-favored-nation treatment: customs unions, free-trade areas, and preferential treatment for trade between a country and its colonies or dominions.

2 The principle that **countries must use tariffs rather than nontariff means** (such as quotas) to protect their domestic industry. There are, however, two important exceptions to this principle: First, countries may use quotas to protect their domestic agriculture; and second, countries may use nontariff measures (such as quotas and export subsidies) to deal with balance-of-payments difficulties.

3 The **principle of consultation** in solving disputes among nations over commercial policy. Indeed, GATT has provided the institutional framework within which the nations of the world have conducted important multilateral negotiations on tariff reductions.

Note also that GATT has two special provisions for the developing countries: (1) The developing countries receive preferential treatment by the industrial nations (which actually is a violation of the most-favored-nation principle), and (2) they obtain all concessions exchanged among industrial nations without any reciprocity.

Under the aegis of GATT, nations have successfully negotiated significant tariff cuts during the post-World War II era. The first major tariff cut occurred in 1947, when the average U.S. tariff dropped by about 20 percent. In each of the following four rounds of negotiations (1947–1962) there were small tariff reductions (4 percent or less).

Economists cite several factors for the meager tariff cuts at these multilateral negotiations. First, in 1947 many tariffs were abnormally high. After these high tariffs were negotiated down to normal levels, import-competing producers began to complain against further cuts, and governments became reluctant to bargain further significant cuts. This lobbying effort actually suited the purposes of governments that wanted to maintain some tariffs for future bargaining. Further, countries whose tariffs were already reduced to low levels could not induce foreigners to negotiate further cuts—they had very little to offer in exchange. Also, the formation of the European Community in 1957 complicated matters further—the members of the Community were reluctant to reduce their common external tariff on a product-by-product basis. Finally, the U.S. Congress attached restrictive provisions (escape clause and peril point provisions) to renewals of the Trade Agreements Act of 1934, which made it very difficult for the President to negotiate significant tariff reductions.

Escape Clause and Peril Point Provisions

As we have just seen, the trend toward trade liberalization that began in the 1930s was suppressed in the 1950s by the protectionist devices that the U.S. Congress tagged onto renewals of the Trade Agreements Act. These protectionist devices were of two types: general and specific. General protectionist devices were those that offered protection to all domestic industries "injured" by import competition. The general devices included the **escape clause** and the **peril point provisions.** Specific protectionist devices were those that offered protection to particular industries, such as agriculture.

Incidentally, an important example of a specific protectionist device is the **national security clause,** which blocks action to reduce a duty and even permits withdrawal of concessions when the import-competing industry is essential to national defense. But as noted in Chapter 8, the best policy for achieving a production goal is a direct production subsidy to the affected industry, not tariff protection.

Peril point provisions essentially prevented the President from negotiating reductions that could bring the U.S. tariff rates to such low levels as to cause serious damage to the domestic industry. The escape clause went further. *After* the negotiations were concluded, the escape clause permitted any domestic industry that claimed injury from import competition to petition the U.S. Tariff Commission (now known as the International Trade Commission) for relief. In those cases in which the Tariff Commission determined that serious injury had occurred, it recommended to the President to raise the tariff again. (Actually, until 1962, domestic industries could claim serious injury on the basis of a shrinking market share alone, irrespective of whether their absolute volume of production had also *in*creased.)

The escape clause dealt a devastating blow to the trade liberalization process. In essence, the escape clause was promising foreign nations no less than this: that no tariff concessions would be permitted to remain effective unless such concessions were considered to be insignificant.

The 1962 Trade Expansion Act and the Kennedy Round

Partly because of the no-injury doctrine that was embodied in the peril point provisions and the escape clause and partly because of the formation of the European Community, which created a new situation and posed a new negotiating challenge, the U.S. Congress in 1962 passed the Trade Expansion Act, which had two important features:

1 The act gave the President the authority to negotiate *across-the-board* tariff reductions of as much as 50 percent of their 1962 level. This across-the-board approach replaced the product-by-product approach of the Trade Agreements Act that was choking tariff negotiations.

2 The act also launched, for the first time, an **adjustment assistance program** to relocate and retrain workers who became unemployed because of tariff concessions and to provide aid (such as low-interest loans, technical assistance, and tax relief) to eligible firms. The 1962 act recognized the superiority of direct adjustment assistance over import restriction to those workers and firms injured by increased imports. For this reason, the act did not include any peril point provisions.

The principle of adjustment assistance is most significant. Free trade improves the potential welfare of the world as well as the welfare of each trading country. However, free trade necessarily hurts some domestic groups, as the Stolper-Samuelson theorem reminds us, even though the welfare of the entire nation improves. In principle, those who gain from free trade can indeed compensate those who lose so that free trade can improve the welfare of everybody. Until 1962 such compensation was discussed as a theoretical possibility only. In actual practice, the losers had to swallow their pride and their losses and move along to other, more profitable ventures while the rest of the society enjoyed the benefits of free trade. No wonder, then, that there have always been groups that opposed free trade and lobbied for trade restriction. The main objective of the adjustment assistance program was to correct this anomaly.

The adjustment assistance program that was launched by the 1962 act did not become a success overnight, particularly because of the narrow eligibility criteria used by the Tariff Commission. Indeed, until 1969, nobody qualified for aid, and frustrated labor unions complained that the displaced workers had been betrayed. In the following years the eligibility criteria were relaxed, and adjustment assistance was provided generously.

Under the aegis of GATT and the authority of the 1962 Trade Expansion Act, the United States and other industrial nations negotiated wide-ranging tariff reductions in the **Kennedy Round,** which was completed in 1967. In particular, the industrial nations of the world agreed to cut their 1962 tariff rates an average of approximately 35 percent. Although this agreed-upon reduction fell short of the maximum reduction of 50 percent that was authorized by Congress, the Kennedy Round was justifiably considered to be a remarkable achievement.

The Trade Reform Act of 1974 and the Tokyo Round

The 1962 Trade Expansion Act was replaced in 1974 by the Trade Reform Act, which gave the President the authority to negotiate tariff reductions up to a maximum of 60 percent of the post-Kennedy Round rates (and to eliminate completely rates of 5 percent or less). In addition, the act authorized the President to negotiate the reduction of nontariff barriers—a major innovation.

Several other provisions of the 1974 act are also noteworthy. The new legislation considerably liberalized the eligibility criteria for adjustment assistance. Indeed, the 1974 act reaffirmed the superiority of adjustment assistance over trade restrictions and did not include any peril point provisions. Further, it changed the antidumping provisions to conform with the rules of GATT. (Essentially this means that countervailing duties can be imposed only after determining that the domestic producers have actually been injured by foreign price discrimination.) The act also authorized the President to extend most-favored-nation treatment to foreign countries that in 1974 did not enjoy such treatment (such as communist China). Finally, the act offered a "Generalized System of Preferences" to "beneficiary" developing nations with respect to "eligible" products. In particular, it granted duty-free entry to the exports of developing countries with respect to manufactures, semimanufactures, and selected other products. However, the definitions of "beneficiary country" and particularly "eligible product" are quite restrictive. For instance, duty-free treatment cannot be given to textiles and apparel, watches, shoes, certain kinds of electronic products, steel, and glass products, nor to any other article subject to import-relief measures. Indeed, the act requires the withdrawal of preferential treatment from any article that becomes subject to import-relief or national security actions.

Under the authority of the Trade Reform Act of 1974, the United States participated in the **Tokyo Round** of multilateral trade negotiations. These negotiations, which were concluded in Geneva in April 1979, were conducted within the framework of GATT. (The Tokyo Round received its name from the fact that these negotiations were formally inaugurated in Tokyo in September 1973, even though the actual negotiations took place in Geneva.) The Tokyo Round negotiations were conducted on the basis of broad commodity categories rather than on a product-by-product basis. The negotiated tariff cuts averaged 31 percent for the United States, 27 percent for the European Community, 28 percent for Japan, and 34 percent for Canada. Most of the cuts were phased in over a period of eight years beginning January 1, 1980, mainly because every country, including the United States, took special care to protect certain "sensitive" industries from sharp tariff reductions. For example, U.S. tariff cuts on textiles, steel, and some chemical products did not take place until January 1, 1982.

The Trade Bill of 1988

The persistent U.S. trade deficit (see Section 12-7) intensified protectionist pressures, which threatened to disrupt the world trading system. The protectionist wave was by no means limited to the United States. Following the second oil shock of 1979, the western industrial nations slid into a deep recession. As a result, 30 million workers lost their jobs and world trade slumped. Ironically, nations that in the Tokyo Round pledged themselves to move toward freer trading relations began to move the other way. Autos, steel, and textiles headed a long list of industries that successfully sought import restraints in a multitude of countries. Many U.S. politicians justified their protectionist sentiments by pointing to the protectionist and "unfair" trade practices of Japan, South Korea, Taiwan, and other East Asian economies. These politicians demanded "fair trade," as opposed to "free trade"; they argued that the western nations must break open the labyrinthine distribution networks that these countries weave to keep foreign competition at bay. Several economists also supported the shift toward protectionism.

In August 1988 the U.S. Congress passed, and President Ronald Reagan signed into law, a new trade bill, which is expected by its authors and supporters to be instrumental in opening foreign markets and restoring U.S. competitiveness. The bill tightens U.S. procedures for handling alleged unfair trade practices by foreign countries and narrows presidential discretion to avoid retaliation in such cases. However, the bill's most protectionist features (included in earlier versions) were either scrapped or watered down. Indeed, Congressman Richard Gephardt, who had based his presidential campaign largely on a tough trade stance, voted against the bill because, as he said, he considered it weak.

The 1988 trade bill does not represent a major shift in trade policy. It contains no significant tariff increases or new quotas, and it erects no major new trade barriers. In many cases, the bill lowers tariffs. Some of the important provisions of the 1988 trade bill are as follows:

1 The bill requires presidential action against countries with consistent patterns of unfair trade practices. The administration must begin unfair-trade investigations of such countries but has some discretion in deciding whether to retaliate and how.

2 The bill directs the President to initiate expedited unfair-trade actions in certain cases of foreign pirating of U.S. patents and copyrights.

3 The bill expands the President's authority to engage in trade talks. In particular, it authorizes the President to complete, probably by 1990, the current **Uruguay Round** of world trade negotiations, which began in 1986.

4 The bill increases presidential options for relief to domestic industries harmed by imports. To win import relief, a company must show that such relief would help it adjust and become more competitive.

5 The bill authorizes a new program for retraining displaced workers at an annual cost of $980 million. It also expands existing programs to help adjustment of workers who lose jobs to imports.

6 The bill provides additional export subsidies for agricultural products at a total cost of more than $2 billion.

7 The bill reduces or eliminates U.S. duties on dozens of products for which there is no U.S. source.

8 The bill gives a legal mandate for the current U.S. practice of coordinating economic policies and exchange-rate strategies with other major nations.

Average U.S. Tariff Rates

Figure 9-5 gives a bird's-eye view of the history of average U.S. tariff rates during the twentieth century. The dark line represents the behavior of the average tariff rate on dutiable imports only. The light line shows the tariff rate as a percentage of total imports.

The average U.S. tariff rate on dutiable imports peaked at 59.06 percent in 1932 under the Smoot-Hawley Tariff Act of 1930. (The peak attained in 1932 was surpassed only in 1830, when the U.S. tariff rate averaged 61.69 percent under the Tariff of Abominations of 1828.) Since 1971, the average U.S. tariff rate on dutiable imports has remained below 10 percent. Note that the data fail to reflect the dispersion of tariff rates across industries as well as the importance of nontariff barriers.

9-12 SUMMARY

1 To restrict the flow of their imports, nations may impose import duties or import quotas; to restrict the flow of their exports, nations may impose export duties or export quotas.

2 Export subsidies are negative export taxes, and their microeconomic effects are opposite to the corresponding effects of export taxes. The terms-of-trade effect of export subsidies is generally unfavorable.

3 In a long-run, static-equilibrium model, a general export tax has the same effects as a general import tax of the same ad valorem percentage (Lerner's symmetry theorem). A similar symmetry exists between export and import quotas.

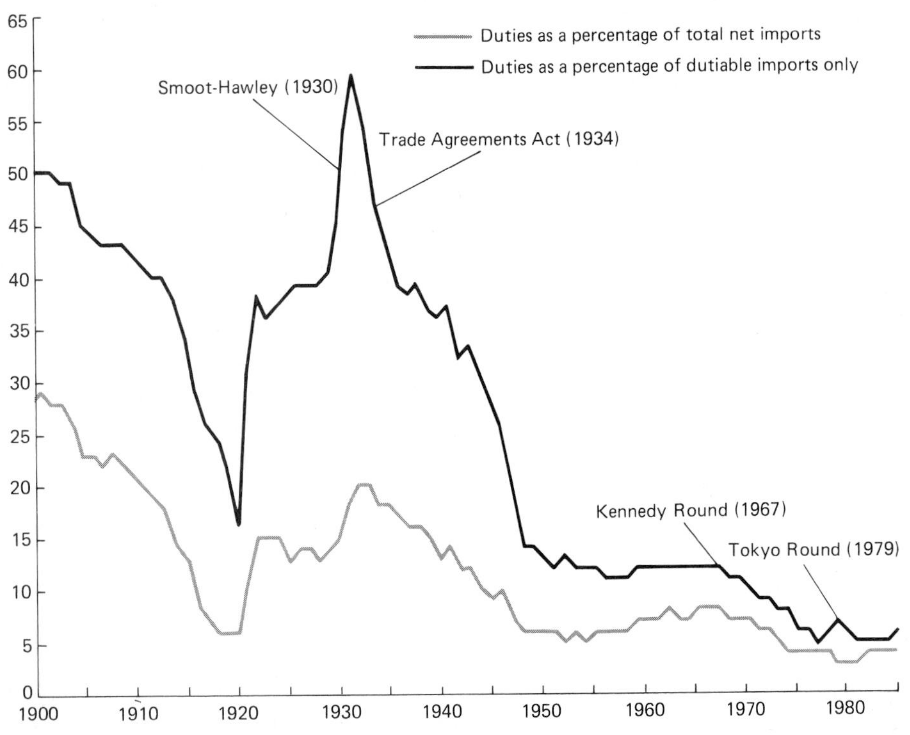

FIGURE 9-5 **Average U.S. tariff rates, 1900–1985.** (*U.S. Department of Commerce, Bureau of the Census,* Historical Abstract of the United States: Colonial Times to 1970, *U.S. Government Printing Office, Washington, D.C., 1976, series U207–212, p. 888; and* Statistical Abstract of the United States, *U.S. Government Printing Office, Washington, D.C., 1987, table 1410, p. 799.*) The average U.S. tariff rate on dutiable imports peaked at 59.06 percent in 1932 under the Smoot-Hawley Tariff Act of 1930 but has remained below 10 percent since 1971.

4 A quota is a quantitative restriction on the volume of imported goods. To avoid the many disadvantages of an open (or global) quota, governments usually issue import licenses.

5 For every import quota there is an equivalent import tax. The microeconomic effects of an import quota are the same as those of an equivalent import tax. However, there are important differences between quotas and tariffs: The quota profit need not accrue to the domestic government; an import quota is more certain than a tariff; when the foreign supply-of-exports schedule is perfectly inelastic, a tariff cannot raise the domestic price; and an import quota may convert a potential into an actual monopoly, while a tariff cannot.

6 Under a voluntary export restraint, the importing country solicits the cooperation of foreign countries to voluntarily curb their exports. The effect on the importing country's welfare is unfavorable—the "tariff-equivalent revenue" usually accrues to the foreigners.

7 Two conditions are necessary for the success of an international cartel: (a) The elasticity of demand for imports by the rest of the world must be low; and (b) the cartel members must adhere to the official set of policies, that is, they must avoid cheating. Condition (a) is a combination of three conditions: (i) The demand elasticity for total consumption by the rest of the world must be low, (ii) the elasticity of supply by the rest of the world must be low, and (iii) the cartel must control a very large share of the world market.

8 Dumping is international price discrimination (that is, selling a commodity to foreign buyers at a price that is lower than the price charged to domestic customers). Dumping is possible because the foreign and domestic markets are separated from each other geographically and by tariff walls or other barriers to trade; hence, the cost of transferring goods from the cheap foreign market to the dearer, domestic market is prohibitive.

9 Dumping can be: (a) persistent (arising from the pursuit of maximum profits and from the fact that the foreign demand elasticity is higher than the domestic); (b) predatory (occurring when a producer sells abroad at reduced prices until control is gained of the foreign market, at which point the producer raises the price substantially); or (c) sporadic (occurring when a producer sells an occasional surplus to foreigners at reduced prices in order to avoid spoiling the domestic market).

10 Dumping violates Pareto-optimality conditions and is harmful to world welfare. At least in the short run, however, dumping benefits the consumers of the importing countries. Yet importing countries typically retaliate against dumping because of the pressure put on them by domestic producers who seek protection.

11 Other nontariff barriers to trade include exchange control, technical and administrative protection, and government procurement policies.

12 The Trade Agreements Act of 1934 was founded on two principles: (a) Tariff reductions should be mutual, and (b) bilateral tariff reductions should be extended to all trading partners (most-favored-nation principle).

13 The General Agreement of Tariffs and Trade (GATT) rests on three principles: (a) nondiscrimination, (b) consultation, and (c) use of tariffs rather than nontariff measures. (This last principle applies to a country's means of protecting its industry, except agriculture; however, the country may use nontariff measures to cope with balance-of-payments difficulties.)

14 In the 1950s the U.S. Congress tagged onto renewals of the Trade Agreements Act two types of protectionist devices: (a) general devices (such as the escape clause and the peril point provisions) and (b) specific devices (such as protection to agriculture and the national security clause).

15 The Trade Expansion Act of 1962 (which replaced the Trade Agreements Act of 1934) had two features: (a) It gave the President the authority to negotiate across-the-board tariff reductions of as much as 50 percent of their 1962 level, and (b) it provided for adjustment assistance to workers and firms injured by increased imports (a major innovation). The act did not include any peril point provisions. Under the aegis of GATT and the authority of the Trade Expansion Act, the United States negotiated tariff cuts of 35 percent of the 1962 tariff rates with other industrial nations (Kennedy Round).

16 The Trade Reform Act of 1974 (which replaced the Trade Expansion Act) gave the President the authority to negotiate: (a) tariff reductions of as much as 60 percent of the post-Kennedy Round rates and (b) the reduction of nontariff barriers (a major innovation). In addition, the 1974 act liberalized the eligibility criteria for adjustment assistance and did not include any peril point provisions. Under the authority of the Trade Reform Act, the United States participated in the Tokyo Round of multilateral trade negotiations. The tariff cuts were similar in form and size to those in the Kennedy Round.

17 The trade bill of 1988 does not represent a major shift in trade policy.

PROBLEMS[1]

1 Liberia's domestic supply and demand functions for timber are as follows:

$$p = 5 + 0.05Q_s \qquad \text{(supply function)}$$

$$p = 100 - 0.90Q_d \qquad \text{(demand function)}$$

where p is price (in dollars), Q_s is quantity supplied, and Q_d is quantity demanded. The world price of timber is $30 per unit.

a Determine the equilibrium price and quantity of timber in autarky.

b Determine the quantity of free-trade domestic output and consumption of timber as well as Liberia's volume of exports.

c The government of Liberia imposes an export tax of $5 per unit of timber. Determine the effects of the export tax on the domestic price, output, and consumption of timber as well as Liberia's exports.

d Determine the effects of the export tax on the distribution of income. What is the deadweight loss of the export tax?

2 Europe's domestic supply and demand functions for wheat are as follows:

$$Q_s = -20 + 2p \qquad \text{(supply function)}$$

$$Q_d = 300 - 8p \qquad \text{(demand function)}$$

where Q_s is quantity supplied, Q_d is quantity demanded, and p is price (in dollars). The foreign supply of exports of wheat to Europe is given by the following function:

$$X = 18p - 100$$

where X is the volume of foreign exports.

a Derive Europe's import demand function.

b Determine Europe's free-trade price and volume of imports of wheat. Determine, also, Europe's domestic volume of output and consumption of wheat.

c Europe imposes an import quota that limits imports to 100 bushels of wheat. De-

[1]Problems that appear with asterisks are more difficult.

termine the effects of the import quota on the domestic price, output, and consumption of wheat as well as Europe's volume of imports.

d Calculate the effects of the quota on consumer surplus and producer surplus. Determine, also, the maximum revenue collected by the government from the auctioning of import licenses.

e Illustrate your answers graphically.

3 Suppose that the marginal cost functions of Brazil and Colombia in the production of coffee are as follows:

$$MC = 2 + 0.01Q_b \qquad \text{(Brazil)}$$

$$MC = 5 + 0.02Q_c \qquad \text{(Colombia)}$$

where MC is marginal cost (in dollars) and Q_b and Q_c are the coffee outputs of Brazil and Colombia, respectively. For simplicity, assume that domestic coffee consumption in Brazil and Colombia is zero. The import demand for coffee by the rest of the world is given by the following equation:

$$D = 1565 - 5p$$

where D is the quantity of imports and p is the price (in dollars).

a Determine the competitive export supply function of coffee by Brazil and Colombia combined.

b Determine the competitive price and volume of exports of coffee.

c Brazil and Colombia form a cartel. At what price and volume of exports are the cartel's profits maximized? What is the total profit? (Note: Assume that fixed costs are zero.)

d How is the profit-maximizing volume of exports divided between Brazil and Colombia? If each country keeps its export revenue, how is the total profit of the cartel distributed between Brazil and Colombia?

e Explain why Brazil (and alternatively, Colombia) would have an incentive to cheat on the cartel agreement.

f Illustrate your conclusions graphically.

***4** Korea's auto production is in the hands of a single corporation, the Hyundai Motor Company. The marginal cost of production of Hyundai is constant at $5,000. Along Korea's domestic demand curve for autos, the elasticity of demand is -2 at all points. The corresponding elasticity of the foreign import demand for autos is -3 at all points.

a Is there any economic reason for Hyundai to practice dumping? Why or why not?

b What prices should Hyundai charge in the domestic and foreign markets in order to maximize its total profit?

SUGGESTED READING

Adams, W., et al. (1979). *Tariffs, Quotas and Trade: The Politics of Protectionism.* Institute for Contemporary Studies, San Francisco.

Baldwin, R. E. (1985). *The Political Economy of U.S. Import Policy.* The MIT Press, Cambridge, Mass.

Baldwin, R. E., and J. D. Richardson (1986). *International Trade and Finance: Readings,* 3rd ed., parts II–V. Little, Brown and Company, Boston.

Bhagwati, J. (1965). "On the Equivalence of Tariffs and Quotas." In R. E. Baldwin et al. (eds.), *Trade, Growth and the Balance of Payments: Essays in Honor of Gottfried Haberler,* Rand McNally & Company, Chicago.

Cline, W. R. (1987). *The Future of World Trade in Textiles and Apparel.* Institute for International Economics, Washington, D.C.

Crandall, R. W. (1984). "Import Quotas and the Automobile Industry: The Costs of Protectionism." *The Brookings Review,* vol. 2 (Summer), pp. 8–16.

Goldstein, J. L., and S. D. Krasner (1984). "Unfair Trade Practices: The Case for a Differential Response." *American Economic Review,* Papers and Proceedings, vol. 74 (May), pp. 282–287.

Golt, S. (1978). *The GATT Negotiations, 1973–79: The Closing Stage.* National Planning Association, Washington, D.C.

Jones, R. W., and P. B. Kenen, eds. (1984). *Handbook of International Economics,* vol. 1. North-Holland, New York, chaps. 11 (A. O. Krueger) and 12 (R. E. Baldwin).

Kindleberger, C. P. (1975). "Quantity and Price, Especially in Financial Markets." *Quarterly Review of Economics and Business,* vol. 15, no. 2 (Summer), pp. 7–19.

Lerner, A. P. (1936). "The Symmetry between Import and Export Taxes." *Economica,* vol. 3, no. 11 (August), pp. 306–313. Reprinted in R. E. Caves and H. G. Johnson (eds.), American Economic Association *Readings in International Economics,* Richard D. Irwin, Inc., Homewood, Ill., 1968.

Tarr, D. G., and M. E. Morkre (1984). *Aggregate Costs to the United States of Tariffs and Quotas on Imports: General Tariff Cuts and Removal of Quotas on Automobiles, Steel, Sugar, and Textiles.* Federal Trade Commission, Washington, D.C.

CHAPTER **10**

CUSTOMS UNIONS

Basically there are two approaches to international trade liberalization: the **international approach** and the **regional approach.** The international approach involves international conferences under the aegis of GATT, such as the Kennedy Round and the Tokyo Round. The purpose of these international conferences is to reduce tariff and nontariff barriers to international trade worldwide. The regional approach involves agreements among small numbers of nations whose purpose is to establish free trade among themselves while maintaining barriers to trade with the rest of the world. The European Community and the recent Free Trade Agreement between Canada and the United States are prominent examples of such **preferential trading arrangements,** as these agreements are collectively known.

Even though the formation of preferential trading arrangements may be influenced more by political factors than by economic factors, such regional trading groups raise a number of interesting economic questions. Does the formation of regional trading groups represent a movement toward freer trade or greater protection? Do preferential trading arrangements enhance the economic efficiency and welfare of the world as a whole? Will the Free Trade Agreement benefit both Canada and the United States? Will the rest of the world lose? Answers to these questions are provided in this chapter, which deals with the partial equilibrium approach to preferential trading. (The general equilibrium approach is beyond the scope of the book.)

10-1 PREFERENTIAL TRADING ARRANGEMENTS: SOME DEFINITIONS

Preferential trading arrangements may assume several forms. We can distinguish among five such arrangements: **preferential trading club, free-trade**

area, customs union, common market, and **economic union**. These trading arrangements start at the lowest degree of economic integration (that is, preferential trading club) and go through progressively higher stages to the most complete degree of economic integration (that is, economic union). In this section we explore the meaning of these forms of regional integration and introduce several terms that have come into fairly standard usage.

Preferential Trading Club

Two or more countries form a *preferential trading club* when they *reduce* their respective duties on imports of all goods (except the services of capital) from each other, that is, when they exchange small tariff preferences. The member countries retain their original tariffs against the outside world.

In 1932, Great Britain and its Commonwealth associates, encompassing approximately one-fourth of the earth's land surface and population, established a system of trade known as the **Commonwealth Preference System.** Under it, the Commonwealth countries lowered their tariff rates on their mutual trade (that is, imports from other Commonwealth countries) but retained their higher tariff rates on imports from the rest of the world. The 48-nation association of Britain and its former colonies is a good historical example of a preferential trading club.

Free-Trade Area (or Association)

Two or more countries form a *free-trade area,* or a **free-trade association,** when they *abolish* all import duties (and all quantitative restrictions) on their mutual trade in all goods (except the services of capital) but retain their original tariffs against the rest of the world.

An example of a free-trade area is the European Free Trade Area (EFTA), which was created by the Stockholm convention in 1960. Originally, EFTA consisted of the *Outer Seven:* Austria, Denmark, Norway, Portugal, Sweden, Switzerland, and the United Kingdom. Finland joined EFTA in 1961, and Iceland in 1970. Since then, the membership to the European Free Trade Area has been shrinking, mainly because several countries joined the European Community: Denmark and the United Kingdom in 1977, and Portugal in 1986. Headquartered in Geneva, EFTA is indeed a free-trade area. It has neither a common external tariff nor a common economic policy, and it does not participate in GATT negotiations as a single bargaining unit. A more recent example of a free-trade area is provided by the Free Trade Agreement between Canada and the United States (see Section 10-11).

When a group of countries forms a free-trade area, a **policing problem** arises: Imports from the rest of the world may enter a high-duty member country through a low-duty member country, thus avoiding the high import duty. This phenomenon is known as **trade deflection.** For instance, consider three countries: A (home country), B (partner country), and C (representing the rest of the world). While trade between A and B is free, imports from C are subject to import duties, say, 60 percent in A but only 10 percent in B. Given the large difference in import duties, there is a strong incentive to import C's products into country A (high-duty member) through country B (low-duty member) and pay an import duty of only 10 percent, since trade between A and B is free.

To correct the problem of trade deflection, member countries must be able to distinguish effectively (perhaps through a detailed examination of the certificates of origin as the commodities cross the national frontiers) between goods originating in the free-trade area and goods originating in the rest of the world. But the problem is not that simple, as illustrated by the case of an outside producer who builds just a "final" assembly plant in the low-duty member country and then exports from that plant to the rest of the free-trade area.

Trade deflection also occurs in the case of preferential trading clubs, which do not have a common external tariff, either. However, because trade among the club members is not completely free—they exchange only *small* tariff preferences—the incentive to beat the system is not as strong as in the case of free-trade areas.

Customs Union

Two or more countries form a *customs union* when they abolish all import duties on their mutual trade in all goods (except the services of capital) and, in addition, adopt a common external tariff schedule on all imports of goods (except the services of capital) from the rest of the world. A customs union is also a free-trade area because trade among the member countries is free. But a free-trade area need not be a customs union because a free-trade area need not have a common external tariff. Because of the adoption of a common external tariff, the phenomenon of trade deflection and the policing problem do not arise in a customs union.

There are many historical examples of customs unions. For instance, in 1834 a large number of sovereign German states formed a customs union known as the **Zollverein.** (The Zollverein would prove significant in Bismarck's unification of Germany in 1870.) A more recent example is the European Community (EC), which was founded by the Treaty of Rome (signed in March 1957). The European Community, also known as the Common Market, originally included six countries: Belgium, France, West Germany, Italy, Luxembourg, and the Netherlands. The membership has increased to 12 as Denmark, Ireland, and the United Kingdom joined the Community in 1977, Greece in 1981, and Spain and Portugal in 1986.

Common Market

Two or more countries form a *common market* when they form a customs union and, in addition, allow free movement of all factors of production among them. Thus, the common-market countries abolish all trade restrictions on their mutual trade and also establish a common external tariff, as a customs union. A common market is also a customs union (and a free-trade area). However, a customs union need not be a common market, because the latter allows free movement of all factors of production (labor and capital) among the common-market countries. The European Community is working toward the implementation of the concept of a common market. The EC has set 1992 as its deadline to achieve this goal.

Economic Union

Two or more countries form an *economic union* when they form a common market and, in addition, proceed to unify their fiscal, monetary, and socioeconomic policies. An economic union is the most complete form of economic integration.

An example of an economic union is **Benelux,** which was the economic union formed by Belgium, the Netherlands, and Luxembourg. (The term Benelux is made up of the first letters of each country's name.) These three countries formed a customs union in 1948; this was converted into an economic union in 1960 (as a result of the 1958 Benelux Treaty). As we noted earlier, Belgium, the Netherlands, and Luxembourg became part of the European Community, which is also moving gradually toward an economic union.

The United States serves as an excellent example of an economic union. Fifty states are joined together in a complete economic union with a common currency (which implies permanently fixed rates of exchange among the 50 states) and a single central bank (that is, the Federal Reserve System). Trade is free among the states, and both capital and labor move freely in pursuit of maximum returns. Fiscal and monetary policy as well as international affairs, military expenditures, retirement and health programs, and so on, are pursued by the federal government. Other programs, such as education, police protection, and cultural affairs, are pursued by state and local governments so that states can maintain their "identity" within the union.

An economic union is the ultimate form of economic integration. Whether the European Community will eventually attain the status of an economic union remains to be seen. The obstacles are great. Unlike the United States, the European Community consists of different sovereign nations with different languages, customs, and heritages. Nationalism runs deep in their peoples' minds, and memories of violent wars still prevent them from discarding their individual national identities and joining hands in the pursuit of a common goal. However, much progress has been made already.

10-2 THE NATURE OF PREFERENTIAL TRADING

The theory of customs unions, which we discuss below, does not deal solely with the economic effects of customs unions narrowly defined. It deals also with the economic effects of free-trade areas, common markets, preferential trading clubs, and even economic unions. In short, the theory of customs unions deals with the economic effects of discriminatory systems in general. We begin our discussion of the theory of customs unions by considering the general nature of preferential trading.

Commodity versus Country Discrimination

The standard theory of tariffs surveyed in Chapter 7 rests on the simplifying assumption that import duties are imposed in a nondiscriminatory fashion, that is, a uniform ad valorem tariff rate is levied on *all* imports irrespective of the imported commodity or the country of origin.

In practice, however, discrimination does occur. It takes one of two forms: (1) **commodity discrimination** or (2) **country** (or **geographical**) **discrimination.** Commodity discrimination occurs when different ad valorem import duties are levied on different commodities (for example, 20 percent on oil and 50 percent on cameras). Country discrimination occurs when different ad valorem import duties are levied on the same commodity imported from different countries (for example, 10 percent on cameras imported from Germany and 60 percent on cameras imported from Japan).

Customs Unions as Country Discrimination

The theory of customs unions is a branch of the theory of tariffs and deals primarily with the effects of geographical discrimination, that is, preferential trading. As we have seen, a group of countries may decide to form a preferential trading arrangement. This means that all member countries agree to lower (or eliminate) their respective tariff rates on imports from each other but not on imports from the rest of the world. Such reciprocal tariff reductions necessarily discriminate against imports from the rest of the world.

How is trade between the union members affected? How is trade between the union members and the rest of the world affected? How is the welfare of the member countries, individually and as a group, as well as the welfare of the rest of the world, affected by this geographical discrimination? All these are important questions, and we will discuss them in the rest of this chapter.

The Two Opposing Tendencies of a Customs Union

The pioneer in the theory of customs unions was Jacob Viner (1950). He put forth the major proposition that a customs union (or any other form of preferential trading) combines elements of freer trade with elements of greater protection, and he argued convincingly that it is not clear that such an arrangement increases (potential) welfare. Viner argued that a customs union gives rise to two opposing tendencies. On the one hand, *a customs union tends to increase competition and trade among the member countries,* and this represents a movement toward freer trade. On the other hand, *a customs union tends to provide relatively more protection against trade and competition from the rest of the world*, and this represents a movement toward greater protection.

In the field of customs unions, free traders and protectionists often agree with each other. This paradoxical agreement between the two opposing camps is actually the result of the strange coexistence of elements of freer trade with elements of greater protection. In their calculations, the free traders tend to exaggerate the elements of freer trade, while the protectionists tend to exaggerate the elements of greater protection.

Customs Unions and Pareto Optimality

The theory of customs unions is *not* concerned with Pareto-optimum conditions, that is, the conditions that lead to maximum welfare. The formation of a customs union necessarily violates Pareto optimality because of the existence of tariffs. In fact, Pareto optimality is violated even before the formation of the customs union—tariffs exist before the customs union is formed. The theory of customs unions deals with nonoptimal situations, and it is therefore a special case of the **theory of the second best.**

10-3 THE THEORY OF THE SECOND BEST: A DIGRESSION

The theory of the second best deals with suboptimal situations, that is, situations in which not all Pareto-optimum conditions are satisfied. Its main theorem is simple. Consider an economy that is prevented from fulfilling one Paretian condition. Then the other Paretian conditions, although still attainable, are in general no longer desirable. That is, when one Paretian condition cannot be fulfilled—and thus maximum welfare cannot be reached—maximization of *attainable* welfare requires in general the violation of the other Paretian conditions.

From the above general theorem follows a very important corollary. Consider an economy in a suboptimal situation in which several Paretian conditions are violated (because of, say, the existence of taxes). Suppose now that one or more, but not all, of the previously violated conditions were to be fulfilled (because, say, some of the initial taxes are now removed). Would welfare increase? One might be tempted to answer yes, since such a change seems to bring the economy closer to Pareto optimality—more Pareto-optimum conditions are satisfied after than before the removal of some taxes. Yet the theory of the second best teaches us that such a conclusion in simply wrong. The precise effect on welfare depends on circumstances. When two suboptimal situations are compared, there are no general rules for judging which is better than the other.

Meade (1955b, p. 7) offers an illuminating analogy. He imagines a person who wishes to climb to the highest point on a range of hills. Not every step upward helps the person reach the summit, however. Walking uphill, the person can reach only the summit of the particular hill the individual happens to be on—not the summit of the highest hill. Similarly, while it may be possible to tell that an infinitesimal change in a tariff actually increases welfare (that is, a small step upward brings the person higher on the particular hill he happens to be on), there is no way of predicting that the elimination of tariffs on trade between the customs union members will actually increase welfare. In other words, there is no way of predicting "in a dense fog and without elaborate instruments"—Meade's phrase—that by switching to another hill the person will actually be higher.

10-4 AN OUTLINE OF THE THEORY OF CUSTOMS UNIONS

What are the effects of customs unions on the international allocation of resources? Does the formation of a customs union improve or worsen resource allocation and welfare? Before the publication of Viner's classic book, it was generally believed that the formation of a customs union was a step toward free trade and that it therefore tended to increase welfare. Viner showed that this view is not necessarily correct. He showed that the formation of a customs union combines elements of freer trade with elements of greater protection and may either improve or worsen resource allocation and welfare.

Viner's main tools of analysis were the concepts of **trade creation** and **trade diversion.** Viner demonstrated that the formation of a customs union may lead to either trade creation or trade diversion; but whereas trade creation is good and tends to increase welfare, trade diversion is bad and tends to decrease welfare. The final effect on welfare depends on which of these two opposing influences, trade creation or trade diversion, is stronger.

What do the terms *trade creation* and *trade diversion* mean? The formation of a customs union, such as the European Community, normally shifts the national locus of production of some commodities. When the shift in the national locus of production of a certain commodity is such as to *create* some *new* trade, we say that the customs union gives rise to trade creation. When the shift in the national locus of production is such as to merely *divert* some *old* trade from one country to another, we say that the customs union gives rise to trade diversion.

For instance, suppose that before the formation of the European Community, France and Germany were self-sufficient in the production of commodity X; neither France nor Germany imported commodity X because of their existing high tariffs. However, suppose that after the formation of the Community and following the elimination of tariffs on intra-Community trade, France finds it cheaper to import commodity X from Germany, presumably because Germany is more efficient than France in the production of X. The national locus of production of commodity X shifts from the *higher*-cost French producers to the *lower*-cost German producers; thus *new* trade is generated between France and Germany. This is a case of trade creation.

Trade creation improves the international allocation of resources by shifting the national locus of production from a high-cost producer to a low-cost producer. Thus, trade creation increases welfare by reducing costs or, alternatively, by increasing world income. It is in this sense that trade creation is conceived to be beneficial to welfare.

Turn now to an illustration of trade diversion. Suppose that before the formation of the European Community, France imported commodity Y from the United States, presumably because the United States was the most efficient (lower-cost) producer of commodity Y in the world. Suppose further that after the formation of the Community and following the elimination of tariffs on intra-Community trade, France finds it cheaper to import commodity Y from Germany because imports from Germany are duty free. Thanks to the newly formed geographical tariff discrimination, the national locus of production of commodity Y shifts from the *lower*-cost producer, (the United States) to the *higher*-cost producer (Germany). France's imports of Y are diverted from the United States to Germany. This is clearly a case of trade diversion.

Trade diversion worsens the international allocation of resources. Thus, trade diversion reduces welfare by increasing costs or, alternatively, by reducing world income. It is in this sense that trade diversion is detrimental to welfare.

In summary, the formation of a customs union causes some products that were formerly produced domestically (say, in France) to be imported from other partner countries (say, Germany)—the tariffs on such imports have been eliminated. Here the shift in production is from a higher-cost domestic producer to a lower-cost producer in a partner country. Result: trade creation. In addition, the formation of a customs union causes some products that were formerly imported from the rest of the world (say, the United States) to be imported from a partner country because of the newly formed geographical tariff discrimination. Here the shift in production is from a lower-cost producer in the rest of the world to a higher-cost producer in a partner country. Result: trade diversion. The final effect on welfare is indeterminate. Welfare improves only when trade creation outweighs trade diversion. When trade diversion outweighs trade creation, welfare deteriorates. Indeed, one partner country may lose even though the other partner countries gain.

10-5 AN ILLUSTRATION OF TRADE CREATION AND TRADE DIVERSION

The concepts of trade creation and trade diversion are best illustrated by a numerical example. Consider three countries: A (home country), B (partner country), and C (representing the rest of the world). Suppose that each country produces commodity X at constant average cost, as shown in Table 10-1.

Under free-trade conditions, country C would export commodity X to both A and B ($30 < $40, $30 < $50). Suppose, however, that country A imposes a 100 percent uniform ad valorem tariff on all imports. While the cost of production of X in A remains at $50, the cost (inclusive of the tariff) of importing X from B and C increases to $80 and $60, respectively, as shown in column (2) of Table 10-1. Since $50 < $80 and $50 < $60, country A will produce commodity X domestically.

Now let countries A and B form a customs union and eliminate all tariffs on imports from each other (but not on imports from C). The relevant costs to A

TABLE 10-1 TRADE CREATION
(Average Cost of Production of Commodity X in Countries A, B, and C and A's Cost of Importing X from B and C; in Dollars)

Country	Average cost of production (1)	A imposes a uniform 100% import duty (2)	A removes the duty on imports from B but not from C (3)
A	50	50	50
B	40	80	40
C	30	60	60

are shown in column (3) of Table 10-1. A's domestic cost of importing X from B falls to $40 (since country A now eliminates the tariff on imports from B), and the cost of importing X from C (inclusive of the tariff) remains at $60. Obviously, after the formation of the customs union, country A ceases to produce X and imports it from country B (the other union member). This is an example of trade creation. Before the formation of the customs union, country A produces X at $50. After the formation of the customs union, country A stops production of X and imports it from B. Since B's cost of production is lower than A's ($40 < $50), such a shift in the national locus of production represents trade creation and improves the allocation of resources.

Table 10-2 gives an example of trade diversion. The cost of production of commodity Y in the three countries is exactly the same as the cost of X in Table 10-1. The only difference from the preceding illustration is that A's initial import duty is 50 percent. Before the formation of the customs union, country A imports Y from C, since $45 < $50 < $60 [see column (2)]. However, after the formation of the customs union, country A imports Y from B, since $40 < $45 < $50 [see column (3)]. The shift in production is now from the low-cost producer, C ($30), to the high-cost producer, B ($40). This shift in production represents trade diversion and is detrimental to resource allocation and welfare.

In this illustration, higher protection is necessarily offered to B's high-cost producers. This is done not in the customary fashion of a reduction in B's imports of Y but rather through price discrimination in country A in B's favor. This

TABLE 10-2 TRADE DIVERSION
(Average Cost of Production of Commodity Y in Countries A, B, and C and A's Cost of Importing Y from B and C; in Dollars)

Country	Average cost of production (1)	A imposes a uniform 50% import duty (2)	A removes the duty on imports from B but not from C (3)
A	50	50	50
B	40	60	40
C	30	45	45

type of protection enables B's producers to extend their sales to country A. Result: a more efficient producer (C) is replaced with a less efficient one (B).

10-6 CONSUMPTION EFFECTS

Viner's innovative analysis of customs unions, as presented in Sections 10-4 and 10-5, deals only with the **production effects** of preferential trading. However, the formation of customs unions gives rise to **consumption effects** also. In this section, we bring together both the production and consumption effects of customs unions.

The Nature of the Consumption Effects

What is the nature of the consumption effects of customs unions? Return to the examples of trade creation and trade diversion given in Tables 10-1 and 10-2. In *both* cases, after country A removes its tariff on imports from B (but not from C), *the price paid by A's consumers falls.* In the trade-creation example of Table 10-1, the price of X falls from $50 (A's domestic cost of X) to $40 (B's average cost of X). In the trade-diversion example of Table 10-2, the price of Y falls from $45 (C's average cost of Y plus import duty) to $40 (B's average cost of Y). Unless A's demand for either X or Y is perfectly inelastic, *A's consumption of both X and Y must increase.* This resultant increase in consumption is actually the consumption effect of customs unions—an element overlooked by Viner. In our discussion of the theory of customs unions, we must take into consideration this new (consumption) effect, since it tends to expand trade and improve welfare.

Trade Creation Again

Figure 10-1 illustrates both the production and consumption effects of customs unions. Downward-sloping line DD' is A's demand schedule (for a certain commodity, say, X). Similarly, upward-sloping line SS' is A's domestic supply schedule (for X). To simplify our analysis, we assume that the supply schedule of B (that is, the partner) is infinitely elastic, as shown by horizontal line PP'. Adding A's tariff to B's supply schedule, we obtain horizontal schedule TT'. Before the formation of the customs union (and assuming that C's average cost of production is higher than OP), country A consumes OQ_3, with OQ_2 produced by A's domestic producers and Q_2Q_3 imported from B. The area of rectangle $G_1F_2F_3G_2$ gives A's tariff revenue.

What happens after the formation of the customs union and the elimination of A's tariff? A's consumption increases to OQ_4, A's domestic production falls to OQ_1, A's imports increase to Q_1Q_4, and A's tariff revenue disappears. A's consumers benefit from the elimination of A's tariff. By how much? By area PF_4G_2T. But not all of this is a net gain to country A. For one thing, area PF_1G_1T is a producer surplus enjoyed by A's producers before the elimination of A's tariff, and it is now lost (to A's consumers). For another, the area of rectangle

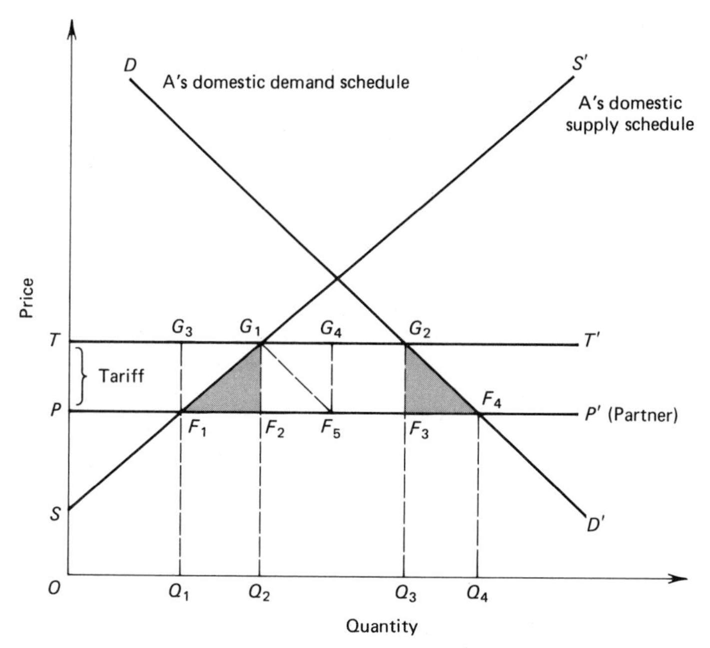

FIGURE 10-1 **Trade creation.** Before the formation of the customs union, country A consumes OQ_3, with OQ_2 produced by A and Q_2Q_3 imported from B (partner). After the formation of the customs union between A and B and the elimination of A's tariff (PT), A's consumption increases to OQ_4, A's domestic production falls to OQ_1, A's imports increase to Q_1Q_4, and A's tariff revenue ($G_1F_2F_3G_2$) disappears. The net gain to A is represented by the areas of the two shaded triangles, $F_1F_2G_1$ (production effect) and $F_3F_4G_2$ (consumption effect).

$G_1F_2F_3G_2$ represents the tariff revenue collected by A's government before the formation of the customs union. This tariff revenue is now lost. The net gain to country A is represented by the areas of the two shaded triangles, $F_1F_2G_1$ and $F_3F_4G_2$.

Shaded triangle $F_1F_2G_1$ represents A's saving of real cost on domestic production that is replaced by imports and illustrates Viner's *production effect* of a customs union that leads to trade creation. Amount Q_1Q_2 was formerly produced domestically at a total cost given by area $Q_1Q_2G_1F_1$. This same amount (Q_1Q_2) is now imported from a lower-cost country at a total cost given by area $Q_1Q_2F_2F_1$. Obviously, there is a net gain of $F_1F_2G_1$. Similarly, shaded triangle $F_3F_4G_2$ represents a net gain in consumer surplus. It is this *consumption effect* that Viner ignored.

The total gain from trade creation is represented in Figure 10-1 by the sum of the areas of the two shaded triangles: $F_1F_2G_1$ and $F_3F_4G_2$. It depends on three parameters: (1) A's initial tariff (that is, distance PT), (2) A's supply elasticity at preunion production point G_1, and (3) A's demand elasticity at preunion consumption point G_2. In general, the total gain from trade creation is significant when the initial level of A's tariff is high and the elasticities of A's domestic supply and demand curves are large.

Draw dashed line G_1F_5 parallel to G_2F_4 (Figure 10-1). The sum of the two shaded triangles is equal to the area of triangle $F_1F_5G_1$, which is half the area of rectangle $F_1F_5G_4G_3$ (that is, the increase in imports times the tariff). This provides a convenient formula for empirical measurement of the trade-creation gains from the customs union. Empirical estimates of this figure run extremely low: 1 or 2 percent of the gross national product of the participating countries—sometimes even less. To understand why, assume that a country whose imports (M) are 30 percent of its gross national product (GNP) imposes a 40 percent tariff (t) on imports. Assume further that the foreign price of imports is p_m and that after the tariff is eliminated, imports increase by 50 percent. The total gain, given by the earlier formula, becomes: $(tp_m\Delta M)/2 = (0.4 \times 0.5Mp_m)/2 = (0.4 \times 0.5 \times 0.3GNP)/2 = 0.03GNP$. Even with such an optimistic example, the total gain amounts to only 3 percent of gross national product.

Trade Diversion Again

Turn now to the case of trade diversion. Before the formation of the customs union, country A imports commodity Y from relatively more efficient country C (representing the rest of the world). However, after the formation of the union, country A imports Y from its partner, country B. The latter, though less efficient than C, can sell Y to A's consumers more cheaply than C, since A's tariff schedule discriminates against C.

Consider Figure 10-2, which illustrates the case of trade diversion. As before, lines DD' and SS' represent A's domestic demand and supply schedules, respectively. Similarly, horizontal lines BB' and CC' represent the infinitely elastic supply schedules (*before* the addition of A's tariff) of countries B and C, respectively. By assumption, C's average cost of production (OC) is lower than B's (OB). Adding A's tariff to C's supply schedule CC', we obtain schedule TT'. (B's supply schedule, including the tariff, is not needed. Why not?) Before the formation of the customs union, country A consumes OQ_3, of which OQ_2 is produced domestically by A's producers and Q_2Q_3 is imported from C. A's tariff revenue is given by area $G_1H_1H_2G_2$.

After the formation of the customs union and the elimination of A's tariff on imports from B, country A finds it cheaper to import Y from B ($OB < OT$). A's consumption increases to OQ_4. A's domestic production decreases to OQ_1, A's imports increase to Q_1Q_4 (that is, A's imports increase by the decrease in domestic production, Q_1Q_2, plus the increase in domestic consumption, Q_3Q_4), and A's tariff revenue vanishes. The consumer surplus increases again by area TBF_4G_2, but the producer surplus decreases by area TBF_1G_1.

Divide A's tariff-revenue loss (that is, area $G_1H_1H_2G_2$) into two parts: $G_1F_2F_3G_2 + F_2H_1H_2F_3$. Subtract the loss of producer surplus (that is, area

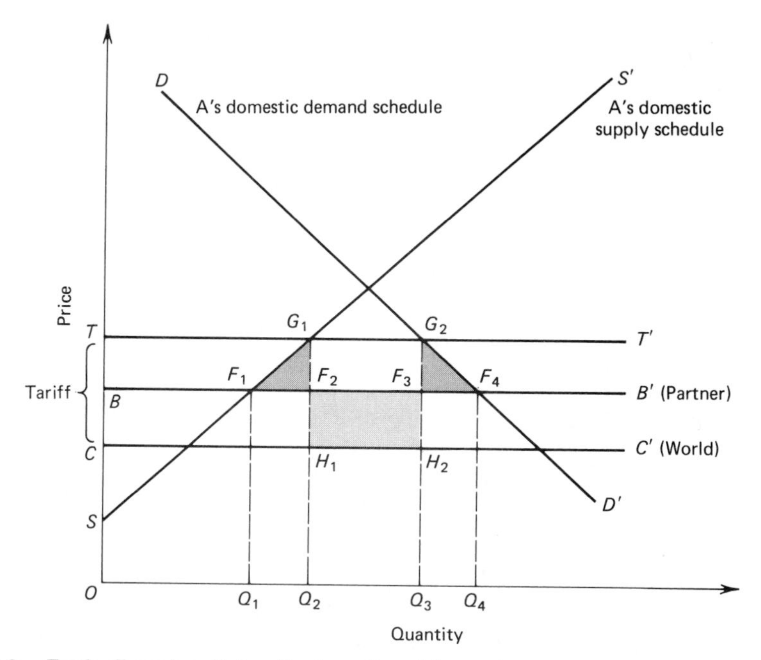

FIGURE 10-2 **Trade diversion.** Before the formation of the customs union, country A consumes OQ_3, of which OQ_2 is produced domestically and Q_2Q_3 is imported from C (representing the rest of the world). After the formation of the customs union and the elimination of A's tariff on imports from B, A diverts its purchases from C to B (because $OB < OT$). A's consumption increases to OQ_4, A's production decreases to OQ_1, A's imports increase to Q_1Q_4, and A's tariff revenue ($G_1H_1H_2G_2$) vanishes. The two shaded triangles, $F_1F_2G_1$ and $F_3F_4G_2$, represent gain. Shaded rectangle $F_2H_1H_2F_3$ represents the loss from diverting the initial amount of imports (Q_2Q_3) from a lower-cost source (C) to a higher-cost source (B).

TBF_1G_1) as well as the first part of the tariff-revenue loss (that is, area $G_1F_2F_3G_2$) from the gain in consumer surplus (that is, area TBF_4G_2) to obtain the two shaded triangles, $F_1F_2G_1$ and $F_3F_4G_2$. The sum of these two shaded triangles represents a gain that we must compare with the remaining loss of the second part of the tariff revenue (that is, shaded area $F_2H_1H_2F_3$). If the sum of the two shaded triangles (that is, $F_1F_2G_1 + F_3F_4G_2$) is larger than shaded rectangle $F_2H_1H_2F_3$, then trade diversion actually results in a net social gain. If $F_1F_2G_1 + F_3F_4G_2 < F_2H_1H_2F_3$, trade diversion results in a net social loss.

What is the meaning of triangles $F_1F_2G_1$ and $F_3F_4G_2$ and of rectangle $F_2H_1H_2F_3$? Well, rectangle $F_2H_1H_2F_3$ represents the net loss from diverting the *initial* amount of imports (Q_2Q_3) from a lower-cost source (country C) to a higher-cost source (country B). This is primarily the detrimental effect of trade diversion referred to by Viner. But as we have just seen, this is not the only effect. Triangles $F_1F_2G_1$ and $F_3F_4G_2$ represent two beneficial effects. Triangle

$F_1F_2G_1$ represents a *production gain*, while triangle $F_3F_4G_2$ represents a *consumption gain*. The production gain reflects the net reduction in social cost that results from shifting the locus of production of the amount Q_1Q_2 from country A, where its total cost is given by area $F_1Q_1Q_2G_1$, to country B, where its total cost is given by area $F_1Q_1Q_2F_2$. The consumption gain denotes the net increase in consumer surplus brought about by the increase of Q_3Q_4 in A's consumption. (Recall that country B produces amount Q_3Q_4 at the total cost given by area $F_3Q_3Q_4F_4$.)

Trade-diverting Customs Unions and Welfare Improvement

Implicit in the preceding analysis is the notion that trade diversion need not have a net detrimental effect on welfare, contrary to Viner's original view. The problem arises from a definition of trade diversion that includes two elements: (1) diversion of *initial* trade from a lower-cost source (country C) to a higher-cost source (partner country B) plus (2) creation of *new* trade between the home country (A) and the partner country (B), resulting both from the adjustment in A's consumption and from the replacement of A's domestic production by B's production. Analytically, these two elements must be kept apart.

The diversion of *initial* trade from a lower-cost source to a higher-cost source is called **pure trade diversion.** In contrast, the creation of *new* trade between the home country and the partner country must be considered as *trade creation and must be added to the trade creation proper.* Once this is done, we can always say that trade creation is a "good thing" (that is, welfare increasing) and trade diversion a "bad thing" (that is, welfare reducing) with the net effect of the customs union depending on which of these two effects (properly defined) is stronger. In terms of Figure 10-2, we can say that the sum of the two shaded triangles, $F_1F_2G_1$ and $F_3F_4G_2$, is actually trade creation, and that only rectangle $F_2H_1H_2F_3$ represents trade diversion.

10-7 DYNAMIC EFFECTS OF CUSTOMS UNIONS

Besides the static effects of trade creation and trade diversion, whose magnitude, as we have seen, is no more than a negligible percentage of the national income of the participating countries, customs unions have some interesting **dynamic effects,** such as **increased competition, stimulation of technical change, stimulation of investment,** and **economies of scale.** These dynamic effects do not lend themselves easily to systematic analysis. As a result, widespread disagreement and controversy surrounds them.

Competition in this context does not mean many firms selling a homogeneous product. Rather, it refers to the *ability and willingness of producers to encroach upon each other's markets.* As tariffs are removed and the market expands, the number of potential competitors increases. Monopolistic and oligopolistic market structures become exposed to outside pressures. Inefficient firms must either become efficient or close down. Competition becomes less personal and more effective and leads to research and development of new products. This creates a climate that is conducive to increased technical change and faster economic growth. Increased competition was very significant among the countries that now constitute the European Community.

The increase in competition and technical change leads to additional investment, which is necessary in order to take advantage of the newly created opportunities. To be sure, certain import-competing industries are hard hit by the extra competition from more efficient producers located in other union countries. In these industries, a certain amount of disinvestment must be expected. This disinvestment must be subtracted from the positive investment activity in other flourishing industries in order to determine the net effect on investment. The latter is very hard to estimate.

Some union countries may also experience an increase in investment from the rest of the world. Existing foreign firms in the union may expand or regroup in order to take advantage of the newly created opportunities. In addition, foreign firms that in the past used to serve the union countries by exports may now decide to build plants in the union countries—after all, as we saw earlier in the discussion of trade diversion, these foreign producers are discriminated against after the formation of the customs union. This actually may have been the reason for the massive U.S. investment in Europe after 1955, although there are those who believe that this phenomenon was due to a sudden awareness on the part of U.S. corporations of the existence of a growing, vigorous market from which they did not wish to be excluded.

The creation of a large market leads to a greater degree of specialization, which results in a reduction in costs for several reasons: fuller utilization of plant capacity, learning by doing, and development of a pool of skilled labor and management. Such economies of scale are particularly important to the developing countries (see Section 10-10).

It has been argued that a great advantage of the U.S. economy is its huge internal market, which facilitates the exploitation of economies of scale. Critics make two observations: (1) Many small companies are efficient while at the same time some large ones are sluggish, and (2) countries with relatively small internal markets, like Sweden and Switzerland, have highly efficient industries and are very affluent.

10-8 THE COMMON EXTERNAL TARIFF

The determination of a common external tariff by a customs union is not always an easy matter. Aside from the real problem of arriving at a common tariff nomenclature, the union members must also reach agreement on the height of the common tariff as well as the distribution of the tariff proceeds among the member countries.

In the case of the European Community, the Treaty of Rome set the common external tariff equal to the arithmetical average of the import duties of the member nations—a procedure that was consistent with the rules of GATT. Initially, this simple average of members' duties resulted in lower tariffs for France and Italy but higher tariffs for Germany and the Benelux countries.

Taking a simple arithmetical average of the import duties of the member nations is not the only way to determine the common external tariff. Perhaps a better approach would be to take a weighted average. But what weights should be used? If the existing import duties are weighted by the *actual* volume of trade, the resultant average would be rather biased: the higher the import duty, the lower the volume of imports and hence its weight. In the extreme case of a prohibitive tariff, its weight would be zero, which is ludicrous. Conceivably, the *free-trade* volume of trade would generate a much better system of weights. Yet the free-trade weights are not available—at least not before the union members complete an enormous amount of econometric work to estimate elasticities.

Turn now to the question of distributing the tariff proceeds among the member countries. How should this be done? Perhaps the simplest solution would be to allow each member country to keep all tariff proceeds it collects when the goods (shipped from the rest of the world to the customs union) cross its borders. Yet this is not necessarily an equitable system. A union member's imports from the rest of the world may have to cross another member's border first, such as Germany's imports, which arrive through either the Netherlands or Italy. A more equitable system would be to distribute the tariff proceeds on the basis of the amount each country actually consumes of the goods imported from the rest of the world. Unfortunately, tracing imported goods to the country of consumption requires a prohibitively costly bureaucratic machinery.

Because the solution to the above problems is vital to the welfare of each member country, negotiations tend to last for a long time. Each individual country's objective in these negotiations is to maximize its own share of the net welfare gains.

10-9 COMMON AGRICULTURAL POLICY

Without question, one of the most difficult problems in the formation of the European Community has been the establishment of a common agricultural policy. Because the national agricultural programs of the original Community members were markedly different from one another, agreement on a common agricultural policy was not easy to achieve.

Eventually, the European Community adopted a unique system known as the **variable levy** (*prélèvement*). The basic idea of the system is simple. First, the Community determines in advance the desired internal price it wishes to maintain for each agricultural product. This support price, known as the **target price** (*prix indicatif*), determines the level of internal consumption and production and, therefore, the volume of imports of each commodity. Second, the Community imposes a **sliding tariff** (or **variable levy**) equal to the difference between the (lowest) price on the world market and the target price. Any change in the world price, or the target price, gives rise to a corresponding change in the variable levy. Apparently, the variable levy shifts the entire burden of adjustment to variations in the Community's consumption and production onto third-country suppliers. In addition, the variable levy discourages foreign countries from subsidizing their exports and discourages foreign producers from absorbing part of the import duty in order to maintain (or increase) their sales.

Agreement on the system of the variable levy was relatively easy. Agreement on the desired levels of the support prices, however, proved much more difficult. Indeed, a direct conflict arose between France and West Germany. In particular, West Germany, which is relatively inefficient in the production of wheat, demanded a high support price for wheat, especially because German farmers were politically powerful. France, with a more efficient agricultural sector, demanded a lower support price for wheat. Eventually, the Community reached agreement on a support price between the two extremes.

The common agricultural policy was also a major obstacle in Britain's entry into the European Community. Britain supported its agricultural sector by direct subsidies to the farmers. Essentially, the British system, known as a **deficiency payment system,** allowed supply and demand conditions to determine food prices. For this reason, British consumers' food prices, as well as the British agricultural incomes, were generally low. Britain then made up the "deficiency" in agricultural incomes by means of direct cash payments to its farmers. Britain's entry into the European Community and the acceptance of the Community's price support system in lieu of Britain's own deficiency payment system generated a sharp rise in the cost of living in Britain. Ironically, the large increase in the price of foodstuffs essentially subsidized French, West German, and Italian farmers.

The deficiency payment system is superior to the price support system for three reasons. First, the deficiency payment system does not generate any unwanted surplus production. Second, the deficiency payment system keeps prices low for consumers. Third, the deficiency payment system makes public the total cost of this form of aid; thus, the system is continuously under budgetary control and public scrutiny.

10-10 PREFERENTIAL TRADING AMONG DEVELOPING ECONOMIES

Among the developing countries there exists an understandable desire to accelerate the pace of their economic development and to raise their standard of living. To achieve this goal, the developing countries often pursue a policy known as **import-substituting industrialization.** This policy often means heavy losses to the countries involved because it goes against the law of comparative advantage and generates economic inefficiency.

An important economic factor that may account for the failure of import-substituting industrialization in many developing countries is the small size of national markets. Developing nations suffer from low per capita incomes. In addition, the populations of many of these countries are very small. For these reasons, each individual developing country is not able to support efficient industries. A modern industry must serve a large market in order to achieve economies of scale and become efficient and viable in the long run.

To overcome the obstacle of their small national markets, the developing countries often resort to regional integration. For instance, suppose that each of five countries, such as Costa Rica, El Salvador, Guatemala, Honduras, and Nicaragua, are too small to support five modern industries, say X_1, X_2, X_3, X_4, and X_5. These five countries could form a customs union and agree to assign only one industry to each country; say, industry X_1 to Costa Rica, industry X_2 to El Salvador, industry X_3 to Guatemala, industry X_4 to Honduras, and industry X_5 to Nicaragua. In this way, each individual country could develop an efficient industry to serve all five countries—a much larger market than that of any of the five national markets.

Actually, in 1960 the preceding five countries did establish the Central American Common Market (CACM), and customs unions and free-trade areas among developing countries have been established in various parts of the world. For instance, the Latin American Free Trade Association (LAFTA) was established in 1960; the Caribbean Free Trade Association (CARIFTA) was formed in 1968 and transformed in 1973 into a common market (CARICOM); the East African Community was established in 1967; the Customs and Economic Union of Central Africa was organized in 1966; and the Economic Community of West Africa was formed in 1974.

The trend toward regional integration among developing economies follows from their awareness that they cannot succeed in their efforts to industrialize unless they achieve economies of scale, which require large markets. The interest of these countries does not lie in trade creation. Indeed, they seem to be more interested in trade diversion! Because of their interest in enlarging the size of their markets, the developing countries are actually interested in diverting at least part of their purchases from the industrial nations to their own partner countries. After all, the labor that goes into the trade-diverting activities is seldom withdrawn from other useful activities. More often than not, such labor is drawn from the ranks of the unemployed or underemployed, and its opportunity cost is very low, near zero.

Unfortunately, regional integration has not been very successful. Various reasons are responsible for this fact. First, there are political difficulties. Governments, especially those of newly founded nations, are not eager to sacrifice their freedom, sovereignty, and autonomy. Second, there is the problem of transportation. Despite their geographical proximity, the developing economies lack adequate transportation facilities for making the enlarged market meaningful. The lack of adequate transportation facilities, plus the fact that the countries' overall market actually remains small even after integration, limits the scope of economies of scale as well as the scope of competition. Third, there is always the apprehension among the relatively poorer countries that the relatively more advanced countries of the group may eventually dominate the entire customs union. That is, the relatively poorer countries feel that once they open their doors to their partners, they will never be able to build their own industry. To cope with this problem, several customs unions, such as the Central American Common Market, tried, with very limited success, the approach of **industrial planning.** This involves the assignment of certain industries to certain countries. But while each country may be happy with its own monopoly, some countries may not resist the temptation to encroach upon the other countries' monopolies. This is actually what happened with the Central American Common Market, where industrial planning broke down even before the outbreak of the dismal "soccer war" between Honduras and El Salvador in 1969.

In conclusion, it may be fair to say that if the developing countries are determined to industrialize irrespective of the social cost, industrialization through regional integration should be preferred where feasible. The reason is simple: Regional integration can support larger and more efficient production units.

10-11 THE FREE TRADE AGREEMENT BETWEEN CANADA AND THE UNITED STATES

On January 2, 1988, President Ronald Reagan and Canadian Prime Minister Brian Mulroney signed the **Free Trade Agreement** (FTA), which is designed to create, by 1999, a vast open market, stretching over 19 million square kilometers and covering more than 265 million consumers.

Table 10-3 provides a profile of the two economies. In terms of national income (or gross domestic product—GDP), the United States is more than 11 times bigger than Canada. Per capita income is more than 20 percent higher in the United States than in

TABLE 10-3 A PROFILE OF THE UNITED STATES AND CANADA, 1985

	United States	Canada
Area (thousands of square kilometers)	9,363	9,976
Population (millions)	239.3	25.4
Life expectancy at birth (years)	76	76
Gross domestic product (billions of dollars)	3,947	346
GNP per capita (dollars)	16,690	13,680
Unemployment	6.2	8.9
Inflation rate (consumer prices)	3.6	4.0
Merchandise exports		
Billions of dollars	213.1	87.5
Percent of GDP	5.4	25.3
Merchandise imports		
Billions of dollars	361.6	81.5
Percent of GDP	9.2	23.6

Source: The World Bank, *World Development Report 1987,* Oxford University Press, New York, 1987, Washington D.C., and International Monetary Fund, *World Economic Outlook,* 1988.

Canada. In absolute terms, total merchandise exports and imports are much larger for the United States than for Canada. But Canada exports more than 25 percent of its GDP compared to about 5 percent for the United States.

The United States and Canada do more trade with each other than any other pair of countries in the world. In 1987 more than $163 billion of goods and services crossed their 4,000-mile border. As shown in Figure 10-3, Canada is America's largest trading partner, accounting for 18.9 percent of total U.S. trade. By contrast, the U.S. share of Canadian trade exceeds 71 percent. From another point of view, U.S. exports to Canada represent only 1.3 percent of U.S. national income, while Canada exports almost 20 percent of its aggregate output to the United States.

FIGURE 10-3 Shares of U.S. and Canadian Merchandise trade in 1986. (Economic Report of the President, *U.S. Government Printing Office, Washington, D.C., February 1988.*)

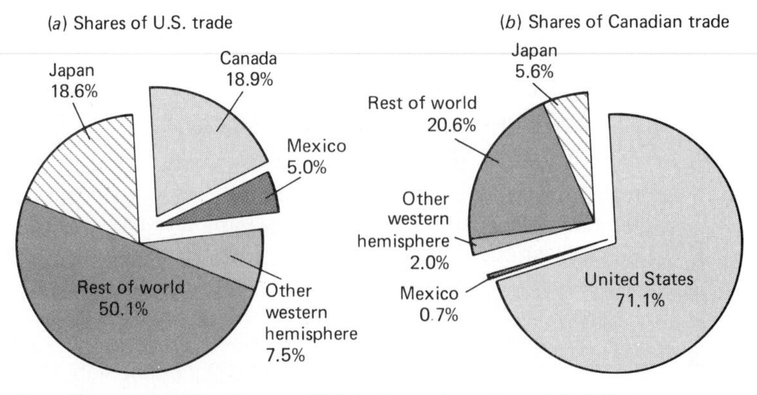

Note: Shares are based on the sum of bilateral exports and imports in dollars.

Among the major achievements of the FTA are:

1 Tariffs. Without exception, all tariffs between the two countries will be eliminated over a 10-year period. On average, tariffs between the two trading partners are already tiny. In 1985, the average tariff rate on dutiable imports was 3.3 percent for the United States and 9.9 percent for Canada. But because three-fourths of U.S.-Canada trade is already duty free, these average tariff rates fall to 0.9 and 2.4 percent, respectively, when duty-free imports are included in the calculation. The averages, however, conceal high tariffs on such items as clothes and timber.

To eliminate the potential problem of "trade deflection," the agreement provides that articles imported from third countries into, say, the United States cannot be exported to Canada duty free before they are sufficiently processed.

2 Government procurement. The FTA will also eliminate national preference (such as "Buy American" provisions of U.S. law) on all government contracts worth more than $25,000 (instead of the current threshold of $171,000). It is estimated that $3 billion of U.S. contracts and $500 million of Canadian contracts will be affected by the new, lower threshold.

3 Energy. The FTA prohibits most restrictions on bilateral energy trade, which totaled about $10 billion in 1987. Reasons for exceptions include national security considerations and prevention of the exhaustion of a finite energy resource. (The FTA places a ceiling, also, on the sales of Alaskan oil to Canada.) From the U.S. perspective, the FTA reduces uncertainties about future energy supplies and benefits U.S. consumers.

4 Agriculture. The United States and Canada are two of the largest grain exporters of the world. Yet their trade in agricultural goods accounts for only 4.5 percent of total bilateral trade, mainly because of extensive quotas and licensing requirements. The FTA eliminates agricultural tariffs and export subsidies; it also liberalizes significant quantitative restrictions. Canada's discriminatory pricing system for distilled spirits will be eliminated; barriers against wine imports will be phased out in seven years; import restrictions on poultry products will be lessened; and trade in fertilizers and other agricultural inputs will be liberalized.

5 Investment. In 1986 the United States had a direct investment of $50 billion in Canada, while Canada had a direct investment of only $18 billion in the United States. The FTA will improve the investment climate in both countries. The two partners will provide **national treatment** to each other's investors (that is, equivalent treatment of foreign and domestic investors). Restrictions on the establishment of new firms will be eliminated. The Canadian threshold for the review of direct acquisitions by U.S. investors will be raised to $150 million by 1992. Canadian screening of indirect acquisitions (where a firm's ownership changes when ownership of its parent firm outside the country changes) by U.S. investors will be phased out.

6 Dispute settlement mechanism. The FTA establishes a Canada-U.S. Commission to supervise the implementation of the agreement and resolve disputes.

Econometric studies indicate that in the long run the FTA will raise real incomes in both Canada and the United States by 2.5 to 3.5 percent. However, these estimates do not take into account the benefits from dynamic effects, such as increased competition, stimulation of technical change, stimulation of investment, and economies of scale. If the experience of the European Community is any guide, these dynamic effects may be very substantial indeed.

The FTA was easily ratified by the U.S. Congress. However, furious debate over the pact forced Prime Minister Brian Mulroney to call new elections on November 21, 1988. The contest gave his Progressive Conservative Party its second straight majority government and a clear mandate to push for passage of the legislation. The pact was finally approved by the Canadian House of Commons on December 24, and by the Canadian Senate on December 30, 1988. The Free Trade Agreement took effect on January 1, 1989, and it represents a victory of free trade over special interests and protectionism.

10-12 SUMMARY

1 The theory of customs unions deals with the economic effects of preferential trading arrangements, such as preferential trading clubs, free-trade areas, customs unions, common markets, and economic unions.

2 While the members of preferential trading clubs exchange small tariff preferences, the members of a free-trade area abolish all import duties on their mutual trade.

3 A customs union is a free-trade area with a common external tariff schedule. The union members must agree on both the height of the common tariff and the distribution of the tariff proceeds.

4 Unlike customs unions, preferential trading clubs and free-trade areas do not have a common external tariff. For this reason, a policing problem arises: Imports from the rest of the world may enter a high-duty member country through a low-duty member country (trade deflection).

5 A common market is a customs union whose members allow, in addition, free movement among them of all factors of production.

6 An economic union is a common market whose members unify their fiscal, monetary, and socioeconomic policies.

7 A preferential trading arrangement gives rise to two opposing tendencies: (a) It increases competition and trade among the member countries (movement toward freer trade), and (b) it increases protection against trade and competition from the rest of the world (movement toward greater protection).

8 The theory of customs unions is a special case of the theory of the second best, whose main proposition states that when one Paretian condition is violated, all other Paretian conditions, although still attainable, are no longer desirable. The theory of the second best warns us that no general conditions can be specified under which the formation of a preferential trading arrangement always leads to an increase in welfare.

9 Viner demonstrated that the formation of a customs union generates two static effects: trade creation and trade diversion. He dealt only with the production effects, which arise from the shift in the national locus of production. Consumption effects arise from the cheapening of goods in member countries.

10 When properly defined, trade creation (diversion) is always beneficial (detrimental) to welfare. Welfare increases (decreases) when trade creation is larger (smaller) than trade diversion.

11 Customs unions also generate dynamic effects, such as increased competition, stimulation of technical change, stimulation of investment, and economies of scale.

PROBLEMS

1 Suppose that the average cost per bottle of wine is \$1.50 in Portugal, \$2.00 in France, \$2.40 in Italy, and \$2.50 in Germany. The current ad valorem import duty for wine is 25 percent in Portugal, 30 percent in France, 100 percent in Italy, and 60 percent in Germany.

a Which countries import wine?

b Which countries export wine?

c Italy and Germany form a free-trade association. They eliminate all import duties on their mutual trade but retain their tariffs on imports from third countries. What is the pattern of the wine trade now? Does the formation of the free-trade area give rise to trade creation or trade diversion? Is there any possibility of trade deflection?

d Italy and Germany convert their free-trade association into a customs union by adopting a common external tariff of 50 percent. What is the new pattern of the wine trade? Does the formation of the customs union give rise to trade creation or trade diversion?

e Suppose that France joins the customs union originally formed by Italy and Germany. As a result, France adopts the common external tariff of 50 percent. The union members eliminate all tariffs on their mutual trade. What is the new pattern for the wine trade? Does the expanded customs union give rise to trade creation or trade diversion?

2 Canada's domestic supply and demand functions for cloth are as follows:

$$Q_s = 100p - 50 \qquad \text{(supply)}$$

$$Q_d = 1500 - 100p \qquad \text{(demand)}$$

The price per yard of cloth is \$3 in the United States and \$2 in the rest of the world. Canada is too small to influence prices in the United States or the rest of the world. Initially, Canada imposes a tariff of 100 percent on imports of cloth from foreign countries.

a Determine Canada's equilibrium price of cloth, domestic production and consumption, imports, and tariff revenue.

b Canada forms a free-trade area with the United States. Determine Canada's new equilibrium, that is, determine again the price of cloth, domestic production and consumption, imports, and tariff revenue.

c Does the free-trade area give rise to trade creation or trade diversion?

d Determine the effect of the free-trade area on Canada's welfare.

3 Britain's domestic supply and demand functions for wine are as follows:

$$Q_s = 25p - 25 \qquad \text{(supply)}$$

$$Q_d = 125 - 5p \qquad \text{(demand)}$$

The price per bottle of wine is \$3 in Portugal and \$4 in France.

a Determine Britain's free-trade equilibrium price of wine, domestic production and consumption, and imports.

b Suppose that Britain imposes a 100 percent ad valorem duty on imports of wine. Determine Britain's new equilibrium price of wine, domestic production and consumption, imports, and tariff revenue.

c Britain forms a customs union with France. Britain eliminates the duty on imports from France but retains the duty on imports from Portugal. Determine Britain's new equilibrium price of wine, domestic production and consumption, imports, and tariff revenue.

d Does the customs union between Britain and France give rise to trade creation or trade diversion?

e What is the effect of the customs union on the welfare of Britain?

SUGGESTED READING

Balassa, B. (1961). *The Theory of Economic Integration.* Richard D. Irwin, Inc., Homewood, Ill.

———(1974). "Trade Creation and Trade Diversion in the European Common Market: An Appraisal of the Evidence." *Manchester School of Economic and Social Studies,* vol. 42 (June), pp. 93–135.

Chacholiades, M. (1978). *International Trade Theory and Policy.* McGraw-Hill Book Company, New York, chaps. 22–23.

Cooper, C. A., and B. F. Massell (1965). "A New Look at Customs Union Theory." *Economic Journal,* vol. 75 (December), pp. 742–747.

Corden, W. M. (1972). "Economies of Scale and Customs Union Theory." *Journal of Political Economy,* vol. 80 (March), pp. 465–475.

Council of Economic Advisers (1988). *Economic Report of the President.* U.S. Government Printing Office, Washington, D.C., chap. 4.

Gehrels, F. (1956). "Customs Union from a Single-Country Viewpoint." *Review of Economic Studies,* vol. 24, pp. 61–64.

Johnson, H. G. (1958). "The Gains from Freer Trade with Europe: An Estimate." *Manchester School of Economic and Social Studies,* vol. 26 (September), pp. 247–255.

———(1962). *Money, Trade and Economic Growth.* Harvard University Press, Cambridge, Mass., chap. 3.

Lipsey, R. G. (1957). "The Theory of Customs Unions: Trade Diversion and Welfare." *Economica,* vol. 24 (February), pp. 40–46.

———(1960). "The Theory of Customs Unions: A General Survey." *Economic Journal,* vol. 70, no. 279 (September), pp. 496–513. Reprinted in R. E. Caves and H. G. Johnson (eds.), American Economic Association *Readings in International Economics,* Richard D. Irwin, Inc., Homewood, Ill., 1968.

———(1970). *The Theory of Customs Unions: A General Equilibrium Analysis.* Weidenfeld and Nicolson, London.

Lipsey, R. G., and K. Lancaster (1956). "The General Theory of the Second Best." *Review of Economic Studies,* vol. 24, pp. 11–32.

Meade, J. E. (1955a). *The Theory of Customs Unions.* North-Holland Publishing Company, Amsterdam.

———(1955b). *The Theory of International Economic Policy,* vol. 2, *Trade and Welfare.* Oxford University Press, London.

Schott, J. J. (1988). *United States–Canada Free Trade: An Evaluation of the Agreement.* Institute for International Economics, Washington, D.C.

Scitovsky, T. (1958). *Economic Theory and Western European Integration.* Stanford University Press, Stanford, Calif.

Viner, J. (1950). *The Customs Union Issue.* Carnegie Endowment for International Peace, New York, especially chap. 4.

PART TWO

INTERNATIONAL FINANCE

CHAPTER **11**

THE FOREIGN EXCHANGE MARKET

The first part of this book dealt with the *real* economic forces that in the long run determine the structure of production, consumption, and trade in the international economy. Throughout, money was seen in its classical role as a veil of real economic phenomena and as such was ignored.

The time has come to put money under special scrutiny. Our main interest now shifts to **international finance.** In this part, we are concerned with the foreign exchange market and the balance of payments. The short-run adjustment processes (which we took for granted in Part One) now assume great significance. Also of central importance are the difficulties of attaining international equilibrium and the economic policies that may be necessary for the achievement of international equilibrium when the automatic processes either are too slow or are not working properly.

International finance is full of strange terms: arbitrage, speculation, hedging, forward contracts, the adjustable peg, the crawling peg, the Snake in the Tunnel, special drawing rights (SDR's), and many, many more. This jargon, combined with tales about international financial markets, creates an atmosphere of mystery, which is mainly responsible for the apprehension of the student who approaches the subject for the first time. It is hoped that this book will eradicate such apprehension. The rest of this book will show how the main principles and tools of economic analysis (with which the student is already familiar) can be applied to the area of international finance.

We begin the story of international finance with a brief account of the foreign exchange market. In particular, this chapter deals with the nature, organization, and functions of the foreign exchange market; the forward market and its relationship to the spot market; and, finally, the Eurodollar market.

11-1 THE BASIS OF THE FOREIGN EXCHANGE MARKET

The foreign exchange market performs three important functions:

1 It transfers purchasing power from one currency to another and from one country to another.
2 It provides credit for foreign trade.
3 It furnishes facilities for hedging foreign exchange risks (as explained in Section 11-5).

The transfer of purchasing power is by far the most important of these functions—it is the fundamental cause for the existence of the foreign exchange market.

The Multitude of National Currencies

What is the **foreign exchange market?** It is the market in which national currencies are bought and sold against one another. Indeed, the foreign exchange market is the largest market in the world. Its daily trading volume often exceeds $100 billion.

Why is the foreign exchange market needed? Because there are as many national currencies as there are sovereign nations. The multitude of national currencies provides an extra dimension to every **international economic transaction** (that is, every economic transaction between a resident of one country and a resident of another). Thus every international economic transaction requires a **foreign exchange transaction,** that is, the conversion of one currency into another. The primary function of the foreign exchange market is to perform this conversion of (or the transfer of purchasing power from) one currency into another. If a single currency were used throughout the world there would be no need for a foreign exchange market, and trade among nations (such as the United States and Japan) would resemble trade among the various states of the United States (such as California and New York).

Exports, Imports, and Foreign Exchange

In general, **the flow of goods and services between countries requires the conversion of the currency of the importing country into the currency of the exporting country.** For instance, consider the case of an American corporation that sells (exports) computers to a British importer. The American corporation must be paid in dollars, while the British importer has pounds sterling only. Somehow the pounds sterling of the British importer must be converted into dollars. It is immaterial, of course, as to whether the

American exporting corporation or the British importer goes to the trouble of actually converting pounds sterling into dollars. (If the American corporation accepts payment in pounds sterling, it is that corporation's responsibility to go into the foreign exchange market and sell pounds for dollars. If the American corporation insists on being paid directly in dollars, the responsibility of selling pounds for dollars, or buying dollars with pounds, is assigned to the British importer.) The important point is that *the flow of goods and services from America to Britain generates a supply of pounds (the importer's currency) and a demand for dollars (the exporter's currency).*

Consider another example. Suppose that an American importer buys British automobiles from a British exporter. If the American importer is allowed to pay in dollars, the British exporter must sell the dollars for pounds in the foreign exchange market. If the British exporter insists on being paid in pounds, it is the American importer who must enter the foreign exchange market and exchange dollars for pounds.

Finally, consider America's exports and imports of goods and services at the same time. America's exports require the conversion of foreign currencies (foreign exchange) into dollars. That is, *America's exports give rise to a supply of foreign exchange and a demand for dollars.* America's imports require the conversion of dollars into foreign exchange. That is, *America's imports give rise to a demand for foreign exchange and a supply of dollars.*

Other International Transactions and Foreign Exchange

The flow of goods and services among sovereign nations generates a large part of the supply and demand for currencies in the foreign exchange market, but it is not the only type of activity that gives rise to foreign exchange transactions. For instance, tourists traveling abroad usually come into contact with the foreign exchange market upon their arrival at the foreign airport, where they rush to the exchange counter to convert their own currency into the foreign currency. Also, many people in Italy and Greece who receive remittances from their relatives who emigrated to the United States, Canada, or Australia enter the foreign exchange market to exchange the foreign currencies for their domestic currency (lire or drachmas, as the case may be). Finally, people may demand foreign currencies because they want to buy assets from foreigners. Indeed, for some economies foreign exchange transactions involving assets and speculation dwarf all other foreign exchange transactions based on the flow of goods and services.

The Need for a Market Mechanism

It would be very difficult for an American importer in need of pounds sterling to seek out an American exporter with the necessary amount of pounds for sale. Surely exporters and importers in all countries are willing to pay a small commission for the convenience of making currency exchanges on a smoothly working, impersonal market. An important function of the foreign exchange market is to bring together all buyers and sellers of each national currency and carry out all currency exchanges quickly and efficiently.

A Hypothetical Clearing House

The foreign exchange market solves the conversion problem by performing an important **clearing function.** We can understand this clearing function by imagining that a clearing house is set up with small working balances of all currencies. To keep the discussion simple, however, assume that there are only two currencies: dollars and pounds. The clearing house announces that it is willing to exchange either currency for the other at a certain rate (say, $2 per £1) and hopes, of course, that the inflow of each currency will approximately match the outflow. The initial cash balances of the clearing house actually become a revolving fund.

The clearing function is shown schematically in Figure 11-1. The initial working balances of the clearing house are represented by the level of the water in the middle tank. Actually, this tank consists of two chambers. The level of the water in chamber 1 shows the initial stock of dollars held by the clearing house, and the level of the water in chamber 2 shows the initial stock of pounds.

Striped arrow *a* at the upper left-hand corner shows the flow of dollars into chamber 1 that results from the activity of American importers, British exporters, American tourists in London, etc. As we saw earlier, this group of people needs to convert dollars into pounds, that is, they supply dollars and demand pounds. The group's demand for pounds is shown by striped arrow *d* at the lower right-hand corner, which represents an outflow of pounds from the clearing house. Note carefully that arrows *a* and *d* (that is, the inflow of dollars and the outflow of pounds, respectively) are similarly striped in order to emphasize the strict correspondence that exists between them—the same group of transactors turn them on and off simultaneously.

Dark arrows *b* and *c* at the upper right-hand and the lower left-hand corners, respectively, represent the conversion of pounds into dollars that is required by British importers, American exporters, British tourists in New York, etc. In particular, arrow *b* shows the inflow (supply) of pounds into chamber 2 of the middle tank, and arrow *c* shows the outflow of (demand for) dollars from chamber 1. Again, both of these arrows bear the same appearance in order to emphasize the strict relationship that exists between them.

When the inflow of a currency into the clearing house does not completely match its outflow, the difference is reflected in the level of the stock of that currency held by the clearing house. When the inflow is larger than the outflow, the stock held by the clearing house tends to rise; when the inflow is smaller than the outflow, the stock tends to fall.

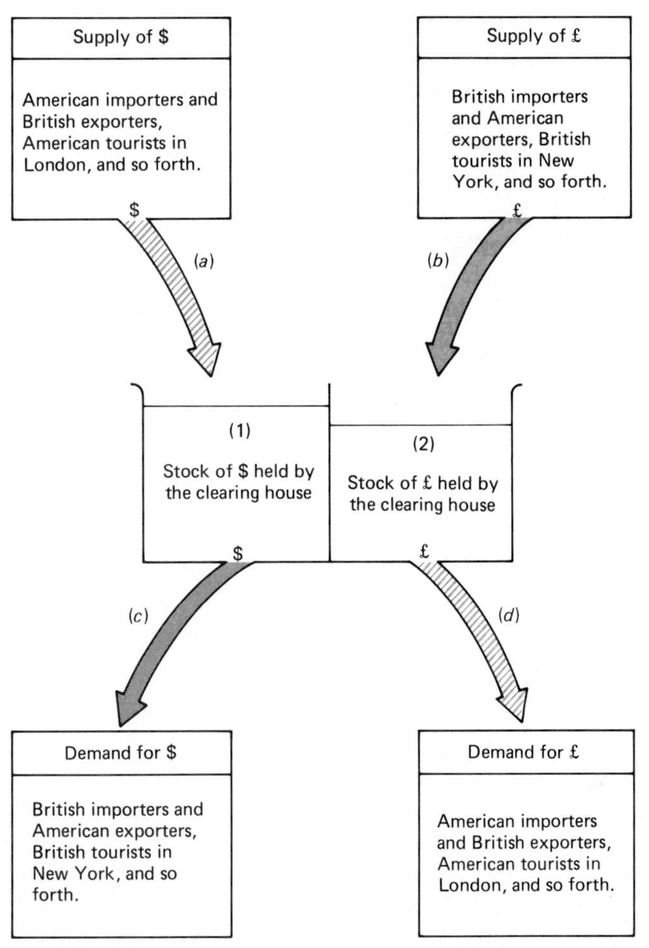

FIGURE 11-1 **The clearing function.** The level of the water in middle chambers 1 and 2 represents the initial stock of dollars and pounds, respectively, held by the clearing house. Striped arrows *a* and *d* show, respectively, the inflow (supply) of dollars into and the outflow of (demand for) pounds from the clearing house. Similarly, dark arrows *b* and *c* show, respectively, the inflow (supply) of pounds into and the outflow of (demand for) dollars from the clearing house. Note the strict correspondence that must exist between arrows *a* and *d*, and between arrows *b* and *c*.

Temporary versus Fundamental Disequilibrium

Besides facilitating currency exchanges, the initial stock of dollars and pounds of the clearing house can be used to bridge *temporary* gaps between the inflow and the outflow of either currency. *Permanent* or *persistent* gaps, however, which may arise from time to time, cannot be dealt with in this manner. When a persistent gap arises, economists say that a **fundamental disequilibrium** exists.

At the risk of oversimplifying, we may say that the rest of the book discusses the various causes and cures of this phenomenon. Essentially, a fundamental disequilibrium can be corrected by means of some adjustment that brings about a better synchronization between the inflows and the outflows of the clearing house.

Means of Payment and Foreign Exchange

So far we used the term **foreign exchange** to mean foreign currencies (bills and coins). In general, however, foreign exchange includes, in addition to foreign currencies, bank deposits and other short-term financial instruments denominated in foreign currencies. In practice, most foreign exchange transactions involve purchases and sales of bank deposits denominated in foreign currencies.

In this book we are not interested in the various means of payment in international transactions (for example, bills of exchange, checks, telegraphic transfers, and cash). The distinctions among them are legal—not economic. It is sufficient for our purposes to note that because of the keen competition that exists among these different means of payment, we can speak of the supply and demand for foreign money without paying much attention to the particular document used.

Credit Function

In addition to its primary function of clearing payments, the foreign exchange market also provides credit. That international trade requires credit follows from the fact that all trade does. It takes time to move goods from seller to buyer, and someone must finance the transaction while the goods are in transit. If the importer pays cash, the importer does the financing. If the exporter provides open-book credit to the importer (or if the exporter holds the accepted bill of exchange until maturity), the exporter furnishes the financing. Typically, however, the credit facilities of the foreign exchange market are used. Thus the exporter discounts the bill of exchange at the foreign department of a commercial bank; the exporter receives cash at once while the bank is paid by the importer when the bill of exchange becomes due.

11-2 ORGANIZATION OF THE MARKET

So far we have used the term *clearing house* to characterize a function rather than a particular institution. In reality, the clearing function is performed by banks, partly because most foreign exchange transactions of any size take the form of an exchange of bank deposits and partly because, in the case of importers who need credit to finance their imports, it is convenient to combine the foreign exchange transactions with the credit transactions.

To understand the actual organization of the foreign exchange market, examine Figure 11-2. The various transactors in the foreign exchange market are presented as four layers of a pyramid. At the bottom (layer 1) we find those businesses and individuals (for example, exporters, importers, and tourists) whose activities generate either a supply of or demand for foreign exchange. As a rule, these ultimate users and suppliers of foreign exchange do not deal directly with one another but use the services of the commercial banks, which are represented by layer 2. For instance, the American corporation that sells computers to a British importer will first receive a promissory note from the importer for the amount of the purchase. Then the American corporation will sell ("discount") the note to an American bank. Similarly, the American importer of British cars may purchase the necessary amount of sterling from an American commercial bank.

To meet the needs of their customers, commercial banks usually maintain deposits with foreign banks. Thus, the American commercial bank will accept the American importer's dollars (or reduce the importer's checking account balance) and at the same time instruct its correspondent bank in London to make a transfer from the American bank's account to the account of the British exporter.

FIGURE 11-2 **Organization of the foreign exchange market.** The four layers of the pyramid portray the four types of transactors and their relationship to one another. In layer 1, we find the ultimate users and suppliers of foreign exchange; these transactors use the services of commercial banks (layer 2). To iron out their net balances, commercial banks use the services of brokers (layer 3). The latter are also the link between commercial banks and central banks (layer 4).

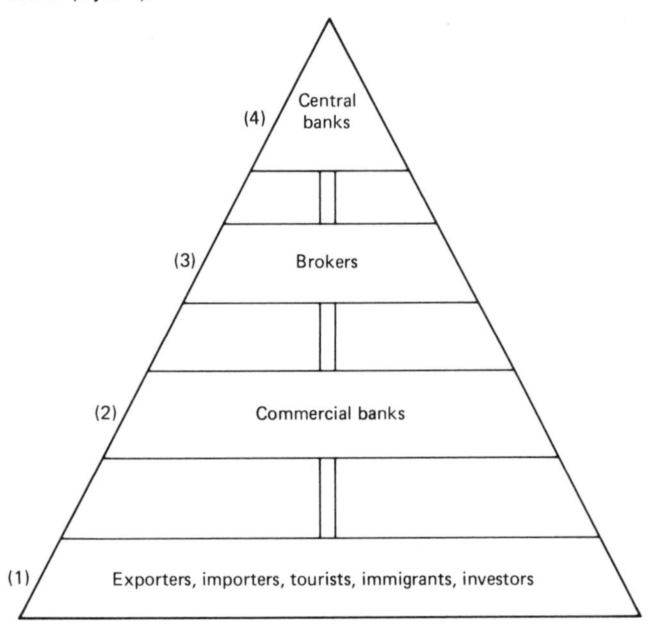

In the course of their foreign exchange dealings, commercial banks purchase foreign exchange from some of their customers while selling it to others. Accordingly, each commercial bank acts to some extent as a clearing house, partially offsetting sales with purchases. However, this clearing process cannot be expected to be perfect because for some banks the total purchases of foreign exchange exceed their sales, while for other banks the total purchases fall short of their sales. To iron out their net balances, commercial banks do not transact directly with one another but rather use the services of foreign exchange brokers. The latter are represented by layer 3 in the pyramid of Figure 11-2. In effect, these brokers offer to commercial banks the same type of services as those offered by commercial banks to the ultimate users and suppliers of foreign exchange. The brokers keep in constant touch with commercial banks. Competition among brokers is rather keen.

The brokers are also the link between commercial banks and central banks. (A nation's central bank controls the supply of money and the banking system in general and serves as the principal banker of the government.) In Figure 11-2, central banks are represented by the top layer. The foreign exchange activities of central banks depend crucially on the existing exchange rate system or regime, as explained in Section 11-3 and the rest of the book.

The student should resist the feeling that the four layers of Figure 11-2 stand for the chronological order of the various transactions. The truth of the matter is that all types of transactions usually take place simultaneously.

11-3 EXCHANGE RATE SYSTEMS

In this section, we define exchange rates and show how they are determined under alternative types of foreign exchange regimes.

Foreign Exchange Rates

The price of one currency in terms of another is called the **rate of foreign exchange** or just the **exchange rate.** There is, of course, some ambiguity in the use of this definition. Consider, for instance, the case of the dollar and the pound sterling. Assume that $2 exchange for £1. Which of the two currencies is to be used as the unit of account, or numéraire? We could calculate the price of the foreign currency (pound sterling) in terms of the domestic currency (dollar), which is $2.00 per pound. Alternatively, we could calculate the price of the domestic currency (dollar) in terms of the foreign currency (pound sterling), which is £0.50 per dollar. Note that $0.50 = 1/2.00$. Because these two prices are reciprocals of each other, it is immaterial which one we use, provided we always remember its meaning. In this book, to avoid confusion we define the exchange rate to mean the price of the foreign currency in terms of the domestic currency. (In practice, when the dollar price of a foreign currency is very small, it is more convenient to use its reciprocal. For instance, we may say that the yen-dollar exchange rate is 125 yen per dollar rather than $0.008 per yen.)

The Flexible Exchange-Rate System

Under the **flexible exchange-rate system** the exchange rate is determined daily in the foreign exchange market by the forces of supply and demand. The exchange rate moves freely in response to market forces, as governments and central bankers refrain from any systematic intervention. This system, which is also known as the **freely flexible (or clean-floating) exchange-rate system,** is illustrated in Figure 11-3.

The demand curve for pounds sterling (*D*) shows the quantity of pounds demanded at alternative exchange rates. It slopes downward; thus as the price of a pound in terms of dollars increases, the quantity of pounds demanded declines. The reason for the negative slope need not concern us at the moment. We return to it in Chapter 14. Briefly, as the pound sterling becomes more expensive, the prices of British goods rise in America; thus Americans import less, causing the quantity of pounds demanded to fall.

The supply curve for pounds sterling (*S*) shows the quantity of pounds supplied at alternative exchange rates. We assume that it slopes upward; thus as the exchange rate rises, the quantity of pounds supplied increases. The assumed positive slope reflects the fact that as the pound becomes more expensive, the prices of American goods *fall* in Britain; hence Britons import more, causing the

FIGURE 11-3 **Equilibrium in the foreign exchange market.** Under a flexible exchange-rate system, equilibrium occurs at *E*, where the supply and demand curves for pounds intersect. Under a fixed exchange-rate system, the monetary authorities can maintain the peg at $1.60 per pound by selling £40 million (corresponding to distance *AB*) per day.

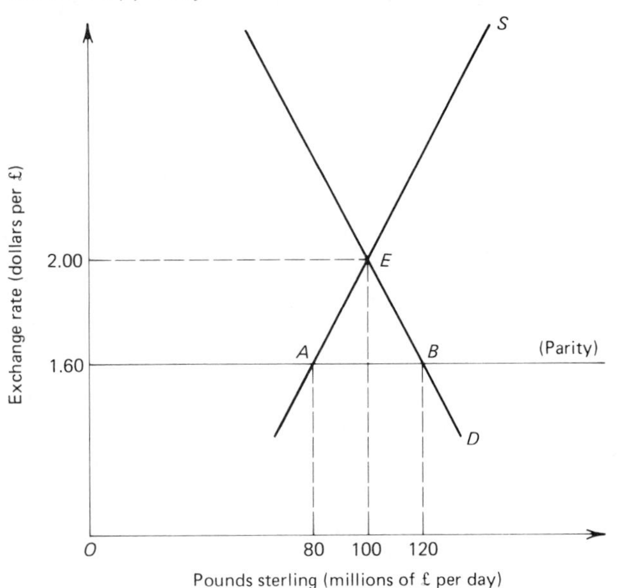

quantity of pounds supplied to increase. (Warning: As Chapter 14 shows, this proposition is not generally true.)

Equilibrium occurs at point *E*, at which the supply and demand curves for pounds intersect. At the equilibrium exchange rate of $2 per pound, £100 million are traded. At a higher exchange rate, the quantity supplied exceeds the quantity demanded; thus the exchange rate tends to fall. At a lower exchange rate, the quantity demanded exceeds the quantity supplied; thus the exchange rate tends to rise.

Shifts in the supply and demand curves for pounds cause the equilibrium rate of foreign exchange to rise or fall depending on circumstances. When the equilibrium exchange rate rises, the pound is said to *appreciate* in terms of the dollar (since the amount of dollars required to buy a pound increases), or the dollar *depreciates* in terms of the pound.

Since 1973 most major currencies have been allowed to "float," but not entirely freely. Central banks do intervene frequently to iron out wide fluctuations in the exchange rate. For instance, if the Federal Reserve, the U.S. central bank, wants to support the dollar, it will sell foreign exchange through one or more foreign exchange brokers. This system has come to be known as *dirty*, or *managed*, floating.

The Fixed Exchange-Rate System

Under a fixed exchange-rate system, the central bank intervenes in the foreign exchange market in an effort to maintain the exchange rate within prescribed limits, or a "band" even if the chosen rate departs from the (free-market) equilibrium rate. The central rate is called the **par value** (or **peg**) of the currency. To maintain the officially declared parity, it is necessary for the central bank to stand ready to fill any gaps between the supply and demand for foreign exchange at the fixed rate. To achieve this goal, the central bank must hold **international reserves** (that is, inventories of foreign currencies), pretty much like the hypothetical clearing house of Section 11-1.

The fixed exchange-rate system is illustrated in Figure 11-3, where it is now assumed that the exchange rate is pegged at $1.60 per pound. (For simplicity, we assume no band around the peg.) Because the peg lies below the equilibrium rate, there exists an excess demand for pounds represented by horizontal distance *AB*. To maintain the exchange rate at the peg, the central bank (of either country) must be willing and able to fill gap *AB*. Thus the central bank must sell (through a broker) £40 million per day at $1.60 per pound. Surely this situation cannot last forever. Eventually, the authorities may have to pursue deliberate policy measures to *shift* the supply and demand curves for foreign exchange (pounds sterling) until they intersect at the fixed parity of $1.60. If such policy measures fail to eliminate the fundamental disequilibrium, the central bank may be forced to change the parity.

If the par value is increased, the domestic currency is said to be **devalued** (because the price of foreign currency rises in terms of domestic currency). If the par value is decreased, the domestic currency is said to be **revalued** (or **upvalued**). Thus **devaluation** and **revaluation** correspond to depreciation and appreciation, respectively, of the domestic currency. The different terminology reflects the different exchange-rate systems. Devaluation and revaluation refer to deliberate government policy response to market forces.

The fixed exchange-rate system has taken several forms. Before World War I, it took the form of an international **gold standard,** according to which all countries tied their monies to gold and allowed the unrestricted import and export of gold. The essence of the gold standard was that the rates of exchange were fixed. For instance, suppose that the American monetary authorities agreed to buy and sell unlimited amounts of gold at $200 per ounce. Assume also that the British authorities agreed to buy and sell gold at £100 per ounce. Then the rate of exchange would be $2 per pound **(mint parity).** Any excess demand for pounds at this rate would merely cause gold to be exported from America to Britain. Thus, economic units in need of pounds would simply turn their dollars in for gold at the Federal Reserve and then sell the gold to the Bank of England for pounds. Similarly, an excess supply of pounds (that is, an excess demand for dollars) would cause gold to be exported from Britain to America.

After World War II, and in particular between 1944 and 1971, the free world sought the advantages of the fixed exchange rate system in the so-called **Bretton Woods system,** also known as the system of the **adjustable peg.**

Under the Bretton Woods system, the dollar was pegged to gold at the fixed parity of $35 per ounce of gold, and the United States was prepared to buy and sell unlimited amounts of gold at the official rate. Dollars held by official monetary institutions were freely convertible into gold. Every other country besides the United States was required to (1) declare the par value (or **parity**) of its currency in terms of gold or the U.S. dollar and (2) stand ready to defend the declared parity in the foreign exchange market by buying or selling dollars, at least in the short run. Accordingly, the currencies of member countries were kept stable in terms of dollars and thus in terms of each other. Exchange rates were thereby *fixed* (but only in the short run).

Between the polar cases of the fixed and flexible exchange-rate systems there are many compromises. For instance, there is the **wide band:** the exchange rate is flexible within wide limits but is prevented from moving outside those limits. There is also the **crawling peg,** according to which the exchange rate changes continuously but by very small amounts, that is, it "crawls."

11-4 THE INTERNATIONAL CHARACTER OF THE FOREIGN EXCHANGE MARKET

What is a market? Does a market have to be housed in a single building? Does a market have to be limited to a particular locality? Certainly, national currencies are traded at many spots on the globe, for example, New York, Chicago, London, Zurich, Hong Kong, Singapore, and Tokyo. Is each one of these geographic places a separate market? If not, why not? These are important questions, and the purpose of this section is to consider them briefly.

The Foreign Exchange Market as an International Market

A market is composed of sellers and buyers. These persons are in close touch with one another in order to sell or buy some commodity. How the buyers and sellers actually keep in touch with one another is not important. If all buyers and sellers are housed in the same building, they can transact business face to face. If they are scattered around the globe, as is the case with the foreign exchange market, they can keep in constant touch with one another and transact business by telephone, telegraph, teletype, or computer.

The foreign exchange dealers of commercial banks are constantly alert to the latest quotations in the various geographic spots of the market. As a result, the foreign exchange market embraces all financial centers of the world. The foreign exchange market is not limited to a particular locality; rather it is an *international* market in which national currencies are traded. Because of its international character, the foreign exchange market is open around the clock. After the New York market closes at 3:00 p.m. eastern standard time, trading continues in San Francisco. When the San Francisco market closes, trading moves to Tokyo, and later on to Hong Kong, Singapore, Zurich, and London, before it returns to New York for a new cycle to begin again.

Arbitrage

The economic force that keeps the various financial centers around the world united as a single market is known as **arbitrage.** By definition, arbitrage is the simultaneous purchase and sale of foreign currencies for the sake of profit. Profitable arbitrage opportunities arise either because the price of one currency in terms of another (that is, the rate of foreign exchange) differs from one financial center to another or because the various rates of exchange are inconsistent, as explained below.

Two-Point (or Spatial) Arbitrage

Two-point arbitrage (also known as **spatial** arbitrage) involves *two* currencies only. Suppose that the pound sterling exchanges for $2 in New York and for $2.10 in London. An arbitrageur (usually a foreign exchange dealer of a commercial bank) can make a profit by buying pounds in New York at $2 and simultaneously selling them in London at $2.10. This kind of arbitrage tends to draw the two prices together by forcing up the dollar price of the pound sterling in New York and depressing it in London. Even small discrepancies between the exchange rates quoted in various financial centers give rise to voluminous arbitrage—which practically wipes out the discrepancies within minutes.

Three-Point (or Triangular) Arbitrage

Three-point arbitrage (also known as **triangular** arbitrage) involves *three* currencies. Its profitability is due to the inconsistency of the uniformly quoted rates. For instance, consider three currencies: the dollar, the pound, and the yen. All three currencies are traded in New York, London, and Tokyo. Suppose that the following prices (or rates of exchange) prevail currently in all three financial centers:

£1 sells for either $2 or 250 yen
$1 sells for 130 yen

Because the same prices prevail in all financial centers, two-point arbitrage is no longer profitable. Nevertheless, the quoted prices (or rates) are inconsistent, and an arbitrageur can make a profit as follows:

1 Sell £1 for $2.
2 Then sell each $1 for 130 yen to collect a total of 260 yen.
3 Finally, buy back the initial £1 for 250 yen, and pocket 10 yen.

There is a simple procedure to determine a profitable sequence. Place each currency at a different corner of a triangle, as shown in Figure 11-4. An arbitrageur starts with any currency and moves in a clockwise direction. For instance, starting with dollars, the arbitrageur can exchange dollars for pounds, then pounds for yen, and finally yen for dollars. If this sequence generates a profit, the arbitrageur has a profitable sequence. If the sequence generates a loss, then moving counterclockwise must generate a profit, and the arbitrageur has a profitable sequence.

FIGURE 11-4 **Three-point arbitrage.** Start with any currency and move in a clockwise direction around the triangle. If this sequence does not generate a profit, then the opposite sequence (in a counterclockwise direction) does.

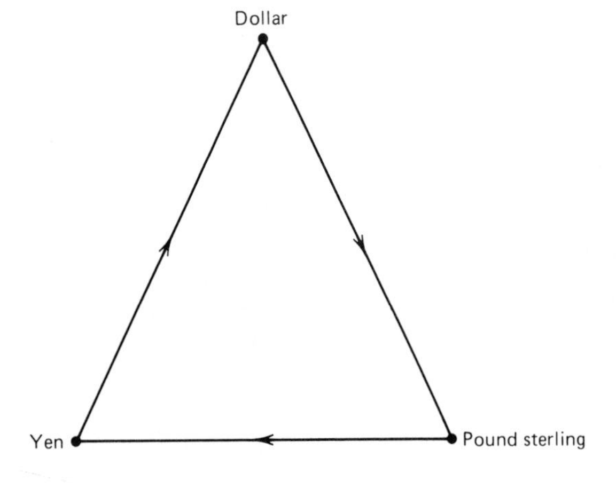

Indirect (or Cross) Rates of Exchange

The rates (or prices) used in the preceding example are usually called *direct*. To gain further insight into the problem of consistency of exchange rates, we pursue the above example of three-point arbitrage a little further.

First, we must introduce the concept of an **indirect** (or **cross**) **rate of exchange.** What is an indirect rate? Suppose you want to convert £1 into yen. The direct rate is the number of yen (250) that a bank can give you in exchange for £1. However, you may obtain yen for your pound by first exchanging it for dollars ($2) and then exchanging the dollars for 260 yen. The number of yen you obtain in this indirect fashion is the indirect rate. In our illustration, the direct rate (250 yen) is lower than the indirect rate (260 yen). Hence, you can make a profit by selling your pound indirectly for 260 yen and buying it back directly for 250 yen.

Many-Currency Arbitrage

In the real world, other, more complicated forms of arbitrage—involving four, five, or more currencies—can take place. Nevertheless, the relatively simple three-currency arbitrage illustrated above is sufficient to establish consistent rates of foreign exchange. Accordingly, when it works well, three-currency (or three-point) arbitrage eliminates the profitability of these more complicated forms of arbitrage, which only rarely take place.

11-5 EXCHANGE RISK

We now turn to the third function of the foreign exchange market, hedging foreign exchange risks. The main distinguishing feature of international finance is not really the multitude of national currencies per se but rather the possibility of exchange-rate fluctuations. Ordinarily, export and import transactions involve periods of waiting, and the slightest unfavorable change in the exchange rate may involve exporters and importers in losses completely unrelated to their normal business. The third function of the foreign exchange market, in addition to clearing and credit, is to provide hedging facilities to exporters and importers against possible losses due to exchange-rate fluctuations.

Some Definitions

The possibility of loss because of an unfavorable change in the exchange rate is usually referred to as **exchange risk.** Covering an exchange risk is called **hedging,** and deliberately assuming an exchange risk is called **speculation.**

In general, foreign assets may appreciate or depreciate in value as the price of the foreign currency increases or decreases, respectively. If my total assets in a foreign currency exactly match my total liabilities in that same currency, I run no exchange risk—my net wealth remains independent of any exchange rate fluctuations because my foreign assets offset my foreign liabilities.

Some people (known as **hedgers**) who dislike exchange risk insist on maintaining an exact balance between their assets and liabilities in foreign currencies. Others (known as **speculators**), who think they know what the future rate of exchange will be and are willing to gamble, hold their assets in that currency which they expect to appreciate in value.

Note that even though we often speak of hedgers and speculators, it is more accurate to refer to the *activities* of hedging and speculation. It is the activities, not the persons, that are important from an economic viewpoint because the same person may actually act as a hedger in some cases while acting as a speculator in others.

The foreign exchange market provides useful services to both hedgers and speculators, as illustrated in the following examples.

Hedging

Consider first the case of an American exporter of computers who has just received £100,000 in the form of a checking deposit at a London bank. Suppose that the American exporter wants to maintain the funds in liquid form for three months but does not wish to run an exchange risk. For instance, if in three months the pound sterling were to fall to $1.80 from its current price of $2, the dollar equivalent of the American exporter's deposit would fall from $200,000 to $180,000—a loss of $20,000 in just three months. To avoid the exchange risk, the American exporter must sell the £100,000 today in the foreign exchange market and invest the dollars ($200,000) in the United States.

As a second illustration, assume that the American exporter expects to receive £100,000 in three months. Since the pounds are not available today, how can the exporter hedge against the possible depreciation of the pound? The answer is implicit in what we said earlier: *The exporter must generate a liability in pounds of exactly the same amount as the expected sales proceeds.* To accomplish this, the exporter borrows £100,000 in London for three months; then the exporter sells the loan proceeds (pounds) in the foreign exchange market for $200,000 and invests the dollars in the United States. Now the exporter has the funds in dollars, as in the first illustration, but in addition has an asset of £100,000 (the expected payment by the British importer) plus a liability of £100,000 (the loan in London). Since both the asset and liability in sterling mature in three months, it follows that *irrespective of what the price of the pound is in three months, the exporter can use the sales proceeds to pay off the loan.* (In this example we ignored the interest charges for the sake of simplicity.)

Note that even though in the above illustration he is able to eliminate the exchange risk, the American exporter is required to have credit facilities in London. This is, of course, a severe drawback, which usually forces the American exporter to work with the forward market, as is explained in the following section.

As a third and final illustration, consider the case of an American importer of British automobiles who must pay the British exporter £100,000 in three months. To hedge against this sterling liability, the importer can buy sterling today in the foreign exchange market, deposit it with a British bank, and use it (along with the interest accrued) in three months to pay off the debt. Of course, this type of hedging requires the importer to have either idle cash or credit facilities. For this reason, the American importer usually prefers to work with the forward market, as is explained in the next section.

Speculation

Speculation is the deliberate assumption of exchange risk in the expectation of a profit. Speculators have definite expectations about future rates of exchange and are interested in making a profit by buying foreign exchange when it is cheap and selling it when it is expensive. Speculators who are right in their expectations make a profit; but if they are wrong, they suffer a loss. The possibility of a loss often restrains speculators in their activities.

Note that speculation is the opposite of hedging. While hedging means some action that tends to eliminate exchange risk, speculation means the deliberate assumption of exchange risk.

Speculation also ought to be distinguished from arbitrage. Arbitrage also involves the principle of buying a currency where it is cheap and selling it where it is expensive. Nevertheless, arbitrage is riskless because for all practical purposes the purchase and sale take place at the same moment and all prices are known to the arbitrageur. The activities of the speculator, however, are necessarily subject to exchange risk. Indeed, the element of exchange risk is *the* characteristic feature of speculation.

Speculators are usually portrayed as greedy and antisocial individuals whose subversive activities generate total chaos in international financial markets from time to time. In fact, these mysterious gnomes of Zurich are supposed to perform their subversive activities during major financial crises. With respect to such tales, the reader must keep in mind two things. First, in the broad form in which we are using the term, speculation can be practiced by many types of individuals and businesses: exporters and importers of goods and services, bankers, tourists, and so on. Anybody whose total assets in a foreign currency do not match that person's liabilities in that same currency is a speculator. Second, whether speculation is responsible for the crises that arise from time to time in the international financial markets is an empirical question. While speculation may be responsible for some crises, it need not, and in fact does not, always create chaos. It is at least theoretically possible for speculation to perform the highly useful function of ironing out exchange rate fluctuations over time. As Milton Friedman points out, speculators will continue in the business only so long as it is profitable. This will be the case if, as a rule, they can buy cheap and sell dear. But to buy cheap and sell dear is to iron out exchange rate fluctuations over time.

A speculator with pessimistic expectations about the future price of a currency is called a **bear;** one with optimistic expectations, a **bull.** For example, bulls on sterling (that is, those who expect the pound sterling to become more expensive in the future) buy sterling now when it is cheap and plan to sell it later on when it becomes expensive. In technical jargon, the bulls on sterling take a **long position** (that is, their sterling assets are larger than their sterling liabilities).

Similarly, bears on sterling (that is, those who expect the price of sterling to fall in the future) take a **short position** (that is, their sterling assets are smaller than their sterling liabilities). For instance, an American speculator who expects the pound sterling to depreciate in the near future can borrow pounds sterling in London and sell them for dollars in the foreign exchange market. In this fashion the speculator creates a sterling liability without a matching sterling asset. The speculator whose expectations are right will buy sterling in the future at a lower price and pay off the debt, in the meantime pocketing a handsome profit in dollars.

Trader Speculation

As noted earlier, exporters and importers who either expect to receive or make payment in a foreign currency in the future are running an exchange risk. These traders can speculate merely by not covering their exchange risk. The decision by a trader not to cover his exchange risk is certainly similar to the decision of a pure speculator to deliberately open a long or a short position in a foreign currency in order to make a profit.

Nevertheless, not covering the exchange risk is not the only form of **trader speculation** (that is, speculation by an importer or exporter). Another important form of trader speculation is what is usually referred to as **leads and lags.** This term refers to the adjustment that importers and exporters make in the timing of payments, the placement of orders, and the making of deliveries for the purpose of avoiding losses or making profits from an anticipated change in the rate of foreign exchange.

Suppose, for instance, that a substantial depreciation of the pound sterling is expected. British exporters of goods invoiced in dollars will be anxious to delay (*lag*) receiving payment in the hope of selling their dollar revenue at an exchange rate that is more favorable than the present one. They can do so merely by extending credit to foreign importers, perhaps at very attractive terms, or by delaying their deliveries.

If the British exports are invoiced in pounds sterling instead of dollars, the outcome is the same except that American importers assume the initiative now. Thus, when a depreciation of the pound sterling is expected, American importers will delay payment and the placement of orders in the hope of buying pounds sterling cheaper in the future.

British importers of goods invoiced in dollars will be anxious to accelerate (*lead*) their payments and placement of orders merely to avoid being caught with dollar obligations in the event of a depreciation of the pound sterling. Again, if the goods are invoiced in pounds sterling, it is the American exporters who will take the initiative to accelerate their receipts. In addition, the American exporters may offer better terms to the British importers and induce the latter to accelerate their orders as well.

11-6 FORWARD EXCHANGE

Foreign exchange transactions are divided into two major classes: **spot** and **forward.** All the foreign exchange transactions we have considered so far are **spot transactions.** Their distinguishing feature is that they require *immediate delivery,* or *exchange of currencies on the spot.* (In practice, the settlement of spot transactions usually requires a couple of days.) The rate of exchange used in the settlement of spot transactions is called the **spot rate;** the market for spot transactions, the **spot market. Forward transactions** are merely agreements for future exchanges of currencies. The rate of exchange used in the settlement of forward transactions is called the **forward rate;** the market for forward transactions, the **forward market.** In this section, we study the mechanics and conventions of forward exchange, and explain the economic significance of the forward market. In the following section, we examine briefly the relationship that exists between spot rates and forward rates.

Forward Transactions

Consider again the case of the American importer of British automobiles who must pay £100,000 to the British exporter in three months, say, on April 10. Suppose that today, January 10, the spot rate of sterling is $2, but the American importer is uncertain what the rate will be in three months. For this reason, he wants to hedge against this sterling liability (that is, cover his exchange risk).

The American importer can cover his exchange risk by using the facilities of the spot market (**spot covering**). Thus, he can buy sterling today in the spot market, deposit it with a British bank, and use it (along with the interest accrued) in three months to pay off his debt. This type of spot covering has a severe drawback: It requires the American importer to have either large amounts of idle cash or credit facilities. The forward market, however, requires neither cash nor credit facilities. In addition, covering the exchange risk through the forward market (**forward covering**) is much simpler and is usually preferred. How can the American importer cover his exchange risk in the forward market?

All the American importer has to do is to sign a contract (known as a **forward contract**) with his bank, according to which the bank agrees to deliver to him £100,000 on April 10. The price per pound (that is, the forward rate) that the American importer agrees to pay his bank may or may not be equal to the current spot rate ($2). The American importer may agree to pay, say, $1.90 or $2.05 per pound to be delivered on April 10, depending on what the current forward rate is. The important thing to note, though, is the fact that by signing the forward contract and agreeing to the forward rate, the American importer removes the uncertainty surrounding his liability. If, for instance, the current forward rate is $2.05, the American importer knows at the very moment he signs the forward contract that on April 10 he will be required to pay $205,000 exactly, irrespective of what the actual spot rate or forward rate is on April 10.

Note that today (January 10) the American importer only signs a contract. Neither pounds nor dollars change hands. (In practice, the commercial bank may set a **margin requirement,** that is, the bank may require the American importer to put up, say, 10 percent of the value of the forward contract as security.) The exchange of currencies will take place three months later, on April 10. In other words, the forward market deals in present commitments to buy and sell currencies at some specified future time.

As a second illustration, consider the case of the American exporter who expects to receive £100,000 in three months, say, on April 10. We have seen how the American exporter can cover her exchange risk in the spot market (spot covering): She can borrow £100,000 in London for three months and sell it in the spot market for, say, $200,000; and on April 10 she can use her sales proceeds of £100,000 to pay off her debt. (For simplicity, we ignore any interest charges.) Spot covering has the drawback that the American exporter must have credit facilities in London. Again, forward covering is much simpler.

The American exporter can cover her risk in the forward market by selling £100,000 forward. She must sign a contract with her bank today, according to which the bank agrees to buy £100,000 from her on April 10. Again, the forward rate need not be, and in general is not, equal to either the current spot rate or the spot rate that will actually prevail in the spot market on April 10. It is conceivable that the American exporter may have to sell her expected sales proceeds of £100,000 at a price that is lower than the current spot rate. But by signing the forward contract today, the American exporter protects herself against the risk of an unfavorable change of the rate of exchange.

In summary, a forward transaction is merely an agreement (called the forward contract) between two parties (either a bank and a customer or two banks) that calls for delivery at some prescribed time in the *future* of a specified amount of foreign currency by one of the parties against payment in domestic currency by the other party at a price (called the forward rate) agreed upon *now* when the contract is signed.

The Basis of the Forward Market

The main function of the forward market, its raison d'être, is to enable businesspeople to cover their exchange risks. The forward covering of exchange risks essentially enables exporters and importers alike to eliminate the uncertainty of the foreign exchange element from international transactions.

Note that the exchange risk is not eliminated if the exporters and importers of one country insist on dealing in terms of their own domestic currency. In that case, the exchange risk is simply shifted to the foreigners. Since this procedure might discourage the foreigners, it is almost certain that some advantageous transactions would be ruled out. Thanks to forward exchange, however, this great loss to the international economy can be averted.

Forward Premium and Forward Discount

The forward rate for a currency, say, the pound sterling, is said to be at a **premium** with respect to the spot rate when £1 buys more units of another currency, say, the dollar, in the forward market than in the spot market. Conversely, the forward rate for pounds is said to be at a **discount** with respect to the spot rate when £1 buys fewer dollars in the forward market than in the spot market. For instance, when the spot rate is \$2 and the three-month forward rate is \$2.025, we say that the pound sterling is at a forward premium because $\$2.025 > \$2$. However, when the spot rate is \$2 and the forward rate is only \$1.975, we say that the pound sterling is at a forward discount, since $\$1.975 < \$2$.

The forward premium or forward discount is usually expressed as a percentage deviation from the spot rate on a per annum basis (like the rate of interest). For instance, when the spot rate is \$2 and the three-month forward rate is \$2.025, the pound sterling is at a 5 percent forward premium:

$$\frac{\$2.025 - \$2}{\$2} \times \frac{12 \text{ (months)}}{3 \text{ (months)}} \times 100 = +5 \text{ (premium)}$$

Similarly, when the spot rate is \$2 and the three-month forward rate is only \$1.975, the pound sterling is at a 5 percent forward discount:

$$\frac{\$1.975 - \$2}{\$2} \times \frac{12 \text{ (months)}}{3 \text{ (months)}} \times 100 = -5 \text{ (discount)}$$

Note that when the pound is at a forward premium, the dollar is necessarily at a forward discount. Similarly, when the pound is at a forward discount, the dollar is at a forward premium.

Actual Exchange-Rate Quotations

Table 11-1 gives the exchange-rate quotations for January 5, 1989 as published in *The Wall Street Journal.* The first two columns give the prices of foreign currencies in terms of the domestic currency (U.S. dollars); the last two columns give the number of units of foreign currency required to buy \$1. The rates given in Table 11-1 were quoted at 3 p.m. eastern standard time, by Bankers Trust Company and used in trading among banks in amounts of \$1 million or more. For instance, the dollar price of the pound was \$1.7960. Similarly, the dollar prices (spot exchange rates) for the Japanese yen and the German mark were \$0.007949 and \$0.5566, respectively. Note that these were wholesale quotes, which differed from the retail rates quoted by banks for tourists, exporters, importers, and other individual users of foreign exchange.

TABLE 11-1 FOREIGN EXCHANGE QUOTATIONS* FROM *THE WALL STREET JOURNAL*, FRIDAY JANUARY 6, 1989

	U.S. $ equiv.		Currency per U.S. $	
Country	**Thurs.**	**Wed.**	**Thurs.**	**Wed.**
Argentina (austral)	.06135	.06135	16.30	16.30
Australia (dollar)	.8647	.8693	1.1565	1.1503
Austria (schilling)	.07909	.07961	12.64	12.56
Bahrain (dinar)	2.6521	2.6521	.37705	.37705
Belgium (franc)				
Commercial rate	.02653	.026695	37.68	37.46
Financial rate	.02644	.026602	37.82	37.59
Brazil (cruzado)	.001336	.001336	748.05	748.05
Britain (pound)	1.7960	1.8095	.5567	.5526
30-day forward	1.7903	1.8038	.5585	.5543
90-day forward	1.7797	1.7933	.5618	.5576
180-day forward	1.7658	1.7794	.5663	.5619
Canada (dollar)	.8408	.8386	1.1893	1.1924
30-day forward	.8398	.8376	1.1907	1.1938
90-day forward	.8374	.8354	1.1941	1.1970
180-day forward	.8336	.8316	1.1996	1.2024
Chile (official rate)	.0040176	.0040176	248.90	248.90
China (yuan)	.268672	.268672	3.7220	3.7220
Colombia (peso)	.002985	.002985	335.00	335.00
Denmark (krone)	.1441	.1450	6.9365	6.8925
Ecuador (sucre)				
Official rate	.004008	.004008	249.50	249.50
Floating rate	.0019762	.0019762	506.00	506.00
Finland (markka)	.2388	.2404	4.1860	4.1595
France (franc)	.1630	.1640	6.1340	6.0945
30-day forward	.1631	.1641	6.1299	6.0906
90-day forward	.1633	.1644	6.1215	6.0820
180-day forward	.1637	.1647	6.1070	6.0695
Greece (drachma)	.006680	.006724	149.70	148.70
Hong Kong (dollar)	.1280	.1280	7.8075	7.8075
India (rupee)	.0665335	.0665335	15.03	15.03
Indonesia (rupiah)	.0005841	.0005841	1712.00	1712.00
Ireland (punt)	1.5182	1.5182	.6586	.6586
Israel (shekel)	.6267	.6267	1.5955	1.5955
Italy (lira)	.0007583	.0007623	1318.75	1311.75
Japan (yen)	.007949	.008005	125.80	124.92
30-day forward	.007982	.008037	125.27	124.41
90-day forward	.008045	.008100	124.29	123.45
180-day forward	.008143	.008199	122.80	121.96
Jordan (dinar)	2.1052	2.1052	.4750	.4750
Kuwait (dinar)	3.5483	3.5483	.2818	.2818
Lebanon (pound)	.001953	.001953	512.00	512.00
Malaysia (ringgit)	.36909	.36968	2.7093	2.7050
Malta (lira)	3.0395	3.0395	.3290	.3290
Mexico (peso)				
Floating rate	.0004378	.0004378	2284.00	2284.00
Netherlands (guilder)	.4945	.4961	2.0220	2.0155

TABLE 11-1 FOREIGN EXCHANGE QUOTATIONS* FROM *THE WALL STREET JOURNAL*, FRIDAY JANUARY 6, 1989 *(continued)*

	U.S. $ equiv.		Currency per U.S. $	
Country	**Thurs.**	**Wed.**	**Thurs.**	**Wed.**
New Zealand (dollar)	.6380	.6360	1.5674	1.5723
Norway (krone)	.1513	.1522	6.6060	6.5675
Pakistan (rupee)	.05405	.05405	18.50	18.50
Peru (inti)	.0006639	.0006639	1506.25	1506.25
Philippines (peso)	.048309	.048309	20.70	20.70
Portugal (escudo)	.006875	.006875	145.45	145.45
Saudi Arabia (riyal)	.2666	.2666	3.7505	3.7505
Singapore (dollar)	.5159	.5154	1.9383	1.9400
South Africa (rand)				
Commercial rate	.4237	.4237	2.3600	2.3600
Financial rate	.2558	.2591	3.9100	3.8600
South Korea (won)	.001461	.001461	684.00	684.00
Spain (peseta)	.008791	.008845	113.75	113.05
Sweden (krona)	.1618	.1627	6.1790	6.1455
Switzerland (franc)	.6508	.6587	1.5365	1.5180
30-day forward	.6531	.6612	1.5310	1.5124
90-day forward	.6572	.6658	1.5214	1.5019
180-day forward	.6637	.6731	1.5065	1.4855
Taiwan (dollar)	.03549	.03549	28.17	28.17
Thailand (baht)	.039777	.039777	25.14	25.14
Turkey (lira)	.0005530	.0005530	1808.10	1808.10
United Arab (dirham)	.2722	.2722	3.6725	3.6725
Uruguay (new peso)				
Financial	.002212	.002212	452.00	452.00
Venezuela (bolivar)				
Official rate	.1333	.1333	7.50	7.50
Floating rate	.0268	.0268	37.20	37.20
W. Germany (mark)	.5566	.5599	1.7965	1.7860
30-day forward	.5584	.5617	1.7907	1.7802
90-day forward	.5619	.5651	1.7796	1.7693
180-day forward	.5672	.5706	1.7629	1.7524
SDR†	1.34137	1.34662	0.745506	0.742602
ECU†	1.16361	1.16792		

*The New York foreign exchange selling rates apply to trading among banks in amounts of $1 million and more, as quoted at 3 p.m. eastern standard time by Bankers Trust Company. Retail transactions provide fewer units of foreign currency per dollar.

†Data on SDRs (special drawing rights) are from the International Monetary Fund and are based on exchange rates for U.S., West German, British, French, and Japanese currencies. ECU (European Currency Unit) data are from the European Community Commission and are based on a basket of EC currencies.

Source: Adapted from *The Wall Street Journal*, Friday, January 6, 1989. Reprinted by permission.

Forward contracts usually have maturities of 30, 90, and 180 days, as illustrated in Table 11-1 for the pound sterling, the Canadian dollar, the French franc, the Japanese yen, the Swiss franc, and the German mark. (Maturities of up to one year are also common.) Note that the pound sterling and the Canadian dollar were at a forward discount, while the French franc, the Japanese yen, the Swiss franc, and the German mark were at a forward premium. For instance, the 90-day forward premium on the German mark was

$$\frac{0.5619 - 0.5566}{0.5566} \times \frac{360}{90} \times 100 = +3.81\%$$

Other forward discounts and premiums could be calculated in a similar fashion.

Forward Speculation

We saw earlier how a speculator can speculate in the spot market. For instance, an American speculator who expects the pound sterling to appreciate in terms of the dollar may buy sterling now in the spot market in the hope of selling it later at a higher price. **Spot speculation** has the drawback that the speculator must have either idle cash or access to credit facilities. **Forward speculation,** however, requires neither command over cash nor access to credit facilities.

The speculator who expects the pound sterling to appreciate in the near future simply buys sterling forward. For instance, if today, January 10, the current *forward rate* for three-month sterling is $2.05 and the speculator expects the *spot rate* to rise to $2.40 on April 10, he can buy £100,000 forward. (The bank may require the speculator to put down 10 percent of the contract as collateral.) On April 10 the speculator must pay $205,000 to the bank in exchange for £100,000. If he is right in his expectations and the spot rate on April 10 is indeed $2.40, the speculator can turn around and sell his £100,000 to the same bank for $240,000. Thus, he can make a profit of $35,000 (that is, $240,000 − $205,000). In fact, on April 10, the speculator can walk into the bank without any cash and merely collect his profit of $35,000, since the bank can combine the two transactions and just pay the difference. Of course, if on April 10 the spot rate is less than $2.05, the speculator will suffer a loss. For instance, if the rate is $1.90, the speculator will lose $15,000.

Similarly, the speculator who expects the pound sterling to depreciate in the near future can sell pounds sterling forward. For instance, suppose that on January 10 the current forward rate is $2.05 and a speculator expects the spot rate to be $1.80 on April 10. She sells, say, £100,000 forward at the current forward rate of $2.05. If she is right in her expectations and the spot rate actually falls to $1.80, on April 10 she can buy £100,000 in the spot market at a total cost of $180,000. Then she can deliver £100,000 to the bank with which she signed the forward contract on January 10 and collect a total of $205,000. Actually, the speculator can do all her business with the same bank. Thus, on April 10 she may walk into the bank and simply collect her profit of $25,000 (that is, $205,000 − $180,000).

Banks and Exchange Risk

How do banks cover the risks they assume as they sign forward contracts? They do it in three steps.

First, forward purchases and sales of a particular currency by a particular bank ordinarily match to a considerable extent. Hence, a large portion of the risk involved is automatically offset.

Second, banks deal among themselves (with the help of brokers) to iron out their net individual positions. Hence, another large portion of risk is canceled by means of trading between banks.

Third, banks use spot covering for any residual amount of forward sales or forward purchases that remains after the first two steps. Suppose, for instance, that a bank finds itself with a residual amount of forward sterling liabilities. The bank can cover its residual exchange risk merely by buying sterling spot and investing it in London. Accordingly, when the forward contracts become due, the bank can use the London funds to honor its forward commitments.

In the same way, banks can cover their working balances of foreign exchange. Essentially, the procedure boils down to a swap of demand deposits between, say, the New York banks and the London banks, with a forward contract to reverse the exchange of deposits in, say, three months. These transactions are repeated, of course, every three months, or whatever the maturity of the forward contract is.

There is an important application of the above principle in the so-called **swaps,** through which the monetary authorities of two countries acquire claims on each other. For instance, suppose that the pound sterling is under heavy pressure and the Bank of England needs foreign exchange (dollars) to support it. For this purpose, the Bank of England may enter into an agreement with the Federal Reserve to exchange ("swap") demand deposits. This swapping of demand deposits places additional foreign exchange reserves in the hands of both monetary authorities. Such swaps may be irreversible; but as a rule they are accompanied by a forward contract that reverses the initial transaction at a future date (usually within a maximum of 12 months).

11-7 COVERED INTEREST ARBITRAGE

Even though we speak of the spot market and the forward market, we must resist regarding these markets as unrelated. On the contrary, they are very closely linked and the spot and forward rates are simultaneously determined. The link between the spot and forward rates is provided by a form of arbitrage known as **covered interest arbitrage.** The theory of covered interest arbitrage was first expounded clearly by John M. Keynes (1923). It rests on the simple proposition that funds available for short-term investments, say, three months, are placed in that center (at home or abroad) which yields the highest return. This is actually part of the normal process of maximizing earnings from investment. The purpose of this section is to elucidate the theory of covered interest arbitrage.

Short-Term Investments and Exchange Risk

In a closed economy with a single national currency the problem of interest arbitrage is trivial: Funds move from the region where the interest rate is low to the region where the interest rate is high until the same interest rate prevails everywhere. In the world economy, the problem of interest arbitrage becomes more complicated because of the existence of exchange risk. In the presence of exchange risk, the comparison between interest rates is no longer a sufficient guide for the allocation of funds between financial centers.

Suppose that the interest rate is 12 percent per annum in London. An American investor who invests her funds in London will not necessarily earn 12 percent per annum, however. She will do so only if the rate of exchange remains constant. If the pound actually depreciates, she will make less; if the pound appreciates, she will make more. For instance, assume that the current spot rate is $2 and the American investor wants to invest $10,000 in London. To do so, she must first sell her dollars for pounds in the spot market (that is, she must buy pounds). Thus, she obtains £5,000, which she invests in London for three months at 12 percent per annum. In three months her investment will grow to £5,150. Indeed, her investment *in pounds* will increase at 12 percent per annum, which is the interest rate in London. But the American investor is not interested in pounds; rather, she is interested in dollars. To obtain dollars, she must sell her £5,150 in the foreign exchange market. If in three months the exchange rate continues to be $2, our investor will obtain $10,300, which means that she will earn 12 percent per annum on her initial investment of $10,000.

Suppose, however, that in three months the pound drops to $1.975, which represents a depreciation of 5 percent per annum. In that case, at the end of the three-month period, the American investor will receive only $5,150 × 1.975 = $10,171.25. Thus the American investor now will make (approximately) 7 percent per annum, which is actually *the difference between the annual interest rate in London (12 percent) and the depreciation of the pound (5 percent).*

Alternatively, suppose that in three months the pound rises to $2.025 (that is, the pound appreciates by 5 percent per annum). In three months the American investor will receive $5,150 × 2.025 = $10,428.75. Now the rate of return is (approximately) 17 percent per annum, which is the sum of the London interest rate (12 percent) and the appreciation of the pound (5 percent).

The preceding results are summarized in the following important proposition:

Proposition 11-1: **The American investor's rate of return on the funds that she invests in London is roughly equal to the rate of interest that prevails in London less any depreciation of the pound (or plus any appreciation of the pound).**

It must be apparent why the rate of return of the American investor consists of two parts, the London interest rate and the appreciation or depreciation of the pound. First, the American investor earns interest at the rate of 12 percent per annum on the funds she invests in London. Second, she enjoys either an exchange gain or suffers an exchange loss by buying pounds at $2 and selling them later at a different price (say, $1.975 or $2.025). It follows that the investor's net return must be equal to the algebraic sum of the London interest rate and the exchange gain (or loss).

In deciding where to invest her funds, the American investor must compare the New York interest rate with the rate of return earned by funds invested in London, *not* the London interest rate. Thus if the New York interest rate is 10 percent per annum, the American investor cannot conclude that it is more profitable to invest her funds in London (where the interest rate is 12 percent). If the pound depreciates by, say, 5 percent, she will earn only 7 percent in London, which is less than the New York interest rate.

The Keynesian Theory of Covered Interest Arbitrage

Investing funds in a foreign financial center involves an exchange risk. To cover the exchange risk, the American investor (usually a bank) has to sell forward the sterling the investor expects to receive in the future (hence the term "covered" interest arbitrage). The percentage sterling depreciation or appreciation used in the previous example is now reflected by the forward discount or forward premium, respectively. If the forward rate is equal to the spot rate, it is profitable for the American to invest funds in London (that is, the center with the higher interest rate). If the pound sterling is at a forward premium, it is even more profitable to do so, because, in addition to the gain due to the favorable interest-rate differential, the investor makes an additional gain by buying sterling in the spot market, where it is cheap, and selling it in the forward market, where it is expensive. However, if the pound is at a forward discount, the gain from the favorable interest-rate differential must be weighed against the loss suffered from buying sterling in the spot market, where it is expensive, and selling it in the forward market, where it is cheap. If the interest-rate differential is higher than the forward discount, it is profitable to transfer funds to London. If the interest-rate differential is smaller than the forward discount, transferring funds to London is not profitable. On the contrary, in the latter case, *it is profitable to transfer funds from London to New York.*

If it is profitable for an American investor to transfer funds to London, it is necessarily profitable for an English investor to do so as well. The only difference between the two is that the American investor starts with dollars and ends with dollars, while the English investor starts with pounds and ends with pounds. Thus, the English investor has to borrow dollars in the New York money market, use the dollars to buy sterling in the spot market, and invest the sterling in London. In addition, the English investor has to sell forward a sufficient amount of sterling to be able to repay the loan (principal plus interest) when it becomes due. Of course, the English investor's profit is in sterling; it is the difference between the amount of sterling received from the loan made to the London money market (principal plus interest) and the amount of sterling sold forward to repay the loan (principal plus interest) received from the New York money market. The significance of this observation is that *it is unnecessary for us to distinguish between arbitrageurs according to their nationality.*

Under normal circumstances, covered interest arbitrage proceeds until the forward difference (premium or discount, as the case may be) equals the interest-rate differential. This means that the interest-rate differential is exactly balanced by the loss (or gain, as the case may be) of buying sterling in, say, the spot market and selling it in the forward market. Under these circumstances, it is no longer profitable to transfer funds from one financial center to another, and we say that the forward rate is at **interest parity,** or simply that interest parity prevails.

The preceding discussion is summarized by the following important propositions:

Proposition 11-2: **If the interest rate differential (that is, the domestic interest rate less the foreign interest rate) is smaller than the forward difference (discount or premium) of the foreign currency (in algebraic terms), it is profitable to transfer funds from the home country to the foreign country. If the interest rate differential is higher than the forward difference of the foreign currency, it is profitable to transfer funds from the foreign country to the home country.**

Proposition 11-3: **Interest parity prevails when the forward difference (discount or premium) of the foreign currency equals the interest rate differential (that is, the domestic interest rate less the foreign interest rate). When interest parity prevails, the rate of return is equalized across countries and it is no longer profitable to transfer funds from one financial center to another.**

The fact that the movement of fully covered funds from one financial center to another depends not only on the interest-rate differential but also on the forward difference is of great significance to economic policy. Mainly because of the role the interest rate plays in maintaining full employment and a healthy rate of economic growth, it is important to know that the movement of arbitrage funds can be influenced through the forward market. For this reason, the forward rate becomes an important instrument of economic policy—it frees the interest rate to attend to other domestic goals.

Appendix 14 presents a brief algebraic formulation of the theory of covered interest arbitrage.

The Efficiency of the Foreign Exchange Market

A market is said to be efficient if prices fully reflect all available information. In the present context, **market efficiency** means that the forward rate is a good predictor of the future spot rate, and spot and forward rates adjust quickly to any new information.

With **perfect foresight,** the forward rate must be equal to the future spot rate. For instance, if everyone knew with absolute certainty that in 90 days the spot rate for sterling would be $1.85, the 90-day forward rate would become equal to $1.85. The reason is simple. If the forward rate were, say, $1.80, profits could be made by buying sterling forward. These purchases would continue until the forward rate rose to $1.85, eliminating all profits. Alternatively, if the forward rate were, say, $2.00, everyone would sell sterling forward until the forward rate dropped to $1.85, again eliminating all profits.

The real world is characterized by uncertainty, not perfect foresight. Thus the future spot rate cannot be predicted perfectly. In the presence of uncertainty, market efficiency implies that the forward rate differs from the *expected* future spot rate by only a **risk premium** (compensation for risk bearing). In an efficient foreign exchange market, there can be no unexploited profit opportunities. Note, however, that market efficiency does not mean that investors never make profits. It only means that they cannot make profits *systematically;* thus, sometimes they win, sometimes they lose.

Finally, note that spot and forward rates adjust quickly to new information. For instance, when the discovery of North Sea oil was announced, people came to believe that the pound sterling would appreciate in the near future. The rise in the expected future spot rate first caused the forward rate to rise (as explained above). In turn, the increase in the forward rate made it profitable to move funds into Britain (through covered interest arbitrage); and the resultant increase in the demand for sterling caused the spot rate to rise.

11-8 THE EURODOLLAR MARKET

We conclude this chapter with a brief discussion of the nature of **Eurodollars** and the **Eurodollar market,** the main causes for the development of the Eurodollar market, how Eurodollars are created, and the issue of whether the Eurodollar market creates dollars.

What Are Eurodollars?

Exactly what are Eurodollars? They are deposit liabilities, denominated in U.S. dollars, of banks located outside the United States. Eurodollars have two basic characteristics: (1) They are *short-term obligations* to pay U.S. dollars, and (2) they are obligations of *banks located outside the United States.* The banks themselves need not be foreign. They are often European branches of major U.S. commercial banks. Further, their depositors may be of any nationality. In fact, the depositors range from European central banks and European and non-European firms and individuals to U.S. banks, corporations, and residents. (Note that there also exists a counterpart long-term market for **Eurobonds,** that is, bonds offered in Europe but denominated in U.S. dollars.)

The term *Eurodollars* has recently come to be a little misleading. In the 1970s the European banks expanded their operations to accept deposits and make loans in currencies other than the dollar. This development led to the use of the more general terms **Eurocurrency, Euromarket,** and **Eurobank** (bank accepting deposits in foreign currencies). But even the latter terms are misleading because the practice of accepting deposits in dollars and other foreign currencies has spread to other parts of the world, such as Hong Kong and Singapore.

Causes of the Eurodollar Market

What were the main causes for the development of the Eurodollar market? Eurodollars originated in the 1950s with the Soviets, who wanted to hang on to their dollar balances but did not want to keep them in the United States out of fear that the U.S. government might one day freeze them. In effect, the Soviets wanted dollar claims that were not subject to any control by the U.S. government. They solved their problem merely by depositing their dollar earnings in special accounts with European banks. These Soviet deposits marked the birth of the Eurodollar market. Through the 1960s and 1970s the Eurodollar market grew very rapidly.

In a deeper sense, the fundamental cause for the development of the Eurodollar market was the special position of the dollar as a **key,** or **vehicle, currency.** The international monetary system revolved around the dollar; the dollar was the main currency that was (and still is) used to carry out international transactions. In addition, governments around the world used the dollar as the main **intervention currency** for the purpose of maintaining the external value of their currency within the so-called **support points,** or **intervention points** (usually set at 1 percent on either side of the official parity). Because of this special role of the dollar, dollar balances were held by both non-U.S. private individuals and corporations (to finance their foreign transactions) and foreign central banks (as part of their international reserves).

The special role of the dollar as a vehicle currency explains why foreign individuals, corporations, and governments would want to hold dollar balances. Nevertheless, this important role by itself does not explain why these funds were deposited with European rather than U.S. banks. What additional reason was there for the rapid development of the Eurodollar market?

The most important additional reason was **Regulation Q,** which was a Federal Reserve regulation fixing a ceiling on the interest rate that member banks could pay on time deposits. As interest rates in Europe grew higher than the ceiling placed by the Federal Reserve, Eurodollar deposits became more profitable than U.S. deposits, and so the Eurodollar market grew rapidly.

The Eurodollar market continued to grow with the increase in world trade. After the oil price increase of 1973, the Eurodollar market experienced phenomenal growth as the oil-exporting countries began to deposit large amounts of dollars in European banks. (Arab members of OPEC were reluctant to deposit their dollars in U.S. banks because of fear of possible confiscation. After all, in 1979 the Iranian assets in the United States—about $12 billion—were frozen by the Carter administration in response to the taking of hostages at the U.S. Embassy in Teheran.) Total Eurodollar deposits (including Eurocurrencies other than the dollar) grew from about $1 billion in 1960 to $3 trillion in 1986.

Creation of Eurodollars

How are Eurodollars created? Do European banks have the capacity to create dollars? These are important questions.

Eurodollars are created when someone who owns dollars deposits them with a European bank. A few examples can illustrate the point. First consider the case of an Arab sheik who transfers $1 million from his checking account with the Morgan Guaranty Trust Company of New York to a bank in London, say, Barclays Bank, which has an account with Morgan Guaranty. The New York bank transfers $1 million from the account of the sheik to the account of Barclays Bank, leaving the total U.S. money supply (which includes deposits of foreign banks and other foreigners) unchanged. Barclays Bank experiences an increase in both its dollar assets (its demand deposits with Morgan Guaranty increase by $1 million) and dollar liabilities (its deposit liabilities to the sheik increase by $1 million). Accordingly, $1 million Eurodollars are created, as reflected by the increase in the deposit liabilities of Barclays Bank.

As a second illustration, consider the case of a European bank that in some way acquires dollar deposits on a New York bank. The European bank may acquire dollar deposits either from a European exporter or from anyone else who happens to own dollars, such as the sheik of the first illustration. The important point now is that the European bank can create Eurodollars by simply lending the acquired dollars to someone else at interest. (In principle, this process of Eurodollar creation is identical to the ordinary process of money creation by commercial banks). For instance, to pursue the first illustration a little further, Barclays Bank could loan $900,000 to a British corporation, keeping as reserve only 10 percent of its newly acquired demand deposits on Morgan Guaranty.

The last illustration shows clearly that the Eurodollar market can potentially create dollars in exactly the same way that commercial banks create money, that is, by making loans which are redeposited in the same banking system. In fact, there are those who believe that the money multiplier in the Eurodollar market is very high because of the absence of any minimum reserve requirements beyond those imposed by prudence. The leading proponent of this view is Milton Friedman. However, other economists have pointed out that the multiplier process to which Friedman refers is fundamentally correct in principle only. Severe leakages weaken substantially the capacity of the Eurodollar market to create dollars, and thus dampen the multiplier process. For instance, the dollars loaned by the Eurobanks are not always deposited back into the system. They are often sold to European central banks for local European currencies. As it turns out, since 1971 European central banks have tended to hold their dollar assets in the form of deposits with U.S. banks or U.S. Treasury bills, thereby cutting the multiplier process short. The view now is that the Eurodollar market can indeed create money but that the **money multiplier** is rather low. The

Eurodollar banks behave more like the savings and loan associations rather than the commercial banks of the United States.

Some Concluding Remarks

We conclude this section with some additional observations on the Eurodollar market.

In the first place, note that a Eurobank is not subject to foreign exchange risk; its dollar assets are equal to its dollar liabilities. This does not mean that Eurobanks cannot speculate. Rather, it means that by merely operating in the Eurodollar market the Eurobanks do not necessarily assume an open position, long or short.

Second, the Eurodollar market is a highly organized capital market that facilitates the financing of international trade and investment. Competition in the Eurocurrency markets is quite keen, with banks carrying on arbitrage operations between the dollar and other markets. Interest parity is usually maintained.

Finally, the Eurodollar market has not been subject to any overall official regulation even though some spotty requirements have marred, from time to time, the rather free character of the market.

11-9 SUMMARY

1 The foreign exchange market performs three functions: It clears payments between countries, it provides credit to foreign trade, and it furnishes hedging facilities for covering exchange risks.

2 The foreign exchange market embraces all financial centers of the world, and it enables all buyers and sellers of each national currency to carry out all currency exchanges quickly and efficiently.

3 The price of one currency in terms of another is called the rate of exchange. Under a flexible exchange-rate system, the exchange rate is determined daily by supply and demand. Under a fixed exchange-rate system, the central bank intervenes in the foreign exchange market to maintain the exchange rate at the declared parity.

4 Arbitrage is the simultaneous purchase and sale of foreign currencies for the sake of profit. Arbitrage is the force that keeps the various financial centers around the world united as a single market. Arbitrage is riskless.

5 Profitable arbitrage opportunities arise because the rates of exchange either differ between financial centers or are inconsistent. Three-point arbitrage is sufficient to establish consistent rates of exchange.

6 Speculation is the deliberate assumption of exchange risk in the expectation of profit. Speculators take a long position (short position) in that currency they expect will appreciate (depreciate) in value.

7 Hedging is the opposite of speculation. Hedgers avoid the exchange risk by maintaining an exact balance between their assets and liabilities in foreign currencies.

8 The term *leads and lags* refers to the adjustment that importers and exporters make in the timing of payments, the placement of orders, and the making of deliveries for the purpose of avoiding losses or realizing profits from an anticipated change in the rate of exchange.

9 Spot transactions require immediate delivery. Forward transactions are agreements (forward contracts) for future exchanges of currencies.

10 The main function of the forward market (that is, the market for forward transactions) is to enable businesspeople to cover their exchange risks.

11 Spot speculation has the drawback that the speculator must have either idle cash or access to credit facilities. Forward speculation requires neither, and for this reason it is preferred.

12 To cover the exchange risks that arise from their forward contracts, banks (with the aid of brokers) deal among themselves to iron out their individual positions. For any remaining balances, banks use spot covering.

13 Swaps are a means by which two central banks acquire claims on each other—they exchange equivalent amounts of their own currencies. Swaps may be irreversible, but as a rule, they are accompanied by a forward contract that reverses the initial transaction at a future date.

14 Covered interest arbitrage provides the link between the spot rate and the forward rate. When the forward difference equals the interest-rate differential, the forward rate is said to be at interest parity.

15 In an efficient foreign exchange market, the forward rate differs from the expected future spot rate by only a risk premium.

16 Eurodollars are deposit liabilities, denominated in U.S. dollars, of banks located outside the United States. In the 1970s the practice of accepting deposits in foreign currencies spread to many parts of the world and applied to currencies besides the dollar.

17 The Eurodollar market can potentially create dollars in the same way commercial banks create money. Because of severe leakages, however, the money multiplier is rather low.

18 A Eurobank is not subject to exchange risk—its dollar assets are equal to its dollar liabilities.

19 The Eurodollar market is a highly organized capital market but is not subject to any overall official regulation.

PROBLEMS

1 You are given the following data:

$$r_a = 0.10, r_b = 0.05, \text{ and } R_s = \$2.00$$

where r_a and r_b are the three-month interest rates in America and Britain, respectively, and R_s is the spot rate (dollars per pound sterling). The costs of transferring funds between countries are zero.

a Assuming interest parity prevails, what is the three-month forward rate?

b The monetary authorities of America disturb the initial equilibrium by reducing their three-month interest rate to $r'_a = 0.08$. Describe the effects on the movement of funds, the spot and forward rates, and the forward premium.

2 In a world of four financial centers and four currencies (dollars, pounds, marks, and yen), you are given only the rates registered in the table below. Assuming that currency arbitrage is profitless, determine all missing rates.

Financial center	Currencies			
	Dollars	Pounds	Marks	Yen
New York (dollars)	1	1.80	—	—
London (pounds)	—	—	0.25	—
Bonn (marks)	—	—	—	—
Tokyo (yen)	125	—	—	—

3 Consider the following rates of exchange:

$$\$1 = £0.50$$

$$1 \text{ mark} = \$0.25$$

$$£1 = 10 \text{ marks}$$

a What is the indirect rate of pounds sterling (£) in terms of marks?
b How can an arbitrageur make a profit?

4 In a model of two countries, France and Germany, the supply and demand functions for marks are as follows:

$$Q_s = 200R - 50 \qquad \text{(supply)}$$

$$Q_d = 925 - 100R \qquad \text{(demand)}$$

where Q_s and Q_d are the quantities of marks supplied and demanded, respectively, and R is the rate of exchange (so many francs per mark).

a Assuming a flexible exchange rate system, determine the equilibrium exchange rate and the quantities of marks and francs traded in the foreign exchange market.
b Alternatively, assume the franc is pegged to the mark at 2 francs per mark. Determine the quantities of francs and marks demanded and supplied at the official parity rate. How can the market exchange rate be maintained at the official parity rate?

SUGGESTED READING

Chacholiades, M. (1971). "The Sufficiency of Three-Point Arbitrage to Insure Consistent Cross Rates of Exchange." *Southern Economic Journal,* vol. 38, no. 1 (July), pp. 86–88.

———(1978). *International Monetary Theory and Policy.* McGraw-Hill Book Company, New York, chap. 1.

Friedman, M. (1969). "The Euro-Dollar Market: Some First Principles." *Morgan Guaranty Survey* (October), pp. 4–14. Reprinted in R. E. Baldwin and J. D. Richardson (eds.), *International Trade and Finance,* Little, Brown and Company, Boston, 1974.

Keynes, J. M. (1923). *A Tract on Monetary Reform.* Macmillan and Company, London, pp. 113–139.

Kubarych, R. M. (1978). *Foreign Exchange Markets in the United States.* Federal Reserve Bank of New York.

Levich, R. M. (1985). "Empirical Studies of Exchange Rates: Price Behavior, Rate Determination and Market Efficiency." In R. W. Jones and P. B. Kenen (eds.), *Handbook of International Economics,* vol. II, North-Holland, New York.

Melvin, M. (1985). *International Money and Finance.* Harper & Row, Publishers, New York.

CHAPTER **12**

THE BALANCE OF PAYMENTS

This chapter deals mainly with the balance of payments, that is, the basic accounting record of a country's economic transactions with the rest of the world. After clarifying the basic balance-of-payments accounting principles and conventions, the chapter uses examples from the actual construction of the U.S. balance of payments to illustrate these principles as well as the usual reporting difficulties. The discussion then moves to the concept of balance-of-payments equilibrium and later to various accounting balances (that is, merchandise balance, balance on goods and services, current-account balance, and official settlements balance). The chapter concludes with a brief discussion of the behavior of the U.S. trade balance during the period 1960–1987, the international investment position (also known as the balance of international indebtedness), and the U.S. foreign debt.

12-1 DEFINITIONS AND CONVENTIONS

The balance of payments of a country is a systematic record of all economic transactions between the residents of the reporting country and the residents of the rest of the world over a specified period of time (usually a year). This definition raises two questions. What is an economic transaction? Who is a resident?

Economic transactions are exchanges of value; they involve transfers of ownership of goods, rendering of services, and transfers of money and other assets from residents of one country to residents of another. **International economic transactions** are economic transactions between residents of different countries.

The concept of a **resident** comprises not only individuals, but also institutions. Obvious examples are citizens of the country living there permanently, central and local governments, and business enterprises and nonprofit organizations located in the country. Residency is not always a clear concept, however, and many cases are decided on the basis of arbitrary rules of thumb. For instance, a corporation is a resident of the country in which it is incorporated, but its foreign branches and subsidiaries are residents of the country where they are located. Tourists, diplomatic and military personnel stationed abroad, temporary migrant workers, and citizens studying or undergoing medical treatment abroad are all considered residents of their country of origin.

Some examples can clarify these conventions. Japanese tourists in the United States are classified as residents of Japan, and their purchases of U.S. goods are treated as U.S. exports. Similarly, Korean students in American universities are viewed as Korean residents, and their expenditures in the United States are regarded as U.S. exports. U.S. troops stationed in Germany are U.S. residents and their purchases of European products are considered as U.S. imports. Mexicans working temporarily in the United States (legally or illegally) are classified as Mexican residents, and their incomes are perceived as U.S. imports of services. Finally, a shipment of computers by IBM to its affiliate in Japan is recorded as U.S. exports, since it involves a sale by a U.S. resident (parent company) to a foreign resident (Japanese affiliate).

International institutions (such as the United Nations, the International Monetary Fund, and the International Bank for Reconstruction and Development) are not considered residents of the country of their location. They are treated instead as international areas outside national boundaries. Therefore, their transactions with residents of the country of their location are considered international and are recorded as such in its balance of payments.

12-2 BALANCE-OF-PAYMENTS ACCOUNTING

In principle, the balance of payments is constructed on the basis of double-entry bookkeeping similar to that used by business firms. Thus, an international economic transaction gives rise to two entries in the balance of payments: a debit entry and a credit entry of equal amounts. This section explains the general principles of balance-of-payments accounting.

As viewed by the reporting (home) country, an international economic transaction (exchange of value) has two sides:

1 An **import of value,** which gives rise to a *payment* to the rest of the world.

2 An **export of value,** which gives rise to a *receipt* from the rest of the world.

The import of value (or payment) is a **debit entry,** which appears as a *negative* item in the balance of payments. The export of value (or receipt) is a **credit entry,** which appears as a *positive* item. (Note: In classifying entries as debits or credits, we can concentrate either on the direction of the flow of value or the direction of the payment.)

In general, the *payments* (debit entries) represent the *actual purchases of foreign exchange* made by residents of the reporting country in order to finance their imports of goods and services, money, and other assets from the rest of the world. Similarly, the *receipts* (credit entries) represent the *actual sales of foreign exchange* received by the residents of the reporting country for their exports of goods and services, money, and other assets. In terms of the "clearing house" of Chapter 11 (see especially Figure 11-1), the payments (debit entries) correspond to the *outflow of foreign exchange* (say, pounds sterling), while the receipts (credit entries) correspond to the *inflow of foreign exchange.*

Table 12-1 illustrates the above principles by means of a so-called T account, which records the debit and credit entries of an international economic transaction. Suppose that IBM (a resident of the home country) exports $50,000 worth of computers to a British customer who pays with a check drawn on his account at Barclays Bank. For simplicity, we assume that both IBM and the British importer hold Eurodollar accounts with Barclays Bank, which transfers $50,000 from the account of the British importer to the account of IBM. The T account records the export of computers as a *credit* entry (merchandise exports) because it represents an *export of value* which gives rise to a *receipt* of $50,000. The transfer of $50,000 to the IBM account at Barclays Bank is an *import of value* which gives rise to a *payment* (in the form of $50,000 worth of computer exports); it is recorded as a *debit* entry (increase in U.S. assets abroad) in the T account. (Note: To avoid confusion, think of the IBM acquisition of a deposit with Barclays Bank as a *purchase* of a foreign asset.) The T account illustrates the basic principle of double-entry bookkeeping: *Every economic transaction gives rise to a debit entry and a credit entry of equal amounts.*

12-3 THE U.S. BALANCE OF PAYMENTS

Table 12-2 is a highly condensed version of the U.S. balance of payments for 1987. This simplified version has been adapted from the more detailed statement of U.S. international transactions for the years 1960–1987 reported by the U.S. Department of Commerce in its *Survey of Current Business* (June 1987 and March 1988), and reproduced in its entirety as Table 12-5 on pages 302–305. To facilitate the comparison of the tables, the numbers in parentheses at the end of each entry in Table 12-2 give the line numbers of the corresponding entries in Table 12-5.

TABLE 12-1 T ACCOUNT FOR THE UNITED STATES

Debit (−)		Credit (+)	
Increase in U.S. assets abroad		Merchandise exports	
Deposits at Barclays Bank	$50,000	Computers	$50,000

TABLE 12-2 SUMMARY OF U.S. BALANCE OF PAYMENTS, 1987
(Billions of Dollars; Numbers in Parentheses Refer to Line Numbers in Table 12-5)

1. Exports of goods and services (1)		420.1
Merchandise (2)	250.8	
Services (3–14)	169.3	
2. Imports of goods and services (16)		−567.3
Merchandise (17)	−410.0	
Services (18–29)	−157.3	
3. Unilateral transfers, net (31)		−13.5
U.S. government grants (32)	−9.9	
U.S. government pensions (33)	−2.2	
Private remittances (34)	−1.3	
4. U.S. assets abroad, net (35) [increase/capital outflow (−)]		−63.8
U.S. official reserve assets (36)	9.2	
U.S. government assets (41)	1.2	
U.S. private assets (45)	−74.2	
5. Foreign assets in the U.S., net (50) [increase/capital inflow (+)]		202.6
Foreign official assets in U.S. (51)	44.3	
Other foreign assets in U.S. (58)	158.3	
6. Allocations of special drawing rights (64)		0
7. Statistical discrepancy (65)		21.9

Source: Adapted from U.S. Department of Commerce, *Survey of Current Business,* March 1988, Table 1-2 (p. 41).

Exports of Goods and Services

The first entry ("Exports of goods and services") is registered as a *credit* (+), because exports represent an **outflow of value** that gives rise to a *receipt* from the rest of the world. In 1987 the United States exported a total of $420.1 billion worth of goods and services. This total was composed of $250.8 billion worth of "Merchandise exports" and $169.3 billion worth of "Exports of services." Merchandise exports included many commodities, such as computers, aircraft, machinery, and agricultural products. Exports of services included "Interest and dividends" received by U.S. residents who held foreign bonds, stocks, and other assets (essentially for the use of U.S. capital that was made available to foreigners); receipts for "Transportation services" provided to foreigners by U.S. residents; and "Fees and royalties" received by U.S. residents for services rendered to foreigners. Service items are usually referred to as **invisibles** or **invisible trade.**

Imports of Goods and Services

The second entry ("Imports of goods and services") is registered as a *debit* (−), because imports represent an **inflow of value** that gives rise to a *payment* to the rest of the world. In 1987 the United States imported a total of $567.3 billion worth of goods and services, composed of $410.0 billion worth of "Merchandise imports" and $157.3 billion worth of "Imports of services." Merchandise imports included many commodities, such as automobiles, stereo equipment, television sets, oil, shoes, and textiles. Imports of services included *payments* for "Travel abroad" by U.S. tourists, "Transportation services" received from foreigners, "Fees and royalties," and "Interest and dividends" to foreign holders of domestic bonds, stocks, and other assets.

Unilateral Transfers

The third major entry in the U.S. balance of payments is "Unilateral Transfers." When a U.S. resident of, say, Greek origin exports commodities to her relatives in Greece as a gift, a credit entry ("Merchandise exports") must be made in the U.S. balance of payments showing the *outflow of value.* Since the U.S. resident receives nothing in return, however, no debit entry can be made. Yet to fulfill the principle of double-entry bookkeeping, which states that for every credit entry there must be a corresponding debit entry and vice versa, a debit entry ("Unilateral transfers to foreigners: private remittances") is made in the U.S. balance of payments. This convention is followed for all one-way transactions (gifts and donations) that do not involve a quid pro quo and thus give rise to only one entry, a debit or a credit, as the case may be.

In 1987 the United States made $13.5 billion worth of *net* unilateral transfers to foreigners. These "gifts" consisted of U.S. government grants, U.S. government pensions to American citizens residing abroad, and private remittances. Note that "unilateral transfers" is the fictitious debit entry made in the balance of payments to fulfill the principle of double-entry bookkeeping. Traditionally the United States has been a net donor to the rest of the world.

U.S. Assets Abroad

The fourth major entry ("U.S. assets abroad, net") shows the *net* purchases of foreign assets by U.S. residents. It is recorded as a debit (−) because it represents an *import of value* that gives rise to a *payment* to the rest of the world. Insofar as balance-of-payments accounting is concerned, a debit entry is made in the U.S. balance of payments whether U.S. residents acquire goods, services, or financial assets from foreigners. Note that this entry does not record all transactions in foreign assets—it records only *net* purchases. This practice is due to the fact that bonds, stocks, and other assets may be sold and bought several times during a year, and the *turnover* is of less interest than the net change. Also, it is difficult to collect data on the gross amounts traded.

In 1987 U.S. residents increased their holdings of foreign assets by $63.8 billion. These foreign assets consisted of three categories, as follows:

1 *U.S. official reserve assets* ($9.2 billion). As Table 12-5 shows, these are mainly *reductions* in the central bank's holdings of international reserves. U.S. holdings of foreign currencies were reduced by $7.6 billion; the U.S. reserve position with the International Monetary Fund was also reduced by $2.1 billion; but U.S. holdings of special drawing rights were increased by $0.5 billion.

2 *U.S. government assets* ($1.2 billion). These are U.S. government loans to foreign countries less repayment of loans by foreigners.

3 *U.S. private assets* ($74.2 billion). These include private **direct investment** abroad by U.S. corporations (such as the establishment of foreign branches and subsidiaries), **portfolio investment** (that is, purchases of foreign securities by U.S. residents), acquisition of demand and time deposits in foreign banks by U.S. residents, and open-book credit extended to foreigners by U.S. corporations.

Direct investment must be distinguished from portfolio investment. Direct investment is investment in enterprises located in one country but effectively controlled by residents of another country. As a rule, direct investment takes the form of investment in branches and subsidiaries by parent companies located in another country. Thus U.S. direct investment abroad consists of U.S.-owned portions of foreign business enterprises in which U.S. residents are deemed to have an important voice in management. Portfolio investment refers to purchases of foreign securities (bonds and stocks) that do not carry any claim on control or ownership of foreign enterprises.

Purchases of foreign assets by U.S. residents are usually referred to as **capital outflows** because they represent loans to foreigners (or outflows of funds).

Foreign Assets in the United States

The fifth major entry in Table 12-2 ("Foreign assets in the United States, net") shows *net* sales of domestic assets to foreigners. It is recorded as a credit (+), because it represents an *export of value* that gives rise to a *receipt* from the rest of the world. These sales of assets to foreigners are usually referred to as **capital inflows** because they involve inflows of funds (or loans from foreigners). Note again that this entry registers only the *net* sales of domestic assets to foreigners, not all transactions. In 1987 foreign residents increased their holdings of domestic assets by $202.6 billion. Out of this total, $44.3 billion were increases in "Foreign official assets in the United States" (such as purchases of Treasury bills by the Bank of England); the rest ($158.3 billion) represented increases in "Other foreign assets in the United States" (such as foreign direct investments in the United States, portfolio investment in the United States by foreign residents, and loans extended to U.S. residents by foreigners).

Allocations of Special Drawing Rights

Special drawing rights (SDRs), also known as **paper gold,** are international reserve assets created by the International Monetary Fund and distributed to member countries. The monetary authorities of member countries accept SDRs from one another in settling debts.

An allocation of SDRs to the United States is a one-way transaction. The actual receipt of the SDRs is registered as a *debit* entry ("U.S. official reserve assets" under "U.S. assets abroad," which is the fourth item in Table 12-2) because it represents an inflow of value. The sixth major entry in Table 12-2 ("Allocations of special drawing rights") is a fictitious *credit* entry, that is made for the purpose of fulfilling the principle of double-entry bookkeeping (like "Unilateral transfers"). During 1987 there were no allocations of SDRs.

Statistical Discrepancy

The fact that the balance of payments is theoretically constructed on the basis of double-entry bookkeeping implies that the sum of total debits must necessarily be equal to the sum of total credits. This is usually expressed by saying that **the balance of payments always balances.** In practice, however, the collection of statistical data for the construction of the balance of payments is inherently imperfect, for reasons given in Section 12-4. Therefore, it is not improbable—in fact it is the rule—to get in practice a sum of debits that is unequal to the sum of credits. To fulfill the accounting principle that total credits equal total debits, an additional entry (called "Statistical discrepancy") is made in the balance of payments to restore the equality between the two sides. This is the nature of the last major entry in Table 12-2.

In 1987 the statistical discrepancy was $21.9 billion (credit), which reflected the extent of unrecorded transactions and measurement errors in the balance of payments. The general belief is that the positive value of the statistical discrepancy represents unrecorded capital inflows (that is, sales of U.S. assets to foreigners).

12-4 REPORTING DIFFICULTIES

Putting together a balance of payments raises questions of **residency** (that is, how to *identify* international transactions), **coverage** (that is, how to accurately collect data on *all* international transactions), **valuation** (that is, how to *value* international transactions, especially those that do not go through the marketplace), and finally, **timing** (that is, *when* to make the necessary entry in the balance of payments). This section examines those problems.

Residency

Theoretically, the balance of payments is defined as a systematic record of all transactions between the residents of the reporting country and foreigners. In practice, there are several exceptions and borderline cases.

For instance, until recently the U.S. Department of Commerce did not include in the U.S. balance of payments the undistributed profits of foreign subsidiaries of U.S. corporations. This practice understated, of course, both investment earnings and capital flows and was abandoned by the U.S. Department of Commerce in June 1978.

However, sales of gold by the U.S. monetary authorities to U.S. residents are included in the U.S. balance of payments (despite the fact that no international transaction is involved) because such purchases and sales affect the stock of international monetary reserves of the United States.

Coverage

In principle, the balance of payments is supposed to record *all* international economic transactions. In practice, however, many international economic transactions are hard to capture through any systematic procedures of data collection. As a result, they go unreported.

Consider, for instance, merchandise trade. This item is usually based on customs returns. There are many reasons why these returns do not, as a rule, cover all transactions of merchandise trade. In the first place, when the formal border procedures are inadequate to cope with the volume of traffic (as is the case of U.S. exports over the Canadian border), several important transactions are of necessity omitted from the statistics. Further, certain items regarded as merchandise (such as goods sent by parcel post; ships and aircraft; and fish and other marine products caught in the open sea and sold directly in foreign ports) are often omitted from the customs reports.

For most service items there are no comprehensive reports of individual transactions as there are for merchandise exports and imports. Therefore, the data on services are usually arrived at by *estimation* rather than *enumeration*. This is the main reason for the imperfect coverage of services. Estimates for tourist expenditures, for example, are based in part on the number of travelers and on a sample of voluntary returns showing destination, length of stay, and expenditures. For a wide variety of other service items (such as commissions and royalties) there are little or no data.

Finally, note that the collection of data on movements of private long-term portfolio capital and short-term capital presents serious problems of coverage. It is usually extremely difficult to obtain reports on all such movements from all individuals and firms engaging in international transactions. As a rule, no estimates of unreported transactions can be made because the universe of transactors and transactions is not known. The size of omissions is not known, even roughly. For this reason it is usually thought that the "Statistical discrepancy" is due to unrecorded capital movements. But even though its coverage is imperfect, the balance-of-payments account is accurate enough and remains a highly useful instrument.

Valuation

Essentially, the balance-of-payments statisticians attempt to measure the value of the resources transferred from one country to another. To the extent that regular market transactions are involved, resource value is best represented by the actual amount paid (or agreed on), with appropriate treatment of transportation and other related expenses. In practice, however, the actual amounts paid are not always easily available.

For instance, a U.S. importer must file an "import-entry" form with the Customs Bureau on the arrival of the goods from abroad. On the basis of this document, the Customs Bureau determines whether the goods are dutiable and, if so, the amount due. In addition, this document forms the basis for the balance-of-payments entry. It is obvious that if the value figure is not involved in the calculation of duty, there is little incentive for accuracy on the part of the importer—especially if the correct figure is not conveniently available.

Even greater valuation difficulties arise when there is no market transaction, as in the case of shipments between affiliated companies or branches, immigrants' household effects, gifts, barter transactions, and so on. Such transactions enter the trade figures at nominal or arbitrary values.

Timing

At what point should merchandise trade be recorded in the balance of payments? When the importer's liability is incurred (that is, when the order is placed or the contract signed)? When the importer actually pays for the goods? Or when the goods actually move from the exporter to the importer—and in this case, should the entry be made when the goods leave the exporter or when they reach the importer? Each of these points has its merits, of course. For instance, the time that payment is made is important to the foreign exchange market and the reserves of the countries involved.

In practice, the entries in the merchandise trade account are based on customs returns, which generally record merchandise as it crosses the customs frontier of the reporting country. Most countries assume that, in general, their customs returns provide a reasonably accurate record of changes in ownership. Further, they assume that services should be recorded when they are actually rendered; unilateral transfers, when the gift is legally made; and capital flows, when the ownership of assets is transferred from residents of one country to residents of another.

12-5 BALANCE-OF-PAYMENTS EQUILIBRIUM

As we saw earlier in this chapter, the balance of payments is constructed on the basis of double-entry bookkeeping. As a result, the balance of payments always balances in an accounting sense, that is, total debits equal total credits. Does this accounting balance mean that the balance of payments is also in equilibrium? In other words, does the identity "total debits = total credits" mean that the reporting country never experiences any balance-of-payments difficulties? Unfortunately, that is not the case, as any casual observer of international affairs would know.

Autonomous versus Accommodating Transactions

In principle, the transactions recorded in the accounting balance can be divided into two major categories: **autonomous** and **accommodating.** Autonomous transactions are those that are undertaken for their own sake, usually in response to business considerations and incentives but sometimes in response to political considerations as well. Their main distinguishing feature is that they take place independently of the balance-of-payments position of the reporting country. All other transactions are called accommodating. Accommodating transactions do not take place for their own sake. Rather, they take place because other (autonomous) transactions are such as to leave a *gap to be filled.*

Examples of autonomous transactions include virtually all exports of goods and services undertaken for profit, unilateral transfers, direct investment, and portfolio investment motivated by a desire either to earn a higher return or to find a safe refuge. Examples of accommodating transactions include the sale of gold or foreign currencies by the central bank in order to fill the gap between the receipts and payments of foreign exchange by the domestic residents and a loan received by the domestic monetary authorities from foreign governments for the express purpose of filling a gap in the autonomous receipts and payments.

Deficits and Surpluses: Definitions

Imagine that a horizontal line is drawn through a balance-of-payments statement. Above this imaginary line, place all autonomous transactions (or entries); below the line, place all accommodating transactions (or entries). When the balance on autonomous transactions is zero (that is, when autonomous payments equal autonomous receipts), the balance of payments is in equilibrium. When the sum of autonomous receipts (credits) is greater than the sum of autonomous payments (debits), there is a **surplus;** and when the sum of autonomous receipts falls short of the sum of autonomous payments, there is a **deficit.** In each case, the accounting measure of disequilibrium (surplus or deficit) is given by the difference between the sum of autonomous receipts and the sum of autonomous payments.

Because the balance of payments is an identity, we always have

Sum of autonomous transactions +
sum of accommodating transactions = 0

or

Sum of autonomous transactions =
− sum of accommodating transactions

Accordingly, the accounting measure of balance-of-payments disequilibrium can also be determined as the *negative* of the difference between accommodating receipts and payments.

Difficulties with Autonomous and Accommodating Transactions

The analytical distinction between autonomous and accommodating transactions, although sound in principle, faces insurmountable difficulties in practical applications.

First, there is the possibility of *international inconsistency*. A transaction may be regarded as autonomous for one country but accommodating for another. This is the case, for instance, when in the face of balance-of-payments difficulties the monetary authorities of a country borrow in the private financial market of another country.

Second, the distinction between autonomous and accommodating transactions is an ex ante concept depending ultimately on *motives*, which cannot be observed in an ex post statistical statement like the balance of payments. The problem would not be as difficult if it were possible to infer the motive either from the type of transaction or the type of transactor. But this is not the case. As a result, in any practical application a subjective judgment must be made regarding the ultimate motive behind each transaction. The subjective element necessarily gives rise to differences of opinion among equally competent and honest people.

A very subtle difficulty arises in relation to monetary policy. For instance, suppose that the U.S. monetary authorities are successful in attracting substantial amounts of short-term capital from foreign financial centers by simply raising their interest rate. What is the nature of this short-term capital inflow: autonomous or accommodating? Certainly from the point of view of private arbitrageurs these transactions are motivated by profit considerations and ought to be classified as autonomous. But their profitability is actually influenced by the action of the U.S. monetary authorities, who presumably are concerned about the state of the U.S. balance of payments. From the viewpoint of the U.S. monetary authorities these transactions are accommodating—they are prompted by monetary policy to fill a gap left by other transactions.

We conclude that the ex post grouping of transactions into autonomous and accommodating is not unambiguous. The horizontal line through the balance-of-payments entries may be drawn in a number of arbitrary ways. Thus there is no unique accounting measure of balance-of-payments disequilibrium, and the feeling must be resisted that a single number can be relied upon to show the precise degree of balance-of-payments disequilibrium.

12-6 ACCOUNTING BALANCES

In this section, we describe several accounting balances in relation to the U.S. balance of payments. These balances and the ensuing discussion highlight some of the difficulties involved in any effort to determine the balance-of-payments deficit or surplus. Each balance provides the analyst with some useful information. Nevertheless, none of these (or any other) balances can adequately describe the international position of the United States during any given period.

For this reason, the most controversial balances have now been abandoned by the U.S. Department of Commerce.

The Structure of the U.S. Balance of Payments

The balance of payments is subdivided into two major accounts: the **current account** and the **capital account.** The capital account registers all international asset transactions; the current account registers all the rest. Thus all changes in U.S. assets abroad and foreign assets in the United States are recorded in the capital account. Exports and imports of goods and services as well as unilateral transfers are posted in the current account. The statistical discrepancy is included in the capital account because it is widely believed that it reflects unreported asset transactions.

Each major account is subdivided further into subaccounts or (sub)balances. Each of these subaccounts deals with a broad class of international transactions. The current account is subdivided into the **balance on goods and services** plus the **balance on unilateral transfers.** The balance on goods and services is further subdivided into the **merchandise trade balance** plus the **invisible trade balance.** Finally, the capital account is subdivided into the **capital account proper** plus the **official reserve account.**

Table 12-3 illustrates the structure of the U.S. balance of payments for the year 1987. (The numbers in parentheses at the end of each entry in Table 12-3 give the line numbers of the corresponding entries in Table 12-5.) The *merchandise trade balance,* or just *trade balance,* is the difference between exports and imports of merchandise (goods). In 1987 the United States exported $250.8 billion and imported $410.0 billion worth of goods. Thus the United States suffered a **trade deficit** of $159.2 billion ($250.8 − $410.0). The trade balance is available on a monthly basis, as the customs officials can rapidly collect and report merchandise trade data. The "trade balance" that we hear about in the news every month is actually the merchandise trade balance.

The *invisible trade balance* is the difference between exports and imports of services. In 1987 the United States enjoyed an invisible trade *surplus* of $12 billion. This means that in 1987 U.S. exports of services ($169.3 billion) exceeded U.S. imports of services ($157.3 billion) by $12 billion.

The sum of the merchandise trade balance and the invisible trade balance is the *balance on goods and services.* In 1987 the U.S. balance on goods and services was equal to −$147.2 billion (− $159.2 + $12.0 = − $147.2). The negative sign means that in 1987 the United States had a *deficit* in the balance on goods and services. Note that the deficit in the balance on goods and services was smaller than the trade deficit because of the invisible trade surplus, which partly offset the trade deficit.

The balance on goods and services provides an important link between the balance of payments and national income. This is explained at some length in Chapter 15. For the moment, note that the balance on goods and services (or

TABLE 12-3 ACCOUNTING BALANCES IN THE U.S. BALANCE OF PAYMENTS, 1987
(Billions of Dollars; Numbers in Parentheses Refer to Line Numbers in Table 12-5)

Current account balance (69)				−160.7
Balance on goods and services (67)			−147.2	
Merchandise trade balance (66)		−159.2		
Merchandise exports (2)	250.8			
Merchandise imports (17)	−410.0			
Invisible trade balance		12.0		
Exports of services (3–14)	169.3			
Imports of services (18–29)	−157.3			
Unilateral transfers (31)			−13.5	
Capital account balance				104.1
U.S. assets abroad, excluding official reserves (41 plus 45)			−72.9	
Foreign assets in U.S., excluding official reserves (55 plus 58)			155.1	
Statistical discrepancy (65)			21.9	
Official reserve account balance				56.7
Increase (−) in U.S. official reserve assets (70)			9.2	
Increase (+) in foreign official assets in U.S. (71)			47.5	
Overall accounting balance				0.0

Source: Adapted from U.S. Department of Commerce, *Survey of Current Business,* March 1988, Table 1-2 (p. 41).

net exports, for short) is a major component of the aggregate demand for (expenditure on) the reporting country's aggregate output.

One of the most important balances is the **current account balance,** which is the sum of the balance on goods and services plus the balance on unilateral transfers. In 1987 the United States had a current account *deficit* equal to $160.7 billion (− $147.2 − $13.5). Because the United States is a net donor to the rest of the world, the current account deficit is larger than the deficit in the balance on goods and services.

The capital account (proper) registers all international asset transactions except those involving official reserve assets. In 1987 the United States had a **capital account surplus** of $104.1 billion, which was equal to the algebraic sum of capital outflows (− $72.9 billion) plus capital inflows ($155.1 billion) plus the statistical discrepancy ($21.9 billion). The positive sign means that in 1987 the United States experienced a **net capital inflow** (equal to the capital account surplus).

The official reserve account registers changes in official reserve assets. These transactions are recorded separately because of their significance to the international monetary reserve position of the United States. In 1987 the balance of the official reserve account was equal to $56.7 billion, which reflected a net reduction in U.S. official reserve assets ($9.2 billion) plus a net increase in U.S. liquid liabilities to foreign central banks ($47.5 billion).

The Official Settlements Balance

The **official settlements balance** views all entries in the official reserve account as accommodating. As noted in Section 12-5, the accounting measure of balance-of-payments disequilibrium is the *negative* of the difference between accommodating receipts and payments. Thus a positive (credit) balance in the official reserve account means that the autonomous transactions "above the line" register a *deficit,* which is known as the official settlements balance *deficit.* In 1987 the official settlements balance deficit was equal to $56.7 billion.

The official settlements balance was introduced in 1965 by the review committee chaired by Edward M. Bernstein. At that time, exchange rates were pegged, and there was concern over the gradually mounting volume of U.S. liquid liabilities to foreigners. The basic rationale for the official settlements balance was that it would serve as a barometer of the ability of U.S. monetary authorities to defend the exchange value of the dollar. But this basic rationale was eliminated in 1973 by the introduction of flexible exchange rates. As a result, the U.S. Department of Commerce abandoned official reporting of the official settlements balance (and other overall balances). Instead, the department now presents the balance of payments in a rather neutral way: It retains as memoranda only the merchandise trade balance, the balance on goods and services, the current account balance, and the changes in U.S. official reserve assets and foreign official assets in the United States.

Under a *freely fluctuating* exchange-rate system there is absolutely no government intervention in the foreign exchange market, and the rate of exchange is left free to equate autonomous supply with autonomous demand for foreign exchange. It is axiomatic that under a freely fluctuating exchange-rate system accommodating transactions are totally absent and the balance of payments can register neither a surplus nor a deficit. Any disturbances, real or monetary, that may give rise to balance-of-payments disequilibria under a *fixed* exchange-rate system are now reflected in exchange-rate fluctuations.

The current regime of "dirty," or managed, floating is a mixture of the fixed and freely fluctuating exchange-rate systems. Here the authorities do intervene to iron out wide fluctuations in the exchange rate, although such intervention is discretionary—not mandatory. For instance, in the presence of an excess demand for yen, the U.S. monetary authorities may supply the needed yen to prevent a depreciation of the dollar. Alternatively, the intervention may be carried out by the Japanese monetary authorities instead, who may purchase dollars with yen. But because the dollar is a **reserve currency,** such dollar purchases by foreign monetary authorities need not always measure the degree of foreign intervention. Rather the purchases may reflect a genuine need for additional international reserves or a switch from another reserve currency to high-yielding dollar assets (such as U.S. Treasury bills). That is, the purchases of dollar assets by foreign monetary authorities need not always be classified as accommodating. For this reason, an official settlements balance deficit must be interpreted with extreme care.

The Economic Meaning of the Current Account

In 1987 the United States had a current account *deficit* equal to $160.7 billion. What is the economic meaning of the current account deficit? In searching for an answer, we get an important clue by looking at the capital account balance.

It is an accounting fact that the current account balance is the mirror image of the capital account balance (*including* official reserves). Thus

Balance of payments = current account balance + capital account balance = 0

or

Current account balance = − capital account balance

(Recall that the balance of payments always balances because the sum of all debit entries equals the sum of all credit entries.) Accordingly, a current account *deficit* of $160.7 billion coincides with a capital account *surplus* (including reserves) of $160.7 billion. As it turns out, we can discover the meaning of the current account deficit by looking at its mirror image, the capital account surplus. What does a capital account surplus (or deficit) mean?

The meaning of the capital account *surplus* (that is, net credit balance) of $160.7 billion which the United States experienced in 1987 is simply that the (net) liabilities of the United States to the rest of the world increased by $160.7 billion. In other words, in 1987 the United States received $160.7 billion of credit from the rest of the world. Why was this credit necessary? To finance the current account deficit of $160.7 billion, that is, the *net* U.S. outpayment for goods, services, and gifts. Accordingly, a **current account deficit is tantamount to an increase in the international indebtedness of the reporting country.** The situation is very much like that of the family which either goes into debt or uses some of its accumulated wealth to finance the excess of its spending over its income.

Conversely, a **current account surplus represents an increase in the net foreign wealth of the reporting country.** The current account surplus is the mirror image of a capital account (including reserves) deficit, that is, net debit balance, which evidently means that the reporting country's *net* foreign assets increase (or its net foreign liabilities decrease). This situation is very similar to that of the family which uses part of its income to increase its assets (or reduce its debts).

In summary, the current account balance shows the change in the reporting country's net foreign wealth. A current account surplus tends to increase the country's net foreign wealth, and it is usually called **net foreign investment.** A current account deficit, however, represents a reduction in the reporting country's net foreign wealth, and it is referred to as **net foreign disinvestment.**

12-7 THE U.S. TRADE BALANCE

Figure 12-1 shows how the U.S. trade balance has behaved since 1960. The pattern is clear: The U.S. trade balance moved gradually from surplus to substantial deficit. Until 1970 the United States enjoyed a trade surplus. Beginning with 1971, however, the trade balance turned negative (deficit), with the exception of the years 1973 and 1975. Until 1976 the trade deficits were mild (below $10 billion). In 1977 the trade deficit jumped to a higher plateau (about $30 billion) and remained roughly at that level until 1982. Since 1982 the trade deficit has exhibited sharp deterioration, rising to $159 billion in 1987.

(Note that both the balance on goods and services and the current account balance displayed a pattern similar to the trade balance, worsening substantially after 1982.)

The deterioration of the U.S. trade deficit in the 1980s was rather general, extending over all categories of goods (such as foods, feeds, and beverages; industrial supplies and materials; capital goods; automobiles; and consumer goods) and most major regions and trading partners (such as industrial countries and developing nations; Europe and East Asia as well as Africa and Latin America). The seriousness of the problem is underscored by the fact that the financial markets have become very sensitive to the monthly announcements by the Department of Commerce concerning the continuing huge trade deficit.

The large trade (and current account) deficits of the 1980s did not translate into large losses of U.S. reserves. In the 1980s the official settlements balance (which in the 1970s exhibited deficits at least as large as the corresponding trade deficits) registered mild deficits or even surpluses. As shown in Figure 12-1, this situation lasted until 1985. For 1986 and 1987 the official settlements balance deficits were $33 and $57 billion, respectively. The main reason for this behavior of the official settlements balance was the substantial amounts of capital inflows that were attracted into the United States during this period.

FIGURE 12-1 The U.S. balance of trade, 1960–1987.

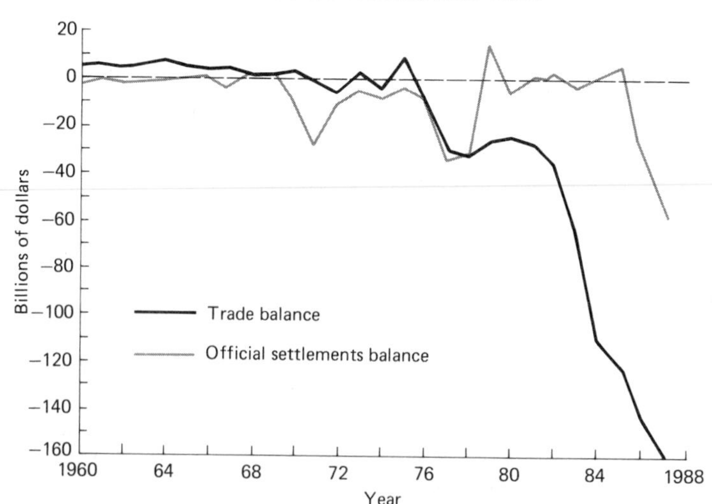

What are the causes of the continuing U.S. trade deficit? This is a complex issue; we shall try to address it in the rest of the book. For the moment, we can mention a few factors that are often discussed by the news media. These are

1 The sharp rise in the price of imported oil in the 1970s.
2 The perceived low quality of U.S. products and the superior quality of foreign (especially Japanese) products.
3 The restrictive trade policies of foreign governments, which tend to exclude U.S. products.
4 The deteriorating position of the United States in the area of international competitiveness due to high U.S. labor costs and the high external value of the dollar.
5 The low rate of saving in the U.S. economy.
6 The huge budget deficits of the federal government during the 1980s. (As will become evident in the next chapter, the federal budget deficit is probably the most important cause of the U.S. trade deficit; yet it has not received the proper attention.)

12-8 THE INTERNATIONAL INVESTMENT POSITION

The **international investment position** (also known as the **balance of international indebtedness**) is a statement of the stock of total foreign assets and liabilities of the reporting country at a particular time. Its usefulness derives mainly from the fact that it provides a basis for projecting future flows of investment income. Unfortunately, there are enormous difficulties in the way of its practical evaluation. Since total foreign assets need not be equal to total foreign liabilities, it is not even possible to say how accurate such a statement is.

The international investment position is, in principle, related to the balance of payments. Essentially, the capital account of the balance of payments records *changes* in the reporting country's stocks of foreign assets and liabilities. Under ideal conditions the international investment position could be derived as a summation of *all* past debits and credits in the capital account of the balance of payments. In practice, however, ideal conditions are never realized, so that the international investment position summarizes, in addition to the combined cumulative effects of international capital flows, the effects of a number of other factors over the years, such as changes in foreign exchange rates and changes in prices of domestic and foreign securities. (Valuation changes in claims and liabilities are not included in the balance of payments because they are not international transactions.)

12-9 THE U.S. FOREIGN DEBT

During the nineteenth century, the United States was a debtor country. At that time, capital imports were essential because the rate of domestic saving was not large enough to sustain the growth of the U.S. economy. Imports of foreign capital enabled the economy to finance productive investments, which expanded its capacity to produce. For instance, foreign capital was imported to finance construction of U.S. railroads. By the 1920s, however, domestic saving had increased substantially, spilling over into foreign investments. So the United States was converted into a creditor country—a title which it held proudly until the mid-1980s.

Table 12-4 presents the international investment position of the United States at year end for the period 1979–1986. Note that by the end of 1985 the United States had become a debtor country with a net foreign debt equal to $112 billion. The sharp deterioration in the U.S. net international investment position reflected the cumulative effect of a string of large current account deficits as well as some valuation changes. If one concludes that the sharp deterioration of the U.S. trade deficit was caused by the federal budget deficits of the Reagan administration, one must also conclude that the recent huge imports of foreign capital were indirectly used to finance excess government spending, not productive investments. This picture is, of course, quite different from that of nineteenth century America.

TABLE 12-4 INTERNATIONAL INVESTMENT POSITION OF THE UNITED STATES AT YEAR END, 1979–1986 (Billions of Dollars)

Type of investment	1979	1980	1981	1982	1983	1984	1985	1986
Net international investment position of the United States	94.5	106.3	141.1	137.0	89.6	3.6	−111.9	−263.6
U.S. assets abroad	510.6	607.1	719.8	824.9	873.9	896.1	949.4	1,067.9
U.S. official reserve assets	19.0	26.8	30.1	34.0	33.7	34.9	43.2	48.5
Gold	11.2	11.2	11.2	11.1	11.1	11.1	11.1	11.1
Special drawing rights	2.7	2.6	4.1	5.3	5.0	5.6	7.3	8.4
Reserve position in the International Monetary Fund	1.3	2.9	5.1	7.3	11.3	11.5	11.9	11.7
Foreign currencies	3.8	10.1	9.8	10.2	6.3	6.7	12.9	17.3
U.S. Government assets, other than official reserve assets	58.4	63.8	68.7	74.6	79.5	84.9	87.7	89.4
U.S. loans and other long-term assets	56.5	62.0	67.2	72.9	77.8	82.9	85.8	88.6
Repayable in dollars	54.1	59.8	65.0	70.9	76.0	80.8	84.1	87.0
Other	2.4	2.2	2.2	1.9	1.8	1.8	1.7	1.6
U.S. foreign currency holdings and U.S. short-term assets	1.9	1.7	1.5	1.7	1.7	2.0	1.8	0.9
U.S. private assets	433.2	516.6	621.1	716.4	760.7	776.3	818.5	929.9
Direct investment abroad	187.9	215.4	228.3	207.8	207.2	211.5	229.7	259.9
Foreign securities	56.8	62.7	63.4	75.5	83.8	89.1	112.8	131.1
Bonds	42.0	43.5	45.8	56.7	57.7	61.8	73.0	80.2
Corporate stocks	14.8	19.2	17.6	18.8	26.1	27.3	39.8	50.9
U.S. claims on unaffiliated foreigners reported by U.S. nonbanking concerns	31.5	34.7	35.9	28.6	35.1	30.1	28.6	32.6
U.S. claims reported by U.S. banks, not included elsewhere	157.0	203.9	293.5	404.6	434.5	445.6	447.4	506.4
Foreign assets in the United States	416.1	500.8	578.7	688.0	784.3	892.5	1,061.3	1,331.5
Foreign official assets in the United States	159.9	176.1	180.4	189.1	194.5	199.2	202.5	240.8
U.S. Government securities	106.6	118.2	125.1	132.6	137.0	143.0	143.4	177.4
U.S. Treasury securities	101.7	111.3	117.0	124.9	129.7	135.5	135.7	170.7
Other	4.9	6.9	8.1	7.7	7.3	7.5	7.7	6.7
Other U.S. Government liabilities	12.7	13.4	13.0	13.6	14.2	14.8	15.6	17.4
U.S. liabilities reported by U.S. banks, not included elsewhere	30.5	30.4	26.7	25.0	25.5	26.1	26.7	27.3
Other foreign official assets	9.9	14.1	15.5	17.9	17.7	15.2	16.7	18.7
Other foreign assets in the United States	256.3	324.8	398.3	498.9	589.8	693.3	858.8	1,090.7
Direct investment in the United States	54.5	83.0	108.7	124.7	137.1	164.6	184.6	209.3
U.S. Treasury securities	14.2	16.1	18.5	25.8	33.8	58.2	83.6	96.0

TABLE 12-4 INTERNATIONAL INVESTMENT POSITION OF THE UNITED STATES AT YEAR END, 1979–1986 (*Continued*)
(Billions of Dollars)

Type of investment	1979	1980	1981	1982	1983	1984	1985	1986
U.S. securities other than U.S. Treasury securities	58.6	74.1	75.1	93.0	113.7	127.3	206.6	309.5
Corporate and other bonds	10.3	9.5	10.7	16.7	17.3	32.8	82.5	142.1
Corporate stocks	48.3	64.6	64.4	76.3	96.4	94.6	124.1	167.4
U.S. liabilities to unaffiliated foreigners reported by U.S. nonbanking concerns	18.7	30.4	30.6	27.5	26.9	31.0	29.4	26.7
U.S. liabilities reported by U.S. banks, not included elsewhere	110.3	121.1	165.4	228.0	278.3	312.2	354.5	449.2

Source: Economic Report of the President, U.S. Government Printing Office, Washington, D.C., 1988, p. 369.

12-10 SUMMARY

1 The balance of payments is a systematic record of all economic transactions between the residents of the reporting country and the residents of the rest of the world over a specified period of time.

2 In principle, the balance of payments is constructed on the basis of double-entry bookkeeping. For this reason, it always balances (that is, total debits equal total credits). Any statistical deficiencies are reported separately as a "statistical discrepancy."

3 A debit (credit) entry is made to represent an import (export) of value, which gives rise to a payment to (receipt from) the rest of the world.

4 The balance of payments is divided into three accounts: the current account (consisting of the entries for exports and imports of goods and services plus unilateral transfers), the capital account (consisting of the entries that indicate the net changes in foreign claims and liabilities), and the official reserve account (consisting of those entries that indicate changes in the official reserve assets).

5 The construction of a balance of payments raises questions of residency, coverage, valuation, and timing.

6 In principle, the transactions recorded in the balance of payments can be divided into autonomous (undertaken for their own sake) and accommodating (undertaken to fill a gap left by the autonomous transactions).

7 When autonomous payments equal autonomous receipts, the balance of payments is in equilibrium. Otherwise, there exists either a deficit (autonomous payments > autonomous receipts) or a surplus (autonomous receipts > autonomous payments).

8 The ex ante distinction between autonomous and accommodating transactions cannot be observed in an ex post accounting balance of payments. Accordingly, several accounting measures of disequilibrium can be developed, each one serving a particular purpose.

9 The merchandise trade balance (available on a monthly basis) is the difference between exports and imports of goods.

10 The balance of goods and services is the difference between exports and imports of goods and services. It provides an important link between the balance of payments and national income.

11 The important current account balance shows the change in the reporting country's net foreign wealth.

12 The official settlements balance places below the line changes in U.S. monetary reserves plus changes in U.S. liquid liabilities to official foreigners (such as foreign central banks) only.

13 The international investment position (or balance of international indebtedness) is a statement of the stock of total foreign assets and liabilities of the reporting country at a particular time. It provides a basis for projecting future flows of investment income but faces enormous difficulties of statistical estimation.

PROBLEMS

1 For each of the following transactions indicate the correct entries in the U.S. balance of payments:

a An American purchases a Toyota in Tokyo for $10,000. The buyer ships the car to the United States at an additional cost of $1,000. Payment for the car and shipping charges is by check drawn on the buyer's account with the Chase Manhattan Bank.

b A U.S. corporation exports $1,000 of merchandise to a German importer on open book credit.

c A U.S. charitable organization sends $1,000 worth of food to Ethiopia.

d A resident of France owes $5,000 to an American corporation. The person borrows $5,000 from a French bank and pays off the debt to the American corporation.

e A Japanese investor purchases the IBM tower in Atlanta for $20 million. The investor pays $2 million in cash and agrees to repay the balance in five years.

2 Explain briefly why you regard each of the following transactions as capital inflow or capital outflow from the point of view of the United States.

a An American settles an old debt by paying $500 in cash to a Mexican corporation.

b A British arbitrageur borrows $2,000 in London. The arbitrageur invests the borrowed funds in the New York money market.

c An American robs the Bank of England and brings into the United States £1 million which the thief sells to the Chase Manhattan Bank.

3 You are given the following hypothetical data (in billions of dollars) concerning the international economic transactions of the United States during a recent year:

Merchandise exports	700
Invisible trade surplus	40
Unilateral transfers deficit	25
Reduction in foreign demand deposits with U.S. banks	10
Increase in foreign currencies held by the Federal Reserve	15

Increase in foreign direct investments in the United States	90
Imports of services	20
Merchandise trade deficit	150

Assume that these are the only international economic transactions of the United States. Compute the following:

a Balance on goods and services.
b Merchandise imports.
c Exports of services.
d Current account balance.
e Official reserve account balance.
f Capital account balance.
g Statistical discrepancy.

4 During his campaign for the presidency of the United States, Governor Michael Dukakis repeatedly expressed concerns about the huge U.S. trade deficit.
a Why should a U.S. President be concerned with the U.S. trade deficit?
b Should the government be concerned with a large trade deficit even if the official reserve account balance is zero? Why or why not?

SUGGESTED READING

Chacholiades, M. (1978). *International Monetary Theory and Policy.* McGraw-Hill Book Company, New York, chap. 2.

Cooper, R. N. (1966). "The Balance of Payments in Review." *Journal of Political Economy* (August), pp. 379–395.

Fieleke, N. S. (1971). "Accounting for the Balance of Payments." *New England Economic Review* (May–June), Federal Reserve Bank of Boston, pp. 3–15.

International Monetary Fund. *Balance of Payments Yearbook,* International Monetary Fund, Washington, D.C.

———(1977). *Balance of Payments Manual,* 4th ed. International Monetary Fund, Washington, D.C.

Kemp, D. S. (1975). "Balance-of-Payments Concepts—What Do They Really Mean?" *Review* (July). Federal Reserve Bank of St. Louis, pp. 14–23.

Kindleberger, C. P. (1965). *Balance-of-Payments Deficits and the International Market for Liquidity.* Princeton Essays in International Finance, no. 46. International Finance Section, Princeton University, Princeton, N.J.

———(1969). "Measuring Equilibrium in the Balance of Payments." *Journal of Political Economy* 77 (November–December), pp. 873–891.

Review Committee for Balance of Payments Statistics (1965). *The Balance of Payments Statistics of the United States: A Review and Appraisal.* Washington, D.C.

Stern, R. M., et al. (1977). *The Presentation of the Balance of Payments: A Symposium.* International Finance Section, Princeton University, Princeton, N.J.

TABLE 12-5 U.S. INTERNATIONAL TRANSACTIONS, 1960–1987 (Millions of U.S. Dollars)

Line	(Credits + ; debits –)	1960	1961	1962	1963	1964	1965	1966	1967	1968	1969	1970	1971
1	Exports of goods and services	28,861	29,937	31,803	34,214	38,826	41,087	44,562	47,314	52,363	57,522	65,674	68,838
2	Merchandise, adjusted, excluding military	19,650	20,108	20,781	22,272	25,501	26,461	29,310	30,666	33,626	36,414	42,469	43,319
3	Transfers under U.S. military agency sales contracts	335	402	656	657	747	830	829	1,152	1,392	1,528	1,501	1,926
4	Travel	919	947	957	1,015	1,207	1,380	1,590	1,646	1,775	2,043	2,331	2,534
5	Passenger fares	175	183	191	205	241	271	317	371	411	450	544	615
6	Other transportation	1,607	1,620	1,764	1,898	2,076	2,175	2,333	2,426	2,548	2,652	3,125	3,299
7	Royalties and license fees from affiliated foreigners	590	662	800	890	1,013	1,199	1,162	1,354	1,430	1,533	1,758	1,927
8	Royalties and license fees from unaffiliated foreigners	247	244	256	273	301	335	353	393	437	486	573	618
9	Other private services from affiliated foreigners												
10	Other private services from unaffiliated foreigners	570	607	585	613	651	714	814	951	1,024	1,160	1,294	1,546
11	U.S. Government miscellaneous services	153	164	195	236	265	285	326	336	353	343	332	347
	Receipts of income on U.S. assets abroad:												
12	Direct investment	3,621	3,823	4,241	4,636	5,106	5,506	5,260	5,603	6,591	7,649	8,169	9,160
13	Other private receipts	646	793	904	1,022	1,256	1,421	1,669	1,781	2,021	2,338	2,671	2,641
14	U.S. Government receipts	349	383	473	499	462	510	599	636	756	925	907	906
15	Transfers of goods and services under U.S. military grant programs, net	1,695	1,465	1,537	1,562	1,340	1,636	1,892	2,039	2,547	2,610	2,713	3,546
16	Imports of goods and services	–23,670	–23,453	–25,676	–26,970	–29,102	–32,708	–38,468	–41,476	–48,671	–53,998	–59,901	–66,414
17	Merchandise, adjusted, excluding military	–14,758	–14,537	–16,260	–17,048	–18,700	–21,510	–25,493	–26,866	–32,991	–35,807	–39,866	–45,579
18	Direct defense expenditures	–3,087	–2,998	–3,105	–2,961	–2,880	–2,952	–3,764	–4,378	–4,535	–4,856	–4,855	–4,819
19	Travel	–1,750	–1,785	–1,939	–2,114	–2,211	–2,438	–2,657	–3,207	–3,030	–3,373	–3,980	–4,373
20	Passenger fares	–513	–506	–567	–612	–642	–717	–753	–829	–885	–1,080	–1,215	–1,290
21	Other transportation	–1,402	–1,437	–1,558	–1,701	–1,817	–1,951	–2,161	–2,157	–2,367	–2,455	–2,843	–3,130
22	Royalties and license fees to affiliated foreigners	–35	–43	–57	–61	–67	–68	–64	–62	–80	–101	–111	–118
23	Royalties and license fees to unaffiliated foreigners	–40	–46	–44	–51	–60	–67	–76	–104	–106	–120	–114	–123
24	Other private services to affiliated foreigners												
25	Other private services to unaffiliated foreigners	–593	–588	–528	–493	–527	–461	–506	–565	–668	–751	–827	–956
26	U.S. Government miscellaneous services	–254	–268	–296	–370	–415	–457	–513	–561	–631	–586	–576	–592
	Payments of income on foreign assets in the United States:												
27	Direct investment	–394	–432	–399	–459	–529	–657	–711	–821	–876	–848	–875	–1,164
28	Other private payments	–511	–535	–586	–701	–802	–942	–1,221	–1,328	–1,800	–3,244	–3,617	–2,428
29	U.S. Government payments	–332	–278	–339	–401	–453	–489	–549	–598	–702	–777	–1,024	–1,844
30	U.S. military grants of goods and services, net	–1,695	–1,465	–1,537	–1,562	–1,340	–1,636	–1,892	–2,039	–2,547	–2,610	–2,713	–3,546
31	Unilateral transfers (excluding military grants of goods and services), net	–2,367	–2,662	–2,740	–2,831	–2,901	–2,948	–3,064	–3,255	–3,082	–3,125	–3,443	–3,856
32	U.S. Government grants (excluding military grants of goods and services)	–1,672	–1,855	–1,916	–1,917	–1,888	–1,808	–1,910	–1,805	–1,709	–1,649	–1,736	–2,043
33	U.S. Government pensions and other transfers	–273	–373	–347	–339	–399	–463	–499	–571	–537	–537	–611	–696
34	Private remittances and other transfers	–423	–434	–477	–575	–614	–677	–655	–879	–836	–939	–1,096	–1,117
35	U.S. assets abroad, net [increase/capital outflow (–)]	–4,099	–5,538	–4,174	–7,270	–9,560	–5,716	–7,321	–9,757	–10,977	–11,585	–9,337	–12,475
36	U.S. official reserve assets, net	2,145	607	1,535	378	171	1,225	570	53	–870	–1,179	2,481	2,349
37	Gold	1,703	857	890	461	125	1,665	571	1,170	1,173	–967	787	866

1972	1973	1974	1975	1976	1977	1978	1979	1980	1981	1982	1983	1984	1985	1986	1987p	Line
77,495	110,241	146,666	155,729	171,630	184,276	219,994	286,796	342,485	376,499	349,570	334,422	360,778	359,458	372,807	420,123	1
49,381	71,410	98,306	107,088	114,745	120,816	142,054	184,473	224,269	237,085	211,198	201,820	219,900	215,935	224,361	250,814	2
1,364	2,559	3,379	4,049	5,454	7,351	7,973	6,516	8,274	10,041	11,986	12,344	9,954	8,670	8,903	11,886	3
2,817	3,412	4,032	4,697	5,742	6,150	7,183	8,441	10,588	12,913	12,393	11,408	11,353	11,675	12,913	15,374	4
699	975	1,104	1,039	1,229	1,366	1,603	2,156	2,591	3,111	3,174	3,037	3,028	3,040	3,562	4,649	5
3,579	4,465	5,697	5,840	6,747	7,090	8,136	9,971	11,618	12,560	12,317	12,590	13,809	14,066	15,190	16,545	6
2,115	2,513	3,070	3,543	3,531	3,883	4,705	4,980	5,780	5,794	3,507	3,597	3,921	4,224	4,715	5,820	7
655	712	751	757	822	1,037	1,180	1,204	1,305	1,490	1,669	1,679	1,724	1,942	2,147	2,281	8
										1,816	2,532	2,483	2,516	3,084	2,197	9
1,764	1,985	2,321	2,920	3,584	3,848	4,296	4,403	5,158	6,577	7,384	7,498	7,985	8,215	9,122	10,254	10
357	401	419	446	489	557	620	520	398	517	576	666	711	876	602	531	11
10,949	16,542	19,157	16,595	18,999	19,673	25,458	38,183	37,146	32,549	21,381	20,499	21,217	32,665	36,697	47,928	12
2,949	4,330	7,356	7,644	8,955	10,881	14,944	23,654	32,798	50,182	58,050	51,920	59,464	50,131	45,191	46,530	13
866	936	1,074	1,112	1,332	1,625	1,843	2,295	2,562	3,680	4,118	4,832	5,229	5,503	6,321	5,314	14
4,492	2,810	1,818	2,207	373	203	236	465	756	679	585	180	153	46	101	94	15
−79,237	−98,997	−137,274	−132,745	−162,109	−193,764	−229,869	−281,659	−333,020	−362,155	−349,292	−371,188	−455,612	−460,550	−498,501	−567,336	16
−55,797	−70,499	−103,811	−98,185	−124,228	−151,907	−176,001	−212,009	−249,749	−265,063	−247,642	−268,900	−332,422	−338,083	−368,700	−410,015	17
−4,784	−4,629	−5,032	−4,795	−4,895	−5,823	−7,352	−8,294	−10,511	−11,224	−12,260	−12,587	−11,896	−12,009	−12,565	−13,965	18
−5,042	−5,526	−5,980	−6,417	−6,856	−7,451	−8,475	−9,413	−10,397	−11,479	−12,394	−13,556	−15,449	−16,482	−17,627	−20,785	19
−1,596	−1,790	−2,095	−2,263	−2,568	−2,748	−2,896	−3,184	−3,607	−4,487	−4,772	−5,484	−6,502	−7,313	−6,842	−8,046	20
−3,520	−4,694	−5,942	−5,708	−6,852	−7,972	−9,124	−10,906	−11,790	−12,474	−11,710	−12,222	−14,843	−15,852	−17,099	−19,363	21
−155	−209	−160	−287	−293	−243	−393	−523	−428	−362	−326	−405	−597	−467	−616	−735	22
−139	−176	−186	−186	−189	−262	−277	−309	−297	−289	−292	−318	−359	−425	−461	−485	23
										403	471	478	696	1,324	793	24
−1,043	−1,180	−1,262	−1,551	−2,006	−2,190	−2,573	−2,822	−2,909	−3,162	−3,957	−4,245	−5,074	−5,983	−6,853	−7,622	25
−589	−640	−722	−789	−911	−951	−1,099	−1,239	−1,214	−1,287	−1,460	−1,567	−1,531	−1,733	−1,696	−1,826	26
−1,284	−1,610	−1,331	−2,234	−3,110	−2,834	−4,211	−6,357	−8,635	−6,898	−3,155	−5,598	−9,229	−6,079	−5,846	−12,632	27
−2,604	−4,209	−6,491	−5,788	−5,681	−5,841	−8,795	−15,481	−20,893	−28,553	−33,443	−28,953	−38,421	−35,516	−38,912	−48,610	28
−2,684	−3,836	−4,262	−4,542	−4,520	−5,542	−8,674	−11,122	−12,592	−16,878	−18,285	−17,825	−19,769	−21,306	−22,607	−24,046	29
−4,492	−2,810	−1,818	−2,207	−373	−203	−236	−465	−756	−679	−585	−180	−153	−46	−101	−94	30
−4,052	−4,103	−7,431	−4,868	−5,314	−5,023	−5,552	−6,128	−7,593	−7,460	−8,956	−9,480	−12,178	−15,301	−15,658	−13,467	31
−2,173	−1,938	−5,475	−2,894	−3,146	−2,787	−3,176	−3,550	−4,731	−4,466	−5,501	−6,288	−8,541	−11,222	−11,773	−9,942	32
−770	−915	−939	−1,068	−1,250	−1,378	−1,532	−1,658	−1,818	−2,041	−2,251	−2,207	−2,193	−2,171	−2,231	−2,247	33
−1,109	−1,250	−1,017	−906	−917	−859	−844	−920	−1,044	−953	−1,204	−985	−1,444	−1,908	−1,654	−1,279	34
−14,497	−22,874	−34,745	−39,703	−51,269	−34,785	−61,130	−64,331	−86,118	−110,951	−121,153	−49,777	−22,291	−31,399	−95,982	−63,796	35
−4	158	−1,467	−849	−2,558	−375	732	−1,133	−8,155	−5,175	−4,965	−1,196	−3,131	−3,858	312	9,151	36
547					−118	−65	−65		(*)							37

TABLE 12-5 U.S. INTERNATIONAL TRANSACTIONS, 1960–1987 (continued)
(Millions of U.S. Dollars)

Line	(Credits + ; debits −)	1960	1961	1962	1963	1964	1965	1966	1967	1968	1969	1970	1971
38	Special drawing rights											-851	-249
39	Reserve position in the International Monetary Fund	442	-135	626	29	266	-94	537	-94	-870	-1,034	389	1,350
40	Foreign currencies		-115	19	-112	-220	-346	-538	-1,023	-1,173	822	2,156	382
41	U.S. Government assets, other than official reserve assets, net	-1,100	-910	-1,085	-1,662	-1,680	-1,605	-1,543	-2,423	-2,274	-2,200	-1,589	-1,884
42	U.S. credits and other long-term assets	-1,214	-1,928	-2,128	-2,204	-2,382	-2,463	-2,513	-3,638	-3,722	-3,489	-3,293	-4,181
43	Repayments on U.S. credits and other long-term assets	642	1,279	1,288	988	720	874	1,235	1,005	1,386	1,200	1,721	2,115
44	U.S. foreign currency holdings and U.S. short-term assets, net	-528	-261	-245	-447	-19	-16	-265	209	62	89	-16	182
45	U.S. private assets, net	-5,144	-5,235	-4,623	-5,986	-8,050	-5,336	-6,347	-7,386	-7,833	-8,206	-10,229	-12,940
46	Direct investment	-2,940	-2,653	-2,851	-3,483	-3,760	-5,011	-5,418	-4,805	-5,295	-5,960	-7,590	-7,618
47	Foreign securities	-663	-762	-969	-1,105	-677	-759	-720	-1,308	-1,569	-1,549	-1,076	-1,113
48	U.S. claims on unaffiliated foreigners reported by U.S. nonbanking concerns	-394	-558	-354	157	-1,108	341	-442	-779	-1,203	-126	-596	-1,229
49	U.S. claims reported by U.S. banks, not included elsewhere	-1,148	-1,261	-450	-1,556	-2,505	93	233	-495	233	-570	-967	-2,980
50	Foreign assets in the United States, net [increase/capital inflow (+)]	2,294	2,705	1,911	3,217	3,643	742	3,661	7,379	9,928	12,702	6,359	22,970
51	Foreign official assets in the United States, net	1,473	765	1,270	1,986	1,660	134	-672	3,451	-774	-1,301	6,908	26,879
52	U.S. Government securities	655	233	1,409	816	432	-141	-1,527	2,261	-769	-2,343	9,439	26,570
53	U.S. Treasury securities	655	233	1,410	803	434	-134	-1,548	2,222	-798	-2,269	9,411	26,578
54	Other			-1	12	-2	-7	21	39	29	-74	28	-8
55	Other U.S. Government liabilities	215	25	152	429	298	65	113	83	-15	251	-456	-510
56	U.S. liabilities reported by U.S. banks, not included elsewhere	603	508	-291	742	930	210	742	1,106	10	792	-2,075	819
57	Other foreign official assets												
58	Other foreign assets in the United States, net	821	1,939	641	1,231	1,983	607	4,333	3,928	10,703	14,002	-550	-3,909
59	Direct investment	315	311	346	231	322	415	425	698	807	1,263	1,464	367
60	U.S. Treasury securities	-364	151	-66	-149	-146	-131	-356	-135	136	-68	81	-24
61	U.S. securities other than U.S. Treasury securities	282	324	134	287	-85	-358	906	1,016	4,414	3,130	2,189	2,289
62	U.S. liabilities to unaffiliated foreigners reported by U.S. nonbanking concerns	-90	226	-110	-37	75	178	476	584	1,475	792	2,014	369
63	U.S. liabilities reported by U.S. banks, not included elsewhere	678	928	336	898	1,818	503	2,882	1,765	3,871	8,886	-6,298	-6,911
64	Allocations of special drawing rights											867	717
65	Statistical discrepancy (sum of above items with sign reversed)	-1,019	-989	-1,124	-360	-907	-457	629	-205	438	-1,516	-219	-9,779
	Memoranda												
66	Balance on merchandise trade (lines 2 and 17)	4,892	5,571	4,521	5,224	6,801	4,951	3,817	3,800	635	607	2,603	-2,260
67	Balance on goods and services (lines 1 and 16)	5,191	6,484	6,127	7,244	9,724	8,378	6,095	5,838	3,693	3,524	5,773	2,423
68	Balance on goods, services, and remittances (lines 67, 33, and 34)	4,496	5,677	5,303	6,331	8,711	7,238	4,941	4,388	2,320	2,048	4,067	610
69	Balance on current account (lines 67 and 31)	2,824	3,822	3,387	4,414	6,823	5,431	3,031	2,583	611	399	2,331	-1,433
	Transactions in U.S. official reserve assets and in foreign official assets in the United States												
70	Increase (−) in U.S. official reserve assets, net (line 36)	2,145	607	1,535	378	171	1,225	570	53	-870	-1,179	2,481	2,349
71	Increase (+) in foreign official assets in the United States (line 51 less line 55)	1,258	741	1,118	1,558	1,362	69	-785	3,368	-759	-1,552	7,364	27,389

P = preliminary for 1987.
Source: U.S. Department of Commerce, *Survey of Current Business,* June 1987, Table 1 (pp. 54–55) and March 1988, Table 1-2 (p. 41).

1972	1973	1974	1975	1976	1977	1978	1979	1980	1981	1982	1983	1984	1985	1986	1987^p	Line
-703	9	-172	-66	-78	-121	1,249	-1,136	-16	-1,824	-1,371	-66	-979	-897	-246	-509	38
153	-33	-1,265	-466	-2,212	-294	4,231	-189	-1,667	-2,491	-2,552	-4,434	-995	908	1,501	2,070	39
-1	182	-30	-317	-268	158	-4,683	257	-6,472	-861	-1,041	3,304	-1,156	-3,869	-942	7,590	40
-1,568	-2,644	366	-3,474	-4,214	-3,693	-4,660	-3,746	-5,162	-5,097	-6,131	-5,006	-5,476	-2,831	-1,920	1,219	41
-3,819	-4,638	-5,001	-5,941	-6,943	-6,445	-7,470	-7,697	-9,860	-9,674	-10,063	-9,967	-9,599	-7,660	-8,915	-6,319	42
2,086	2,596	4,826	2,475	2,596	2,719	2,941	3,926	4,456	4,413	4,292	5,012	4,505	4,716	6,075	7,555	43
165	-602	541	-9	133	33	-131	25	242	164	-360	-51	-382	113	920	-16	44
-12,925	-20,388	-33,643	-35,380	-44,498	-30,717	-57,202	-59,453	-72,802	-100,679	-110,058	-43,576	-13,685	-24,711	-94,374	-74,166	45
-7,747	-11,353	-9,052	-14,244	-11,949	-11,890	-16,056	-25,222	-19,222	-9,624	2,369	-373	-2,821	-17,267	-28,047	-38,194	46
-618	-671	-1,854	-6,247	-8,885	-5,460	-3,626	-4,726	-3,568	-5,699	-7,983	-6,762	-4,756	-7,481	-3,302	-3,654	47
-1,054	-2,383	-3,221	-1,357	-2,296	-1,940	-3,853	-3,291	-3,174	-1,181	6,626	-6,513	5,019	1,361	-3,986	n.a.	48
-3,506	-5,980	-19,516	-13,532	-21,368	-11,427	-33,667	-26,213	-46,838	-84,175	-111,070	-29,928	-11,127	-1,323	-59,039	-33,431	49
21,461	18,388	34,241	15,670	36,518	51,319	64,036	38,752	58,112	83,032	93,746	84,869	102,467	129,872	213,386	202,585	50
10,475	6,026	10,546	7,027	17,693	36,816	33,678	-13,665	15,497	4,960	3,593	5,845	2,987	-1,140	34,698	44,289	51
8,470	641	4,172	5,563	9,892	32,538	24,221	-21,972	11,895	6,322	5,085	6,496	4,703	-1,139	33,301	44,871	52
8,213	59	3,270	4,658	9,319	30,230	23,555	-22,435	9,708	5,019	5,779	6,972	4,690	-838	34,515	43,301	53
257	582	902	905	573	2,308	666	463	2,187	1,303	-694	-476	13	-301	-1,214	1,570	54
182	936	301	1,517	4,627	1,400	2,476	-40	615	-338	605	602	586	823	1,723	-3,227	55
1,638	4,126	5,818	-2,158	969	773	5,551	7,213	-159	-3,670	-1,747	545	555	645	554	3,705	56
185	323	254	2,104	2,205	2,105	1,430	1,135	3,145	2,646	-350	-1,798	-2,857	-1,469	-880	-1,060	57
10,986	12,362	23,696	8,643	18,826	14,503	30,358	52,416	42,615	78,072	90,154	79,023	99,481	131,012	178,689	158,297	58
949	2,800	4,760	2,603	4,347	3,728	7,897	11,877	16,918	25,195	13,792	11,946	25,359	19,022	25,053	40,582	59
-39	-216	697	2,590	2,783	534	2,178	4,960	2,645	2,927	7,027	8,689	23,001	20,433	8,275	-6,088	60
4,507	4,041	378	2,503	1,284	2,437	2,254	1,351	5,457	6,905	6,085	8,164	12,568	50,962	70,802	42,134	61
815	1,035	1,844	319	-578	1,086	1,889	1,621	6,852	917	-2,383	-118	4,704	-450	-2,791	n.a.	62
4,754	4,702	16,017	628	10,990	6,719	16,141	32,607	10,743	42,128	65,633	50,342	33,849	41,045	77,350	77,857	63
710							1,139	1,152	1,093							64
-1,879	-2,654	-1,458	5,917	10,544	-2,023	12,521	25,431	24,982	19,942	36,085	11,154	26,837	17,920	23,947	21,892	65
-6,416	911	-5,505	8,903	-9,483	-31,091	-33,947	-27,536	-25,480	-27,978	-36,444	-67,080	-112,522	-122,148	-144,339	-159,201	66
-1,742	11,244	9,392	22,984	9,521	-9,488	-9,875	5,138	9,466	14,344	278	-36,766	-94,835	-101,093	-125,694	-147,213	67
-3,622	9,078	7,436	21,011	7,354	-11,724	-12,251	2,559	6,604	11,350	-3,177	-39,957	-98,472	-105,171	-129,579	-150,739	68
-5,795	7,140	1,962	18,116	4,207	-14,511	-15,427	-991	1,873	6,884	-8,679	-46,246	-107,013	-116,393	-141,352	-160,681	69
-4	158	-1,467	-849	-2,558	-375	732	-1,133	-8,155	-5,175	-4,965	-1,196	-3,131	-3,858	312	9,151	70
10,293	5,090	10,244	5,509	13,066	35,416	31,202	-13,624	14,881	5,298	2,988	5,243	2,401	-1,963	32,975	47,516	71

CHAPTER **13**

THE BALANCE-OF-PAYMENTS PROBLEM: A BASIC MODEL

The preceding two chapters dealt with the basic concepts of foreign exchange and the balance of payments. These concepts are indispensable when dealing with the great issues of international finance. Throughout Chapters 11 and 12 there were repeated references to exchange rates and balance-of-payments equilibrium. Nevertheless, there was no systematic discussion of the economic forces that keep the foreign exchange market and the balance of payments in equilibrium. The time has come to begin such a discussion.

It is indeed ironic that the complex issues of international finance can be tackled successfully by means of an uncomplicated model. Nevertheless, it is true. Our main objective in this chapter is to describe this model and then use it to illustrate various aspects of the balance-of-payments problem. In that sense this chapter serves as a general introduction to the rest of the book.

The simplified model introduced in this chapter draws on concepts that were developed in Part One of the book, especially in Chapters 2 and 3. Familiarity with that analysis can be helpful but is *not* necessary for understanding the present discussion. All necessary concepts are discussed sufficiently in this chapter. The main concern here is with the general nature of the problem and the issues involved, rather than with any specific solution to the model. For concreteness, however, a numerical illustration is pursued throughout the chapter.

13-1 THE BASIC ASSUMPTIONS

Most of the important issues of international finance can be studied within the context of a simplified two-country model. Assume that there are two countries, America (home country) and Britain (foreign country, or the rest of the world); their respective national currencies are the dollar and the pound sterling. Each country is endowed with a fixed supply of a single homogeneous factor of production, labor, and specializes completely in the production of a single commodity. Thus America produces only A-exportables and Britain produces only B-exportables. For concreteness, we assume throughout that America and Britain are endowed with 900 and 650 units of labor, respectively. We further assume that the units of measurement are such that it takes 1 unit of labor to produce either 1 unit of A-exportables in America or 1 unit of B-exportables in Britain. Tastes in each country are represented by a social indifference map that is qualitatively similar to the indifference map of an individual consumer. The interest rate in each country is given; perfect competition prevails everywhere; and transportation costs as well as barriers to trade (for example, tariffs) are zero. Commodity exports are the only source of supply of foreign exchange, and commodity imports are the only purpose of demand for foreign exchange.

The present model has several limitations. For instance, it excludes the possibility of diversification in production, the existence of nontraded goods, capital markets, and the multiplicity of factors of production, to mention only a few. There are, however, reasons for using this model. First, such simplifications permit us to cut through much detail and go directly to the real issues; any complications can be introduced at a later stage. (Indeed, most of the assumptions enumerated presently are modified in later chapters.) Second, none of the important conclusions of the model are destroyed when any or all simplifying assumptions are dropped. From the point of view of balance-of-payments theory, nothing is gained by unnecessarily introducing more complications into our basic model.

13-2 INTERNATIONAL EQUILIBRIUM

Before commenting on the adjustment process, it is necessary to consider briefly the general equilibrium of our basic model. For this purpose, assume that in each country **aggregate expenditure on commodities (or absorption) equals national income.** (This assumption was also made in Part One in the context of the pure theory of trade.) We drop this restrictive assumption later in the chapter.

Note that the international equilibrium of our basic model is identical to the *exchange equilibrium* between two consumers. Familiarity with the problem of exchange equilibrium can be helpful but is *not* essential to the present discussion. Those who desire a review of exchange equilibrium are referred to Chacholiades (1986, chap. 14).

Wage Rates and Commodity Prices

Let p_a and p_b indicate America's equilibrium prices (in dollars) of A-exportables and B-exportables, respectively. Similarly, let $p_a{}^*$ and $p_b{}^*$ stand for Britain's corresponding prices in pounds sterling. (From now on we shall use asterisks to indicate prices expressed in pounds.) Assume also that the exchange rate is R, that is, £1 sells for $\$R$. In the absence of transportation costs, tariffs, and other barriers to trade, **commodity arbitrage** establishes the equalities $p_a = Rp_a^*$, $p_b = Rp_b^*$. The latter equalities illustrate the **law of one price: A commodity commands the same price everywhere.**

In equilibrium, commodity prices are equal to per-unit labor costs. For instance, consider the price of A-exportables. In equilibrium, p_a must be equal to the cost of labor that is needed to produce 1 unit of A-exportables. In turn, this labor cost is equal to the amount of labor needed for the production of 1 unit of A-exportables (that is, **the labor coefficient of production**) times the money-wage rate in America. Now recall that for simplicity we have assumed that the labor coefficient of A-exportables is unity; hence the average labor cost of production of A-exportables (in dollars) coincides with America's money-wage rate (w_a), that is, $p_a = w_a$. Finally, the price of A-exportables in pounds is equal to $p_a^* = p_a/R = w_a/R$.

The same principle holds for the price of B-exportables. In equilibrium, p_b^* must be equal to Britain's average labor cost of production. Because the labor coefficient is by assumption unity, p_b^* must coincide with Britain's money-wage rate (w_b^*), that is, $p_b^* = w_b^*$. The price of B-exportables in dollars is obtained from the relationship $p_b = Rp_b^* = Rw_b^*$.

The price ratio $p_a/p_b = p_a^*/p_b^*$ (or relative price of A-exportables) is called America's **terms of trade.** It shows the number of units of B-exportables that exchange for 1 unit of A-exportables.

Equilibrium in the Factor and Commodity Markets

General equilibrium prevails when the terms of trade are such that supply equals demand in all markets—the labor markets, the commodity markets, and the foreign exchange market. America's labor market is in equilibrium when America produces 900 units of A-exportables per year. (Recall that America is endowed with 900 units of labor and that each unit of A-exportables requires 1 unit of labor.) Similarly, Britain's labor market is in equilibrium when Britain produces 650 units of B-exportables per year. (Recall that Britain is endowed with 650 units of labor and that each unit of B-exportables requires 1 unit of labor.) The commodity markets are in equilibrium when, at the current prices, America and Britain wish to purchase (or absorb) 900 units of A-exportables and 650 units of B-exportables. We return to the foreign exchange market in the next subsection.

For concreteness, assume that general equilibrium occurs when $p_a = w_a = \$10$; $p_b^* = w_b^* = £5$; and $R = \$2$. It follows that $p_a^* = p_a/R = 10/2 = £5$, and $p_b = Rp_b^* = 2 \times 5 = \$10$. At these prices, America's *national income* (that is, the total wage bill) is $Y_a = \$9000$ (that is, $w_a \times 900 = \$10 \times 900$). America's *national product* (that is, the value of A-exportables produced) is also equal to $9,000 (that is, $p_a \times 900 = \$10 \times 900 = \$9000$).

America's national income (or product) in pounds is equal to $Y_a^* = Y_a/R = \$9000/2 = £4500$.

Similarly, Britain's national income is $Y_b^* = w_b^* \times 650 = £5 \times 650 = £3250$, which is also equal to Britain's national product (that is, $p_b^* \times 650 = £5 \times 650 = £3250$). Britain's national income in dollars is equal to $Y_b = R \times Y_b^* = 2 \times £3250 = \$6500$.

By assumption, in each country aggregate expenditure on A-exportables and B-exportables equals national income. Hence, America spends \$9,000, and Britain £3,250 (or \$6,500). We assume that tastes are such that America purchases 700 units of A-exportables and 200 units of B-exportables at a total cost of \$9,000; that is $(\$10 \times 700) + (\$10 \times 200) = \$9000$. Britain purchases 200 units of A-exportables and 450 units of B-exportables at a total cost of \$6,500; that is $(\$10 \times 200) + (\$10 \times 450) = \$6500$.

The preceding solution is illustrated in Figure 13-1. First consider panel (*a*), which describes the situation of America. Straight line NE_a is America's budget line. It is the locus of all combinations of A-exportables and B-exportables whose market value equals \$9,000 (that is, America's national income). For instance, America could purchase 900 units of A-exportables only, at a total cost of $\$10 \times 900 = \$9000$, as shown by point E_a. Alternatively, America could

FIGURE 13-1 **Production, absorption, and trade.** In panel (*a*), America produces at point E_a (that is, 900 units of A-exportables) and absorbs bundle Z_a (that is, 700 units of A-exportables and 200 units of B-exportables), where budget line NE_a is tangent to the highest possible social indifference curve. In panel (*b*), Britain produces at E_b (that is, 650 units of B-exportables) and absorbs bundle Z_b (that is, 200 units of A-exportables and 450 units of B-exportables).

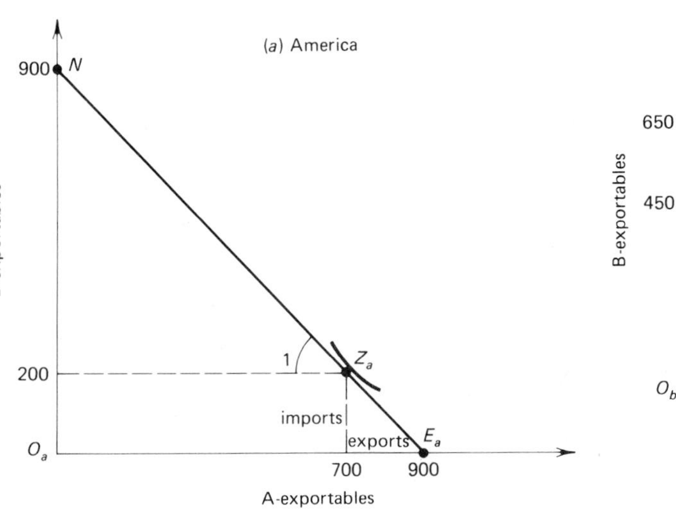

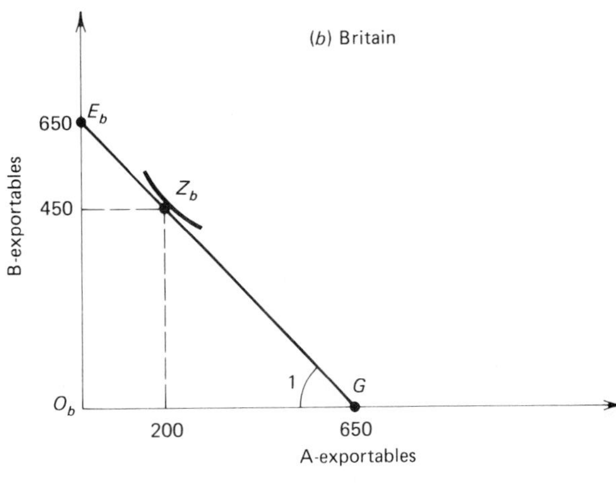

purchase 900 units of B-exportables only, at a total cost of $10 × 900 = $9000, as shown by point *N*. Actually, America purchases bundle Z_a at a total cost of $9,000; that is ($10 × 700) + ($10 × 200). At Z_a America's budget line is tangent to the highest social indifference curve, as shown.

America imports 200 units of B-exportables from Britain. Out of its total production of 900 units of A-exportables, America uses 700 units for domestic consumption and investment (that is, domestic **absorption**) and exports 200 units to Britain, as shown. Essentially, America exchanges 200 units of A-exportables for 200 units of Britain's B-exportables. Note that the slope of budget line NE_a is unity; it gives America's terms of trade (that is, the relative price of A-exportables).

Panel (*b*) illustrates the position of Britain. Line E_bG is Britain's budget line; it is the locus of all bundles of A-exportables and B-exportables that exhaust Britain's national income ($6,500). Britain purchases bundle Z_b (where budget line E_bG is tangent to the highest social indifference curve) at a total cost of $6,500; that is ($10 × 450) + ($10 × 200). Thus Britain imports 200 units of A-exportables. Out of its total production of 650 units of B-exportables, Britain uses 450 units for domestic absorption and exports the rest (that is, 200 units) to America. Note again that the slope of budget line E_bG gives the relative price of A-exportables.

We now wish to combine the information contained in the two separate panels of Figure 13-1. Imagine that Britain's diagram is drawn on a separate piece of paper so that we can freely move it around as we please. Superimpose it on America's diagram, so that the "endowment" points E_a and E_b coincide, calling the common endowment point *E*. Place a pin at *E*, holding points E_a and E_b together at all times, and then turn Britain's diagram around the pin by 180°, as shown in Figure 13-2.

The dimensions of the resultant rectangle O_aEO_bH (known as the **Edgeworth box**) give the full-employment outputs of America (900 units of A-exportables) and Britain (650 units of B-exportables). Any point within the box (such as *Z*) represents a specific allocation of the full-employment outputs of A-exportables and B-exportables between America and Britain. The coordinates of the point (say, *Z*) with respect to O_a give the quantities absorbed by America, while its coordinates with respect to O_b show the amounts absorbed by Britain.

In Figure 13-2 the budget lines of America and Britain coincide. Further, the absorption points (Z_a and Z_b of Figure 13-1) also coincide. This is illustrated by point *Z*, which represents the equilibrium allocation of A-exportables and B-exportables between the two countries.

Note that the coordinates of *Z* with respect to the southeast corner, *E*, give America's volumes of exports and imports. America and Britain start at *E* and through international exchange shift to *Z*. The movement from *E* to *Z* represents international trade. Figure 13-2 brings together production, absorption, and trade for America and Britain simultaneously.

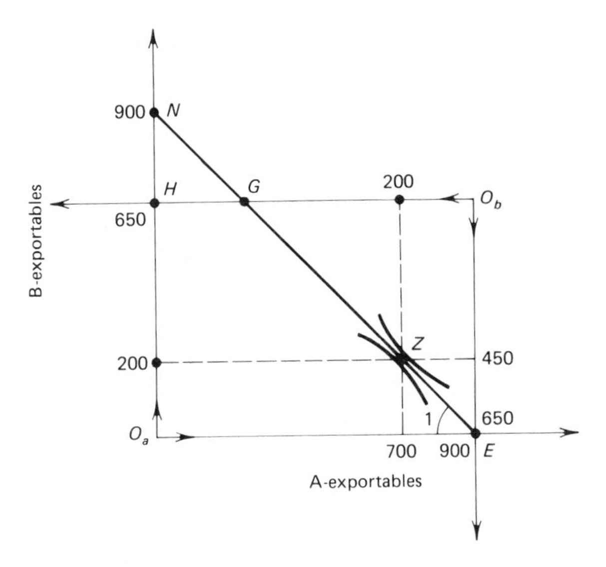

FIGURE 13-2 **International equilibrium.** Britain's diagram is turned around by 180° and is superimposed on America's diagram so that the production (or "endowment") points coincide, as shown by *E*. Rectangle O_aEO_bH is the Edgeworth box, whose dimensions measure the full-employment outputs of A-exportables and B-exportables. International equilibrium occurs at *Z*, where America absorbs 700 units of A-exportables and 200 units of B-exportables, and Britain absorbs 200 units of A-exportables and 450 units of B-exportables. The coordinates of *Z* with respect to *E* measure America's exports and imports.

Equilibrium in the Foreign Exchange Market

General equilibrium point *Z* (Figure 13-2) exhibits equilibrium in the commodity and labor markets. (Recall that America and Britain produce the *full-employment* outputs of A-exportables and B-exportables, respectively.) What is the status of the foreign exchange market?

By assumption, the quantity of foreign exchange (pounds) supplied coincides with the value (in pounds) of American exports; and the quantity of foreign exchange demanded coincides with the value (in pounds) of American imports. At general equilibrium point *Z*, America exports 200 units of A-exportables and imports 200 units of B-exportables. Consequently,

$$\text{Quantity of pounds supplied} = p_a^* \times 200 = £5 \times 200 = £1000$$

$$\text{Quantity of pounds demanded} = p_b^* \times 200 = £5 \times 200 = £1000$$

Evidently, general equilibrium point *Z* implies equilibrium in the foreign exchange market as well, because the supply of pounds (£1,000) equals the demand for pounds (£1,000).

13-3 THE ADJUSTMENT PROCESS: (1) INCOME = ABSORPTION

Can the long-run equilibrium of Figure 13-2 be attained automatically? That is, does a disequilibrium state automatically generate forces that tend to restore equilibrium? If such automaticity exists, what is the precise adjustment process? If such automaticity does not exist, what policy measures must be pursued to restore equilibrium? These are important questions. The rest of the book is devoted to them. This chapter gives only tentative answers and prepares the ground for subsequent discussion.

Types of Disequilibria

We are concerned primarily with the problems of equilibrium and adjustment in the foreign exchange market. The foreign exchange market is not an ordinary market, because it provides the link among the economies of the world. *Long-run* equilibrium in the foreign exchange market is akin to general equilibrium; long-run equilibrium in the foreign exchange market requires that all other markets also be in equilibrium. The adjustment process of the foreign exchange market is inherently much more complicated than the adjustment process of any other market, such as the wheat market or the shoe market.

Disequilibrium in the foreign exchange market may coincide with (or reflect) a disequilibrium in some other market or markets. But this is not necessary. As shown in Section 13-4, disequilibrium in the foreign exchange market may exist even when all other markets are in equilibrium. The present section deals with disequilibrium states in which, in addition to the foreign exchange market, some other market is out of equilibrium.

Disequilibrium in the Commodity Markets

In this section, we describe the type of balance-of-payments disequilibrium that reflects disequilibrium in the commodity markets. The discussion of this section is based on a crucial assumption: **national income equals desired spending** (or **absorption**) in each country.

Consider Figure 13-3, which is similar to Figure 13-2. The current price ratio is 1.5, as shown by the slope of common budget line *ET*. By assumption, the relative price of A-exportables is higher than the long-run equilibrium price ratio. This is clearly a disequilibrium situation. There are many types of disturbances (for example, changes in tastes, technology, and factor supplies) that can cause a system to be out of long-run equilibrium. For our present purposes, the cause of disequilibrium is irrelevant. For concreteness, assume now that $p_a = w_a = \$15$, $p_b^* = w_b^* = £5$, and $R = \$2$; thus $p_a/p_b = p_a/Rp_b^* = 15/(2 \times 5) = 1.5$. Further, $p_a^* = p_a/R = 15/2 = £7.5$, and $p_b = Rp_b^* = 2 \times 5 = \$10$.

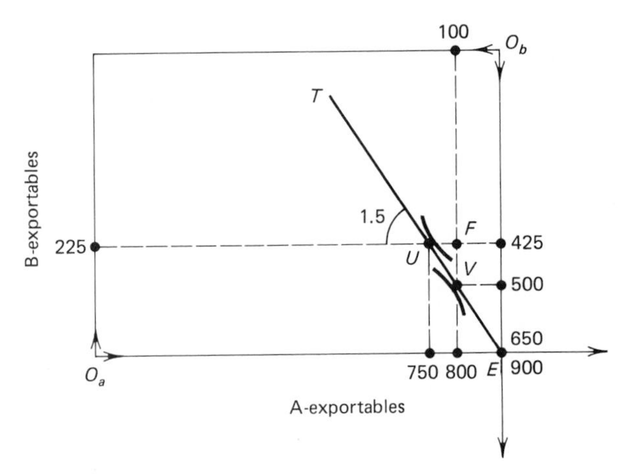

FIGURE 13-3 **Disequilibrium in the commodity markets and the foreign exchange market.** At the current terms of trade indicated by *ET*, America wants to buy (absorb) bundle *U*, and Britain bundle *V*. Assuming that all buyer plans are realized, both countries end up at *F*, where America runs a balance-of-trade deficit of *UF* (in A-exportables) or *VF* (in B-exportables). America's inventories of A-exportables increase by *UF*, and Britain's inventories of B-exportables decrease by *VF*, per unit of time.

What is the nature of the disequilibrium state portrayed in Figure 13-3? That is, what markets are out of equilibrium? Clearly, the labor markets are in equilibrium—each country continues to employ all available labor. However, at the current price ratio, America wants to buy bundle *U* (that is, 750 units of A-exportables and 225 units of B-exportables) and Britain wants to buy bundle *V* (that is, 100 units of A-exportables and 500 units of B-exportables). Alternatively, America wants to export 150 units of A-exportables in exchange for 225 units of imports of B-exportables, while Britain wants to export only 150 units of B-exportables in exchange for 100 units of imports of A-exportables. Thus, America's desired volume of trade, *EU*, exceeds Britain's desired volume of trade, *EV*. As a result, there exists an **excess demand** for B-exportables (given by vertical distance *VF* = 75 units) and an **excess supply** of A-exportables (given by horizontal distance *UF* = 50 units).

For the moment assume that *all buyer plans are realized.* America imports 225 units of B-exportables, even though Britain planned to export 150 units only. Britain's producers meet the *excess demand for B-exportables (75 units) out of inventory.* Similarly, Britain imports 100 units of A-exportables, even though America planned to export 150 units. *America's producers use the excess supply of A-exportables (50 units) to increase their inventory.* Thus, the disequilibrium in the commodity markets reflects **unplanned inventory changes.**

Note that each country's *actual* absorption is given by point *F*. First consider America, which produces 900 units of A-exportables and exports 100 units to

Britain. This means that America actually absorbs 800 units of A-exportables, even though 50 units (distance *UF*) represent *unplanned* inventory accumulation. Further, America desires and actually imports 225 units of B-exportables. Now 800 units of A-exportables and 225 units of B-exportables are the coordinates of point *F* with respect to O_a. Instead of buying its desired bundle, *U*, America actually absorbs bundle F, which lies *beyond* America's budget line, *ET*.

Similarly, Britain produces 650 units of B-exportables and exports 225 units to America. This means that Britain absorbs 425 units of B-exportables plus 100 units of A-exportables. Again, 100 units of A-exportables and 425 units of B-exportables are the coordinates of point *F* with respect to O_b. Britain's actual absorption point, *F*, is the same as America's actual absorption point. Point *F* lies *inside* Britain's budget line, *ET*.

Disequilibrium in the Foreign Exchange Market

What is the situation in the foreign exchange market? The quantity of pounds demanded exceeds the quantity of pounds supplied. We can confirm this conclusion as follows:

$$\text{Quantity of pounds supplied} = p_a^* \times 100 = £7.5 \times 100 = £750$$

$$\text{Quantity of pounds demanded} = p_b^* \times 225 = £5 \times 225 = £1125$$

$$\text{Excess demand for pounds} = £1125 - £750 = £375$$

Note that America is running a balance-of-trade deficit equal to the excess demand for pounds sterling. Further, America's balance-of-trade deficit (in pounds) is equal to the value of America's unplanned inventory accumulation: $(p_a^* \times UF) = £7.5 \times 50 = £375$. It is also equal to the value of Britain's unplanned inventory decumulation: $p_b^* \times VF = £5 \times 75 = £375$. America's deficit mirrors Britain's balance-of-trade surplus.

The preceding results are special cases of a more general identity:

$$\textbf{Balance of trade} = \textbf{national income} - \textbf{actual absorption} \qquad (13\text{-}1)$$

For instance, America's national income (or value of output produced) is equal to $p_a^* \times 900 = £7.5 \times 900 = £6750$, while America's actual absorption (that is, value of bundle *F*) is £7125; that is, $(£7.5 \times 800) + (£5 \times 225) = £7125$; hence, balance of trade $= £6750 - £7125 = -£375$. Alternatively, America's actual absorption exceeds America's national income by $UF = 50$ units of A-exportables, or $VF = 75$ units of B-exportables, which is America's balance-of-trade deficit. Equation (13-1) is studied further in Chapter 15.

Perhaps the analogy of a family may be instructive. A family's income is equal to the value of factor services (such as labor) it sells (or "exports") to the rest of the economy. The family uses its income to buy (or "import") food, clothing, shelter, transportation, medical care, and so on. When the expenditure on goods and services (that is, "imports") exceeds income (that is, "exports"), the family experiences a balance-of-trade *deficit*. When income ("exports") exceeds spending ("imports"), the family has a balance-of-trade *surplus*.

Summary of Disequilibrium Signs

In summary, the disequilibrium portrayed in Figure 13-3 implies disequilibrium in the markets for A-exportables, B-exportables, and foreign exchange. In particular, there exist:

1 An excess supply of A-exportables ($UF = 50$ units), which is reflected in an increase in American inventories.

2 An excess demand for B-exportables ($VF = 75$ units), which is reflected in a decrease in British inventories.

3 An excess demand for pounds sterling ($p_b^* \times VF = p_a^* \times UF = £5 \times 75 = £7.5 \times 50 = £375$), which is reflected in a decrease (increase) in America's (Britain's) foreign exchange reserves. In effect, America converts its foreign exchange reserves into unwanted inventories of A-exportables; and Britain reluctantly transforms its commodity inventories of B-exportables into foreign exchange reserves.

How can this disequilibrium be corrected?

Tendencies toward General Equilibrium

The disequilibrium of Figure 13-3 could be corrected if America's terms of trade (that is, the relative price of A-exportables) were allowed to fall. Then the world economy would return to the international equilibrium of Figure 13-2. Are there any economic forces that may automatically bring about this result?

Write America's terms of trade (p) as follows:

$$p = \frac{p_a}{R \cdot p_b^*} \tag{13-2}$$

(Note that in forming the terms of trade—a ratio of money prices—we must express both money prices in terms of the *same* currency.) A reduction in p may be accomplished by any one of the following three ways (or any combination):

1 A reduction in the dollar price of A-exportables (p_a).
2 An increase in the pound sterling price of B-exportables (p_b^*).
3 An increase in the rate of exchange (R).

Are there any economic signs that may lead us to believe these changes will actually take place?

Based on the disequilibrium states in the markets for A-exportables, B-exportables, and foreign exchange (pounds sterling), a classical economist would hasten to point out that in the current disequilibrium state there are indeed strong economic forces at work that will restore international equilibrium. Perhaps the classical economist would argue as follows: The excess supply of A-exportables would cause their price (p_a) to fall; the excess demand for B-exportables would cause their price (p_b^*) to rise; and the excess demand for pounds sterling would cause the rate of exchange (R) to rise. Accordingly, in the classical world of **perfect price flexibility** one would expect the price system to adjust quickly and restore equilibrium promptly. In fact, we accepted this much ourselves in Part One of this book! Unfortunately, the world economy of today does not justify such optimism. Let us consider each one of these prices separately.

Exchange-Rate Adjustment

The disequilibrium state illustrated in Figure 13-3 involves an excess demand for pounds. Will the rate of exchange rise sufficiently to restore general equilibrium?

The question of an exchange-rate adjustment depends largely on the institutional arrangement of the foreign exchange market. As we learned in Chapter 11, there are two basic systems: (1) the *fixed exchange-rate system* and (2) the *flexible exchange-rate system.* If the foreign exchange market is organized on the basis of a fixed exchange-rate system, the rate of exchange will not change even though there may exist an excess demand for pounds. What if a flexible exchange-rate system is actually adopted or if the monetary authorities of the deficit country (America) devalue their currency? Will the system then return smoothly to long-run equilibrium? It certainly seems plausible. However, there are reasons to believe that general equilibrium cannot be restored by a mere exchange-rate adjustment.

In the first place, an exchange-rate adjustment may affect aggregate spending. If this is so, the system will not move to general equilibrium because aggregate spending will not remain equal to full-employment income in either country.

More important, a devaluation (or depreciation) of the dollar is equivalent to a reduction in America's real income because of the deterioration of America's terms of trade. Such real-income reductions are usually resisted by workers. Thus, American workers would probably attempt to negotiate higher money wages in order to recover their losses caused by the devaluation. If the American workers are successful in raising their money wages, the cost of production (and thus the price) of A-exportables will increase and offset completely the adverse effect of the devaluation of the dollar on the American terms of trade. [Equation (13-2) shows that as p_a and R increase by the same percentage, America's terms of trade (p) remain constant.]

Alternatively, in a more general context, foreign producers might resist the devaluation (or depreciation) of the dollar by lowering their prices. For instance, in terms of equation (13-2), if p_b^* fell by, say, 10 percent as R increased by 10 percent, America's terms of trade (p) would remain constant. Without a deterioration in the American terms of trade, there can be no movement toward the long-run equilibrium point, Z, of Figure 13-2.

We conclude that adjustment through exchange-rate variations is not that simple. Later in the book, we shall pursue the influence of the exchange rate and its variations on the behavior of the world economy.

Adjustment in the Commodity and Labor Markets

As we have seen, the disequilibrium state illustrated in Figure 13-3 involves a positive excess *supply* of A-exportables plus a positive excess *demand* for B-exportables. Ordinarily, the price of A-exportables (p_a) would tend to fall, and the price of B-exportables (p_b^*) would tend to rise. Or would they?

Consider the price of A-exportables. In equilibrium, the price of A-exportables (in dollars) coincides with America's money-wage rate (w_a); that is, $p_a = w_a$. Consequently, *a reduction in the price of A-exportables requires a prior reduction in the American money-wage rate.* Is a reduction in the American money-wage rate possible? Unfortunately, reductions in money-wage rates are always resisted by powerful labor unions. Indeed, it is a common observation that the money-wage rate is notoriously inflexible in the downward direction. We must conclude that the assumed tendency for the price of A-exportables (p_a) to fall is an illusion.

Finally, turn to the price of B-exportables (p_b^*). In equilibrium, p_b^* must coincide with Britain's money-wage rate (w_b^*); that is, $p_b^* = w_b^*$. Thus an increase in the price of B-exportables would reflect an increase in the British money-wage rate. Surely, the British workers would be delighted with a wage increase. Should we then conclude that general equilibrium will be restored through an increase in w_b^* and p_b^*? Think again.

There are two constraints on the foregoing solution. First, because of fear of *inflation* the British authorities may want to intervene to prevent the money-wage rate from rising. Second, even if w_b^* and p_b^* were allowed to rise, America's terms of trade would not necessarily fall! The reason should be evident from our discussion of exchange-rate adjustment. *A deterioration of America's terms of trade is equivalent to a reduction in America's real income.* As noted earlier, a real-income reduction will most certainly be resisted by American workers, who will again try to negotiate higher money wages in order to recover their income losses due to the terms-of-trade deterioration. If w_a and p_a rise at the same rate as w_b^* and p_b^*, America's terms of trade will remain constant and the disequilibrium will persist.

The Tendency toward Unemployment

As we have just seen, the classical optimism for a three-way convergence toward general equilibrium has vanished. But this is not all, as economic forces could still conspire to dispatch the system into an abyss of Keynesian unemployment.

Return to the market for A-exportables, where there exists an excess supply reflected in the unplanned inventory accumulation of America's producers. If the money-wage rate cannot be reduced, then America's producers will simply have to cut their production of A-exportables—they cannot be expected to accumulate inventories indefinitely. Thus, America's producers will start laying off workers. America's rate of unemployment will start rising as production and national income fall.

The student probably knows already that when a country's national income falls, the demand for commodities in general (that is, aggregate expenditure) also falls. The reduction in America's national income will cause a *reduction in America's demand for both A-exportables and B-exportables.* If allowed to proceed far enough, *such a process can restore equilibrium in both the commodity markets and the foreign exchange market.* However, because of the massive unemployment that emerges in America, this process cannot restore general equilibrium.

For instance, suppose that at the current disequilibrium terms of trade ($p = 1.5$), America absorbs the two commodities in the proportion indicated by point U in Figure 13-3, irrespective of the level of aggregate spending. This means that America's absorption basket always contains A-exportables and B-exportables in the proportion 10:3. If we allow America's production to fall to 600 units, America would want to absorb 500 units of A-exportables and 150 units of B-exportables; hence America would desire to export 100 units of A-exportables (that is, $600 - 500 = 100$) in exchange for 150 units of B-exportables. America's desired volume of trade would then match precisely Britain's wishes for trade, as revealed by point V in Figure 13-3. Note that America's national income (that is, $\$15 \times 600 = \$9000$) would be equal to America's absorption; that is $(\$15 \times 500) + (\$10 \times 150) = \$9000$.

The preceding solution is illustrated in Figure 13-4. Vector ET and points U and V of Figure 13-3 are transferred to Figure 13-4. At the current disequilibrium terms of trade indicated by the slope of vector ET, the consumption behavior of America is illustrated by straight line O_aU, whose slope shows the fixed proportion in which America absorbs the two commodities. [Line O_aU is known as America's **income-consumption curve** (ICC_a) which is the locus of points at which America's marginal rate of substitution (or absolute slope of America's indifference curves) is equal to the given terms of trade.] Allow America's production to fall by 300 units, and shift America's origin from O_a to O'_a and America's income-consumption curve (O_aU) to O'_aV. After these changes are completed, point V (Britain's desired absorption point) becomes America's desired absorption point as well. In other words, point V becomes an equilibrium point similar to point Z of Figure 13-2. At V both the commodity markets and the foreign exchange market are in equilibrium. Of course, massive unemployment prevails in America now, and unfortunately there exists no automatic mechanism to eliminate it.

Once equilibrium is established in the commodity markets and the foreign exchange market, there will be no further tendency for either the price of B-exportables or the rate of exchange to change.

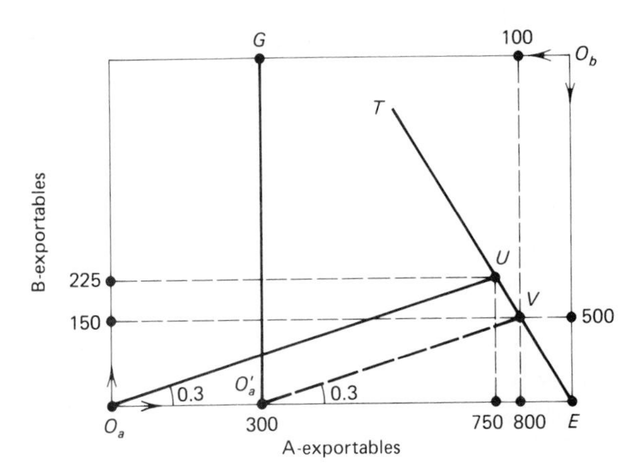

FIGURE 13-4 **Balance-of-payments equilibrium established by means of changes in production and income.** As America's production of A-exportables falls by 300 units, the box diagram shrinks to O'_aEO_bG, and America's income-consumption curve passes through Britain's absorption point, V, as shown by dashed curve O'_aV. Balance-of-payments equilibrium now prevails at V, but America suffers from massive unemployment.

13-4 THE ADJUSTMENT PROCESS: (2) INCOME ≠ ABSORPTION

So far we have assumed that in each country national income equals desired absorption (or spending). The time has come to drop this assumption. This opens the way for a new type of balance-of-payments disequilibrium—a disequilibrium in the foreign exchange market that does not coincide with a disequilibrium in any other market.

Policies for Internal Balance

Return to the initial disequilibrium of Figure 13-3. In the market for A-exportables there exists an excess supply that leads to an unplanned accumulation of American inventories. In the market for B-exportables there exists an excess demand that leads to an unplanned decumulation of British inventories. These unintended changes in inventories tend to reduce production and employment in America and possibly generate inflation in Britain. (In the preceding section we saw how a cut in America's production and employment can restore equilibrium in the foreign exchange market.) How will the American and British authorities react to this situation?

The American authorities, fearing unemployment, may increase aggregate spending by means of expansionary fiscal and monetary policies. For example, the American authorities may encourage domestic investment by reducing the rate of interest. Or they may encourage domestic consumption by reducing income taxes, thus placing more purchasing power in the hands of the consumers. Or finally, they may step up government purchases of goods and services. The British authorities, fearing inflation, may reduce aggregate spending by means of deflationary fiscal and monetary policies. For instance, they may raise the interest rate and/or income taxes, and they may also reduce government spending on goods and services.

Under certain conditions, which are specified below, such policies for **internal balance** (that is, full employment without inflation) pursued by America and Britain simultaneously can restore equilibrium in the commodity markets and eliminate unintended inventory changes. Nevertheless, they give rise to a **fundamental disequilibrium** in the foreign exchange market (and, of course, the balance of payments).

Fundamental Disequilibrium

Suppose that at the current disequilibrium terms of trade ($p = 1.5$), America and Britain absorb the two commodities roughly in the proportions indicated by points U and V (Figure 13-3), respectively, at all levels of aggregate spending. Thus the proportion of A-exportables and B-exportables is about 10:3 in the American absorption basket, and 1:5 in the British basket, as illustrated in Figure 13-5 by the income-consumption curves of America (ICC_a) and Britain

FIGURE 13-5 **Fundamental disequilibrium.** At the current terms of trade ($p = 1.5$), America wants to purchase bundle U, and Britain bundle V. America, fearing unemployment, increases spending to $p_a \times 984 = \$14,760$. Britain, fearing inflation, cuts spending to $p_b \times 524 = \$5,240$. Equilibrium occurs at K, where America runs a balance-of-payments deficit equal to an export deficit of 84 units of A-exportables (shown by horizontal distance ED), which also indicates America's excess spending over national income.

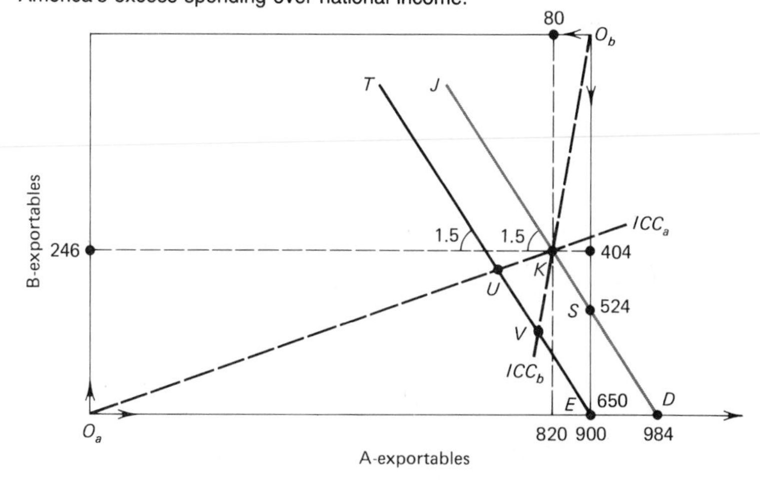

(ICC_b). These income-consumption curves intersect at *K*.[1] Vector *ET* and points *U* and *V* correspond to vector *ET* and points *U* and *V* of Figure 13-3. Recall that at the current terms of trade and levels of spending, America desires bundle *U* and Britain desires bundle *V*.

Let America *increase* its spending to $14,760, which is the value of American bundle *K* at the current disequilibrium prices; that is, $(p_a \times 820) + (p_b \times 246) = (\$15 \times 820) + (\$10 \times 246) = \$14,760$. America's budget line would shift to *DJ*. (Note that the value of American bundle *D* is equal to America's new level of spending: $p_a \times 984 = \$15 \times 984 = \$14,760$.) America's desired absorption would shift from *U* to *K*.

At the same time, let Britain *reduce* its spending to $5,240, which is the value of British bundle *K* at the current disequilibrium prices; that is, $(p_a \times 80) + (p_b \times 404) = (\$15 \times 80) + (\$10 \times 404) = \$5240$. Britain's budget line would shift to *SJ*. (Note that the value of British bundle *S* is equal to Britain's new level of spending: $p_b \times 524 = \$10 \times 524 = \$5240$.) Britain's desired absorption would also shift from *V* to *K*.

We conclude that with the preceding changes in American and British spending, point *K* will indicate both countries' desired absorption; thus both commodity markets will clear. At point *K* equilibrium will exist in the commodity markets and the labor markets.

Is there also equilibrium in the foreign exchange market at *K?* Unfortunately, that is not the case. At *K*, America exports 80 units of A-exportables and imports 246 units of B-exportables. Clearly, at the current terms of trade ($p = 1.5$), the value of 80 units of A-exportables equals the value of only 120 units of B-exportables. Hence, America suffers from an *import surplus* of 126 units of B-exportables, shown by vertical distance *ES*. Alternatively, we can say that America suffers from an *export deficit* of 84 units of A-exportables, shown by horizontal distance *ED*.

Note again that America's deficit is equal to the excess of America's absorption over America's income, as illustrated by horizontal distance *ED*. Similarly, Britain's surplus is equal to the excess of Britain's income over Britain's absorption, as illustrated by vertical distance *ES*.

Since both the commodity and labor markets are in equilibrium at point *K*, there is no reason to expect any change in either commodity prices or money-wage rates. Further, at point *K* there are no unintended inventory changes. Accordingly, neither the American nor the British producers have any incentive to change their production plans. Every consumer and every producer is in equilibrium. Yet the foreign exchange market is out of equilibrium: *The American monetary authorities lose reserves to the British authorities in every period.* Since re-

[1]In Figure 13-5 we took it for granted that an intersection of the two income-consumption curves exists above and to the right of vector *ET*, as illustrated by point *K*. But this is the case only when America's income-consumption curve is flatter than Britain's, as shown in the figure. When America's income-consumption curve happens to be steeper than Britain's, no intersection exists above and to the right of *ET*, although one may exist below and to the left of *ET*. In general, the two income-consumption curves may intersect any number of times, or not at all.

serves are limited, this situation cannot continue for long. Can a devaluation (or depreciation) of the dollar restore general equilibrium? No, even though it is the commonsense medicine that is often applied to cure a fundamental balance-of-payments disequilibrium.

Expenditure Adjusting versus Expenditure Switching

How can America and Britain correct the disequilibrium of Figure 13-5? First, both America and Britain must reverse the earlier expenditure changes and return to the disequilibrium state of Figure 13-3. This means that both countries must pursue an **expenditure-adjusting policy** (that is, a policy that affects aggregate expenditure) to shift the budget line of Figure 13-5 from *DJ* to *ET*. Second, America and Britain must pursue an **expenditure-switching policy** (that is, a policy that "switches" expenditures from B-exportables to A-exportables), such as a devaluation of the dollar, to restore full general equilibrium at *Z* (Figure 13-2).

The above prescription may sound easy, but it is not. In addition to the difficulties (discussed in Section 13-3) associated with a deterioration of the deficit country's (America's) terms of trade, there is another complication: Normally, expenditure-adjusting policies also have an element of expenditure switching and expenditure-switching policies have an element of expenditure adjusting. The art of economic policy is to determine the correct mix of expenditure-adjusting and expenditure-switching policies, as is shown in Chapters 15 and 17.

The discussion of this chapter leads to an important conclusion: **Adjustment may proceed either through prices (such as exchange-rate adjustments and money-wage changes) or through incomes (that is, aggregate spending, production, and employment).** The next few chapters deal with both of these aspects of the international adjustment mechanism. In particular, Chapter 14 discusses exclusively the price-adjustment mechanism, while Chapter 15 concentrates mainly on the income-adjustment mechanism.

13-5 COUNTERTRADE

Countertrade refers to a variety of international trade practices in which the exporter agrees to receive goods or services as total or partial payment for the exports. When the payment (in goods or services) precedes the delivery of exports (that is, when the exporter first buys from the importing country goods and services which are then credited to the counterpurchase), the transaction is referred to as **reverse countertrade.**

The array of countertrade transactions reported in the trade press is intriguing. In 1982 the U.S. government is said to have acquired $13.6 million of Jamaican bauxite in exchange for powdered milk and butter oil. The same year General Motors and the Chrysler Corporation swapped trucks and cars for Jamaican bauxite. In 1985 Peru and Brazil signed a $600 million countertrade deal to exchange Peruvian oil and mining products for Brazilian capital goods, manufactures, and replacement parts. Indonesian rubber has been countertraded for Canadian railway freight cars. New Zealand's lamb and Uruguay's meat have been traded for Iran's oil. Coca Cola has traded its syrup for cheese from a factory it built in the Soviet Union, for oranges from an orchard it planted in Egypt, for tomato paste from a plant it installed in Turkey, and for soft drink bottles from Hungary; and Boeing exchanged 10 of its 747 line of jumbo jets for 34 million barrels of Saudi Arabian oil.

Countertrade is not a new phenomenon. Its oldest form is **barter** (that is, direct exchange of goods and services without the use of money). In the immediate post-World War II period countertrade arrangements were common in Europe and Latin America (in the form of bilateral trade and payments agreements), due to the dollar shortage. Countertrade has also been routine among the centrally planned economies of the Soviet bloc and has been practiced regularly in East-West trade.

In the 1980s countertrade grew rapidly and spread to nearly every country in the world. Some observers, particularly in the press, estimate that countertrade represents between 20 and 40 percent of world trade. Such estimates appear to be inflated, particularly because official estimates tend to be low (6 to 8 percent). Perhaps a realistic figure is about 10 percent.

Many reasons account for the rise of countertrade. To a great extent, however, the 1980s surge in countertrade is attributed to the balance-of-payments difficulties of developing nations. Perhaps it is no coincidence that countertrade experienced tremendous growth in a period of sluggish world economic growth and trade combined with a rising tide of protectionism. During this period many developing countries faced severe economic difficulties: growing debt service burdens (aggravated by the dramatic decline in the inflow of new funds, particularly after the Mexican debt crisis of 1982), a drop in demand for their exports, and a decline in the prices of primary products. Because of these difficulties, developing nations turned to countertrade as a means of securing much needed imports of intermediate goods, spare parts, and foreign consumer goods.

Many countries and firms often use countertrade as a tool to open markets for their products. Countertrade is also used to circumvent foreign exchange controls—exporting a product that has a low priority in foreign exchange allocations becomes easier when the exporter is willing to accept countertrade. Countries lacking marketing skills and international distribution networks often use countertrade as a means of marketing their products abroad. Governments may use countertrade either to control imports or to acquire technical know-how.

Countertrade can take many forms. Its most common form is the **counterpurchase,** in which each party agrees to buy goods and services from the other for hard currency. Counterpurchase arrangements have been common among centrally planned economies and in East-West trade. Recently, such arrangements have spread to trade between developed countries. Often one side of the deal involves some homogeneous bulk product, agricultural or mineral. During the 1980s oil has become the most important commodity in countertrade. Some OPEC countries started countertrading oil when their production quotas were cut; and under the veil of countertrade they frequently offered their oil at prices below the official OPEC price.

Buy-back is a form of countertrade that is used to finance direct investment. Typically, in buy-back arrangements a developed country builds a plant in the buyer country, provides technology and equipment, and agrees to buy back all or a portion of the future output of the project. The Soviet Union, the prime initiator of this type of transaction, has signed a number of such agreements with developing countries, such as Egypt and

India. Another common form of countertrade among industrialized countries is the **offset,** which refers to compensatory transactions involving aircraft and military equipment.
For further discussion of countertrade arrangements, see Alexandrides and Bowers (1987).

13-6 TEMPORARY VERSUS FUNDAMENTAL DISEQUILIBRIA

In this section, we discuss briefly the all-important distinction between temporary and fundamental balance-of-payments disequilibria. We show that temporary disequilibria must be financed, while fundamental disequilibria require true adjustment. Indeed, the rest of the book deals mainly with the problem of how to handle fundamental disequilibria.

Some Broad Definitions

As we saw earlier, an external disequilibrium reflects in the first instance a gap between "autonomous" purchases and sales of foreign exchange. This gap is closed by "accommodating" sales or purchases (as the case may be) of foreign exchange by the monetary authorities. But not every gap between autonomous international receipts and payments need present serious problems. In this connection, the distinction between *temporary* and *fundamental* (or persistent) balance-of-payments disequilibria is important.

In principle, **temporary balance-of-payments disequilibria** (deficits or surpluses) tend to last for a short period of time; they are prompted by exogenous disturbances that are of either a purely *transitory* nature (for example, a strike or crop failure) or a *reversible* nature (for example, seasonal or cyclical). **Fundamental disequilibria,** on the other hand, are chronic in nature; that is, they tend to persist. The causes of fundamental disequilibria are deep-seated imbalances in the international economy.

Financing Temporary Disequilibria

The main implication of the distinction between temporary and fundamental disequilibria is this: **Temporary disequilibria can and should be financed, while fundamental disequilibria call for true adjustment.**

The argument for financing temporary disequilibria is similar to the argument for justifying the transactions demand for money. Neither individual economic units nor nations enjoy perfect synchronization between their streams of revenue and their streams of expenditure. To bridge temporary gaps between their streams of revenue and expenditure, economic units need money. When their revenue exceeds their expenditure, economic units let their stock of money absorb their surplus; and when their expenditure exceeds their revenue, economic units use their stock of money to finance their deficit.

Nations use their stocks of international reserves in the same way that individual economic units use their stocks of money. Thus, a nation whose autonomous international payments temporarily exceed its autonomous international receipts can finance its deficit by running down its international reserves. Similarly, a nation may finance a temporary surplus merely by increasing its stock of international reserves.

We can strengthen the argument for financing temporary disequilibria by considering the welfare implications of this policy. Suppose America is an agricultural country, exporting grain, such as corn, which is harvested at only one season of the year. America's exports of corn (which are made during the harvest season only) must pay for America's imports of other commodities throughout the year. Without any financing of temporary disequilibria by America's monetary authorities, the rate of exchange would fluctuate from, say, \$1 (during the harvest season), to \$3 (during nonharvest seasons). Financing, however, stabilizes the rate at, say, \$2, and improves America's welfare.

How does financing external disequilibria improve America's welfare? Merely by effecting a better allocation of resources through time. In the absence of financing, foreign exchange is less valuable during the harvest season than during nonharvest seasons. Consequently, commodities (domestic and foreign) are more plentiful and cheaper during the harvest season than during nonharvest seasons. Apparently, consumer welfare would increase if America were to transfer some consumption from the harvest season (when consumption is plentiful and its marginal utility is low) to nonharvest seasons (when it is less plentiful and its marginal utility is high). Financing accomplishes just this.

During the harvest season, America's monetary authorities buy foreign exchange and raise its price from \$1 to \$2. In turn, the rise in the exchange rate increases the prices of *all* commodities, American and foreign, cajoling America's consumers to consume less. Note that the prices of foreign products rise because they are originally given in terms of foreign exchange, say, pounds sterling, which become more expensive. For instance, the price of a British car (say, a Jaguar) which costs £20,000 in Britain will rise from \$20,000 to \$40,000 in America, as the price of pounds sterling rises from \$1 to \$2. The prices of American commodities rise because the depreciation of the dollar enhances foreign demand. For instance, consider the case of an IBM personal computer that sells for \$10,000 in America. As the price of pounds sterling rises from \$1 to \$2, the cost of the IBM computer in Britain will *fall* from £10,000 to £5,000, encouraging additional purchases.

During nonharvest seasons, America's monetary authorities sell foreign exchange and prevent its price from rising all the way to \$3. Accordingly, the prices of all other commodities (domestic and foreign) remain low, and consumers consume more (compared to the case of no financing).

Thus financing temporary external disequilibria is indeed a sound policy that tends to raise economic welfare by effecting a better allocation of resources through time.

Temporary Disequilibria and Speculation

It is interesting to note that under the ideal conditions of the preceding example, private speculation may indeed accomplish the same result as official financing. As long as the balance on autonomous transactions follows a predictable pattern, such as the one postulated above for America, private speculators will soon realize that they can make a profit by buying foreign exchange during the harvest season and selling it during nonharvest seasons. Such **stabilizing speculation** will tend to reduce the amplitude of exchange-rate fluctuations and improve economic welfare in the same way as official financing. In fact, stabilizing speculation reduces substantially, and in the limiting case eliminates completely, the need for official financing of temporary disequilibria.

Difficulties of the Distinction between Temporary and Fundamental Disequilibria

The rule that temporary disequilibria ought to be financed, while fundamental disequilibria call for true adjustment is simple enough in principle. Its practical application, however, faces insurmountable difficulties.

Whether an existing balance-of-payments disequilibrium is fundamental or temporary depends on future events. Economists can, of course, make a prediction as to the future course of the balance of payments, but they can never be absolutely sure that their prediction will indeed be right. In fact, different people are likely to make different predictions and thus reach different policy recommendations. But even in cases of general unanimity among forecasters, the world economy is under no obligation to follow the common forecast; it may very well prove all forecasters wrong. There are events (such as the 1973–1974 Arab oil embargo) that defy all crystal balls.

Some Risks of Temporary Financing

Because of the inherent difficulty of identifying the true nature of an existing payments imbalance, policymakers are bound to make costly mistakes in the application of economic policy. For instance, financing a "temporary" deficit that turns out to be fundamental may involve the authorities (and the economy) in huge losses. Essentially, the monetary authorities sell large amounts of their international reserves at the existing, low price only to have to buy them back later (after they realize that the deficit is fundamental and thus devalue their domestic currency) at a much higher price. The postwar era is full of such policy errors.

Similarly, financing a "temporary" surplus that turns out to be fundamental may involve the authorities in huge losses. In this case, the monetary authorities buy large amounts of foreign exchange at the current, high price only to have to sell it back at a lower price—after they revalue their domestic currency.

13-7 SUMMARY

1 Most issues of international finance can be clarified by a simple model of two countries, say, America and Britain. America produces only A-exportables with labor (which is in fixed supply) and under constant returns to scale. Britain produces only B-exportables. Each country's tastes are given by a social indifference map.

2 General equilibrium requires that supply equals demand in all markets: the labor markets, the commodity markets, and the foreign exchange market. A necessary condition for general equilibrium is that national income equals aggregate expenditure in each country. When this condition is satisfied, general equilibrium can be portrayed graphically by means of a box diagram, as in a two-consumer exchange economy.

3 Assuming that national income equals desired spending (or absorption) in each country, a balance-of-payments disequilibrium must reflect disequilibrium in the commodity markets and (when all buyer plans are realized) unplanned inventory changes, with the deficit country converting its foreign exchange reserves into unwanted inventories of goods, and the surplus country converting its commodity inventories into foreign exchange reserves. This disequilibrium can be corrected by allowing the deficit country's terms of trade to worsen sufficiently, but without disturbing the equality between national income and desired absorption.

4 A reduction in America's terms of trade can be accomplished in one of three ways: (a) a reduction in the money price of A-exportables, (b) an increase in the money price of B-exportables, or (c) a depreciation of America's currency.

5 A reduction in the money prices of the deficit country's exportables requires a reduction in that country's money-wage rate. Since the latter is inflexible in the downward direction, production and income in the deficit country will fall instead—producers cannot be expected to accumulate inventories indefinitely. Such income reduction can restore equilibrium in both countries' commodity markets as well as the foreign exchange market, but at the expense of massive unemployment in the deficit country.

6 Whether the currency of the deficit country depreciates or not depends on the existing exchange-rate system. A depreciation of the deficit country's currency need not restore equilibrium for two reasons: (a) The depreciation may affect aggregate spending and thus destroy the equality between national income and desired spending; (b) it may induce the deficit country's workers to demand higher money wages, which neutralizes the effect of currency depreciation on the terms of trade. (Alternatively, foreign producers may resist the depreciation by lowering their prices.)

7 When the (deficit) country with unplanned inventory accumulation increases its spending (by means of expansionary fiscal and monetary policies), while at the same time the (surplus) country with unplanned inventory decumulation decreases its spending, equilibrium in the commodity markets could be restored; but a *fundamental* disequilibrium would arise in the foreign exchange market. Actual absorption would be equal to desired absorption in each country, but absorption would be different from national income. A deterioration in the deficit country's terms of trade (brought about by devaluation or otherwise) would no longer restore general equilibrium, because income does not equal absorption.

8 In principle, external disequilibria are classified into temporary (lasting for a short time) and fundamental (lasting for a long time). In practice, predicting the nature of an existing disequilibrium is inherently difficult.

9 Fundamental disequilibria require true adjustment. To correct a fundamental disequilibrium, the two countries must combine expenditure-adjusting policies (to bring their expenditures into equality with their respective full-employment incomes) with expenditure-switching policies (to shift the terms of trade to their equilibrium value).

10 Temporary disequilibria should be financed, however, in order to achieve a better allocation of resources through time and to raise welfare. Such financing can be done by either the monetary authorities or private speculators.

PROBLEMS

1 America uses 1 unit of labor to produce 1 bushel of wheat. Europe uses 1 unit of labor to produce a gallon of wine. America is endowed with 1,000 units of labor. Europe is endowed with 750 units of labor. America consumes commodities in the fixed proportion of 2 bushels of wheat per gallon of wine. Europe, however, has a strong preference for wine and consumes 2 gallons of wine per bushel of wheat. The wage rate is $10 in America and £5 in Europe.

a How many gallons of wine can Europe produce with all available labor?
b How many bushels of wheat can America produce with all available labor?
c Assume that in each country full employment prevails and that aggregate expenditure on commodities equals aggregate income. Determine the equilibrium terms of trade, America's exports of wheat, Europe's exports of wine, and the equilibrium rate of exchange (dollars per pound).
d Illustrate your results graphically.

2 Return to the scenario of Question 1. Assume that the rate of exchange is fixed at £1 = $2.

a Describe the disequilibrium states prevailing in the commodity markets. (Determine precisely the excess demand or supply for wheat and wine.)
b What is the excess supply or demand for pounds?

3 Return to the scenario of Question 1 and again assume that the exchange rate is fixed at £1 = $2.

a What should America and Europe change their aggregate expenditure to in order to re-establish equilibrium in the wheat and wine markets?
b What is America's balance-of-trade deficit or surplus?

4 Return to the disequilibrium state reached in Question 3.

a Can a devaluation of the dollar restore general equilibrium? Why or why not?
b What policy mix should America and Europe pursue in order to restore general equilibrium?
c Illustrate your results graphically.

SUGGESTED READING

Alexander, S. S. (1952). "Effects of a Devaluation on a Trade Balance." *IMF Staff Papers*, vol. 2 (April), pp. 263–278. Reprinted in H. G. Johnson and R. E. Caves, eds., American Economic Association *Readings in International Economics*, Richard D. Irwin, Inc., Homewood, Ill., 1968.

Alexandrides, C. G., and B. L. Bowers (1987). *Countertrade: Practices, Strategies, and Tactics.* John Wiley & Sons, New York.

Chacholiades, M. (1978). *International Monetary Theory and Policy.* McGraw-Hill Book Company, New York, chaps. 9 and 12.

———(1986). *Microeconomics.* Macmillan Publishing Company, New York, chap. 14.

Organization for Economic Co-operation and Development (1985). *Countertrade: Developing Country Practices.* OECD, Paris.

Pearce, I. F. (1970). *International Trade.* W. W. Norton and Company, New York, chaps. 1–6.

CHAPTER **14**

THE PRICE-ADJUSTMENT MECHANISM

This chapter deals exclusively with the **price-adjustment mechanism.** As noted in Chapter 13, price adjustment may take different forms depending on the institutional arrangement of the foreign exchange market. Under a **flexible exchange-rate system,** price adjustment operates through *exchange-rate changes.* Under a **fixed exchange-rate system** (such as the gold standard), price adjustment works through *price-level changes* (that is, general *inflation* and *deflation*), which is the essence of David Hume's **price-specie-flow mechanism.**

We begin with a detailed discussion of the effects of exchange-rate changes on the balance of payments and the terms of trade. Later we show briefly how to extend the analysis of exchange-rate changes to price-level changes under fixed exchange rates.

14-1 THE PARTIAL EQUILIBRIUM MODEL

The analysis of this chapter rests heavily on the so-called **partial equilibrium model.** [The main architects of the partial equilibrium model were Bickerdike (1920), Robinson (1947), and Machlup (1939, 1940), even though others have generously contributed to its development.] What are the assumptions of this model?

As before, assume that there are two countries, America (home country) and Britain (foreign country, or rest of the world) and that their respective national currencies are the dollar and the pound sterling. Aggregate America's exports into a single homogeneous commodity and call it for convenience A-exportables. Similarly, aggregate Britain's exports into another homogeneous commodity and call it B-exportables. Observe that A-exportables and B-exportables are *different* commodities. In contrast to the model of Chapter 13, assume that each country produces *both* A-exportables and B-exportables. This last assumption provides greater generality, of course.

Also, in order to concentrate on commodity trade only, assume as before that the net balance of capital movements plus unilateral transfers is always zero.

We now come to the heart of the partial equilibrium model. In complete contrast to the model of Chapter 13, assume that each country has supply and demand schedules showing the quantities of A-exportables and B-exportables supplied by domestic producers and demanded by domestic consumers, respectively, at alternative prices expressed in the *domestic* currency. It is this assumption that is mainly responsible for the name *partial equilibrium* model.

Panel (*a*) of Figure 14-1 illustrates America's domestic supply and demand schedules for B-exportables. In particular, supply schedule *SS′* shows the quantities of B-exportables supplied by American producers at alternative *dollar* prices. This supply curve slopes upward because American producers can produce larger quantities of B-exportables only at higher costs. For instance, when the unit price of B-exportables is $60, American producers as a group are willing to supply 14,000 units; when the price rises to $120, American producers are willing to supply the larger quantity of 18,000 units.

FIGURE 14-1 Derivation of America's demand-for-imports schedule. Panel (*a*) shows America's domestic supply schedule (*SS′*) and demand schedule (*DD′*) for B-exportables. Panel (*b*) gives America's demand-for-imports schedule. For each price below $120 (say, $60), determine in panel (*a*) America's domestic supply (14,000) and demand (20,000) of B-exportables. America's excess demand for B-exportables (that is, 20,000 − 14,000 = 6,000) is America's demand for imports at the selected price ($60), as shown in panel (*b*).

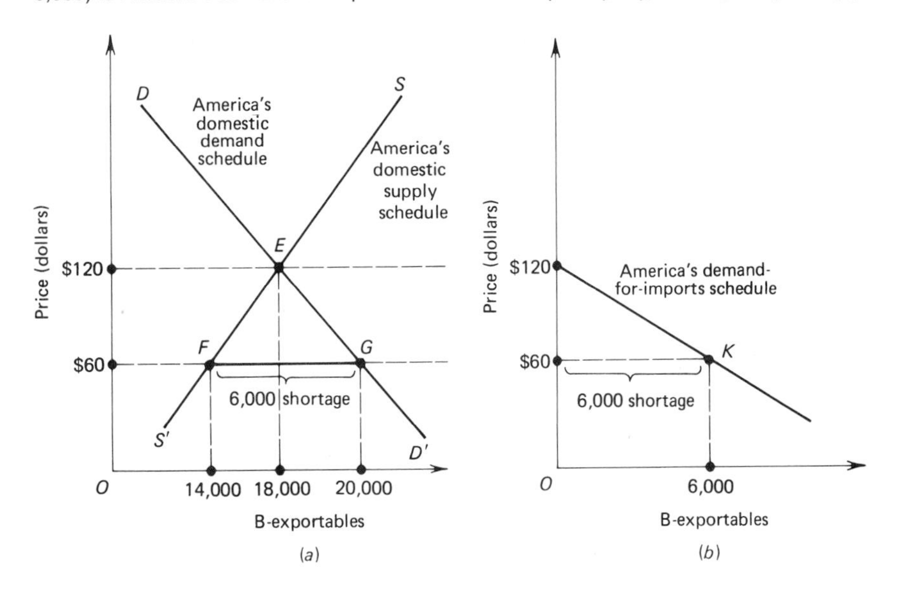

Similarly, America's domestic demand schedule, DD', shows the quantities of B-exportables that American consumers are willing to purchase at alternative *dollar* prices. This demand curve slopes downward because American consumers are willing to purchase larger quantities of B-exportables only at lower prices. For instance, when the price is $120, American consumers are willing to buy 18,000 units of B-exportables; when the price falls to $60, American consumers are willing to purchase the larger quantity of 20,000 units.

Similar domestic supply and demand schedules exist in America for A-exportables. Also, such domestic schedules for A-exportables and B-exportables exist in Britain. The only difference is that Britain's schedules give prices in *pounds,* not dollars.

An important assumption of the partial equilibrium model is that the various domestic supply and demand schedules are largely independent of each other. For instance, we must insist that the demand schedules for A-exportables remain unaltered as the price of B-exportables changes, even though in reality one commodity may be substituted for another as *relative* prices change. This is, of course, a drawback of the partial equilibrium model that we can justify by assuming that such substitution, if any, is rather negligible.

This is the basic skeleton of the partial equilibrium model. Before we can put it to work, we must go through the preliminary exercise of deriving the demand-for-imports and supply-of-exports schedules, as shown in the next section.

14-2 SCHEDULES FOR IMPORTS AND EXPORTS

A commodity market is in equilibrium when the price is such that one country's desired volume of imports matches the other country's desired volume of exports. For this reason, we cannot show international equilibrium in the commodity markets unless we have each country's **demand-for-imports schedule** and **supply-of-exports schedule.** We can obtain these from the domestic supply and demand schedules, as explained below.

The demand-for-imports schedule is part of what is ordinarily called in price theory the **excess-demand curve.** Similarly, the supply-of-exports schedule is part of what is ordinarily known as the **excess-supply curve.** The only new element is that America's consumers and producers are interested in prices expressed in dollars, while Britain's consumers and producers are interested in prices expressed in pounds. Fortunately, this is not an insurmountable difficulty.

The Demand-for-Imports Schedule

Return to Figure 14-1, which shows how to derive America's demand-for-imports schedule. Panel (*a*) shows America's domestic supply and demand schedules for B-exportables. Panel (*b*) gives America's demand-for-imports schedule.

Consider panel (*a*) first. When the price of B-exportables is $120, American consumers are willing to buy 18,000 units, which is exactly the number of units

American producers are willing to sell at that price. Therefore, when the price is $120, America's demand for imports is zero. When the price drops below $120, America develops a shortage (excess demand) of, or a *demand for imports* of, B-exportables. For instance, when the price drops to $60, American consumers are willing to purchase 20,000 units of B-exportables, but American producers are willing to sell 14,000 units only; thus, America develops a shortage (demand for imports) of 6,000 units. Panel (*b*) gives the information directly; it shows that America's demand for imports is zero when the price is $120 but increases to 6,000 units when the price falls to $60.

In general, America's demand-for-imports schedule in panel (*b*) gives directly the horizontal differences between the domestic demand and supply schedules of panel (*a*) for all prices below $120. Because it is derived from the domestic demand *and* supply schedules, the demand-for-imports schedule depends on all those parameters that lie behind the domestic demand *and* supply schedules. Thus like America's domestic demand for B-exportables, the demand-for-imports schedule depends on tastes, incomes, and other prices. But unlike America's domestic demand for B-exportables, the demand-for-imports schedule depends also on technology and factor prices—the parameters that lie behind America's domestic supply schedule.

In the same way, we can derive Britain's demand-for-imports schedule (for A-exportables). There is no compelling reason to repeat this exercise. We must only remember that Britain's demand-for-imports schedule gives the quantities of A-exportables that Britain is willing to import at alternative prices *expressed in pounds*.

The Supply-of-Exports Schedule

Turn now to Figure 14-2, which shows how to derive America's supply-of-exports schedule. Panel (*a*) shows again America's domestic supply (SS') and demand (DD') schedules for A-exportables. Panel (*b*) gives America's supply-of-exports schedule.

Consider panel (*a*) first. When the price of A-exportables is $54, American consumers are willing to buy 2,000 units, which is exactly the amount American producers are willing to sell at that price. Therefore, when the price is $54, America's supply of exports is zero, as shown in panel (*b*). As the price rises above $54, however, America develops a *surplus* of A-exportables. For instance, when the price rises to $90, America's consumers reduce their consumption of A-exportables to 1,200 units, while America's producers increase their production to 3,000 units. Accordingly, when the price rises to $90, America develops a surplus of 1,800 units of A-exportables. Put differently, at $90 America is willing to export 1,800 units of A-exportables, as shown again in panel (*b*). Panel (*b*) gives directly all the information concerning America's surpluses of A-exportables at prices higher than $54.

In general, America's supply-of-exports schedule in panel (*b*) gives directly the horizontal differences between the domestic supply and demand schedules

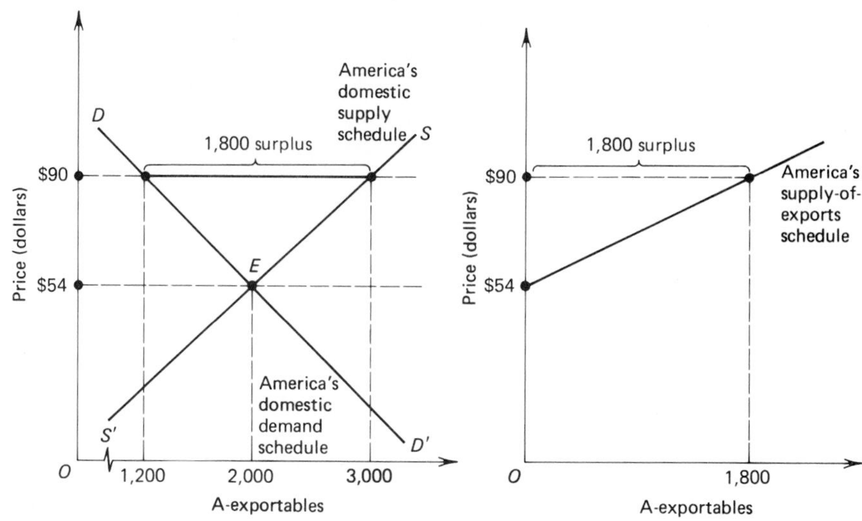

FIGURE 14-2 **Derivation of America's supply-of-exports schedule.** Panel (*a*) shows America's domestic supply schedule (*SS'*) and demand schedule (*DD'*) for A-exportables. Panel (*b*) gives America's supply-of-exports schedule. For each price above $54 (say, $90), determine in panel (*a*) America's domestic supply (3,000) and demand (1,200) of A-exportables. America's excess supply of A-exportables (that is, 3,000 − 1,200 = 1,800) is America's supply of exports at the selected price ($90), as shown in panel (*b*).

of panel (*a*) for all prices above $54. Note again that America's supply-of-exports schedule does not depend only on those parameters that lie behind the domestic supply schedule in panel (*a*)—that is, technology and factor prices. It depends also on all those parameters that lie behind America's domestic demand schedule—that is, tastes, incomes, and prices of other commodities.

We could follow the above procedure to derive Britain's supply-of-exports schedule, but there is no need to do so. We must always remember, however, that Britain's supply-of-exports schedule gives the quantities of B-exportables that Britain is willing to export at alternative prices *expressed in pounds.*

14-3 EQUILIBRIUM IN THE COMMODITY MARKETS

Given America's and Britain's demand-for-imports and supply-of-exports schedules, we can proceed to determine equilibrium in the commodity markets. We must do this before we can find out whether the balance of payments is in equilibrium. When we know the equilibrium volumes of exports and imports as well as the equilibrium prices of A-exportables and B-exportables, we can determine each country's export revenue and expenditure on imports (in either dollars or pounds). The difference between a country's export revenue and expenditure on imports is, of course, the country's balance-of-trade deficit or surplus, as the case may be.

The Need to Express All Prices in Terms of the Same Currency

As we pointed out earlier, a commodity market is in equilibrium when the price of the commodity is such that one country's desired volume of imports matches the other country's volume of exports.

If America and Britain were two *regions* of a single country using a common currency, we could easily determine equilibrium in a commodity market: We could superimpose one country's (region's) demand-for-imports schedule on the other country's (region's) supply-of-exports schedule and then determine the point of intersection of the two schedules.

However, America and Britain are different *nations* with different national currencies. As a result, our search for commodity-market equilibria is now slightly complicated by the fact that America's schedules express all prices in dollars, and Britain's schedules express all prices in pounds sterling. Before we can determine the commodity-market equilibria, we must express all prices in terms of the same currency. We can choose either currency for this purpose, although here we choose to express all prices in terms of pounds mainly because of our interest in the supply of and demand for foreign exchange (pounds).

Conversion of American (Dollar) Prices into Pounds

Britain's demand-for-imports and supply-of-exports schedules give prices in pounds to begin with. Accordingly, in Figure 14-3 we have drawn Britain's schedules as they were originally derived. The rate of foreign exchange simply has no influence on Britain's schedules, which remain unaltered throughout our discussion.

However, the original demand-for-imports and supply-of-exports schedules of America (see Figures 14-1 and 14-2) give all prices in dollars. We must transform America's schedules so that they will give prices in pounds. For this transformation, we must know the rate of foreign exchange.

Suppose that the rate of exchange is $2, that is, £1 sells for $2. How can we convert the dollar prices given by the original demand-for-imports and supply-of-exports schedules of America into pounds? Simply by dividing each dollar price by 2, since $2 is equivalent to £1. This is actually shown by America's schedules in Figure 14-3.

On the assumption that £1 sells for $2, the schedules of America's demand-for-imports and supply-of-exports in Figure 14-3 give exactly the same information as the corresponding schedules in Figures 14-1 and 14-2. For instance, America's demand-for-imports schedule in Figure 14-1, panel (*b*), shows that America is willing to import 6,000 units of B-exportables *at $60 per unit.* In Figure 14-3, panel (*a*), America's demand-for-imports schedule shows that America is willing to import 6,000 units of B-exportables *at £30 per unit.* Since £1 sells for $2, by assumption, the price of $60 is equivalent to the price of £30 and vice versa.

The same relationship holds, of course, between all prices along America's demand-for-imports schedule in Figure 14-1, panel (*b*), and the corresponding

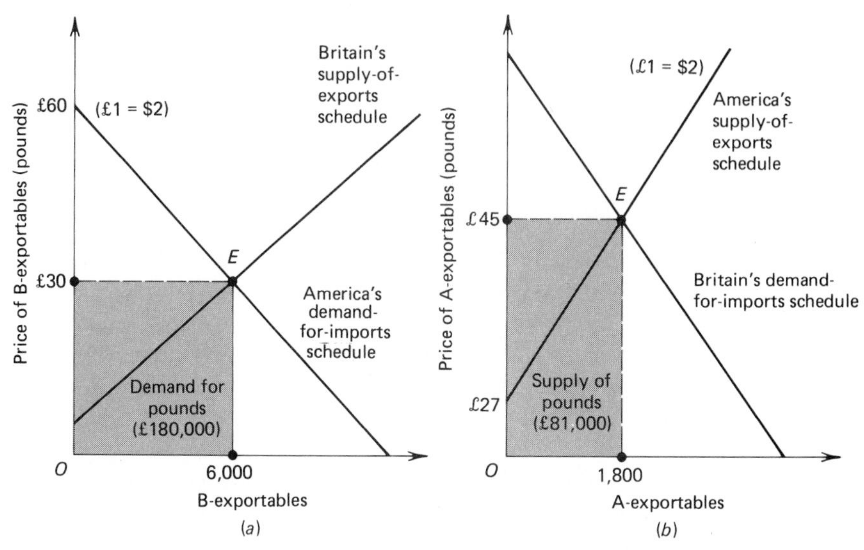

FIGURE 14-3 **Equilibrium in the commodity markets.** After transforming America's schedules in Figures 14-1(*b*) and 14-2 (*b*) to obtain prices in pounds, we superimpose them on Britain's schedules to determine equilibrium in the commodity markets. Panel (*a*) shows that equilibrium in the market for B-exportables occurs at *E*, at which the price of B-exportables is £30, and that the quantity imported by America is 6,000 units. America's expenditure on imports (that is, £30 × 6,000 = £180,000) is the quantity of pounds demanded (or demand for pounds, for short), as shown by the shaded rectangle.

Panel (*b*) shows that equilibrium in the market for A-exportables occurs at *E*, at which the price of A-exportables is £45 and the quantity exported by America is 1,800 units. America's export revenue (that is, £45 × 1,800 = £81,000) is the quantity of pounds supplied (or supply of pounds, for short), as shown by the shaded rectangle.

prices along America's schedule in Figure 14-3, panel (*a*). For any volume of imports, the dollar price (Figure 14-1) is *twice* as high as the price in pounds (Figure 14-3), because $2 is equivalent to £1.

Similarly, America's supply-of-exports schedule in Figure 14-2, panel (*b*), shows that America is willing to export 1,800 units of A-exportables at $90 per unit; and America's supply-of-exports schedule of Figure 14-3, panel (*b*), shows that America is willing to export 1,800 units of A-exportables at £45 per unit. Again, since £1 sells for $2, by assumption, the price of $90 is equivalent to the price of £45 and vice versa.

Again the same relationship holds between all prices along America's supply-of-exports schedule in Figure 14-2, panel (*b*), and the corresponding prices along America's schedule in Figure 14-3, panel (*b*). For any volume of exports, the dollar price (Figure 14-2) is *twice* as high as the price in pounds (Figure 14-3), because $2 is worth £1.

Note that America's demand-for-imports and supply-of-exports schedules in Figure 14-3 are good only when £1 sells for $2. If the rate of exchange were different, these schedules would also be different, as shown in Section 14-4. To remind the reader of this important truth, the equation £1 = $2 is printed next to America's schedules.

Commodity-Market Equilibrium with Prices in Pounds

We are finally ready to determine equilibrium in the markets for A-exportables and B-exportables. This is shown in Figure 14-3. Panel (*a*) illustrates the market for B-exportables, and panel (*b*) the market for A-exportables.

Consider panel (*a*) first. Equilibrium occurs at the intersection (*E*) of Britain's supply-of-exports schedule and America's demand-for-imports schedule. At the equilibrium price of £30, Britain exports 6,000 units of B-exportables to America. This means that America spends £180,000 on imports (shown by the shaded rectangle), which is the quantity of pounds demanded in the foreign exchange market at the current rate of exchange (£1 = $2).

Turn now to panel (*b*), which shows the market for A-exportables. Equilibrium occurs at the intersection (*E*) of America's supply-of-exports schedule and Britain's demand-for-imports schedule. At the equilibrium price of £45, America exports 1,800 units of A-exportables to Britain. America's export revenue is £81,000, which is actually the amount of pounds supplied in the foreign exchange market at the current rate of exchange ($2 = £1).

Knowing the equilibrium prices in pounds and the rate of foreign exchange, we can easily infer the equilibrium prices in dollars as well as America's export revenue and expenditure on imports in dollars. Thus, the equilibrium prices of A-exportables and B-exportables are, respectively, $\$2 \times 45 = \$90$ and $\$2 \times 30 = \$60$. Similarly, America's export revenue is $\$2 \times 81{,}000 = \$162{,}000$, while America's expenditure on imports is $\$2 \times 180{,}000 = \$360{,}000$.

We should also emphasize that given the equilibrium prices, we can go back to each country's domestic supply and demand schedules to determine each country's domestic production and consumption of A-exportables and B-exportables. We leave this as an exercise for the reader.

In the current illustration, America suffers from an import surplus of £99,000 (that is, £180,000 − £81,000). Will a devaluation (or depreciation) of the dollar reduce (or eliminate) America's import surplus? This is a critical question, and we consider it in the next section.

14-4 THE EFFECTS OF DEVALUATION

Exchange-rate adjustments have very profound effects on the international economy. A change in the exchange rate throws all commodity markets out of equilibrium. As the commodity markets adjust slowly to a new equilibrium, each country experiences dramatic changes in domestic production, consumption, exports, imports, supply of foreign exchange, demand for foreign exchange, and terms of trade. Indeed, the effects of an exchange-rate adjustment are so extensive that they sooner or later filter down to each and every citizen. For instance, as a result of the depreciation of the dollar during the period 1985–1988, many families of American soldiers stationed in Germany had to return to the United States because they could no longer make ends meet; foreign products, such as Japanese cars, cameras, and VCRs, became more expensive in the United States; foreign tourists found a lot of bargains in America; and according to the headlines, the European aerospace industry scrambled to stay aloft.

The purpose of this section is to enable the reader to obtain a general understanding of the multifarious effects of exchange-rate adjustments. The discussion is deliberately cast in very general terms, simply because it is immaterial whether an exchange-rate change is the result of government policy (such as devaluation or revaluation under the adjustable peg) or reflects market supply and demand conditions. The economic effects of, say, a 10 percent devaluation under the adjustable peg are identical to the economic effects of a 10 percent depreciation under the flexible exchange-rate system.

Effects of Commodity-Market Equilibria

Return to Figure 14-3, where America is running a balance-of-trade deficit (or import surplus). Under a flexible exchange-rate system, the dollar will depreciate automatically; that is, the price of the pound in terms of dollars will tend to rise. Even under the adjustable peg, America may decide to devalue the dollar, or Britain may decide to revalue the pound. In any case, the rate of exchange (dollars per pound) will increase. For concreteness, suppose that the rate of exchange rises to \$3. What happens to the initial commodity market equilibria?

When the dollar depreciates, the equilibria (E) shown in the two panels of Figure 14-3 can no longer persist. This must be clear from our earlier discussion. America's demand-for-imports and supply-of-exports schedules are drawn on the assumption that £1 = \$2. *When the dollar depreciates, America's schedules become obsolete and must be redrawn.* As a result, the commodity market equilibria will shift to new points along the unmodified schedules of Britain.

Consider the market for B-exportables. Before the depreciation of the dollar, equilibrium occurs at E, where Britain exports to America 6,000 units of B-exportables at £30 per unit. Of course, we know from Figure 14-1, panel (b), that America is willing to import 6,000 units of B-exportables at \$60 per unit; since \$2 = £1, it follows that America is indeed willing to pay £30 (that is, \$60/2) per unit. When the dollar depreciates, say to \$3 = £1, Britain will no longer export 6,000 units of B-exportables to America. For this volume (6,000 units), Britain demands £30 per unit and America offers \$60 per unit. Since now \$3 = £1, it follows that America is willing to pay only £20 (that is, \$60/3) per unit, which is, of course, less than the £30 per unit that Britain wants. Alternatively, Britain can receive £30 per unit only if America pays \$90 (that is, 3 × £30 instead of 2 × £30) per unit. But America is not willing to import 6,000 of B-exportables at \$90 per unit. At that high price, America is willing to import much *less* (see Figure 14-1).

Similarly, America's volume of exports of A-exportables cannot remain at 1,800 units—it will tend to increase. The reason is simple. For the volume of 1,800 units of A-exportables, America is willing to accept $90 per unit, while Britain is willing to offer £45. When £1 = $2, Britain's offer of £45 is equivalent to America's demand for $90. However, when the exchange rate rises to £1 = $3, the price of £45 that Britain is willing to pay becomes much higher than $90 (the price America is willing to accept). In fact, after the dollar depreciates, America is willing to export 1,800 units of A-exportables at only £30 (that is, $90/3) per unit; but at this low price (£30), Britain is willing to import much *more* (see Figure 14-2).

We therefore reach the following important conclusion:

The depreciation of the dollar disturbs the initial commodity market equilibria. In particular, America's *volume of imports tends to fall as the British goods become more expensive in dollars*; but America's *volume of exports tends to rise as the American goods become cheaper in pounds.*

How can we determine the new commodity market equilibria after the dollar depreciates? We must first redraw America's demand-for-imports and supply-of-exports schedules on the assumption that the rate of exchange is £1 = $3. This is shown in Figure 14-4, which gives all the schedules shown in Figure 14-3 plus America's new schedules (see dashed lines) for the new rate of exchange (£1 = $3). Once America's schedules are redrawn, the commodity market equilibria are determined as before, as illustrated by points *G* in both panels.

Note that as the dollar depreciates, America's new schedules (dashed lines) necessarily lie below the corresponding initial schedules. The reason must be clear: The dollar prices along America's schedules (see Figures 14-1 and 14-2) are now divided by $3—not $2—to obtain the corresponding prices in pounds.

Summary of the Effects of Devaluation

Having determined the postdevaluation commodity market equilibria, we can use Figure 14-4 to identify clearly the various effects of devaluation. In general, we can expect the following eight effects:

1 The Effect on Commodity Flows In general, the volume of imports of the devaluing country (America) decreases, while the volume of exports increases. In Figure 14-4, America's volume of imports decreases from 6,000 to 5,600 units of B-exportables, while the nation's volume of exports increases from 1,800 to 3,000 units of A-exportables.

2 The Effect on Foreign Prices In general, devaluation depresses foreign prices. In Figure 14-4 the prices of A-exportables and B-exportables expressed in pounds (foreign currency) fall. The price of B-exportables falls from £30 to £25, and the price of A-exportables falls from £45 to £36.

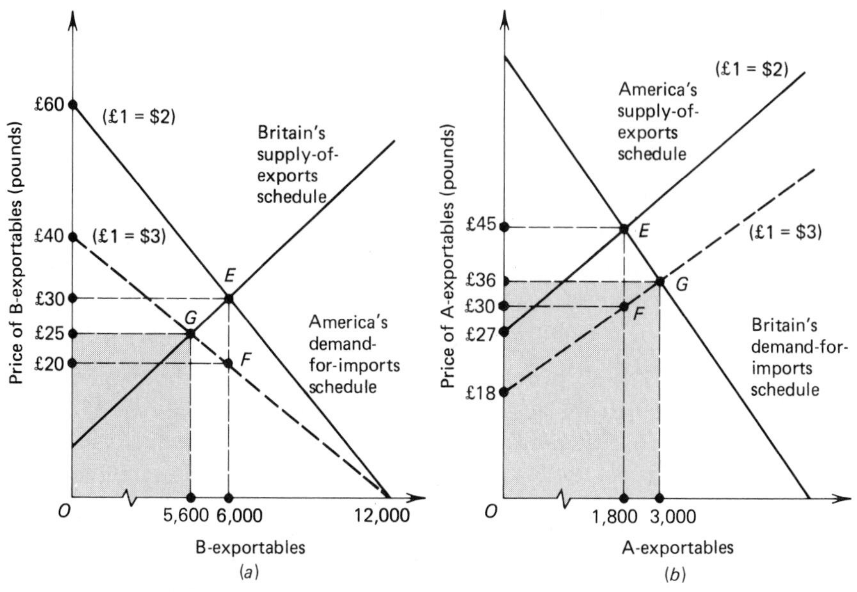

FIGURE 14-4 **Effects of devaluation.** As the rate of exchange increases from \$2 to \$3 per pound (that is, as the dollar depreciates), America's schedules shift downward, as illustrated by the dashed schedules in both panels. Equilibrium shifts from *E* to *G* in both panels. The quantity of pounds demanded (that is, America's expenditure on imports of B-exportables) decreases from £30 × 6,000 = £180,000 to £25 × 5,600 = £140,000. The quantity of pounds supplied (that is, America's export revenue) increases from £45 × 1,800 = £81,000 to £36 × 3,000 = £108,000, because the elasticity of Britain's demand for imports is greater than unity.

3 The Effect on Domestic Prices In general, devaluation has an *inflationary effect* on domestic prices. Even though Figure 14-4 does not directly show the dollar prices of A-exportables and B-exportables, we can easily infer that both these dollar prices increase with the devaluation of the dollar.

How can we infer that the dollar price of B-exportables rises with devaluation (even though the price of B-exportables in pounds actually falls)? By observing that America's volume of imports falls. At a lower volume of imports, America must be paying a higher dollar price (see America's downward-sloping demand-for-imports schedule in Figure 14-1).

How can we infer that the dollar price of A-exportables also rises with devaluation (even though the price of A-exportables in pounds actually falls)? By observing that America's volume of exports increases. At a higher volume of exports, America must be receiving a higher dollar price (see America's upward-sloping supply-of-exports schedule in Figure 14-2).

4 The Effect on the Quantity of Foreign Exchange Demanded What does the quantity of pounds (foreign exchange) demanded signify? It signifies America's expenditure on imports (expressed in pounds). Now both America's volume of imports and the price of B-exportables (in pounds) fall. Therefore, America's expenditure on imports, and thus the quantity of pounds demanded, must also fall. In Figure 14-4, panel (*a*), America's expenditure on imports falls from £180,000 (that is, £30 × 6000) to £140,000 (that is, £25 × 5,600).

5 The Effect on the Quantity of Foreign Exchange Supplied Unfortunately, this effect is indeterminate. Essentially because of this, the analysis of the foreign exchange market as well as the effect of devaluation on the balance of trade becomes complicated.

The quantity of pounds (foreign exchange) supplied coincides with America's export revenue (in pounds): the price of A-exportables in pounds times America's volume of exports. As the dollar depreciates, the price of A-exportables (in pounds) falls, while America's volume of exports increases. Hence, America's export revenue (and thus the supply of pounds) may increase, decrease, or remain constant.

In Figure 14-4 America's export revenue actually increases from £81,000 (that is, £45 × 1,800) to £108,000 (that is, £36 × 3,000). However, this favorable outcome is the result of an implicit assumption: that the elasticity of Britain's demand for imports is greater than unity.

As the dollar depreciates, equilibrium shifts from *E* to *G* along Britain's demand-for-imports schedule. As we already know (see Section 3-6), such a movement along a demand curve causes the total revenue to increase only when the elasticity of demand is greater than unity. If Britain's demand-for-imports schedule were actually inelastic, such a movement would have caused America's export revenue to fall.

6 The Effect on America's Terms of Trade Does a devaluation (or depreciation) of the dollar improve or worsen America's terms of trade? Anything is possible.

As we saw earlier, the devaluation of the dollar causes the prices of *both* A-exportables *and* B-exportables to rise in America (where they are expressed in dollars) and fall in Britain (where they are expressed in pounds). Therefore, it is not possible to predict the effect of devaluation on America's terms of trade, that is, the ratio of the price of A-exportables to the price of B-exportables. In the example of Figure 14-4, the relative price of A-exportables falls from 45/30 to 36/25.

Appendix 15 shows rigorously that the effect of devaluation on America's terms of trade depends on the various import-demand elasticities and export-supply elasticities. In particular, America's terms of trade improve, deteriorate, or remain constant according to whether the product of the supply elasticities of exports is respectively smaller than, larger than, or equal to the product of the demand elasticities for imports.

7 The Effect on the Balance of Trade This is the most important effect of devaluation. A country devalues its currency because its balance of trade (or, in general, balance of payments) is in deficit. Does devaluation improve the balance of trade? Not always. The effect of devaluation on the balance of trade is indeterminate.

We can easily understand why the balance-of-trade effect of devaluation is indeterminate. As we saw earlier, an increase in the rate of exchange (that is, devaluation of the dollar) decreases America's expenditure on imports expressed in pounds (quantity of pounds demanded), which works in the direction of reducing America's deficit. However, before we can say whether America's balance of trade improves, we must also know what happens to America's export revenue (quantity of foreign exchange supplied). If the export revenue increases, we must unequivocally conclude that the deficit falls. But the export revenue may fall (when Britain's demand for imports is inelastic). Evidently, when export revenue falls, it is not at all obvious that America's deficit decreases with devaluation. If the reduction in export revenue is larger than the fall in expenditures on imports, America's deficit actually becomes larger.

Economists have shown that the balance-of-trade effect of devaluation depends in a rather complex fashion on the import-demand and export-supply elasticities. Nevertheless, there is an important and less complicated condition, known as the **Marshall-Lerner condition,** whose satisfaction guarantees that devaluation actually improves the balance of trade, that is, reduces the deficit. (For a proof of the Marshall-Lerner condition, see Appendix 15.)

Marshall-Lerner Condition: **When the sum of the two demand elasticities for imports (that is, America's and Britain's), in absolute terms, is greater than unity, devaluation reduces the balance-of-trade deficit.**

We have already met an example in which the Marshall-Lerner condition is satisfied and devaluation reduces the deficit. This is the example of Figure 14-4, where Britain's demand elasticity for imports is greater than unity (and thus the Marshall-Lerner condition is satisfied irrespective of what America's demand elasticity for imports is). The devaluation of the dollar reduces America's deficit from £99,000 (that is, £45 $\times$ 1,800 $-$ £30 $\times$ 6,000) to £32,000 (that is, £36 $\times$ 3,000 $-$ £25 $\times$ 5,600).

As an example in which the Marshall-Lerner condition is *not* satisfied and devaluation *increases* the deficit, return to Figure 14-4 and assume that each country's elasticity of demand for imports is zero, that is, each country's demand-for-imports schedule is vertical. When the dollar depreciates, America's schedules [that is, America's import-demand schedule in panel (*a*) and America's supply-of-exports schedule in panel (*b*)] shift downward. In the market for A-exportables, equilibrium shifts from E to F since Britain's demand-for-imports schedule is now assumed to be given by the vertical line through E. Thus, America's export revenue falls from £81,000 to £54,000. Equilibrium in the market for B-exportables, in panel (*a*), remains at E, since a vertical shift of a vertical line will leave the vertical line in the same position. Accordingly, the demand for pounds remains at its initial value of £180,000 and America's deficit *increases* by the loss of America's export revenue. In particular, America's balance-of-trade deficit *increases* from £99,000 (that is, £81,000 − £180,000) to £126,000 (that is, £54,000 − £180,000).

Unfortunately, even when the Marshall-Lerner condition is indeed satisfied, the beneficial effect of devaluation on the balance of trade may be frustrated by labor union demands for higher money wages. Recall our earlier conclusion that devaluation has an inflationary impact on domestic prices. When labor unions are successful in maintaining their *real* wages at the predevaluation level (by forcing the same percentage increase in their money-wage rates as the percentage increase in the rate of foreign exchange), the beneficial effects of devaluation are completely wiped out. When America experiences **cost-push inflation** at the same percentage rate as the devaluation of the dollar, America's dashed schedules in Figure 14-4 will shift back to the initial positions shown by the solid lines.

8 The Effect on Domestic Consumption and Production Devaluation has some predictable effects on domestic production and consumption of both countries. As we saw, the devaluation of the dollar causes the prices of A-exportables and B-exportables to rise in America (where they are expressed in dollars) and to fall in Britain (where they are expressed in pounds). In general, we must expect the consumption of both A-exportables and B-exportables to fall in America (where they become more expensive) and rise in Britain (where they become cheaper). We must also expect the production of both A-exportables and B-exportables to rise in America and fall in Britain.

14-5 PRICE ELASTICITIES OF DEMAND FOR IMPORTS AND EXPORTS

Table 14-1 summarizes the empirical estimates of price elasticities of demand for total imports and exports of 18 industrial market economies. Column (4) gives for each country the sum of the elasticities of total imports and total exports listed in columns (2) and (3). The Marshall-Lerner condition is satisfied for all industrial countries. Indeed, with the possible exception of Australia and the United Kingdom, the sum of the price elasticities of demand for imports and exports is invariably much higher than unity. These estimates suggest that relative prices play an important role in the balance-of-payments adjustment mechanism. Thus expenditure-switching policies (such as exchange-rate adjustments, the imposition of new tariffs, and the reduction or elimination of old tariffs) exert a strong influence on the balance of trade.

14-6 THE J-CURVE EFFECT

Following a devaluation (or depreciation) of the domestic currency, the balance of trade typically *worsens* for several months before it eventually improves. This phenomenon is known as the **J curve,** because the trade balance traces a J-shaped curve through time, as shown in Figure 14-5. Empirical studies show that the time lag involved in the balance-of-trade improvement of devaluation varies considerably from country to country.

(Perhaps the persistence of the U.S. trade deficit following the sharp depreciation of the dollar since 1985 may be partly due to the J-curve effect. However, the time lag appears to be too long—the U.S. trade deficit began to show signs of improvement only in the first quarter of 1988. Thus one may surmise that the U.S. trade deficit may reflect, in addition, other fundamental imbalances in the U.S. economy.)

What causes the J-curve phenomenon? *Low short-run elasticities!* The price elasticities of demand for imports and exports presented in Table 14-1 are *long-run* elasticities; they describe the effects of a devaluation after enough time (at least two years) has elapsed for consumers and producers to adjust to the new economic reality. Empirical studies suggest that the long-run elasticities are roughly twice as high as the corresponding short-run elasticities, and that about 50 percent of the final relative price adjustment takes place within one year. (See Goldstein and Khan, 1985, pp. 1076–1086.) Thus the short-run elasticities do not always satisfy the Marshall-Lerner condition; hence the J-curve effect.

There are several reasons why the short-run elasticities are lower than the long-run elasticities. For example, immediately following a devaluation, the course of export revenue and expenditure on imports is determined by contracts (usually denominated in the currency of the exporter) signed before the devaluation. Further, consumers react slowly to price changes because it takes time for habits to adjust. Finally, switching suppliers also takes time—traders are likely to wait until they are reasonably convinced that the benefits will last long enough to make the switch worthwhile.

The J-curve effect poses a serious problem for the functioning of the flexible exchange-rate system: A flexible exchange rate can *overshoot* its long-run value. Suppose that the domestic currency depreciates because of an autonomous increase in the

TABLE 14-1 PRICE ELASTICITIES OF DEMAND FOR TOTAL IMPORTS AND EXPORTS

Country (1)	Imports (2)	Exports (3)	Sum of cols. (2) + (3) (4)
Australia	−0.42	−0.74	−1.16
Austria	−1.32	−0.93	−2.25
Belgium-Luxembourg	−0.83	−1.02	−1.85
Canada	−1.30	−0.79	−2.09
Denmark	−1.05	−1.28	−2.33
Finland	−0.50	−0.78	−1.28
France	−1.08	−1.31	−2.39
Germany	−0.88	−1.11	−1.99
Ireland	−1.37	−0.86	−2.23
Italy	−1.03	−0.93	−1.96
Japan	−0.78	−1.25	−2.03
Netherlands	−0.68	−0.95	−1.63
New Zealand	−1.12	−0.70	−1.82
Norway	−1.19	−0.81	−2.00
Sweden	−0.79	−1.96	−2.75
Switzerland	−1.22	−1.01	−2.23
United Kingdom	−0.65	−0.48	−1.13
United States	−1.66	−1.41	−3.07

Source: R. M. Stern, J. Francis, and B. Schumacher, *Price Elasticities in International Trade: An Annotated Bibliography,* Macmillan and Company, London, 1976, Table 2.2 (p. 20).

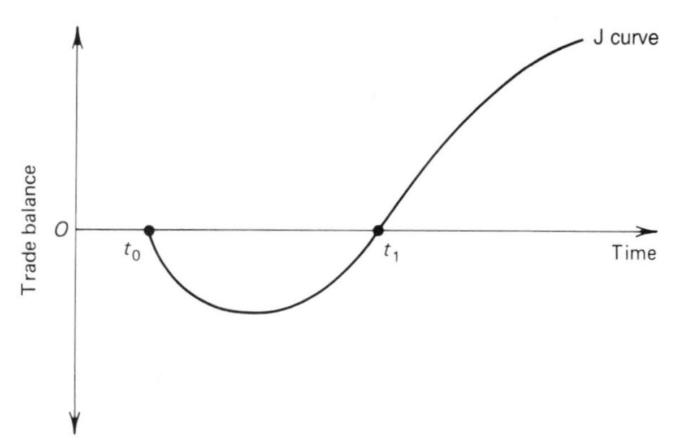

FIGURE 14-5 The J curve. Devaluation occurs at time t_0 but has no immediate effect on the volumes of exports and imports. Because exports are invoiced in the exporter's currency, the export revenue (in foreign exchange) falls, while the expenditure on imports (in foreign exchange) remains the same. Thus the balance of trade deteriorates. By time t_1 the initial balance-of-trade deterioration is totally reversed. The positive effects of devaluation occur after t_1.

demand for foreign exchange. If the balance of trade worsens in the short run, the excess demand for foreign exchange will get bigger, not smaller; thus the domestic currency may continue to depreciate beyond its long-run equilibrium value, causing an unnecessary and wasteful reallocation of resources.

14-7 SUPPLY AND DEMAND FOR FOREIGN EXCHANGE

In Sections 14-3 and 14-4 we learned how to determine the quantities of foreign exchange demanded and supplied at any given rate of exchange and how these quantities are likely to change as the rate of exchange changes. This section completes that analysis by introducing explicitly the supply and demand schedules for foreign exchange. These schedules show the various quantities of foreign exchange demanded and supplied at alternative rates of exchange.

Supply and Demand Schedules for Foreign Exchange

Figure 14-6 gives the supply and demand schedules for pounds sterling. Consider first the *demand schedule for foreign exchange* (pounds), which is derived from America's demand-for-imports schedule and Britain's supply-of-exports schedule summarized in Figure 14-4, panel (*a*). For each rate of exchange, we determine the quantity of foreign exchange demanded, as we did in Section 14-4. This information enables us to determine a point on the demand schedule for

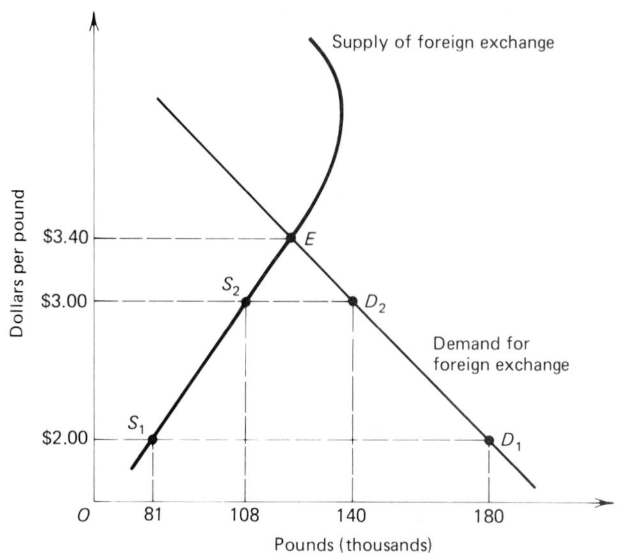

FIGURE 14-6 **Supply and demand schedules for foreign exchange.** Points D_1 and D_2 on the demand schedule for foreign exchange (pounds) correspond to points *E* and *G*, respectively, in Figure 14-4 (*a*). Points S_1 and S_2 on the supply schedule for foreign exchange correspond to points *E* and *G*, respectively, in Figure 14-4 (*b*).

foreign exchange. For instance, when £1 = $2, the quantity of pounds demanded (America's expenditure on imports) is equal to £180,000, that is, £30 × 6,000, as shown by point *E* in Figure 14-4(*a*); and this information fixes point D_1 on the demand schedule for foreign exchange in Figure 14-6. Similarly, when the rate of exchange is $3 per pound, the quantity of pounds demanded (America's expenditure on imports) becomes equal to £140,000 [see point *G* in Figure 14-4(*a*)]; and this information determines point D_2 on the demand schedule for foreign exchange depicted in Figure 14-6. By repeating this exercise many times, we can determine as many points as we wish on the demand schedule for foreign exchange. When we have enough points, we can trace the continuous curve shown in Figure 14-6.

Normally, *the demand curve for foreign exchange slopes downward.* This is implicit in our earlier conclusion that a devaluation of the dollar (that is, an *increase* in the rate of exchange) *decreases* the quantity of foreign exchange (pounds) demanded.

Turn now to the *supply schedule for foreign exchange,* which is derived from America's supply-of-exports schedule and Britain's demand-for-imports schedule summarized in Figure 14-4, panel (*b*). For each rate of exchange, we determine the quantity of foreign exchange (pounds) supplied, as we did in Section 14-4. This information enables us to determine a point on the supply schedule for foreign exchange. For example, when £1 = $2 the quantity of pounds supplied (America's export revenue) is equal to £81,000, as shown by point E in Figure 14-4(b) and point S_1 on the supply schedule for foreign exchange in Figure 14-6. Similarly, when £1 = \$3 the quantity of pounds supplied (America's export revenue) becomes equal to £108,000, as shown by point G in Figure 14-4(b) and point S_2 in Figure 14-6. By repeating this exercise many times, we can determine as many points as we wish on the supply schedule for foreign exchange.

The supply curve for foreign exchange is normally *backward bending*. This is again consistent with our earlier conclusion that a devaluation of the dollar may cause the quantity of pounds supplied to either *increase* (when Britain's demand for imports is *elastic*) or *decrease* (when Britain's demand for imports is *inelastic*).

For low values of the rate of exchange, America's supply-of-exports schedule intersects Britain's demand-for-imports schedule very high up on the curves, closer to the vertical than to the horizontal axis, where Britain's demand for imports is elastic. Thus, for low values of the rate of exchange, the supply schedule for pounds slopes upward. For high values of the rate of exchange, America's supply-of-exports schedule intersects Britain's demand-for-imports schedule very low down on the curves, closer to the horizontal than to the vertical axis, where Britain's demand for imports is inelastic. Thus, for high values of the rate of exchange, the supply schedule for pounds bends backward. [Return again to Figure 14-4, panel (b), and verify these conclusions.] This explains why the supply schedule for foreign exchange is normally backward bending, as shown in Figure 14-6.

Equilibrium and Stability in the Foreign Exchange Market

Equilibrium in the foreign exchange market occurs when the rate of exchange is such that the quantity of foreign exchange demanded equals the quantity supplied. Graphically, equilibrium occurs at the point of intersection of the supply and demand schedules for foreign exchange, as illustrated by point E in Figure 14-6. When a market is in equilibrium, each potential buyer can find a seller and each seller can find a buyer. All the market participants do what they desire to do, and neither buyers nor sellers have any incentive to change their behavior. If not disturbed, equilibrium can last forever. But is there any guarantee that a market will be in equilibrium if it is not already? What happens when a market is out of equilibrium? Will the market return to equilibrium?

The behavior of a market (or a system of markets) out of equilibrium is the subject matter of **stability analysis.** Are there economic forces at work that will automatically bring the market back to equilibrium? If there are such forces and the market does tend to return to equilibrium, then that equilibrium is called **stable;** otherwise, the equilibrium is called **unstable.** Clearly, the concept of stability is an important one because equilibrium cannot be taken seriously unless it is stable.

How can we tell whether an equilibrium point is stable or unstable? To answer this question, we need to know how the buyers and sellers react when the current price is not an equilibrium one.

It is commonly believed that if the quantity supplied is larger than the quantity demanded, the price will tend to fall, presumably because the suppliers who are unable to sell all they want to sell at the current price will lower their bids. If the quantity supplied is smaller than the quantity demanded, the price will tend to rise, presumably because the buyers who are unable to buy all they want at the current price will raise their bids.

The equilibrium illustrated in Figure 14-6 is stable. A rate of exchange lower than $3.40 per pound will tend to rise because the quantity of pounds demanded exceeds the quantity of pounds supplied. For instance, when £1 = $2 the quantity of pounds demanded is £180,000 but the quantity of pounds supplied is only £81,000. A rate of exchange higher than $3.40 will tend to fall because the quantity of pounds supplied exceeds the quantity of pounds demanded (as indicated by the fact that above the equilibrium rate of $3.40 the supply schedule for foreign exchange lies to the right of the demand schedule for foreign exchange).

14-8 NONTRADED GOODS: A DIGRESSION

As we saw in Section 14-4, a devaluation of the dollar causes the prices of A-exportables *and* B-exportables to rise in America and fall in Britain. Accordingly, the production of both A-exportables and B-exportables expands in America and falls in Britain. The partial equilibrium model does not explain where the American producers of A-exportables and B-exportables find the additional resources that are necessary for the expansion of their production. Similarly, our model fails to explain what actually happens to the resources that Britain's producers of A-exportables and B-exportables release as they reduce their production.

If we allow unemployment in each country as a possibility, we could argue that America's producers bring into the production process resources (such as labor) that were previously unemployed, while the resources the British producers release remain idle (or unemployed). We shall explore this possibility further in the next chapter. For the moment, we would like to concentrate on a different explanation—an explanation that is consistent with full employment in both countries.

An implicit assumption of the partial equilibrium model is that each country possesses another industry (in addition to the industries of A-exportables and B-exportables). This third industry (or sector) produces other goods and services, such as haircuts and houses, that are not traded internationally because of prohibitive transportation costs. These goods and services are usually called **domestic** or **nontraded goods.**

Given the existence of nontraded goods, it appears that we could argue that a devaluation of the dollar causes American resources to shift out of the **nontraded goods sector** and into the export and import-competing sectors (or the **traded goods sector**), that is, into the industries of A-exportables and B-exportables. In Britain, of course, where the production of A-exportables and B-exportables falls, we could argue that the released resources flow into the nontraded goods sector. But there is a difficulty with this argument that calls for further clarification. Our analysis in Part One of this book shows clearly that such transfers of resources can take place only if the prices of the traded goods (that is, A-exportables and B-exportables) rise in America and fall in Britain relative to the prices of nontraded goods. Is it reasonable to expect such relative-price changes after the devaluation of the dollar? Yes it is, provided that devaluation is combined with the appropriate expenditure changes in the countries involved, as explained in the rest of this section.

Immediately after the devaluation of the dollar, the money prices of the traded goods rise in America and fall in Britain. Accordingly, there seems to be a tendency for the traded goods to become more expensive relative to the nontraded goods in America, and cheaper in Britain. These are, of course, the relative price changes that are necessary in both countries for the transfer of resources between sectors, as explained in the preceding paragraph. But are such relative price changes viable in the long run? Will America's and Britain's markets for nontraded goods continue to remain in equilibrium at these altered relative prices?

Consider America's market for nontraded goods first. As America transfers resources from the nontraded goods sector to the traded goods sector, *America's output of nontraded goods necessarily falls.* What happens to America's demand for nontraded goods? *The quantity of nontraded goods demanded in America must rise.* As the nontraded goods become relatively cheaper, rational Americans substitute nontraded goods for traded goods. (Recall that the devaluation of the dollar also causes America's consumption of A-exportables and B-exportables to fall.) Evidently America's market for nontraded goods cannot remain in equilibrium *because their supply falls while their demand increases.* Thus the initial reduction in the relative price of nontraded goods generates an excess demand for nontraded goods that tends to push their relative price back to its initial level. (By definition, equilibrium in the market for nontraded goods requires that the domestic demand be equal to the domestic supply—there can be no exports or imports of nontraded goods.) But without a permanent reduction in the relative price of nontraded goods, no permanent transfer of resources can take place from the nontraded goods sector to the traded goods sector.

We observe exactly the opposite tendencies in Britain. Initially, the devaluation of the dollar causes the traded goods to become cheaper relative to the nontraded goods. Such a relative price change is, of course, necessary for the needed transfer of resources from the traded goods sector to the nontraded goods sector. But again this relative price change is not viable in the long run, as it generates forces for its elimination. The initial increase in the relative price of nontraded goods causes their supply to increase and their demand to fall, and the resultant excess supply of nontraded goods tends to force their relative price down to its initial level.

Our analysis seems to have reached an impasse. After the devaluation of the dollar, the relative price of nontraded goods must change in both America and Britain in order to facilitate the transfer of resources between sectors (in each country separately). Yet such relative price changes do not seem to be viable in the long run. Without permanent relative price changes, no permanent transfers of resources can take place. How can we resolve this apparently difficult issue?

The solution is implicit in our discussion in Chapter 13. Recall that devaluation alone cannot restore balance-of-payments equilibrium and maintain full employment at the same time. The deficit country (whose absorption exceeds that nation's national income) must, in addition, reduce its aggregate spending. The surplus country (whose national income is higher than its absorption) must, in addition, increase its spending. This is necessary because balance-of-payments equilibrium requires that each country's aggregate spending equals that country's national income.

Thus, simultaneously with the devaluation of the dollar, America must *reduce* its aggregate spending on *all* goods and services (including nontraded goods). In turn, this expenditure reduction eliminates the excess demand for nontraded goods, which we observed earlier, and removes the tendency for the reversal of the initial reduction in the relative price of America's nontraded goods. Similarly, Britain must *increase* its spending on *all* goods and services (including nontraded goods). In turn, this increase in Britain's spending eliminates the excess supply of nontraded goods, which we observed earlier, and removes the tendency for the reversal of the initial increase in the relative price of Britain's nontraded goods.

We therefore conclude that when devaluation is combined with the appropriate expenditure changes in the countries involved, the necessary relative price changes can indeed take place and facilitate the required transfer of resources between sectors (in each country separately) as envisaged by the partial equilibrium model.

14-9 THE PRICE-SPECIE-FLOW MECHANISM

So far we have discussed the price adjustment mechanism in relation to exchange-rate changes. How does price adjustment work under a fixed exchange-rate system, such as the gold standard?

Two centuries ago, the Scottish philosopher David Hume argued that there was an automatic self-correcting **price-specie-flow mechanism** at work that guaranteed balance-of-payments equilibrium. Hume's explanation was that gold flows tended to produce price-level changes (according to the **quantity theory of money**), which in turn tended to restore equilibrium in the balance of payments and eventually check the flow of gold.

For instance, suppose that America and Britain are on the gold standard and that at the existing rate of exchange of $2 per pound America runs a balance-of-payments deficit. Because the rate of exchange cannot rise (to, say, $3), America's import surplus will lead to a gold flow from America to Britain, as shown in Figure 14-7 (see distance *CD*). According to the **rules of the game,** America's money supply will contract, while Britain's money supply will expand. (The precise changes in the money supplies will depend, of course, on the structures of the banking systems of the two countries.) Given the classical world of complete wage and price flexibility (and full employment), the reduction in the American money supply will cause, according to the quantity theory of money, America's cost structure and prices to fall. Similarly, the expansion in the British money supply will cause Britain's cost structure and prices to rise. In terms of our partial equilibrium model, this means that America's demand-for-imports and supply-of-exports schedules will shift downward and that Britain's schedules will shift upward. With *high elasticities,* these shifts will

1 Increase America's exports (as America becomes a cheaper place in which to buy) and cause the supply-of-pounds schedule to shift to the right, as shown by the dashed supply curve in Figure 14-7.

2 Reduce America's imports and cause the demand-for-pounds schedule to shift to the left, as shown by the dashed demand curve in Figure 14-7.

FIGURE 14-7 **The price-specie-flow mechanism.** At the fixed rate of $2 per pound, America is running a deficit given by distance *CD.* America finances its deficit by exporting gold to Britain. Britain's money supply expands, causing Britain's cost structure and prices to rise. Similarly, America's money supply contracts, causing America's cost structure and prices to fall. As a result, America's exports increase, causing the supply-of-pounds schedule to shift to the right, as shown by the dashed supply line; and America's imports decrease, causing the demand-for-pounds schedule to shift to the left, as shown by the dashed demand line. Equilibrium is finally re-established at *E* (that is, at the fixed rate of $2).

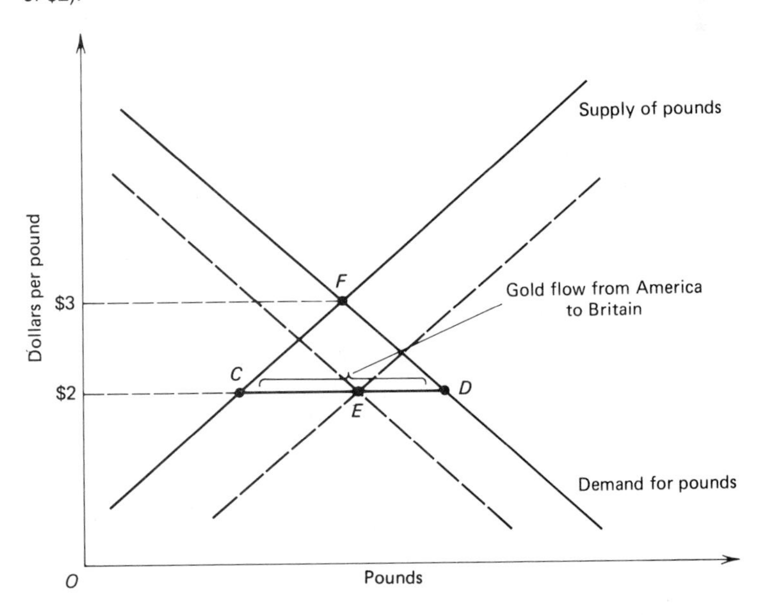

In this way, the flow of gold will cease and equilibrium in the foreign exchange market will occur at the existing rate of exchange (see point *E*).

It is often erroneously stated that there is a presumption in the price-specie-flow mechanism that the gold-losing country will experience a worsening in its terms of trade. This conclusion is wrong. Inflation and deflation, as implied by the classical economists, are equivalent to exchange-rate changes. As we have seen, the terms-of-trade effect of an exchange-rate adjustment is indeterminate. The same must be true for the price-specie-flow mechanism as well. The explanation for this phenomenon is simple. While it is true that America's gold exports to Britain cause prices to fall in America and rise in Britain, it is the prices of *both* A-exportables *and* B-exportables that fall in America and rise in Britain. Thus, it is unwarranted to jump to the conclusion that A-exportables become cheaper relative to B-exportables.

Modern economists emphasize that national income changes play a major stabilizing role in the adjustment process under an international gold standard. This fact was widely recognized after Keynes published his *General Theory* in 1936. There is no particular urgency to discuss the importance of national income changes at this point. The next chapter studies the income-adjustment mechanism in detail.

14-10 EFFECTIVE EXCHANGE RATES

So far we have dealt with only two currencies. Yet in the real world there are more than 100 different national currencies. In addition, the dollar does not depreciate (or appreciate) uniformly relative to all other currencies. Rather, the dollar may appreciate (at different rates) relative to some currencies as it depreciates (at different rates) relative to other currencies. For instance, Figure 14-8 shows that during the 1973–1986 period the dollar appreciated against the British pound, the Canadian dollar, the French franc, and the Italian lira but depreciated relative to the Japanese yen and the Swiss franc; the dollar was about the same in 1986 as it was in 1973 against the German mark. In what sense, then, can we claim that the external value of the dollar increased (the dollar became stronger) or decreased (the dollar became weaker)?

The problem of measuring changes in the external value of the dollar is similar to the problem of measuring *inflation.* With the passage of time, the prices of some goods rise faster than others; indeed some prices may even fall. To measure the average increase in prices (that is, inflation), we use a **price index,** such as the **Consumer Price Index** issued by the U.S. Bureau of Labor Statistics.

Likewise, to measure the average change in the external value of the dollar, we construct an index known as the **effective exchange rate,** which is a weighted average of the **bilateral exchange rates** of the dollar, such as the dollar-yen rate, the dollar-mark rate, and the dollar-pound rate. (The exchange rate between any two currencies is called the bilateral exchange rate.)

The construction of an effective exchange rate involves two issues:

1 Which currencies should be included?
2 How should the included currencies be weighted?

Note: The exchange rates in this diagram register the prices of the dollar in terms of foreign currencies.

FIGURE 14-8 Nominal Dollar Exchange Rates for G-7 Countries and Switzerland. (*From Ott, 1987, p. 6.*)

Obviously, it is cumbersome to include all bilateral rates. For this reason, only the currencies of the most important trading partners are included in the index. For instance, it makes little sense to include the drachma in the effective exchange rate of the U.S. dollar, because Greece is not a major trading partner of the United States. However, the yen, the deutsche mark, and the Canadian dollar must be included because Japan, Germany, and Canada are major trading partners of the United States. Further, the weights assigned to the included currencies must reflect the relative importance of each trading partner. In practice, there exist various weighting schemes depending on whether trade is measured on the basis of imports, exports, or total trade (that is, exports plus imports). Figure 14-9 presents two versions of the Atlanta Federal Reserve Bank's dollar index for the period 1980–1987.

14-11 REAL EXCHANGE RATES

A **nominal exchange rate** gives the price of a foreign currency in terms of the domestic currency. The bilateral exchange rates published in the daily press are nominal exchange rates. So far we have used nominal exchange rates only.

Nominal exchange rates are not always good indicators of the home country's international competitiveness. Suppose that the dollar depreciates relative to the pound sterling. Does that mean that American producers gain a price advantage over British producers? Not necessarily. If because of domestic inflation the prices of American goods are rising faster than the price of the pound sterling, the U.S. producers will actually develop a price *dis*advantage (that is, the American producers will lose price competitiveness).

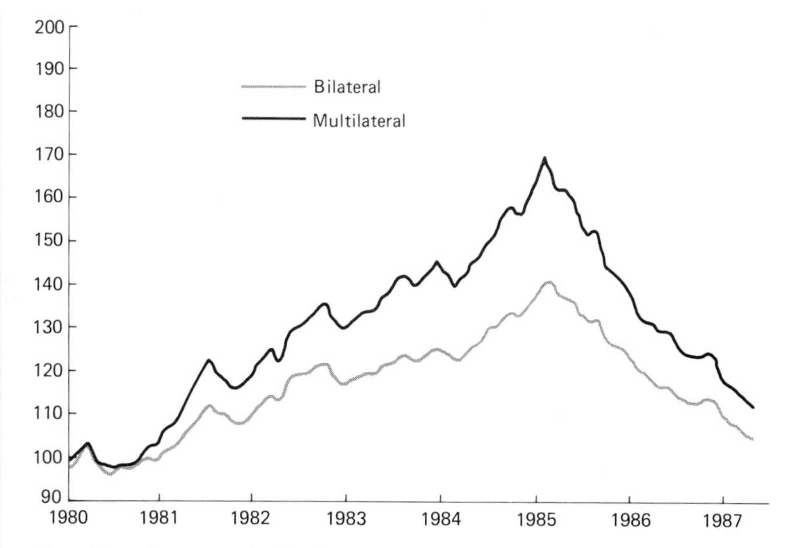

Note: The exchange rates in this diagram measure the prices of the dollar in terms of foreign currencies.

FIGURE 14-9 Two Versions of the Atlanta Fed Dollar Index. (*Reprinted by permission from the Federal Reserve Bank of Atlanta, from Jeffrey A. Rosenweig, "Constructing and Using Exchange Rate Indexes,"* Economic Review, *vol. LXXII, No. 3/4, Summer 1987, p. 10.*)

Changes in a country's competitiveness relative to a foreign nation are best captured by a **real exchange rate,** which is a price-adjusted nominal exchange rate. Specifically, the real exchange rate is equal to the nominal exchange rate (R) times the ratio of the foreign price level (P^*) to the domestic price level (P), that is,

$$\text{Real exchange rate} = \frac{RP^*}{P}$$

The term RP^* gives the foreign price level in terms of the home currency. Thus the real exchange rate essentially denotes the ratio of the prices of foreign and domestic goods, both expressed in dollars (home currency). When the real exchange rate increases, the home country becomes more competitive relative to the foreign country.

Typically, we are not interested in the competitiveness of the United States relative to just one foreign country. Rather, we are interested in some measure of competitiveness of the United States relative to its major trading partners (or the rest of the world). For this purpose, we can use a **real effective exchange rate,** which is a nominal effective exchange rate multiplied by an appropriate price index for the major U.S. trading partners and divided by a U.S. price index.

14-12 THE EFFECT OF DOLLAR APPRECIATION ON U.S. TEXTILE AND APPAREL IMPORTS

The U.S. textile and apparel industries are highly competitive. Each is composed of a large number of small manufacturers. In 1984 the U.S. apparel industry comprised about 23,000 establishments employing 1.2 million workers, and the U.S. textile industry consisted of about 6,000 firms employing 724,000 workers.

The textile industry weaves fiber into fabric and processes fabric into intermediate products. About one-third of textile production is used by the apparel industry. Textile products are more standardized than apparel products. Textile and apparel products are labor intensive, giving a competitive edge to producers in low-wage foreign countries.

Figure 14-10, panel (*a*), gives U.S. textile and apparel imports from 1977 to 1986. During this period the volume of textile imports increased 256 percent and the volume of apparel imports increased 380 percent. Panel (*b*) presents the behavior of a trade-weighted real exchange rate specially constructed for the textile and apparel industry. This index is based on data from countries that accounted for an average of 84 percent

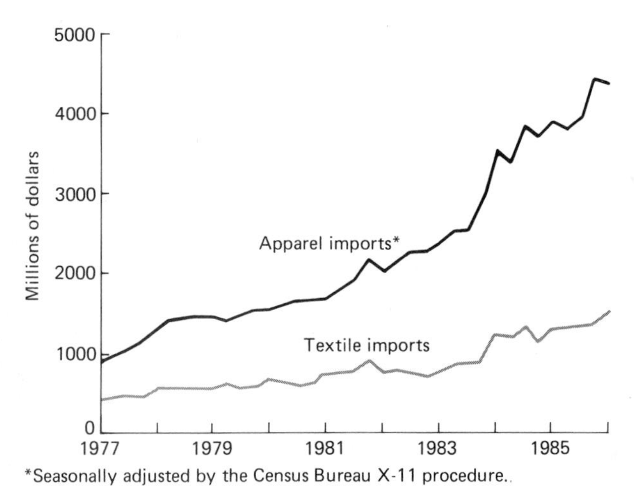

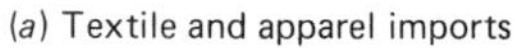
(*a*) Textile and apparel imports

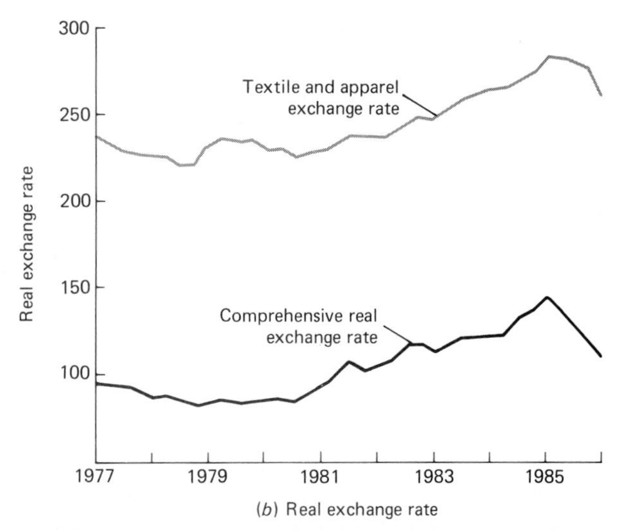

(*b*) Real exchange rate

FIGURE 14-10 U.S. Textile and Apparel Imports and Real Exchange Rates, 1977–1986. (*From Chmura, 1987.*)

of U.S. textile and apparel imports during the period 1977–1986. (The Federal Reserve's comprehensive index designed to cover all goods is also shown for comparison.)

Christina Chmura (1987) calculates that a 1 percent increase in the exchange rate (dollar appreciation) is associated with about a 1.4 percent increase in imports of both textiles and apparel.

Source: Adapted from Chmura (1987).

14-13 SUMMARY

1 The partial equilibrium model assumes that each country has supply and demand schedules giving the quantities of goods supplied by domestic producers and demanded by domestic consumers, respectively, at alternative prices expressed in the domestic currency. These schedules are assumed to be independent of each other.

2 A country's demand-for-imports schedule gives the quantities (domestic shortages) that the country is willing to import at alternative prices expressed in the domestic currency. This schedule depends on both the parameters that lie behind the domestic demand schedule (that is, tastes, incomes, and other commodity prices) and those that lie behind the domestic supply schedule (that is, technology and factor prices).

3 A country's supply-of-exports schedule gives the quantities (domestic surpluses) that the country is willing to export at alternative prices expressed in the domestic currency. This schedule also depends on the parameters that lie behind the domestic supply and demand schedules.

4 A commodity market is in equilibrium when the price of the commodity is such that one country's desired volume of imports matches the other country's desired volume of exports.

5 Before determining the commodity market equilibria, it is necessary to express all prices in the same currency. For this purpose, it is necessary to know the rate of foreign exchange.

6 A country's export revenue (expenditure on imports) is given by the product of the country's equilibrium volume of exports (imports) and their equilibrium price in either the domestic currency or foreign exchange. The difference between a country's export revenue and expenditure on imports gives that country's balance-of-trade deficit or surplus.

7 A change in the rate of exchange disturbs an initial commodity market equilibrium by causing one country's demand-for-imports and supply-of-exports schedules to shift.

8 A devaluation has many effects: The devaluing country's volume of imports decreases and its volume of exports increases; the prices of traded goods fall in the rest of the world and rise in the devaluing country; the production of traded goods falls in the rest of the world and expands in the devaluing country; the consumption of traded goods falls in the devaluing country and expands in the rest of the world; the demand for foreign exchange (that is, the devaluing country's expenditure on imports expressed in foreign currency) falls; the supply of foreign exchange (that is, the devaluing country's export revenue expressed in foreign exchange) may increase, decrease, or remain constant according to whether the foreign demand for imports is elastic, inelastic, or unit elastic, respectively.

9 The devaluing country's terms of trade may improve, deteriorate, or remain constant according to whether the product of the export-supply elasticities is respectively smaller than, larger than, or equal to the product of the import-demand elasticities.

10 Devaluation improves the balance of trade when the sum of the two import-demand elasticities (in absolute terms) is greater than unity. This is the Marshall-Lerner condition.

11 By plotting the quantities of foreign exchange supplied (demanded) against alternative rates of exchange, we obtain the supply (demand) schedule for foreign exchange. Usually, the demand schedule is downward sloping, while the supply schedule is backward bending.

12 Equilibrium in the foreign exchange market occurs at the intersection of the supply and demand schedules for foreign exchange.

13 The partial equilibrium model becomes consistent with full employment when each country possesses an additional industry producing nontraded goods. However, devaluation must then be combined with appropriate expenditure adjustments in both countries: The deficit country must reduce, and the surplus country must increase, aggregate spending.

14 Hume's automatic, self-correcting price-specie-flow mechanism rests on the idea that gold flows between countries tend to produce price-level changes, which in turn tend to restore equilibrium in the balance of payments. The mechanism assumes wage and price flexibility and high elasticities. The gold-losing country need not experience a terms-of-trade deterioration.

PROBLEMS

1 Consider a partial equilibrium model of two countries (France and Germany) and two commodities (wine and steel). France exports wine to Germany in exchange for German steel. France's supply of exports of wine is perfectly inelastic and given by the equation

$$Q_F = 1000$$

where Q_F = France's volume of exports of wine. Germany's supply of exports of steel is also perfectly inelastic and is given by the equation

$$Q_G = 400$$

where Q_G = Germany's volume of exports of steel. France's demand for imports of steel is given by the equation

$$D_F = 1400 - 10p_s$$

where D_F = France's quantity of imports of steel and p_s = price of steel in French francs. Finally, Germany's demand for imports of wine is given by the equation

$$D_G = 1200 - 20p_w^*$$

where D_G = Germany's quantity of imports of wine and p_w^* = price of wine in German marks. Use asterisks (*) to indicate prices in German marks; omit asterisks for prices in French francs.

a Determine the supply schedule for German marks.
b Determine the demand schedule for German marks.
c Determine the equilibrium exchange rate (francs per mark).
d Determine the equilibrium prices of wine and steel in both francs and marks.
e Illustrate your results graphically. (Along the vertical axis measure the price of marks in terms of francs.)

2 Starting from an initial equilibrium configuration in a partial equilibrium model, the home country (America) makes a unilateral transfer to the foreign country (Japan). Both countries' export supply elasticities are infinite. Determine the effects of the transfer on the following economic variables:

a The rate of exchange (yen per dollar).
b The prices of America's and Japan's exportables in dollars and yen.
c America's and Japan's outputs and consumption of commodities.
d America's volume of exports to Japan, and Japan's volume of exports to America.
e America's terms of trade.

3 Suppose that America and Britain are on a gold standard. The fixed rate of exchange (mint parity) is \$2 = £1. America's supply of exports of A-exportables and demand for imports of B-exportables are given by the equations

$$S_a = 2p_a \qquad \text{(America's supply of exports)}$$

$$D_a = 300 - 7p_b \qquad \text{(America's demand for imports)}$$

where S_a = America's volume of exports, D_a = America's volume of imports, p_a = price of A-exportables in dollars, and p_b = price of B-exportables in dollars. Similarly, Britain's corresponding functions are

$$S_b = 200 + 4p_b^* \qquad \text{(Britain's supply of exports)}$$

$$D_b = 500 - 6p_a^* \qquad \text{(Britain's demand for imports)}$$

where asterisks (*) indicate prices in pounds.

a Determine the quantity of pounds demanded at mint parity.
b Determine the quantity of pounds supplied at mint parity.
c Determine the flow of gold between America and Britain at mint parity.
d Suppose that Britain devalues the pound to £1 = \$1. Determine the effects on the quantities of pounds demanded and supplied and the flow of gold.

4 In each of the following cases, decide whether the supply schedule for foreign exchange is upward sloping, vertical, or backward bending. Illustrate each case graphically.

a The home country is a price taker in world markets.
b The home country's supply of exports is perfectly inelastic (vertical).
c Foreign demand for the home country's exports is perfectly inelastic (vertical).
d Foreign demand for the home country's exports is inelastic.
e Foreign demand for the home country's exports is unit elastic.

SUGGESTED READING

Bickerdike, C. F. (1920). "The Instability of Foreign Exchange." *Economic Journal,* vol. 30 (March), pp. 118–122.

Chacholiades, M. (1978). *International Monetary Theory and Policy.* McGraw-Hill Book Company, New York, chaps. 3–8.

Chmura, C. (1987). "The Effect of Exchange Rate Variation on U.S. Textile and Apparel Imports." Federal Reserve Bank of Richmond *Economic Review,* vol. 73.

Goldstein, M., and M. S. Khan (1985). "Income and Price Effects in Foreign Trade." In R. W. Jones and P. B. Kenen (eds.), *Handbook of International Economics,* vol. 2, North-Holland, New York, 1985.

Hume, D. (1752). "Of the Balance of Trade." *Essays, Moral, Political and Literary,* vol. 1, Longmans Green, London, 1898. Reprinted in W. R. Allen (ed.), *International Trade Theory: Hume to Ohlin,* Random House, Inc., New York, 1965.

Machlup, F. (1939 and 1940). "The Theory of Foreign Exchanges." *Economica,* vol. 6 (new series), November 1939 and February 1940. Reprinted in H. S. Ellis and L. A. Metzler (eds.), American Economic Association *Readings in the Theory of International Trade,* Richard D. Irwin, Inc., Homewood, Ill., 1950.

Ott, M. (1987). "The Dollar's Effective Exchange Rate: Assessing the Impact of Alternative Weighting Schemes." Federal Reserve Bank of St. Louis *Economic Review,* vol. 69.

Robinson, J. (1947). "The Foreign Exchanges." In J. Robinson, *Essays in the Theory of Employment,* 2nd ed. Macmillan and Company, London. Reprinted in H. S. Ellis and L. A. Metzler (eds.), American Economic Association *Readings in the Theory of International Trade,* Richard D. Irwin, Inc., Homewood, Ill., 1950.

Rosensweig, J. A. (1987). "Constructing and Using Exchange Rate Indexes." Federal Reserve Bank of Atlanta *Economic Review,* vol. 72.

CHAPTER **15**

THE INCOME-ADJUSTMENT MECHANISM

The income-adjustment mechanism is a direct outgrowth of Keynes's *General Theory,* even though Keynes himself had little to do with it. This powerful mechanism yields two important propositions:

1 *International trade is a significant vehicle for the transmission of business cycles between countries.*

2 *Balance-of-payments disturbances that affect the circular flow of income give rise to national income changes that tend to bring about partial (not complete) adjustment in the balance of payments.*

This chapter deals mainly with the **income-adjustment mechanism.** It also examines the policy issue of how to achieve internal and external balance simultaneously. The discussion rests on the simplifying assumption that all commodity prices, money-wage rates, and the interest rate remain constant.

15-1 INCOME DETERMINATION IN A CLOSED ECONOMY

This section provides a brief review of the basic Keynesian model of income determination in a closed economy. For simplicity, we ignore the government sector.

Three Basic Economic Flows

In any closed economy, we can distinguish among three economic flows, as follows:

1 Gross national product *(GNP)*—the total money value of the flow of final goods and services produced by the economy.

2 National income (Y)—the sum of all factor earnings (wages, interest, rents, and profits).

3 Aggregate expenditure (or absorption)—the sum of total spending on consumption (C) and investment (I).

It is an accounting fact that gross national product (value of output produced) is identically equal to national income (costs of production). Because of this fundamental identity, we shall use the symbol Y to represent both gross national product and national income.

Determination of National Income

We may recall from introductory economics that national income equilibrium occurs when *desired* (or *planned*) aggregate expenditure ($C + I$) equals national income (Y), that is, when

$$Y = C(Y) + I \tag{15-1}$$

We assume that desired investment is exogenous (that is, independent of the level of national income). Desired consumption, however, depends on national income; that is, $C = C(Y)$. This is the crucial **consumption function** that plays a significant role in the Keynesian macroeconomic system.

The part of national income that is not spent on consumption is called **saving** (S), that is, $S = Y - C(Y) = S(Y)$. Using the definition of saving, we can rearrange Equation (15-1) as follows:

$$S(Y) = Y - C(Y) = \bar{I} \tag{15-2}$$

If we think of saving as a **leakage** from the income stream (that is, as a portion of national income that is not spent and that is therefore lost to the income stream) and of investment as an exogenous **injection** into the income stream, we can then say that *national income equilibrium occurs when the injections* (I) *match the leakages* (S). National income equilibrium is illustrated in Figure 15-1; it occurs at E, where the saving schedule, $S(Y)$, intersects the investment schedule, $\bar{I}$. The equilibrium level of income is 900. Investment and saving are both equal to 200.

The Marginal Propensities to Consume and Save

As national income increases, desired consumption increases also, but the increase in consumption ΔC is always smaller than the increase in income ΔY. The extra income that is not spent on consumption, that is, $\Delta Y - \Delta C$, represents additional saving, ΔS. Thus $\Delta Y = \Delta C + \Delta S$. The fraction of each extra dollar of income that goes into consumption, that is, $\Delta C/\Delta Y$, is called the **marginal propensity to consume** (MPC); and the fraction that goes into saving, that is, $\Delta S/\Delta Y$, is the **marginal propensity to save** (MPS). The identity $\Delta Y = \Delta C + \Delta S$

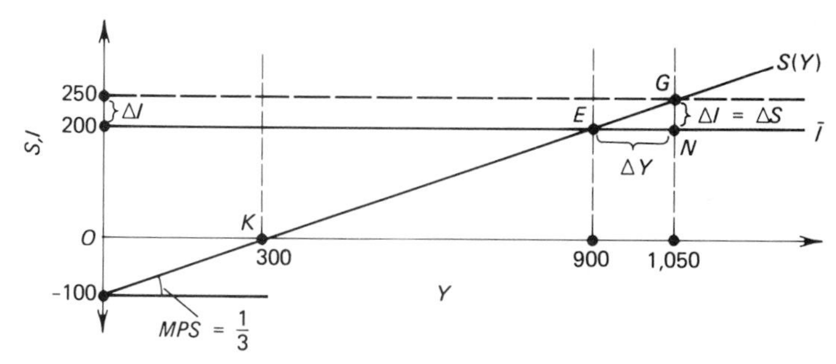

FIGURE 15-1 **National-income equilibrium in a closed economy.** Equilibrium occurs at *E*, where saving schedule *S*(*Y*) intersects horizontal investment schedule $\bar{I}$. The equilibrium level of income is 900. Investment and saving are both equal to 200. When investment spending rises to 250, the investment demand schedule shifts upward, as shown by the dashed line, and equilibrium shifts to *G*, at which national income is 1,050.

implies that **the sum of the marginal propensity to consume plus the marginal propensity to save equals unity;** that is, $MPC + MPS = 1$. The marginal propensity to save is given by the slope of the saving schedule, as illustrated in Figure 15-1. (The marginal propensity to consume is given by the slope of the consumption function.)

Stability of the National Income Equilibrium

Return to Figure 15-1. Is the national income equilibrium at *E* stable? It certainly is. When *Y* is below 900, desired investment $\bar{I}$ exceeds desired saving, $S(Y)$, which means that **sales** $(C + I)$ exceed **production** (Y). Business firms will experience an **unplanned inventory decumulation,** which will cause them to revise their production plans upward. National income will rise. When *Y* is above 900, desired saving exceeds desired investment, which means that $C + I < Y$ (or sales < production). Business firms will be unable to sell all they want; they will experience an unplanned inventory accumulation that will eventually force them to revise their production plans downward. National income will fall. Thus the national income equilibrium at *E* is indeed stable.

Note that the stability of the national income equilibrium is guaranteed by the fact that the marginal propensity to consume is less than 1. When $MPC < 1$, the saving schedule is positively sloped $(MPS > 0)$, as shown in Figure 15-1.

The Multiplier

Suppose now that desired investment rises from 200 to 250. What happens to the equilibrium level of national income? Apparently income will rise. But that is not the whole story. Income will not rise by just the increase in investment; it will rise by much more than the increase in investment. How can that be?

Return again to Figure 15-1. The increase in investment causes the investment schedule to shift upward, as shown by the dashed horizontal line. Equilibrium shifts to point *G*, where the saving schedule intersects the new investment schedule. National income increases by 150 (that is, 1,050 − 900), which is 3 times as large as the increase in investment. The number 3 is called the (closed economy) **multiplier.**

What determines the multiplier? Why is the multiplier greater than unity? To answer these questions, consider Figure 15-1 again. Note that as investment increases by ΔI, equilibrium is re-established only when national income rises sufficiently to generate additional saving, ΔS (leakage), to match precisely the autonomous increase in investment (injection). By how much should income increase? Because $\Delta S = MPS \times \Delta Y$, we must have

$$\Delta I = \Delta S = MPS \times \Delta Y \qquad \text{or} \qquad \Delta Y = \frac{1}{MPS}\Delta I$$

Therefore

$$\text{Multiplier} = \frac{\Delta Y}{\Delta I} = \frac{1}{MPS} \tag{15-3}$$

That is, **the multiplier is equal to the reciprocal of the marginal propensity to save.** Since $0 < MPS < 1$, it follows that the multiplier is higher than 1. In Figure 15-1, the marginal propensity to save is 1/3; therefore, the multiplier is 3.

The commonsense meaning of the multiplier is not difficult to capture. As businesses build more factories and buy more equipment, they generate extra income. This extra income goes to those factors (such as workers) who actually produce the additional factories and equipment. In turn, these income recipients, who find their incomes increased, spend part of their new revenues on consumption. How large their increase in consumption will be depends, of course, on their marginal propensity to consume. The crucial consideration, however, remains the fact that extra consumption means extra production and, therefore, extra income, which leads again to further consumption, and so on, ad infinitum. Thus national income does not rise just by the increase in investment; it rises by much more. When does this process end? When national income rises by the increase in investment times the multiplier.

15-2 INCOME DETERMINATION IN AN OPEN ECONOMY

This section extends the analysis of national income equilibrium to an open economy that is "small" in the sense that changes in its imports do not have any appreciable effect on total world income. This means that for the moment we shall ignore all foreign repercussions of induced changes in total world income.

Aggregate Absorption versus Aggregate Demand

In a closed economy, aggregate demand for the economy's output coincides with aggregate expenditure (or absorption) by the economy's residents. This is not so in an open economy. Accordingly, we must first clarify the distinction between **aggregate absorption** and **aggregate demand.**

First, consider aggregate absorption (or spending), which is simpler. As with the closed economy, aggregate absorption (Z) is the sum of consumption and investment expenditures; that is, $Z = C + I$. (When the government sector is included, Z must include government expenditure, G, as well; that is, $Z = C + I + G$). As before, we shall assume that desired investment is exogenous, while desired consumption depends on national income.

What is aggregate demand (D) for the open economy's aggregate output? When the economy is open, the aggregate demand is the sum of two major components: a domestic demand component plus a foreign demand component. The foreign demand component is merely the open economy's *exports (X)* to the rest of the world. The domestic demand component is that portion of aggregate absorption (Z) that is spent on domestic products.

The domestic demand component does not coincide with the economy's aggregate expenditure (Z) because part of that expenditure goes to purchase foreign products (imports). To arrive at the domestic demand component, we must subtract from Z the open economy's expenditure on imports; that is, domestic demand component $= Z - M$.

Thus the aggregate demand (D) for the open economy's output is equal to $D = Z + (X - M) = C + I + (X - M)$; that is, *$D$ equals the economy's aggregate absorption ($C + I$, or Z) plus the economy's balance of trade ($X - M$).*

Note that imports (M) act as "leakages," just like saving. Exports act as exogenous "injections" into the expenditure stream, just like investment. Because our present interest is with a "small" open economy, we take exports of goods and services as exogenous, like investment. Exports depend on foreign economic conditions that our open economy is too small to influence. Imports, however, depend positively on domestic national income. The important relationship between imports (M) and national income (Y) is known as the **import function.**

The Import Function

In general, an open economy imports goods and services from the rest of the world for two different reasons.

1 An open economy may import foreign goods for direct domestic consumption or investment. For instance, a country may import final consumption goods (such as food and clothing) as well as capital goods (such as machinery).

2 An open economy may also import raw materials (such as oil, steel, and lumber) for use as inputs into the domestic production of goods and services.

Each of these reasons provides some economic justification for the observed positive dependence of imports (M) on national income (Y).

Figure 15-2 illustrates a hypothetical import schedule. The desired level of imports (M) depends on the current level of national income (Y). The import schedule slopes upward because, in general, imports tend to increase as national income increases. For instance, when national income is 700, the desired level of imports is 75; when national income increases to 800, the desired level of imports increases to 85. Thus, as income increases by 100, imports increase by 10.

Of special significance is the ratio of the change in imports (ΔM) to the change in national income (ΔY); that is, $\Delta M/\Delta Y$. This ratio is known as the **marginal propensity to import** (MPM) and gives the extra amount of imports caused by a one-unit increase in national income. For instance, in Figure 15-2 imports increase by 10 when national income increases by 100. This means that the marginal propensity to import is 0.10; that is, for each dollar increase in national income ($\Delta Y = \$1$), the economy increases its spending on imports by 10 cents. The marginal propensity to import (MPM) is given graphically by the slope of the import function, as illustrated in Figure 15-2.

National Income Equilibrium

As with a closed economy, national income equilibrium in an open economy occurs when desired aggregate demand $C(Y) + \bar{I} + \bar{X} - M(Y)$ equals aggregate output Y. Or

FIGURE 15-2 **The import function.** When national income is 700, the desired level of imports is 75; and when national income increases to 800, the desired level of imports increases to 85. Thus, as income increases by 100, imports increase by 10. The ratio 10/100 is the *marginal propensity to import* (*MPM*); it is given graphically by the slope of the import function.

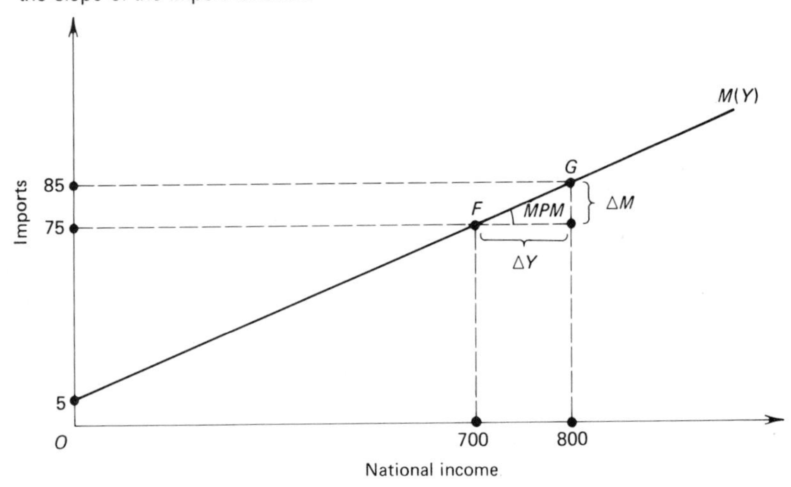

$$Y = C(Y) + \bar{I} + \bar{X} - M(Y) \tag{15-4}$$

In what follows, we find it more convenient to use Equation (15-4) in either of the following forms:

$$S(Y) - \bar{I} = \bar{X} - M(Y) \tag{15-5}$$

$$S(Y) + M(Y) = \bar{I} + \bar{X} \tag{15-6}$$

where saving function $S(Y)$ is given by the difference $Y - C(Y)$, as before. We obtain equation (15-5) by subtracting $C(Y) + \bar{I}$ from both sides of Equation (15-4). Next we obtain Equation (15-6) by adding $M(Y) + \bar{I}$ to both sides of Equation (15-5).

Mathematically, Equations (15-4), (15-5), and (15-6) are all equivalent. They all determine the same equilibrium level of national income. Equation (15-6) relates the endogenous leakages, $S(Y)$ and $M(Y)$, from the income stream to the exogenous injections, $\bar{I}$ and $\bar{X}$, into the income stream. National income equilibrium occurs when the injections match the leakages. Equation (15-5) relates the excess of saving over domestic investment (that is, the *net* domestic leakage) to the balance-of-trade surplus (that is, the *net* foreign injection), or the excess of domestic investment over saving (that is, the *net* domestic injection) to the balance-of-trade deficit (that is, the *net* foreign leakage). (The excess of saving over domestic investment is called **hoarding;** and the excess of investment over saving is called **dishoarding.**) The virtue of equation (15-5) is that it gives directly the balance-of-trade surplus or deficit.

Figure 15-3 illustrates the determination of national income equilibrium in a small open economy. The top panel gives the solution in terms of Equation (15-6). The lower panel gives the solution in terms of Equation (15-5). In both panels, the equilibrium level of income is Y_0.

In panel (*a*), we first add vertically exogenous exports $\bar{X}$ to exogenous investment $\bar{I}$ to obtain horizontal schedule $\bar{I} + \bar{X}$. We also add import function $M(Y)$ vertically to saving function $S(Y)$ to obtain upward-sloping schedule $S(Y) + M(Y)$. National income equilibrium occurs at intersection E of the $\bar{I} + \bar{X}$ schedule and the $S(Y) + M(Y)$ schedule. At that equilibrium point, the economy's saving S_0 and imports M_0 are given, respectively, by vertical distances Y_0G and GE. The economy's balance of trade is in deficit, as shown by vertical distance GF, which is equal to both $M_0 - \bar{X}$ and $\bar{I} - S_0$.

Note that the slope of the $S(Y) + M(Y)$ line is equal to the sum of the marginal propensity to save (*MPS*) plus the marginal propensity to import (*MPM*), that is, the sum of the individual slopes of the saving function and the import function. This observation becomes important in the next section, which deals with the foreign-trade multiplier.

In the lower panel, we arrive at national income equilibrium as follows. First, we subtract import function $M(Y)$ vertically from exogenous exports $\bar{X}$ to obtain downward-sloping schedule $\bar{X} - M(Y)$. We further subtract exogenous invest-

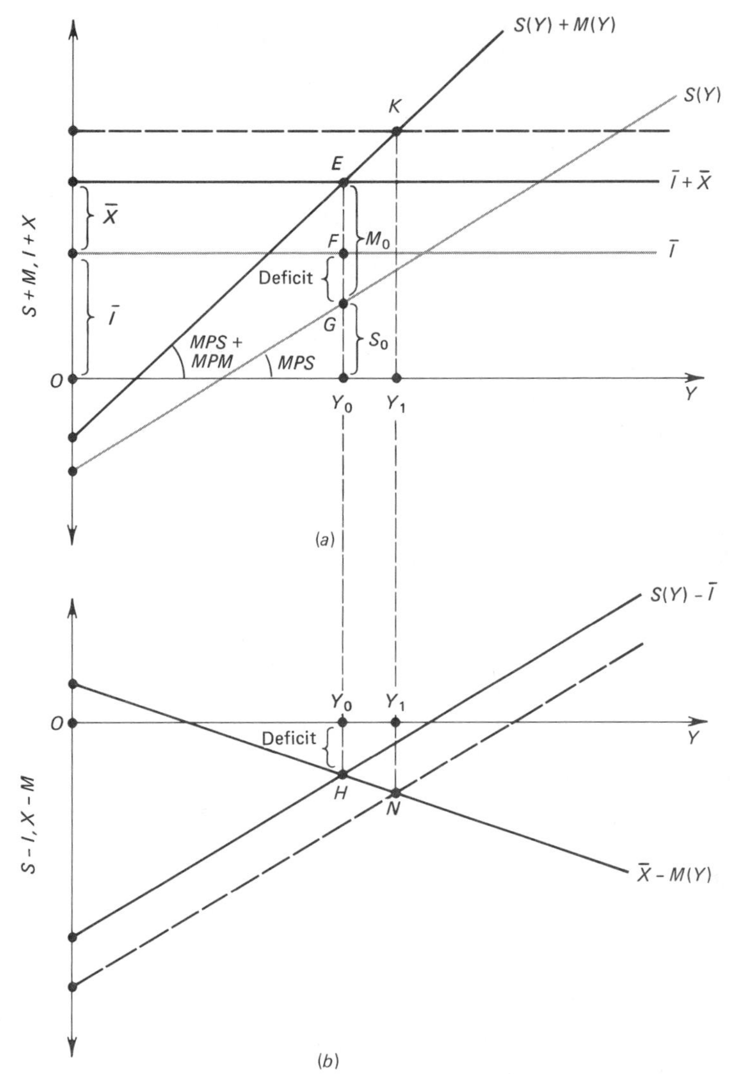

FIGURE 15-3 **National income equilibrium in a small, open economy.** In panel (*a*) we add exogenous exports $\bar{X}$ vertically to exogenous investment $\bar{I}$ to obtain horizontal schedule $\bar{I} + \bar{X}$. We also add import function $M(Y)$ vertically to saving function $S(Y)$ to obtain schedule $S(Y) + M(Y)$, whose slope gives the sum of the marginal propensity to save (*MPS*) plus the marginal propensity to import (*MPM*.) Equilibrium occurs at the intersection of the $\bar{I} + \bar{X}$ schedule and the $S(Y) + M(Y)$ schedule. In panel (*b*) we subtract import function $M(Y)$ vertically from exogenous exports, $\bar{X}$, to obtain downward-sloping schedule $\bar{X} - M(Y)$. We also subtract exogenous investment $\bar{I}$ vertically from saving function $S(Y)$ to obtain upward-sloping schedule $S(Y) - \bar{I}$. Equilibrium occurs at H, which is the intersection of schedules $\bar{X} - M(Y)$ and $S(Y) - \bar{I}$. In both panels, the equilibrium level of income is Y_0. The balance-of-trade deficit is given in panel (*a*) by distance $\overline{GF}$ and in panel (*b*) by distance HY_0, with $GF = HY_0$. An increase in investment ΔI causes the $\bar{I} + \bar{X}$ schedule in panel (*a*) to shift upward and the $S(Y) - \bar{I}$ schedule in panel (*b*) to shift downward, as illustrated by the dashed lines. National income increases to Y_1 in both panels, and the balance-of-trade deficit increases to NY_1, as shown in panel (*b*.)

ment $\bar{I}$ vertically from saving function $S(Y)$, that is, we shift the saving function downward by the amount of exogenous investment, to obtain upward-sloping schedule $S(Y) - \bar{I}$. National income equilibrium occurs at intersection H of the $\bar{X} - M(Y)$ schedule and the $S(Y) - \bar{I}$ schedule. Again national income is Y_0; and vertical distance HY_0 shows the balance-of-trade deficit that coincides with the deficit shown in the top panel.

Compare Figure 15-3 to Figure 15-1, and argue, as before, that national income equilibrium is "stable." That is, for levels of national income *below* Y_0, show that business firms will experience **involuntary inventory decumulation** and that they will revise their production plans upward, causing national income to *rise*. For levels of national income *above* Y_0, show that business firms will experience **involuntary inventory accumulation** and that they will revise their production plans downward, causing national income to *fall*. Only when national income is equal to Y_0 will the business firms be content with their production plans.

Note that the equilibrium level of income (Y_0) need not coincide with the full employment level of income. National income equilibrium may indeed coincide with widespread unemployment. Also there is no need for the balance of trade to be in equilibrium when national income is at its equilibrium level. The national income equilibrium condition, as illustrated by Equation 15-5, is *not* the same thing as the balance-of-trade equilibrium condition ($X - M = 0$). Therefore, national income equilibrium may coexist with balance-of-trade disequilibrium. This is actually the case in Figure 15-3.

15-3 THE FOREIGN-TRADE MULTIPLIER

How do exogenous disturbances, such as autonomous changes in domestic investment, exports, and imports, affect the open economy's national income and balance of trade? This section deals exclusively with that crucial question.

Derivation of the Foreign-Trade Multiplier

On the basis of the discussion of the closed economy in Section 15-1, it must be clear that any autonomous disturbance that causes aggregate demand $D = C(Y) + \bar{I} + \bar{X} - M(Y)$ to change by, say, ΔD, must also cause national income to change. In particular, the change in national income (ΔY) must be a *multiple* of the change in aggregate demand, ΔD. The ratio $\Delta Y/\Delta D$ is the **open-economy multiplier,** also known as the **foreign-trade multiplier.**

We have seen that national income equilibrium occurs when the leakages, $S(Y) + M(Y)$, out of the income stream exactly match the exogenous injections, $\bar{I} + \bar{X}$, into the income stream. When an exogenous disturbance causes aggregate demand to increase by ΔD at *every* level of income, there emerges, at the *initial* level of income, an excess of autonomous injections over leakages equal to the autonomous increase in aggregate demand. Equilibrium is restored when an increase in income ΔY *induces* the leakages, $S(Y) + M(Y)$, to increase by ΔD, so that total endogenous leakages equal total exogenous injections once again. For any change in income ΔY, the leakages change by $(MPS + MPM)\Delta Y$. (Recall that MPS stands for the marginal propensity to save, and MPM for the marginal propensity to import.) Accordingly, national income equilibrium is restored when

$$\Delta D = (MPS + MPM)\Delta Y \tag{15-7}$$

A simple rearrangement of Equation (15-7) gives:

$$\text{Foreign-trade multiplier} = \frac{\Delta Y}{\Delta D} = \frac{1}{MPS + MPM} \tag{15-8}$$

The foreign-trade multiplier is smaller than the closed economy multiplier. This result is mathematically trivial because

$$\frac{1}{MPS} > \frac{1}{MPS + MPM}$$

What is the commonsense explanation for this result? The obvious reason is that the open economy has an extra leakage for imports. But there is a deeper reason. From the point of view of the world economy as a whole, imports are *not* a leakage—only saving is a leakage. The world is indeed a closed economy! As autonomous spending increases in our economy, a new equilibrium is established only when a corresponding amount of saving is generated in the world economy. But whereas in a closed economy the additional saving is generated only at home, in an open economy the additional saving is generated both at home and abroad. Thus the increase in the closed economy's national income must be larger than the income increase of a corresponding open economy because the closed economy must generate more saving than the open economy.

The Balance-of-Trade Effect

An exogenous disturbance may have two effects on the balance of trade:

1 *Autonomous effect:* The disturbance may originate in the foreign sector and thus affect the balance of trade directly (or autonomously). This **autonomous effect** occurs when either exports or imports change autonomously (at each level of income), as explained below.

2 *Induced effect:* Whether it originates in the foreign sector or not, a disturbance also *induces* a further change in the balance of trade through its effect on national income. This **induced effect** occurs when a disturbance causes the aggregate demand to change by, say ΔD, which in turn causes national income to change (by a multiple of ΔD); and the change in income (ΔY) induces a change in imports ($MPM \times \Delta Y$).

The overall effect of a disturbance on the balance of trade is the sum of the autonomous effect (if any) and the induced effect. When a disturbance originates in the foreign sector the induced effect tends to work against the autonomous effect; thus the overall balance-of-trade effect of the disturbance is much smaller than its initial direct (or autonomous) effect. In other words, the **national income adjustment mechanism is a powerful stabilizing mechanism of the balance of payments.**

Specific Illustrations

To gain further insight into the above propositions, we now turn to concrete examples. In particular, we wish to consider briefly the effects on national income and the balance of trade of the following disturbances:

1 An increase in desired investment
2 An increase in exports
3 A decrease in imports

Throughout our discussion, we assume that the marginal propensity to save is 0.10 and that the marginal propensity to import is 0.15. Therefore, the foreign-trade multiplier is $1/(0.10 + 0.15) = 4$. In all examples, we assume that the open economy's national income is in equilibrium before the disturbance.

1 An Increase in Desired Investment Suppose that domestic investment increases by $100 million. Determine the effect on national income and the balance of trade.

Since the foreign-trade multiplier is 4, the increase in national income must be $4 \times \$100 = \$400$ (million).

In terms of Figure 15-3, the increase in investment, ΔI, causes the $\bar{I} + \bar{X}$ curve—panel (*a*)—to shift upward by ΔI, as illustrated by the dashed schedule. Alternatively, in the lower panel, the increase in investment ΔI causes the $S(Y) - \bar{I}$ schedule to shift downward, as shown again by the dashed schedule. Equilibrium shifts from E to K in the top panel and from H to N in the lower panel. The increase in national income, ΔY, is the same in both panels, as it should be.

The increase in investment causes the balance of trade to deteriorate. In the present case there is only the induced effect. (The autonomous effect is missing because the change in investment does not affect the balance of trade directly.) The increase in investment causes imports to increase by

$$MPM \times \Delta Y = 0.15 \times \$400 = \$60 \text{ (million)}$$

This is illustrated in Figure 15-3, panel (*b*), by the fact that distance NY_1 is greater than distance HY_0.

2 An Increase in Exports Suppose that exports increase by $100 (million). Determine the effect on national income and the balance of trade.

The effect on national income is again equal to 4 × \$100 = \$400 (million). The balance-of-trade effect consists now of the autonomous effect (that is, the increase in exports by \$100 million) plus the induced effect (that is, the increase in imports induced by the increase in income). Thus,

$$\begin{aligned}\text{Balance-of-trade effect} &= \Delta X - \Delta M \\ &= \Delta X - MPM \times \Delta Y \\ &= \$100 - (0.15 \times \$400) = \$100 - \$60 = \$40 \text{ (million)}\end{aligned}$$

Note that the overall improvement in the balance of trade (that is, \$40 million) is much smaller than the initial autonomous effect (that is, \$100 million). This is an important result, and it confirmes our earlier conclusion that the income-adjustment mechanism acts as a powerful stabilizing mechanism.

The preceding result is illustrated in Figure 15-4, which is similar to Figure 15-3, panel (*b*). National income equilibrium occurs initially at *E*, where the $S(Y) - \bar{I}$ schedule intersects the $\bar{X} - M(Y)$ schedule. The balance of trade is zero: point *E* lies on the horizontal axis. Exports increase autonomously by *EH*, causing the $\bar{X} - M(Y)$ schedule to shift upward, as shown by the dashed schedule. Equilibrium shifts to *F*. Note that the final balance-of-trade improvement, shown by distance *GF*, is necessarily smaller than the initial, autonomous improvement, shown by distance *EH*.

FIGURE 15-4 **Effects of an increase in exports.** Equilibrium occurs initially at *E*, where the balance of trade is zero. Exports increase by *EH* and cause the $\bar{X} - M(Y)$ schedule to shift upward, as shown by the dashed line. Equilibrium shifts to *F*. The final balance-of-trade improvement (*GF*) is smaller than the initial improvement (*EH*.)

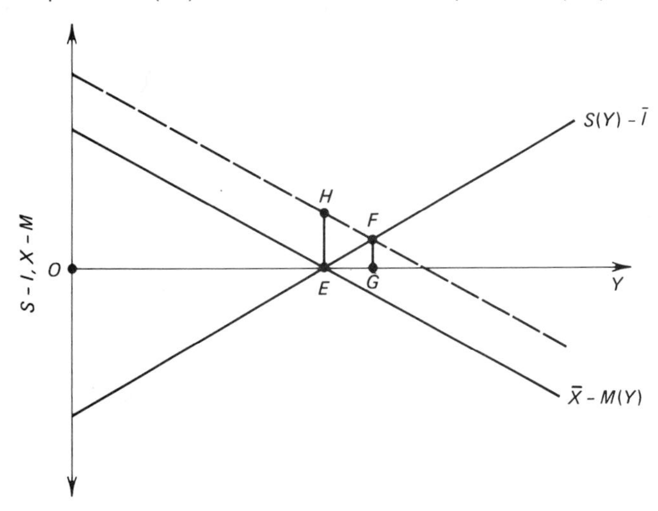

3 A Decrease in Imports Suppose that the open economy imposes a tariff and thus causes domestic consumers to divert \$100 (million) of their consumption expenditures from foreign to domestic products. Determine the effect on national income and the balance of trade.

The shift from foreign to domestic products causes the aggregate demand for domestic output to rise by the decrease in imports (\$100 million). Thus, national income increases by $4 \times \$100 = \$400$ (million).

The overall balance-of-trade improvement is again less than the initial autonomous reduction in imports. This is due to the increase in national income, which induces an increase in imports equal to $MPM \times \Delta Y = 0.15 \times \$400 = \$60$ (million). Accordingly, the overall balance-of-trade improvement is only $\$100 - \$60 = \$40$ (million). Figure 15-4 illustrates this case also.

15-4 DEVALUATION: ABSORPTION VERSUS ELASTICITIES

How does devaluation affect the balance of trade? In Chapter 14, Section 14-4, we discussed this issue in the context of the partial equilibrium model, also known as the **elasticities approach.** According to this approach, the balance of trade (T) is the difference between the value of exports (X) and the value of imports (that is, $T = X - M$); and devaluation improves the balance of trade when the **Marshall-Lerner condition** is satisfied (that is, when the sum of the import-demand elasticities, in absolute terms, is greater than unity).

But the balance of trade is also equal to the difference between national income (Y) and absorption (Z); that is, $T = Y - Z$. This point was emphasized by Alexander (1952), who claimed that under conditions of full employment devaluation can improve the balance of trade only through reduction in absorption (Z); hence the elasticities play no role! Initially, the **absorption approach** was thought to be at odds with the elasticities approach. Later it was realized that this impression is misleading; the two approaches are complementary to each other, not rival.

The difference between income and absorption is equal to the difference between saving and investment: $Y - Z = Y - C - I = S - I$. We already know that the $S - I$ schedule is insufficient to determine either national income, Y, or the balance of trade, T. For this purpose, we must also add the $X - M$ schedule, as in Figure 15-4. The elasticities approach focuses on the $X - M$ schedule; the absorption approach concentrates on the $S - I$ schedule. Both blades of the analytical scissors are needed.

Consider Figure 15-5. Equilibrium occurs initially at E_0, where the balance of trade registers a deficit equal to E_0Y_0. Suppose that the open economy devalues its currency. Assuming that the Marshall-Lerner condition is satisfied, the devaluation will have a favorable **autonomous effect** on the balance of trade, as illustrated by E_0H. *This autonomous effect is provided by the elasticities approach.* The $\overline{X} - M(Y)$ schedule shifts upward, as shown by the dashed line. Equilibrium shifts to E_1. National income increases by Y_0Y_1. The increase in national income induces an additional flow of imports; hence the final improvement is

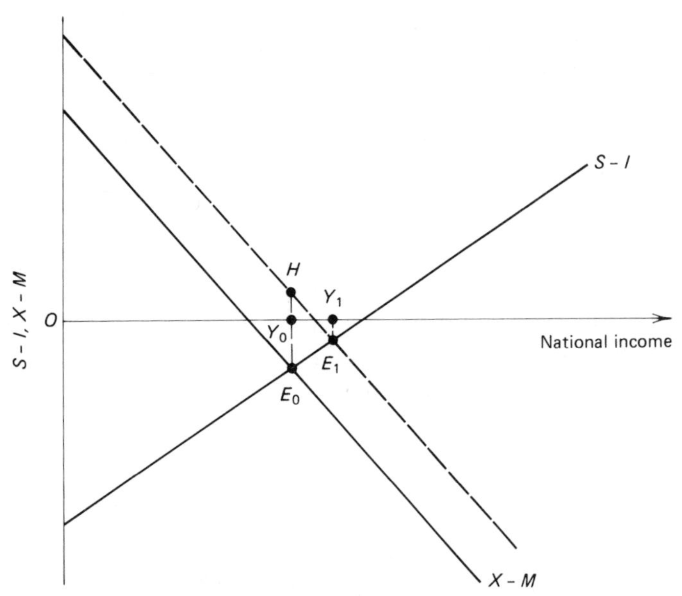

FIGURE 15-5 **The effects of devaluation.** Starting from an initial equilibrium at E_0, a devaluation shifts the $X - M$ schedule upward (see dashed line through E_1), causing national income to increase to Y_1 and the deficit to fall to E_1Y_1.

smaller than the initial autonomous improvement, $E_0 H$. Note that as national income increases, absorption increases also, and the final balance of trade improvement is necessarily equal to $\Delta Y - \Delta Z$, or ΔS (because I is exogenous). Thus, there is no contradiction between the elasticities approach and the absorption approach.

15-5 POLICY MIX FOR INTERNAL AND EXTERNAL BALANCE

This section deals with the problem of how to apply two **policy instruments** (government spending and exchange-rate adjustments) in order to simultaneously achieve full employment (**internal balance**) and balance-of-trade equilibrium (**external balance**). Throughout our discussion, we assume that the Marshall-Lerner condition is satisfied.

Attaining Internal and External Balance

Consider Figure 15-6. External balance prevails when the balance of trade is zero. This occurs only along the "heavy" horizontal axis which we call the **external balance schedule.** If a nonzero balance happened to be the target, external balance would occur along a horizontal line whose height would be determined by the size of the desired deficit or surplus. There is no qualitative

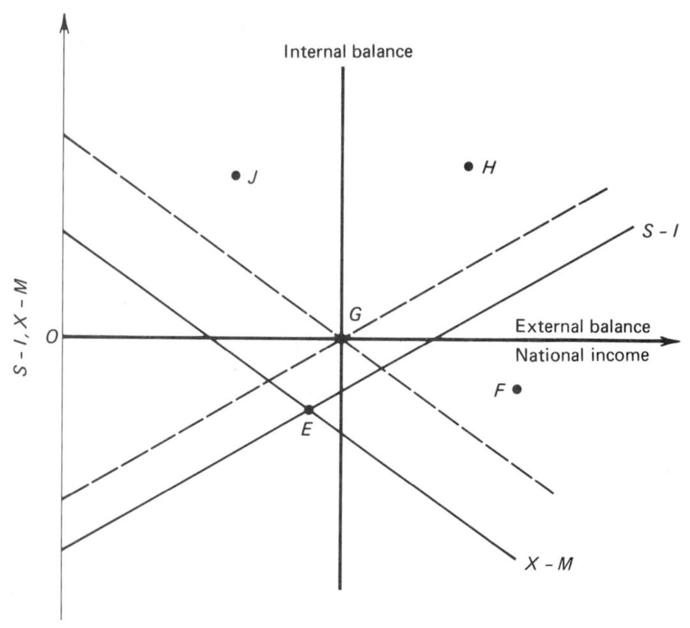

FIGURE 15-6 **Policies for internal and external balance.** External balance prevails along the "heavy" horizontal axis. Assuming that *OG* is the full-employment income, internal balance prevails along the "heavy" vertical line through *G*. Internal and external balance prevail simultaneously at point *G* only. To achieve general balance, the authorities must choose that policy mix which causes the $S - I$ and $X - M$ schedules to pass through point *G*, as illustrated by the dashed lines.

difference in policy-making between the case of aiming at a balance-of-trade surplus or deficit and the case of aiming at a zero balance. Assume that full employment (internal balance) exists when national income is *OG*. This occurs along the heavy vertical line through *G*, which we call the **internal balance schedule.** Evidently, internal and external balance occur simultaneously at the intersection, *G*, of the internal and external balance schedules.

Suppose that equilibrium occurs initially at the intersection, *E*, of the $S - I$ and $X - M$ schedules. Thus the open economy suffers from unemployment and a trade deficit. How can the open economy simultaneously attain internal and external balance? By means of a policy mix that will cause both the $S - I$ and $X - M$ schedules to pass through point *G*, as illustrated by the dashed lines. The correct policy mix is a *cut* in government spending combined with a *devaluation* of the domestic currency. The reduction in government spending is similar to a decrease in investment; it shifts the $S - I$ schedule upward, as shown. The devaluation shifts the $X - M$ schedule upward, as shown.

Question: What policy mixes can restore internal and external balance when the economy starts from an initial equilibrium position at points *F*, *H*, or *J*?

The Trade Deficit of the United States Again

As noted in Section 14-6, the U.S. dollar has experienced sharp depreciation since 1985. Yet the U.S. balance-of-trade deficit has persisted, even though the Marshall-Lerner condition seems to be satisfied (see Table 14-1). (Recall also that we ruled out the J-curve effect as a possible explanation for this paradoxical phenomenon; see Section 14-6.) Can the present analysis shed any light on this puzzle? We believe it can.

Figure 15-6 seems to illustrate the case of the United States during the late 1980s. While the depreciation of the dollar may have caused the $X - M$ schedule to shift upward, the $S - I$ schedule may have shifted downward because of the failure of the Reagan administration to reduce the federal budget deficit. Thus starting from a point such as *E*, the U.S. economy could not move to general balance point *G*. That would require a cut in government spending or an increase in taxes (or a combination of lower government spending and increased taxes) in order to shift the $I - S$ schedule upward and make it pass through point *G*. *Without a drastic reduction in the federal budget deficit, there can be no substantial improvement in the U.S. balance of trade.*

Tinbergen's Rule

The preceding discussion illustrates an important principle known as **Tinbergen's rule:** *To achieve* n *policy targets, we must apply* n *independent policy instruments*. For instance, to achieve two targets, such as internal and external balance, we need two policy instruments, such as an expenditure-adjusting policy and an expenditure-switching policy. These two instruments are independent: each affects a different schedule. Thus the expenditure-adjusting policy affects the location of the $S - I$ schedule only; the expenditure-switching policy influences the position of the $X - M$ schedule only. As shown, a judicious mix of government spending (expenditure-adjusting policy) and exchange-rate adjustment (expenditure-switching policy) can bring about internal and external balance.

15-6 FOREIGN REPERCUSSIONS

In our discussion so far, we have assumed that imports are a leakage, while exports are given exogenously on the argument that exports depend on events that occur in the rest of the world. This assumption works well for a "small" country, whose exports and imports of goods and services are actually negligible fractions of total world output. For a "large" country, such as the United States, whose exports and imports of goods and services are respectable percentages of world income, our analysis needs drastic modification.

A country's imports are the exports of the rest of the world. Similarly, a country's exports are the imports of the rest of the world. Accordingly, an open economy is economically interdependent with the rest of the world; we cannot ignore this interdependence, especially when the open economy is large. In a large country economic events, such as investment booms or recessions, influence the economies of other nations; similarly, such events occurring in the rest of the world exert an influence on an open economy. As the saying goes, when America sneezes, Europe and Japan catch cold (and nowadays vice versa). This was illustrated vividly by the great depression of the 1930s. The sharp reduction in U.S. national income, which was caused by a severe decline in U.S. investment, induced a large decline in U.S. imports (that is, foreign exports) and threw the world economy into a tailspin.

As should be expected, foreign repercussions give rise to rather complicated multiplier formulas, which are best derived separately (see Appendix 16).

15-7 MACROECONOMIC INTERDEPENDENCE IN THE REAL WORLD

Table 15-1 presents some estimates of macroeconomic interdependence among the seven major OECD (Organization for Economic Co-operation and Development) countries: the United States, Japan, Germany, France, the United Kingdom, Italy, and Canada. These estimates are those reported for the Japanese EPA (Economic Planning Agency) World Econometric model; they are based on the assumption that both the exchange rates and the domestic interest rates are fixed.

The numbers in Table 15-1 are not exactly comparable to the foreign-trade multipliers derived in Appendix 16. They show only *second-year* effects of fiscal policy rather than the full multiplier effects. In addition, they include certain other effects, such as price changes caused by income changes. Nevertheless, these estimates are indicative of the degree of macroeconomic interdependence among the seven OECD countries.

How do we interpret Table 15-1? All numbers in this table measure percentage changes in real gross national product (GNP). The autonomous increase in expenditure

TABLE 15-1 MACROECONOMIC INTERDEPENDENCE AMONG SEVEN OECD COUNTRIES, 1974–1977
(Percentage Change in Real GNP)

Country where government spending changes (1)	Effect on income in: Canada (2)	France (3)	Germany (4)	Italy (5)	Japan (6)	United Kingdom (7)	United States (8)
Canada	(1.97)	0.06	0.06	0.05	0.06	0.07	0.06
France	0.05	(3.02)	0.24	0.19	0.05	0.21	0.01
Germany	0.12	0.66	(1.98)	0.42	0.14	0.34	0.02
Italy	0.08	0.43	0.30	(1.39)	0.08	0.15	−0.02
Japan	0.12	0.11	0.11	0.08	(2.17)	0.15	0.02
United Kingdom	0.11	0.30	0.23	0.15	0.09	(0.78)	0.02
United States	0.83	0.27	0.25	0.20	0.33	0.56	(2.60)

Source: Adapted from Helliwell and Padmore (1985, Table 3.1). The estimates are second-year effects of fiscal policy reported for the Japanese EPA World Econometric model.

in any of the seven countries is always set equal to 1 percent of that country's GNP. For instance, suppose that the United States, the last country in column (1), increases its government spending by 1 percent of its GNP. The effects on the real gross national products of the seven countries are given across the last line of figures. Thus Canadian real income rises by 0.83 percent, as shown in the column for Canada, that is, column (2); French real income rises by 0.27 percent, as shown in column (3); German real income increases by 0.25 percent; and so on. Similarly the effects of an increase in spending by the Canadian government are given across the first line; by the French government, across the second line; and so on.

The own-country effects are circled for easy identification. They are larger than the cross-country effects. But some cross-country effects are strong, especially those of U.S. fiscal policy. Evidently macroeconomic interdependence is not insignificant.

15-8 DIRECT CONTROLS

Exchange-rate adjustments are *general* switching policies that influence the balance of payments indirectly, that is, through their effects on national income and the price mechanism. Their primary aim is to divert (or switch) expenditure, *both domestically and in the rest of the world,* from foreign goods to domestic goods.

This section deals with **direct controls,** that is, *selective* expenditure-switching policies, whose aim is to control particular elements in the balance of payments. Usually direct controls are imposed on *imports* in an attempt to switch *domestic* expenditure away from foreign goods to home goods. Less common is the use of controls to stimulate *exports* by switching *foreign* spending to domestic products. (Controls may also be imposed on capital flows in an effort to either curb excessive capital outflows or induce capital inflows.) Direct controls are classified into **fiscal controls, commercial controls,** and **monetary controls.**

Fiscal Controls

Fiscal controls include all taxes and subsidies that affect particular items in the balance of payments—usually the exports and imports of merchandise. The reason is simple: Merchandise exports and imports lend themselves more readily to the fiscal devices of taxes and subsidies. Invisible balance-of-payments items, such as tourist expenditure, are more difficult to cover by fiscal controls. Indeed, in the case of capital movements, fiscal controls tend to break down completely unless they are reinforced by an effective system of exchange control.

The most prominent fiscal devices are the import tax and the export subsidy. The object of the import tax is to switch domestic expenditure from imports to domestic output. Similarly, the object of an export subsidy is to stimulate exports by switching foreign spending to domestic output.

An important feature of direct controls, as opposed to general switching policies (such as exchange-rate adjustment), is their flexibility in operating differently on exports and imports of particular commodities or on exports to, and imports from, particular countries. For instance, export subsidies and import taxes are not normally levied indiscriminately on all imports or on all exports. Different ad valorem import duties may be levied on different commodities (for example, 20 percent on oil but 50 percent on cameras). Also, different ad valorem import duties may be levied on the same commodity imported from different countries (for example, 10 percent on cameras imported from Germany but 60 percent on cameras imported from Japan). This flexibility of direct controls enhances their effectiveness as an instrument of balance-of-payments adjustment.

Note that insofar as commodity trade is concerned, an x percent depreciation (or devaluation) of the domestic currency is equivalent to an x percent ad valorem tax on all imports plus an x percent ad valorem subsidy to all exports.

Commercial Controls

Commercial controls are quantitative restrictions on the physical volume or value of imports or exports. The most common commercial device is the import quota. Recall from Chapter 9 that when the government, for one reason or another, desires to control directly the volume (or value) of imports, it may decree that only a given quantity (**import quota**) may be imported per unit of time. Similarly when a country desires to control directly the volume (or value) of exports, it may decree that only a given quantity (**export quota**) may be exported per unit of time. Typically, import and export quotas are administered through a system of import and export licenses, which the government either sells to importers and exporters at a competitive price (or a license fee) or just gives away on a first-come, first-served basis.

Imports may also be restricted by means of a **tariff quota.** Under this scheme a certain amount of the commodity is imported free of any duty (or is imported on payment of a low import duty), while a heavier import duty is imposed on additional quantities. Thus, the ordinary tariff is a special case of the tariff quota, in which the quota part is zero. Similarly, the ordinary import quota is a special case of the tariff quota in which the import duty on any quantities greater than the quota amount is prohibitively high.

Monetary Controls

A deficit country may attempt to solve its balance-of-payments problem by means of **exchange control,** that is, by arbitrarily *rationing* the limited supply of foreign exchange among all potential buyers at the prevailing rate of exchange. For this purpose, the deficit country may establish an **exchange control authority.** Then the deficit country may proceed to require by law that all citizens who receive payment from abroad must sell their foreign currency to the exchange control authority at the official rate and that all citizens who make payments abroad must buy the foreign currency they need from the exchange control authority at the official rate.

The administration of an effective system of exchange control is not an easy matter. An elaborate bureaucratic machinery is required to oversee *all* foreign exchange dealings. Both exporters and importers have an interest in evading the law—a situation that often leads to **black markets,** where the domestic currency is traded against foreign exchange at depreciated rates. An elaborate **postal control** is also needed to prevent foreign exchange transactions by mail. Tourists and other travelers cannot be allowed to carry currency out of, or into, the country, except in limited amounts. Similarly, all barter transactions must be banned. For this reason, an extensive bureaucratic inquiry at the ports is needed to determine the way all imports and exports are financed. Further, the exchange control authority must make sure that licensed importers actually use their foreign exchange allotment for the legal purpose for which it is approved. Importers cannot be allowed to overstate the price of imported goods and then use the surplus of foreign exchange for illegal purposes. Also, exporters cannot be permitted to declare an artificially low price for the exported commodities. Finally, transfers between **nonresident accounts** (that is, accounts with the domestic banking system held by foreigners, which are freely convertible) and **resident accounts** (that is, accounts with the domestic banking system held by domestic residents, which are not convertible) must also be controlled. Domestic importers cannot be allowed to pay for their imports by means of a transfer to nonresident accounts, unless such a transfer is consistent with the objectives of the exchange control. Similarly, exporters who are paid by means of a transfer from nonresident to resident accounts, and therefore have no foreign exchange to surrender to the exchange control authority, must provide proof that they were actually paid by means of such a transfer. Nevertheless, such measures can never plug all loopholes. For instance, how can the exchange control authority prevent all **leads and lags** in international payments?

The preceding discussion assumes that all foreign exchange transactions with the exchange control authority are carried out at a single official rate of exchange. But there is no logical necessity for a uniform rate. The exchange control authority may establish different rates for different transactions. For instance, it may set relatively high rates for imported luxury goods and relatively low rates for necessities. Similar arrangements may be established for different classes of exports. A system of **multiple exchange rates** is equivalent to a system of trade taxes and subsidies.

Imports may also be discouraged by requiring importers to deposit funds in a commercial bank in an amount equal to some specified percentage of the value of the imported goods for some specified period prior to the receipt of the goods. Such **advance-deposit requirements,** as they are known, impose an additional cost on importers, who must tie up their funds or borrow the necessary amount. Hence, the requirements are similar to import taxes. One important reason for the adoption of this device is the comparative ease with which it can be administered, especially when international agreements hamper manipulation of other direct controls.

15-9 SWITCHING POLICIES DURING THE GREAT DEPRESSION

During the 1930s, the years of the great depression, countries sought to at least partially solve their problem of domestic unemployment by diverting expenditure from foreign products toward their own domestic products. For this purpose, countries used a whole arsenal of policy weapons. Such measures are now known as **switching policies** because they *switch* expenditure away from the products of one country and channel it toward the products of another country. These switching policies can range from devaluation and tariff and nontariff barriers to international trade to mere political propaganda, which may take the form of such slogans as "Buy American," "Buy French," "Buy British," and so on.

The distinguishing feature of expenditure-switching policies is that they primarily affect the aggregate demand for the products of the country pursuing such policies *through changes in the country's balance of trade.* Such policies tend to expand domestic income and employment at the expense of foreign incomes and employment. In effect, the country adopting an expenditure-switching policy is exporting unemployment to the rest of the world. For this reason, expenditure-switching policies are usually referred to as **beggar-thy-neighbor** policies. When all countries suffer from the same ills, beggar-thy-neighbor policies usually provoke retaliation. Thus, as soon as one country succeeds in increasing its balance of trade, other countries retaliate, with the result that the volume of international trade relative to world activity continually shrinks. Political, strategic, and sentimental considerations add fuel to the fire, and the flames of economic nationalism blaze ever higher and higher.

Figure 15-7 vividly illustrates the contracting spiral of world trade. In January 1929, the total monthly imports of 75 countries, valued in terms of the old U.S. gold dollars, stood at $2,998 million. By January 1933, the same total had spiraled down to only $992 million—a whopping reduction of 67 percent.

The strong theoretical justification for free trade is based fundamentally on the assumption of full employment. In the presence of severe unemployment, the argument for free trade seems suspect. During the great depression of the 1930s, the main concern was not with the possibility that some resources were not optimally allocated. The problem was that a large portion of the economic resources were not allocated at all! Under these circumstances, the first order of business was to increase the level of employment. Improving the allocation of resources was less of a problem. Because aggregate-demand management was not well developed at that time, countries sought to solve their problem of severe unemployment by means of expenditure-switching policies, such as tariffs and devaluations. Such policies prompted, of course, an avalanche of foreign retaliation that led to the competitive devaluations of the early 1930s.

15-10 SUMMARY

1 In a closed economy, national income equilibrium occurs when desired aggregate spending, $C(Y) + \bar{I}$, equals national income, Y; that is, $Y = C(Y) + \bar{I}$. Alternatively, national income equilibrium occurs when the leakages, $S(Y)$, are

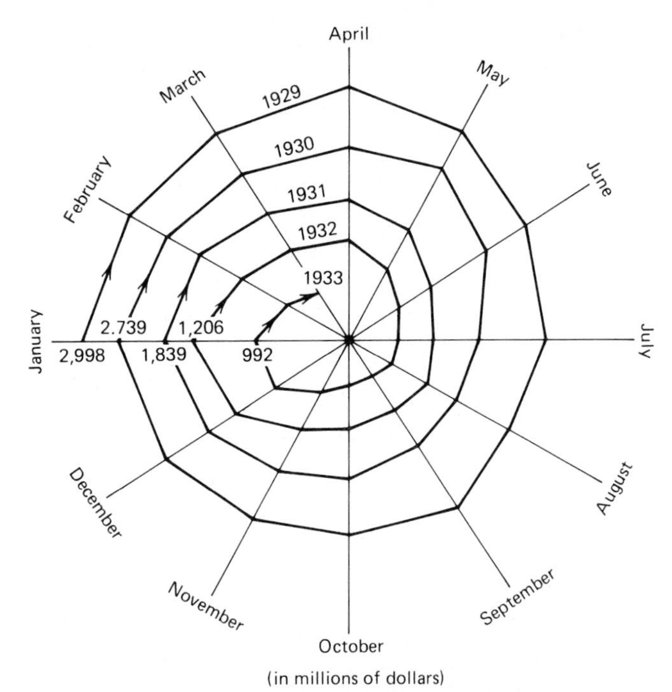

FIGURE 15-7 **The contracting spiral of world trade, January 1929 to March 1933.** This diagram illustrates the behavior of the total monthly imports of 75 countries valued in terms of millions of old U.S. gold dollars. (*From C.P. Kindleberger,* The World in Depression 1929-1939, *1975, p. 172, © 1986 by The Regents of the University of California.*)

equal to injections ($\bar{I}$); that is, $S(Y) = \bar{I}$. Because the marginal propensity to consume is less than 1, equilibrium is stable.

2 The closed economy multiplier is equal to the reciprocal of the marginal propensity to save (MPS). Since MPS < 1, the multiplier is higher than 1.

3 Aggregate demand for an open economy's output equals the economy's aggregate absorption ($Z = C + I$) plus its balance of trade ($T = X - M$).

4 The marginal propensity to import (that is, the ratio of the change in imports to the change in national income) is given graphically by the slope of the import schedule.

5 In a "small" open economy, national income equilibrium prevails when aggregate output equals desired aggregate demand, that is, when $Y = C(Y) + \bar{I} + \bar{X} - M(Y)$. The last equation can take either of the following forms: (a) $S(Y) + M(Y) = \bar{I} + \bar{X}$ (that is, leakages equal injections) or (b) $\bar{X} - M(Y) = S(Y) - \bar{I}$ (that is, the balance of trade equals excess saving).

6 National income equilibrium may coexist with a balance-of-trade disequilibrium ($X - M \neq 0$) or unemployment or both.

7 The foreign-trade multiplier without foreign repercussions (''small'' open economy) is given by $1/(MPS + MPM)$.

8 The overall effect of a disturbance on the balance of trade is the sum of two effects: (a) the induced effect (which works through national income and the resultant change in imports) plus (b) the autonomous effect (which exists only when the disturbance originates in the foreign sector and results in a change in exports or imports at the *initial* level of national income).

9 The induced effect of a disturbance that originates in the foreign sector tends to work against the autonomous effect with the result that the overall balance-of-trade effect is much smaller than the initial autonomous effect. (This is true both in the presence and absence of foreign repercussions.) Thus, the national income adjustment mechanism is a powerful stabilizing mechanism of the balance of payments.

10 Full employment (internal balance) and balance-of-payments equilibrium (external balance) are policy objectives (or targets) that must be pursued by means of deliberate economic policy measures.

11 The policy approach takes the targets as given and solves for the required values of the instruments, such as government spending and the exchange rate. To achieve n targets, we need at least n independent and effective instruments (Tinbergen's rule).

12 In a fixed price model, full employment (internal balance) and balance-of-trade equilibrium (external balance) can be achieved simultaneously by a combination of expenditure-adjusting and expenditure-switching policies.

13 The commonsense rule for policy-making—namely, that the authorities should increase (decrease) government spending in the presence of unemployment (inflation) and devalue (revalue) in the presence of an external deficit (surplus)—does not always work.

14 For a ''large'' country, it is necessary to take into account foreign income repercussions, which give rise to rather complicated multiplier formulas.

15 Expenditure-switching policies (also known as beggar-thy-neighbor policies) switch (that is, divert) expenditure from the products of one country to the products of another country. When all countries suffer from the same ills, beggar-thy-neighbor policies provoke retaliation.

16 General switching policies (such as exchange-rate adjustments) switch expenditure, both domestically and in the rest of the world, from foreign goods to domestic goods.

17 Direct controls are selective expenditure-switching policies whose aim is to control particular elements in the balance of payments. They are divided into fiscal controls (such as import taxes and export subsidies), commercial controls (mainly quotas), and monetary controls (such as exchange control, multiple exchange rates, and advance-deposit requirements).

18 An important feature of direct controls is their flexibility in operating differently on exports and imports of particular commodities or on exports to, and imports from, particular countries. This flexibility of direct controls enhances their effectiveness as an instrument of balance-of-payments adjustment.

PROBLEMS[1]

1 You are given the following information about the home country (say, Sweden):

$$C = 50 + 0.7Y \qquad \text{(consumption function)}$$

$$M = 10 + 0.2Y \qquad \text{(import function)}$$

$$X = 200 \qquad \text{(exports)}$$

$$I = 100 \qquad \text{(investment)}$$

a Determine Sweden's equilibrium level of national income.
b Determine Sweden's saving, consumption, imports, and balance of trade at the equilibrium you determined in part *a* of this problem.
c Show that at the equilibrium you determined in part *a*, $S - I = X - M$.
d Illustrate your results graphically.

2 Suppose that Korea's marginal propensity to consume is 0.90 and its marginal propensity to import is 0.15.
a What is Korea's foreign-trade multiplier?
b Suppose that Korea switches spending of $1,000 from foreign to domestic goods. What are the precise effects on Korea's national income, balance of trade, saving, consumption, and imports?
c Suppose that Korea's autonomous investment increases by $500. What are the precise effects on Korea's national income, balance of trade, saving, consumption, and imports?

3 Suppose that Italy's marginal propensities to save and import are 0.2 and 0.3, respectively. Full employment is attained when Italy's national income reaches $400 billion. Italy's exports and investment remain fixed at $60 billion and $80 billion, respectively. Italy's autonomous consumption and autonomous imports are $30 billion and $20 billion, respectively. External balance occurs when the balance of trade is zero.
a What is Italy's foreign-trade multiplier?
b Show graphically Italy's internal and external balance schedules.
c Determine Italy's equilibrium level of national income and balance-of-trade deficit or surplus. Illustrate your results graphically.
d Suppose that every percentage point of devaluation of the lira (Italy's currency) results in a $4 billion balance-of-trade improvement. What precise policy mix should Italy pursue in order to attain internal and external balance simultaneously?

*4 Consider a model of two countries, America (home country) and Britain (foreign country). America's marginal propensities to consume and import are $3/4$ and $1/12$, respectively. The corresponding propensities in Britain are $4/5$ and $1/20$. Investment is exogenous in both countries.
a Determine America's and Britain's foreign-trade multipliers *without* foreign repercussions.
b Determine America's and Britain's foreign-trade multipliers *with* foreign repercussions.

[1] Problems that appear with asterisks are more difficult.

c Suppose that America's investment rises by $100 billion. What are the effects on the national incomes of America and Britain? What is the effect on America's balance of trade?

d Suppose that America removes a tariff; as a result, America diverts $100 billion from home products to British products. What are the effects on national incomes and America's balance of trade?

SUGGESTED READING

Alexander, S. S. (1952). "Effects of a Devaluation on a Trade Balance." *IMF Staff Papers,* vol. 2 (April), pp. 263–278. Reprinted in R. E. Caves and H. G. Johnson (eds.), American Economic Association *Readings in International Economics,* Richard D. Irwin, Inc., Homewood, III., 1968.

Bhagwati, J. (1978). *Anatomy and Consequences of Exchange Control Regimes.* Ballinger Publishing Company, Cambridge, Mass.

Chacholiades, M. (1978). *International Monetary Theory and Policy.* McGraw-Hill Book Company, New York, chaps. 10 and 14.

Goldstein, M., and M. S. Khan (1985). "Income and Price Effects in Foreign Trade." In R. W. Jones and P. B. Kenen (eds.), *Handbook of International Economics,* vol. 2, North-Holland, New York, 1985.

Helliwell, J. F., and T. Padmore (1985). "Empirical Studies of Macroeconomic Interdependence." In R. W. Jones and P. B. Kenen (eds.), *Handbook of International Economics,* vol. 2, North-Holland, New York, 1985.

Kindleberger, C. P. (1975). *The World in Depression, 1929–1939.* University of California Press, Berkeley.

Machlup, F. (1943). *International Trade and the National Income Multiplier.* The Blakiston Company, Philadelphia.

Meade, J. E. (1951). *The Theory of International Economic Policy,* vol. 1, *The Balance of Payments.* Oxford University Press, New York, parts 2, 3, and 5.

Robinson, R. (1952). "A Graphical Analysis of the Foreign Trade Multiplier." *Economic Journal* (September), pp. 546–564.

Swan, T. W. (1955). "Longer-Run Problems of the Balance of Payments." Paper presented to Section G of the Congress of the Australian and New Zealand Association for the Advancement of Science, Melbourne. In R. E. Caves and H. G. Johnson (eds.), American Economic Association *Readings in International Economics.* Richard D. Irwin, Inc., Homewood, Ill., 1968.

Tinbergen, J. (1952). *On the Theory of Economic Policy.* North-Holland Publishing Company, Amsterdam.

CHAPTER 16

THE WORLD DEBT CRISIS

The world debt crisis is a ticking bomb that threatens the prosperity of developed and developing countries alike. It has been in the making since the beginning of the energy crisis in the early 1970s; but it became visible only after the dramatic announcement of Mexico, on August 12, 1982, that it could no longer meet previously scheduled payments on its external debt. Since then many other developing nations (particularly in Latin America) have announced similar difficulties. In the ensuing years no widespread default has erupted, but the apparent calm should not be taken as a sign that the problem is under control. Behind the facade, the situation has worsened. Since 1982, the total foreign debt of developing countries (DCs) has increased by about 50 percent. The bomb is still ticking; it must be defused before it explodes. This chapter deals with the dimensions, causes, and consequences of the debt crisis; it also discusses alternative policy options in dealing with the crisis.

16-1 THE DIMENSIONS OF THE DEBT CRISIS

There are two sides to the world debt: the borrowing side and the lending side. We consider the borrowing side first. In 1973 the total external debt of the Third World stood at the comfortable level of $100 billion. Now the situation is so bad that many developing nations find it necessary to borrow money just to cover the interest payments on their loans.

Table 16-1 shows how the total world debt grew for the period 1979–1988. Note that by 1982 the total debt had increased to about $850 billion. Today (1988) it exceeds $1.2 trillion. As a percentage of exports of goods and services, the world debt increased from 90.8 percent in 1979 to 160.7 percent in 1988.

TABLE 16-1 TOTAL EXTERNAL DEBT OF DEVELOPING COUNTRIES, 1979–1988
(In Billions of U.S. Dollars; Figures in Parentheses in Percent of Exports; Figures in Brackets in Percent of GDP)

	1979	1980	1981	1982	1983	1984	1985	1986	1987	1988‡
Total debt	533.4	633.9	745.5	849.6	898.4	946.8	1,009.1	1,094.9	1,183.8	1,222.9
(end-of-year)	(90.8)	(81.6)	(94.6)	(120.1)	(133.3)	(133.7)	(147.8)	(167.5)	(168.6)	(160.7)
By region										
Africa	84.8	97.0	107.0	122.2	130.8	133.2	140.0	156.3	169.8	175.3
	(107.1)	(90.2)	(116.3)	(153.8)	(170.4)	(170.1)	(181.0)	(219.6)	(227.7)	(220.0)
Asia	114.4	137.8	157.6	184.2	204.2	216.7	243.6	272.3	300.1	313.9
	(75.7)	(71.9)	(74.5)	(88.4)	(93.6)	(88.1)	(100.0)	(101.6)	(100.0)	(95.8)
Europe	81.0	93.6	102.0	106.8	107.4	112.0	127.1	138.2	146.3	149.3
	(130.1)	(127.4)	(136.7)	(147.0)	(150.0)	(146.4)	(161.9)	(160.7)	(156.8)	(148.6)
Middle East	65.2	74.1	90.5	102.8	113.2	123.0	130.4	144.8	158.7	166.5
	(32.6)	(26.6)	(33.2)	(45.7)	(59.8)	(69.7)	(82.2)	(120.4)	(129.0)	(127.3)
Latin America	188.0	231.3	288.4	333.5	342.8	361.9	368.0	383.2	408.9	417.9
	(197.7)	(183.5)	(210.3)	(273.8)	(290.3)	(277.1)	(295.5)	(354.7)	(367.6)	(342.2)
Countries with recent debt-servicing problems*	317.6	383.3	461.3	528.1	546.4	571.2	588.0	623.5	671.7	691.4
	[34.0]	[33.6]	[38.5]	[45.5]	[50.0]	[51.1]	[52.2]	[54.8]	[57.5]	[54.7]
Fifteen heavily indebted countries†	218.2	269.3	330.8	383.1	394.2	410.9	417.2	434.4	464.9	473.9
	(182.3)	(167.1)	(201.4)	(269.8)	(289.7)	(272.1)	(284.2)	(337.9)	(349.6)	(324.7)
	[30.2]	[30.8]	[34.6]	[41.7]	[47.0]	[46.8]	[46.3]	[48.4]	[50.8]	[47.9]

*Countries that have experienced debt-servicing problems are defined as those countries that incurred external payments arrears during 1985 or rescheduled their debt during the period from end-1983 to end-1986 as reported by the IMF in its *Annual Report on Exchange Arrangements and Exchange Restrictions.*

†The group of 15 heavily indebted countries comprises Argentina, Bolivia, Brazil, Chile, Colombia, Ivory Coast, Ecuador, Mexico, Morocco, Nigeria, Peru, Philippines, Uruguay, Venezuela, and Yugoslavia.

‡Projected.

Source: International Monetary Fund, *World Economic Outlook,* April 1987, Tables A46, A47, A48, and A50.

The table also shows how the debt grew for each of the regions, for countries with recent debt-servicing problems, and for the 15 most heavily indebted countries. In absolute terms the debt is concentrated in two regions: Asia and Latin America (western hemisphere). As a percentage of exports, however, the Latin American debt is much more onerous than the Asian debt. Whereas the Asian debt increased from 75.7 percent of exports in 1979 to 95.8 percent in 1988, the corresponding percentages for the Latin American debt are 197.7 and 342.2, respectively. Relative to exports, the external debt has increased substantially for Africa as well.

The 15 most heavily indebted countries have been carrying 38 to 45 percent of the total debt during the period from 1979 to 1988. Yet as a percentage of their exports, the debt of these countries almost *doubled,* rising from 182.3 percent in 1979 to 349.6 percent in 1987. Another measure of the difficulties facing the 15 most heavily indebted countries is provided by the ratio of their total debt to their gross domestic product (GDP). This ratio increased from 30.2 percent in 1979 to 50.8 percent in 1987—an increase of almost 70 percent.

Table 16-2 provides further insights into the world debt problem in terms of **debt service** (interest plus amortization) and interest payments relative to exports of goods and services. These are indicators of the debt burden. Debt service payments as a percentage of exports increased from 14.1 percent in 1979 to 20.0 percent in 1988. But there are striking differences among the five regions. Latin America's debt burden (fluctuating around 40 percent) has been much larger than the debt burdens of any of the other four regions throughout the period. Africa's debt burden has doubled during the period (rising from 15.3 percent in 1979 to 29.9 percent in 1988) and can no longer be viewed as insignificant. By contrast, Asia's debt burden has not experienced any significant increase but has remained within a range of about 9 to 13 percent.

Turn now to the lending side. Here the main issue concerns the degree of commercial bank involvement. Bank loans have constituted a large and rising portion of Third World debt. From about 25 percent in 1970, the share of bank loans increased to 40 percent in 1982. By 1987, one-half of Third World debt was financed by banks. These aggregates conceal, of course, large differences both among developing countries and among banks. Thus some Latin American countries are much more dependent on bank finance than African nations; and most private loans to Latin American countries are held by a few large U.S.

TABLE 16-2 DEBT SERVICE RATIOS OF DEVELOPING COUNTRIES, 1979–1988
(Part 1 as labeled; Parts 2, 3, and 4 in Percent of Exports)

	1979	1980	1981	1982	1983	1984	1985	1986	1987	1988§
1. Debt service payments*										
% of exports	14.1	12.9	16.2	19.5	18.9	20.1	20.5	22.4	20.7	20.0
U.S.$ billions	82.6	100.5	127.4	138.1	127.6	142.1	140.3	146.5	145.6	152.4
Interest payments										
% of exports	6.0	6.7	9.1	11.4	11.4	11.8	11.5	11.3	10.1	9.5
U.S.$ billions	35.4	52.4	72.1	80.7	76.8	83.4	78.7	74.0	71.0	72.4
2. By region										
Africa	15.3	15.2	18.0	22.1	24.3	26.8	28.7	30.2	27.0	29.9
Asia	9.4	8.7	10.0	11.9	11.4	12.1	12.9	13.0	11.2	10.6
Europe	18.2	20.0	24.0	25.2	23.6	25.0	27.2	26.7	24.7	24.2
Middle East	3.7	3.8	5.3	6.9	8.0	10.0	10.6	14.8	15.4	14.9
Western Hemisphere	39.6	33.4	41.9	51.0	43.9	41.7	38.7	45.6	44.9	40.9
3. Countries with recent debt-servicing problems†	27.7	25.2	32.6	39.9	35.5	35.5	34.3	37.6	36.2	35.1
4. Fifteen heavily indebted countries‡	34.7	29.6	39.0	49.4	42.5	41.1	38.7	43.9	40.7	39.5

*Interest plus amortization.

†Countries that have experienced debt-servicing problems are defined as those countries which incurred external payments arrears during 1985 or rescheduled their debt during the period from end-1983 to end-1986 as reported by the IMF in its *Annual Report on Exchange Arrangements and Exchange Restrictions.*

‡The group of 15 heavily indebted countries comprises Argentina, Bolivia, Brazil, Chile, Colombia, Ivory Coast, Ecuador, Mexico, Morocco, Nigeria, Peru, Philippines, Uruguay, Venezuela, and Yugoslavia.

§Projected.

Source: International Monetary Fund, *World Economic Outlook,* April 1987, Table A51.

banks. For these banks the situation is critical; their Third World loans substantially exceed their capital. Figure 16-1 illustrates the rapid increase in bank lending to developing countries and the large share of Latin American debtor countries. Surely the sharp shift toward bank finance is a major factor in the debt drama of the Third World.

16-2 INTERNATIONAL CAPITAL MOVEMENTS

Relative to the advanced nations of the world, the developing countries suffer from a scarcity of capital and low saving rates. To satisfy their relatively abundant investment opportunities, the developing countries rely on capital inflows from the advanced countries. In this section, we discuss briefly the nature of international capital movements and emphasize the crucial distinction between debt and equity finance.

The Nature of Capital Movements

When we speak of international capital movements, we do *not* mean the sale of capital goods, such as machines and tools, by one country to another. Like sales of consumption goods, sales of capital goods by one country to another consti-

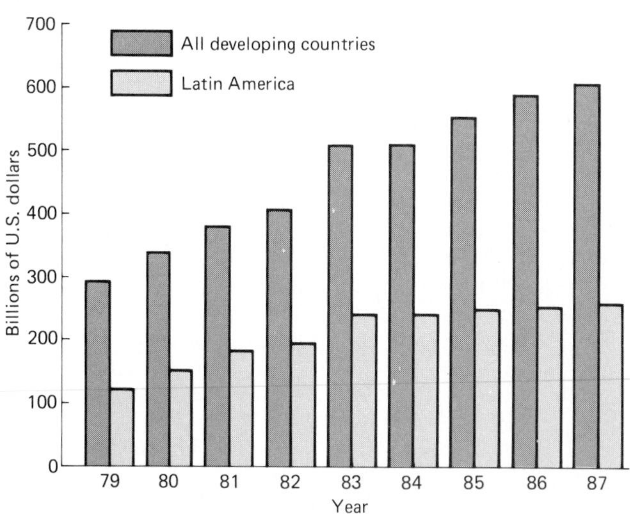

FIGURE 16-1 **Bank exposure to developing countries.** This diagram shows the behavior of bank lending to developing countries and the share of Latin American debtor countries for the period 1979–1987. The data cover the activity of those banking institutions that report to the Bank for International Settlements (BIS). (*From Michel Henry Bouchet,* The Political Economy of International Debt: What, Who, How Much, and Why? *(Quorum Books, a division of Greenwood Press, Inc., Westport, CT, 1987), p. 29. Copyright © 1987 by Michel Henry Bouchet. Reprinted with permission of author and publisher.)*

tute international *trade,* not international capital movements. Thus sales of capital goods are recorded in the payments balances of the relevant countries as flows of exports and imports of goods.

The term **international capital movements** refers to *borrowing* and *lending* between countries. These are the transactions that are recorded in the capital account of the balance of payments. Capital movements are divided into short-term and long-term flows, depending on the nature of the credit instruments involved. **Short-term capital movements** are embodied in credit instruments with *original* maturity of one year or less, such as demand deposits, commercial and financial paper and acceptances, loans and commercial book credits, and items in the process of collection. **Long-term capital movements** consist of credit instruments with original maturity greater than one year (such as long-term securities and mortgages) plus ownership instruments (such as equity holdings of shares and real estate). Long-term capital movements are further divided into direct investment and portfolio investment. **Direct investment** is investment in enterprises located in one country but effectively controlled by residents of another country. Typically, direct investment takes the form of investment in branches and subsidiaries by parent companies located in another country, such as the IBM subsidiary in France. Any other long-term capital movement is classified as **portfolio investment.**

Debt versus Equity Finance

Analytically, international capital movements can be classified into **debt finance** and **equity finance.** Debt finance includes all short-term capital movements plus portfolio investment. Equity finance coincides with direct investment.

Debt finance requires the debtor country to repay the face value of the loan plus interest, usually in a fixed stream of money payments, regardless of the state of the domestic or world economy. This is similar to the monthly mortgage payments that a homeowner has to make to the local savings and loan association. Thus even in a recession, the debtor country must continue to make the agreed upon payments, just like the homeowner who must continue making the mortgage payments even when unemployed. Under adverse conditions, it may become painful for the debtor country to continue honoring its foreign obligations.

Equity finance does not present the same problem. Foreign owners of a direct investment are partners of the debtor country; they have a claim only to a share of the net output of their investment, not a claim to a fixed stream of money payments. When adverse economic conditions in the debtor country reduce the earnings of direct investment, the dividends paid out to foreigners automatically fall. This reduction in dividends does not involve any violation of any loan agreement or law; it merely reflects the fact that the foreign investors (partners) have agreed to share in both the good *and* the bad times of the debtor country.

The world debt crisis was precipitated by the fact that developing countries had acquired too much debt and not enough direct investment. As a result, debtor countries were saddled with huge interest payments that had to be made irrespective of changes in the world economy. Falling export prices rendered unprofitable some of the uses to which the borrowed funds had been put; they also impaired the ability of the debtor countries to meet their loan obligations.

16-3 THE CAPITAL TRANSFER PROCESS

An international capital movement gives rise to the need to *transfer* purchasing power from the lender to the borrower within the current period. Eventually, the transaction is completed when the borrower, through a *reverse transfer* (or sequence of transfers), returns the principal and interest (or dividends) to the lender.

In general, transfers of purchasing power, or **transfer payments,** from one country to another may occur for the following various reasons:

1 *Borrowing* by economic units in a poor country from economic units in richer countries

2 *Reparations* made to the victors by defeated countries (for example, by France after the Franco-Prussian War of 1870–1871 and by Germany after World War I)

3 *Grants* supplied by developed nations to developing countries

4 Settlement of old debts

5 Transfer payments by immigrants

The difficulties that arise when a country needs to transfer purchasing power to another country form the main elements of the **transfer problem,** which is merely an inversion of the balance-of-payments problem studied in Chapter 13.

Financial Transfer versus Real Transfer

In discussing the transfer problem, we must distinguish between two concepts: the **financial transfer** and the **real transfer.** The financial transfer refers to the movement of financial assets from the transferor to the transferee, and the conversion of the currency of the transferor into the currency of the transferee through the foreign exchange market. The real transfer refers to the induced movement of goods between countries. The financial transfer and the real transfer are interrelated. In general, the real transfer may precede, accompany, or follow the financial transfer.

A crucial question that has attracted much attention is whether a financial transfer of, say, $1 million from America to Britain will result in the subsequent movement of $1 million worth of goods from America to Britain. When this is actually the case (that is, when $1 million worth of goods are actually shipped from America to Britain), we say that the transfer is **effected.** When the financial transfer induces a *smaller* flow of goods (say, $800,000), we say that the transfer is **undereffected.** And when the financial transfer induces a *larger* flow of goods (say $1,300,000), we say that the transfer is **overeffected.**

When the transfer is actually effected, there is no transfer problem; that is, an effected transfer results in no balance-of-payments difficulties—the financial flows match the commodity trade flows precisely. When a transfer is either undereffected or overeffected, there is a transfer problem; that is, a transfer that is not exactly effected creates a balance-of-payments disequilibrium, which must be corrected somehow.

The degree to which a transfer is actually effected depends on the manner in which the financial assets are raised in the transferor country and also how they are used in the transferee country. For instance, if the funds come out of past savings in the transferor country and go into savings in the transferee country, there will be no effect on the commodity flows. The same will be true if the transferor country actually prints new money that finds its way into the transferee's stockpile of foreign currency. But if the funds are actually raised by taxation in the transferor country and spent on goods and services in the transferee country, there will be definite repercussions on the flows of goods and services between the two countries, and the transfer may be effected, undereffected, or overeffected, depending on circumstances.

The Real Transfer and the Current Account

The real transfer is actually effected when the transferor country develops an export surplus, and the transferee country an import surplus, equal to the transfer. Thus, the real transfer may take the form of either *increased exports* or *reduced imports* by the transferor country, or both. This is the only way in which real capital may be transferred between countries.

Note that the goods transferred need not be capital goods, even though the transfer may be the result of a long-term loan by a rich country to a poor country for the purpose of assisting the poor country to build a factory, a dam, or some other project. Even in such cases consumption goods and services may indeed by transferred by the transferor country to the transferee. These consumption goods and services enable the transferee country to free resources and channel them into the production of capital goods (for example, a dam or a factory). Thus the nature of the goods transferred is immaterial. In general, these goods reflect the comparative advantages and disadvantages of the countries involved.

The Transfer Problem as the Inversion of the Balance-of-Payments Problem

The transfer problem may be viewed as the inversion of the balance-of-payments problem. Any actual balance-of-payments disequilibrium involves a real transfer from the surplus country to the deficit country. The correction of the balance-of-payments disequilibrium, brought about either automatically or by means of planned government policies, can be viewed as the problem of generating either a real transfer of equal amount in the opposite direction (that is, from the deficit to the surplus country) or a money transfer from the surplus to the deficit country. The latter case is illustrated in Section 16-4 with the recycling of petrodollars.

Consider the balance-of-payments disequilibrium illustrated in Figure 16-2, which is similar to Figure 13-5. America is running a deficit of OC (measured in A-exportables). America's expenditure on goods and services is given by O_aC, while America's income is given by O_aO (both aggregates measured in A-exportables). The difference between America's income and expenditure, that is, $OC = O_aC - O_aO$, is made possible by the import surplus. Britain is actually transferring to America OC units of A-exportables per unit of time. This is a real transfer. Nevertheless, we have a balance-of-payments problem because the real transfer from Britain to America is not accompanied by a financial transfer.

The balance-of-payments problem can be solved in one of two ways: (1) by reversing the real transfer or (2) by inducing a financial transfer from the surplus country (Britain) to the deficit country (America). As noted in Chapter 13, the reversal of the real transfer (that is, the elimination of America's import surplus) requires a combination of expenditure-adjusting policies (in both countries) and expenditure-switching policies. The inducement of a financial transfer involves a loan (or grant) from Britain to America. The reversal of the real transfer implies a return to the long-run equilibrium portrayed in Figure 16-3, which is identical to Figure 13-2. The loan from Britain to America maintains the state of Figure 16-2 by making America able to finance its deficit (without running out of reserves).

Consider now the transfer problem proper. Starting from the long-run equilibrium of Figure 16-3, let Britain make a financial transfer to America. The

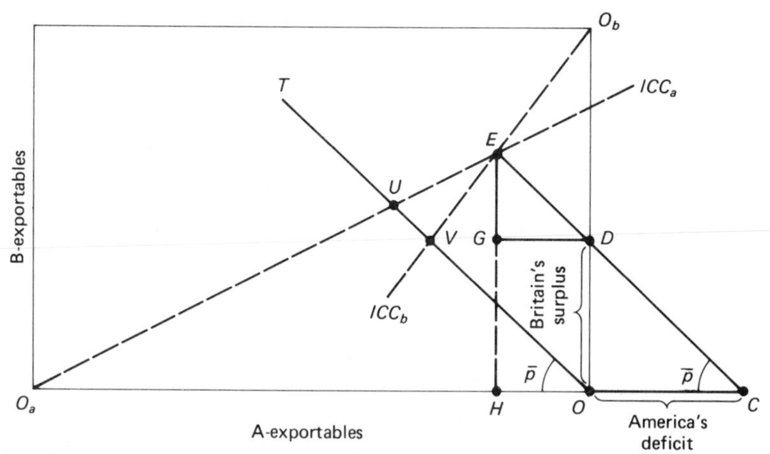

FIGURE 16-2 **Balance-of-payments disequilibrium and the real transfer.** America is running a deficit of OC (measured in A-exportables). This means that America is receiving a real transfer, OC, from Britain. There will be a balance-of-payments problem if the real transfer is not accompanied by a financial transfer.

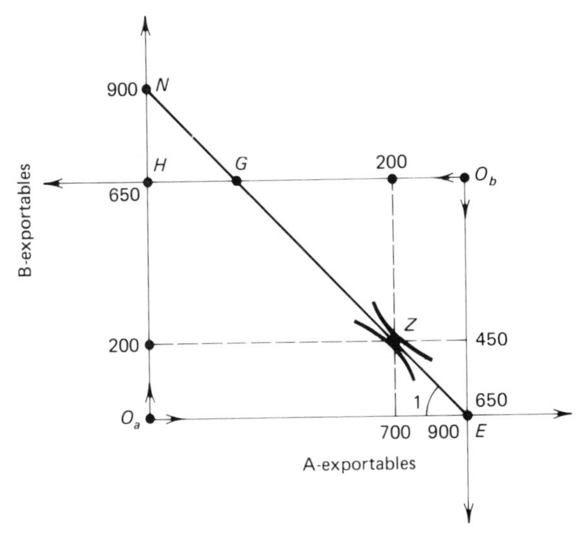

FIGURE 16-3 **Reversal of the real transfer.** To reverse the real transfer implied by Figure 16-2, we must return to the general equilibrium illustrated by point *Z*.

transfer will be totally effected only when a new state of equilibrium is reached in which America develops an import surplus equal to the transfer, as illustrated in Figure 16-2. Accordingly, effecting a transfer means that we shift from the equilibrium of Figure 16-3 to that of Figure 16-2. This is exactly the opposite, of course, of what we must do in the absence of any transfer to correct the balance-of-payments disequilibrium portrayed in Figure 16-2.

The Secondary Burden of the Transfer: Digression

In general, effecting a transfer requires (1) an adjustment in each country's aggregate expenditure and (2) a change in relative prices. The required change in relative prices (terms of trade) attracted too much attention in the past, especially in relation to the German reparations.

It may be recalled that after World War I Germany was made at Versailles to pay war reparations to the Allies. John M. Keynes upheld the so-called **orthodox position,** namely, the view that the transfer problem causes the terms of trade of the transferor to deteriorate. Keynes claimed that Germany would have to experience a severe terms-of-trade deterioration in order to generate the necessary export surplus and effect the transfer. He even expressed fears that Germany would not be able to make the transfer at all because of the low elasticity of demand for the nation's exports. Bertil Ohlin opposed Keynes by advocating that a transfer need not necessarily worsen the terms of trade of the transferor country.

The issue of whether the terms of trade of the transferor country deteriorate with the transfer is clearly an empirical one. No amount of a priori reasoning can tell us what will actually happen in any particular situation. Each case must be studied on its own by means of patient econometric work.

When the transfer actually causes the terms of trade to deteriorate, the transferor country apparently suffers a **secondary burden.** Nevertheless, the whole question of secondary burdens (and benefits, for that matter) seems semantic or artificial. What is important is the total effect of the transfer on the economic welfare of the transferor country and the transferee. One would then expect governments engaged in negotiating reparations payments to take into consideration the effects of the transfer on the terms of trade, although this argument need not apply to transfers effected by private economic units, which behave as price takers.

Long-Run Effects of Capital Movements

As noted in Chapter 4, the equalization of real factor rewards between countries is an important Pareto-optimality condition for the efficient allocation of resources worldwide. In the same way that efficient resource allocation within a closed economy requires that all workers earn the same real wage and all capital earn the same return, efficient resource allocation in the world economy requires complete factor-price equalization. Because factor prices are not equalized in the real world, factor movements can enable the world to reap large gains in potential welfare—in addition to the gains from trade in commodities. Thus the real capital flow from the capital-abundant countries of the North, where its marginal productivity is relatively low, to the capital-scarce countries of the South, where its marginal productivity is relatively high, can benefit *all* countries.

One hopes that as foreign capital flows into the developing countries, their production-possibilities frontier will shift outward, causing their gross national product to rise and that even after they pay interest (or dividends) on the foreign capital, their income (both in the aggregate and per capita) will remain higher than what it would be without the capital inflow.

It is ironic that this mechanism has not worked well in the 1970s and 1980s. Today, the Third World countries, especially those in Latin America, find themselves handicapped by huge debts and by service payments that they are unable to make. What went wrong? What caused the present crisis?

16-4 THE RECYCLING OF PETRODOLLARS

As a result of the oil price increases of the 1970s (see Section 9-6), hundreds of billions of dollars (or "petrodollars") were transferred from the oil-importing countries to the oil-exporting countries. In 1974 alone, the members of OPEC developed a current account surplus of almost $60 billion. Surely the oil-exporting countries could not convert this tremendous influx of funds into imports of goods and services, because their economies lacked the necessary capacity to absorb such vast amounts of resources; hence they faced the paradoxical problem of what to do with their windfall.

The surplus funds of the oil-exporting countries mirrored the current account *deficits* of the rest of the world. As the oil-exporting countries were seeking alternatives for their surpluses, the rest of the world was searching for ways to finance its deficits. Most Third World countries, which were hit hard by the oil price increases, were desperate for new sources of development capital. Essentially, the *recycling* of petrodollars concerned the distribution of oil-surplus monies back to the deficit countries in order to close the cycle.

Petrodollar recycling became a problem because there was no coincidence of wants between surplus and deficit countries. On the one hand, OPEC had a strong preference for liquidity and wanted to place its surpluses in highly liquid, low-risk investment. The Third World, on the other hand, sought to finance its deficits by liquidating longer-term and riskier assets. Some kind of international financial intermediation was necessary; thus a heavy recycling burden fell upon the international financial community.

As it turned out, the Eurodollar market did most of the recycling. OPEC countries deposited their surplus funds in the Eurodollar market. (For instance, during the period 1976–1982 over $750 billion were placed by OPEC with American and European banks.) In turn, the banks used the newly acquired funds to make loans to the Third World, especially to Latin America.

Petrodollar recycling is shown schematically in Figure 16-4. OPEC countries exported oil to Japan, Europe, and the United States (arrow 1) in exchange for dollars (arrow 2), which they deposited in the Eurodollar market (arrow 3). In turn, the Eurodollar market made loans to the Third World (arrow 4), which used the loan proceeds to pay (arrow 5) for the net imports of goods and services from Japan, Europe, and the United States (arrow 6). For a while the cycle seemed closed and everyone was happy. Yet the recycling of petrodollars gave birth to the **debt crisis** which came to haunt the world during the 1980s.

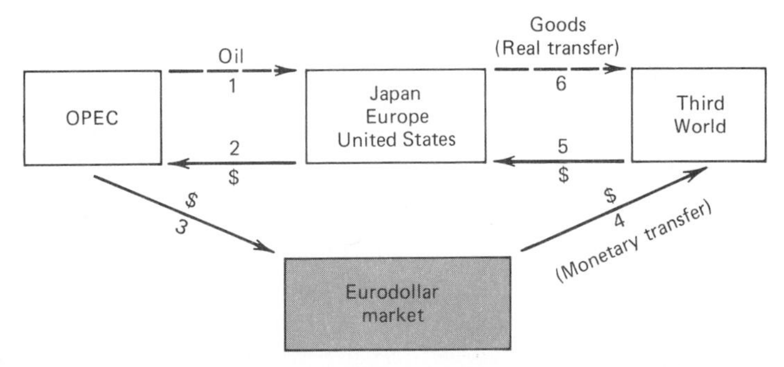

FIGURE 16-4 Petrodollar recycling. OPEC countries export oil to Japan, Europe, and the United States (arrow 1); the latter group of countries exports goods and services to the Third World (arrow 6). OPEC receives dollars from Japan, Europe, and the United States (arrow 2). OPEC deposits its funds in the Eurodollar market (arrow 3), which makes loans to the Third World (arrow 4). Finally, the Third World uses the loan proceeds to pay for its net imports (arrow 5).

16-5 THE CAUSES OF THE WORLD DEBT CRISIS

With the magnificent wisdom of hindsight, analysts attribute the world debt crisis to three major factors: (1) the sharp increase in interest rates, starting in 1978; (2) the world recession of the early 1980s; and (3) the strong appreciation of the dollar. We consider each of these factors separately. We also comment on the phenomenon of capital flight.

The Rise in Interest Rates

In the late 1970s, a large portion of the debt of developing countries (particularly that of Latin American countries) carried **floating** (or **adjustable**) **interest rates.** This institutional feature of bank lending turned out to be an important contributor to the world debt crisis.

Under a floating rate loan contract, the lender is allowed to adjust the interest rate on the loan as market interest rates change—very much like the adjustable-rate mortgages. Typically, the floating rate bank loans to developing countries were tied to the so-called LIBOR (or London interbank offered rate). These variable rates were adjusted every six months.

To curb inflation, the Federal Reserve in 1979 initiated a tight monetary policy. Interest rates rose sharply. The U.S. prime rate (used for loans to Latin American countries) eventually peaked in 1981 at 20.5 percent. LIBOR rose from 9.5 percent in 1978 to 16.6 percent in 1981, as shown in Table 16-3.

The sharp rise in interest rates had a dramatic impact on developing countries' debt service for two reasons: (1) New borrowing became more expensive, and (2) interest payments on old loans increased rapidly because of the floating rate loan contracts. As a result, debt service of developing countries increased substantially (recall Table 16-2).

The World Recession

The higher interest rates propelled the world economy into the worse recession since the 1930s. By 1981 the average unemployment rate in seven major industrial countries surpassed 8 percent while real GDP growth became negative. This is illustrated in Figure 16-5, which conceals major differences among the seven industrial nations.

TABLE 16-3 SIX-MONTH DOLLAR LIBOR
(Percent Per Year)

1978	1979	1980	1981	1982	1983	1984	1985
9.5	12.1	14.3	16.6	13.3	9.9	11.2	8.7

LIBOR = London interbank offered rate.
Source: The World Bank, *World Development Report 1986*, Oxford University Press, New York, 1986, Table 2.10 (p. 32).

FIGURE 16-5 Growth, inflation, and unemployment rates in seven major industrial countries, 1965–1985. Data are for Canada, France, Germany, Italy, Japan, the United Kingdom, and the United States. (*The World Bank,* World Development Report 1986, *Oxford University Press, New York, 1986, p. 16.*)

The world recession of 1980–1982 reduced the incomes of the developing countries for two reasons: (1) It caused their exports to fall, and (2) the reduction in demand caused the prices of their products to fall. (Recall from Chapter 6, Table 6-4, that the export prices of the developing nations declined sharply during this period.) The recession intensified protectionist pressures in the industrial countries (and in the developing nations as well). The increased protection made it even more difficult for the developing countries to sell their products in the markets of the industrialized world. At the same time, the second OPEC oil price increase, in 1979, put an extra demand on the dwindling foreign exchange earnings of the Third World. All this was happening at a time when the supply of petrodollars was diminishing rapidly—the current account surplus of the oil-exporting countries actually turned into a deficit in 1982. Thus the capacity of the developing nations to service their growing external debt was severely impaired.

The Appreciation of the Dollar

The higher interest rates, which were prompted by the tight monetary policy of the Federal Reserve, caused the dollar to appreciate considerably. The link between the interest rate and the external value of the dollar was provided by the interest-arbitrage mechanism studied in Chapter 11. As the U.S. interest rate rose significantly above rates in Britain, France, Germany, and Japan, large flows of financial capital moved into the United States and the increased demand for dollars in the spot market raised the external value of the dollar (recall Figure 14-9).

The appreciation of the dollar raised the real value of the developing countries' debt service because much of that debt was denominated in dollars. Not only did interest payments escalate because of the rising interest rates, but also debt service became much more expensive because of the appreciating dollar.

Capital Flight

During this period, the external debt outlook of the developing nations, particularly in Latin America, worsened significantly because of extensive **capital flight**—the transfer of money from one country to another by private individuals or firms in search of a safe refuge. It is extremely difficult to determine how large capital flight is. One estimate suggests that by 1985 the total capital flight out of developing nations was about $200 billion.

Table 16-4 shows that capital flight considerably augmented the growth in the external indebtedness of many major debtor countries. From 1976 to 1985 the portion of external debt growth due to capital flight was 62 percent for Argentina, 13 percent for Brazil, 71 percent for Mexico, and 115 percent for Venezuela.

Figure 16-6 illustrates the overall effect of capital flight on the total external

TABLE 16-4 ESTIMATED NET CAPITAL FLIGHT, 1976–1985

	Capital flight, U.S. $ billions	Change in external debt, U.S. $ billions	Flight as percent of debt growth
Latin America			
Argentina	26	42	62
Bolivia	1	3	33
Brazil	10	80	13
Ecuador	2	7	29
Mexico	53	75	71
Uruguay	1	4	25
Venezuela	30	26	115
Other countries			
India	10	22	45
Indonesia	5	27	19
Korea	12	40	30
Malaysia	12	19	63
Nigeria	10	18	56
Philippines	9	23	39
South Africa	17	16	106

Source: Adapted from Morgan Guaranty Trust Company of New York, *World Financial Markets,* March 1986, Table 10 (p. 13).

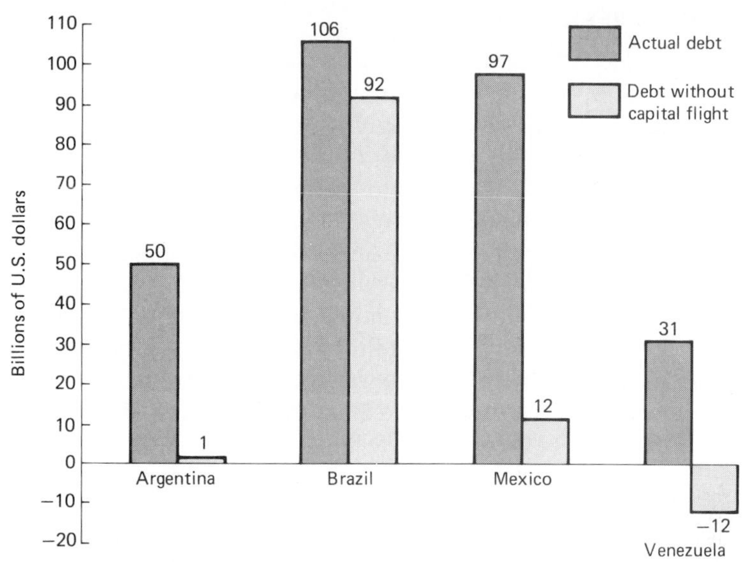

FIGURE 16-6 **The external indebtedness of Argentina, Brazil, Mexico, and Venezuela with and without capital flight, end-1985.** To get the external indebtedness of a country without capital flight, we subtract from the actual debt not only the capital flight but also the interest payments that would have been saved in the absence of capital flight. (*Morgan Guaranty Trust Company of New York,* World Financial Markets, *March 1986, Table 12, p. 15.*)

debt of Argentina, Brazil, Mexico, and Venezuela. In the absence of capital flight, the external indebtedness of Argentina and Mexico would be insignificant, while Venezuela would be a creditor country.

What caused the enormous capital flight? Probably the unsettled economic conditions in the developing countries: overvalued exchange rates, lax fiscal and monetary policies, interest-rate ceilings, inflation, taxes on domestic financial assets, and so on. As a result, many residents of developing countries used their savings to purchase assets in the more efficient financial markets of foreign countries, such as the United States. Until the outbreak of the debt crisis, the outflow of private savings was generally returned to the developing countries, often in the form of bank loans to the public sector. Thus there was no need for the outflow of domestic savings to be matched by a real transfer from the developing to the developed countries. Yet the substitution of external finance for domestic savings set the stage for the debt crisis. As interest rates inched upward, debt service became a serious problem.

After the debt crisis erupted in 1982, circumstances changed radically. The banks that received the inflows of private savings were no longer willing to relend the money to the governments of countries with debt-servicing problems. Hence, capital flight began to have real resource transfer implications.

16-6 THE COSTS OF SOVEREIGN DEFAULT

Independent nations are **sovereign,** which means **subject to no one.** Most debt of developing countries is **sovereign debt;** it reflects either borrowing by the governments of developing countries or loans guaranteed by these governments. Sovereign borrowers cannot be forced to repay their debts if they do not wish to do so. **Sovereign default** (that is, a government decision to suspend the payments specified in the loan contract) is not subject to the legal sanctions that can be invoked in cases of private default. For instance, Manufacturers Hanover cannot foreclose on Argentina in the same way that a local savings and loan association can seize the house of a delinquent debtor. The doctrine of sovereign immunity means that governments cannot be sued even for their commercial activities. Courts cannot pass judgment on acts of a foreign state because they cannot encroach upon the making of foreign policy, which is not the function of the judiciary.

Several distinguished economists have suggested that debtor nations should default. The immediate benefit of sovereign default is that the defaulting debtor nation will no longer have to repay its loans. (Default would be equivalent to a financial transfer from creditor countries to debtor countries.) Why, then, are the developing countries reluctant to default? Because even sovereign borrowers cannot default without impunity. Sovereign default involves important costs, which may outweigh the benefits.

Suppose that a Latin American country, such as Brazil, defaults. U.S. banks that hold large loans against Brazil (such as the Bank of America, Bankers Trust, Chase Manhattan, Citibank, Chemical, and Morgan Guaranty) may convince the U.S. government to seize any Brazilian assets located in the United States. (This threat may explain, for example, why the government of Peru in 1986 repatriated about $700 million worth of gold and silver that it had been holding abroad.) However, given the small magnitude of assets held abroad relative to the total world debt, seizure of assets is not a major deterrent to default.

Note that the United States may also seize the defaulting country's exports. However, the sovereign defaulter could arrange for its exports to become the property of the importer before the goods cross its own border.

Alternatively, the United States could impose trade restrictions or ban all trade with the defaulting country. Such trade restrictions may work in an isolated case. However, in a general default (by, say, all Latin American countries) it would be rather difficult for the United States to sever all trade relations with all defaulters.

Next, the defaulting country may be excluded from new borrowing. Such exclusion from the international capital market need not be based on any organized sanctions imposed by the creditor countries, such as the United States. Rather, the sovereign defaulter will be viewed as a bad risk by prospective lenders. Prior to 1982, the specter of being cut off from the international capital market was an important deterrent to default. After 1982, when the debtor nations were already cut off from the world capital markets, the threat was kept alive by the initiatives of the International Monetary Fund (IMF), which has managed to keep the flow of new finance at a high enough level to avert default.

Finally, the sovereign defaulter may experience substantial reductions in the gains from trade. As we noted earlier, creditor countries may cut off trade relations with the defaulter. They may also seize, or threaten to seize, both the defaulter's exports and assets (such as demand deposits and trade credits) that are located within their jurisdiction. The immediate effect of all these impediments would be a reduction in the volume and gains of trade. Potentially, these losses could be severe.

16-7 THE SECONDARY MARKET FOR DEBT OF DEVELOPING COUNTRIES (DC)

In the last few years, a new secondary market in discounted DC debt has developed. In this section, we briefly review the size and functions of this market.

The Nature of the Secondary Market

The secondary market for DC debt is still small but growing rapidly. It is estimated that the debt may have totaled $1 billion in 1984, $3 billion in 1985, $6 billion in 1986, and $10 billion in 1987. It is expected to rise above $15 billion in 1988.

Typically, large discounts are applied to the debt's face value, as illustrated in Table 16-5. For instance, in May 1988 Argentine debt was quoted at less than 30 cents on the dollar, compared with about 60 cents a year earlier; Brazilian and Mexican debt sold for about 55 cents on the dollar; and Peruvian and Nicaraguan debt sold for less than 5 cents on the dollar. The debt of most big Latin American debtor nations plummeted after Brazil declared a moratorium on an estimated $67 billion of its foreign bank debt in February 1987.

TABLE 16-5 PRICE QUOTES FOR DEBT OF VARIOUS COUNTRIES (Cents on the Dollar)

	May 1988		12-Month	
	Bid	**Ask**	**High**	**Low**
Argentina	28.0	29.0	60.5	25.0
Bolivia	10.5	12.0	12.0	6.0
Brazil	55.0	56.0	65.5	38.0
Chile	61.0	62.0	72.5	50.0
Mexico	53.5	54.5	59.5	46.5
Nicaragua	2.0	4.0	6.0	2.0
Nigeria	29.0	30.0	35.0	25.0
Peru	4.0	9.0	15.0	4.0
Philippines	50.0	51.0	72.0	49.0
Venezuela	55.0	56.0	74.0	49.5

Source: Adapted from *The Wall Street Journal,* May 17, 1988, p. 41. Reprinted by permission.

The risks are at least as large as the discounts. Some debtors may never pay back their loans. Certain nations with deep debt discounts are not paying any interest now and have not done so for years. Even with more solvent nations, interest payments are often in doubt. Yet courageous buyers—mainly banks and corporations with Third World business interests—are ready to purchase what sellers are glad to unload. Most individual investors are either from the debtor nations themselves or know the countries well. For individuals, the minimum face value of investments in Third World debt is $1 million.

The secondary market is the best available indicator for establishing the current value of the various loans. The market serves three additional purposes:

1 Private banks use the market to readjust their portfolios by reshuffling loans.
2 Debtor countries use the market to retire debt.
3 Debtor countries encourage investors to use discounted debt to make new investments (debt-equity swaps), as explained below.

Debt-Equity Swaps

Debt-equity swaps (or **debt capitalization**) are schemes designed to convert some of the existing debt into equity. Banks themselves may convert some of their own debt into local investment. For example, Bankers Trust converted some of its Chilean debt into shares in a pension management company. Typically, however, the debt-equity swap is carried out by multinational corporations. For example, Fiat bought Brazilian debt at a discount, exchanged it at the central bank for the cruzado equivalent of the face value of the debt, and used the proceeds to expand its plant in Brazil. Nissan Corporation has arranged a similar deal in Mexico; and the Dow Chemical Company has executed one in Chile. Nissan and Dow actually shared the discounts with the respective central banks. Such schemes retire debt and transform it into equity, in the process stimulating new investment. It is at least conceivable that such debt-equity swaps may reverse the capital flight by inducing Latin Americans to bring back home the funds they are holding abroad.

Monkeys in Bolivia and the World Debt Crisis

The Wall Street Journal (January 20, 1988) published the following story under the provocative title, "What Do Monkeys in Bolivia Have to Do with the Debt Crisis?"

Conservation International is a Washington-based nonprofit group that helps operate the biological station in El Porvenir, Bolivia. In 1987, after obtaining the approval of the Bolivian government, Conservation International purchased $650,000 of Bolivia's deeply discounted foreign bank debt from a Swiss bank for about $100,000 and then swapped the debt with the Bolivian government. In return, the Bolivian government created conservation areas covering almost 4 million acres around the El Porvenir station, adding them to an already established reserve of 334,000 acres.

The Bolivian government also set aside $250,000 in local currency to help administer the entire reserve and retained Conservation International as an adviser. Thus Bolivia's debt was reduced by $650,000 and important steps were taken in conservation.

When Peter Truell, the author of the article, arrived at the El Porvenir station, he was "greeted by a smiling man with a squeaking night monkey on his head." This episode plus some additional confrontations with the monkeys prompted Truell to ask rhetorically: "Is this the way to handle Latin America's $400 billion foreign-debt crisis?" The answer may be yes: Other heavily indebted countries (such as Brazil, Chile, and Peru), international banks, and conservation groups are contemplating transactions similar to the El Porvenir experiment.

16-8 ALTERNATIVE POLICY OPTIONS

In this concluding section, we discuss the policy alternatives available to international policymakers in dealing with the debt crisis.

The World Debt Problem as a Transfer Problem

The world debt crisis is a classic case of the transfer problem. During the 1970s the developing countries were the beneficiaries of a massive transfer of resources from the rest of the world. At that time, the financial transfer accommodated the real transfer and there appeared to be calm in the world community. The problem of the 1980s is how to reverse the transfer of the 1970s. This is an oversimplification of the problem, but it is useful.

Following the discussion in Section 16-3, the current debt problem can be solved in one of two ways: (1) by effecting a *real* transfer (or a series of transfers) from the debtor countries to the creditor countries or (2) by inducing a financial transfer from the creditor countries to the debtor countries. Both options face difficulties. The first option works against the proposition that capital should flow from the capital-abundant countries of the North to the capital-scarce countries of the South, and *not* the other way around. The second option would merely perpetuate, and even worsen, the current state of affairs if by a financial transfer we mean debt rescheduling.

Muddling Through

So far, the crisis has been contained by means of country-by-country **rescheduling agreements** and the provision of some *new* credits. Debt rescheduling involves a postponement of principal repayments but not of interest payments. The new credits help the debtor countries meet their interest obligations and finance smaller current-account deficits. Bank finance has been supplemented by loans from some governments and the IMF.

This muddling-through strategy has left a lot of scars in the debtor nations. As a precondition for debt rescheduling, debtor nations were required to accept **IMF conditionality,** that is, the austere economic surveillance of the International Monetary Fund. Thus debtor nations were forced to pursue policies that would sharply cut their current account deficits. Such policies involved reductions in wages and public-sector deficits, devaluations, and the like. In effect, the debtor nations were asked to carry out the needed adjustment by themselves. The results were dramatic. By 1984 the current account deficits of the developing countries had been reduced substantially but at a great cost. Per capita incomes dropped, unemployment soared, and hyperinflation ran rampant in many countries (for example, 1,200 percent in Argentina and 500 percent in

Brazil before their recent monetary reforms). The 1980s have been described as a "lost decade" for the economies of most Latin American countries.

It is ironic that after so much suffering, the debt crisis has actually worsened. Obviously, the muddling-through strategy is not a viable option in the long run. This conclusion seems to have been reached also by the banks and the U.S. government. Thus major U.S. and British banks have set aside reserves against 25 to 30 percent of their doubtful Third World debt, while other major European banks have made provisions for debt losses of as much as 70 percent or more. Japanese banks, which have the second-largest exposure to Third World debt after the U.S. banks, are now increasing loan-loss reserves from 5 percent to 10 percent.

Treasury Secretary James Baker announced in June 1988 that while the United States itself would not grant any debt relief, it would not prevent other countries from doing so for the poorest debtor countries. In the past, the Reagan administration feared that debt relief for the poor nations would prompt demands for similar concessions by Argentina, Brazil, Mexico, and other much wealthier nations. Now the feeling is that a clear enough distinction can be made among the debtors so that debt forgiveness will not necessarily spread to large Latin American countries. Following the announcement by the Reagan administration, France and West Germany made it clear that they plan to forgive some loans to the world's poorest countries (mainly sub-Saharan ones) as part of their efforts to ease the burden of those debtor nations.

Generalized Default

As noted in Section 16-6, many distinguished economists have suggested that the debtor nations should default. Is default a viable option? We must reject sovereign default, because it is a unilateral and irresponsible act that would undermine the legal and ethical fabric of the world community. Surely, nobody was twisting any arms when the developing countries took out such unprecedented foreign loans in the 1970s. But neither was the debt crisis manufactured by the debtor countries alone. The debt crisis was brought about by a complex interplay of economic events; thus the crisis should be the joint responsibility of both debtor and creditor countries alike. The debtor countries should not be asked to carry out the necessary adjustment by themselves. They should not be encouraged to default, because a unilateral action taken by the debtor countries to abrogate their responsibilities will have devastating effects on the world community. How can individuals be asked to behave in an ethical and moral manner if their governments do not?

Toward a Viable Solution

The world debt crisis has exposed major weaknesses in the international capital transfer mechanism. By now it must be clear that a viable solution to the world debt crisis must address two issues: (1) the sharing of adjustment costs by all interested parties and (2) the creation of conditions that are conducive to a continuous flow of capital from the capital-rich countries of the North to the capital-poor countries of the South.

To be successful, adjustment must be viewed as a joint responsibility. Thus the advanced countries must take steps to increase their imports of goods and services from the developing nations. At the same time, the debt discounts must somehow be passed on to the debtor countries. The secondary market for DC debt has already demonstrated that the market value of the debts is much lower than the face value—a fact that is implicitly recognized by the banks as evidenced by their increased reserves. These two measures alone would go a long way toward restoring tranquillity in the world financial markets.

The governments of the developing nations have some responsibilities also. These governments must pursue economic policies that will create a climate of stability, hope, and optimism. They should create an environment that is attractive to foreign capital. Foreign investors should feel welcome in the developing countries, so that capital inflow will replace capital flight. This is another reason why default is disruptive—it may solve the problem in the short run but aggravate the situation in the long run.

These ideas are presented as a challenge to international policymakers. In the next few years, we shall find out whether policymakers will accept the challenge and meet the crisis head on.

16-9 SUMMARY

1 The Third World debt has increased considerably both absolutely and relative to exports. About one-third is owed by Latin America. By 1987 one-half of Third World debt was financed by banks.

2 International capital movements refer to borrowing and lending between countries. Capital flows are divided into short-term and long-term capital movements. The latter are subdivided into portfolio investment and direct investment.

3 Debt finance requires the debtor country to repay the face value of the loan plus interest, typically in a fixed stream of money payments. With equity finance, dividends are paid out to the foreign owner only when profits exist. The developing countries have acquired too much debt and little direct investment.

4 The transfer problem concerns the difficulties with which, and manner in which, real capital is transferred between countries as a result of borrowing, reparations, aid, and so on. It is the inverse of the balance-of-payments problem.

5 The transfer is effected, overeffected, or undereffected when the flow of goods (real transfer) from the transferor to the transferee is equal to, larger than, or smaller than the financial transfer that induces it. The nature of the goods transferred is immaterial. There is a transfer problem (that is, balance-of-payments difficulties) when the transfer is not exactly effected.

6 The degree to which a transfer is actually effected depends on the manner in which the financial assets are raised in the transferor country and used in the transferee country.

7 In general, effecting a transfer requires (a) an adjustment in each country's aggregate spending and (b) a change in the terms of trade.

8 The orthodox (Keynesian) position holds that the transfer causes the terms of trade of the transferor to deteriorate (secondary burden). The modern position (Ohlin's) holds that the transfer need not worsen the transferor's terms of trade.

9 Because factor prices are not equalized in the real world, all countries benefit when capital flows from the capital-rich countries of the North to the capital-poor countries of the South.

10 The world debt crisis is attributed to three causes: (1) the sharp increase in interest rates, (2) the world recession of 1980–1982, and (3) the appreciation of the dollar.

11 Massive capital flight from the developing countries was a major contributor to the debt crisis.

12 Sovereign default involves costs, such as seizure of assets and exports, exclusion from new borrowing, and reductions in the gains from trade.

13 The muddling-through strategy has worked so far, but it is not a viable solution in the long run.

14 Sovereign default must be rejected because it is too disruptive—it is an irresponsible act that would undermine the legal and ethical fabric of the world economy. It will hurt the debtor countries in the long run.

15 Any viable solution to the debt crisis must meet two criteria: (1) Costs must be shared by all parties, and (2) the developing countries, with help from the developed nations, must pursue policies that are conducive to the creation of an environment of stability and hope.

PROBLEMS

1 Suppose that the United States decides to provide $1 million in foreign aid to Turkey for the construction of a road. The aid is "tied"; that is, Turkey is required to use the funds to purchase the necessary construction equipment, machinery, and materials from the United States rather than from other foreign countries, such as Japan and Germany.

- **a** Will the tied foreign aid to Turkey give rise to a transfer problem?
- **b** Will the tied foreign aid to Turkey worsen the U.S. balance of payments?
- **c** Will the tying of foreign aid be beneficial to the United States?
- **d** Alternatively, suppose that Turkey borrows the funds from the international capital market (through the sale of bonds). How will the U.S. balance of payments differ now from the case of tied foreign aid?

2 "A large portion of the external debt of many Latin American countries is the result of the tremendous capital flight, which is due to fears of currency devaluations. Yet through such capital flight the private citizens of these countries acquired assets in other countries, such as the United States. Thus the net Latin American debt to the rest of the world (including assets held by Latin American citizens in foreign countries) remained the same. Evidently, debtor nations have nothing to fear from capital flight because they lose nothing—the additional foreign debt is matched by the additional foreign assets acquired by their citizens."

a Do you agree with this statement?
b Can a country face a debt crisis even though its citizens are doing well?
c In what way did capital flight aggravate the world debt crisis?

3 a How does debt finance differ from equity finance?
b In what way did debt finance contribute to the world debt crisis?
c How could equity finance have eased the world debt crisis?

4 a What is the relationship between the world debt crisis and the transfer problem?
b Should we conclude from the world debt crisis that all borrowing is bad? Why or why not?
c Domestic borrowing in the United States is at an all-time high; yet no debt crisis exists. Is international borrowing different from domestic borrowing?

SUGGESTED READING

Baldwin, R. E., and J. D. Richardson, eds. (1986). *International Trade and Finance.* Little, Brown and Company, Boston, chaps. 27–29.

Balassa, B., G. M. Bueno, P. Kuczynski, and M. H. Simonsen (1986). *Toward Renewed Economic Growth in Latin America.* Institute for International Economics, Washington, D.C.

Bouchet, M. H. (1987). *The Political Economy of International Debt.* Greenwood Press, Westport, Conn.

Elliot, J. M., ed. (1988). *Third World 88–89.* Dushkin Publishing Group, Guilford, Conn., chaps. 38–43.

Keynes, J. M. (1929). "The German Transfer Problem." *Economic Journal,* vol. 39 (March), pp. 1–7. Reprinted in H. S. Ellis and L. A. Metzler (eds.), American Economic Association *Reading in the Theory of International Trade,* Richard D. Irwin, Inc., Homewood, Ill., 1950.

Ohlin, B. (1929). "The Reparations Problem: A Discussion, I, Transfer Difficulties, Real and Imagined." *Economic Journal,* vol. 39 (June), pp. 172–178. Reprinted in H. S. Ellis and L. A. Metzler (eds.), American Economic Association *Readings in the Theory of International Trade,* Richard D. Irwin, Inc., Homewood, Ill., 1950.

Pool, J. C., and S. Stamos (1987). *The ABCs of International Finance.* D. C. Heath and Company, Lexington, Mass.

CHAPTER **17**

FISCAL AND MONETARY POLICY FOR INTERNAL AND EXTERNAL BALANCE

Tinbergen's rule (Chapter 15) warns us that to achieve two mutually independent targets, such as internal and external balance, we need two mutually independent and effective instruments, such as an **expenditure-adjusting policy** and an **expenditure-switching policy.** However, expenditure-switching policies are often avoided by policymakers for various reasons, some rational and some irrational. For instance, devaluation is usually identified with loss of national prestige and with failure; exchange control and multiple exchange rates are abhorred because they call for an elaborate bureaucratic machinery to oversee all foreign exchange dealings; and import taxes and quotas are dreaded because of the fear of the foreign retaliation they may provoke.

If expenditure-switching policies are excluded, how could internal and external balance be attained simultaneously? If the world insists on a fixed exchange-rate system with free international trade (which, as we have seen, promotes world welfare), do nations have to make the unpleasant choice between the Scylla of unemployment (and inflation) and the Charybdis of balance-of-payments disequilibrium? The possibility of such a conflict was perceived by Meade (1951), but Mundell (1968, pp. 152–176 and 217–271) showed that internal and external balance may still be attained through an appropriate use of fiscal and monetary policies. Mundell's solution is possible *only in the presence of capital mobility.* When capital flows are responsive to interest-rate changes, fiscal and monetary policies affect national income and the balance of payments (*including* the capital account) differently, mainly because of their opposite effects on the rate of interest; thus policymakers can find a combination of fiscal and monetary policy that is consistent with both internal and external balance simultaneously. The object of this chapter is to elucidate the Mundellian approach.

17-1 THE *IS-LM* MODEL

The main framework of analysis for the Mundellian thesis is the ***IS-LM* model,** which we review in this section.

Equilibrium in the Goods Market: The *IS* Curve

As we saw in Chapter 15, the goods market is in equilibrium when aggregate demand ($C + I + X - M$) equals the economy's current level of output or national income (Y). This fundamental equilibrium condition reduces to

$$I + X = S + M \tag{17-1}$$

That is, national income equilibrium occurs when the exogenous injections (investment, I, and exports, X) just match the endogenous leakages (saving, S, and imports, M). We assume again that desired exports, X, are exogenous, while desired saving, S, and imports, M, depend positively on the level of national income. But now we wish to incorporate the influence of the rate of interest on aggregate spending, particularly desired investment, I. In this way, we shall be able to establish an important link between the money market and the goods market. It is essentially through this link that the money supply exerts its influence on national income and the balance of trade.

Investment depends negatively on the rate of interest. As the rate of interest falls, the desired level of investment increases (as additional projects become profitable), causing national income to increase (through the multiplier). The ***IS* curve** summarizes this important relationship between the rate of interest and the equilibrium level of income. In particular, *the IS curve is the locus of all combinations of interest rate, r, and national income, Y, that keep the commodity market in equilibrium, that is, those combinations of r and Y that satisfy Equation (17-1).*

Equilibrium in the Money Market: The *LM* Curve

We now turn to the money market. Equilibrium in the money market prevails when the demand for money equals the supply of money. Initially, we assume that the money supply is exogenous; it is under the control of the monetary authorities. (This assumption is relaxed in Sections 17-7 and 17-8.) The demand for money depends positively on the level of national income and negatively on the rate of interest.

Keynes (1936) suggested three motives for holding money: (1) the **transactions motive,** (2) the **precautionary motive,** and (3) the **speculative motive.** The transactions motive refers to the use of money as a medium of exchange and represents money in *active* circulation. It arises from the fact that economic units do not usually enjoy perfect synchronization between their streams of revenue (income) and their streams of expenditure. Economic units do not normally pay all their bills on payday; thus they need money for executing transactions on the days between paydays. In other words, each economic unit needs money to bridge the gap between its income stream and its expenditure stream. The *aggregate demand for transactions balances is roughly proportional to national income.*

The precautionary and speculative motives represent money held as **inactive** balances. The precautionary motive for holding money emanates from the uncertainty that exists in the real world. It is usually a wise precaution to guard against unforeseen events by holding extra cash instead of planning to spend the last dollar just before payday. Precautionary balances enable people to meet unanticipated increases in expenditure prompted by such adverse developments as illness, a car breakdown while on a trip, and the like. In addition, precautionary balances enable people to take advantage of unanticipated bargains and other opportunities. *The total amount of money held for precautionary purposes is primarily a function of national income.* For this reason, we can *combine the precautionary balances with the transactions balances and consider their sum to be roughly proportional to national income.*

Uncertainty is also responsible for the speculative motive for holding money. Even though money does not earn interest, it may still constitute a particularly attractive investment outlet at times of uncertainty. At such times, money provides protection against capital losses that could be brought about by adverse market conditions. Economic units hold speculative balances because they are uncertain about the future prices of securities and also about the exact time they will have to sell the securities, that is, when they will need liquidity. The demand for speculative balances arises from the fear of capital loss; *it is negatively* (or *inversely*) *related to the rate of interest.*

The prices of securities depend profoundly on the rate of interest. To appreciate this dependence, consider one particular type of security—the British Consol—which pays a fixed coupon return to the bearer but never matures. For instance, a 10 percent British Consol of £1,000 denomination is in effect a promise to pay the bearer £100 each year forever! Thus, those who buy this British Consol for £1,000 earn 10 percent per year on their investment. However, if the market rate of interest is less than 10 percent, the price of the British Consol must increase so that the coupon rate equals the rate of interest. For example, if the interest rate falls from 10 percent to 5 percent, the price of the British Consol must rise from £1,000 to £2,000 so that the person who buys it continues to earn the market rate of interest. Of course, if the rate of interest rises, the price of the British Consol must fall. In general, the price of the British Consol is equal to the ratio of the fixed coupon (£100) to the rate of interest. Thus there exists an inverse relationship between the price of the British Consol and the rate of interest. When the interest rate is high, the price of the British Consol is low; and when the interest rate is low, the price of the British Consol is high. This inverse relationship is typical between the prices of securities and the rate of interest. When the interest rate appears to be low, that is, when economic units *expect* the interest rate to rise (and thus the prices of securities to fall), they shift from securities to money because of the fear of capital losses.

After all, these capital losses could easily outweigh the interest the securities yield. When the interest rate appears to be high, that is, when economic units expect the rate of interest to fall (and thus the prices of securities to rise), they shift from money to securities because, in addition to the interest they earn by holding securities, they also expect capital gains.

Equilibrium in the money market prevails when the level of national income and the interest rate are such that the demand for money equals the given supply of money. Evidently *there are infinitely many combinations of income levels and interest rates that make the demand for money equal to the supply of money. The locus of all such combinations is known as the* **LM curve.**

General Macroeconomic Equilibrium

Figure 17-1 brings together the *IS* curve (which represents equilibrium in the goods market) and the *LM* curve (which reflects equilibrium in the money market). Typically, *the IS curve slopes downward.* As the rate of interest falls, desired investment increases, causing national income to increase (through the multiplier). *The LM curve slopes upward.* As the interest rate increases, speculative de-

FIGURE 17-1 **General macroeconomic equilibrium.** The equilibrium rate of interest (8 percent) and the equilibrium level of national income (300) are simultaneously determined by intersection *E* of the *IS* and *LM* curves.

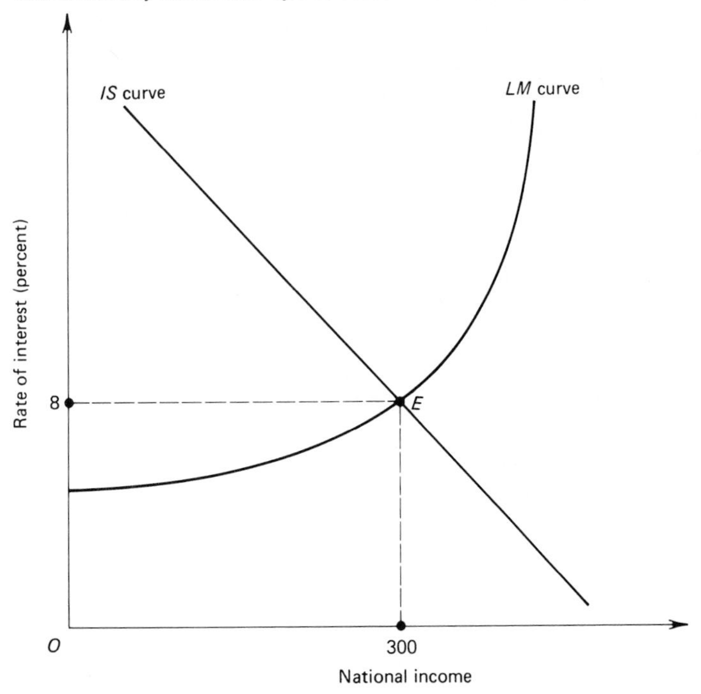

mand decreases and makes more money available for transactions purposes. The economy can absorb the higher transactions balances only if national income rises. Accordingly, an increase in the interest rate requires an increase in the level of national income in order to preserve equilibrium in the money market.

General macroeconomic equilibrium occurs at the intersection, *E*, of the *IS* and *LM* curves. The goods market is in equilibrium because *E* lies on the *IS* curve, and the money market is in equilibrium because *E* lies on the *LM* curve. At *E* the equilibrium interest rate is 8 percent and the equilibrium level of national income is 300. Note that equilibrium point *E* need not coincide either with full employment or balance-of-payments equilibrium.

17-2 BALANCE-OF-PAYMENTS EQUILIBRIUM: THE EXTERNAL BALANCE SCHEDULE

We now bring into focus the last piece of the puzzle: the balance of payments. Under what conditions is the balance of payments in equilibrium?

External Balance: Definition

We already know (see Chapter 12) that the balance of payments consists of three major accounts: the current account, the capital account, and the official reserve account. By accounting necessity, the balance of payments always balances, that is, the sum of the three accounts is always zero. This is the same as any family's personal finances. The family can spend more than it earns (a current account deficit) provided it can borrow (a capital account surplus); otherwise it must use its savings (reserves) to bridge the gap.

Balance-of-payments equilibrium, or **external balance,** prevails when the monetary authorities neither gain nor lose reserves (that is, when the official reserve account balance is zero). Evidently external balance is attained when the following condition is satisfied:

$$\text{Current account balance} + \text{capital account balance} = 0 \qquad (17\text{-}2)$$

The current account balance is the sum of two separate balances: (1) the balance on goods and services (that is, exports less imports) and (2) the balance on unilateral transfers. To simplify our exposition, we assume that the balance on unilateral transfers is zero; hence the current account balance coincides with the balance on goods and services, and we refer to it as the balance of trade. External balance prevails when an *export surplus* (that is, a *positive* current account balance) matches a *net capital outflow* (that is, a *negative* capital account balance); or when an *import surplus* (that is, a *negative* current account balance) matches a *net capital inflow* (that is, a *positive* capital account balance).

The Determinants of External Balance

Turn now to the determinants of the current account balance and the capital account balance. Recall the *assumption that the rate of foreign exchange is fixed.*

As we saw in Chapter 15, the balance of trade ($X - M$) depends on the level of national income (Y). As national income rises, imports tend to increase, causing the balance of trade to deteriorate. We have nothing more to add to that discussion.

The capital account balance depends primarily on the rate of interest. As the domestic rate of interest rises, people tend to substitute domestic securities (which tend to become cheaper) for foreign securities (whose prices remain unchanged), and the capital account improves. As the domestic rate of interest falls, people tend to substitute foreign securities for domestic securities, and the capital account deteriorates.

Economists distinguish among three types of capital mobility:

1 *Perfect capital mobility:* In this case, the domestic securities are perfect substitutes for foreign securities, and their prices (and thus the rate of interest) are determined in world markets. The rate of interest that prevails in the world markets must also prevail in our small, open economy.

2 *Perfect capital immobility:* In this case, our open economy's capital market is totally disconnected from the world capital markets. The capital account balance is always zero, irrespective of the domestic rate of interest.

3 *Imperfect capital mobility:* In this case, which we consider as typical, the domestic securities are only imperfect substitutes for foreign securities. The capital account balance is now a function of the interest-rate differential. As the domestic interest rate rises (assuming that the foreign interest rate remains constant), the capital account improves.

The External Balance Schedule

Given that the balance of trade is primarily a function of national income, while the net capital flow (that is, capital account balance) is primarily a function of the rate of interest, it is evident that external equilibrium prevails when the level of national income and the interest rate are such that the net capital flow matches the balance of trade. Indeed, there are infinitely many combinations of income levels and interest rates that are consistent with external balance. The locus of all such combinations is known as the **external balance schedule.**

The external balance schedule is illustrated in Figure 17-2, which also reproduces the *IS* and *LM* curves of Figure 17-1. To the extent that capital inflow is an increasing function of the domestic interest rate, the external balance schedule must be upward sloping, as shown. Thus, as the domestic interest rate rises, the net capital outflow falls (or the net capital inflow rises), and a surplus appears in the balance of payments. To restore external balance, national income must rise in order to induce an increase in imports equal to the reduction in the net capital outflow. Accordingly, an increase in the interest rate must be accom-

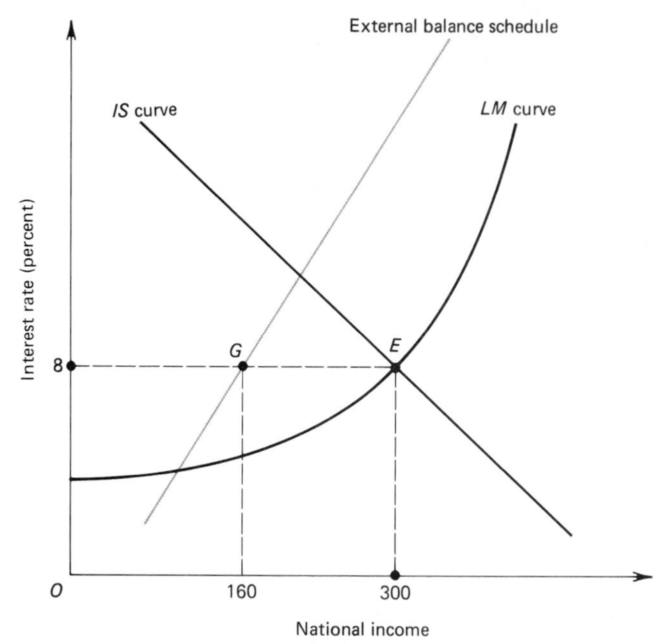

FIGURE 17-2 **The *IS-LM* model with the external balance schedule.** The intersection of the *IS* and *LM* curves determines the equilibrium level of national income (300) and the interest rate (8 percent). Since point *E* lies to the right of the external balance schedule, the balance of payments is in deficit. The deficit is actually proportional to horizontal distance *GE*, with the marginal propensity to import being the factor of proportionality.

panied by an increase in national income, that is, the external balance schedule must be upward sloping. This is the case of imperfect capital mobility. (When capital is perfectly immobile between countries, the external balance schedule becomes vertical at that level of income at which the balance of trade is zero; and when capital is perfectly mobile, the external balance schedule becomes horizontal at the world interest rate.)

The external balance schedule divides the whole quadrant into two regions:

1 The **region of external deficit,** which lies to the right of the external balance schedule. For any point within this region, the level of national income is too high and/or the rate of interest is too low for external balance. The balance of payments is in deficit, and the economy loses international reserves.

2 The **region of external surplus,** which lies to the left of the external balance schedule. For any point in this region, the level of national income is too low and/or the rate of interest is too high for external balance. The balance of payments is in surplus, and the monetary authorities gain international reserves.

The primary function of the external balance schedule is to show whether, at the current equilibrium indicated by the intersection, *E*, of the *IS* and *LM* curves, the balance of payments is in deficit or in surplus. In the example of Figure 17-2, the balance of payments must be in deficit because point *E* lies to the right of the external balance schedule, that is, point *E* lies within the region of external deficit.

How can we determine the size of the deficit illustrated in Figure 17-2? Merely by calculating the change in imports that is necessary to restore external balance, assuming that the rate of interest, and thus the capital account balance, remains constant. For instance, freezing the rate of interest at 8 percent and allowing national income to drop from 300 to 160 (that is, $\Delta Y = -140$), we can restore external balance (see point *G*). Suppose now that the marginal propensity to import is 0.10. By how much do imports fall as income falls by 140? Imports fall by 14 (that is, 0.10×140). Hence, the balance-of-payments deficit at *E* must be 14 also.

17-3 THE EFFECTS OF FISCAL AND MONETARY POLICY

How do fiscal and monetary policies (that is, autonomous changes in government spending or income taxes and the supply of money) affect national income and the interest rate as well as the balance of payments? We must answer this question before we consider the use of fiscal and monetary policies for the attainment of internal and external balance.

The Effects of Monetary Policy

Consider the effects of monetary policy first. An increase in the money supply causes the *LM* curve to shift to the right: At any interest rate, the larger money supply can support a higher income. This is shown by the dashed curve in Figure 17-3. Equilibrium shifts from E_0 to E_1; national income increases from 300 to 340 and the interest rate falls from 8 to 7 percent.

What is the effect on the balance of payments? The *increase* in the money supply *worsens* the balance of payments for two reasons: (1) through the additional imports that are induced by the increase in national income and (2) through the reduced capital inflow caused by the reduction in the interest rate. In terms of Figure 17-3, the deterioration of the balance of payments is illustrated by the fact that horizontal distance HE_1 (which shows the needed reduction in national income for the restoration of external balance *after* the increase in the supply of money) is necessarily larger than horizontal distance GE_0 (which shows the needed reduction in income for the restoration of external balance *before* the increase in the money supply).

Reversing the above argument, we conclude that a decrease in the money supply causes national income to fall, the interest rate to rise, and the balance of payments to improve (since imports tend to fall and capital inflow tends to rise).

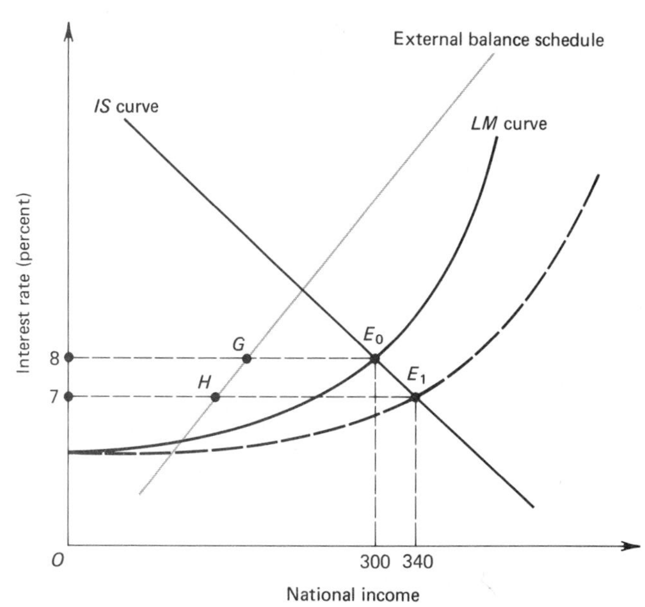

FIGURE 17-3 **The effects of monetary policy.** An increase in the money supply causes the *LM* curve to shift to the right, as shown by the dashed curve. Equilibrium shifts from E_0 to E_1. National income increases from 300 to 340, and the rate of interest falls from 8 to 7 percent. The balance of payments deteriorates because of higher imports and lower net capital flows. The balance-of-payments deterioration is illustrated by the fact that distance HE_1 is greater than distance GE_0.

The Effects of Fiscal Policy

Turn now to fiscal policy. An increase in government spending causes the *IS* curve to shift to the right: At any interest rate, national income is larger by the increase in government spending times the multiplier. This is shown by the dashed line in Figure 17-4. Equilibrium shifts from E_0 to E_1; national income increases from 300 to 400 and the interest rate rises from 8 to 12 percent.

What is the effect on the balance of payments? It is indeterminate. An expansionary fiscal policy gives rise to two conflicting effects: (1) It increases the level of national income, which *worsens* the balance of trade (because of increased imports), and (2) it raises the interest rate, which *improves* the capital account. The final outcome depends on which of these effects is stronger. This indeterminacy is illustrated in Figure 17-4 by the fact that horizontal distance HE_1 can be either smaller or larger than distance GE_0, depending on the relative slopes of the *LM* curve and the external balance schedule.

Reversing the above argument, we conclude that a decrease in government spending causes both national income and the interest rate to fall, but the effect on the balance of payments is again indeterminate.

17-4 THE COMPATIBILITY OF INTERNAL AND EXTERNAL BALANCE

As we have just seen, *fiscal and monetary policies have diametrically opposite effects on the interest rate* even though they have similar effects on national income. This is the key to the use of fiscal and monetary policies for the attainment of internal and external balance. The only important proviso is that the *capital flows must be responsive to interest-rate differentials.* The purpose of this section is to elucidate this.

The Internal and External Balance Schedules

Consider Figure 17-5, which illustrates our two targets: internal and external balance. As before, external balance occurs along the upward-sloping external balance schedule. Internal balance occurs along the vertical line drawn at the full-employment level of national income, Y_f. Evidently, internal and external balance occur simultaneously at point *F,* which is the only point that lies on both schedules.

To attain internal and external balance simultaneously, the authorities must take two steps, as follows:

FIGURE 17-4 **The effects of fiscal policy.** An increase in government spending causes the *IS* curve to shift to the right, as shown by the dashed line. Equilibrium shifts from E_0 to E_1. National income increases from 300 to 400, while the interest rate rises from 8 to 12 percent. The balance-of-payments effect is indeterminate, as horizontal distance HE_1 can be either smaller or larger than GE_0, depending on the relative slopes of the *LM* curve and the external balance schedule.

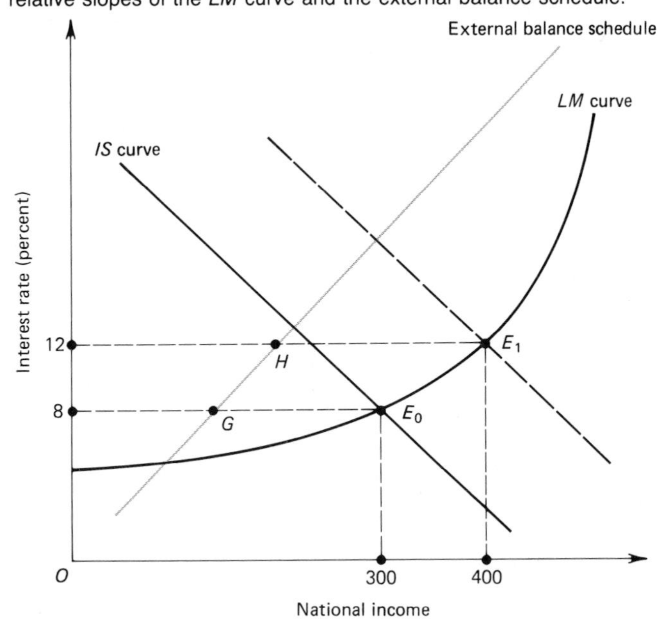

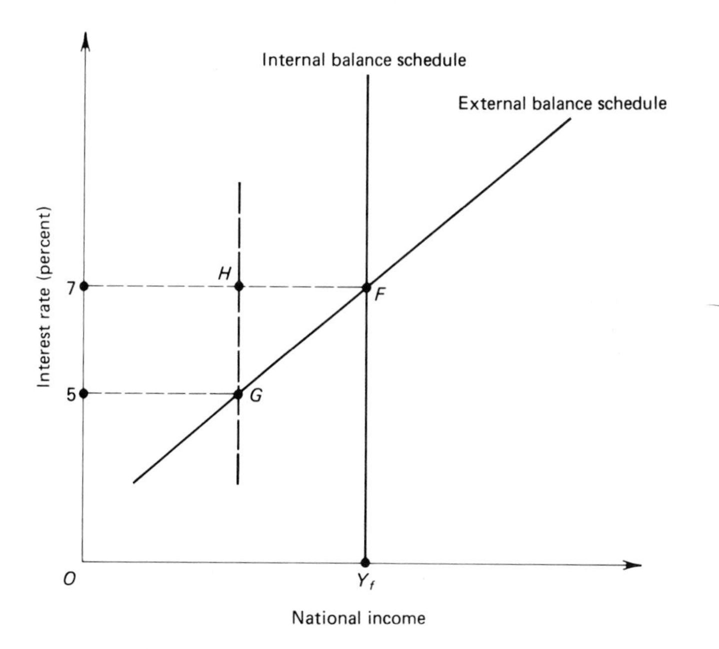

FIGURE 17-5 **The two targets: internal and external balance.** External balance occurs along the upward-sloping external balance schedule. Internal balance occurs along the vertical line drawn at full-employment income (Y_f). Internal and external balance prevail simultaneously at point *F* only. Policymakers must choose that fiscal-monetary mix that causes the *IS* and *LM* curves to pass through the general balance point (*F*).

1 They must fix the money supply at an appropriate level so that the *LM* curve passes through general balance point *F*.

2 They must fix government spending at an appropriate level so that the *IS* curve also passes through general balance point *F*.

The Importance of Capital Mobility

We can now clarify the implications of the proviso that capital flows are responsive to interest-rate differentials. Consider point *G* on the external balance schedule. At *G* the balance of payments is in equilibrium. If we shift the economy from *G* to *H* by raising the interest rate from 5 to 7 percent, the balance of payments will register a surplus, *but only when the higher interest rate attracts additional capital inflows.* In that case, we can restore external balance at the higher interest rate by allowing national income to increase. Thus, starting at *H,* we can restore external balance by moving to point *F,* which lies on the solid upward-sloping external balance schedule. If capital flows are *not* responsive to interest-rate differentials (perfect capital immobility), the balance of payments must remain in equilibrium at *H*. This means that when capital flows are not responsive to interest-rate differentials, the external balance schedule becomes a *vertical* line (as shown by dashed line *GH*), just like the internal balance schedule.

When the external balance schedule is vertical, the economy cannot possibly attain internal and external balance simultaneously by means of fiscal and monetary policies alone. The reason is simple: The internal and external balance schedules do not cross, as they are parallel vertical lines. At any particular time, the economy can be on either the internal or the external balance schedule *but not on both*. Hence a conflict arises between internal and external balance.

How can the economy simultaneously attain internal and external balance in the presence of a conflict? By an appropriate combination of expenditure-adjusting policies (for example, fiscal and monetary policies) and expenditure-switching policies (for example, exchange-rate adjustment and direct controls), as we saw in Chapter 15. In general, expenditure-switching policies cause the external balance schedule to shift. An appropriate expenditure-switching policy can make the vertical external balance schedule coincide with the vertical internal balance schedule and thus remove the potential conflict between internal and external balance. Then, *any* combination of fiscal and monetary policies that brings about internal balance also generates external balance.

Difficulties in the Practice of Policy

Consider Figure 17-6, which is similar to Figure 17-5. The internal and external balance schedules divide the whole quadrant into four disequilibrium zones, or **zones of economic unhappiness.** These zones are as follows:

Zone I: Unemployment and balance-of-payment surplus. This zone lies to the left of both the internal balance schedule and the external balance schedule.

Zone II: Potential inflationary pressure and balance-of-payments surplus. This zone lies to the left of the external balance schedule but to the right of the internal balance schedule.

Zone III: Potential inflationary pressure and balance-of-payments deficit. This zone lies to the right of both the internal balance schedule and the external balance schedule.

Zone IV: Unemployment and balance-of-payments deficit. This zone lies to the left of the internal balance schedule and to the right of the external balance schedule.

At any given time, the economy operates in one of the above four zones—at the intersection of the *IS* and *LM* curves. The authorities cannot be sure of the exact location of the *IS* and *LM* curves or of the external balance schedule, but they can easily infer the zone in which the economy happens to be from the actual data on unemployment, inflation, and the balance of payments. Is this knowledge sufficient for the correct formulation of economic policy? The answer is no!

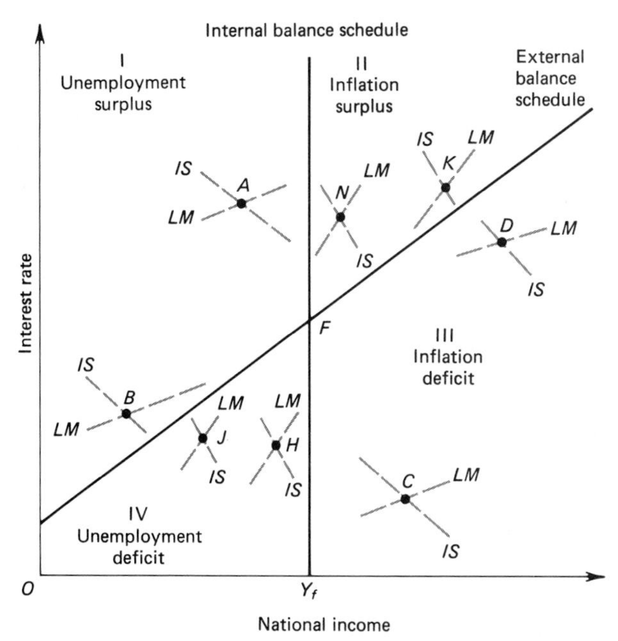

FIGURE 17-6 **The four zones of economic unhappiness.** The internal and external balance schedules divide the diagram into four disequilibrium zones. Knowledge of the zone in which the economy happens to be is not sufficient information for the formulation of economic policy.

In zones I and III, the authorities are completely in the dark. For instance, points *A* and *B* lie in zone I. If the economy is at point *A*, the authorities must reduce government spending (to shift the *IS* curve downward and to the left) and increase the money supply (to shift the *LM* curve to the right). However, if the economy is at point *B*, which also lies in zone I, the authorities must do the *opposite;* that is, they must increase government spending (to shift the *IS* curve to the right) and reduce the money supply (to shift the *LM* curve to the left). Similarly, points *C* and *D* in zone III imply diametrically opposite policies.

The situation is a little better in zones II and IV. In these two zones the direction of change in government spending is known. For instance, in zone II (see points *K* and *N*) the authorities must always reduce government spending (to shift the *IS* curve to the left). Similarly, in zone IV (see points *J* and *H*) the authorities must increase government spending (to shift the *IS* curve to the right). Unfortunately, the direction of change in the money supply continues to be uncertain. For instance, points *K* and *N* lie in zone II, but the authorities must increase the money supply at *N* and reduce it at *K*. Similarly, points *H* and *J* lie in zone IV, but the authorities must increase the money supply at *J* and reduce it at *H*. The indeterminacy of monetary policy in zones II and IV is completely removed when the *LM* curve is *flatter* than the external balance schedule, but then monetary policy becomes indeterminate in zones I and III. Unfortunately, the policymakers do not know whether the *LM* curve is flatter or steeper than the external balance schedule.

We conclude that without additional information on the precise location (and slope) of the *IS* and *LM* curves and the external balance schedule, mere knowledge of the zone in which the economy happens to be is not sufficient for the formulation of economic policy.

17-5 THE ASSIGNMENT PROBLEM

Our discussion so far points to a rather gloomy conclusion: Even though the simultaneous attainment of internal and external balance by means of fiscal and monetary policy is in principle feasible, policymakers lack the necessary information for the formulation of the correct policy mix. Are there any policy rules to assist policymakers in their quest for internal and external balance in a world of imperfect information? Indeed there are. This section deals with the famous **assignment problem,** whose proper solution leads to internal and external balance.

Nature of the Assignment Problem

If full information were available to policymakers, a centralized decision-making process under a unified policy authority for the simultaneous attainment of internal and external balance would be possible. But information is scarce. Policymakers have only data on national income, unemployment, inflation, the rate of interest, and the state of the balance of payments. Under these circumstances, the fiscal authorities may strongly disagree with the monetary authorities as to the proper policy mix. Differences in political persuasions and ethical beliefs intertwined with imperfect knowledge of the economic system could make the discussion more lively and the disagreement stronger and thus lead to a policy stalemate. Is there an alternative? Yes. It is **policy assignment.**

The assignment problem is a product of decentralized decision making and involves the *pairing of a particular policy instrument with a particular policy target.* For instance, the monetary authorities (which control the money supply) may be instructed to attain external balance only, ignoring any side effects of their actions on the level of employment. Similarly, the fiscal authorities may be instructed to use fiscal policy (changes in government spending and taxes) to attain internal balance, ignoring any possible side effects of their actions on the balance of payments.

When each arm of policymaking is assigned to a single policy target, the economy does not move to the general balance point in a single stroke. Instead, an adjustment process takes place. The monetary authorities may adjust the money supply to achieve external balance. In so doing, however, they may frustrate the plans of the fiscal authorities, who must adjust their policy in accordance with the new situation. But this action of the fiscal authorities may throw monetary policy off target. Thus, the monetary authorities must again make a change, and so on in an infinite regression. The assignment problem is successfully solved only when this adjustment process leads eventually to the attainment of both targets simultaneously. In technical jargon, the assignment must be "stable."

Mundell's Assignment

Mundell (1968, pp. 152–176 and 233–239) developed the **principle of effective market classification** according to which *the policy assignment is stable when each policy instrument is assigned to that target on which it has relatively the most influence.* The mathematical underpinnings of this principle are beyond the scope of this book. For our present purposes, we only need to know that *monetary policy should be assigned to external balance and fiscal policy to internal balance* (because monetary policy has a comparative advantage in working on external balance and fiscal policy has a comparative advantage in working on internal balance).

Mundell's assignment rule implies the following prescriptions for specific imbalances:

Zone*	State of the economy	Monetary policy	Fiscal policy
I	Unemployment and surplus	Expansionary	Expansionary
II	Inflation and surplus	Expansionary	Contractionary
III	Inflation and deficit	Contractionary	Contractionary
IV	Unemployment and deficit	Contractionary	Expansionary

*See Figure 17-6.

Advanced treatises on this subject show that when the policy authorities carry out the indicated policy changes smoothly and without lags, Mundell's assignment rule leads to the attainment of internal and external balance. In the presence of lags and discrete policy changes, however, Mundell's assignment rule may become unstable. These problems are illustrated in Appendix 17.

17-6 CRITICISM OF THE FISCAL-MONETARY POLICY MIX

The use of fiscal and monetary policy to attain internal and external balance has been criticized on several points, as follows.

First, fiscal and monetary policies may be subject to constraints, particularly political constraints. For instance, governments may not be willing to either reduce government spending to a low level or raise interest rates to high levels.

Second, even in the absence of political constraints, capital flows may fail to be sufficiently sensitive to interest-rate differentials. In addition, destabilizing speculation may complicate the problem tremendously.

Finally, some economists argue that Mundell's approach is not a true adjustment mechanism. They view the fiscal-monetary mix as a method of *financing* the payments imbalances. The short-term capital flows that are prompted by monetary policy are classified as *accommodating*—not autonomous. These capital flows simply fill a gap left by other transactions. More important, however, the short-term capital flows may be ephemeral. In principle, the short-term capital flows reflect an adjustment in the allocation of *stocks* of assets. When the adjustment proceeds far enough, so that the stocks are optimally allocated, the short-term capital flows must cease. (Nevertheless, in a growing world economy, the short-term capital flows may continue forever because the stocks tend to increase over time.) In addition, interest payments on the mounting stock of liabilities to foreigners may eventually sabotage Mundell's solution by reversing the short-term capital flow (that is, by converting an inflow into an outflow), thus further aggravating the payments imbalance.

17-7 PAYMENTS IMBALANCES AND THE SUPPLY OF MONEY

There is a mutual interaction between the money supply and the balance of payments. So far we examined how changes in the money supply affect the balance of payments. In this section, we wish to complete the circle by studying how payments imbalances influence the money supply. This means that we now drop the assumption that the money supply is exogenous.

Alternative Banking Systems and the Money Supply

The simplest banking system, although not necessarily the best, is that system in which the money supply is always equal to the stock of international reserves. The best example of this system is the **gold-specie standard,** where the actual currency in circulation consists of gold coins of a certain fixed gold content. The coins are freely minted at standard rates. They are also freely meltable and exportable. Under the gold-specie standard, payments imbalances (deficits or surpluses) give rise to gold movements (gold exports or imports, as the case may be). In turn, *gold movements imply changes in the money supply on a one-to-one basis.*

Modern banking systems are much more complicated than the gold-specie standard. For instance, in the United States there are three major types of money: **coins, paper money,** and **checking deposits** (or **demand deposits** in commercial banks). Coins are only a negligible percentage of the total money supply. Paper money (mostly Federal Reserve notes) accounts for roughly 25 percent of the total U.S. money supply. Demand deposits in commercial banks account for the rest of the U.S. money supply; they are by far the largest component of the U.S. money supply.

Commercial banks operate on the **fractional reserve principle:** Member banks are required to maintain reserves in the form of deposits at the Federal Reserve. A bank's reserve deposits must be equal to a certain percentage of that bank's demand liabilities. When it is unable to meet its reserve requirements, a member bank can borrow from the Federal Reserve. The rate of interest the Federal Reserve charges member banks is called the **discount rate.** The maximum volume of demand deposits the commercial banks can create depends on (1) the volume of bank reserves and (2) the required reserve ratio:

$$\text{Demand deposits} = \frac{\text{reserves}}{\text{required reserve ratio}} \tag{17-3}$$

The reciprocal of the required-reserve ratio is usually referred to as the **money multiplier.** Equation (17-3) can also be written as:

$$\text{Demand deposits} = \text{money multiplier} \times \text{reserves} \tag{17-4}$$

The Federal Reserve can control the total volume of demand deposits by controlling its determinants, that is, the reserve ratio and the volume of bank reserves. For instance, to *increase* the money supply, the Federal Reserve must either *reduce* the required reserve ratio, *lower* the discount rate, or *purchase* government securities from the public. The reduction in the required reserve ratio leaves commercial banks with *excess* reserves and induces the banks to make additional loans, which cause demand deposits to increase. The reduction in the discount rate tends to increase the member banks' *borrowed* reserves because borrowing from the Federal Reserve becomes more profitable for those banks. The purchase of government bonds increases the member banks' *un*borrowed reserves—the seller of the securities obtains a demand deposit in a commercial bank, which in turn experiences an increase in its reserve deposit with the Federal Reserve. Federal Reserve purchases and sales of U.S. securities are called **open-market operations.** Varying the required reserve ratio is a drastic measure. For this reason, the Federal Reserve Board relies primarily on the discount rate and open-market operations, changing reserve requirements only infrequently.

Payments Imbalances and Demand Deposits

How do balance-of-payments deficits and surpluses affect the supply of money when a modern banking system, such as that of the United States, is in operation? We shall answer this question within the context of a rather simplified modern banking system.

Assume that the total supply of money consists of demand deposits only. The exclusion of coins and paper money merely simplifies matters without affecting seriously any fundamental conclusions. Assume further that all international reserves, such as gold and foreign currencies, are in the hands of the central bank, even though in practice commercial banks may also hold international reserve assets.

Broadly speaking, the assets of commercial banks consist of (1) **reserve deposit accounts** with the central bank and (2) **domestic assets,** such as stocks, bonds, and loans to corporations. The liabilities of commercial banks are the demand deposits we have already identified with the total money supply. By accounting necessity, the total assets of commercial banks are equal to their total liabilities; hence we have the identity

$$\text{Money supply} = \text{bank reserves} + \text{domestic assets} \tag{17-5}$$

Unlike Equations (17-3) and (17-4) which are valid only when the commercial banks are fully loaned up, Equation (17-5) is always true.

Payments imbalances have two effects on the money supply: (1) a **direct effect,** which concerns the *change in bank reserves* due to the change in international reserves, and (2) an **indirect effect,** which captures the *induced change in domestic assets.* The indirect effect is implied by the direct effect. *If* the commercial banks are always fully loaned up, the change in bank reserves (that is, in the monetary base) will induce the commercial banks to adjust their holdings of domestic assets as well.

Consider a concrete example. Suppose that the required reserve ratio is 0.2 (that is, the money multiplier is 5) and the country suffers from a balance-of-payments deficit of $100. In particular, assume that the exporters receive $1,900 (in foreign exchange), which they sell to the central bank through their commercial banks. The importers pay $2,000 (in foreign exchange) for their imports. The importers buy the foreign exchange they need from the central bank through their commercial banks.

The above transactions result in the following direct changes:

Change in demand deposits in commercial banks	− $100
(The exporters' demand deposits *increase* by $1,900 while the importers' demand deposits *decrease* by $2,000.)	
Change in international reserves	− $100
(The central bank purchases $1,900 and sells $2,000.)	
Change in bank reserves	− $100
(The commercial banks' reserve deposit account in the central bank increases by $1,900 and decreases by $2,000.)	

The above are only the direct effects of the deficit. Assuming that all commercial banks were fully loaned up to begin with, a multiple contraction process of the money supply would follow as the commercial banks reduced their holdings of domestic assets in order to satisfy the legal reserve requirements. Eventually, the money supply would *fall* by $500 (reduction in bank reserves of $100 + reduction in bank domestic assets of $400). The reduction in the money supply would be equal to the reduction in bank reserves ($100) times the money multiplier (5).

Of course, it is conceivable that initially the commercial banks may have excess reserves. In that case, the multiple contraction process of the money supply will not take place. The commercial banks will merely experience a reduction in their excess reserves and the money supply (demand deposits) will fall by $100 (direct effect) only.

We have established the following important conclusion:

Payments imbalances have definite effects on the supply of money. A balance-of-payments deficit tends to reduce the money supply of the deficit country, and a balance-of-payments surplus tends to increase

the money supply of the surplus country. The precise changes in the money supply depend on the specific structure of the banking system.

Sterilization Operations

The preceding discussion shows how payments imbalances affect the money supply *when the monetary authorities react passively, that is, do nothing.* However, the money supply is under the control of the monetary authorities; and the monetary authorities may actively seek to *sterilize* the payments imbalance, that is, prevent the payments imbalance from having any net effect on the money supply.

Historically, such **sterilization operations** were not uncommon even during the gold-standard era (1870–1914). Nevertheless, they became widespread in the 1920s, and especially after World War II, when full employment became a primary objective of economic policy. Thus, monetary policy, the main instrument of the balance-of-payments adjustment process under the gold-standard rules of the game, was diverted from its initial function of keeping the balance of payments in equilibrium (external balance) and redirected toward the achievement of full employment (internal balance).

How do the monetary authorities carry out their sterilization operations? To sterilize a balance-of-payments deficit, they must purchase government bonds in the open market, reduce the discount rate, or lower reserve requirements. To sterilize a balance-of-payments surplus, they must do the opposite, that is, they must either sell government securities, raise the discount rate, or raise reserve requirements.

Apparently, there are limits to the ability of the monetary authorities to sterilize payments imbalances. For instance, the monetary authorities cannot continue sterilizing a chronic (or fundamental) deficit indefinitely, because they will sooner or later run out of international reserve assets. Similarly, the monetary authorities cannot continue sterilizing a chronic surplus indefinitely—sooner or later their stock of international reserve assets will become equal to the domestic money supply, and further surpluses will raise the money supply on a one-to-one basis, as in the case of the gold-specie standard.

We conclude that in the long run chronic payments imbalances are likely to affect the money supply. In the short run, however, the monetary authorities have plenty of leeway, and they actually do offset payments imbalances by means of their sterilization operations.

17-8 THE MONETARY PROCESS

In our earlier discussion of the *IS-LM* model, we assumed that the monetary authorities keep the money supply constant essentially by sterilizing the effects of payments imbalances. Nevertheless, under the gold-standard rules of the game, the deficit country must allow its money supply to fall, and the surplus country must allow its money supply to rise. Indeed, the new monetary approach to the balance of payments (summarized in Chapter 19) is built on the premise that the monetary flows associated with payments imbalances are not sterilized—or cannot be, within the relevant time period—but instead influence the money supply. How does the removal of sterilization operations affect our results?

The *IS-LM* Model Again

Consider Figure 17-7, which is similar to Figure 17-2. Assume that the economy suffers from a balance-of-payments deficit, as indicated by the intersection, *E,* of the *IS* and *LM* curves. When the balance of payments is allowed to exert its influence on the money supply (as, for instance, in the case of the gold-specie standard), the equilibrium at *E* cannot last. Rather, it becomes a *temporary* equilibrium. As the monetary authorities lose international reserves, the money supply falls and the *LM* curve shifts continuously to the left—at the same interest rate but with a smaller supply of money, the money market can remain in equilibrium at a lower level of national income. This process eventually comes to an end when the *LM* curve shifts sufficiently to the left and passes through the intersection, *F,* of the *IS* curve and the external balance schedule.

Under the present circumstances of no sterilization operations, the long-run

FIGURE 17-7 **The monetary process.** In the absence of sterilization, the money supply ceases to be exogenous and the equilibrium at *E* cannot last. As the monetary authorities lose reserves, the money supply falls and the *LM* curve shifts continuously to the left until long-run equilibrium is attained at the intersection (*F*) of the *IS* curve and the external balance schedule.

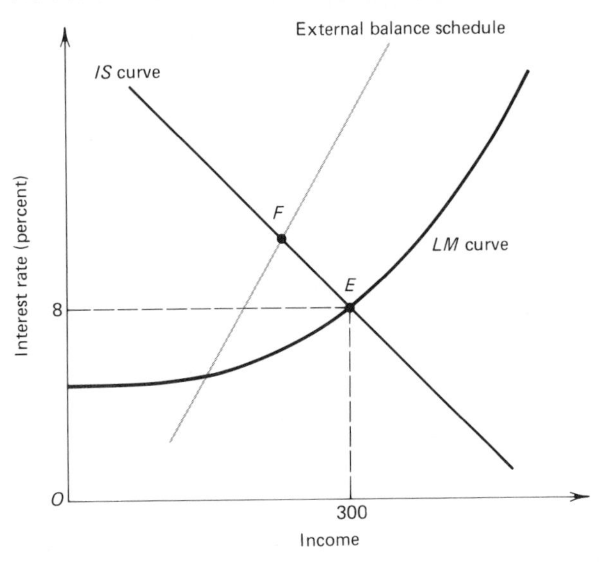

equilibrium of the system is at *F*, the intersection of the unchanging *IS* curve and the external balance schedule—not at *E*, the intersection of the *IS* and *LM* curves. The money supply ceases to be exogenous. Rather, it becomes an important endogenous variable whose value stabilizes only when the system reaches long-run equilibrium at point *F*.

Assuming that the economy enjoys full employment at *E*, the passive policy of the monetary authorities creates unemployment. Thus, by suspending their sterilization operations, the monetary authorities allow the system to move from *E* to *F*. In effect, the monetary authorities sacrifice the goal of full employment at the altar of external balance. This explains why monetary authorities refuse to remain passive but instead actively pursue sterilization operations in an effort to "immunize" the money supply against payments imbalances. To restore full employment at *E*, the economy must apply expenditure-switching policies to shift the external balance schedule to the right.

Perfect Capital Mobility

Finally, consider the extreme case of perfect capital mobility. This means that financial capital is perfectly mobile between countries. Investors do not mind which country's securities they hold. If the domestic interest rate rises above the foreign interest rate, funds will flow into the country until rates are again the same. In equilibrium, the domestic interest rate cannot differ from the world interest rate. The external balance schedule becomes *horizontal* at the world interest rate. In this extreme case, monetary policy becomes totally ineffective. Full employment can be achieved only through fiscal policy (as well as expenditure-switching policies). This is illustrated in Figure 17-8.

The external balance schedule (*EBS*) is horizontal at the world interest rate (8 percent). Suppose that the economy starts at full equilibrium at *E* and the authorities try to raise income with an expansionary fiscal policy. The *IS* curve shifts to the right, as shown by the dashed *IS'* curve. In the absence of perfect capital mobility, equilibrium would move to the intersection, *F*, of the *LM* curve and the dashed curve *IS'*. But at *F* the domestic interest rate (10 percent) would be higher than the world interest rate (8 percent). That would attract a large flow of capital from abroad. In the absence of sterilization, the incipient balance-of-payments surplus would expand the money supply and cause the *LM* curve to shift to the right (as shown by the dashed curve *LM'*). This process will continue until equilibrium is re-established at *G*. Thus, in the presence of perfect capital mobility, *fiscal policy can effectively increase output and employment.*

Turn now to monetary policy. Can the monetary authorities increase national income with an increase in the money supply? The answer is no! Suppose again that the initial equilibrium at *E* is disturbed by an expansionary monetary policy. Initially, the *LM* curve shifts to the right, as shown by the dashed curve *LM'*. The domestic interest rate tends to fall to 6 percent, as shown by *H* at the intersection of the dashed curve *LM'* and the *IS* curve, and financial capital leaves the country. If the monetary authorities attempt to sterilize the

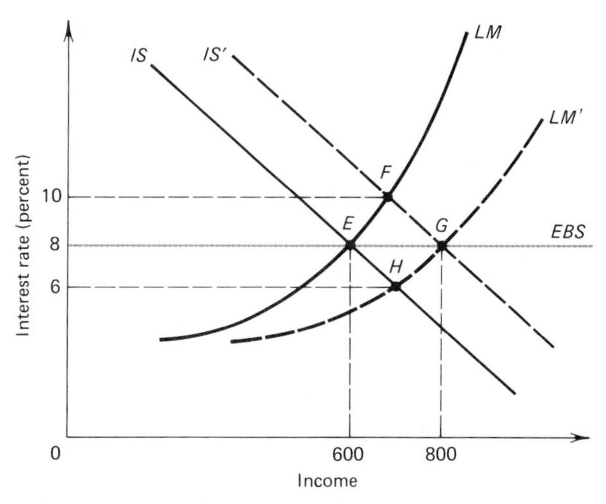

FIGURE 17-8 **Perfect capital mobility.** Full equilibrium occurs initially at *E*. An expansionary fiscal policy causes the *IS* curve to shift to the right, as shown by the dashed curve *IS′*. The interest rate tends to rise (see point *F*), which causes an inflow of foreign capital. The incipient balance-of-payments surplus expands the money supply, causing the *LM* curve to shift to the right, as shown by the dashed curve *LM′*. Equilibrium is re-established at *G*. By contrast, monetary policy is totally ineffective. An increase in the money supply causes the interest rate to fall (see point *H*); and the incipient deficit forces the money supply to return to its original level. Equilibrium returns to *E*.

balance-of-payments deficit, they will soon run out of reserves. Equilibrium can be re-established only when the money supply is allowed to fall to its original level, causing the *LM* curve to shift back to its initial position. Thus the economy returns to *E*, where nothing has changed; only the stock of international reserves is now lower. *In the presence of perfect capital mobility, monetary policy is totally ineffective in raising income and employment.*

17-9 SUMMARY

1 Fiscal and monetary policies have diametrically opposite effects on the interest rate (even though they have similar effects on national income). This difference is the key to their potential use for the attainment of internal and external balance. The only important proviso is that capital flows must be responsive to interest-rate differentials.

2 The *IS* curve is the locus of all combinations of income levels and interest rates that satisfy the equation $I(r) + \overline{X} = S(Y) + M(Y)$, which is the commodity-market-equilibrium condition. The *IS* curve is either downward-sloping or vertical according to whether aggregate spending (particularly investment) is responsive to the interest rate or not, respectively.

3 The demand for money depends positively on the level of national income (transactions plus precautionary balances) and negatively on the interest rate (speculative demand). The *LM* curve is the locus of all combinations of income levels and interest rates that keep the demand for money equal to the supply of money.

4 The external balance schedule is the locus of all combinations of income levels and interest rates that are consistent with balance-of-payments equilibrium (external balance), that is, those combinations that satisfy the equation: balance of trade + capital account balance = 0 (assuming that the balance on unilateral transfers is zero). The external balance schedule is vertical, upward-sloping, or horizontal, according to whether capital is perfectly immobile, imperfectly mobile, or perfectly mobile, respectively. Further, the external balance schedule divides the whole quadrant into two regions, the region of external deficit (located to its right) and the region of external surplus (located to its left).

5 Assuming that the supply of money is exogenous, the equilibrium interest rate and national income are determined simultaneously by the intersection of the *IS* and *LM* curves. The balance of payments registers a deficit or surplus according to whether the intersection of the *IS* and *LM* curves lies in the region of external deficit or surplus, respectively.

6 An increase in the money supply worsens the balance of payments for two reasons: (a) it lowers the interest rate (which worsens the capital account), and (b) it increases national income and imports (which worsens the balance of trade). A decrease in the money supply has symmetrical effects.

7 An increase in government spending (or a reduction in taxes) raises both the interest rate and national income. Hence, it improves the capital account and worsens the balance of trade. Its overall balance-of-payments effect is indeterminate. A decrease in government spending (or an increase in taxes) has symmetrical effects.

8 Internal and external balance occur simultaneously at the general balance point, which coincides with the intersection of the internal balance schedule (a vertical line drawn at the point of full-employment income) and the external balance schedule.

9 To achieve internal and external balance simultaneously, policymakers must set the money supply and government spending at such levels as to make the *LM* and *IS* curves pass through the general balance point.

10 When the external balance schedule is vertical, fiscal and monetary policies alone cannot achieve internal and external balance simultaneously (since a general balance point does not exist). Expenditure-switching policies, however, can shift the vertical external balance schedule and make it coincide with the internal balance schedule. Then any combination of fiscal and monetary policies that brings about internal balance generates external balance also.

11 The internal and external balance schedules divide the diagram into four zones of economic unhappiness. At any time, the economy operates in one of these zones (at the intersection of the *IS* and *LM* curves). Indeed, the statistical data on inflation-unemployment and the balance of payments indicate the relevant zone. However, there is always uncertainty as to which policy mix is the correct one.

12 The assignment problem is a product of decentralized decision making and involves the pairing of a policy instrument with a policy target. Under this scheme, the economy does not move to the general balance point in a single stroke. Instead, an adjustment process takes place. The assignment problem is successfully solved only when this adjustment process is stable.

13 Mundell proposed to assign monetary policy to external balance and fiscal policy to internal balance because monetary policy has a comparative advantage in working on external balance and fiscal policy has a comparative advantage in working on internal balance.

14 The use of fiscal and monetary policy to attain internal and external balance has been criticized on several points: (a) It ignores political constraints; (b) capital flows may not be sufficiently sensitive to interest-rate differentials, or they may dry up quickly (since short-term capital flows reflect an adjustment in the allocation of stocks of assets), or interest payments may sabotage the solution; and (c) the fiscal-monetary mix is not a true adjustment—it is merely a method of financing payments imbalances.

15 A payments imbalance leads to a direct change in bank reserves, which, in turn, induces the commercial banks to adjust their holdings of domestic assets. Assuming the banks are always fully loaned up, the change in the money supply (demand deposits) is equal to the change in bank reserves times the money multiplier.

16 The monetary authorities can, and often do, sterilize payments imbalances, even though there are limits to such operations. To sterilize a deficit (surplus), the monetary authorities must either purchase (sell) government bonds in the open market, reduce (raise) the discount rate, or lower (raise) reserve requirements.

17 In the absence of sterilization operations, the intersection of the *IS* and *LM* curves corresponds to a temporary equilibrium because the money supply ceases to be exogenous. Long-run equilibrium of the system occurs at the intersection of the unchanging *IS* curve and the external balance schedule—the supply of money stabilizes at that point only.

18 With perfect capital mobility, fiscal policy can effectively increase income and employment. By contrast, monetary policy is totally ineffective.

PROBLEMS[1]

1 You are given the following hypothetical economic relationships pertaining to the open economy of Canada:

$$S = -50 + 0.2Y \qquad \text{(saving function)}$$

$$I = 100 - 50r \qquad \text{(investment function)}$$

[1]Problems that appear with asterisks are more difficult.

$$M = 20 + 0.05Y \qquad \text{(import function)}$$

$$X = 80 \qquad \text{(exogenous exports)}$$

$$M_s = 203 \qquad \text{(money supply)}$$

$$M_d = 0.25Y - 20r \qquad \text{(demand for money)}$$

Canada enjoys perfect capital mobility. Its interest rate (r) remains equal to the world interest rate, which currently stands at 0.10.

a Determine Canada's *IS* and *LM* curves.
b What is Canada's equilibrium national income?
c What is Canada's balance of trade?
d What is Canada's capital inflow or capital outflow?
***e** Suppose that Canada's investment increases autonomously by 50. (The new investment function takes the form $I' = 150 - 50r$.) What are the effects on Canada's national income, balance of trade, capital inflow (or capital outflow), and money supply?
***f** Alternatively, suppose that Canada's central bank increases the money supply to 303. What will be the effects on Canada's national income, balance of trade, and capital inflow (or outflow)?

2 Return to the scenario of problem 1, but assume that Canada's capital inflow (K) is an increasing function of the domestic interest rate (r). In particular, assume that

$$K = 100r - 4$$

a What is Canada's balance-of-payments deficit or surplus at the initial national income equilibrium?
b Suppose again that Canada's investment increases by 50. What will be the effects on Canada's national income, balance of trade, and capital inflow (or outflow)?
c Alternatively, suppose that Canada's money supply decreases to 150. What will be the effects on Canada's national income, balance of trade, and capital inflow (or outflow)?

3 Assume that the monetary authorities of Egypt do not sterilize payments imbalances. Capital inflow is totally insensitive to changes in the domestic interest rate. Egypt's marginal propensity to import is 0.20. For each of the following disturbances, determine the effects on Egypt's national income, interest rate, and balance of payments. (If you are unable to provide a numerical answer to any question, indicate the direction of change.)

a Investment increases autonomously by 100.
b Imports increase autonomously by 100.
c Exports increase autonomously by 100.
d Capital inflow increases autonomously by 100.
e The monetary authorities increase the money supply by 100.
f The demand for money increases autonomously by 100.

4 You are given the following hypothetical data pertaining to Spain:

$$X = 100 \qquad \text{(exogenous exports)}$$

$$M = 20 + 0.1Y \qquad \text{(import function)}$$

$$K = -80 + 500r \qquad \text{(capital-inflow function)}$$

$$Y_F = 600 \qquad \text{(full-employment income)}$$

a Derive the external balance schedule and the internal balance schedule.
b At what interest rate can Spain attain internal and external balance simultaneously?
c In each of the following cases (identified with current income, Y, and current interest rate, r) give the fiscal-monetary policy mix that is necessary for attaining internal and external balance. (In each case, indicate only whether fiscal and monetary policy should be contractionary or expansionary or whether some type of uncertainty prevails.)

(i) $Y = 400$, $r = 0.10$
(ii) $Y = 550$, $r = 0.09$
(iii) $Y = 700$, $r = 0.13$
(iv) $Y = 650$, $r = 0.14$

d Illustrate your results graphically.

SUGGESTED READING

Chacholiades, M. (1978). *International Monetary Theory and Policy.* McGraw-Hill Book Company, New York, chaps. 17, 18, and 19.

Fleming, J. M. (1962). "Domestic Financial Policies Under Fixed and Under Floating Exchange Rates." *International Monetary Fund Staff Papers,* vol. 9, pp. 369–379. Reprinted in R. N. Cooper (ed.), *International Finance,* Penguin Books, Baltimore, 1969.

Kenen, P. B. (1985). "Macroeconomic Theory and Policy: How the Closed Economy Was Opened." In R. W. Jones and P. B. Kenen (eds.), *Handbook of International Economics,* vol. 2, North-Holland, New York, 1985.

Keynes, J. M. (1936). *The General Theory of Employment, Interest and Money.* Macmillan and Company, London.

Marston, R. C. (1985). "Stabilization Policies in Open Economies." In R. W. Jones and P. B. Kenen (eds.), *Handbook of International Economics,* vol. 2, North-Holland, New York, 1985.

Meade, J. E. (1951). *The Theory of International Economic Policy,* vol. 1, *The Balance of Payments.* Oxford University Press, New York.

Mundell, R. A. (1968). *International Economics.* Macmillan Publishing Company, New York.

Whitman, M. v. N. (1970). *Policies for Internal and External Balance.* Special Papers in International Economics, no. 9, International Finance Section, Princeton University, Princeton, N.J.

CHAPTER 18

FLEXIBLE VERSUS FIXED EXCHANGE RATES

This chapter deals with the economics of the flexible exchange-rate system and the continuing debate over fixed and flexible exchange rates. Under flexible exchange rates, the rate of foreign exchange is determined daily in the foreign exchange market by the forces of supply and demand. The daily movements of the exchange rate are not restricted in any way by government policy, although monetary authorities may intervene in the foreign exchange market to iron out wide fluctuations. The advocates of flexible exchange rates argue that the freedom of the exchange rate to move daily in response to market forces does not necessarily imply that it will actually move significantly or erratically from day to day. It will do so only if the underlying economic forces are themselves erratic, causing erratic shifts in the supply and demand curves for foreign exchange. By clearing the foreign exchange market, the flexibility of the exchange rate maintains external balance. The authorities may then use other macroeconomic policies to achieve internal balance.

When the industrial countries adopted flexible exchange rates early in 1973, most economists thought that the conflicts between internal and external balance that often prevailed under the adjustable peg would be removed and that harmony would rule in the foreign exchange market. Instead, because of the exchange-rate volatility that prevailed in the ensuing years, economists and policymakers alike are now skeptical about the long-run viability of flexible exchange rates. Critics insists that the current system (or perhaps "nonsystem") is badly in need of reform.

18-1 THE THEORY OF EMPLOYMENT WITH FLEXIBLE EXCHANGE RATES

In Chapter 16 we studied the income-adjustment mechanism under a regime of fixed rates of exchange and reached the important conclusion that international trade is a significant vehicle for the transmission of business cycles between countries—a boom (depression) in one country brings about an expansion (contraction) in the rest of the world. We must now broaden the scope of our investigation by considering the theory of employment under a regime of flexible exchange rates. Under this regime, the rate of foreign exchange adjusts instantaneously and maintains equilibrium in the foreign exchange market continuously. Would such a flexible exchange-rate system act as a buffer and "insulate" an open economy from disturbances that occur in the rest of the world? Would a country now be able to maintain an independent fiscal and monetary policy to stabilize domestic income and employment, ignoring repercussions from foreign disturbances? These are important questions, and we analyze them in this section. (See also Section 18-5.)

National Income Equilibrium under Flexible Exchange Rates

Recall that under a fixed exchange-rate system, national income equilibrium in a small, open economy prevails when desired aggregate demand $C(Y) + \bar{I} + \bar{X} - M(Y)$ equals aggregate output or national income, Y. That is, national income equilibrium occurs when the level of national income is such that the following equation is satisfied:

$$Y = C(Y) + \bar{I} + \bar{X} - M(Y) \tag{18-1}$$

Under a flexible exchange-rate system, the foreign exchange market is constantly in equilibrium. On the simplifying assumption that the net balance on capital flows and unilateral transfers is zero, equilibrium in the foreign exchange market means that the balance of trade is always zero, that is, $X - M(Y) = 0$. Accordingly, Equation (18-1) reduces to:

$$Y = C(Y) + \bar{I} \tag{18-2}$$

Equation (18-2) is exactly the same as the national income equilibrium condition for a closed economy. Evidently, the flexibility of the rate of exchange cuts off the *direct* link between national income and the balance of payments and tends to insulate the open economy from disturbances that occur in the rest of the world. Insofar as the equilibrium level of national income is concerned, an open economy that adopts the flexible exchange-rate system appears to behave like a closed economy.

The Open-Economy Multiplier under Flexible Exchange Rates

What is the size of the open-economy multiplier under flexible exchange rates? For all those autonomous changes that affect the open economy's desired level of spending at each level of income, such as autonomous changes in the desired flow of either investment, I, or consumption, $C(Y)$, expenditure (as well as government spending), the open-economy multiplier with flexible exchange rates is equal to the closed economy multiplier (that is, equal to the reciprocal of the marginal propensity to save). For other autonomous changes, such as changes in exports or imports (see specific illustrations below), the open-economy multiplier with flexible exchange rates is zero.

We can understand the truth of the above proposition and also gain further insights into the mechanism of national income determination under flexible exchange rates by considering a few specific examples. We should reconsider briefly the effects on national income of the following disturbances, which we studied in Section 15-3:

1 An autonomous increase in desired investment
2 An autonomous increase in exports
3 An autonomous decrease in imports

Throughout our discussion, we assume that the marginal propensity to save is 0.10 and that the marginal propensity to import is 0.15. This is the same assumption we made earlier in relation to the examples of Section 15-3. However, those examples were based on the assumption that the rate of exchange remains fixed always. The present examples are based on the assumption that the rate of exchange is flexible, that is, the rate of exchange adjusts instantaneously and maintains equilibrium in the foreign exchange market constantly. Readers may want to review their understanding of the examples of Section 15-3 before proceeding to the rest of this section because the discussion presupposes familiarity with that analysis.

1 An Increase in Desired Investment Suppose that domestic investment, $\bar{I}$, increases by \$100. What is the effect on national income?

As we saw in Section 15-3, under fixed exchange rates an increase in domestic investment (\$100) causes aggregate demand for domestic output to increase by the same amount. National income *increases* by the change in investment times the open-economy multiplier; that is, $4 \times \$100 = \$400$. [Recall that the open-economy multiplier with fixed rates of exchange is $1/(0.10 + 0.15) = 4$.] What happens when the rate of exchange adjusts instantaneously and maintains equilibrium in the foreign exchange market continuously?

Consider Figure 18-1, which is similar to Figure 15-4. Equilibrium occurs initially at E, where the $S(Y) - \bar{I}$ schedule intersects the $\bar{X} - M(Y)$ schedule along the horizontal axis. (Under flexible exchange rates, national income equilibrium occurs always along the horizontal axis. Why?) At E, desired saving, $S(Y)$, equals desired investment, $\bar{I}$; and exports, $\bar{X}$, equal desired imports, $M(Y)$. That is, at initial national income equilibrium E, the foreign exchange market is also in equilibrium and the rate of exchange has no tendency to change from its current level.

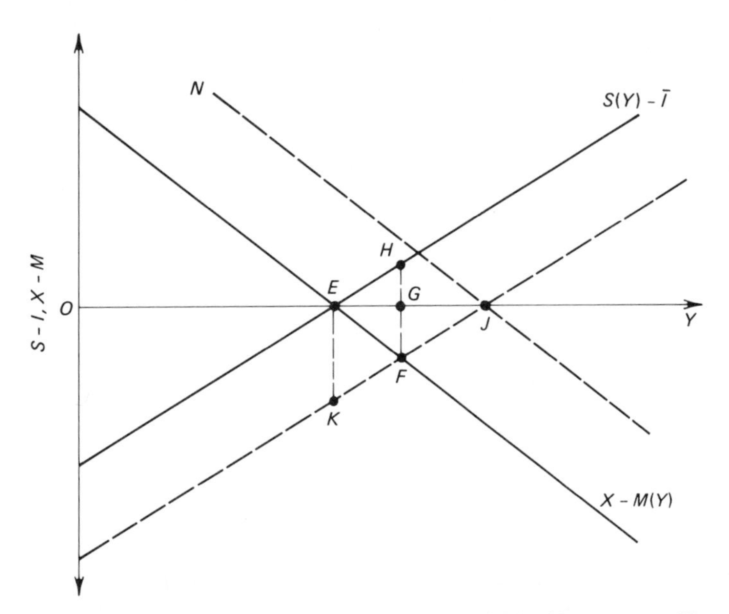

FIGURE 18-1 **The national income effect of an increase in desired investment.** The initial equilibrium at E is disturbed by an increase in investment (FH), which causes the $S(Y) - \bar{I}$ schedule to shift downward, as shown by dashed line FJ. Under fixed exchange rates, equilibrium shifts from E to F, and national income increases by EG. Under flexible exchange rates, the economy cannot remain at F: the deficit at F causes the rate of exchange to increase until the $\bar{X} - M(Y)$ schedule shifts upward to intersect the new $S(Y) - \bar{I}$ schedule along the horizontal axis, as shown by dashed line NJ. Thus, national income increases from OE to OJ. The national income multiplier is now equal to the reciprocal of the marginal propensity to save (closed economy multiplier).

Under fixed exchange rates, the increase in investment causes the $S(Y) - \bar{I}$ schedule to shift downward, as shown by the dashed line running through points F and J. Equilibrium shifts from E to F, and national income *increases* by EG. (In our numerical illustration, FH = increase in investment = \$100, and EG = increase in income = \$400.)

Under flexible exchange rates, the open economy cannot remain at point F. The reason is simple: At F there is a balance-of-trade deficit (FG), and the excess demand for foreign exchange pulls the rate of exchange up. The upward trend in the rate of exchange (depreciation of the domestic currency) continues until the $\bar{X} - M(Y)$ schedule shifts upward and to the right and intersects the new $S(Y) - \bar{I}$ schedule along the horizontal axis, as shown by dashed line NJ. Consequently, the national income equilibrium moves from E to J.

The increase in national income, EJ, under flexible exchange rates is necessarily larger than the corresponding increase, EG, under fixed exchange rates. What is the precise magnitude of the national income multiplier under flexible exchange rates? *It is equal to the reciprocal of the marginal propensity to save, as in the case of a closed economy*. Note that in Figure 18-1, the slope of the $S(Y) - \bar{I}$ schedule (which is equal to the marginal propensity to save, *MPS*) is given by the ratio *EK*/*EJ*. Since *EK* = increase in investment, ΔI; and *EJ* = increase in income, ΔY, we have

$$MPS = \Delta I / \Delta Y$$

or

$$\Delta Y = (1/MPS) \Delta I \qquad (18\text{-}3)$$

In our numerical illustration, the marginal propensity to save is 0.10. Therefore, the national income multiplier under flexible exchange rates is 1/0.10 = 10. When desired investment increases by \$100, the equilibrium level of national income increases by 10 × \$100 = \$1,000.

2 An Increase in Exports Suppose that exports increase by \$100. What is the effect on national income?

As we saw in Section 16-3, under fixed exchange rates the national income multiplier is 4 [that is, 1/(0.10 + 0.15) = 4] and thus national income tends to rise by 4 × \$100 = \$400. Under flexible exchange rates, however, the change in exports cannot have any permanent effect on national income, that is, the multiplier with respect to changes in exports must be zero.

Consider Figure 18-2, which is similar to Figure 18-1. Initially, equilibrium occurs at *E*, where the $S(Y) - \bar{I}$ schedule intersects the $\bar{X} - M(Y)$ schedule along the horizontal axis. Under fixed rates of exchange, the increase in exports causes the $\bar{X} - M(Y)$ schedule to shift upward, as shown by the dashed line. Equilibrium shifts from *E* to *F*, and national income increases by *EG*. (In our numerical illustration, *EH* = increase in exports = \$100, and *EG* = increase in income = \$400.)

Under flexible exchange rates, the system cannot settle down at point *F*, for at *F* there is a balance of trade surplus, that is, an excess supply of foreign exchange. In fact, under flexible exchange rates, the economy never moves from initial equilibrium point *E*. Immediately after the increase in exports, the rate of exchange starts falling because of initial trade surplus *EH*. As we saw in Chapter 15, a revaluation of domestic currency (that is, a reduction in the price of foreign exchange in terms of the domestic currency) causes the $\bar{X} - M(Y)$ schedule to shift downward. The fall in the rate of exchange continues until the dashed $\bar{X} - M(Y)$ line returns to its initial position through *E*. National income equilibrium remains at point *E*. Thus, we reach the following conclusion:

Under flexible exchange rates, autonomous changes in exports do not have any permanent effects on national income—the open-economy multiplier with respect to autonomous changes in exports is zero under flexible exchange rates.

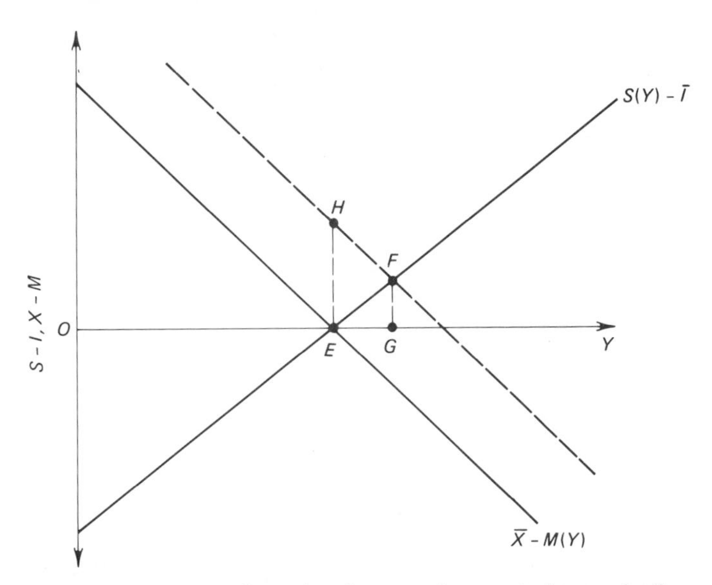

FIGURE 18-2 **The national income effect of an increase in exports (or a reduction in imports).** National income equilibrium occurs initially at *E*, where the $S(Y) - \bar{I}$ schedule intersects the $\bar{X} - M(Y)$ schedule along the horizontal axis. Under fixed rates of exchange, an autonomous increase in exports (say, *EH*) causes the $\bar{X} - M(Y)$ schedule to shift upward, as shown by the dashed line, shifting equilibrium from *E* to *F* and increasing national income by *EG*. Under flexible exchange rates, equilibrium remains at *E* because the initial balance-of-trade surplus (*EH*), causes the rate of exchange to fall until the $\bar{X} - M(Y)$ schedule returns to its initial position through *E*. The open-economy multiplier is now zero.

The preceding conclusion holds irrespective of whether or not the Marshall-Lerner condition is satisfied at the initial equilibrium. The reason is simple: If the Marshall-Lerner condition is not satisfied and the initial equilibrium of the foreign exchange market is indeed unstable, the rate of exchange will continue falling until the system arrives at a new stable equilibrium at which the Marshall-Lerner condition is satisfied. (For further discussion on this point, see Chacholiades, 1978, pp. 244–251.) For this reason, we shall simplify our discussion from now on by assuming that the initial equilibrium is unique and stable.

3 A Decrease in Imports Suppose that the open economy imposes a tariff and thus causes its domestic consumers to divert \$100 of their consumption expenditures from foreign to domestic products. What is the effect on national income?

As we saw in Section 16-3, under fixed exchange rates the shift from foreign to domestic products causes the aggregate demand for domestic output to rise by the reduction in imports (\$100). National income increases by the open-economy multiplier times the reduction in imports; that is, $4 \times \$100 = \$400$. [Recall that the open-economy multiplier with fixed rates of exchange is $1/(0.10 + 0.15) = 4$.] Flexible exchange rates, on the other hand, insulate the domestic economy and prevent the shift from foreign to domestic products from having any permanent effect on national income.

Figure 18-2 illustrates this case also. We merely interpret the upward shift of the $\overline{X} - M(Y)$ schedule as caused by the reduction in imports instead of the earlier increase in exports. Under fixed exchange rates, equilibrium shifts from *E* to *F* and national income rises by *EG*. Under flexible exchange rates, the system cannot reach equilibrium at *F*. As with the second illustration (increase in exports), the economy never moves from *E*. Immediately after the reduction in imports, the rate of exchange starts falling because of balance-of-trade surplus *EH*. This downward trend in the rate of exchange continues until the dashed $\overline{X} - M(Y)$ schedule returns to its initial position through *E*. The national income equilibrium remains at point *E*. Thus, we reach the following important conclusion:

***Under flexible exchange rates, changes in exports and autonomous shifts in domestic expenditure from foreign to domestic products, and vice versa, have no permanent effects on national income.* The rate of exchange acts as a perfect *automatic stabilizer* of the domestic economy.**

18-2 THE *IS-LM* MODEL WITH FLEXIBLE EXCHANGE RATES

We now proceed to consider briefly the functioning of the flexible exchange-rate system within the context of the *IS-LM* model of Chapter 17. In particular, we wish to find out how fiscal and monetary policies affect the level of national income under flexible exchange rates. Are fiscal and monetary policies relatively more effective under flexible than under fixed exchange rates?

The *IS-LM* Model Again

We can easily expand the *IS-LM* model to incorporate flexible exchange rates. The only modification we must make concerns the state of the equilibrium. The flexibility of the rate of exchange guarantees equilibrium in the foreign exchange market. Accordingly, the open economy must always operate on the external balance schedule. This means that general equilibrium cannot prevail unless the external balance schedule passes through the intersection of the *IS* and *LM* curves. Otherwise, in the presence of an external disequilibrium (whether a deficit or a surplus), the rate of exchange will continue to change until external balance is restored, as explained below.

Recall that the external balance schedule is the locus of all combinations of income levels and interest rates that are consistent with equilibrium in the balance of *payments* (not balance of *trade*, unless capital movements are absent). Accordingly, *along the external balance schedule the open economy may experience either a balance-of-trade deficit or a balance-of-trade surplus*, depending on whether the net capital flow (which depends on the interest rate only) is positive or negative. Unlike the model of the previous section, the balance of trade does exert a direct influence on national income, and exogenous changes in exports or imports apparently may affect the equilibrium level of income. That this is *not* so is explained in Section 18-5.

The Effects of Monetary Policy

Consider Figure 18-3. An expansionary monetary policy disturbs the initial equilibrium at point 1 (see solid schedules) by shifting the *LM* curve to the right, as shown by dashed curve *LM'*. Under fixed exchange rates, the economy would move to point 2, where national income is higher, the interest rate is lower, and the balance of payments develops a deficit (because point 2 lies to the right of the initial external balance schedule—see solid line *EBS*). What happens under flexible exchange rates?

Under flexible exchange rates, the incipient deficit at point 2 causes the domestic currency to depreciate. How does this currency depreciation affect the

FIGURE 18-3 **The effects of monetary policy.** Equilibrium occurs initially at point 1. An expansionary monetary policy shifts the *LM* curve to the right, as shown by dashed curve *LM'*. Under fixed exchange rates, the economy moves to point 2, at which there is a balance-of-payments deficit. Under flexible exchange rates, the deficit at point 2 causes the domestic currency to depreciate, which, in turn, causes the *IS* curve and the external balance schedule to shift to the right, as shown by dashed lines *IS'* and *EBS'*. Equilibrium is finally restored at point 3 (between points 2 and 4), at which national income is higher than at point 2.

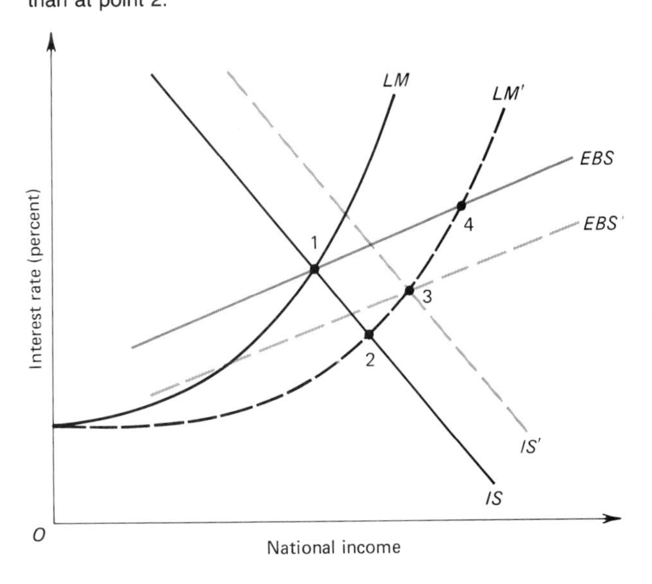

various schedules in Figure 18-3? We must answer this question before we can determine the final equilibrium under flexible exchange rates. Although the *LM'* curve may shift slightly to the left (because of the increase in domestic prices that results from the depreciation of the domestic currency), we shall simplify our analysis by assuming that the currency depreciation leaves curve *LM'* unchanged. However, both the *IS* and *EBS* curves shift to the right, as shown by dashed lines *IS'* and *EBS'*. As the domestic currency depreciates, the balance of trade improves, assuming only that the Marshall-Lerner condition is satisfied. This means that *external balance schedule EBS shifts to the right:* At any given interest rate (and thus given net capital flow), external balance is attained at a higher income level since an external surplus exists at the initial, lower income level. The balance-of-trade improvement caused by the depreciation of the domestic currency also means that *the IS curve shifts to the right:* At every interest rate, the aggregate demand for the open economy's output tends to increase because of the balance-of-trade improvement.

Where is final equilibrium established? Somewhere along curve *LM'* between points 2 and 4, as illustrated by point 3. The open economy reaches a new equilibrium when its currency depreciates sufficiently so that the new *IS* curve and the new external balance schedule intersect along dashed curve *LM'*. At point 3, the economy reaches a lasting equilibrium. The foreign exchange market is in equilibrium, and the rate of exchange is stabilized at its new higher level. Thus we reach the following important conclusion:

Monetary policy is more powerful (insofar as its effects on national income and employment are concerned) under flexible than under fixed exchange rates. **National income is higher at point 3 (equilibrium point with flexible exchange rates) than at point 2 (equilibrium point with fixed exchange rates).**

The Effects of Fiscal Policy

Turn now to fiscal policy. How does an increase in government spending (or a reduction in taxation) affect the level of national income and employment under a flexible exchange-rate system? Is fiscal policy more or less powerful under flexible exchange rates than under fixed exchange rates?

The case of fiscal policy is a little more complicated than the case of monetary policy. As we saw in Chapter 17, the effect of fiscal policy on the balance of payments is indeterminate under fixed exchange rates, depending on whether the external balance schedule is steeper or flatter than the *LM* curve. Accordingly, under flexible exchange rates, fiscal policy may cause the rate of exchange to either increase or decrease. We illustrate both cases in this section.

Figure 18-4 shows how fiscal policy works when the external balance is steeper than the *LM* curve. An increase in government spending disturbs the initial equilibrium at point 1 (see solid schedules) by shifting the *IS* curve to the

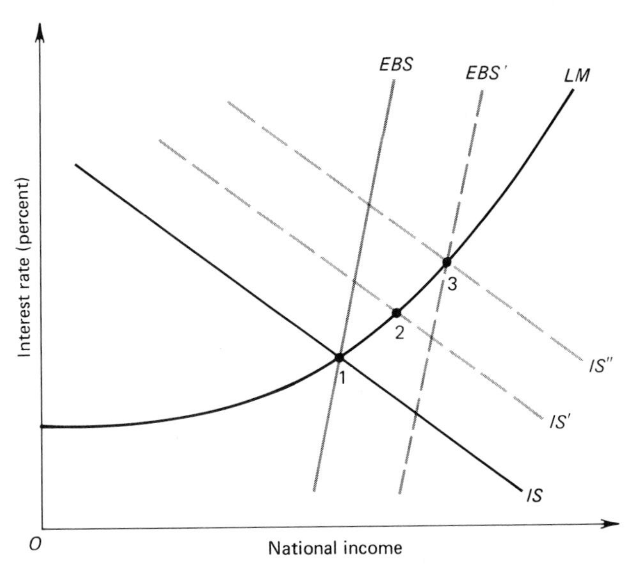

FIGURE 18-4 The effects of fiscal policy when the external balance schedule is steeper than the *LM* curve. Equilibrium occurs initially at point 1. An expansionary fiscal policy shifts the *IS* curve to the right, as shown by dashed curve *IS'*. Under fixed exchange rates, the economy moves to point 2, at which there is a balance-of-payments deficit. Under flexible exchange rates, the deficit at point 2 causes the domestic currency to depreciate; and this depreciation, in turn, causes curve *IS'* and external balance schedule *EBS* to shift to the right, as shown by dashed lines *IS''* and *EBS'*. Equilibrium is finally restored at point 3, at which national income is higher than at point 2.

right, as shown by dashed curve *IS'*. Under fixed exchange rates, the economy would move to point 2, where national income and the interest rate are higher (relative to the initial equilibrium at point 1), and the balance of payments develops a deficit (because point 2 lies to the right of the initial external balance schedule—see solid line *EBS*).

With flexible exchange rates, the incipient deficit at point 2 causes the domestic currency to depreciate. As we saw earlier in this chapter, the currency depreciation causes both the external balance schedule and curve *IS'* to shift to the right until a new equilibrium is re-established, as shown by the dashed lines through point 3. By comparing point 2 (equilibrium point under fixed exchange rates) with point 3 (equilibrium point under flexible exchange rates), we reach the following conclusion:

When the external balance schedule is steeper than the LM curve, fiscal policy has a larger effect on national income and employment under flexible than under fixed exchange rates.

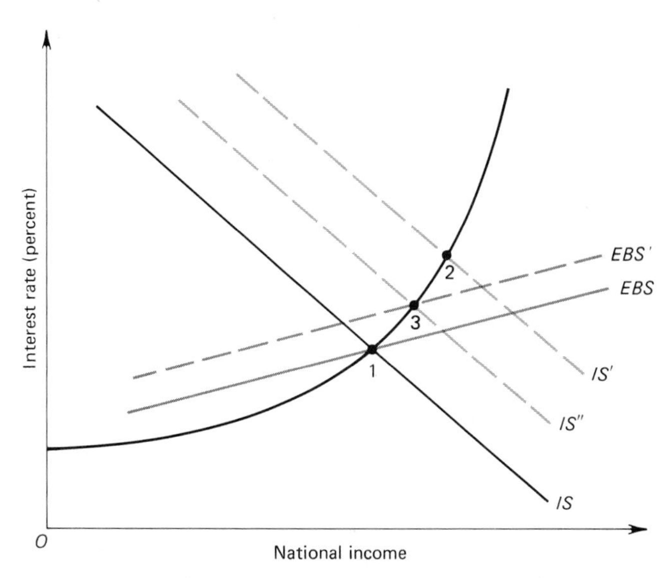

FIGURE 18-5 **The effects of fiscal policy when the external balance schedule is flatter than the *LM* curve.** Equilibrium occurs initially at point 1. An expansionary fiscal policy shifts the *IS* curve to the right, as shown by dashed curve *IS'*. Under fixed exchange rates, the economy moves to point 2, at which there is a balance-of-payments surplus. Under flexible exchange rates, the surplus at point 2 causes the domestic currency to appreciate; and this appreciation, in turn, causes curve *IS'* and external balance schedule *EBS* to shift to the left, as shown by dashed lines *IS''* and *EBS'*. Equilibrium is finally restored at point 3, at which national income is lower than at point 2 (but higher than at point 1).

Consider now Figure 18-5, which illustrates how fiscal policy works when the external balance schedule is flatter than the *LM* curve. Again an expansionary fiscal policy disturbs the initial equilibrium at point 1 by shifting the *IS* curve to the right, as shown by dashed curve *IS'*. Under fixed exchange rates the economy moves to point 2. With flexible exchange rates, the incipient balance-of-payments *surplus* at point 2 causes the domestic currency to *appreciate* in the foreign exchange market. In turn, the appreciation of the domestic currency causes both the external balance schedule (*EBS*) and dashed curve *IS'* to shift to the left—the effects of currency appreciation are symmetrical to the effects of currency depreciation. The economy eventually reaches equilibrium at some point on the *LM* curve between points 1 and 2, as shown by point 3, where dashed lines *IS''* and *EBS'* intersect. By comparing point 2 (equilibrium point under fixed exchange rates) with point 3 (equilibrium point under flexible exchange rates), we reach the following conclusion:

When the external balance schedule is flatter than the* LM *curve, fiscal policy has a smaller effect on national income and employment under flexible than under fixed exchange rates.

We can summarize the preceding discussion as follows: Whether fiscal policy is more powerful (insofar as its effects on national income and employment are concerned) under flexible than under fixed exchange rates depends on circumstances. If an expansionary fiscal policy causes a depreciation of the domestic currency (*low* capital mobility), then fiscal policy is more effective under flexible exchange rates; but if an expansionary fiscal policy causes an appreciation of the domestic currency (*high* capital mobility), then fiscal policy is more effective under fixed exchange rates.

Perfect Capital Mobility

In Chapter 17 we concluded that under conditions of perfect capital mobility and fixed exchange rates, a fiscal boost can effectively increase income and employment while a monetary boost cannot. Now we wish to show that *the relative effectiveness of fiscal and monetary policy is reversed if exchange rates are flexible rather than fixed.*

Consider Figure 18-6, which is similar to Figure 17-8. The external balance schedule (*EBS*) is horizontal at the world interest rate (10 percent). The initial

FIGURE 18-6 The relative effectiveness of fiscal and monetary policy under perfect capital mobility. An expansionary monetary policy shifts the *LM* curve to the right, as shown by curve *LM'*. The domestic currency depreciates, causing the *IS* curve, also, to shift to the right, as shown by curve *IS'*. Equilibrium moves from point 1 to point 3. By contrast, an expansionary fiscal policy is ineffective. The fiscal boost causes the *IS* curve to shift to the right; but the domestic currency appreciates, and the reduction in net exports pushes the system back to its initial equilibrium at point 1 as the *IS* curve returns to its original position.

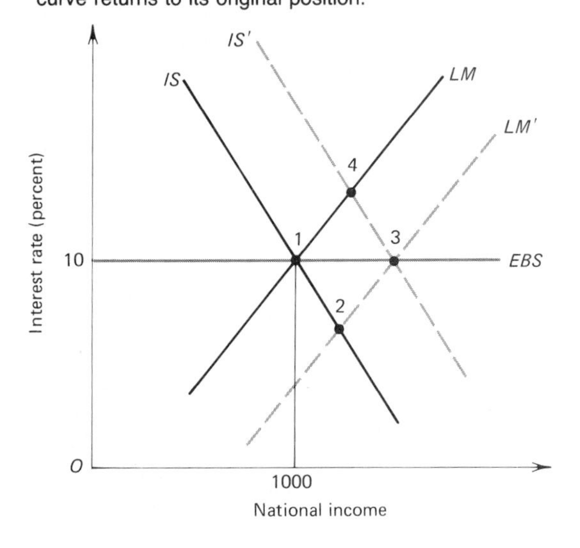

full equilibrium at point 1 is disturbed by an expansionary monetary policy. The *LM* curve shifts to the right, as shown by dashed curve *LM'*. Under fixed exchange rates, the system tends to move to the intersection (point 2) of the *LM'* and *IS* curves but actually returns to point 1 instead, because the incipient capital outflow forces the money supply back to its original level. Under flexible exchange rates, the deficit at point 2 causes the domestic currency to depreciate, which, in turn, forces the *IS* curve to shift to the right until it intersects curve *LM'* on the horizontal external balance schedule, as shown by dashed curve *IS'*. Thus equilibrium moves to point 3. The effectiveness of monetary policy is restored.

By contrast, flexible exchange rates render fiscal policy ineffective. Return again to the initial equilibrium at point 1. A fiscal boost shifts the *IS* curve to the right, as shown by dashed curve *IS'*. Under fixed exchange rates, the system settles at point 3—the massive capital inflow increases the money supply and shifts the *LM* curve to the right, as shown by dashed curve *LM'*. Under flexible exchange rates, the economy returns to its initial equilibrium at point 1. The incipient balance-of-payments surplus due to the capital inflow causes the domestic currency to appreciate, and the reduction in net exports pushes dashed curve *IS'* back to its original position. Fiscal policy is now totally ineffective.

Attaining Internal and External Balance

Under flexible exchange rates, external balance prevails constantly as a result of the interplay of free-market forces. In other words, the flexibility of the rate of exchange is sufficient to maintain external balance. To attain internal balance as well, the open economy may use either fiscal or monetary policy or any combination of the two. For instance, in the presence of unemployment the authorities must pursue an expansionary fiscal-monetary policy; and in the presence of inflationary pressures, the authorities must pursue a contractionary fiscal-monetary policy. (In the extreme case of perfect capital mobility, of course, the authorities must rely on monetary policy alone because fiscal policy is ineffective.) Economists usually count the abundance of policy instruments as a positive advantage of flexible exchange rates.

18-3 EXCHANGE-RATE OVERSHOOTING

When the fixed exchange-rate system collapsed in the early 1970s, most economists expected flexible exchange rates to restore tranquillity in the foreign exchange market. Instead, the currencies of the major industrial countries have fluctuated wildly. How can we explain the great volatility of exchange rates experienced during the 1970s and 1980s? To answer this question, we must briefly examine exchange rate dynamics over the short run.

Consider Figure 18-7, which is similar to Figure 18-6. Assume again that the initial full equilibrium at point 1 is disturbed by an increase in the money supply. The *LM* curve shifts to the right, as shown by dashed curve *LM'*. As shown

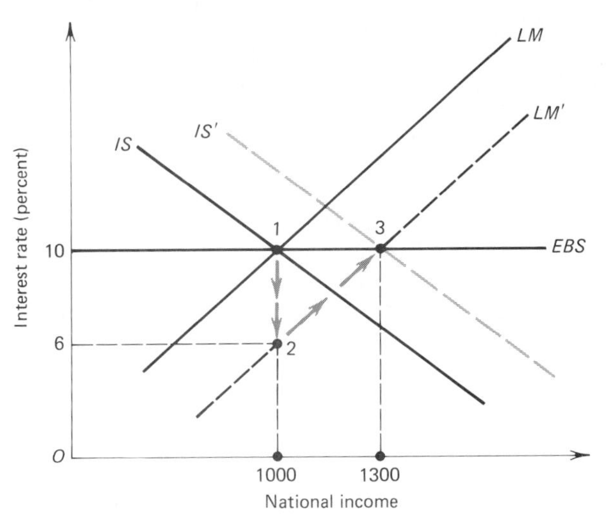

FIGURE 18-7 **Exchange rate overshooting.** The initial equilibrium at point 1 is disturbed by an increase in the money supply that shifts the *LM* curve to the right, as shown by dashed curve *LM*′. In the long run, equilibrium is re-established at point 3. In the short run, the system moves quickly to point 2 (because national income cannot increase instantaneously) and then travels gradually to point 3, as shown by the arrows. At the temporary equilibrium at point 2, the exchange rate is necessarily higher than its long-run equilibrium value at point 3 because the domestic interest (6 percent) is lower than the world rate (10 percent).

earlier, in the long run the domestic currency will depreciate sufficiently until full equilibrium is re-established at point 3—the currency depreciation will shift the *IS* curve to the right, as shown by dashed curve *IS*′. But national income cannot increase instantaneously. Instead, immediately after the increase in the money supply, the domestic interest rate and the exchange rate will adjust to maintain temporary equilibrium in the money market. Evidently, the domestic interest rate must drop from 10 to 6 percent to keep the money market in equilibrium, as shown by point 2. But how can equilibrium be maintained even temporarily when the domestic interest rate dips below the world rate (10 percent)?

To understand how, we must recall from Chapter 11 the interest parity relation. Equilibrium in the foreign exchange market can prevail when interest arbitrageurs come to expect the domestic currency to appreciate by the amount of the interest rate differential (that is, in this example, by 10 − 6 = 4 percent). (This is the so-called *un*covered interest parity condition.) Suppose that at the initial equilibrium at point 1, the exchange rate is \$2.00 per pound sterling and it is expected to rise to \$2.50 at the final equilibrium at point 3. What should the exchange rate be now, in the short run, so that the domestic currency will *ap-*

preciate by 4 percent in the long run? It must be \$2.60, that is, (\$2.50 − \$2.60)/\$2.50 = − 0.04. Thus equilibrium in the asset markets can be maintained temporarily when heavy capital outflow causes the exchange rate to rise from \$2.00 to \$2.60. This means that in the short run the exchange rate will *overshoot* its long-run equilibrium value (\$2.50).

In summary, the economy travels from point 1 to point 2, and then to point 3, as shown by the arrows. The exchange rate rises immediately from \$2.00 to \$2.60 and then declines gradually to \$2.50. The phenomenon of **overshooting** explains at least part of the observed volatility of exchange rates.

18-4 STABILIZATION POLICY: A DIGRESSION

Even a casual observer of economic affairs knows that stabilization policy is a rather complicated and often frustrating art. Fiscal and monetary policies are complicated by lags and uncertainties, and as a rule they do not smoothly stabilize the economy at "full employment." As it turns out, some economic institutions facilitate more than others the task of macroeconomic policy. In fact, the choice of economic institutions is crucial to the success or failure of stabilization policy.

After reviewing in this section the difficulties of stabilization policy, we shall return, in Section 18-5, to the question of whether fixed or flexible exchange rates make stabilization policy easier.

Economic Disturbances

Because of incessant disturbances, no economy remains permanently stable at full employment. Rather, a real-world economy tends to fluctuate continuously around its steady-state equilibrium. The main purpose of stabilization policy is to reduce these fluctuations.

Economic disturbances (or autonomous shocks) take place continuously in an economic system. These disturbances usually cause shifts in the various components of aggregate demand. The consumption function may shift as a result of a change in tastes between consumption and saving. The investment function may shift as a result of a change in the optimism (animal spirits) of investors. Government spending and taxes may change either because of wars or because the government wishes to pursue some socially desirable project(s), such as building a national railroad or highway system or even sending a person to the moon.

Ironically, policymakers themselves may also introduce further disturbances either because of mistakes (the art of policy-making is extremely difficult) or because of political reasons, as exemplified by the so-called **political business cycle**—an incumbent president may attempt to improve economic conditions right before the election even though such action may destabilize the economy after the election.

The Difficulties of Stabilization Policy

What are the requirements for a successful stabilization strategy? First, the authorities must be able to recognize quickly the occurrence of a disturbance and, more important, predict its effects with sufficient accuracy. Second, they must be able to quickly put into effect economic policy measures that completely neutralize the effects of the disturbance, now and in the future.

Unfortunately, neither requirement is met in the real world. This is due partly to the fact that our knowledge of how the economy actually works is rather limited and partly to the existence of lags in recognizing a disturbance and formulating and implementing the correct policy response as well as lags in the effects of that policy itself on the economy.

For instance, following an autonomous reduction in aggregate demand, policymakers must first collect data and attempt to make a prediction concerning the ultimate effects of the disturbance on the economy. For this purpose, policymakers must decide whether the disturbance is temporary or permanent. A temporary disturbance, such as a strike, does not usually require any action. Assuming that the disturbance is permanent, however, policymakers must use a sufficiently accurate model of the economy to predict how disruptive the disturbance will be. Then they must decide on the appropriate strategy to minimize the impact of the disturbance. Suppose they decide on fiscal policy action. As the reader may well know, fiscal policy requires new legislation, which must be approved by both houses of Congress. This is often a rather lengthy process. After Congress approves the necessary legislation, it may take some additional time before the policy change goes into effect. For instance, suppose the government decides to build a new highway. It must first survey possible routes, acquire land, listen to public protests, solicit bids, and so on. Ironically, by the time spending starts flowing, a deflationary policy may be needed instead.

Monetary policy action may go into effect much more quickly, of course, than fiscal policy. Nevertheless, the effect on aggregate demand (and specifically investment spending) of an increase in the money supply may take several months, perhaps a year.

The existence of large and variable lags as well as our imperfect knowledge of the workings of the economy and our inability to predict disturbances, such as the 1973–1974 oil embargo, make the task of stabilization policy rather formidable. To appreciate this, simply imagine that you own a car whose brakes and gas pedal take effect only after a significant, but variable, lag. Suppose that you are driving this car along a street full of traffic lights. Suppose further that pedestrians can cross this street any time they want to. Can you really drive this car for long at a reasonable speed without either getting a ticket or running into somebody?

Automatic Stabilizers

Given the difficulties of discretionary macroeconomic policy, it is a great relief to know that modern economies possess **built-in,** or **automatic, stabilizers.**

These automatic stabilizers tend to reduce the size of the multiplier and add stability to the economy. Their most important advantage is their automaticity. Immediately after the occurrence of a disturbance, the automatic stabilizers go into action—they are not constrained by any decision lags.

The most important automatic stabilizer is the income tax. For instance, following an inflationary increase in investment, the income tax immediately increases the leakages out of the income stream and provides some cushioning of the upswing. Clearly, a *progressive* income tax is a much stronger automatic stabilizer than a flat income tax rate applying to all income and taxpayers. Another important automatic stabilizer is unemployment compensation.

Because of the difficulties of discretionary stabilization policy, it is understandable that macroeconomists may want to improve the automatic stabilizers. This concern actually extends all the way to international economics. Thus, international economists are concerned with the problem of choosing the "best" exchange-rate system among various alternatives. Surely in this choice the question of stabilization is of paramount importance.

18-5 EXCHANGE-RATE REGIMES AND STABILIZATION

An open economy may be subject to any number of economic disturbances, such as autonomous shifts in exports, imports, domestic investment, and consumption. Which exchange-rate system better shields the open economy against the vagaries of such exogenous shocks? That is the central concern of this section. As we show below, sometimes the fixed exchange-rate system and sometimes the flexible exchange-rate system may act as an automatic stabilizer, depending on the nature of the economic disturbances that afflict the open economy.

A General Proposition

The essence of the ensuing discussion can be summarized in the following general proposition.

In general, *flexible exchange rates provide more stability to the open economy in relation to disturbances that originate in the foreign sector,* such as autonomous changes in exports and imports. *Fixed exchange rates provide more stability to the open economy in the presence of disturbances that originate in the domestic flow of spending,* such as autonomous changes in domestic investment, consumption, and government spending.

This general proposition is a useful first approximation, even though there may be some exceptions to it.

Disturbances in the Foreign Sector

Consider first the case of disturbances that originate in the foreign sector, such as autonomous shifts in exports and imports. Clearly, the preceding proposition is consistent with our discussion in Sections 18-1 and 18-2.

For instance, the analysis of Section 18-1 shows clearly that in the absence of any capital movements, flexible exchange rates insulate the domestic economy perfectly from autonomous shifts in exports or imports, while fixed exchange rates allow such autonomous shocks in the foreign sector to exert their full influence on the domestic economy through the open-economy multiplier. Indeed, as we can easily demonstrate, this conclusion remains valid in more general models, such as the *IS-LM* model with interest-sensitive capital movements.

Consider Figure 18-8. Initially, the open economy is in equilibrium at point *E*, where, by assumption, it also enjoys full employment and balance-of-payments equilibrium. Suppose now that the initial equilibrium is disturbed by an autonomous reduction in exports. (Exactly the same analysis holds for an autonomous increase in imports.) How does this autonomous reduction in exports affect the various schedules?

At the initial rate of exchange, the *IS* curve shifts to the left, as shown by dashed curve *IS'*—at any interest rate, the commodity market can be in equilibrium at a lower income level. This is not all. External balance schedule *EBS*

FIGURE 18-8 **Disturbances in the foreign sector.** A reduction in exports disturbs the initial equilibrium at *E* by causing the *IS* curve and external balance schedule *EBS* to shift to the left, as shown by dashed lines *IS'* and *EBS'*. Under a fixed exchange-rate system, equilibrium shifts to *F*. Under a flexible exchange-rate system, however, the economy eventually returns to the initial equilibrium at point *E*.

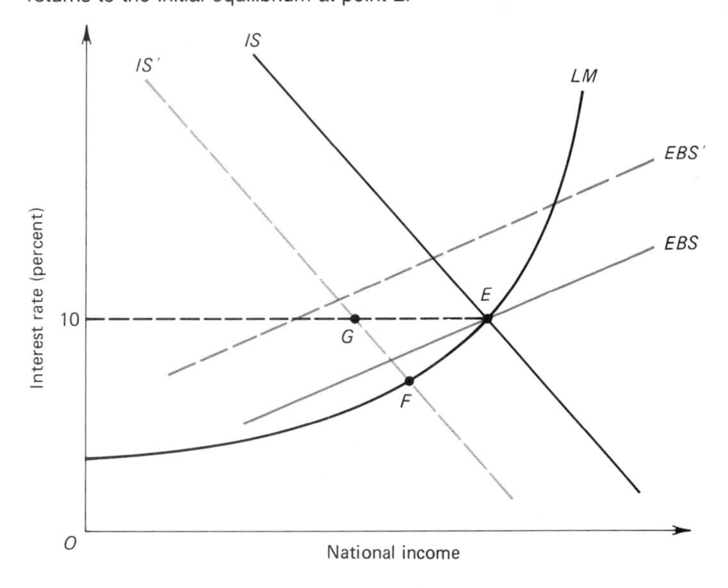

also shifts to the left, as shown by dashed line *EBS'*. Note that the leftward shift of the external balance schedule is necessarily larger than the leftward shift of the *IS* curve. *At the initial rate of interest (10 percent) and the initial rate of exchange,* national income falls by *GE* (which actually represents the leftward shift of the *IS* curve), but the balance of payments develops a deficit: the net capital flow remains the same while the balance of trade deteriorates (see example 2 in Section 15-3, even though that example deals with an *in*crease in exports). Thus point *G* must now lie in the deficit zone, that is, to the right of the dashed *EBS'* line.

Under fixed exchange rates, equilibrium shifts to point *F*, where income is lower than at *E*. Under flexible exchange rates, the economy eventually returns to point *E*. Immediately after the reduction in exports, the incipient deficit causes the domestic currency to depreciate. The depreciation of the domestic currency continues until the external deficit disappears. Evidently, the economy will reach a new equilibrium only when the domestic currency has depreciated sufficiently to offset completely the initial reduction in exports. Under these circumstances both the *IS* curve and the external balance schedule will return to their initial positions through *E*.

Therefore, we reach the following important conclusion:

Countries suffering from export instability (such as countries which export only a small number of products that happen to be susceptible to the vagaries of the business cycle in importing countries) can stabilize their domestic economies by adopting flexible exchange rates. This argument is usually made for countries that export metals, such as Chile (copper) and Malaysia (tin).

Disturbances in the Domestic Flow of Spending

Turn now to internal shocks, such as autonomous shifts in investment spending, government spending, liquidity preference, and the supply of money. We are already familiar with the implications of these autonomous shifts from our discussion in Section 18-2. There we saw that monetary policy has a larger impact on national income and employment under flexible than under fixed exchange rates. Accordingly, internal monetary shocks, such as autonomous shifts in liquidity preference and in changes in the money supply, are likely to be more disruptive (or destabilizing) under flexible than under fixed exchange rates. A country that suffers from these internal monetary shocks can facilitate its stabilization policy by adopting fixed exchange rates.

The effects of internal shocks in domestic spending (such as government spending, investment spending, and consumption spending) are similar to the effects of fiscal policy. As we saw in Section 18-2, whether fiscal policy is more powerful under flexible than under fixed exchange rates depends on the degree of capital mobility. With low capital mobility, fiscal policy is more powerful under flexible exchange rates (see Figure 18-4). But with high capital mobility, fiscal policy is more powerful under fixed exchange rates (see Figure 18-5). Accordingly, internal shocks in domestic spending are likely to be more disruptive under flexible exchange rates only when the degree of capital mobility is relatively low. When the degree of capital mobility is relatively high, internal shocks in domestic spending tend to be more disruptive under fixed exchange rates. Thus we reach the following important conclusion:

Countries that suffer from internal shocks in domestic spending and at the same time experience a *low degree of capital mobility* can facilitate their stabilization policy by adopting *fixed* exchange rates. Countries that suffer from internal shocks in domestic spending and at the same time experience a *high degree of capital mobility* can facilitate their stabilization policy by adopting *flexible* exchange rates.

Disturbances in International Capital Movements

Finally, we wish to mention the case of autonomous shifts of funds from one financial center to another that are prompted by political upheavals, rumors, and so on. Assuming that the monetary authorities can sterilize the effects of such movements of funds on the domestic money supply (as explained in Chapter 17), it must be clear that fixed exchange rates insulate the domestic economy perfectly in this case. Therefore, we have the following conclusion:

Countries that experience sudden inflows or outflows of funds should, when feasible, adopt fixed exchange rates and sterilize any payments imbalances.

18-6 THE POLICY MIX OF THE FIRST REAGAN ADMINISTRATION

Reaganomics provides an important application of the effects of fiscal and monetary policy under flexible exchange rates. When the Reagan administration took office, in January 1981, inflation was above 12 percent and there was growing realization that the U.S. economy was sliding into another recession. Monetary policy was already tight, as the Federal Reserve was determined to conquer inflation. Fiscal policy was also tight, a legacy of the Carter administration.

President Reagan set out to reduce the size of the federal government by cutting both taxes and spending. (The government's share of GNP increased from 18.5 percent in 1960 to 22.5 percent in 1980.) But the tax cuts were far larger than any conceivable cuts in government spending. On July 31, 1981, Congress passed the Economic Recovery Tax Act of 1981, which included President Reagan's proposals with some modifications. Income taxes for individuals were reduced in three installments: 1.25 percent on October 1, 1981; 10 percent on July 1, 1982; and 10 percent on July 1, 1983. (Income tax rates were also indexed to inflation, beginning in 1985.) Business taxes were reduced mainly through accelerated depreciation allowances. Even though at that time President Reagan's policy was thought to be inflationary, fiscal policy actually remained tight until mid-1982. With tight fiscal and monetary policy the results were predictable: The economy stumbled in 1981 and fell in the winter of 1981–1982. Inflation dropped from 12.4 percent in 1980 to 8.9 percent in 1981, and all the way down to 3.9 percent in 1982. Unemployment jumped to almost 11 percent in 1982. Instead of a boom (promised by the Reagan administration) or a mild recession (expected by the Federal Reserve), the U.S. economy suffered a near depression. Recovery did not begin until 1983.

President Reagan's tax cuts and the acceleration of defense spending combined with the worsening recession caused the federal deficit to balloon from $58 billion in 1981 to $111 billion in 1982, and to nearly $200 billion in 1983. The large increase in government borrowing was met by domestic lending in 1981 and 1982. Households provided about one-third (primarily because housing was weak) and business saving provided the rest (because the recession killed business investment while at the same time the business sector was enjoying the benefits of accelerated depreciation allowances). But by 1984, the federal deficit was predominantly financed by means of foreign lending. The current account deficit increased from a little over $8 billion in 1982 to $46 billion in 1983, and then jumped to $107 billion in 1984 (see Table 12-5). Table 18-1 shows U.S. monetary growth, the budget surplus, and interest rates between 1979 and 1987.

As predicted by our theory of Sections 18-2 and 18-3, the expansionary fiscal policy combined with tight monetary policy caused the dollar to greatly appreciate in the foreign exchange market (see Figure 14-9). Indeed the strong and persistent appreciation of the dollar surprised most observers. The balance on goods and services deteriorated promptly: from a surplus of about $14 billion in 1981 to a deficit of almost $95 billion in 1984 (see Table 12-5). In a sense, the tax cuts crowded out exports through the appreciation of the mighty dollar. In addition, the dollar appreciation reduced the annual inflation rate by as much as two percentage points.

TABLE 18-1 U.S. MONETARY GROWTH, BUDGET SURPLUS, AND INTEREST RATES, 1979–1987

Year	Monetary growth rate, % per year	Budget surplus, % of GNP	Interest rates	
			Short-term	Long-term
1979	7.8	0.5	11.2	9.4
1980	6.2	−1.3	13.1	11.5
1981	7.0	−1.0	15.9	13.9
1982	6.6	−3.5	12.4	13.0
1983	11.1	−3.8	9.1	11.1
1984	7.0	−2.8	10.4	12.4
1985	9.2	−3.3	8.0	10.6
1986	13.4	−3.5	6.5	7.7
1987	11.2	−2.4	6.9	8.4

Source: International Monetary Fund, *World Economic Outlook*, April 1987 and April 1988, Tables A14, A15, and A17.

18-7 FURTHER ARGUMENTS FOR AND AGAINST FLEXIBLE EXCHANGE RATES

We conclude this chapter by summarizing briefly some additional arguments in the continuing debate over fixed and flexible exchange rates. Our discussion begins with the case for flexible exchange rates. We then consider the important issues of uncertainty, destabilizing speculation, and price "discipline."

The Case for Flexible Exchange Rates

Under flexible exchange rates external balance is brought about by the free interplay of market forces. The rate of exchange moves freely to equate supply and demand, continuously eliminating external deficits and surpluses. This simplicity in maintaining external balance is an important advantage of flexible exchange rates. We illustrate the implications of this advantage by considering two alternative situations—a model with flexible domestic prices and a model with fixed domestic prices.

Consider first a classical world in which prices (including factor prices, such as the wage rate) are flexible in both directions. In this classical world, the flexibility of prices alone can maintain internal and external balance. The rate of exchange can remain fixed permanently. Economic disturbances, internal or external, affect prices only. In this case (which we may call the "ideal gold standard"), the argument for flexible exchange rates rests on the notion that changing one price (that is, the rate of exchange) is much simpler (and perhaps more economical) than changing millions of commodity and factor prices in the economy. This argument is similar to the adoption of daylight saving time during the summer months. Instead of rescheduling every single event to occur one hour earlier, it is simpler to move the clock one hour ahead, leaving all schedules unchanged.

Turn now to a Keynesian world of rigid prices. As we saw earlier, a fixed rate of exchange gives rise to external deficits and surpluses because there is no automatic mechanism to achieve external balance. Since their ability to finance external imbalances is rather limited, the authorities must ultimately use deliberate economic policy measures (such as monetary and fiscal policy, direct controls, and exchange-rate adjustment) to restore external balance. Besides any economic inefficiencies that direct controls may entail, the use of discretionary policy to maintain external balance creates additional difficulties for stabilization policy. Essentially, the maintenance of a fixed rate of exchange gives rise to an extra policy target: external balance. To achieve internal and external balance simultaneously, the authorities must use two effective and mutually independent instruments. This increases the inherent difficulties of stabilization policy.

In contrast, the adoption of flexible exchange rates automatically ensures the preservation of external balance and thereby reduces the tasks of monetary, fiscal, and other policy instruments. The authorities can now direct these instruments toward the preservation of internal balance alone.

The removal of the balance-of-payments motive for restrictions on international trade and payments is an important advantage of flexible exchange rates. Thus, the world can move toward free trade. Each country can be free to specialize in those commodities in whose production the country has a comparative advantage. Such international division of labor is fundamental to the maximization of world welfare.

Finally, the adoption of flexible exchange rates provides autonomy to individual countries with respect to their use of public policy. For instance, under fixed exchange rates countries cannot choose their own desired inflation rates. Instead they must passively adopt the inflation rate established abroad. The adoption of flexible exchange rates eliminates the need to coordinate public policy (and particularly monetary policy) among countries. Under flexible exchange rates, countries have more freedom to pursue public policy independently of balance-of-payments considerations.

Uncertainty

The first argument against flexible exchange rates relates to uncertainty. The critics argue that flexible exchange rates would be highly unstable—exchange rates would fluctuate wildly from day to day. Such instability would lead to increased uncertainty, which, in turn, would seriously reduce the flows of international trade and investment.

The critics usually cite two factors that may account for the alleged instability in the foreign exchange market: elasticity pessimism and destabilizing speculation. (Discussion of destabilizing speculation is postponed until the next subsection.) Elasticity pessimism refers to fears that the price elasticities of import demand for internationally traded goods are very low and that the Marshall-Lerner condition is not generally satisfied. Indeed, when the elasticities are low, balance-of-payments disturbances can still cause wide fluctuations in the exchange rate even though the Marshall-Lerner condition may be satisfied (see Appendix 15).

The proponents of flexible exchange rates have three main counterarguments: (1) Fixed exchange rates are not free of risk and uncertainty; (2) flexible exchange rates are not necessarily unstable; and (3) any resultant risk and uncertainty under flexible exchange rates need not have the detrimental effects claimed by the critics. We consider these arguments below.

To the extent that each country cannot, as a practical matter, attain internal and external balance by means of an appropriate use of fiscal and monetary policies (without exchange-rate adjustment), permanently fixed rates impose heavy adjustment costs. Deficit countries must either deflate their economies and generate widespread unemployment or impose restrictions on trade and capital movements. Similarly, surplus countries must eventually accept unwanted inflation. The adjustable-peg system substantially reduces the risk of unemployment and inflation (as well as restrictions on trade and capital movements) by allowing countries in fundamental disequilibrium to use exchange-rate adjustment. But occasional devaluations and revaluations also involve traders and investors in unexpected losses (and gains). Thus the risks and adjustment costs are not necessarily any smaller under fixed than under flexible exchange rates.

On the positive side, the proponents of flexible exchange rates argue that the freedom of the exchange rates to move daily in response to market forces does not necessarily imply that they will actually move significantly and erratically from day to day. They will do so only if the underlying economic forces are themselves erratic, causing erratic shifts in the supply and demand schedules for foreign exchange. But in that case no international monetary system can function smoothly. The fact of the matter is that the exchange rates will move gradually and predictably, providing gradual adjustment and averting crises. Stabilizing speculation will keep the exchange-rate fluctuations within narrow limits.

Further, risk-averse traders and investors can actually cover their exchange risks in the forward-exchange markets at a moderate cost, as explained in Chapter 11. This is, of course, true for short-term transactions. Admittedly, for long-term transactions, the forward markets are very thin (if they exist at all) and the cost of coverage is very high. Nevertheless, the exchange risk for long-term transactions is highly exaggerated—the world economy tends to provide a substantial amount of automatic hedging. A country whose currency depreciates steadily over time is likely to be experiencing a steady inflation relative to the rest of the world. [This will become evident from our discussion of the purchasing-power-parity theory (see Section 19-5).] For foreign direct investments, this means that any losses due to the depreciation of the foreign currency are likely to be balanced by the increase in foreign earnings due to the higher foreign price level. The same is true of foreign portfolio investments, since the foreign rate of interest is likely to rise to compensate investors for the inflation.

Destabilizing Speculation

Does speculation tend to depress or amplify exchange-rate fluctuations through time? This is an extremely important question. On it depends the success or failure of flexible exchange rates. As one would expect, the proponents of flexible exchange rates argue that speculation is *stabilizing,* that is, speculation depresses exchange-rate fluctuations. The critics claim that speculation is *destabilizing,* that is, speculation amplifies exchange-rate fluctuations.

Figure 18-9, panel (*a*), illustrates the case of **stabilizing speculation.** The solid sinewave curve shows the movement of the exchange rate in the absence of speculation. Presumably this cyclical behavior of the exchange rate reflects the influence of cyclical factors on the foreign sector. For simplicity, the trend line is a horizontal straight line. The dashed sine curve shows how the exchange rate would fluctuate in the presence of stabilizing speculation. The important assumption is that once the rate rises above the trend line, speculators expect the rate to fall and therefore sell foreign exchange (here the pound). Thus they prevent the rate from rising too much. Similarly, once the rate falls below the trend line, speculators expect the rate to rise and therefore buy foreign ex-

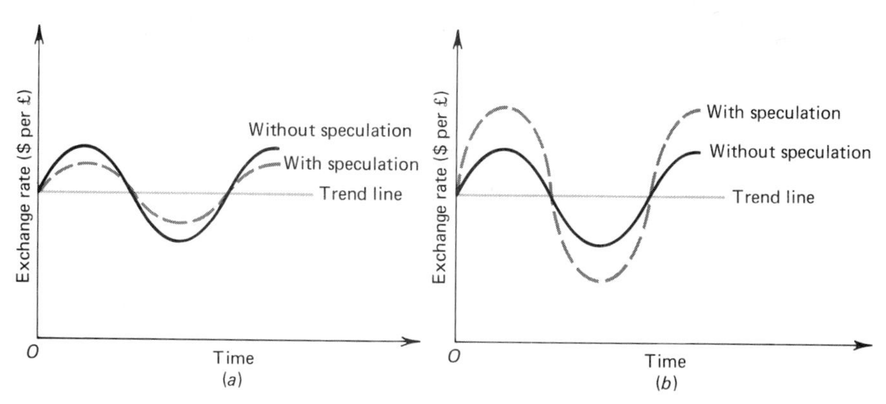

FIGURE 18-9 **Stabilizing and destabilizing speculation.** Panel (*a*) illustrates the case of stabilizing speculation. Once the rate rises above (falls below) the trend line, speculators expect it to fall (rise) and they therefore sell (buy) foreign exchange. This stabilizing speculation depresses exchange-rate fluctuations, as shown by the dashed curve. Panel (*b*) illustrates the case of destabilizing speculation. Here, once the rate rises above (falls below) the trend line, speculators expect it to rise (fall) even further and they therefore buy (sell) foreign exchange. This destabilizing speculation amplifies exchange-rate fluctuations, as shown by the dashed curve.

change. Thus they prevent the rate from falling too much. This sort of stabilizing speculation depresses exchange-rate fluctuations around the trend line, as shown by the dashed curve.

Consider now panel (*b*), which illustrates the case of **destabilizing speculation.** The solid sine curve and the trend line are exactly the same as those of panel (*a*). But here, once the rate begins to rise above the trend line, speculators expect it to rise even further. As a result, speculators now *buy* foreign exchange in the hope of selling it in the future at a higher rate. These speculative purchases intensify the rise in the rate of exchange. Conversely, when the rate falls below the trend line, speculators expect it to fall even further. As a result, speculators now *sell* foreign exchange, and they precipitate the fall in the rate. This sort of destabilizing speculation amplifies exchange-rate fluctuations around the trend line, as shown by the dashed curve.

How does speculation actually behave under flexible exchange rates? Friedman (1953, p. 175) had a powerful theoretical argument that speculation must be stabilizing. He claimed that "people who argue that speculation is generally destabilizing seldom realize that this is largely equivalent to saying that speculators lose money, since speculation can be destabilizing in general only if speculators on the average sell when the currency is low in price and buy when it is high." Thus, according to Friedman, speculators will continue in the business only so long as it is profitable. This will be the case if they buy cheap and sell dear. But to buy cheap and sell dear is to stabilize.

Friedman's analysis has provoked an interesting controversy as to whether profitable speculation is necessarily stabilizing. Several economists have offered counterexamples in which they attempt to show that destabilizing speculation may be profitable. Other critics have argued that the question of whether destabilizing speculation is profitable or unprofitable is irrelevant. For instance, in the great crash of the New York Stock Exchange in October 1929, as well as the more recent crash of October 1987, destabilizing speculators suffered severe losses; but these losses did not prevent them from behaving the way they actually did, precipitating a catastrophe.

The question of whether speculation is stabilizing or destabilizing cannot be settled by recourse to theoretical arguments. Although there may be a presumption that speculation is stabilizing, the question is at bottom an empirical one. Only actual experience with truly flexible exchange rates can resolve the issue.

Price Discipline

Another argument against flexible exchange rates concerns fears that the flexibility of the exchange rate generates excessive inflation. The critics of flexible exchange rates claim that fixed exchange rates impose a price "discipline" on the domestic authorities because of the balance-of-payments constraint. Inflationary policies under fixed exchange rates cause external deficits and losses of international monetary reserves. The loss of reserves plus the loss of national prestige in the event of devaluation prevent governments from pursuing inflationary policies. Under flexible exchange rates governments are no longer subject to the discipline, as the flexibility of the exchange rate automatically maintains external balance.

The proponents of flexible exchange rates argue that fixed exchange rates do not really guarantee price stability. To avoid balance-of-payments problems when the exchange rate is fixed, a country must maintain at home that rate of inflation which prevails in the rest of the world. Further, the rate of world inflation, which need not be zero, is likely to be different from what the country really wants. In addition, under the adjustable-peg system, countries may avoid the discipline by using owned or borrowed reserves, by imposing direct controls on trade and payments (which interfere with economic efficiency), and, in the last resort, by devaluing their currencies, as the postwar record shows.

Moreover, the consequences of inflationary policies are more readily apparent to the general public under flexible exchange rates: The domestic currency would depreciate in the foreign exchange market, and the domestic price level would rise.

Finally, the proponents of flexible exchange rates make the valid point that a country must be free to choose that rate of domestic inflation its citizens desire. Flexible exchange rates make it possible for the authorities to pursue the public's choice of the right mixture of unemployment and inflation because flexible rates remove the balance-of-payments constraint.

18-8 SUMMARY

1 Under the flexible exchange-rate system, the exchange rate adjusts instantaneously and maintains external balance constantly. When the net balance on international capital flows and unilateral transfers is zero, external balance means that $X - M = 0$. The national income equilibrium condition $Y = C + I + X - M$ reduces to $Y = C + I$ (closed economy equilibrium condition). The multiplier becomes equal to the closed economy multiplier ($1/MPS$) for all autonomous changes in C, I (and G); it becomes zero for changes in exports and imports (that is, shifts in domestic expenditure between domestic and foreign products).

2 The *IS-LM* model can be modified to incorporate flexible exchange rates. General macroeconomic equilibrium occurs now at the point of intersection of three schedules: the *IS* and *LM* curves plus the external balance schedule.

3 Along the external balance schedule, the open economy may experience a balance-of-*trade* surplus or deficit, depending on whether the net capital flow is negative or positive. Thus, the balance of trade may now exert a direct influence on national income. Yet exogenous changes in exports and imports continue to leave the equilibrium level of income unchanged.

4 Insofar as its effects on national income are concerned, monetary policy is more powerful under flexible than under fixed exchange rates; but it causes the exchange rate to *overshoot* its long-run equilibrium value.

5 When the external balance schedule is steeper (flatter) than the *LM* curve—that is, when expansionary fiscal policy causes a depreciation (appreciation) of the domestic currency because of low (high) capital mobility—fiscal policy has a larger effect on national income under flexible (fixed) exchange rates.

6 In general, flexible exchange rates provide more stability to the open economy in relation to disturbances that originate in the foreign sector, such as autonomous changes in exports and imports. Countries that suffer from export instability can stabilize their domestic economies by adopting flexible exchange rates.

7 Internal monetary shocks, such as autonomous shifts in liquidity preference and changes in the money supply, are more disruptive (or destabilizing) under flexible than under fixed exchange rates. Countries that suffer from such internal shocks can facilitate their stabilization policy by adopting fixed exchange rates.

8 Internal shocks in domestic spending are more disruptive under flexible (fixed) exchange rates when the degree of capital mobility is low (high). Countries that suffer from such internal shocks in domestic spending and at the same time experience a low (high) degree of capital mobility can facilitate their stabilization policy by adopting fixed (flexible) exchange rates.

9 Countries that experience sudden inflows or outflows of funds should, when feasible, adopt fixed exchange rates and sterilize any payments imbalances.

10 The case for flexible exchange rates rests on their simplicity in maintaining external balance. In a classical world of price flexibility, it is simpler to change the exchange rate than millions of commodity and factor prices. In a Keynesian world of rigid prices, fixed exchange rates give rise to an extra policy target (external balance) and increase the difficulties of stabilization policy. Flexible exchange rates reduce the tasks of monetary and fiscal policy, remove the balance-of-payments motive for restrictions on international trade and payments, and provide autonomy to individual countries with respect to their use of public policy (particularly monetary policy).

11 One argument against flexible exchange rates is that they are highly unstable (because of low import-demand elasticities and/or destabilizing speculation), reducing seriously the flows of international trade and investment. Proponents counter that flexible exchange rates need not be unstable, fixed exchange rates are not free of risk and uncertainty, exchange risk on short-term transactions can be covered in the forward market, and the world economy tends to provide automatic hedging for long-term transactions.

12 Whether speculation under flexible exchange rates is stabilizing or destabilizing is at bottom an empirical question, even though there may be a presumption that it is stabilizing.

13 Critics argue that flexible exchange rates generate excessive inflation because governments are not subject to the price discipline imposed by fixed exchange rates and the balance-of-payments constraint. The proponents counter that fixed exchange rates do not guarantee price stability: A country must maintain at home that rate of inflation which prevails in the rest of the world, and under the adjustable-peg system countries may avoid price discipline by using reserves (owned or borrowed), by imposing direct controls, or finally by devaluing their currencies.

PROBLEMS

1 You are given the following hypothetical data about Finland:

$$MPS = 0.3 \qquad \text{(marginal propensity to save)}$$

$$MPM = 0.2 \qquad \text{(marginal propensity to import)}$$

Exports and investment are exogenous. A change in Finland's tastes redistributes \$1,000 worth of spending from domestic products to foreign products.

a Assume that the exchange rate is fixed. What are the effects of the change in tastes on Finland's national income and balance of trade?

b Alternatively, assume that the exchange rate is flexible. What are the effects on Finland's national income and balance of trade?

c Provide a commonsense explanation for any differences between parts *a* and *b*.

2 Why is it that monetary policy is more powerful (insofar as its effects on national income and employment are concerned) under flexible than under fixed exchange rates?

3 a Under what circumstances is fiscal policy more powerful (insofar as its effects on national income and employment are concerned) under flexible than under fixed exchange rates?

b Why is it that the effects of fiscal policy on national income and employment depend crucially on the degree of capital mobility?

4 For each of the following countries (together with the specified features), indicate which exchange-rate regime provides more stability:

a *Chile.* The price of copper (one of Chile's major export commodities) fluctuates significantly in world markets.

b *Mexico.* Monetary policy is erratic while capital mobility is low.

c *Argentina.* The economy often experiences sudden inflows or outflows of capital.

SUGGESTED READING

Chacholiades, M. (1978). *International Monetary Theory and Policy.* McGraw-Hill Book Company, New York, chaps. 5, 6, 11, 17, and 19.

Dornbusch, R. (1976). "Expectations and Exchange Rate Dynamics." *Journal of Political Economy,* vol. 84, pp. 1161–1176.

Friedman, M. (1953). "The Case for Flexible Exchange Rates." In M. Friedman. *Essays in Positive Economics,* University of Chicago Press, Chicago. Reprinted in R. E. Caves and H. G. Johnson (eds.), American Economic Association *Readings in International Economics,* Richard D. Irwin, Inc., Homewood, Ill., 1968.

Johnson, H. G. (1970). "The Case for Flexible Exchange Rates, 1969." In G. N. Halm (ed.), *Approaches to Greater Flexibility of Exchange Rates,* Princeton University Press, Princeton, N.J.

Mundell, R. A. (1968). *International Economics.* Macmillan Publishing Company, New York, chaps. 17 and 18.

Shafer, J. R., and B. E. Loopesko (1983). "Floating Exchange Rates After Ten Years." *Brookings Papers on Economic Activity,* 1:1983, pp. 1–70.

Sohmen, E. (1969). *Flexible Exchange Rates.* 2d ed. University of Chicago Press, Chicago.

CHAPTER **19**

THE MONETARY APPROACH

The **monetary approach** to the balance of payments is an outgrowth of domestic **monetarism** and the intellectual grandchild of David Hume's **price-specie-flow mechanism** (although there are important differences between the two theories). Stemming mainly from the work of Robert A. Mundell and Harry G. Johnson, the monetary approach views the balance of payments as a largely monetary phenomenon. This recent addition to our intellectual stock of international-adjustment theories leads to predictions and policy implications that seem to be diametrically opposite to those of the more traditional approaches. The present chapter reviews the monetary approach under both fixed and flexible exchange rates; it also offers a reconciliation between the monetary approach and the traditional theories.

19-1 AN OUTLINE OF THE MONETARY APPROACH

The monetary approach rests on the mutual interaction between the money supply and the balance of payments. Payments imbalances (deficits or surpluses) represent net flows of money between nations and tend to affect each nation's money supply; and conversely, changes in the money supply affect the balance of payments, as we saw earlier in our discussion of the price-specie-flow mechanism (Chapter 14) and the *IS-LM* model (Chapter 17).

According to the monetary approach, *payments imbalances (deficits and surpluses) reflect stock disequilibria between the supply of money and the demand for money*. Indeed, the monetary approach views the balance of payments as a safety valve that opens automatically to either release an excess supply of money in the form of a balance-of-payments deficit or allow into the country an additional amount of money in the form of a balance-of-payments surplus in order to satisfy an existing excess demand for money.

A fundamental premise of the monetary approach is that the monetary authorities cannot, and actually do not, sterilize the monetary flows associated with surpluses and deficits but instead allow the flows to influence the domestic money supply. As we saw in Section 17-7, there are indeed limits to the ability of the monetary authorities to sterilize payments imbalances; and in the long run, chronic payments imbalances are likely to affect the money supply. However, in the short run, the monetary authorities have plenty of leeway and they do offset payments imbalances by means of sterilization operations.

Given the premises of the monetary approach, it must be clear that payments imbalances must be *transitory* phenomena that tend to correct themselves—payments imbalances can last until the supply of money becomes equal to the demand for money. In other words, a payments imbalance (reflecting a disequilibrium between the supply of and demand for money) brings about an adjustment in the supply of money that tends to eliminate the initial disequilibrium in the money market and thus correct the balance-of-payments disequilibrium.

The monetary approach concentrates mostly on the official reserve account of the balance of payments, lumping together all other entries into a single autonomous, above-the-line category. Thus the monetary approach makes no effort to explain the behavior of individual entries above the line or the behavior of partial balances, such as the balance on goods and services, the current account balance, and so on. Rather, it views the balance of payments "from the bottom up."

The monetary approach is reminiscent of Hume's price-specie-flow mechanism, particularly because both theories deal with a self-correcting mechanism based on the monetary flows associated with deficits and surpluses. However, the two theories differ in at least one important respect: *Hume's mechanism works through commodity prices, while the monetary approach works through the supply and demand for money*. Thus, the price-specie-flow mechanism starts at the top of the balance of payments, whereas the monetary approach begins at the bottom. As a result, the import-demand elasticities, which are so important for the smooth functioning of the price-specie-flow mechanism, are irrelevant to the monetary approach.

The policy implications of the monetary approach are far-reaching. Viewing payments imbalances as temporary, self-correcting phenomena, the monetary approach leads practically to the conclusion that policy measures to correct balance-of-payments disequilibria are generally unnecessary. If the authorities are patient enough and remain passive, a balance-of-payments disequilibrium will automatically correct itself sooner or later. The trouble, of course, is that such correction may occur much later; and, in the meantime, the economy may suffer from unnecessary adjustment costs.

19-2 THE BASIC MODEL OF THE MONETARY APPROACH

The self-correcting monetary process that forms the foundation of the monetary approach can be applied to many models. For instance, in Section 17-8 we applied it to the *IS-LM* model. In this section, we discuss the basic model that is usually associated with the monetary approach.

The Supply and Demand for Money

We already know from Section 17-1 that the **demand for money** (M_d) depends positively on the level of national income (Y) and negatively on the rate of interest (r). The monetary approach assumes that both the interest rate and national income are exogenous. This means that the quantity of money demanded is also exogenous, changing only when autonomous changes occur in the rate of interest and national income. The assumed exogeneity of national income is rationalized by asserting that the open economy is at full employment and that national income changes only through growth.

As in Section 17-7, we can identify the total money supply with demand deposits in commercial banks. Thus, the open economy's **supply of money** (M_s) is equal to the **money multiplier** times the **volume of commercial bank reserves** (that is, deposits at the Federal Reserve). By accounting necessity, the volume of bank reserves (or *liabilities* of the Federal Reserve) is equal to the assets of the Federal Reserve, which consist of *domestic assets* (such as U.S. government securities) and *international reserves* (such as gold). Thus the supply of money (M_s) is given by

$$M_s = g(DA + IR) \qquad (19\text{-}1)$$

where g = money multiplier
DA = domestic assets held by the Federal Reserve (or domestic component of the monetary base)
IR = international reserves (or foreign component of the monetary base)

(Note: In this oversimplified picture, we ignore the Federal Reserve's capital and nonreserve liabilities, such as Treasury deposits.) The sum of domestic assets and international reserves held by the Federal Reserve, that is, $DA + IR$, is called the **monetary base** of the nation, or **high-powered money.**

The money supply schedule (M_s) of Figure 19-1 illustrates Equation (19-1). We assume that the money multiplier is 5 and that the domestic component (DA) of the monetary base is kept constant at \$100 million. In the absence of international reserves, the money supply would be \$500 million (that is, 5×100), as shown by the horizontal line. This is the **domestic component** of the money supply. To obtain the total money supply, we add to the domestic component ($g \cdot DA$) the **international component** ($g \cdot IR$), which is an increasing function of the volume of international reserves. For instance, when the volume of international reserves is \$120 million, the international compo-

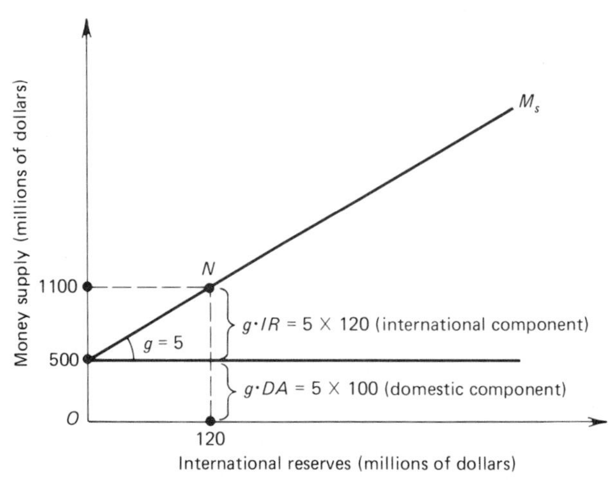

FIGURE 19-1 **The money supply schedule.** The total money supply is an increasing function of international reserves, as shown by schedule M_s. The domestic component of the money supply is equal to the money multiplier times the domestic component of the monetary base, as shown by the horizontal line. The foreign component of the money supply is equal to the money multiplier times the volume of international reserves, as shown by the upward-sloping schedule starting at \$500 million.

nent of the money supply is \$600 million; thus the total money supply is \$1,100 million, as shown by point *N*. Note that the slope of the money supply schedule is equal to the money multiplier.

The Payments Imbalance Schedule

According to the monetary approach, a payments imbalance (B) is equal to the excess demand for money; that is,

$$B = M_d - M_s \tag{19-2}$$

Equation (19-2) is the starting point of the monetary approach. This important equation is illustrated in Figure 19-2.

The top panel superimposes the money demand schedule (M_d) on the money supply schedule of Figure 19-1. We assume that the exogenous income (Y) and interest rate (r) are such that the quantity of money demanded is equal to \$1,500 million. Because the demand for money is independent of the volume of international reserves, the money demand schedule is *horizontal.*

The lower panel illustrates the **payments imbalance schedule.** The latter shows the external imbalance (which is equal to the excess demand for money) at alternative volumes of international reserves. In other words, the payments imbalance schedule registers directly the vertical differences between the money demand and supply schedules. For instance, when international reserves are \$100 million, the quantity of money demanded is \$1,500 million (point *B*) and the quantity of money supplied is \$1,000 million (point *A*); thus the excess demand for money is \$500 million, as shown by vertical distance *AB* (top panel) or point *A*′ (lower panel). The payments imbalance schedule slopes downward—as the volume of international reserves increases, the supply of money expands, causing the excess demand for money (and thus the payments imbalance) to decrease.

When the volume of international reserves is \$200 million, the money market is in equilibrium (point *E*, top panel) and the payments imbalance is zero

FIGURE 19-2 **The self-correcting monetary process.** The top panel superimposes the horizontal money demand schedule (M_d) on the money supply schedule (M_s). The lower panel gives the payments imbalance schedule, which shows the excess money demand at alternative levels of international reserves. When the reserves are \$300 million, the nation runs a deficit (point *F*′) and the money supply falls. When the reserves are \$100 million, there is a surplus (point *A*′) and the money supply rises. Equilibrium occurs at *E* (top panel) or *E*′ (lower panel).

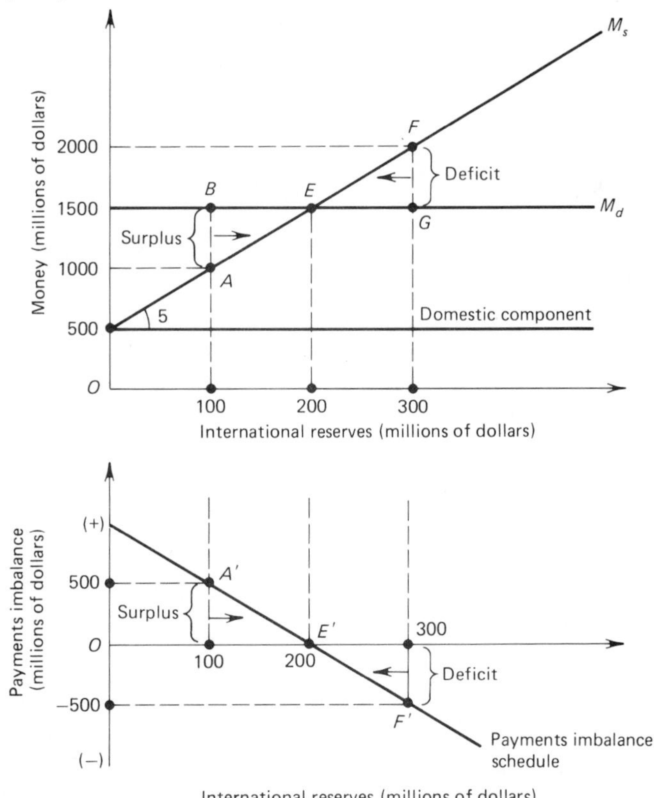

(point E', lower panel). When the volume of international reserves is less than \$200 million, there exists an excess demand for money and a balance-of-payments surplus. For instance, when the volume of international reserves is \$100 million, there exists an excess demand for money equal to \$500 million (distance AB, top panel) and a balance-of-payments *surplus* equal to \$500 million (point A', lower panel). When the volume of international reserves exceeds \$200 million, there exists an excess supply of money and a balance-of-payments deficit. For example, when the volume of international reserves is \$300 million, there exists an excess demand for money equal to −\$500 million (distance GF, top panel) and a balance-of-payments *deficit* equal to \$500 million (point F', lower panel).

The Monetary Stock-Flow Adjustment Process

Turn now to the self-correcting monetary process itself. Payments imbalances give rise to either a loss (deficit) or gain (surplus) of international reserves; thus they bring about an adjustment in the supply of money that tends to eliminate the initial disequilibrium in the money market and the balance of payments.

Return to Figure 19-2. Suppose that the current volume of international reserves is only \$100 million. The nation enjoys a balance-of-payments surplus of \$500 million (per year), as shown by point A'. As time goes by, the balance-of-payments surplus gives rise to a gradual gain of international reserves. In turn, the gain of reserves increases the money supply; thus it reduces the excess demand for money and the balance-of-payments surplus. The system moves toward equilibrium point E (or E'), as shown by the arrows. When the volume of international reserves increases to \$200 million, equilibrium is restored in the balance of payments and the money market.

Alternatively, suppose that the current volume of international reserves is \$300 million. The nation suffers from a balance-of-payments deficit, as shown by point F'. But the deficit cannot last for long; it is only transitory, thanks to the monetary stock-flow adjustment process. As the nation loses international reserves, the money supply falls gradually and the system moves again toward equilibrium point E (or E'), as shown by the arrows. Thus the monetary stock-flow adjustment process restores equilibrium in both the money market and the balance of payments.

Sterilization Operations

The self-correcting monetary stock-flow adjustment mechanism restores external balance automatically unless the process is interrupted by sterilization operations. This is shown in Figure 19-3, which is similar to Figure 19-2, top panel. (There is no need to reproduce the payments imbalance schedule also.)

At the current level of international reserves (\$300 million), the nation is running a *deficit* (illustrated by distance FG = \$500 million). Suppose that the deficit causes the level of international reserves to fall to \$250 million (implying

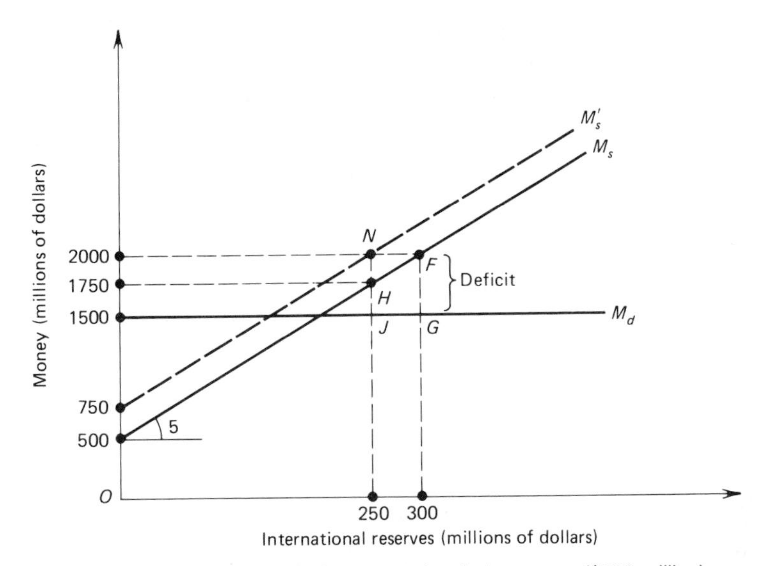

FIGURE 19-3 **Sterilization operations.** At the current level of reserves ($300 million), the nation is running a deficit (*FG*). When the reserves fall to $250 million, the monetary authorities purchase $50 million worth of securities in the open market, causing the money supply schedule to shift upward, as shown by dashed line M'_s. The money supply is temporarily restored to its original level ($2,000 million) as the external deficit persists at the initial rate ($NJ = FG$).

a loss of reserves equal to $50 million). If the monetary authorities react passively and allow the money supply to fall, the deficit will shrink to $250 million, as shown by vertical distance *JH*.

Suppose, however, that the monetary authorities sterilize the external deficit by means of open-market operations. This means that the monetary authorities purchase $50 million worth of securities in the open market—an amount equal to the loss of reserves. The domestic component of the money supply increases by $250 million; that is, money multiplier (5) × open-market operations ($50 million). As a result, the money supply schedule shifts upward by $250 million, as shown by the dashed line M'_s, and the external deficit is preserved at $500 million, as indicated by *JN*. Such sterilization operations (and the external deficit) can persist until the monetary authorities run out of reserves.

19-3 POLICY IMPLICATIONS OF THE MONETARY APPROACH

Because of the fundamental premise embodied in Equation (19-2), a policy measure can affect the balance of payments only through its influence on the supply and demand for money. In addition, the balance-of-payments effect is only transitory, because of the underlying self-correcting monetary stock-flow adjustment process. Indeed, as noted earlier, policy measures to correct external disequilibria are not necessary, provided the authorities remain passive long enough for the monetary process to bring about the desired result automatically. To clarify these far-reaching policy implications, we consider a few specific cases.

Monetary Policy

In the monetary model, an *expansionary* monetary policy generates an excess supply of money that leads to a *deficit* in the balance of payments. A *contractionary* monetary policy gives rise to an excess demand for money and a *surplus* in the balance of payments. These conclusions are in agreement with those reached in Chapter 17 in the context of the *IS-LM* model.

Consider Figure 19-4, which is similar to Figure 19-3. The initial equilibrium at E is disturbed by an expansionary monetary policy: The monetary authorities purchase \$50 million worth of securities in the open market. As a result, the domestic component of the money supply increases to \$750 million, causing the money supply schedule to shift upward, as shown by the dashed line M'_s. Immediately after the increase in the money supply, a deficit emerges in the balance of payments, as illustrated by vertical distance EF. But the deficit is transitory. Eventually the system moves to G, where the supply of money returns to its original level (\$1,500 million). Note, however, that at G the stock of international reserves is lower (\$150 million instead of \$200 million). In essence, the monetary authorities exchange international reserves for domestic securities. Everything else remains the same.

Devaluation

In the monetary model, a devaluation of the domestic currency improves the balance of payments always. Consider Figure 19-5, which exhibits the same initial equilibrium as Figure 19-4. As the nation devalues its currency, the domestic price level rises—imported *and* exported goods become more expensive. As a result, the demand for money rises from \$1,500 million to, say, \$2,000 million, as shown by the dashed line that depicts the new money demand schedule (M'_d). Immediately after the devaluation, the balance of payments registers a surplus illustrated by vertical distance EF. But again the surplus is transitory; it lasts only for as long as it takes the system to move to new equilibrium point G. At G, the monetary authorities have a larger stock of international reserves (\$300 million versus \$200 million), the quantity of money is larger (\$2,000 million versus \$1,500 million), and the price level is higher. Everything else is the same.

Note that *the monetary approach claims implicitly that the import-demand elasticities and the Marshall-Lerner condition are totally irrelevant to the effect of devaluation.* In the monetary model, the devaluation works through the demand for money alone.

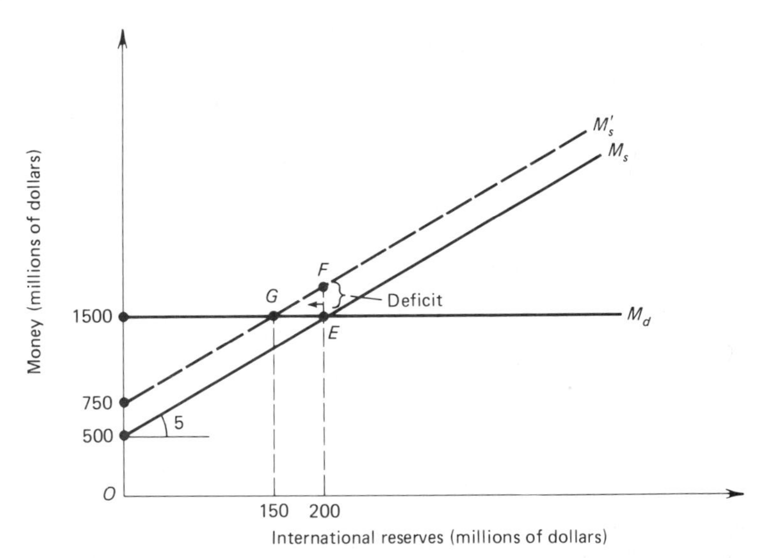

FIGURE 19-4 **The effects of an expansionary monetary policy.** The monetary authorities disturb the initial equilibrium, at *E*, with a $50 million purchase of securities in the open market. The money supply schedule shifts upward, as shown by dashed line M'_s, and a deficit (*EF*) emerges in the balance of payments. Eventually, the system moves to a new equilibrium at *G*, at which the stock of international reserves is lower ($150 million versus $200 million).

Tariffs, Quotas, and Money Wages

Figure 19-5 can also be used to study the effects of tariffs, quotas, or even *autonomous increases in the domestic money-wage rate.* Any one of these changes raises domestic prices, which in turn cause the demand for money to increase. The excess demand for money translates into a balance-of-payments surplus, which allows international reserves to flow into the country until a new equilibrium is attained. Note that *the monetary approach leads to a balance-of-payments effect of an increase in the domestic money-wage rate that is diametrically opposite to the conclusion reached by more traditional approaches.*

National Income and the Interest Rate

In the context of the basic model of the monetary approach, national income and the interest rate are exogenous. Autonomous changes in these variables affect the balance of payments through their effects on the demand for money. For instance, an increase in income and/or a reduction in the interest rate cause the demand for money to increase, and the resultant excess demand for money generates a *surplus* in the balance of payments. This conclusion, which contradicts the results of the traditional approach (Chapters 15 and 17), has been presented by the advocates of the monetary approach as a major challenge to orthodoxy.

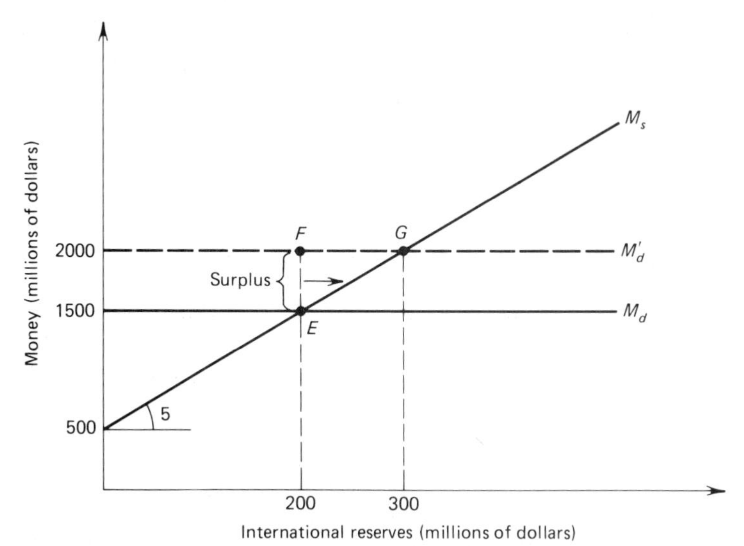

FIGURE 19-5 **The effects of devaluation.** The initial equilibrium, at *E*, is disturbed by a devaluation of the domestic currency. The domestic price level rises, causing the money demand schedule to shift upward, as shown by dashed line M'_d. Immediately after the devaluation, a temporary surplus (*FE*) emerges in the balance of payments. Eventually, the system moves to *G*.

There is no need for a new diagram. Figure 19-5 illustrates this case also. Merely interpret the upward shift of the money demand schedule, shown by dashed line M'_d, as due to the increase in income or the reduction in the interest rate.

19-4 RECONCILIATION BETWEEN THE MONETARY AND TRADITIONAL APPROACHES

As we have seen, the monetary approach leads to conclusions that are often diametrically opposite to those of the more traditional approaches. For instance, according to the monetary approach the balance of payments develops a *surplus* in each of the following cases: (1) an autonomous increase in the domestic money-wage rate, (2) an autonomous increase in national income, and (3) an autonomous reduction in the interest rate. In these cases, the demand for money rises, and the balance-of-payments safety valve opens to allow into the country an additional amount of money to satisfy the excess demand for money. Yet this conclusion contradicts common sense and the traditional theory, which predicts a deficit in the balance of payments in each of the three cases. How do we resolve this dilemma?

The monetary approach makes the valid point that the monetary stock-flow adjustment process cannot be ignored. The monetary authorities cannot sterilize payments imbalances forever. Sooner or later, the authorities will be forced to allow the external deficit or surplus to exert its influence on the money supply. But the monetary stock-flow adjustment mechanism can be applied to any model, and the selection of the model is crucial. What actually accounts for the contradiction between the monetary approach and the more traditional approaches is *not* the monetary stock-flow adjustment mechanism itself, but rather *the underlying models.*

The basic monetary model discussed in this chapter can be interpreted as dealing with long-run equilibrium states. In emphasizing the monetary process, the proponents of the monetary approach ignored completely the short-run processes of the traditional approach, perhaps because of the rising tide of "monetarism." The key to the reconciliation between the two opposing camps lies in the recognition that the exogeneity of national income inadvertently turned the monetary approach into a long-run theory, despite the short-run illusion provided by the monetary stock-flow adjustment mechanism. Once the long-run nature of the monetary approach is accepted, its reconciliation with the traditional short-run approach is immediate.

International economists have long been familiar with paradoxes concerning the diametrically opposite effects of policy measures in the long run versus the short run. For instance, Lerner's symmetry theorem (Section 9-1) states that a general export tax has the same effects as a general import tax of the same ad valorem percentage. But the theorem is valid in the context of long-run equilibrium only. In the short run, an import tax tends to operate in an *expansionary* fashion that leads to an *improvement* in the balance of payments, while an export tax tends to operate in a *contractionary* manner that leads to a *deterioration* of the balance of payments. Neither proposition is wrong; they merely address different issues.

The monetary approach *is* valid when we compare equilibrium states. (This is the method of **comparative statics.**) For instance, *if* national income is higher in equilibrium state A than in state B (while the interest rate and all prices are constant), the equilibrium quantity of money must be higher in state A than in state B; and *if* the domestic component of the money supply is the same in the two states, *then* we can infer that the economy must have experienced a balance-of-payments surplus in moving from state B to state A. Surely this interpretation is valid both in the context of the monetary model and the *IS-LM* model of Chapter 17. But the monetary model does *not* explain how the model moves from state B to state A.

A similar interpretation can be provided for all other cases considered by the advocates of the monetary approach. Instead of "changes" (in interest rates or money wage rates) think in terms of "differences" between two equilibrium states. Remember always that the monetary approach does *not* deal with short-run cause-effect relationships. The advocates of the monetary approach are wrong if they think that their model explains the behavior of the open economy in the short run.

19-5 THE PURCHASING-POWER-PARITY THEORY

The purchasing-power-parity (PPP) theory is an attempt to explain, and perhaps more importantly measure statistically, the equilibrium rate of exchange and its variations by means of the price levels and their variations in different countries. This theory, which is usually associated with the Swedish economist Gustav Cassel, is based on the simple idea that a certain amount of money should purchase the same representative bundle of commodities in different countries—hence Cassel's term **purchasing power parity.** The PPP theory has been severely criticized through the years.

There are two versions of the purchasing-power-parity theory: the *absolute* version and the *relative* (or *comparative*) version. While the absolute version is useless, the relative version does have some validity, as explained below. This section deals with both versions.

The Absolute Version of the PPP Theory

Consider two countries, America (home country) and Britain (rest of the world). The absolute version of the PPP theory declares that the equilibrium rate of exchange (R), that is, dollars per pound, is equal to the ratio of America's price level (P) to Britain's (P^*), that is, $R = P/P^*$. How valid is this proposition? Can we really abandon our supply-and-demand analysis of the foreign exchange market and use instead the ratio of price levels to determine the equilibrium rate of exchange? Unfortunately, that is not the case.

In our discussion of the partial equilibrium model (Chapter 14), we pointed out that for *any* rate of exchange (whether it is the equilibrium rate or not), the dollar price of each traded good equals its price in pounds times the rate of exchange. For instance, if the rate of exchange is \$2 (per pound) and the price of A-exportables in Britain is £5, the price of A-exportables in America is \$10 (that is, $\$10 = \$2 \times £5$). In the absence of transportation costs and trade impediments (such as tariffs and quotas), this strict relationship holds for each traded good. When all goods are traded internationally, it follows that the same strict relationship must hold trivially between any *equally weighted* price index numbers for America and Britain.

For instance, suppose that the current rate of exchange is \$2 (per pound) and that the prices of A-exportables and B-exportables, respectively, are \$10 and \$40 in America and £5 and £20 in Britain. For simplicity, suppose that the weights of A-exportables and B-exportables are equal in the construction of America's and Britain's price index numbers. America's price index number (P) is \$25 [that is, $(0.5 \times \$10) + (0.5 \times \$40)$], and Britain's price index number (P^*) is £12.5 [that is, $(0.5 \times £5) + (0.5 \times £20)$]. Obviously, $\$2 = \$25/£12.5$, that is, rate of exchange $R = P/P^*$.

The relationship $R = P/P^*$ must hold trivially for *any* rate of exchange—not just the equilibrium rate. Thus, we cannot use the equation $R = P/P^*$ to determine *the* equilibrium rate. This is a devastating blow to the absolute version of the PPP theory.

In the real world there are, of course, transportation costs, trade impediments, and extensive product differentiation. In fact, as we pointed out in Section 14-8, there are *nontraded* (purely domestic) goods in each country that are not traded internationally because of prohibitive transportation costs. Now there is no simple relationship between the prices of these nontraded goods in the various countries. Thus in general, the equation $R = P/P^*$ cannot hold even when the current rate of exchange (R) happens to be the equilibrium rate.

Yet a small but influential group of international economists, aptly called **global monetarists** by Marina Whitman (1975), asserts the **law of one price.** According to the global monetarists, the world consists, not of separate national economies, but of a single integrated world economy. Goods produced by domestic producers and foreign competitors behave as if they were perfect substitutes. Their prices are equalized by commodity arbitrage. Thus the global monetarists claim that the law of one price and the purchasing-power-parity theory hold. Global monetarism is no longer in fashion.

The Relative Version of the PPP Theory

The relative version of the PPP theory, which incidentally received more attention than the absolute version, is a comparative statics proposition. It is concerned with *the effects of inflation on an initial equilibrium rate of exchange.* Essentially, Cassel invoked the quantity theory of money and proposed that money is neutral.

We can again use our partial equilibrium model to illustrate the relative version of the PPP theory. Suppose that at the current rate of exchange of, say, \$2 (per pound), the value of American exports of A-exportables equals the value of American imports of B-exportables, as shown in Figure 19-6 by the initial equilibrium points, *E,* in the two panels. Now let America increase its money supply by, say, 50 percent, and wait until the international economy reaches a new equilibrium. What will be the relationship between the new equilibrium rate of exchange and the initial rate of \$2? Cassel's theory predicts that the new equilibrium rate must be higher than the old by the percentage rate of inflation in America, that is, 50 percent. The new equilibrium rate of exchange must be \$3, that is, $\$2 + (0.50 \times \$2)$. Let us see why.

As we learned in our discussion of the price-specie-flow mechanism (see Section 14-9), the expansion in the American money supply causes America's cost structure and prices to rise. Accordingly, America's demand-for-imports and supply-of-exports schedules shift upward, as illustrated by the dashed lines. Because of inflation, America's prices (in both pounds and dollars) increase by 50 percent at all volumes of exports and imports. For instance, at the initial volume of imports of 5,000 units of B-exportables, America is now willing to pay £30, which is 50 percent higher than the initial price of £20. Similarly, for the initial volume of exports of 20,000 units of A-exportables, America now demands £7.5, which is also 50 percent higher than the initial price of £5.

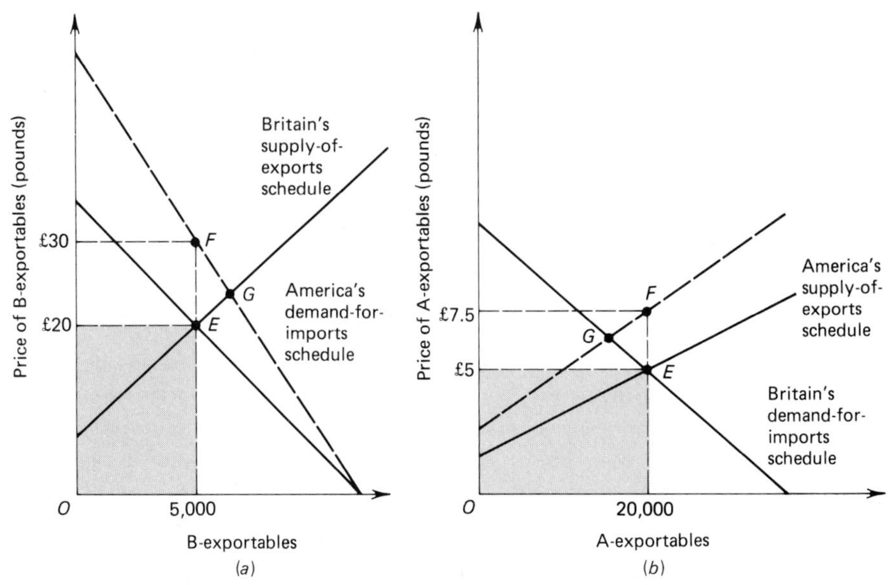

FIGURE 19-6 The purchasing-power-parity theory. At the current rate of exchange ($2 = £1), the value of American exports ($5 × 20,000) equals the value of American imports (£20 × 5,000). As America undergoes 50 percent inflation, the nation's demand-for-imports and supply-of-exports schedules shift upward, as shown by the dashed lines. By itself, the American inflation would cause the commodity market equilibria to shift from *E* to *G* in both panels and generate a deficit in America's balance of payments. However, when the rate of exchange also increases by 50 percent, that is, from $2 to $3, the American schedules return to their original position and equilibrium returns in both panels to *E*, at which America's balance of payments is in equilibrium again.

If the rate of exchange remains constant at $2 (per pound), equilibrium in the markets for A-exportables and B-exportables will shift to point *G* in both panels, and America's balance of trade will register a deficit (assuming that each country's elasticity of demand for imports is higher than unity). Is it possible to change the rate of exchange and shift America's schedules (the dashed lines) back to their initial position? If this is actually done, equilibrium in the markets for A-exportables and B-exportables will return to points *E*, where America's balance of trade is zero. As it turns out, America's schedules will shift back to their initial position when the rate of exchange also rises by 50 percent, that is, from $2 to $3, as the student should be able to verify. Note that the existence of nontraded commodities does *not* affect this conclusion at all.

A problem similar to the above actually occurred after World War I. The war had disrupted trade between allies and had halted it completely between enemies. When the war was finally over and trade started to flow again, there was a need to establish new rates of exchange. Many countries thought they could return to the prewar rates. But the prewar rates were inappropriate, particularly because the various countries had experienced quite different degrees of inflation. Cassel suggested that the prewar rates of exchange must be adjusted by these divergent degrees of inflation. For the case of two countries, say, America and Britain, he suggested the following formula:

$$R_t = \frac{P_t/P_0}{P_t^*/P_0^*} R_0 \qquad (19\text{-}3)$$

where R_0 = rate of exchange before the war
R_t = recommended rate of exchange after the war
P_0, P_t = America's price level before and after the war, respectively
P_0^*, P_t^* = Britain's price level before and after the war, respectively

It must be clear by now that the relative version of the PPP theory is no longer a truism. It makes the valid point that monetary conditions exert an important influence on the rate of exchange. Yet this theory suffers from a severe drawback: Aside from difficulties of statistical verification, it rests on the crucial assumption that technology, tastes, factor supplies, levels of employment, trade impediments, and capital movements do not change during the transition period. Such changes no doubt take place incessantly in the international economy and do exert a profound influence on the rate of exchange. This is especially true when the transition involves a major war.

19-6 BIG MACS AND THE PPP THEORY

In an amusing attempt to "test" the PPP theory, *The Economist* conducted a survey in 1986 on the prices of Big Mac hamburgers at McDonald's restaurants throughout the world. Because in the meantime some readers "developed an appetite for another helping," the magazine repeated the survey in 1988; "so *The Economist*'s correspondents have been gorging themselves on big Macs—all in the cause of research."

According to the (absolute version) of the PPP theory, exchange rates should equalize the prices of a basket of goods and services across countries. Since the Big Mac hamburger is itself a basket of goods, the magazine argued, exchange rates should equalize the price of Big Macs throughout the more than 40 countries hosting McDonald's restaurants. Hence, dividing the foreign price by the dollar price of a Big Mac, the magazine obtained the implied Mac PPP of the dollar, which it compared to the actual exchange rate.

In both surveys, the implied Mac PPP rates of the dollar turned out to be quite different from the actual rates. For instance, on March 28, 1988, the dollar was *undervalued* 33 percent against the Danish krone, 22 percent against the Japanese yen, and 24 percent against the Swedish krona. The dollar was *overvalued* 66 percent against the Australian dollar, 44 percent against the Canadian dollar, 145 percent against the Hong Kong dollar, 71 percent against the Singapore dollar, and 46 percent against the Yugoslav dinar.

Note: Adapted from "Junk Currencies," *The Economist*, April 2, 1988.

19-7 THE MONETARY APPROACH TO EXCHANGE-RATE DETERMINATION

After the widespread resumption of floating exchange rates in 1971, the purchasing-power-parity theory was revived once again but with a new twist added by the monetary approach. The idea was to combine the **quantity theory of money** with the purchasing-power-parity theory in order to arrive at a theory of exchange-rate determination.

We begin with the familiar **equation of exchange:**

$$M_s V = PQ \tag{19-4}$$

where M_s = nominal quantity of money
V = velocity of circulation of money
P = domestic price level
Q = real output

The velocity of circulation of money (V) may be a function of other variables, such as the interest rate and national income. For simplicity, we assume that V is exogenous. We also assume that real output (Q) is constant at the full-employment level.

We can solve Equation (19-4) for the price level to obtain

$$P = \frac{M_s V}{Q} \tag{19-5}$$

Equation (19-5) states that for any given V and Q, the price level is directly proportional to the quantity of money. For instance, when M_s increases by 10 percent, P increases by 10 percent also.

Equation (19-5) holds for each country separately. Thus, using asterisks (*) to indicate the foreign variables, we have the following equation for the foreign country (Britain):

$$P^* = \frac{M_s^* V^*}{Q^*} \tag{19-6}$$

Equations (19-5) and (19-6) can be combined with the purchasing-power-parity theory to get a theory of the exchange rate.

Consider the absolute version of the purchasing-power-parity theory:

$$R = \frac{P}{P^*} \tag{19-7}$$

Equation (19-7) states that the rate of exchange (dollars per pound) is equal to the ratio of our price level (P) to the foreign price level (P^*). Substituting Equations (19-5) and (19-6) into Equation (19-7), we finally obtain

$$R = \left(\frac{M_s}{M_s^*}\right)\left(\frac{V}{V^*}\right)\left(\frac{Q^*}{Q}\right) \tag{19-8}$$

Equation (19-8) shows that the rate of exchange depends on *relative* money supplies, relative velocities, and relative real outputs in the two countries. Other things equal, an increase in the domestic quantity of money relative to the foreign quantity of money leads to a rise in the exchange rate (that is, a depreciation of the domestic currency). Recent empirical evidence does not provide much support for the monetary approach to exchange-rate determination.

19-8 SUMMARY

1 The monetary approach to the balance of payments maintains that payments imbalances are temporary phenomena that reflect stock disequilibria between the supply and demand for money.

2 A fundamental premise of the monetary approach is that the monetary authorities do not sterilize payments imbalances.

3 Unlike the price-specie-flow mechanism, the monetary approach views the balance of payments "from the bottom up."

4 The supply of money has two components: a domestic component and a foreign component.

5 According to the monetary approach, a payments imbalance is equal to the excess demand for money; that is, $B = M_d - M_s$.

6 Payments imbalances give rise to either a loss (deficit) or gain (surplus) of international reserves and lead to changes in the money supply. This monetary stock-flow adjustment process restores balance-of-payments equilibrium automatically, unless it is temporarily interrupted by sterilization operations.

7 Policy measures and exogenous changes affect the balance of payments only through their influence on the supply and demand for money.

8 An expansionary monetary policy generates an excess supply of money, which leads to a balance-of-payments deficit.

9 Any changes (such as devaluation of the domestic currency, increase in the domestic money-wage rate, and imposition of import tariffs and import quotas) that raise domestic prices cause the demand for money to increase; and the excess demand for money leads to a balance-of-payments surplus.

10 An increase in income and/or a reduction in the interest rate generate an excess demand for money, which leads to a balance-of-payments surplus. This conclusion contradicts traditional theories.

11 The monetary approach can be reconciled with the traditional approaches when we realize that the underlying monetary model deals mainly with long-run equilibrium states.

12 The absolute version of the purchasing-power-parity theory asserts that the equilibrium rate of exchange is equal to the ratio of the price levels of the countries involved, that is, $R = P/P^*$. This theory is useless. In the absence of transportation costs and other trade impediments, the equation $R = P/P^*$ holds trivially for any rate of exchange—not just the equilibrium rate. In the presence of transportation costs, the equation $R = P/P^*$ cannot hold even when R is the equilibrium rate.

13 The relative version of the PPP theory has some validity. This version is concerned with the effects of inflation on an initial equilibrium rate of exchange and rests on the quantity theory and the neutrality of money. Its drawback is that it also rests on the assumption that technology, tastes, etc., do not change during the transition period.

14 The quantity theory of money can be combined with the purchasing-power-parity theory to produce a theory of exchange-rate determination.

15 The global monetarists assert that the world consists of an integrated, closed economy in which the law of one price and the PPP theory hold.

PROBLEMS

1 You are given the following hypothetical data pertaining to the economy of Denmark:

$$\text{Money multiplier} = 10$$
$$\text{Monetary base} = \$1000$$
$$\text{International reserves} = \$400$$

$$M_d = 0.25Y - 1000r \qquad \text{(demand for money)}$$

a What is Denmark's money supply?
b What is Denmark's domestic component of the monetary base?
c In each of the following cases, determine Denmark's balance-of-payments deficit or surplus:
(i) $Y = 50{,}000$, $r = 0.10$ **(ii)** $Y = 32{,}000$, $r = 0.08$ **(iii)** $Y = 39{,}800$, $r = 0.05$

2 Return to the scenario of Question 1. Denmark currently enjoys balance-of-payments equilibrium. In each of the following cases, determine the total gain or loss of international reserves.
a Denmark's monetary authorities increase the money supply by \$500.
b Denmark's national income rises by \$4,000.

3 Consider a hypothetical model of two countries, America and Japan. The equation of exchange holds in each country. You are given the following data:

	America	Japan
Money supply	\$1,000	300,000 yen
Velocity of circulation	2	3
Real output	5,000	15,000

a What is the equilibrium exchange rate (yen per dollar)?
b What is the effect on the rate of exchange in each of the following cases:
(i) America's output increases by 10 percent as Japan's output increases by 20 percent. **(ii)** America's money supply increases by 15 percent as Japan's money supply increases by only 2 percent.

4 Assume that the monetary authorities of Greece attempt to sterilize payments imbalances. Currently, Greece's hypothetical monetary base is $1,000, of which 80 percent represents international reserves. The money multiplier is 5, and the demand for money is given by the equation

$$M_d = 0.2Y - 200r$$

In each of the following cases, determine Greece's balance-of-payments deficit or surplus and indicate how long the monetary authorities will be able to continue sterilizing payments imbalances:

a $Y = 24{,}400,\ r = 0.10$

b $Y = 25{,}350,\ r = 0.15$

SUGGESTED READING

Chacholiades, M. (1972). "The Classical Theory of International Adjustment: A Restatement." *Econometrica*, pp. 463–485.

———(1978). *International Monetary Theory and Policy*. McGraw-Hill Book Company, New York, chap. 15.

———(1980). "The Stability of the Price-Specie-Flow Mechanism." *Greek Economic Review*, pp. 191–206.

Dornbusch, R. (1979). "Monetary Policy under Exchange Rate Flexibility." In J. R. Artus et al. (eds.), *Managed Exchange-Rate Flexibility*, Federal Reserve Bank of Boston, 1979.

———(1980). *Open Economy Macroeconomics*. Basic Books, New York, chap. 7.

———(1983). "Exchange Rate Economics: Where Do We Stand?" In J. S. Bhandari and B. H. Putnam (eds.), *Economic Interdependence and Flexible Exchange Rates*, The MIT Press, Cambridge, Mass., 1983.

Frankel, J. A., and H. G. Johnson, eds. (1976). *The Monetary Approach to the Balance of Payments*. George Allen and Unwin, London.

———(1978). *The Economics of Exchange Rates*. Addison-Wesley Publishing Company, Reading, Mass.

Johnson, H. G. (1961). "Towards a General Theory of the Balance of Payments." In H. G. Johnson, *International Trade and Economic Growth: Studies in Pure Theory*, Harvard University Press, Cambridge, Mass., 1961. Reprinted in R. E. Caves and H. G. Johnson (eds.), American Economic Association *Readings in International Economics*, Richard D. Irwin, Inc., Homewood, Ill., 1968.

Krueger, A. O. (1983). *Exchange-Rate Determination*. Cambridge University Press, New York.

Officer, L. H. (1976). "The Purchasing-Power-Parity Theory of Exchange Rates: A Review Article." *International Monetary Fund Staff Papers*, vol. 23, pp. 1–60.

Polak, J. J. (1957). "Monetary Analysis of Income Formation and Payments." *International Monetary Fund Staff Papers*, vol. 6, pp. 1–50.

Putnam, B. H., and D. S. Wilford, eds. (1986). *The Monetary Approach to International Adjustment*. Rev. ed., Praeger Publishers, New York.

Whitman, M. v. N. (1975). "Global Monetarism and the Monetary Approach to the Balance of Payments." *Brookings Papers on Economic Activity*, 3:1975, pp. 491–536.

CHAPTER 20

THE INTERNATIONAL MONETARY SYSTEM

This final chapter deals with those special problems that arise in connection with the international monetary system, that is, the rules and conventions that govern the international financial conduct of nations. In addition to discussing general principles, this chapter deals with the actual systems that have existed over the last century or so, such as the gold standard (as well as the interwar attempts to restore the classical gold standard and the general instability of this period), the Bretton Woods system, the present system of managed flexibility, and the new European Monetary System.

20-1 TYPES OF INTERNATIONAL MONETARY SYSTEMS

The term **international monetary system**[1] refers to the framework of rules, regulations, and conventions that govern the financial relations among nations. The foreign financial conduct of nations can be organized in many different ways. Accordingly, the international monetary system can assume many different forms. All international monetary systems, whatever their form, have much in common and differ only in certain respects. Economists usually use several alternative criteria for classifying the various possible international monetary systems. For our purposes, it is sufficient to concentrate on only two of these criteria (or dimensions): (1) the role of exchange rates and (2) the nature of the reserve asset(s).

[1]Some authors prefer the terms **international monetary *order*** or **international monetary *regime*** to **international monetary *system*.**

Exchange-Rate Regimes (or Systems)

From one point of view, international finance deals with the difficulties of international money changing—difficulties of turning one money into another. It is for this reason that the exchange rates play a crucial role in all international monetary systems. Indeed, we can classify the various possible international monetary systems according to the degree of flexibility (or rigidity) of foreign exchange rates.

We are already familiar with the two polar alternatives of permanently fixed or absolutely flexible exchange rates. Between these two extremes, there is a large array of possible compromises. The most widely discussed compromises include the **adjustable peg** (in which nations may alter their "fixed" par values whenever necessary to correct a fundamental disequilibrium); the **wide band** (in which the exchange rate is flexible within wide limits—known as the "wide band"—but is prevented from moving outside the band); the **crawling peg** (in which the exchange rate changes continuously but by very small amounts each time; that is, it is "crawling"); and **managed floating** (in which there are no fixed parities, but the monetary authorities do intervene in the foreign exchange market to limit the frequency and amplitude of fluctuations of exchange rates around their long-term trend).

A recent addition to the list of possible exchange-rate systems is the **target zone approach,** which is favored by many economists and policymakers. Under this arrangement, the major economies (the United States, West Germany, and Japan) would establish a set of mutually consistent *targets* for real, trade-weighted exchange rates, not nominal ones. (The nominal central rates would change continuously to reflect differences in inflation rates between the countries.) Given the targets, the participating countries would use monetary policy to keep the market exchange rates within a band, or *zone,* of 10 percent of either side of the targets. The limits would be "soft" in the sense that in exceptional circumstances countries would let their rates move outside the zones.

Monetary Standards

Another important dimension of international monetary systems is the nature of the reserve asset(s). In general, international monetary reserves are divided into two major categories: (1) commodity reserves and (2) fiduciary (or fiat) reserves. Commodity reserves (such as gold) do have some intrinsic value quite apart from their value as money. By contrast, fiduciary reserves (such as special drawing rights and national currencies that are inconvertible into commodity reserves) have no intrinsic value.

Based on the nature of the reserve asset(s), we can classify international monetary systems into the following three categories:

1 Pure commodity standards, in which all reserves consist of commodity reserves, as in the case of the gold standard

2 Pure fiduciary standards, in which all reserves are fiduciary reserves, as illustrated by the "inconvertible-paper standard"

3 Mixed standards, in which the reserves are a mixture of commodity reserves and fiduciary reserves, as illustrated by the gold exchange standard

During the course of time, the term **monetary standard** has undergone a fundamental change. Originally, when gold (or silver) was used as a standard, a certain quantity of the metal served as a unit of account. Thus, it was possible to express the exchange values of all goods and services in terms of the standard commodity (gold or silver), which in turn facilitated the comparison of different quantities of goods and services. Today the term *standard* refers to any monetary system, even though no "standard commodity" may be present.

The various exchange-rate regimes and monetary standards refer to the same population of international monetary systems. The difference lies in the fact that these two classifications use different criteria in grouping the total population of international monetary systems into different sets. This explains why economists may often use different names to refer to the same international monetary system. For instance, economists may refer to the gold standard as either a fixed exchange-rate system (when they want to emphasize that under this system the exchange rates are fixed) or a pure commodity standard (when they want to emphasize that gold is a commodity reserve asset).

20-2 THE CHARACTERISTICS OF A GOOD INTERNATIONAL MONETARY SYSTEM

We now turn to the choice of an international monetary system. What is a good international monetary system? How can we tell whether a certain system is good or bad? What criteria should we use for this purpose? These are extremely important questions. To answer them, we must first identify what the international monetary system does, or what it is supposed to do.

The Ultimate Objectives of the International Monetary System

The international monetary system is not an end in itself. Its main function is to enable the fundamental economic processes of production and distribution to operate as smoothly and efficiently as possible. It is mainly for this reason that Adam Smith called the international monetary system the "great wheel." When the wheel turns effortlessly, international monetary relations become inconspicuous, taken for granted, as the attention turns to the resultant large, constant flow of goods and services that go to satisfy human wants in every corner of the globe. But when the wheel turns badly, the international flow of goods and services is interrupted, with grave consequences for the economic welfare of nations. It is particularly during such crises that most people become aware of the existence and significance of the international monetary system (the wheel).

It follows that the ultimate objectives of the international monetary system are (1) the maximization of total world output and employment and (2) the achievement of a desirable distribution of economic welfare among nations as well as among different groups within each nation.

A well-organized international monetary system can lead to the maximization of total world output (by permitting the fullest use of efficient division of labor among the nations of the world) and to an acceptable distribution of that output among the members of the world community. This, of course, presupposes the free flow of goods and services, capital, labor, and even ideas, among nations. Direct controls for balance-of-payments reasons have no place in a well-organized international monetary system.

Cooperation and Rivalry among Nations

Before going any further, we should draw attention to the elements of cooperation and rivalry that exist among nations. The element of cooperation emanates from the common policy objective of maximizing total world output and thus promoting the highest level of global welfare. The element of rivalry arises from the divergent policy objectives of nations concerning the distribution of economic welfare among nations.

The element of rivalry may lead to serious policy conflicts. Like selfish individuals, nations usually prefer a bigger slice of the pie even though such preference may lead to a smaller overall pie, with the result that all nations become worse off in absolute terms than they need be. An example of this is provided by the optimal tariff. A large country imposes an optimal tariff in order to exploit its monopolistic position in international trade. Such a selfish policy may lead to a tariff war, as other countries retaliate in an attempt to maximize their own national welfare. The tariff war comes to an end only when no country can gain further through unilateral action. As we already know, such a tariff war may leave all countries worse off. Put differently, all countries may benefit by agreeing to remove all tariffs. Similar examples in the monetary realm are presented later on in this chapter.

It must be clear by now that a good international monetary system which minimizes the element of rivalry among nations can be beneficial to the entire world community, since it can preserve the joint gain that the world economy can achieve through an efficient international division of labor.

We conclude that a good international monetary system is one that reconciles the elements of cooperation and rivalry which exist among nations. Some minimum degree of consistency among the policies of nations is absolutely necessary for the preservation of the joint gains that spring from an efficient division of labor among nations.

Autarky versus Anarchy

One possible way of minimizing the element of rivalry is to adopt the system of **autarky.** Each nation could seal off its borders and prohibit the inflow and outflow of goods and services, capital, and labor. Thus, each nation could become self-sufficient. The absurdity of this solution must be clear: It eliminates the element of rivalry by sacrificing all the benefits that emanate from international trade and investment. We reject it.

At the other extreme, there is the alternative of **anarchy.** In this case, there would be no rules or conventions at all, and each nation would be free to do what it thought best. We reject anarchy also. Such a system (if we could call it that) would allow large, powerful nations to exploit smaller, weaker nations. It would disorganize markets as various nations pursued inconsistent policy objectives. For instance, suppose that the Bank of Canada started buying U.S. dollars in order to force a depreciation of the Canadian dollar. Assume further that the United States did not like the idea and preferred the current exchange rate. It must be clear that the United States (the stronger country) could frustrate the Canadian plan by purchasing Canadian dollars at the same rate as Canada (the weaker country) issued them.

20-3 ADJUSTMENT, LIQUIDITY, AND CONFIDENCE

To appraise the actual performance of the international monetary system, economists have developed three important tests: **adjustment, liquidity,** and **confidence.** Adjustment refers to the capacity of nations to maintain or restore equilibrium in their international payments. Liquidity refers to the adequacy of international reserves. Confidence refers to the absence of destabilizing (panicky) shifts from one reserve asset to another when there are many reserve assets. The purpose of this section is to clarify the meaning and significance of these three concepts.

Adjustment

We are already familiar with the problem of balance-of-payments adjustment, which involves a marginal reallocation of resources prompted by changes in incomes, relative prices, and/or exchange rates (see especially Chapter 13). The essence of the adjustment problem is that every adjustment policy involves economic costs. For instance, to correct its external deficit, a country may have to deflate its economy and accept domestic unemployment. A surplus country may eliminate its unwanted surplus by having to accept inflation. If adjustment costs are inevitable and adjustment is unavoidable, the role of the international monetary system must surely be to enable countries to choose those policies (or combinations of policies) that (1) minimize the overall cost of adjustment and (2) distribute that minimum cost equitably among all nations.

Unfortunately, the designing of rules, regulations, and conventions (that is, the drafting of the constitution of the international monetary system) that meet the above objectives is not an easy matter, as the history of international monetary relations shows. There are several reasons for this pessimistic view. First, there is the real problem that the costs associated with each policy are not easily predictable—indeed, these costs may be high or low depending on circumstances (such as the state of economy). In addition, there is the fundamental difficulty that each nation, in the final analysis, is concerned with its own responsibilities and costs of adjustment, not the aggregate costs of the world community. It is mainly for this reason that nations do not adjust willingly. Deficit countries ordinarily refuse to accept the intolerable cost of domestic unemployment, while surplus countries refuse to accept the consequences of domestic inflation. Indeed, for prestige and political reasons, every nation ordinarily wants other nations to take the initiative in restoring external balance—usually governments interpret such initiative as failure on their part.

The adjustment process is further complicated by the fact that groups within each nation are apt to lobby vigorously against any policies that they perceive to be detrimental to their own interests. For instance, labor unions in deficit countries may oppose deflationary fiscal and monetary policies. Similarly, the foreign-trade sector of a nation may lobby against exchange-rate flexibility and direct controls.

Liquidity

International economists use the term **liquidity** to refer to the volume of gross international monetary reserves. A good international monetary system must provide an adequate supply (and growth) of reserves. (In our current international monetary system, reserves consist of total official holdings of gold, convertible foreign currencies, special drawing rights, and net reserve positions in the International Monetary Fund.)

What is the main function of reserves (or liquidity)? We may recall from our earlier discussion that temporary external disequilibria call for financing—not adjustment. Only permanent (or fundamental) disequilibria require real adjustment. Nevertheless, even in the case of permanent disequilibria, the availability of financing gives the authorities some desirable leeway in choosing among the various policy options. The availability of financing often enables the authorities to adopt a slow-working policy whose adjustment costs are lower than the corresponding costs of other policy alternatives. The main purpose of reserves is to make financing of external disequilibria possible. Indeed, the optimal volume (and rate of growth) of reserves is that which ensures the most efficient mix of financing and adjustment.

Seigniorage

The creation of international liquidity generates benefits and costs. Nations often find themselves in conflict over the distribution of these benefits and costs. The main bone of contention in this connection is the profit from issuing money, known as **seigniorage.**

Seigniorage is a technical term in monetary economics. Originally seigniorage referred to the difference between the cost of producing money (that is, the cost of bullion plus the cost of minting) and the value of money in exchange. This difference represented a once-and-for-all gain to the issuer of money, the king or *seigneur*.

Today seigniorage means the profit from issuing any kind of money, including international money. Domestically, all governments (through their central banks) have a monopoly power in issuing currency and thus enjoy all seigniorage (monopoly profit). Internationally, governments similarly have a strong desire to benefit from any seigniorage arising from the issue of international money.

Whether the amount of seigniorage arising from the issue of international money is large or small depends crucially on the type of monetary standard that happens to be in operation. For instance, a pure commodity standard, such as the gold standard, implies a relatively small amount of seigniorage because of the higher cost of producing and storing gold. Under a pure fiduciary standard, such as the dollar standard, international money is costless to produce and there is a relatively large amount of seigniorage, which must be distributed in some way among nations. When the issuer of the fiduciary reserve asset pays no interest on reserve holdings, then all the seigniorage gains accrue to the issuer. But when the issuer is obliged to pay interest on the liabilities, part (or all) of seigniorage gains accrue to the holders of reserves in the form of interest income.

Confidence

When several reserve assets coexist, there is always the danger of destabilizing shifts from one reserve asset to another, as predicted by **Gresham's law:** "Bad money drives out good."

The confidence needed for the smooth functioning of the international monetary system refers to the willingness of the holders of the various reserve assets to continue holding them. Confidence essentially means the absence of panicky shifts from one reserve asset to another.

A crisis of confidence arises when the holders of the various reserve assets become discontented with the composition of their portfolios and attempt to switch from one asset to another. A good international monetary system must have safeguards against the occurrence of crises of confidence or at least must be able to cope satisfactorily with such crises. As we shall see in Section 20-6, the danger of crises of confidence was particularly serious under the Bretton Woods system.

20-4 THE GOLD STANDARD (1870–1914)

Under an international gold standard, each country ties its money to gold and allows the unrestricted import and export of gold. In particular, the central bank of each gold-standard country stands ready to buy and sell gold (and only gold) freely at a fixed price in terms of the domestic currency, while its private residents are entirely free to export or import gold. The essence of an international gold standard is that the rates of exchange are fixed.

Even though the use of gold coins dates back to antiquity, the international gold standard was a relatively brief episode in world history. It emerged during the 1870s and lasted until the outbreak of World War I in 1914. This period is often described as the "golden age" of the gold standard. During these four decades world trade and investment flourished, promoting international specialization and global welfare. The balance-of-payments mechanism appeared to be working smoothly. Conflicts of policy among nations were extremely rare. Consequently, after World War I, it was quite natural for nations and scholars to look back on the prewar gold standard with nostalgia.

At the center of the gold-standard stage was Great Britain because of its leading role in commercial and financial affairs. At that time, Britain was the supreme industrial nation, a significant importer of foodstuffs and raw materials, the biggest exporter of manufactured goods, and the largest source of long- and short-term capital. London was the financial center of the world. Britain had been on the gold standard since 1821, half a century before other major countries joined the bandwagon. As a result, sterling came to be identified with gold and was freely accepted and widely used. Indeed, a substantial proportion of world trade was financed with sterling, and as a consequence sizable sterling balances were held in London. Furthermore, Britain pursued a free-trade policy and also acted as lender of last resort in times of exchange crisis.

The pre-1914 gold standard did not really encompass the entire world. Only a core of major European countries were actually on the gold standard and maintained fixed exchange rates. The exchange rates of other, less developed, primary-producing countries outside of the British empire, particularly in Latin America, fluctuated widely during the 1870–1914 period in response to shifts of foreign demand for their exports as well as sudden interruptions of capital inflows.

What accounts for the apparent success of the pre-1914 gold standard? In retrospect, its success was clearly a myth. The fact is that during the 1870–1914 period, the world economy did not really experience any dramatic shocks (such as World Wars I and II, the great depression of the 1930s, or even the 1973–1974 OPEC oil price increase). On the contrary, during this period the major trading countries experienced a broad synchronization of fluctuations in their economic activity as well as a parallel movement of their exports and imports, both individually and as a group. Thus, the gold standard existed during a rather tranquil period and was not really put to the test.

The myth of the golden age reflected two serious misconceptions: (1) that the price-specie-flow mechanism (see Chapter 14) worked smoothly and maintained external balance automatically and (2) that the monetary authorities of the gold-standard countries followed the "rules of the game," allowing gold flows to exert their full influence on the domestic money supplies and price levels. These misconceptions, in turn, generated the belief that the gold standard was an impersonal, automatic, and politically symmetrical system.

Historical data show that during the 1870–1914 period, prices in the major trading countries moved in a parallel fashion rather that in a divergent fashion as required by the price-specie-flow mechanism. This fact actually puzzled contemporary economists, who were unable to reconcile their observations with the predictions of the price-specie-flow mechanism. For instance, in the 1920s Frank Taussig and his Harvard students studied historical examples of balance-of-payments adjustment and expressed surprise at the observed smoothness and speed of adjustment in many countries before World War I. Essentially, they observed that small gold flows and relative price changes seemed to restore equilibrium in the balance of payments quite promptly. This result was too good to believe and led Taussig to suspect that some important economic forces were ignored by classical theory. Indeed, after the publication of Keynes's *General Theory* the missing link was recognized to be the income-adjustment mechanism.

In addition, Bloomfield (1959) demonstrated convincingly that the pre-1914 central banks did not really follow the rules of the game. In the majority of cases, central banks did not administer the classical medicine. Rather, they sterilized payments imbalances, effectively shielding their money supplies from the balance of payments and thus short-circuiting the adjustment mechanism.

What, then, did maintain and restore external balance during the pre-1914 period? In the case of Great Britain, the main instrument was the **bank rate** (analogous to the discount rate of the Federal Reserve banks in the United States). In the presence of a deficit, the Bank of England raised its bank rate, rendering London a relatively more attractive place to which to lend and a relatively less attractive place from which to borrow. As a result, large amounts of funds flowed into London, strengthening sterling in the foreign exchange market and discouraging the outflow of gold. Similarly, in the presence of a surplus, the Bank of England lowered its bank rate. The lower bank rate, in turn, encouraged a capital outflow and suspended the need to import gold. Accordingly, in the case of Great Britain, stabilizing capital movements maintained external balance.

The other "core" countries did not have any major degree of monetary independence. They followed the lead of the Bank of England. To maintain external balance, the major central banks (for example, that of France) often used their reserves, and on many occasions they simply resorted to the manipulation of gold points, intervention in the foreign exchange market, borrowing from foreigners, and so on.

20-5 THE INTERWAR PERIOD

If the pre-1914 gold-standard era is viewed as the golden age of international monetary relations, the interwar period may be viewed as the "dark age," a nightmare. With the outbreak of World War I, the golden age came to an end. Initially, the belligerent nations suspended convertibility of their currencies into gold and put an embargo on gold exports in order to protect their gold reserves. Soon after, most other nations adopted the same policy. The classical gold standard was dead.

In the foreign exchange market, private individuals could still trade one paper currency against another but at prices determined by supply and demand conditions. Thus, a purely floating exchange-rate regime succeeded the fixed exchange-rate system of the gold standard. In the ensuing years, exchange rates gyrated chaotically, particularly in response to two great disturbances: World War I and the great depression.

For a few years after World War I (1919–1923), currency values fluctuated violently in the foreign exchange market. However, most nations viewed the regime of fluctuating exchange rates as a temporary arrangement. Thus, they immediately turned their attention to the problem of reforming the international monetary system. Lulled by the myth of the golden age, nations were determined to restore the classical gold standard. However, gold was still valued at its old prewar parities; and in view of the rapid price inflations that almost all countries had experienced during and immediately after the war, there was an obvious shortage of gold.

To overcome this shortage, the Financial Committee of the Genoa Conference, which took place in 1922, recommended worldwide adoption of a **gold exchange standard.** The major financial centers (for example, London) were to maintain **convertibility** of their currencies into gold, while the monetary authorities of the rest of the countries were to maintain convertibility of their currencies into "gold exchange" (that is, currencies convertible into gold, such as sterling). Gold was to be concentrated in the major financial centers as the monetary authorities of the rest of the countries proceeded to convert their unnecessary gold holdings into gold exchange. In this way, the world would economize on the use of gold.

In 1925 Britain re-established the convertilibity of sterling into gold and removed all restrictions on the export of gold. Soon after the British action, country after country restored convertibility at the prewar parities. The gold exchange standard was born. Unfortunately, the experiment did not last long. In 1931 the British had to suspend convertibility once again because of a run on their reserves. The system collapsed, and all the king's horses could not put it together again. From that moment on, the world was divided into three competing and hostile blocks: (1) the **sterling block** (organized around Great Britain), (2) the **dollar block** (organized around the United States), and (3) the **gold block** (organized around France). In addition, many other countries, such as Germany and eastern European countries, abandoned convertibility altogether and imposed exchange control.

The decade of the great depression was a period of open economic warfare. As the depression deepened, governments pursued in vain the game of **competitive depreciations** in the hope of eliminating their domestic unemployment and restoring external balance. During the five-year period 1931–1935, international cooperation reached its nadir.

In 1936 there appeared some sign of cooperation as Britain, France, and the United States signed the **Tripartite Agreement,** which permitted France to devalue its overvalued franc without retaliation. But even this trace of cooperation was abruptly interrupted by World War II. Meaningful international monetary reform had to be postponed until the end of the war.

Why did the interwar experiment fail? Economic historians give two reasons: (1) the golden age was actually a myth, and (2) the world economy had experienced very significant changes because of World War I and the great depression. In particular, the prewar parities were totally inappropriate, particularly because various countries had experienced quite different degrees of inflation (see the discussion of the purchasing-power-parity theory in Chapter 19). Thus, most currencies were either overvalued or undervalued by significant amounts. The great depression further disrupted the world economy to a considerable degree. Prices and money wages were becoming increasingly rigid, especially in the downward direction. Concerned with domestic stability, countries also tended to sterilize their payments imbalances. Finally, London had ceased to be the single dominant financial center of the world. As other competitive financial centers (such as Paris and New York) came into existence, there emerged a growing tendency (after 1931) for short-term funds to move from one country to another (''hot money'' movements) in search of security and in response to political alarms and rumors—the familiar confidence problem.

20-6 THE BRETTON WOODS SYSTEM (1944–1971)

In 1944, delegates of 44 noncommunist nations held a conference at Bretton Woods, New Hampshire. The main objective of the conference was to reform the international monetary system. For this purpose, the delegates considered two rival plans: a British plan developed by Lord Keynes and an American plan developed by Harry Dexter White of the U.S. Treasury.

Keynes proposed the creation of a **clearing union** with overdraft facilities (virtually an automatic line of credit) and the ability to create reserves. In addition, he proposed the creation of a new international unit of account (to be called **bancor**), which was to be used only on the books of the clearing union. Another important feature of the Keynes plan was that not only bancor borrowers but also bancor creditors would pay interest on their balances—an attempt to place at least part of the adjustment responsibility on surplus countries.

The system the delegates finally endorsed, however, was akin to the White plan. It later became known as the **Bretton Woods system.** It served the world from 1944 to 1971, a period of 27 years that was known as the Bretton Woods era.

The most important features of the Bretton Woods system were as follows:

1 *International institutions.* International monetary cooperation requires the creation of an international agency with defined functions and powers.

2 *Exchange-rate regime.* Exchange rates should be fixed in the short run but adjustable from time to time in the presence of ''fundamental disequilibria.''

3 *International monetary reserves.* For the smooth functioning of the adjustable-peg system, countries (individually and as a group) require a large volume of reserves. Accordingly, there must be some augmentation of gold and currency reserves.

4 *Currency convertibility.* In the interests of political harmony and economic welfare, all countries must adhere to a system of unfettered multilateral trade and convertible currencies.

In this section, we review the above principles. In addition, we provide some insights into the inherent drawbacks of the system, as economic observers saw them unfold during the Bretton Woods era.

International Institutions

The Bretton Woods conferees agreed that international monetary cooperation required the creation of an international agency with defined functions and powers. They felt that a permanent institution was necessary to serve as a forum for international consultation and cooperation on monetary matters. For this purpose, they created the **International Monetary Fund** (IMF), which has provided the framework and determined the code of behavior for the postwar international monetary system.

The Adjustable-Peg System

The negotiators at Bretton Woods sought an exchange-rate system that would combine the advantages of both fixed and flexible exchange rates. For this purpose, they adopted the system of the **adjustable peg,** which provides for exchange-rate stability in the short run (and in this respect is similar to the gold standard) but allows for the possibility of exchange-rate adjustment when a country's balance of payments is in fundamental disequilibrium (and in this respect is similar to the flexible exchange-rate system under which external equilibrium is maintained by exchange-rate adjustments). Unfortunately, the adjustable-peg system lacked the stability, certainty, and automaticity of the gold standard and the flexibility of the flexible exchange-rate system, a fact that led to its downfall.

The system of the adjustable peg is similar to the gold standard with respect to the determination and maintenance of the spot exchange rates in the short run. According to the initial agreement, the dollar was pegged to gold at the fixed parity of $35 per ounce of gold, and dollars held by official monetary institutions were freely convertible into gold, as the United States was prepared to buy and sell unlimited amounts of gold at the official price. In this sense, the dollar became the **key currency.** Every other country was required to (1) declare the **par value** (or **parity**) of its currency in terms of gold or the U.S. dollar and (2) stand ready to defend the declared parity in the foreign exchange market by buying and selling dollars, at least in the short run. In this sense, the dollar became the primary **intervention currency.** (For practical reasons the operative standard for most countries was the dollar as such.) Exchange rates could vary only within the so-called **support points** or **intervention points,** which were initially set at 1 percent above or below parity.

Only the United States was not required to intervene in the foreign exchange market. It was up to the other countries to maintain fixed dollar prices. In a world of n countries only $n - 1$ external policies (be they adjustment or liquidity policies) can be independently formulated (a technical difficulty that is known as the **redundancy problem**). The United States followed a policy of "benign neglect" in order to ensure consistency among national policies. This policy came back to haunt the United States during the final years of the Bretton Woods era.

Incidentally, while the monetary authorities of member countries were required to intervene in the **spot market** and to maintain the **spot rates** within the support points, no such requirement was stipulated with respect to the **forward market** and the **forward rates.** Individual countries were free to choose whether or not to intervene in the forward market at their discretion. Forward rates occasionally moved outside the limits ("band") set for the spot rates. This was mainly the result of heavy speculation.

Member countries retained the right to alter par values to correct any fundamental disequilibrium. However, the negotiators at Bretton Woods did not spell out a precise definition of the concept of fundamental disequilibrium.

International Monetary Reserves

With the interwar experience still vivid in their memories, the negotiators at Bretton Woods were convinced that the adjustable-peg system required an adequate supply of international monetary reserves. For this purpose, they developed the IMF system of quotas and subscriptions.

Each member country was assigned a **quota.** (This quota was actually based on a complicated formula that was supposed to reflect each country's relative significance in world trade.) Then each member country had to place a subscription equal to its quota with the IMF. In particular, each member country had to contribute 25 percent of its quota in gold or currency convertible into gold (mainly U.S. dollars) and 75 percent in the member's own currency. (Since 1978 convertible foreign currencies have been substituted for gold.)

In turn, a member's quota determined the maximum amount of loans that the member was eligible to receive from the Fund when short of reserves. In particular, each member's borrowing rights were limited to five **tranches** (or shares). Each tranche was equal to 25 percent of the member's quota. Thus, a member's maximum borrowing was restricted to 125 percent of its quota.

The first tranche was referred to as the **gold tranche,** because it was equal to the member's gold subscription. (The gold tranche is now called the **reserve tranche.**) With respect to its gold tranche, the member's drawing rights were unconditional (that is, the member could borrow within the gold tranche with no questions asked). The remaining four tranches were referred to as **credit**

tranches. With respect to the credit tranches, the member's drawing rights were conditional (that is, required approval by the Fund).

From another point of view, a member could "purchase" (that is, borrow) foreign exchange from the Fund in return for equivalent amounts of the member's own currency. Such purchases could proceed up to the point at which the Fund's holdings of the member's currency equaled 200 percent of its quota. Thus, maximum purchases of foreign exchange by a member were set equal to 125 percent of that member's quota because of the member's initial 75 percent subscription of its own currency. However, in the event that the Fund's holdings of a member's currency were less than 75 percent of that member's quota (presumably because other members had purchased that currency from the Fund), the member's borrowing capacity was correspondingly increased. The resultant increase in the member's borrowing capacity was referred to as the **supergold tranche.** With respect to the supergold tranche, the member's drawing rights were unconditional, just as in the case of the gold tranche. In the event the Fund ran out of a currency altogether, it was supposed to declare that currency "scarce" and permit other countries to discriminate against it. This provision reflected the view of the negotiators that adjustment was the joint responsibility of both deficit and surplus countries.

A member's **net reserve position** with the IMF equaled its gold tranche plus its super-gold tranche, if any (or minus any borrowings by the country from the Fund). In other words, a member's net reserve position with the IMF equaled its quota minus the Fund's holdings of the member's own currency. Countries now add their net reserve positions with the IMF to their official reserve assets.

As it turned out, the Fund's initial pool of international liquidity was totally inadequate. As a result, the United States became the main source of international liquidity growth through its balance-of-payments deficits. In this way, the dollar became the primary **reserve currency,** and observers soon began to refer to the postwar monetary system as a **dollar standard.**

Currency Convertibility and Multilateral Trade

In the interests of political harmony and economic welfare, all countries agreed to a system of unfettered multilateral trade and convertible currencies. Members agreed to refrain from imposing any restrictions on *current* international transactions. Members were not permitted to engage in any discriminatory currency arrangements or exchange control. All currencies were to be freely convertible into one another at official rates. However, because most countries were simply devastated by the war (with huge import needs and exhausted monetary reserves), it was agreed that the dismantling of controls and the return to convertibility should be gradual. Indeed, Europe's currencies did not return to convertibility until 1958.

The principle of multilateral trade and currency convertibility carried with it the necessity of a real adjustment mechanism, something that the Bretton

Woods system lacked. Because of the chaotic experience of the 1930s, the system exhibited a bias against frequent exchange-rate adjustments—governments had to demonstrate the existence of a fundamental disequilibrium before they could adjust their par values. Further, nations became increasingly concerned with domestic employment and removed the link between the balance of payments and the money supply by sterilizing payments imbalances. Thus, deficit countries were left with the possibility of regulating capital account transactions only. (Such capital controls were even encouraged because of the experience of the 1930s.)

Speculation

One major drawback of the adjustable-peg system is that speculation becomes at times destabilizing because of the possibility of parity changes. The main reason for this phenomenon is the **one-way option** offered to speculators. When a currency is under suspicion, there is some doubt as to whether it will be devalued and to what extent; but there is practically no doubt about the direction of change.

For instance, assume that speculators observe that a country is persistently running huge deficits and that they come to expect the country to devalue its currency. To benefit from the expected devaluation, the speculators sell the currency in the hope of buying it later at a lower price. If the country actually devalues, the speculators make substantial profits. If the country does not devalue, their potential losses are minimal, since the narrow band around the par value prevents the currency from appreciating significantly.

Such destabilizing speculation can force the deficit country to devalue its currency by bleeding its reserves, even in cases in which the country could have weathered the storm in the absence of destabilizing speculation. The lower the reserves fall, the stronger the incentive becomes for continued bear speculation.

Defects in the Liquidity-Creation Mechanism

Triffin (1960) was the first to notice that international monetary reserves under the Bretton Woods system were not growing fast enough. He even expressed doubts as to whether the system could indeed generate reserves in sufficient amounts without undermining its very foundations.

Triffin's reasoning was relatively simple. He argued that given the slow growth of the stock of monetary gold (less than 1 percent a year), world reserves could increase only if the key-currency countries (mainly the United States) ran huge balance-of-payments deficits in order to pump into the world monetary system sufficient amounts of reserve-currency deposits (the fiduciary element). But this, he continued, would undermine confidence in the dollar because the stock of U.S. liabilities to the rest of the world would grow larger and larger relative to the U.S. stock of gold. Soon, foreign central banks and private holders would become restless and find the dollar weak and redundant. A switch from dollars to gold would cause the system to collapse.

According to Triffin, the world faced a difficult dilemma: To avoid a liquidity shortage, the United States would have to run deficits, and this would undermine confidence in the dollar; to avoid speculation against the dollar, the U.S. deficits would have to cease, but this would create a liquidity shortage. Consequently, Triffin concluded, a way must be found to increase international reserves without breeding instability into the system.

The Triffin dilemma is illustrated in Figure 20-1. From the late 1950s until the late 1960s the stock of U.S. liabilities to foreign official institutions was increasing steadily while at the same time U.S. gold reserves were declining. During 1970 and 1971 the huge amounts of international liquidity provided by the United States dramatized the inherent conflict anticipated by Triffin.

During the 1960s a series of ad hoc measures was initiated in an effort to contain the mounting speculation against the dollar. These measures included currency **swaps** between the Federal Reserve and other central banks; enlarge-

FIGURE 20-1 **The Triffin dilemma.** From the late 1950s to the late 1960s, U.S. gold reserves declined steadily. In contrast, U.S. liabilities to foreign official institutions continued to increase throughout the period, until they exploded in 1970 and 1971. (*The International Monetary Fund,* International Financial Statistics, *1972.*)

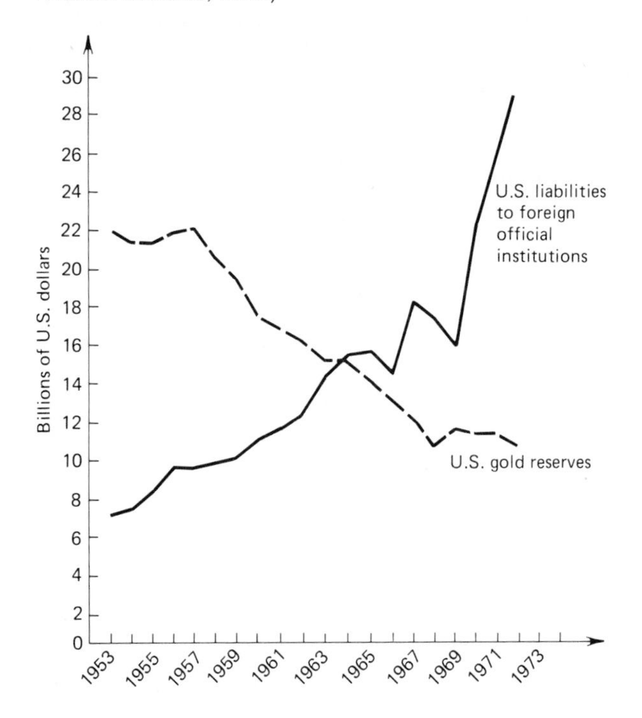

ment of the potential lending authority of the IMF (through the General Agreements to Borrow); a **gold pool** among the major financial powers to stabilize the price of gold in private markets; a **two-tier gold-price system** (with the price for the private market to be determined by supply and demand and the official price of $35 to be maintained for transactions between central banks), which actually replaced the gold pool in 1968; and, finally, the creation of **special drawing rights** (SDRs).

Special Drawing Rights

Awareness of the Triffin diagnosis eventually led to the creation of special drawing rights. Often called "paper gold," SDRs are a new form of international reserve assets whose creation was authorized in 1968 by the first amendment to the Articles of Agreement of the International Monetary Fund. Some $9.5 billion in special drawing rights were first distributed in 1970, 1971, and 1972, and further allocations were made in the 1979–1981 period. No SDR allocations have been made since 1981.

How was the IMF to allocate the newly created SDRs among the member countries? This was a question of seigniorage. Many proposed to "link" the mechanisms of liquidity creation and development finance and thus deliberately direct all the benefits of SDR creation toward the developing countries (**link proposal**). However, this proposal was rejected. The method the IMF finally adopted was to allocate the newly created SDRs among member countries in proportion to their quotas. The justification was that this method of distribution was neutral: It broadly conformed to the pattern of demand for reserves to hold rather than to the demand for reserves to spend.

Special drawing rights are transferable among member countries (and certain eligible international organizations), and they form a genuine supplement to the volume of international monetary reserves. SDRs constitute resources freely available to member countries and are thus added to the list of assets included in official monetary reserves. Consequently, since 1970 the list of reserve assets has included gold, convertible foreign currencies (that is, foreign exchange, such as dollars, pounds sterling, yen, and marks), net reserve positions with the IMF, and SDRs.

Each SDR unit was initially defined in terms of gold to equal one 1970 U.S. dollar. After the two devaluations of the dollar, one in 1971 and another in 1973 (see below), each SDR unit became equal to $1.20 (approximately). Beginning in 1974, after the collapse of the Bretton Woods system and the widespread use of fluctuating exchange rates, the IMF calculated daily the value of each SDR unit as a weighted average of a "basket" of 16 representative currencies. In 1981 the International Monetary Fund greatly simplified the composition of the SDR by moving to a five-currency basket, as follows:

U.S. dollar	(42 percent)
German mark	(19 percent)

Japanese yen	(13 percent)
French franc	(13 percent)
British pound	(13 percent)

The numbers in parentheses show the weights assigned to each currency.

The Road to Collapse

The Bretton Woods era can be conveniently divided into two periods: (1) the period of the "dollar shortage" (1944–1958) and (2) the period of the "dollar glut" (1959–1971).

The period of the dollar shortage, which was actually the heyday of the dollar standard, was characterized by mild U.S. deficits (beginning in 1950, following a round of devaluations of European currencies in 1949). Those early U.S. deficits were, on average, about $1 billion annually, and they served the useful purpose of providing the world with much needed liquidity.

However, in 1958 the annual U.S. deficit jumped to about $3.5 billion, followed by even larger deficits in the following years. At the same time the European economies felt saturated with dollars and began to convert a large portion of their dollar balances into gold. (Recall that the European currencies returned to convertibility in 1958.) The U.S. Congress responded by eliminating the federal gold-reserve requirement for all domestic currency (except notes) in order to free the U.S. stock of gold to meet the increasing world demand. In addition, the U.S. government adopted several other ad hoc measures, such as the interest equalization tax and export promotion. (In this respect, you may also recall our earlier reference to swaps, the gold pool, and the two-tier gold-price system.)

In retrospect, it seems ironic that in the late 1960s the IMF created the SDRs in response to an alleged "shortage" of international liquidity. As it turned out, the first allocations of SDRs occurred in those years (1970, 1971, and 1972) in which international liquidity was growing at an alarming rate.

The most serious adjustment problem during the period of the dollar glut was the persistent payments imbalance between the United States and the surplus countries of Europe (particularly Germany) and Japan. Germany and Japan were resisting the obvious solution to the problem, that is, revaluation of the mark and the yen, respectively. Instead, they argued that it was the responsibility of the United States "to put its house in order" (that is, take appropriate steps to restore external balance). More important, the European countries and Japan felt that the United States was exploiting the rest of the world because of the nation's privilege of financing its payments deficits by issuing dollars (the problem of seigniorage), a privilege no other country had. President Charles de Gaulle of France called this privilege "exorbitant" and claimed that the dollar standard required France to finance the U.S. involvement in the Vietnamese war. Indeed, it was felt that the dollar deposits held by foreigners were involuntary and thus any interest paid by the United States to official holders of dollar balances was like "meals served to a kidnap victim, hardly an offset to the loss of liberty."

The United States felt severely constrained, particularly in its use of exchange-rate policy, because of an inherent *asymmetry* in the dollar standard. Because other nations were using the dollar as their primary intervention currency, the United States could not effectively change the prices of other currencies in terms of dollars, that is, the United States lacked exchange-rate autonomy. Accordingly, the United States argued that it was up to the surplus countries of Europe and Japan to revalue their currencies, since the United States simply could not devalue the dollar.

The European countries and Japan could, of course, put more pressure on the United States by converting their accumulated dollar balances into gold, or at least by threatening to do so. They did not (with the singular exception of France). The reason was simple: The dollar "overhang" was much larger than the U.S. gold stock, and any attempt at conversion would have caused the entire system to collapse—a fact that was not in their best interests.

The agony ended on August 15, 1971, when President Nixon announced his "new economic policy," which in effect suspended the link between the dollar and gold and withdrew the U.S. promise to exchange gold for dollars. Once the dollar was declared inconvertible and the U.S. gold window was firmly closed, the United States regained its exchange-rate autonomy and the Bretton Woods era came to a close.

20-7 THE PRESENT SYSTEM OF MANAGED FLEXIBILITY

Following the dramatic events on August 15, 1971, almost all major currencies began to float freely in the foreign exchange market. Nevertheless, the major financial nations of the world were not yet ready to accept the regime of freely floating exchange rates. On December 18, 1971, the **Group of Ten** (Belgium, Canada, France, Germany, Italy, Japan, the Netherlands, Sweden, the United Kingdom, and the United States) reached an agreement at the Smithsonian Institution in Washington, D.C. This agreement became known as the **Smithsonian Agreement.** The three major provisions of the Smithsonian Agreement were as follows:

1 The United States agreed to raise the official price of gold to $38 an ounce from the $35 price that had prevailed since 1934. However, the United States refused to restore the free convertibility of dollars into gold.

2 Other nations agreed to realign their exchange rates upward in an effort to cope with the problem of the overvalued dollar. This fundamental realignment effectively amounted to a devaluation of the dollar of about 12 percent (on the basis of a weighted average).

3 Exchange rates were permitted to fluctuate within a wide band—2.25 percent on either side of the new parities, instead of the initial 1 percent.

Even though President Nixon called it "the greatest monetary agreement in the history of the world," the Smithsonian Agreement did not really solve any of the fundamental defects of the Bretton Woods system. Within six months, the pound sterling had to return to a floating rate. In February 1973, the United States raised the price of gold for a second time, to $42.22 an ounce, but again without restoring the free convertibility of dollars into gold. Finally, in March 1973, all the major currencies of the world started floating again. What emerged was a new exchange-rate regime: a system of "managed" floating.

Actually, the members of the European Community (plus some non-EC countries) pegged their currencies to each other and floated jointly against the dollar. This experiment of joint European float is referred to as the "snake" within the "tunnel," because the resulting movement of the jointly floating currencies within a narrow band (the tunnel, which is actually a spread of 2.25 percent between the dollar rates of the strongest and weakest currencies) produces a snake-crawling-in-a-tunnel pattern. This arrangement did not last long, however, as Britain, Italy, and France soon allowed their currencies to drop well below the tunnel.

The widespread floating that replaced the Bretton Woods par value system in 1973 was not actually legalized until the conference in Kingston, Jamaica, on January 7–9, 1976. At the Jamaica conference, the Interim Committee of the Board of Governors of the IMF formulated the second amendment to the IMF's Articles of Agreement, which established (or perhaps legalized) the current international monetary framework.

The Jamaica accord abolished the official price of gold and took several steps toward the demonetization of gold (such as eliminating the obligation of Fund members to use gold in certain transactions with the Fund and permitting the Fund to sell part of its stock of gold). Further, the Jamaica conference raised the Fund quotas by 33 percent. Nevertheless, the key feature of the conference was the agreement that countries were free to choose the type of exchange-rate system that best suited their own individual needs. Pegged and floating rates were given equal legal status. Countries were no longer compelled to maintain specific par values for their currencies. Instead, they were urged to pursue domestic economic policies that would be conducive to stability, in the belief that exchange-rate stability is a result of underlying economic and financial stability. In addition, countries were admonished to refrain from such practices as competitive depreciations in order "to gain an unfair competitive advantage over other members."

The new regime of managed floating rates reflected a compromise between France (which was seeking a return to the adjustable peg) and the United States (which was advocating a totally unrestricted regime of floating exchange rates). This diplomatic compromise was achieved at an economic summit meeting among Britain, France, Germany, Italy, Japan, and the United States at Rambouillet, France, in November 1975.

The major problem of the Jamaica accord was how to ensure that countries would actually refrain from competitive depreciations and other similar practices. For this purpose, the second amendment empowered the Fund to "exercise firm surveillance over the exchange rate policies of members" and to "adopt specific principles for the guidance of all members with respect to those policies." Unfortunately, however, "unfair competitive advantage" was not defined, nor were specific functions for the Fund stipulated to give substance to the term "firm surveillance."

In practice, the IMF member countries have adopted widely different exchange-rate regimes. Table 20-1 presents the exchange-rate arrangements that prevailed as of March 31, 1988.

When the present international monetary system was introduced in 1973, the proponents of flexible exchange rates expected tranquility in international payments. Instead, over the 15 years of its operation, the system of managed flexibility has led to huge international imbalances and severe currency misalignments. Today most economists would agree that managed flexibility has failed in three major areas:

1 *Currency misalignment.* Managed flexibility has permitted a large misalignment of the dollar, the system's key currency. The dollar was undervalued in the late 1970s before it became grossly overvalued in the early 1980s. The yen and German mark gyrated in opposite directions from the dollar. Contrary to the expectations of the advocates of flexible exchange rates, misalignments have been the rule rather than the exception.

2 *Lack of policy autonomy.* Floating rates have failed to cut the policy links between countries. Recent experience shows that economic policy leads to effects that are transmitted abroad, mainly because prices change more slowly than nominal exchange rates after a switch in economic policy. Yet the present system does not compel countries to consider the external impact of their own actions. As a result, national policies are much less likely to be internationally compatible in a world where interdependence has been growing steadily. (Since 1960, the volume of world trade has grown at an average rate of 5.7 percent per year compared with only 4.0 percent annual growth in real output.) Economic cooperation is again thought necessary for the smooth functioning of the international monetary system. Policy autonomy has proved to be a mirage.

3 *Protectionism.* Managed flexibility has failed at its basic task of supporting an open trading system. Due to their gradual liberalization, increased international capital movements have dominated trade flows in the determination of exchange rates. In turn, the resultant currency misalignments have distorted the international competitive positions of nations and have led to strong pressures for trade restrictions.

20-8 INTERNATIONAL COOPERATION: FROM THE PLAZA TO THE LOUVRE

On September 22, 1985, the finance ministers of the United States, Japan, West Germany, Britain, and France, the so-called **Group of Five,** held their celebrated meeting at the Plaza Hotel in New York. These industrial countries publicly agreed that the

TABLE 20-1 EXCHANGE-RATE ARRANGEMENTS, MARCH 31, 1988

Pegged					Flexibility limited vis-à-vis a single currency or group of currencies		More flexible		
Single currency			Currency composite						
U.S. dollar	French franc	Other	SDR	Other	Single currency	Cooperative arrangements	Adjusted according to a set of indicators	Other managed floating	Independently floating
Afghanistan	Benin	Bhutan (Indian rupee)	Burma	Algeria	Bahrain	Belgium	Brazil	Argentina	Australia
Antigua and Barbuda	Burkina Faso	Kiribati (Australian dollar)	Burundi	Austria	Qatar	Denmark	Chile	China	Bolivia
The Bahamas	Cameroon	Lesotho (South African rand)	Iran, Islamic Republic of	Bangladesh	Saudi Arabia	France	Colombia	Costa Rica	Canada
Barbados	Central African Republic	Swaziland (South African rand)	Jordan	Botswana	United Arab Emirates	Germany, Federal Republic of	Madagascar	Dominican Republic	The Gambia
Belize	Chad	Tonga (Australian dollar)	Libya	Cape Verde		Ireland	Portugal	Egypt	Ghana
Djibouti	Comoros		Rwanda	Cyprus		Italy		Greece	Guinea
Dominica	Congo		Seychelles	Fiji		Luxembourg		Guinea-Bissau	Japan
Ecuador	Ivory Coast			Finland		Netherlands		Iceland	Lebanon
El Salvador	Equatorial Guinea			Hungary				India	Maldives
Ethiopia	Gabon			Israel				Indonesia	New Zealand
Grenada	Mali			Kenya				Jamaica	Nigeria
Guatemala	Niger			Kuwait				Korea	Philippines
Guyana	Senegal			Malawi				Mauritania	South Africa
Haiti	Togo			Malaysia				Mexico	Spain
Honduras				Malta				Morocco	United Kingdom
Iraq				Mauritius				Pakistan	United States
Laos People's Democratic Republic				Nepal				Singapore	Uruguay
Liberia				Norway				Sri Lanka	Zaire
Mozambique				Papua New Guinea				Tunisia	
Nicaragua				Poland				Turkey	
Oman				Romania				Yugoslavia	
Panama				Sao Tome and Principe					
Paraguay				Solomon Islands					
Peru				Sweden					
St. Kitts and Nevis				Tanzania					
St. Lucia				Thailand					
St. Vincent				Vanuatu					
Sierra Leone				Western Samoa					
Somalia				Zimbabwe					
Sudan									
Suriname									
Syrian Arab Republic									
Trinidad and Tobago									
Uganda									
Venezuela									
Viet Nam									
Yemen Arab Republic									
Yemen, People's Democratic Republic of									
Zambia									

Source: International Monetary Fund, *Annual Report, 1988,* p. 87.

dollar was overvalued and announced that they planned to drive it down by concerted intervention in the foreign exchange market. Although the **Plaza Accord** lacked specific details, its goal was to reduce global trade imbalances and protectionist pressures by sharply cutting the externa! value of the dollar.

The depreciation of the dollar actually began seven months before the Plaza Accord—in February 1985. By the time of the Plaza meeting, the dollar had already experienced a substantial drop. From its peak of 261 yen or 3.47 German marks in February 1985, the dollar fell to 240 yen or 2.84 German marks in September 1985. The Plaza Accord maintained the momentum of the dollar's fall. By the beginning of 1987, the dollar had fallen to 158 yen—a fall of almost 40 percent from its peak. (Many economists believe that the dollar would have followed a trend of steady depreciation even if the Plaza meeting had never taken place.)

In November 1986 the United States and Japan agreed that the dollar had fallen far enough. But the new agreement entailed no clear commitments, and the dollar kept falling. As a result, a quarrel broke out between the United States, on one side, and Japan and West Germany, on the other side. The United States attributed the continuing depreciation of the dollar to the tight fiscal policy pursued by Japan and West Germany. Unless Japan and West Germany absorbed more U.S. exports (through faster growth), warned the Reagan administration, the dollar would fall much further (because of the continuing U. S. trade deficit). But even though Japanese and German exporters were experiencing a tight squeeze because of the dollar depreciation, their governments claimed that they were doing as much as they safely could to promote growth without risking inflation. Japan and Germany actually went a step further: They blamed the United States for the existing tensions, suggesting that the United States ought to cut its budget deficit as it had promised. The quarrel continued until February 1987, when the Group of Five plus Canada and Italy (also known as the **Group of Seven**) met at the Palais du Louvre in Paris.

At the Louvre meeting, the Group of Seven agreed that the then prevailing external value of the dollar (153 yen or 1.82 German marks) was about right. U.S. Secretary of the Treasury James Baker promised to stop "talking the dollar down" and recognized that a reduction in the U.S. budget deficit was a necessary element of the adjustment process. Moreover, at the Venice summit (June 1987), the Group of Seven reaffirmed the **Louvre Accord;** in addition, Japan agreed to stimulate its economy with a $35 billion package of extra spending and tax cuts. So the spirit of the Plaza Accord began to revive.

In 1987 central bank intervention was massive. On most estimates, the central banks of the main industrial countries purchased roughly $100 billion in order to prop up the dollar.

20-9 THE EUROPEAN MONETARY SYSTEM

In March 1979, the European Community (EC) put into operation the **European Monetary System** (EMS). All EC members, except Portugal and Spain, have joined the EMS, but Britain and Greece have opted not to participate in the **exchange-rate mechanism** (ERM). The main purpose of the EMS was to foster monetary stability in Europe—a necessary step toward monetary union.

The EC created a new reserve asset called the **European Currency Unit** (ECU). The ECU is a composite currency that is defined as a "basket" of nine EC currencies (like the SDR), as shown in Figure 20-2. In addition to being a reserve asset, the ECU also functions as a unit of account and as an official means of payment between central banks.

Each ERM member determines a *central* exchange rate for its currency against the ECU. (For instance, following the most recent realignment, on January 12, 1987, some of the ECU central rates are: 2.05853 German marks, 6.90403 French francs, and 1,483.58 Italian lire.) These central rates establish a **parity grid** of bilateral exchange rates among the currencies. The ERM limits each member currency to fluctuations of 2.25 percent on either side of these bilateral exchange rates (6 percent in the case of the Italian lira). When a currency's market exchange rate against the ECU diverges sufficiently from its central rate, a **divergence indicator** provides an early warning signal that some corrective action may be necessary. As a result, much intervention takes place within the EMS exchange-rate margins.

To enable member countries to maintain the external values of their currencies within the permissible limits (or **margins**), the EC created a large credit fund known as the European Monetary Cooperation Fund. Member countries contributed into this fund 20 percent of their gold and dollar reserves in exchange for ECUs. When a currency is under pressure, the system provides short-term credit to pay for intervention on the foreign exchange markets.

West Germany plays the role of hegemonic power and gives the EMS an anti-inflationary backbone. The average rate of inflation in the ERM countries fell from 10.7 percent per year in 1974–1978 to 8.9 percent in 1979–1985. But despite Germany's role, the EMS has found it necessary to adjust central rates 11 times since its establishment.

FIGURE 20-2 The composition of the ECU (European Currency Unit), in September 1987. (*The Economist,* September 19, 1987, p. 94.)

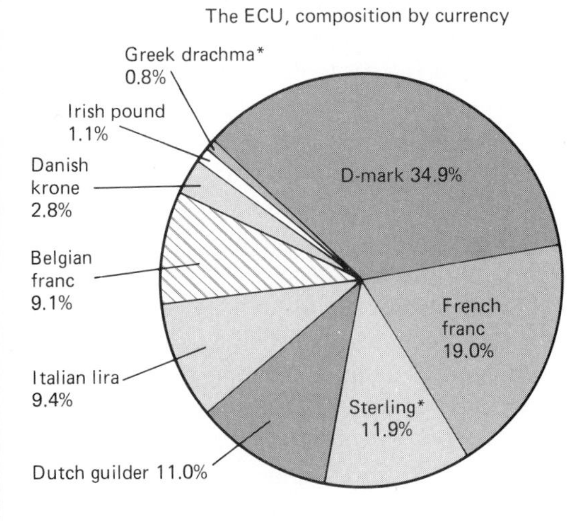

20-10 SUMMARY

1 The term *international monetary system* refers to the framework of rules, regulations, and conventions that govern the financial relations among nations.

2 Economists often classify international monetary systems according to the degree of exchange-rate flexibility. Between the polar cases of permanently fixed and absolutely flexible exchange rates there are many compromises, such as the adjustable peg, the wide band, the crawling peg, managed floating, and target zones.

3 International monetary reserves are divided into commodity reserves (that is, those reserve assets, such as gold, that have intrinsic value) and fiduciary (or fiat) reserves (that is, those that have no intrinsic value, such as special drawing rights, or SDRs).

4 Based on the nature of the reserve asset(s), economists classify international monetary systems into three categories: (a) pure commodity standards, (b) pure fiduciary standards, and (c) mixed standards.

5 The two ultimate objectives of the international monetary system are: (a) the maximization of total world output and (b) the achievement of a desirable distribution of economic welfare among nations.

6 A good international monetary system is one that reconciles the elements of cooperation and rivalry that exist among nations. However, neither autarky nor anarchy is acceptable.

7 To appraise the actual performance of an international monetary system, economists use three tests: adjustment, liquidity, and confidence.

8 Every adjustment policy involves costs. The international monetary system must (a) enable countries to choose those policies that minimize the overall adjustment cost and (b) distribute that minimum cost equitably among nations. Designing rules that meet these objectives is very difficult.

9 A good international monetary system must provide an adequate supply of reserves (liquidity) in order to make the financing of external disequilibria possible. The availability of financing is necessary not only for temporary disequilibria but also for fundamental disequilibria, because it gives the authorities desirable leeway in choosing among the various policy options.

10 Originally, seigniorage referred to the difference between the cost of producing money and its value in exchange. Today seigniorage means the profit from issuing any kind of money, including international money. All nations want to benefit from seigniorage arising from the issuing of international money, and they often find themselves in conflict.

11 Confidence means absence of panicky shifts from one reserve asset to another (when several reserve assets coexist). A good international monetary system must have safeguards against crises of confidence.

12 The international gold standard, with Great Britain at its center, emerged during the 1870s and lasted until 1914—a relatively tranquil period. The myth of the so-called golden age of the gold standard reflected two misconceptions: (a) that the price-specie-flow mechanism worked smoothly and (b) that the gold-standard countries followed the "rules of the game."

13 The interwar attempts to restore the gold standard failed because (a) the image of the golden age was a myth, and (b) the world economy had experienced significant changes as a result of World War I and the great depression.

14 The Bretton Woods system (1944–1971) adopted the adjustable peg. Each country (except the United States) had to defend the declared parity of its currency in terms of gold or the U.S. dollar, adjusting it only in the presence of fundamental disequilibria. In addition, the Bretton Woods conference created the International Monetary Fund (IMF) and the IMF system of quotas and subscriptions (which later proved to be a totally inadequate liquidity mechanism). Finally, all countries agreed to refrain from imposing restrictions on *current* international transactions.

15 The Bretton Woods system (a) lacked a real adjustment mechanism; (b) offered a one-way option to speculators, which meant that speculation was at times destabilizing; and (c) suffered from a defective liquidity-creation mechanism.

16 According to Triffin, the world faced a dilemma: To avoid a liquidity shortage, the United States would have to run deficits, undermining confidence in the dollar; but to maintain confidence in the dollar, the U.S. deficits would have to cease, creating a liquidity shortage. He concluded that a way must be found to increase reserves without breeding instability into the system. Awareness of the Triffin diagnosis led eventually to the creation of SDRs, which are a genuine supplement to the volume of international reserves.

17 The IMF calculates daily the value of each SDR unit as a weighted average of a "basket" of five currencies: the U.S. dollar, the German mark, the Japanese yen, the French franc, and the British pound.

18 The Smithsonian Agreement reached by the Group of Ten on December 18, 1971, did not repair the fundamental defects of the Bretton Woods system. By March 1973 all major currencies were floating. What emerged was the new regime of managed flexibility, which was legalized in 1976 at the Jamaica conference.

PROBLEMS

1 Some economists and politicians favor a return to the gold standard.
- **a** What is a gold standard? How does it work?
- **b** What are the perceived advantages and disadvantages of a gold standard?
- **c** Would you recommend adoption of a gold standard? Why or why not?

2 L. Robbins once noted that "balance of payments difficulties are essentially difficulties of money changing—difficulties of turning one money into another. And if there is only one money then, obviously, no such difficulties arise."
- **a** Would the creation of a world central bank (issuing a single currency) eliminate all balance-of-payments problems?
- **b** Can you foresee any difficulties in any attempt to create a world central bank?

3 According to Triffin, under the Bretton Woods system the world faced a dilemma. Awareness of the Triffin diagnosis led to the creation of special drawing rights (SDRs).
- **a** What dilemma did the world face during the Bretton Woods era?

b What are SDRs?

c If the SDRs were intended to correct the basic instability of the dollar standard, why did the system collapse shortly after their creation?

4 a What similarities and differences can you identify between the Bretton Woods system and the European Monetary System?

b Do you anticipate that the European Monetary System will face difficulties similar to those that led to the collapse of the Bretton Woods system? Why or why not?

SUGGESTED READING

Adams, J. (ed.) (1979). *The Contemporary International Economy: A Reader.* St. Martin's Press, New York, part 4.

Aliber, R. Z. (1979). *The International Money Game.* 3d ed. Basic Books, New York.

Black, S. W. (1985). "International Money and International Monetary Arrangements." In R. W. Jones and P. B. Kenen, *Handbook of International Economics,* vol. 2. North-Holland, New York, 1985.

Bloomfield, A. I. (1959). *Monetary Policy under the International Gold Standard: 1880–1914.* Federal Reserve Bank of New York, New York.

Cohen, B. J. (1977). *Organizing the World's Money.* Basic Books, New York.

Cooper, R. N. (1975). "Prolegomena to the Choice of an International Monetary System." *International Organization,* vol. 29, no. 1 (Winter), pp. 64–97.

———(1986). *Economic Policy in an Interdependent World: Essays in World Economics.* The MIT Press, Cambridge, Mass.

Hawtrey, R. G. (1947). *The Gold Standard in Theory and Practice.* Longmans, London.

Machlup, F. (1975). *International Monetary Systems.* General Learning Press, Morristown, N.J.

Mundell, R. A., and A. Swoboda, eds. (1968). *Monetary Problems of the International Economy.* University of Chicago Press, Chicago.

Officer, L. H., and T. D. Willett, eds. (1969). *The International Monetary System: Problems and Proposals.* Prentice-Hall, Inc., Englewood Cliffs, N.J.

Tew, B. (1977). *The Evolution of the International Monetary System, 1945–77.* John Wiley & Sons, New York.

Triffin, R. (1960). *Gold and the Dollar Crisis.* Yale University Press, New Haven, Conn.

———(1968). *Our International Monetary System: Yesterday, Today, and Tomorrow.* Random House, New York.

Williamson, J. (1985). *The Exchange Rate System.* Institute for International Economics, Washington, D.C.

APPENDIXES

APPENDIX 1
(CHAPTER 2)

MANY COMMODITIES AND MANY COUNTRIES

In this appendix, we extend the results of Chapter 2 to many commodities and many countries. We find it convenient to explain this important generalization with concrete examples.

MANY COMMODITIES AND TWO COUNTRIES

Table A1-1 gives the alternative outputs of five commodities that America [column (1)] and Britain [column (3)] can produce with one unit of labor. The five commodities have been arranged in the order of comparative advantage of America over Britain. Thus, taking two commodities at a time, we can say (following the analysis of Chapter 2) that America is relatively more efficient (or has a comparative advantage) in the production of X_1 compared with X_2, because $5 \div 1 > 4 \div 2$. Similarly, America is relatively more efficient in X_2 compared with X_3, because $4 \div 2 > 3 \div 3$; X_3 compared with X_4, because $3 \div 3 > 2 \div 4$; and X_4 compared with X_5, because $2 \div 4 > 1 \div 5$. These relationships are transitive. For instance, since America is relatively more efficient in X_1 compared with X_2, and in X_2 compared with X_3, America must also be relatively more efficient in X_1 compared with X_3.

Columns (2) and (4) give the prices of the five commodities in America and Britain, respectively, on the assumption that the money wage rate is $W_A = \$120$ in America and $W_B = £60$ in Britain. Columns (5), (6), and (7) translate Britain's prices into dollars at three alternative exchange rates: $R_L = \$0.40$, $R_0 = \$2$, and $R_U = \$10$. Evidently, the rate of foreign exchange (dollars per pound) cannot fall below $R_L = \$0.40$, because then the prices of all commodities would be lower in Britain. Similarly, the rate of exchange cannot rise above

TABLE A1-1 ALTERNATIVE OUTPUTS PER UNIT OF LABOR AND COMMODITY PRICES

	America		Britain				
					Prices		
		Prices					
	Outputs	(W_A = \$120)	Outputs	(W_B = £60)	R_L = \$0.40	R_0 = \$2	R_U = \$10
Commodity	(1)	(2)	(3)	(4)	(5)	(6)	(7)
X_1	5	\$ 24	1	£60	\$24.00	\$120	\$600
X_2	4	30	2	30	12.00	60	300
X_3	3	40	3	20	8.00	40	200
X_4	2	60	4	15	6.00	30	150
X_5	1	120	5	12	4.80	24	120

R_U = \$10, because then all commodities would be cheaper in America. Assuming that the current exchange rate is R_0 = \$2, America will export X_1 and X_2, and Britain will export X_4 and X_5. The direction of trade of X_3 cannot be predicted without additional information on demand, because at R_0 = \$2 the cost of X_3 is \$40 in both America and Britain.

The equilibrium exchange rate will settle at some level between R_L = \$0.40 and R_U = \$10. At that point, *trade will be balanced* (that is, the value of American exports will be equal to the value of American imports). At the final equilibrium, each country will enjoy a comparative advantage (over the other country) in all its export commodities relative to all its import commodities.

TWO COMMODITIES AND MANY COUNTRIES

Consider now the case of two commodities (food and clothing) and five countries (A, B, C, D, and E). Table A1-2 gives the opportunity cost of food in terms of clothing in each country. The five countries have been arranged in order of comparative advantage of food. Thus, taking two countries at a time, we can say that A has a comparative advantage in food relative to B, B relative to C, C relative to D, and D relative to E. Again these relationships are transitive.

With free trade, the equilibrium relative price of food will settle somewhere between 2 (A's opportunity cost of food) and 6 (E's opportunity cost of food). The precise level of the equilibrium terms of trade depends, of course, on demand in addition to the data presented in Table A1-2.

TABLE A1-2 OPPORTUNITY COST OF FOOD IN TERMS OF CLOTHING

Country	A	B	C	D	E
Opportunity cost of food	2	3	4	5	6

For concreteness, suppose that the equilibrium terms of trade are equal to 4 (C's opportunity cost of food). Then countries A and B will export food and import clothing, while countries D and E will export clothing and import food. The trade structure of country C will be indeterminate. Country C will play here the role of the "large" country discussed in Section 2-4. Because in this case the terms of trade are equal to C's opportunity cost of food, country C will gain nothing from free trade. What is more, small shifts in demand will merely affect C's internal allocation of resources without having any effect on the terms of trade.

Finally, note that there is no need for trade to be balanced bilaterally. For instance, country A's value of exports to D may exceed the value of exports of D to A. The only requirement of international equilibrium is that the value of exports of, say, A to *all* countries be equal to the value of imports of A from *all* countries.

MANY COMMODITIES AND MANY COUNTRIES

The general case of many countries and many commodities requires the application of mathematical tools that go beyond the scope of this book. Therefore, no attempt will be made here to discuss this generalization. The interested reader may consult Ronald W. Jones, *International Trade: Essays in Theory* (North-Holland Publishing Company, Amsterdam, 1979, chaps. 3 and 18).

APPENDIX 2
(CHAPTER 3)

SOME SPECIAL CASES OF SOCIAL INDIFFERENCE CURVES

Even though, in general, social indifference curves do not exist, there are some special cases in the literature where the use of social indifference curves can be justified. This appendix provides a brief review of these cases.

A ROBINSON CRUSOE ECONOMY

The simplest, and at the same time most trivial, case is a Robinson Crusoe economy, that is, an economy composed of a single individual. Here the problem of aggregation of indifference maps does not arise. There exists only one indifference map, which is also the social indifference map. This case cannot be taken seriously.

A TOTALITARIAN ECONOMY

In a totalitarian economy, or even when a planning bureau exists, the indifference map of the dictator, or of the planning bureau, becomes the social indifference map. Here, as in the preceding case, the problem of aggregation does not arise.

IDENTICAL TASTES AND FACTOR ENDOWMENTS

A more realistic case is that of a country inhabited by individuals having identical tastes and factor endowments. Thus, these individuals must be equally endowed capitalists (or landowners) and also equally productive workers. In the present case, the aggregate consumption of each commodity is always a multiple of the consumption of the **representative citizen.** Therefore, the social indifference map is a blown-up version of the representative citizen's indifference map. Alternatively, the indifference map of the representative citizen can be converted into a social indifference map by an appropriate change in the scales of the two axes: Merely multiply all quantities along each axis by the number of representative citizens.

Note that because of the assumed identity of tastes and factor endowments, when one individual becomes better off, all do; and social welfare clearly increases. Hence, a movement from a lower to a higher social indifference curve does imply, in the present case, an increase in social welfare.

The identity of tastes is not very unrealistic, particularly within a single nation and culture. However, the identity of factor endowments is most certainly violated in the real world.

IDENTICAL AND HOMOTHETIC TASTES

Another case is that of a country inhabited by individuals having identical indifference maps which are also *homothetic.* **Homothetic indifference maps** have the property that any straight line through the origin intersects all indifference curves at points of equal slope. What this really means is this: All consumers divide their respective incomes between food and clothing in the same way (say, 60 percent on food and 40 percent on clothing), no matter how high or how low an individual's income happens to be. Accordingly, any redistribution of income leaves the aggregate consumption of food and clothing unchanged, that is, the reduction in the amounts of food and clothing by those whose incomes are reduced is always matched exactly by the increase in the amounts of food and clothing by those whose incomes are increased. Hence, the aggregate amounts of food and clothing depend on relative prices only—*not* the distribution of income. In this case, the social indifference map coincides with the indifference map of any one of the many identical individuals.

Homotheticity of tastes runs against the famous **Engel's law.** As the reader will recall, Ernst Engel (not to be confused with Karl Marx's friend, Friedrich Engels) was a nineteenth century German statistician who asserted that if demographic factors are held constant, an increase in income will lower the proportion of income spent on food. This proposition, known as Engel's law, has been tested empirically and found valid. But if Engel's law is accepted, we must reject the homotheticity of tastes, which actually denies the law.

In the case of identical and homothetic tastes, no information is given on the distribution of income. Thus the present indifference map cannot be used to measure changes in welfare—a movement from a lower to a higher social indifference curve can very well be associated with a reduction in social welfare, provided, of course, that such a movement worsens the distribution of income sufficiently.

OPTIMIZING INCOME-REDISTRIBUTION POLICY

The final case is when a *specific social welfare function* is known and the government always redistributes income in such a way as to maximize social welfare. The **social welfare function** summarizes the ethical beliefs of some observer and shows systematically how one person's welfare is to be "added" to another's.

To understand how the maximization of a social welfare function can lead to the construction of a social indifference map, recall our earlier observation that a given combination of food and clothing would represent many levels of welfare because there are many possible ways to distribute income. What the present procedure suggests is to remove the indeterminacy by merely choosing that income distribution which *maximizes* the amount of social welfare for each combination of food and clothing. Once this is done, we can assign a unique level of welfare to each point in the commodity space. Then we can draw social indifference curves merely by connecting all points that represent the same amount of welfare.

APPENDIX 3
(CHAPTERS 3 AND 4)

THE NEOCLASSICAL THEORY OF PRODUCTION: REVIEW

This appendix provides a brief survey of the neoclassical theory of production, which is of vital importance to the theory of international trade.

THE PRODUCTION FUNCTION AND THE ISOQUANT MAP

A production function is a statement of the maximal physical quantity of output that can be produced with any specified physical quantities of factors of production, such as labor and capital. It is usually illustrated by means of **isoquants.** An isoquant, or **equal product curve,** is the locus of alternative combinations of labor and capital that yield the same amount of output. The general properties of isoquants are analogous to those of indifference curves.

Isoquants are negatively sloped (at least in the economically relevant middle region) because additional units of any factor produce additional positive amounts of output—no producer will ever employ a factor up to the point where its marginal product becomes negative, or even zero, since factors do cost something. Thus, if a firm reduces one input, it must simultaneously increase the second input in order to remain on the same isoquant. Because larger quantities of inputs produce more output, higher isoquants imply larger output than lower isoquants. Isoquants do not intersect, because an intersection would represent two different levels of maximal output—a logical contradiction. Finally, isoquants are convex to the origin.

THE MARGINAL RATE OF TECHNICAL SUBSTITUTION

The number of units of capital that can be replaced by one extra unit of labor, assuming that output remains at its initial rate, is called the **marginal rate of**

technical substitution of labor for capital ($MRTS_{LK}$) and is given graphically by the absolute slope of the isoquant. The convexity of isoquants implies that the marginal rate of technical substitution *diminishes* as one factor is substituted for another along an isoquant. This phenomenon, known as the **law of diminishing marginal rate of technical substitution,** means that as the substitution of one factor for the other proceeds, that substitution becomes progressively more difficult.

The marginal rate of technical substitution of labor for capital is equal to the ratio of the marginal physical product of labor (MPP_L) to the marginal physical product of capital (MPP_K). (The **marginal physical product** of a factor, say, labor, is the extra amount of output that can be secured by increasing labor by 1 unit while leaving all other factors unchanged.) For instance, if $MPP_L = 6$ and $MPP_K = 2$, an additional unit of labor can replace 3 units of capital; that is, $MRTS_{LK} = MPP_L \div MPP_K = 6 \div 2 = 3$.

RETURNS TO SCALE

The term **returns to scale** refers to the relationship between a change in the physical quantity of output and a proportionate change in the physical quantity of all inputs. **Constant returns to scale** prevail when the physical quantity of output changes by the same percentage as all inputs. When the physical quantity of output increases by a larger (smaller) percentage than all inputs, we have **increasing (decreasing) returns to scale.** Whether returns to scale are constant, increasing, or decreasing is an empirical question. Most, but not all, of the theory of international trade is based on the assumption that returns to scale are constant.

For a whole industry, as opposed to a firm, constant returns to scale is not an unrealistic assumption. The presumption is that a factory can be duplicated. Suppose that following an increase in demand, the food industry must increase its output by 10 percent. The assumption of constant returns to scale (at the industry level) means that the *number of active farmers will increase* by 10 percent, with each new farmer employing the same inputs and producing the same output as the old farmers. As the number of firms (and thus all inputs) increase by 10 percent, industry output also increases by 10 percent, as is required by constant returns to scale.

PROPERTIES OF CONSTANT RETURNS TO SCALE

When returns to scale are constant, the production function has the following properties:

1 *The average and the marginal physical products of each factor as well as the marginal rate of technical substitution depend only on the proportion in which labor and capital are used.* This property underscores the fact that the average and marginal products of, say, labor depend on how many units of labor and capital are employed by each firm, not the total quantities of factors employed by the entire industry.

2 *The whole isoquant map is a blown-up version of the unit isoquant.*

3 *The total output is exactly exhausted by the distributive shares of all factors when each factor is paid its marginal physical product.* This proposition is known as **Euler's theorem.** Sometimes it is also referred to as the **adding-up theorem,** or the **exhaustion-of-the-produce theorem.**

4 *When the isoquants are convex to the origin, the marginal physical products of labor and capital are diminishing* (that is, the **law of diminishing returns** holds).

THE ISOCOST MAP

An **isocost line** shows all combinations of labor and capital that a firm can purchase with a given total outlay at fixed factor prices—very much like the budget line of a consumer. For instance, suppose that the wage rate is $w = \$20$, the rental rate (that is, the price for 1 unit of capital) is $r = \$10$, and the total outlay of the firm is \$500. The firm can hire either $25L$ or $50K$ or any other factor combination satisfying the *linear* equation $20L + 10K = 500$, or $K = 50 - (20/10)L$. An isocost line is a straight line whose absolute slope (20/10 in our example) gives the constant wage-rent ratio. As the total outlay increases, the firm shifts to a parallel isocost line that lies farther from the origin.

FIGURE A3-1 **The isocost map, cost minimization, and the expansion path.** Costs are minimized at points of tangency between isocost lines and convex isoquants, as illustrated by points *E* and *F*. The locus of all such tangencies is the expansion path (see dashed line through *E* and *F*).

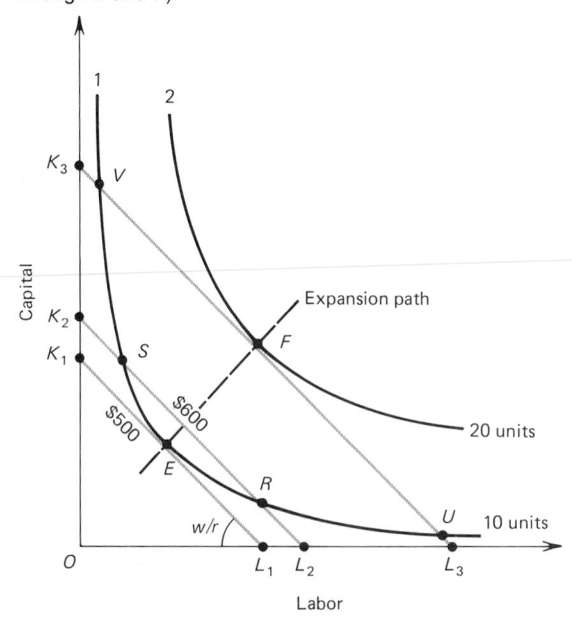

COST MINIMIZATION

To minimize the total cost of producing a specified amount of output (say, 10 units) a firm must choose that factor combination at which the relevant isoquant is tangent to the lowest possible isocost line, as shown by point E in Figure A3-1 for 10 units of output. Anywhere else, cost is higher. Thus the necessary condition for cost minimization is

$$MRTS_{LK} = \frac{MPP_L}{MPP_K} = \frac{w}{r} \tag{A3-1}$$

The locus of all cost-minimization points (such as E) is called the **expansion path.** This is illustrated in Figure A3-1 by the dashed line passing through points E and F. In the presence of constant returns to scale, the expansion path is necessarily a straight line through the origin.

APPENDIX **4**

(CHAPTERS 3 AND 4)

ALLOCATION OF FACTORS BETWEEN INDUSTRIES AND PRODUCTION POSSIBILITIES

THE EDGEWORTH-BOWLEY PRODUCTION BOX

Figure A4-1 presents an **Edgeworth-Bowley production box.** The dimensions of the production box represent the total amounts of homogeneous labor and homogeneous capital available to the economy. The isoquants of the clothing industry are drawn with respect to the origin O_c as illustrated by isoquants 1, 2, and 3, which represent 20, 35, and 40 units of clothing, respectively. The isoquants of the food industry are drawn (turned upside down) with respect to the origin O_f, as illustrated by isoquants 1′, 2′, and 3′, which represent 50, 75, and 100 units of food, respectively. Any arbitrary point in the box corresponds to a definite allocation of labor and capital between the two industries and gives rise to definite production levels of both commodities. For instance, at Z the economy produces $20C$ and $75F$.

Resources are allocated *efficiently* (or optimally) when it is not possible to increase the output of one commodity without reducing the output of the other. Efficient allocations are identified by *points of tangency* between the isoquants of the food and clothing industries. For instance, allocation G is efficient: Producing more than $20C$ (that is, moving to an isoquant such as 2) necessarily reduces the output of food (that is, puts the economy on a lower isoquant for food, such as 2′). Allocation Z, however, is inefficient—the economy can move to, say, G, where the output of clothing continues to be $20C$ but the output of food is larger ($100F$). The locus of all tangencies between the two sets of isoquants, as illustrated by curve O_cGHKO_f, is called the **contract curve.**

Perfect competition leads to the efficient allocation of resources. As explained in Appendix 3, each industry minimizes costs by employing factors in such proportions as to render the marginal rate of technical substitution of labor for cap-

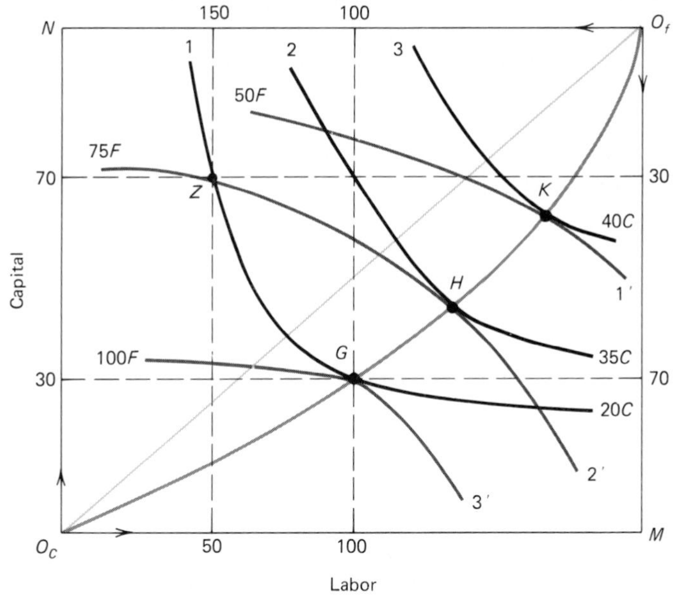

FIGURE A4-1 **The box diagram and the contract curve.** The locus of tangencies between the two sets of isoquants defines the **contract curve.** Resources are allocated optimally along the contract curve only. By moving from Z to some point on the contract curve between G and H, the economy can increase the output of both commodities.

ital equal to the wage-rent ratio. Since factors are homogeneous and factor prices are uniform throughout the economy, the marginal rates of technical substitution will be equalized across industries, that is, the economy will be operating on the contract curve.

THE PRODUCTION-POSSIBILITIES FRONTIER

When the economy allocates its resources along the contract curve, it is impossible to increase the output of one commodity without decreasing the output of the other commodity. Hence, each point on the contract curve corresponds to a point on the production-possibilities frontier, and vice versa. For instance, points K, H, and G on the production-possibilities frontier of Figure A4-2 correspond to the same-named points on the contract curve of Figure A4-1.

When the contract curve coincides with the diagonal of the production box, the production-possibilities frontier is necessarily a straight line. This should not come as a surprise. Along the diagonal, the two factors are used in the same fixed pro portion (say, 2 units of labor per unit of capital) in both industries. Technically, the mixture of 2 units of labor and 1 unit of capital may be viewed as a unit of a composite factor of production, very much like a tablet of a medicine that is composed of a precise combination of chemical elements. The existence of a single factor combined with constant returns to scale generates a linear production frontier exhibiting constant opportunity costs, as in the classical theory.

Normally the contract curve will lie on one side of the diagonal, as shown in Figure A4-1. When this happens, the production-possibilities frontier becomes concave to the origin, exhibiting increasing opportunity costs, as in Figure A4-2. Why should this be so? First, note that the economy can always reach dashed straight line *UV* by allocating its resources *arbitrarily* along the diagonal of the production box. Thus, the production frontier cannot be totally convex to the origin. Second, we can also rule out any convex regions (such as dashed curve *KG*) of the production frontier. Points *K* and *G* correspond to two *different* production techniques. By allocating resources *arbitrarily* to these two techniques, we can always reach points along straight-line segment *KMG*. For instance, when *half* of all resources are allocated to technique K, the outputs of food and clothing will be half of what the economy produces with *all* resources at *K*, as shown by *Q*. When the other *half* of all resources are allocated to technique G, the economy will produce half the outputs at *G*, as shown by *R*. Vector addition of points *Q* and *R* generates point *M*, which lies on straight-line segment *KG*, *halfway* between *K* and *G*.

FIGURE A4-2 The production-possibilities frontier derived from the box diagram. Points *G*, *H*, and *K* on the production-possibilities frontier correspond to the same-named points on the contract curve of Figure A4-1. Points *K* and *G* correspond to two different techniques. By allocating resources arbitrarily to these two techniques, we can always reach points along straight line *KMG*. For instance, when half of all resources are allocated to *K* and the other half to *G*, technique *K* yields combination *Q*; and technique *G*, combination *R*. Addition of *Q* and *R* (by means of the parallelogram rule) yields point *M*.

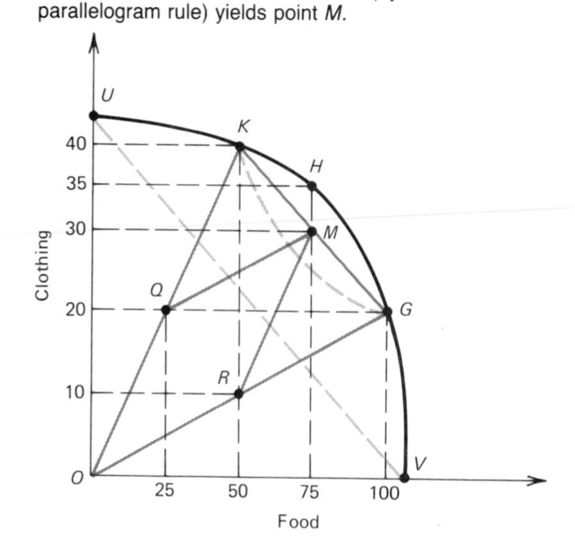

APPENDIX 5
(CHAPTER 3)

MEADE'S GEOMETRIC TECHNIQUE

In the early 1930s, Leontief (1933) and Lerner (1934) provided a geometric technique for obtaining a country's offer curve from its social indifference curves and production-possibilities frontier. Two decades later the Leontief-Lerner technique was finally perfected by James E. Meade in his *Geometry of International Trade* (1952). Meade's ingenious geometric technique is the subject of this appendix.

TRADE INDIFFERENCE CURVES

The crucial first step in Meade's approach is the derivation of the **trade indifference map,** as shown in Figure A5-1. Following Meade's notation, measure A-exportables along the horizontal axis, and B-exportables along the vertical axis. Meade's terms, A-exportables and B-exportables, correspond to the "food" and "clothing" that we have been using so far. Note that for reasons that will become evident as we proceed, the horizontal axis measures positive quantities from right to left—not from left to right. Accordingly, the economy's (America's) production-possibilities frontier is drawn in the second (upper-left) quadrant, as shown by *MPN.* The social indifference map is similarly drawn in the second quadrant, as shown by the curves I_1, I_2, and I_3. Before trade, America produces and consumes at point *P,* enjoying the level of social welfare implied by social indifference curve I_1.

Now think of production set *OMPN* as a block that can be moved anywhere on the diagram. Slide block *OMPN* along social indifference curve I_1 so that curve *MPN* remains tangent to I_1 at all times and line *MO* remains in a horizontal position. During this process, the origin of the block (that is, point *O*) traces

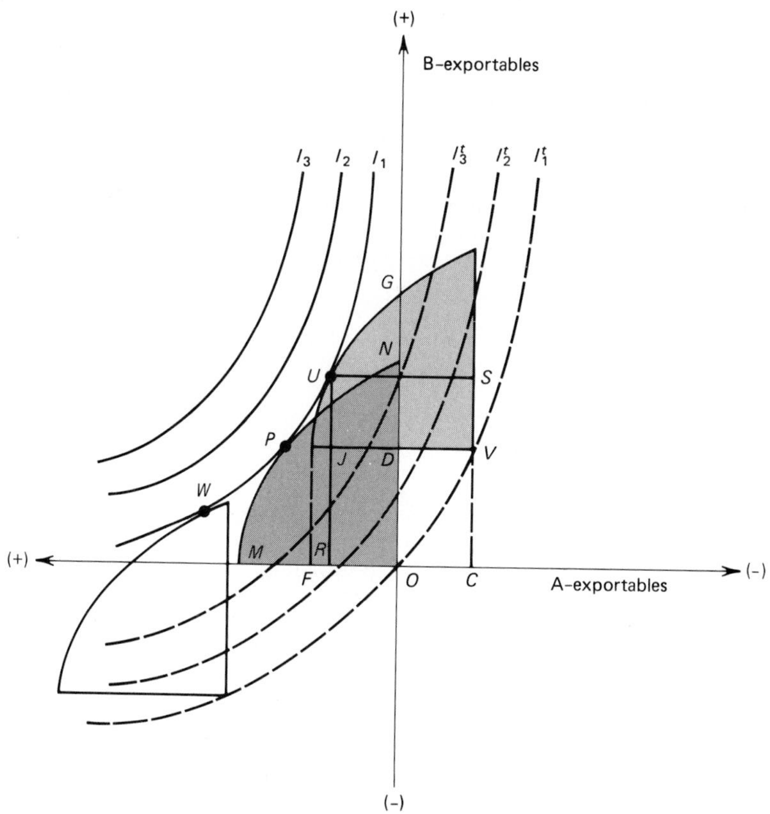

FIGURE A5-1 **Trade indifference curves.** Trade indifference curves are derived from the social indifference map and the production-possibilities frontier.

out dashed curve I_1^t, which is known as a **trade indifference curve.** What is the significance of trade indifference curve I_1^t? It merely gives all the alternative export-import combinations that enable America to reach social indifference curve I_1. For instance, consider point *V*, at which America exports $OC(=DV)$ units of A-exportables in exchange for $OD(=CV)$ units of imports of B-exportables. To verify that this export-import combination enables America to reach social indifference curve I_1 (and not a higher one), first let America make the exchange of *OC* units of A-exportables for *OD* units of B-exportables. After this exchange, America can consume only along curve *FHUG*, where straight line *FH* is perpendicular. Accordingly, America will consume at *U*, where the production block is tangent to I_1. In particular, America will produce *JV* units of A-exportables, out of which it will export *DV* units and consume only *JD*. Similarly, America will produce $VS(=JU)$ units of B-exportables, which along with the imports of $CV(=RJ)$ units make up the total consumption *RU* of B-exportables. Similar reasoning applies to all other points lying on I_1^t.

In general, a trade indifference curve can be derived for each social indifference curve (or consumption indifference curve, as Meade calls it). Thus, as we slide production block *OMPN* along social indifference curve I_2, the origin of the block traces a new trade indifference curve, as illustrated by I_2^t. Observe that I_2^t lies consistently above and to the left of I_1^t, since I_2 lies consistently above and to the left of I_1. In general, one trade indifference curve corresponds to one social indifference curve; and the higher the social indifference curve, the higher the corresponding trade indifference curve.

Under increasing opportunity costs, the trade indifference curves have the same convexity as the social indifference curves. In addition, the slope of a trade indifference curve at any point is equal to the slope of the corresponding social indifference curve and the slope of the production-possibilities frontier at the corresponding point. For instance, the slope of I_1^t at V is equal to the common slope of I_1 and the production block at U.

THE OFFER CURVE

With the trade indifference map at hand, we proceed now with the derivation of the offer curve, which is the locus of tangencies between terms-of-trade lines and trade indifference curves, as shown in Figure A5-2.

Terms-of-trade line TOT_1, which is tangent to trade indifference curve I_1^t at

FIGURE A5-2 The offer curve. America's offer curve is derived from the trade indifference map.

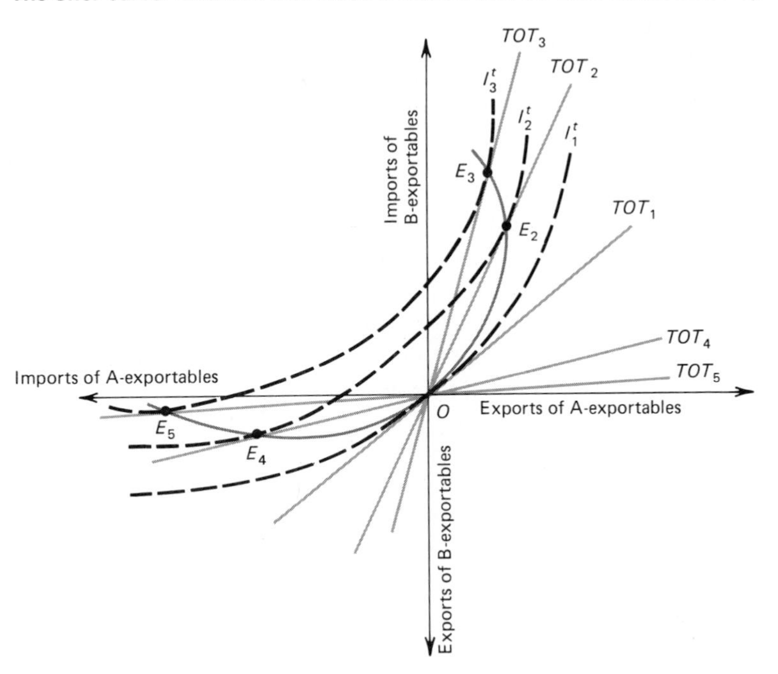

the origin, corresponds to America's pretrade equilibrium price ratio. Imagine that A-exportables become progressively more expensive in the international market, causing the terms-of-trade line to become steeper and steeper, as illustrated by terms-of-trade lines TOT_2 and TOT_3. Trace out the tangencies between the various terms-of-trade lines and the trade indifference curves. The locus of all these tangencies, as illustrated by curve $OE_2 E_3$, is the first part of America's offer curve.

Alternatively, we could allow terms-of-trade line TOT_1 to rotate clockwise (as A-exportables become cheaper and cheaper in the international market) and trace out the remaining part of the offer curve in the third quadrant, as illustrated by curve $OE_4 E_5$. Thus, America's full offer curve is given by solid curve $E_5 E_4 O E_2 E_3$.

It must be clear from the construction of Figure A5-2 that the offer curve has two important properties: (1) It passes through the origin and lies totally above and to the left of terms-of-trade line TOT_1 (whose slope gives the pretrade price ratio); and (2) terms-of-trade line TOT_1 is tangent to the offer curve at the origin, that is, the slope of the offer curve at the origin shows the pretrade price ratio.

INTERNATIONAL EQUILIBRIUM

The same procedure can be repeated to derive the offer curve of a second country, say, Britain. International equilibrium can then be shown in terms of the two offer curves by superimposing one diagram on the other, after Britain's diagram has been rotated by 180° to match the axes of America's diagram, as illustrated in Figure A5-3.

International equilibrium occurs at point E, in the first quadrant, where the two offer curves intersect each other. America exports OR units of A-exportables to Britain, and Britain exports OS units of B-exportables to America. The equilibrium terms of trade are given by the slope of terms-of-trade line TOT, which is equal to the ratio OS/OR. Note that line TOT lies between lines OA and OB, which give, respectively, America's and Britain's autarkic prices. Further, America consumes at C_A, in the second quadrant (that is, at OV units of A-exportables and VC_A units of B-exportables). Similarly, Britain consumes at C_B in the fourth quadrant (that is, at OD units of B-exportables and DC_B units of A-exportables). Finally, America produces EU units of A-exportables and UC_A units of B-exportables, while Britain produces EZ units of B-exportables and ZC_B units of A-exportables. Thus, the total production of A-exportables by both countries is given by $EU + ZC_B = GZ + ZC_B = GC_B$, and the total production of B-exportables is given by $EZ + UC_A = GU + UC_A = GC_A$.

The sides of rectangle $GC_B HC_A$ show the world production of A-exportables and B-exportables. But the sides of the same rectangle also show the world consumption of A-exportables and B-exportables, because $SU + DC_B = GD + DC_B = GC_B$ and $VC_A + RZ = VC_A + GV = GC_A$. In other words, rectangle $GC_B HC_A$ can be thought of as a *production box*. The coordinates of point E with respect to corner C_A show America's production (or endowments) of A-

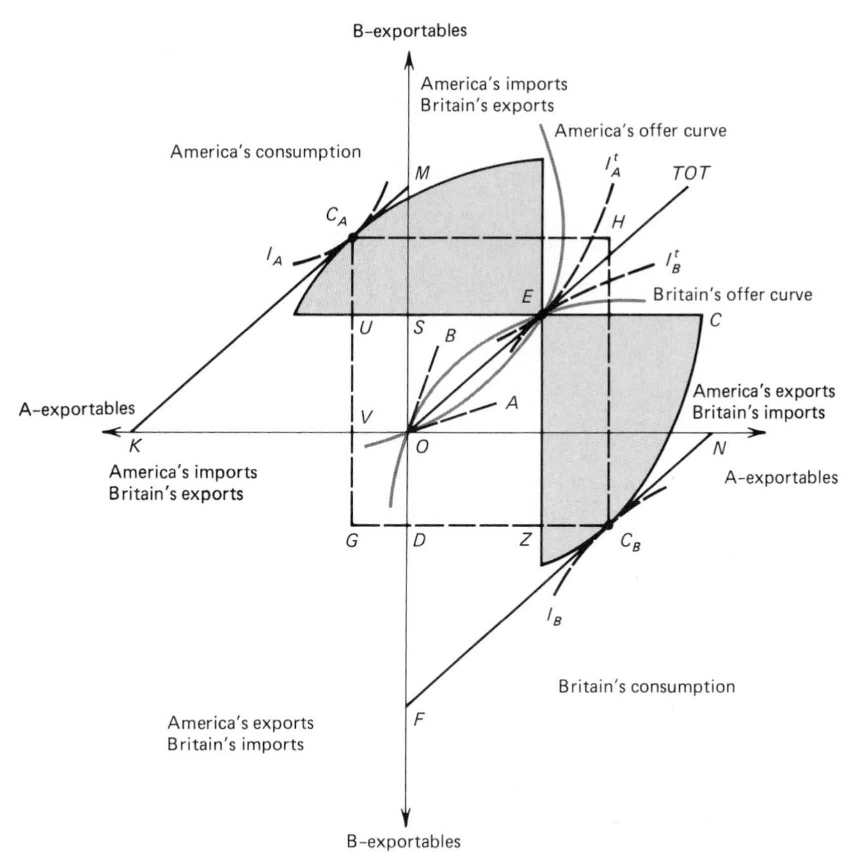

FIGURE A5-3 Meade's demonstration of international equilibrium. Production, consumption, and trade are brought together.

exportables and B-exportables, while the coordinates of E with respect to C_B show Britain's production of A-exportables and B-exportables. Similarly, the coordinates of point O with respect to C_A (C_B) show America's (Britain's) consumption of A-exportables and B-exportables, and the coordinates of O with respect to E show America's exports of A-exportables and imports of B-exportables.

Note that terms-of-trade line TOT is tangent to both America's and Britain's trade indifference curves at E. Further, America's consumption-possibilities frontier KC_AM is tangent to America's social indifference curve at C_A, and Britain's consumption-possibilities frontier NC_BF is tangent to Britain's social indifference curve at C_B. Therefore, all equilibrium conditions are indeed satisfied.

Figure A5-3 brings together production, consumption, and trade in an ingenious way and illuminates a multitude of relationships. This diagram, which we owe to Meade, is the culmination of the neoclassical model.

APPENDIX 6
(CHAPTER 3)

PRODUCTION, INCOME, AND SUBSTITUTION EFFECTS

Typically, a reduction in the relative price of the imported commodity causes the desired quantity of imports to increase. This important proposition involves more than the ordinary **law of demand**—the offer curve combines elements of both demand and supply.

By definition, the imports of, say, food are given by the difference between the domestic consumption and production of food. In general, as food becomes cheaper, three effects can be recognized, as follows:

1 The **production effect** (or **output effect**). As food becomes cheaper, the domestic production of food falls (because of increasing opportunity costs), causing the demand for imports to increase.

2 The **income effect.** As food becomes cheaper, the economy's real income (or welfare) increases for two reasons: (a) The terms of trade improve (that is, more imports of food can be obtained per unit of exports of, say, clothing), and (b) domestic production is readjusted to maximize income—resources are transferred from the food industry to the clothing industry. Unless food is an inferior commodity, the increase in real income causes the domestic consumption of food to increase; and this, in turn, causes the demand for imports to increase *pari passu.* (An **inferior good** is a good whose demand falls as income increases. A **superior,** or **normal,** good is a good whose demand increases as income increases. Finally, a **neutral good** is a good whose demand is not influenced by any income change.)

3 The **substitution effect.** As food becomes cheaper, consumers substitute food for clothing until the marginal rate of substitution of food for clothing is reduced to the lower level of the relative price of food. Thus, the consumption of food increases, causing the demand for imports to increase.

These three effects of a terms-of-trade improvement are illustrated in Figure A6-1. At the initial terms of trade given by line *ST*, the economy produces at P_0 and consumes at C_0, importing *EF* units of food. Suppose now that food becomes cheaper, as shown by line *MN*. The economy's production and consumption points move to P_1 and C_1, respectively, and the imports of food increase to *DK*. What is the increase in imports composed of?

First, the domestic production of food falls by *DE*, as the production point shifts from P_0 to P_1. Hence, the imports of food must increase by *DE* to fill up the gap left by the reduction in the domestic production. The amount *DE* illustrates the production (or output) effect of the terms-of-trade improvement.

Second, the terms-of-trade improvement involves not only a cheapening of food but also an increase in the economy's real income, as revealed by the shift from social indifference curve 1 to social indifference curve 2. One way to isolate the increase in real income embedded in the terms-of-trade improvement is to argue as follows. The economy could move to social indifference curve 2 not by a terms-of-trade improvement but rather by means of an **equivalent in-**

FIGURE A6-1 **Substitution, income, and production effects.** At the initial terms of trade given by line *ST*, the economy produces at P_0 and consumes at C_0, importing *EF* units of food. As food becomes cheaper (see line *MN*), the economy shifts its production and consumption to points P_1 and C_1, respectively. The total increase in imports is composed of (a) a production effect, *DE*; (b) an income effect, *FJ*; and (c) a substitution effect, *JK*.

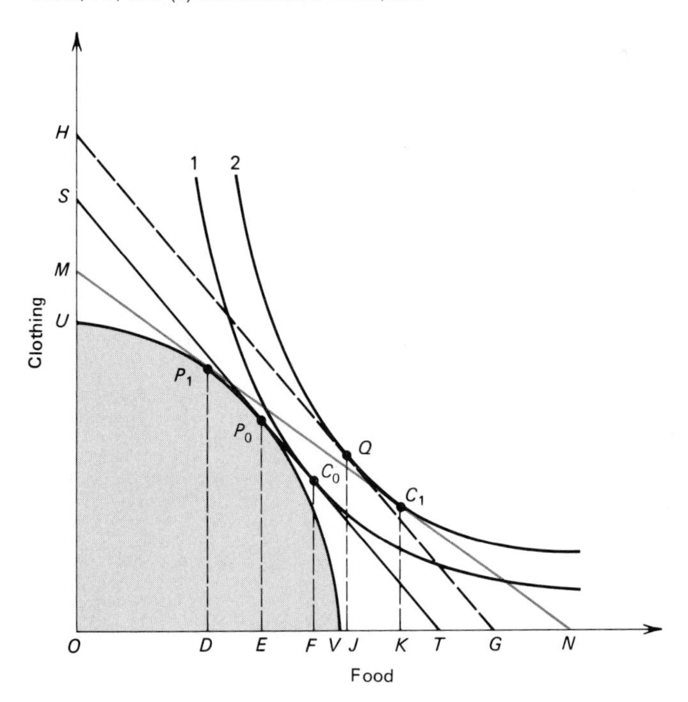

crease in income, as shown by dashed line *HG*, which is parallel to *ST* and tangent to social indifference curve 2 at *Q*. Now if this *equivalent* increase in income had taken place instead, the economy's consumption point would have shifted from C_0 to Q, and both the domestic consumption of food and imports of food would increase by *FJ*. The amount *FJ* is the income effect of the terms-of-trade improvement.

Finally, the economy's consumption point cannot remain at the auxiliary position *Q*; it must shift to C_1, where the marginal rate of substitution of food for clothing is reduced to the new, lower relative price of food. Thus, both the domestic consumption of food and the demand for imports of food increase by additional amount *JK*. Since the movement along indifference curve 2 from *Q* to C_1 involves merely a substitution of food for clothing, the quantity *JK* illustrates the substitution effect.

In summary, then, the reduction in the relative price of food from *ST* to *MN* causes imports to increase by: (a) a production effect (*DE*), (b) an income effect (*FJ*), and (c) a substitution effect (*JK*).

Both the production effect and the substitution effect always cause the demand for imports to increase as imports become cheaper. There is a limit, though, to the production effect: After the country becomes completely specialized, the production effect drops to zero.

It is well known from microeconomics that the income effect is not so reliable as the production and substitution effects. When the imported commodity is inferior, the increase in income will cause both the domestic consumption of food and imports of food to fall. However, such a perverse income effect cannot be expected to occur for the whole class of imported commodities. Even if it did, it could not be very strong; anyway, it cannot outweigh the favorable production and substitution effects. Therefore, we can safely conclude that, in general, a terms-of-trade improvement increases the demand for imports.

APPENDIX **7**

(CHAPTER 5)

FACTOR-INTENSITY REVERSALS

This appendix deals briefly with the theoretical implications of the phenomenon of factor-intensity reversals.

FACTOR-INTENSITY REVERSALS IN TERMS OF ISOQUANTS

The phenomenon of factor-intensity reversals is illustrated in Figure A7-1. At the wage-rent ratio indicated by the absolute slope of *DE*, steel's expansion path is given by dashed line *OE*, and cloth's by *OD*. Since *OE* is flatter than *OD*, steel is labor intensive relative to cloth. However, at wage-rent ratio *GH*, steel's expansion path (*OG*) is steeper than cloth's *OH*, and therefore steel is capital intensive relative to cloth. Because of the assumed smooth substitutability between labor and capital, at the intermediate wage-rent ratio shown by the slopes at *M* and *N*, steel and cloth display the same factor intensity.

FACTOR PRICES AND COMMODITY PRICES

The immediate implication of factor-intensity reversals is the breakdown of the one-to-one correspondence between factor prices and commodity prices. This is shown in Figure A7-2, which is based on Figure A7-1.

Wage-rent ratio *OM* in Figure A7-2 corresponds to the common slope at *M* and *N* in Figure A7-1. For wage-rent ratios higher than *OM* (such as *DE* in Figure A7-1), steel is *labor intensive* relative to cloth. As the wage-rent ratio falls, steel becomes relatively cheaper in accordance with the basic proposition we studied in Section 4-8. This accounts for the positive slope of curve *PW* in Figure A7-2 for all wage-rent ratios higher than *OM*.

For wage-rent ratios lower then *OM* (such as *GH* in Figure A7-1), steel becomes *capital intensive* relative to cloth. Now as labor becomes cheaper, steel becomes relatively more expensive. Thus, curve *PW* has a negative slope in this region.

Given curve *PW* of Figure A7-2, it is no longer possible to associate only one wage-rent ratio with each commodity price ratio. Thus, steel's relative price *OC* is consistent with two wage-rent ratios, *CA* and *CB*. This is the fundamental reason we can no longer be sure that commodity price equalization (brought about by means of free commodity trade) necessarily leads to factor-price equalization. At common commodity price ratio *OC*, it is now *possible* for America's wage-rent ratio to be given by *CA*, and Britain's by *CB*, *even though* neither country specializes completely.

In addition, the validity of the Heckscher-Ohlin theorem is uncertain. When America's post-trade equilibrium wage-rent ratio is given by *CA*, and Britain's by CB, steel is labor intensive in America but capital intensive in Britain. With such a contradictory factor-intensity ranking of commodities, one country must always exhibit a "Leontief paradox." For instance, if America is capital abundant relative to Britain, the country that exports steel must exhibit a Leontief paradox.

FIGURE A7-1 **Factor-intensity reversals.** At the wage-rent ratio, indicated by the absolute value of the slope of *DE*, steel's expansion path is given by dashed line *OE* and cloth's by *OD*. Hence, at *DE*, steel is labor intensive relative to cloth. However, at wage-rent ratio *GH*, steel is capital intensive relative to cloth.

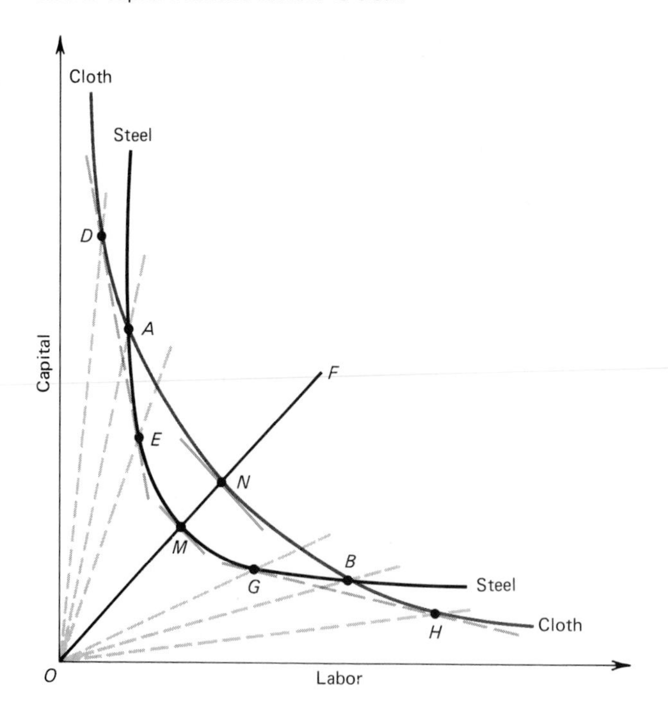

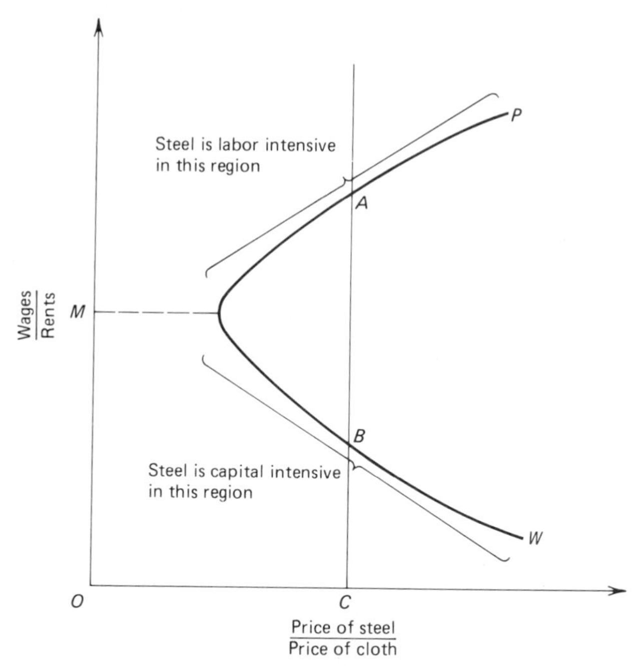

FIGURE A7-2 Factor prices and commodity prices in the presence of factor-intensity reversals. Factor-intensity reversals destroy the one-to-one correspondence between factor prices and commodity prices. At wage-rent ratios *higher* than *OM*, steel is labor intensive relative to cloth, and the relative price of steel *falls* as the wage-rent ratio falls. Curve *PW* slopes *upward* in this area. At wage-rent ratios *lower* than *OM*, steel is capital intensive relative to cloth, and curve *PW* slopes *downward*. The same relative price of steel, say, *OC*, corresponds now to two different wage-rent ratios, *CA* and *CB*.

BOX DIAGRAMS AND FACTOR-INTENSITY REVERSALS

Consider Figure A7-3, which is constructed on the basis of the information given earlier in Figure A7-1. In particular, Figure A7-3 is a combination of three box diagrams: America's *ORA'Q*, Britain's *OKB'M*, and the auxiliary box diagram *ORNM*. The diagonals of these three diagrams—that is, *OA'*, *OB'*, and *ON'*—correspond to the vectors *OA*, *OB*, and *ON*, respectively, in Figure A7-1. Also, cloth's unit isoquant as well as points *A*, *B*, and *N* in Figure A7-3 are exactly the same as those in Figure A7-1.

When the overall capital-labor ratio is given by *ON* (as shown by box diagram *ORNM*), the marginal rates of technical substitution of labor for capital of the steel and cloth industries are necessarily equal along diagonal *ON*—the unit isoquants are by assumption tangent to each other at *N*. Hence, the contract curve must coincide with diagonal *ON* in this case.

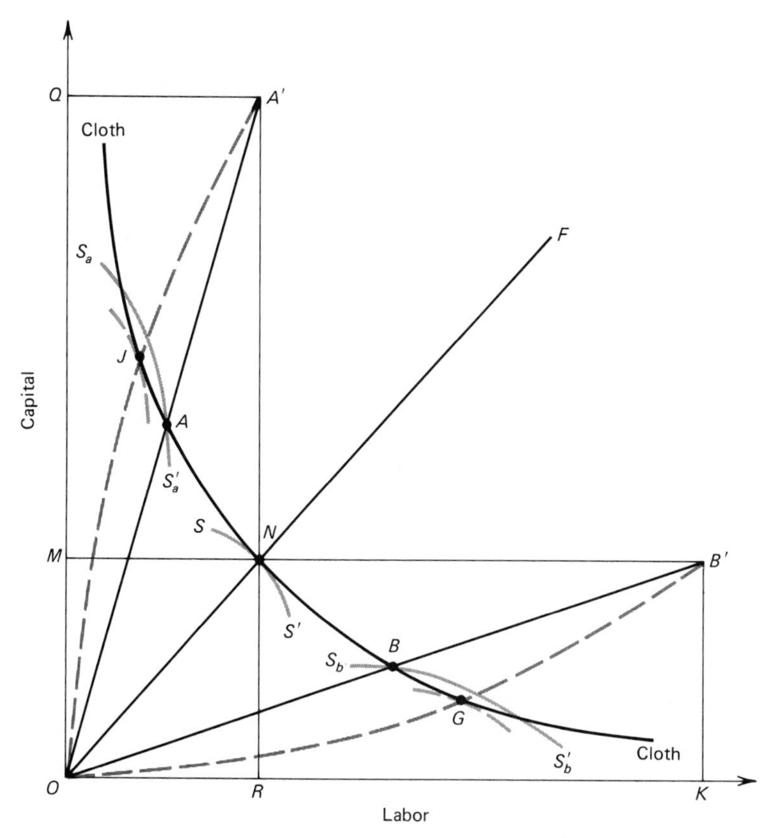

FIGURE A7-3 Factor-intensity reversals and the Leontief paradox. America's box diagram is given by *ORA'Q* and Britain's by *OKB'M*. Cloth's isoquant as well as points *A*, *B*, and *N* are the same as those of Figure A7-1. The overall capital-labor ratios of America (*OA'*) and Britain (*OB'*) are separated by a factor-intensity reversal (ray *OF*). As a result, steel is labor intensive in America but capital intensive in Britain; and one of the two countries *must* exhibit a Leontief paradox. Also, the wage-rent ratios along America's contract curve (*OJA'*) are all higher than all wage-rent ratios along Britain's contract curve (*OGB'*). Hence, no factor-price equalization is possible.

However, when the overall capital-labor ratio is given by *OA'* (that is, America's factor proportions), the contract curve must lie *above* the diagonal, as shown by America's box diagram *ORA'Q*. Nevertheless, when the overall capital-labor ratio is given by *OB'* (that is, Britain's factor proportions), the contract curve must lie *below* the diagonal, as shown by Britain's box diagram *OKB'M*. All this can be easily verified by inspecting Figure A7-3 carefully after recalling an important conclusion reached in Appendix 4, namely, that *the contract curve never crosses the diagonal.*

Under the circumstances of Figure A7-3 steel is labor intensive in America, but capital intensive in Britain, relative to cloth. This conclusion illustrates a general proposition: When the overall capital-labor ratios of America and Britain are separated by vector *OF* (along which the factor-intensity reversal occurs), then the factor-intensity rankings of steel and cloth are contradictory between countries. As a result one of the two countries must exhibit a Leontief paradox, causing the Heckscher-Ohlin theorem to break down.

Finally, note that factor prices cannot be equalized between America and Britain. Thus, the wage-rent ratios along America's contract curve *OJA′* are all higher than the wage-rent ratios along Britain's contract curve *OGB′*. This becomes obvious when we notice that in Figure A7-3 the isoquants of the cloth industry are common to both America's and Britain's box diagrams. Therefore, America and Britain must always operate along different expansion paths of the cloth industry. From this observation we infer that the marginal rate of technical substitution of labor for capital, and thus the wage-rent ratio, must always be different between the two countries. In fact, the reader should verify from Figure A7-3 that the wage-rent ratio must be higher in America than Britain, both before and after trade.

We conclude that when a factor-intensity reversal separates the overall capital-labor ratios of the two countries, neither the Heckscher-Ohlin theorem nor the factor-price equalization theorem is valid. Nevertheless, when the capital-labor ratios of America and Britain are *not* separated by a factor-intensity reversal (that is, when the factor proportions of both countries lie either below or above vector *OF*), the factor-intensity reversal is totally harmless.

APPENDIX 8
(CHAPTER 7)

METZLER'S PARADOX

A tariff typically protects the import-competing industry. **Metzler's paradox** occurs when the price of the imported commodity falls by more than the tariff in the world market, with the result that the imported commodity becomes cheaper in the tariff-levying country also. In this paradoxical case, the tariff provides *negative* protection to the import-competing industry.

Metzler's paradox is illustrated in Figure A8-1. The home country (America) disturbs the free-trade equilibrium at E by imposing a 50 percent tariff on imports of cloth. America's offer curve is displaced toward the origin, as shown by the dashed tariff-distorted offer curve. Consider first the limiting case in which the relative price of steel rises to $p = 3$ in the world market, as indicated by terms-of-trade line TOT_1. In this case, America's relative price of steel remains at its pretariff level of 2, as depicted by terms-of-trade line TOT_0. Thus

$$
\begin{aligned}
\text{America's price of cloth} &= \text{world price of cloth} + \text{tariff} \\
&= p_c + 0.50 \times p_c \\
&= 1.50p_c
\end{aligned}
$$

$$
\begin{aligned}
\text{America's relative price of steel} &= p_s \div 1.50p_c \\
&= 3 \div 1.50 \\
&= 2
\end{aligned}
$$

where p_s and p_c are the world money prices of steel and cloth, and $p_s \div p_c = 3$ by assumption. Metzler's paradox occurs when the world relative price of steel (p_s/p_c) rises above 3. For instance, suppose it rises to 4.5, as implied by vector OR (not drawn). Then America's relative price of steel would be 3 (that is, $4.5 \div 1.50$), as shown by vector TOT_1. Under what circumstances is this result

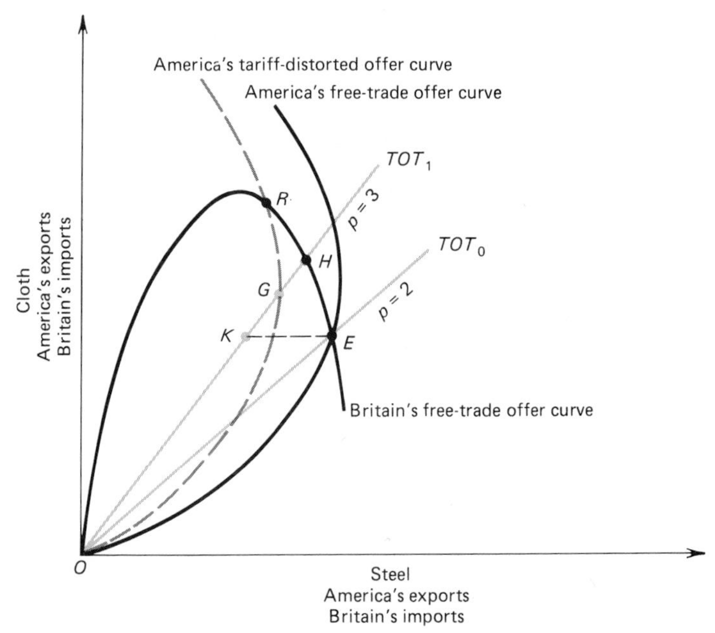

FIGURE A8-1 **Metzler's paradox.** America disturbs the initial equilibrium at E by imposing a 50 percent tariff on the import of cloth, displacing the nation's offer curve as illustrated by the dashed, tariff-distorted offer curve. When the relative price of steel is 3 in the world markets (as shown by TOT_1) and 2 in America (as shown by TOT_0), there emerges a shortage of steel and a surplus of cloth (compare points G and H) causing the relative price of steel to rise further in both Britain and America. Cloth is cheaper in both countries at the post-tariff equilibrium point (R) relative to the free-trade equilibrium point (E).

possible? Metzler's paradox occurs only if at $p = 3$, Britain's offer (H) is larger than America's (G), as illustrated. At $p = 3$ there is a shortage of steel and a surplus of cloth (compare points G and H); thus the world relative price of steel rises above 3, as shown by post-tariff equilibrium point R. Note that H can lie beyond G along TOT_1 (as required by Metzler's paradox) if, and only if, Britain's offer curve is very inelastic in the neighborhood of free-trade equilibrium point E.

The closer G lies to the origin, the greater becomes the likelihood of Metzler's paradox (assuming that Britain's offer curve is inelastic at E). What determines the location of G? Suppose again that the relative price of steel is 3 in world markets and 2 in America. If we ignored the tariff revenue, America's offer would coincide with E. As the tariff revenue is redistributed to the private sector and then spent on steel and cloth, America's offer would shift to G—the exports of steel and the imports of cloth must be adjusted by the additional purchases made possible by the tariff revenue. Thus the location of G depends on how the tariff revenue is spent on steel and cloth. The most favorable case for Metzler's paradox occurs when the marginal propensity to import cloth is zero and the entire tariff revenue is spent on steel, shifting America's offer to K.

In summary, the location of America's offer (G) depends on America's marginal propensity to import (MPM_a), and the location of Britain's offer (H) depends on Britain's import-demand elasticity (e_b). The precise mathematical condition for the occurrence of Metzler's paradox is $MPM_a + |e_b| < 1$. For further details, see Chacholiades, *International Trade Theory and Policy* (McGraw-Hill Book Company, New York, 1978, chap. 18).

APPENDIX 9

(CHAPTER 7)

THE THEORY OF EFFECTIVE PROTECTION

With very little effort and a little high school algebra, we can formalize the theory of effective protection. By so doing, we shall be able easily to derive some important conclusions.

The effective rate of protection gives the percentage increase in domestic value added over the free-trade level, an increase made possible by the country's tariff structure. The effective rate of protection (*ERP*) depends on three parameters:

1 the nominal tariff rate on the final product (t)

2 the nominal tariff rate on imported inputs (t_m)

3 the share of the imported inputs in the total value of the final product in the absence of tariffs (α)

Suppose that the fixed world price of a final imported commodity (for example, shoes) is p. The domestic production of shoes requires a fixed amount of an imported intermediate product (for example, leather) whose price on world markets is also fixed. In the absence of tariffs, the value of imported leather that goes into the domestic production of one pair of shoes is αp. Accordingly, under free-trade conditions the value added in the shoe industry is

$$v = p - \alpha p = p(1 - \alpha) \qquad \text{(A9-1)}$$

Suppose now that the country taxes the imports of both shoes and leather. The domestic price of shoes rises to $(1 + t)p$, and the cost of imported leather per pair of shoes rises to $(1 + t_m)\alpha p$. Accordingly, the value added in the domestic shoe industry changes to

$$v' = (1 + t)p - (1 + t_m)\alpha p \tag{A9-2}$$

By definition, the effective rate of protection (*ERP*) is

$$ERP = \frac{v' - v}{v} \tag{A9-3}$$

Substituting Equations (A9-1) and (A9-2) into Equation (A9-3) and simplifying, we obtain

$$\begin{aligned} ERP = \frac{v' - v}{v} &= \frac{(1 + t)p - (1 + t_m)\alpha p - p(1 - \alpha)}{p(1 - \alpha)} \\ &= \frac{(1 + t) - (1 + t_m)\alpha - (1 - \alpha)}{1 - \alpha} \\ &= \frac{1 + t - \alpha - \alpha t_m - 1 + \alpha}{1 - \alpha} \\ &= \frac{t - \alpha t_m}{1 - \alpha} \end{aligned} \tag{A9-4}$$

In the first numerical example in Section 7-8, we had $t = .25$, $t_m = 0$, and $\alpha = .75$. The effective tariff rate was 100 percent, which is consistent with Equation (A9-4): $ERP = (.25 - 0)/(1 - .75) = 1$. Similarly, in the second numerical example, we had $t = .25$, $t_m = .1$, and $\alpha = .75$. The effective tariff rate was 70 percent, which is again consistent with the equation

$$ERP = \frac{.25 - (.75 \times .1)}{1 - .75} = \frac{.175}{.25} = .7$$

We can now use Equation (A9-4) to establish some important propositions concerning the theory of effective protection, as follows:

1 When the nominal tariff rates on the final product and the imported inputs are equal (that is, when $t = t_m$), the effective tariff rate becomes equal to the nominal rate. Thus, when $t = t_m$, Equation (A9-4) becomes

$$ERP = \frac{t - \alpha t}{1 - \alpha} = \frac{t(1 - \alpha)}{1 - \alpha} = t$$

2 When the nominal tariff rates on the final product and the imported inputs are not equal (that is, $t \neq t_m$), then we distinguish between two cases, as follows:

In the first case, **the effective tariff rate is higher than the nominal tariff rate on the final product (that is, $ERP > t$) when the nominal tariff rate on the final product exceeds the rate levied on the imported inputs (that is, when $t > t_m$).**

In the second case, **the effective tariff rate is lower than the nominal tariff rate on the final product (that is, $ERP < t$) when the nominal tariff rate on the imported inputs exceeds the nominal rate levied on the final product (that is, when $t_m > t$).**

This proposition is easily proved. Rewrite Equation (A9-4) as follows:

$$ERP = \frac{t - \alpha t_m}{1 - \alpha} = \frac{t - \alpha t + \alpha t - \alpha t_m}{1 - \alpha} = t + \frac{\alpha}{1 - \alpha}(t - t_m) \qquad \text{(A9-5)}$$

Since $0 < \alpha < 1$, it follows that $\alpha/(1 - \alpha) > 0$.

Accordingly, when $t > t_m$, the term $[\alpha/(1 - \alpha)]\ (t - t_m)$ is positive, causing the effective rate (ERP) to be larger than the nominal rate (t). For instance, return for a moment to the second numerical illustration, in which $t = .25 > .10 = t_m$, and $\alpha = .75$. In this case, the effective rate is necessarily higher than the nominal rate:

$$ERP = .25 + \frac{.75}{1 - .75}(.25 - .10) = .25 + 3(.15) = .70 > .25 = t$$

However, when $t < t_m$, the term $[\alpha/(1 - \alpha)](t - t_m)$ is negative, causing the effective rate (ERP) to be lower than the nominal rate (t). For instance, assume that $t = .25 < .30 = t_m$, and $\alpha = .75$. Now the effective rate is necessarily lower than the nominal rate:

$$ERP = .25 + \frac{.75}{1 - .75}(.25 - .30) = .25 + 3(-.05) = .10 < .25 = t$$

3 *The effective tariff rate may even become negative!* This occurs when $\alpha t_m > t$, as can be easily seen from Equation (A9-4). In other words, **negative effective protection occurs when the nominal tariff rate on the final product is lower than the nominal tariff rate on key imported inputs weighted by the share of imported inputs in the total value of the final product.** For instance, assume again that $t = .25$ and $\alpha = .75$, but let $t_m = .50$ so that $\alpha t_m = (.75)(.50) = .375 > .25 = t$. A simple application of Equation (A9-4) gives:

$$ERP = \frac{.25 - (.75 \times .50)}{1 - .75} = \frac{-.125}{.25} = -.5$$

Thus, even though the nominal tariff rate is 25 percent, in the final analysis the industry is provided with a *negative* effective rate of protection of 50 percent, that is, the industry's "value added" is cut in half. Many instances of negative effective protection have been observed in developing countries, such as Brazil, Colombia, Chile, Nigeria, Pakistan, and the Philippines.

4 The effective tariff rate increases either when the nominal tariff rate on the final product (t) increases or when the nominal tariff rate on the imported input (t_m) decreases. This proposition must be obvious from Equation (A9-4). Thus, when either t increases or t_m decreases, the numerator $t - \alpha t_m$ increases, causing the effective rate to increase. The reader may wish to return to our earlier numerical illustrations and try different values for t and t_m in order to verify this proposition.

APPENDIX **10**

(CHAPTER 8)

THE OPTIMAL TARIFF RATE

In this appendix, we show how to determine graphically the optimal tariff rate. Consider Figure A10-1. Free-trade equilibrium occurs at *E*, which is the intersection of America's and Britain's free-trade offer curves. At *E*, America attains trade indifference curve I_1^a. Note that terms-of-trade line *TOT* is tangent to America's trade indifference curve (I_1^a) at *E*. This means, of course, that America's marginal rate of substitution (and transformation) of steel for cloth equals America's **average terms of trade.** Assume that Britain remains a free-trade country irrespective of America's commercial policy. What is America's optimal tariff policy?

America maximizes its social welfare by trading not at free-trade point *E* but at the point at which Britain's offer curve becomes tangent to America's highest possible trade indifference curve. This occurs at *G*, at which America reaches trade indifference curve I_2^a. At *G*, America's marginal rate of substitution (given by the slope of trade indifference curve I_2^a) equals America's **marginal terms of trade** (given by the slope of Britain's offer curve). Note that I_2^a is higher not only than I_1^a but also than any other trade indifference curve intersected by Britain's offer curve. On the assumption that Britain remains a free-trade country and therefore continues to trade along its free-trade offer curve, America can impose an optimal tariff and force Britain to trade at *G*, at which America's welfare is maximized. What is the optimal tariff rate?

We can infer the optimal tariff rate by first determining America's and Britain's price ratios at *G*. America's relative price of steel (p_a) is given by the slope of line *HG*, which coincides with America's marginal rate of substitution (and transformation). Britain's relative price of steel (p_b) is given by the slope of vector *OG*, which is the post-tariff terms-of-trade line. Thus p_a coincides with

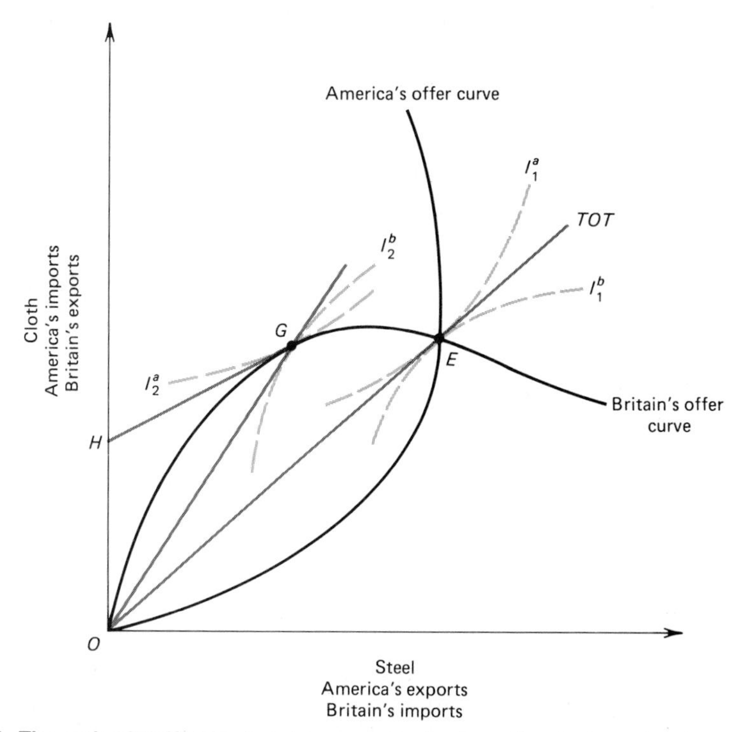

FIGURE A10-1 The optimal tariff rate. America can maximize its welfare by imposing that (optimal) tariff rate which causes the nation's offer curve to pass through point *G*, at which Britain's offer curve is tangent to America's highest possible trade indifference curve, I_2^a. At *G*, America's domestic price ratio is given by the slope of *HG*, which is actually America's marginal terms of trade; and Britain's price ratio is given by the slope of *OG*, which is America's average terms of trade.

America's *marginal* terms of trade (M), and p_b with the *average* terms of trade (A).

There exists a strict relationship between the two price ratios (p_a and p_b) and the optimal tariff rate (t), which is summarized by the formula

$$p_a = p_b \div (1 + t) \quad \text{(A10-1)}$$

By definition, $p_b = p_s \div p_c$, where p_s and p_c are Britain's prices of steel and cloth, respectively. Hence, $p_a = p_s \div (1 + t)p_c = p_b \div (1 + t)$, because America's prices of steel and cloth must be p_s and $(1 + t)p_c$, respectively. Solving Equation (A10-1) for the optimal tariff rate (t), we obtain

$$t = (p_b - p_a) \div p_a \quad \text{(A10-2)}$$

$$= (A - M) \div M \quad \text{(A10-2)}'$$

Britain's offer curve may be viewed as a **total revenue curve,** which is obtained from Britain's demand for imports of steel. In that case, the average (A) and marginal (M) terms of trade can be interpreted as the **average** and **marginal revenue** associated with British purchases of American steel. We may now recall from microeconomics that the elasticity of demand in absolute terms is given by the formula

$$\text{Elasticity of demand} = \frac{A}{A - M} \tag{A10-3}$$

For a proof of Equation (A10-3), see Chacholiades, *Microeconomics* (Macmillan Publishing Company, New York, 1986, pp. 258–261).

Given this interpretation, we can use Equation (A10-3) to express the optimal tariff rate in terms of Britain's elasticity of demand for imports (e_B). Thus

$$t = \frac{A - M}{M} = \frac{A - M}{A} \cdot \frac{A}{M} = \frac{1}{e_B} \cdot \frac{e_B}{e_B - 1} = \frac{1}{e_B - 1} \tag{A10-4}$$

[Note that $A \div M = e \div (e - 1)$. This result follows from Equation (A10-3).]

Note that Equations (A10-2) and (A10-4) are identities: They hold at each point on Britain's offer curve. Thus, we can use Equation (A10-4) or Equation (A10-2) to determine America's optimal tariff rate only if we know the precise point at which Britain's offer curve becomes tangent to America's highest possible trade indifference curve. This is analogous to the use of Equation (A10-3), which holds at every point on an ordinary demand curve and can be used to calculate the elasticity of demand, but only after a point is specified.

APPENDIX **11**

(CHAPTERS 6 AND 8)

IMMISERIZING GROWTH AND DISTORTIONS

In Chapter 6 we considered the paradoxical phenomenon known as **immiserizing growth,** in which a country actually becomes worse off with growth. We pointed out at the time that, in general, immiserizing growth occurs because of the existencc of a distortion (either foreign or domestic) that *is not offset by an optimal policy.* In Chapter 6 we considered only the case of a large, growing country (with monopoly-monopsony power in international trade) that does not pursue an optimal tariff policy. Here, we consider briefly the case of a "small" country (with no monopoly-monopsony power in international trade) that either provides tariff protection to the country's import-competing industry before and after growth or suffers from a production externality.

TARIFF PROTECTION

Consider Figure A11-1. Before growth, the "small" country, Austria, which provides tariff protection to its clothing industry, produces at P_0 and consumes at C_0. Thus, Austria's domestic relative price of food (given by the absolute slope of parallel dashed lines 1, 2, 3, and 4) is lower than the fixed world price of food (given by the absolute slope of parallel lines P_0K and P_1N). Note that both Austria's marginal rate of transformation (that is, the slope of the production-possibilities frontier at P_0) and Austria's marginal rate of substitution of food for clothing (that is, the slope of social indifference curve I_0 at C_0) are equal to Austria's domestic relative price of food. Note also that Austria consumes along line P_0K, where the value of exports of the rest of the world is equal to the value of imports of the rest of the world. Finally, because of the tariff, Austria is *not* maximizing its social welfare.

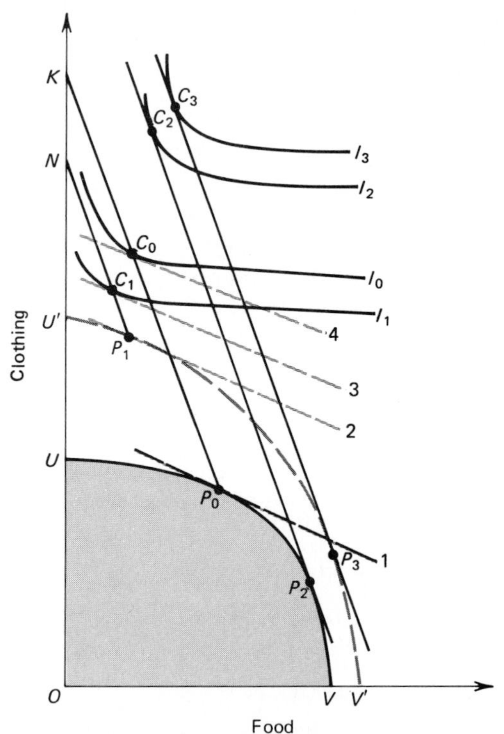

FIGURE A11-1 Immiserizing growth in the presence of tariff protection. Because of a tariff on imports of clothing, Austria produces initially at P_0 (on production frontier UV) and consumes at C_0. Technical progress, predominantly concentrated in the import-competing industry (clothing), causes the production frontier to shift to $U'V'$. Production shifts to P_1, at which the value of Austria's production at the fixed world prices (given by P_0K and P_1N) is lower than before growth (at P_0). Consumption shifts to C_1, which lies on a lower social indifference curve than C_0. If the tariff did not exist, production and consumption would have occurred at P_2 and C_2, respectively, before growth; and growth would have shifted them to P_3 and C_3, respectively.

Suppose now that because of technical progress, Austria's production-possibilities frontier shifts outward, as illustrated by dashed curve $U'V'$. In particular, assume that *Austria's technical progress is now predominantly concentrated in the import-competing industry (clothing).* This assumption is opposite to the assumption we made earlier in Chapter 6 in relation to immiserizing growth experienced by a "large," laissez-faire country. There the technical progress was assumed to be concentrated predominantly in the export sector.

What happens to Austria's production, consumption, and welfare after growth? Austria's production shifts from P_0 to P_1 (where the opportunity cost of food is again equal to Austria's relative price of food); and Austria's consumption shifts from C_0 to C_1 (where the marginal rate of substitution of food for clothing equals Austria's domestic relative price of food and the value of exports equals the value of imports at world prices). Our diagram illustrates the case in which *the value of Austria's production at world prices is lower after growth (at P_1) than before (at P_0);* line P_1N lies closer to the origin than P_0K. As a result, Austria consumes at a lower indifference curve (I_1) after growth than before (I_0). That is, growth reduces Austria's welfare.

FIGURE A11-2 Immiserizing growth due to a distortion in domestic production. Because of a production externality, Austria produces initially at P_0 and consumes at C_0. Technical progress, which is predominantly concentrated in the import-competing industry (clothing), causes production frontier UV to shift to $U'V'$. Production shifts from P_0 to P_1, and consumption from C_0 to C_1. Austria's welfare falls with growth because C_1 lies on a lower social indifference curve than C_0.

Had Austria pursued an optimal policy (production subsidy) throughout, production and consumption would have shifted from their respective pregrowth points, P_2 and C_2, to P_3 and C_3. Thus, Austria's welfare would have increased with growth instead of declining.

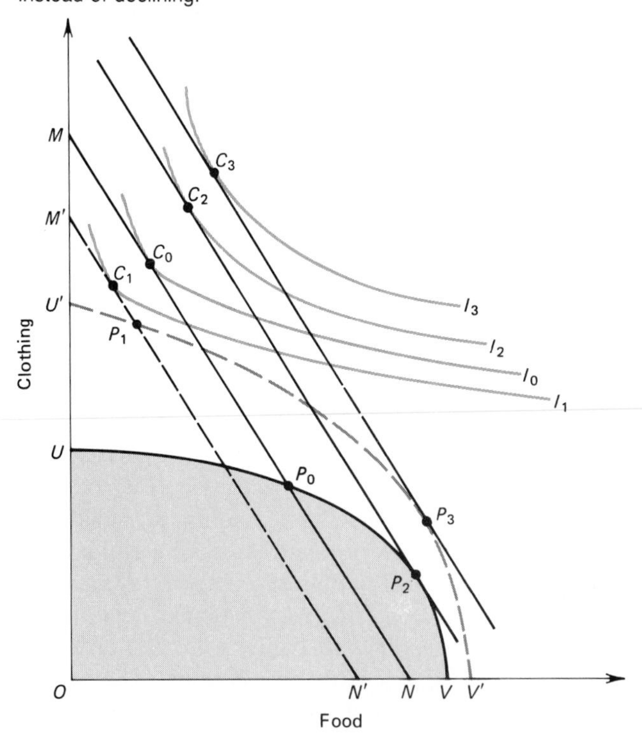

DISTORTION IN DOMESTIC PRODUCTION

Immiserizing growth can also be experienced by a small country in the presence of a distortion in domestic production (or even a distortion in the domestic employment of factors). This is illustrated in Figure A11-2. Before growth, Austria again produces at P_0 and consumes at C_0. Because of a production externality (either an external economy in the production of food or an external diseconomy in the production of clothing), Austria's opportunity cost of food at P_0 (given by the slope of production-possibilities frontier UV at P_0) is less than the fixed world price of food (given by the slope of MN or $M'N'$). However, because foreign prices are equal to domestic prices, Austria's marginal rate of substitution of food for clothing at C_0 equals the relative price of food—line MN is tangent to social indifference curve I_0 at C_0.

Technical progress, which is predominantly concentrated in the import-competing industry (clothing), shifts Austria's production-possibilities frontier outward, as illustrated by dashed curve $U'V'$. Austria's production shifts from P_0 to P_1, and Austria's consumption from C_0 to C_1. As in the preceding case, the value of Austria's production at P_1 (after growth) is lower than at P_0 (before growth). Consequently, Austria's welfare falls—C_1 lies on a lower social indifference curve than C_0.

CONCLUSION

Immiserizing growth is a phenomenon that occurs only when a distortion, foreign or domestic, is not offset by means of an optimal policy. If the distortion is actually corrected by means of an optimal policy, as explained in Chapter 8, then immiserizing growth cannot occur.

For instance, consider the cases illustrated in Figures A11-1 and A11-2. An optimal policy (either removing an existing tariff, as in Figure A11-1, or imposing an optimal production tax, as in Figure A11-2) shifts production and consumption, before growth, to P_2 and C_2, respectively (in both diagrams). Similarly, after growth, production and consumption shift to P_3 and C_3, respectively. Note that while C_2 lies on a higher social indifference curve than C_0(or C_1), C_3 lies on a still higher social indifference curve than C_2.

We conclude that economic growth may become immiserizing only if a distortion, foreign or domestic, exists. When the distortion is corrected by means of an optimal policy, economic growth always improves welfare.

APPENDIX 12
(CHAPTER 9)

A FORMULA FOR A CARTEL MARKUP

A monopoly markup is defined as follows:

$$\text{Markup} = \frac{\text{price } \textit{minus} \text{ marginal cost}}{\text{price}} \qquad \text{(A12-1)}$$

For instance, if the monopoly price is \$10 and the marginal cost (of the last unit sold) is only \$2, the markup is 80 percent.

There is a close relationship between the markup and the elasticity of demand, which is related to the price and the marginal revenue by the formula

$$\text{Elasticity} = \frac{\text{price}}{\text{price } \textit{minus} \text{ marginal revenue}} \qquad \text{(A12-2)}$$

For instance, if the price is \$10 and the marginal revenue (which is always lower than the price) is only \$8, the elasticity is 5, that is, $10/(10 - 8) = 10/2 = 5$.

Further, at the point at which monopoly profits are maximized, marginal revenue equals marginal cost. Combining the equality "marginal cost = marginal revenue" with Equations (A12-1) and (A12-2), we finally obtain

$$\text{Markup} = \frac{1}{\text{elasticity}} \qquad \text{(A12-3)}$$

In other words, the monopoly markup is equal to the reciprocal of the elasticity of demand (in absolute terms). Thus, to achieve a high markup, the elasticity of demand must be low. For instance, when the elasticity of demand is 20, the markup is only 5 percent (that is, 1/20 = .05 = 5 percent). But when the elasticity of demand falls to 2, the markup increases to 50 percent (that is, 1/2 = .5 = 50 percent).

For an international cartel (such as OPEC), the relevant elasticity is, of course, the elasticity of demand for imports by the rest of the world (e_m), which depends on three parameters: (1) the elasticity of the demand for total consumption by the rest of the world (e_c), (2) the elasticity of supply by nonmember countries (e_s), and (3) the cartel's share (k) of the total consumption of the cartelized commodity (such as oil), as summarized by the equation

$$e_m = \frac{e_c + (1 - k)\, e_s}{k} \tag{A12-4}$$

How is Equation (A12-4) derived? First, note that the demand for imports by the rest of the world (M) equals the difference between total consumption (C) and total production (S) by the rest of the world, that is,

$$M = C - S \tag{A12-5}$$

Further, any change in imports (ΔM) that follows a change in price (ΔP) must also reflect changes in total consumption (ΔC) and production (ΔS) by the rest of the world. More specifically,

$$\Delta M = \Delta C - \Delta S \tag{A12-6}$$

Accordingly,

$$\frac{\Delta M}{\Delta P} = \frac{\Delta C}{\Delta P} - \frac{\Delta S}{\Delta P} \tag{A12-7}$$

Now recall the following definitions of elasticities:

$$e_m = -\frac{\Delta M}{\Delta P} \cdot \frac{P}{M} \tag{A12-8}$$

$$e_c = -\frac{\Delta C}{\Delta P} \cdot \frac{P}{C} \tag{A12-9}$$

$$e_s = \frac{\Delta S}{\Delta P} \cdot \frac{P}{S} \tag{A12-10}$$

(All demand elasticities—that is, e_m and e_c—are given in absolute terms, that is, as positive numbers.)

Substituting from Equations (A12-8) to (A12-10) into Equation (A12-7) and simplifying, we obtain

$$Me_m = Ce_c + Se_s$$

or

$$e_m = \frac{e_c + (S/C)\, e_s}{(M/C)} \tag{A12-11}$$

Finally, note that the cartel's share (k) in total world consumption is defined by the equation

$$k = \frac{M}{C} \tag{A12-12}$$

Substituting Equation (A12-12) into Equation (A12-11) and keeping in mind that $S = C - M$, we obtain Equation (A12-4).

Given Equations (A12-3) and (A12-4), we conclude that the cartel markup is given by the formula

$$\text{Cartel markup} = \frac{k}{e_c + (1 - k)\, e_s} \tag{A12-13}$$

This last formula is important because it summarizes for us the factors that determine the optimal cartel markup. Thus, a high markup requires a low demand elasticity for total consumption (e_c), a low supply elasticity by nonmembers (e_s), and a high cartel share (k) in the world market.

APPENDIX **13**

(CHAPTER 9)

THE THEORY OF PERSISTENT DUMPING

Profit maximization under persistent dumping is achieved in two steps: (1) For any fixed output, total revenue is maximized when the marginal revenue of the last unit sold in the domestic market (MR_d) equals the marginal revenue of the last unit sold in the foreign sector (MR_f); and (2) for variable output, profit is maximized when the common marginal revenue equals the marginal cost of the last unit of output produced. For instance, if $MR_d < MR_f$, the monopolist can increase total revenue (and thus profit) by transferring sales from the domestic market to the foreign. Similarly, if $MR_d = MR_f > MC$, the discriminating monopolist can increase profit by expanding output, as in the case of pure monopoly. The theory of persistent dumping is illustrated in Figure A13-1.

Given the domestic and foreign demand schedules (or average revenue curves) AR_d and AR_f, we derive the corresponding marginal revenue curves, as shown by dashed lines MR_d and MR_f in panels (*a*) and (*b*), respectively. To solve the revenue maximization problem for all "fixed" outputs once and for all, we add horizontally the domestic and foreign marginal revenue curves, as shown in panel (*c*) by dashed curve MR. Now for any fixed output, such as Q_e, the monopolist determines the common marginal revenue $Q_e E$, which is then carried into panels (*a*) and (*b*), as shown by the arrows, to determine the optimal allocation between domestic sales (Q_d) and foreign sales (Q_f. Note that, by construction, the sum of distance AB (that is, quantity Q_d) plus GH (that is, Q_f) equals distance CE (that is, Q_e). Note also that in this specific case the prices the monopolist must charge are P_d (domestic price) and P_f (foreign price), with $P_d > P_f$.

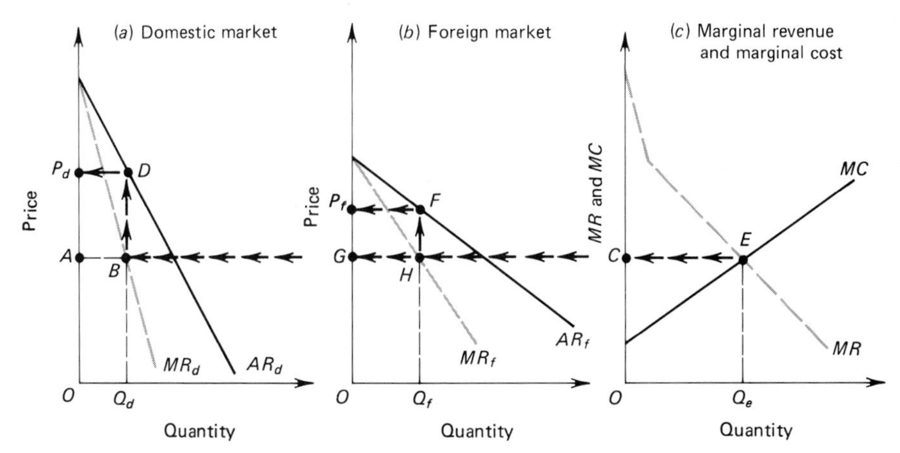

FIGURE A13-1 International price discrimination. Panel (*a*) shows domestic average revenue schedule AR_d along with the corresponding marginal revenue curve, MR_d. Panel (*b*) shows foreign average revenue schedule AR_f along with its marginal revenue curve, MR_f. Panel (*c*) gives the monopolist's marginal cost curve, *MC*, plus the "total" marginal revenue curve, *MR*, which is the horizontal summation of MR_d and MR_f. The monopolist maximizes profits at point *E* in panel (*c*), at which the marginal cost curve intersects the total marginal revenue curve. Thus, the monopolist produces Q_e units; Q_d units are sold to domestic buyers at price P_d, while Q_f units are sold to foreign buyers at the lower price of P_f.

Consider now the general case in which production is also variable. To maximize profit, the monopolist must produce output Q_e indicated by intersection *E* of marginal cost curve *MC* and total marginal revenue curve *MR*. Then the monopolist can treat that amount as a fixed output and proceed, as above, to determine its optimal allocation between the two markets. Note that **the price is necessarily higher in the market with the lower demand elasticity,** which is usually the domestic market.

APPENDIX **14**

(CHAPTER 11)

COVERED INTEREST ARBITRAGE

This appendix provides a brief algebraic formulation of the **theory of covered interest arbitrage,** which was discussed in Section 11-7.

Let r_a = three-month interest rate in New York (America)
r_b = three-month interest rate in London (Britain)
R_s = spot rate (that is, the dollar price of £1 in the spot market)
R_f = three-month forward rate for sterling

Consider an **interest arbitrageur** who borrows $\$R_s$ in New York. In three months the person's *debt* will accumulate to $\$(1 + r_a)R_s$. Suppose that the interest arbitrageur uses the loan proceeds ($\$R_s$) to purchase £1 (in the spot market) and invests the money in London. In three months the *investment* will grow to $£(1 + r_b)$. To be rid of the exchange risk, the interest arbitrageur sells $£(1 + r_b)$ forward; thus in three months the arbitrageur will receive $\$(1 + r_b)R_f$. The interest arbitrageur will make a profit if the *revenue* $\$(1 + r_b)R_f$ from the action exceeds the *cost;* that is, if

$$\$(1 + r_a)R_s < \$(1 + r_b)R_f \qquad \text{(A14-1)}$$

Note that if inequality (A14-1) is reversed, an interest arbitrageur can make a profit by transferring funds from London to New York as follows:

1 The arbitrageur borrows £1 in London. In three months the debt will accumulate to $£(1 + r_b)$.

2 To cover the exchange risk, the arbitrageur buys $£(1 + r_b)$ forward and thus in three months will pay $\$(1 + r_b)R_f$, which is the person's *cost.*

3 The arbitrageur sells £1 (the loan proceeds) in the spot market for $\$R_s$.

4 The arbitrageur invests $\$R_s$ in New York. In three months the investment will accumulate to $\$(1 + r_a)R_s$, which is the person's *revenue.*

The interest arbitrageur makes a profit when

$$\$(1 + r_a)\, R_s > \$(1 + r_b)\, R_f \tag{A14-2}$$

Interest parity prevails when the profitability in London is equal to the profitability in New York, that is, when

$$\$(1 + r_a)\, R_s = \$(1 + r_b)R_f \tag{A14-3}$$

Define the **forward difference** (d) as follows:

$$\mathrm{d} = \frac{R_f - R_s}{R_s} = \frac{R_f}{R_s} - 1 \tag{A14-4}$$

The pound sterling is at a **forward premium** when $d > 0$; it is at a **forward discount** when $d < 0$.

Finally, we use the definition of forward difference to reorganize Equation (A14-3), and by implication inequalities (A14-1) and (A14-2), as follows:

$$\begin{aligned} 1 + r_a &= (1 + r_b)\frac{R_f}{R_s} \\ r_a &= (1 + r_b)(d + 1) - 1 \\ &= r_b + d + r_b d \\ &\cong r_b + d \end{aligned} \tag{A14-3}'$$

Note that the term $r_b d$ is dropped in the last step because it is negligible—it is the product of what are usually two very small fractions.

Equation (A14-3)′ shows clearly that when interest parity prevails, *the currency of the low-interest country is at a forward premium.* For instance, when $r_a > r_b$, $d = r_a - r_b > 0$; that is, when the interest rate is lower in London than in New York, the pound sterling is at a forward premium.

APPENDIX **15**

(CHAPTER 14)

THE MARSHALL-LERNER CONDITION

This appendix deals with two issues: (1) the effects of devaluation on the balance of trade and (2) the stability of the foreign exchange market. These issues are inextricably intertwined. We study them in the context of the partial equilibrium model. Central to our discussion is the Marshall-Lerner condition.

EQUILIBRIUM IN THE FOREIGN EXCHANGE MARKET

To keep our mathematical analysis within manageable proportions, we adopt the simplifying assumption that the supply-of-exports schedules of both America (home country) and Britain (foreign country) are infinitely elastic (that is, horizontal). The implication of this assumption is that both the dollar price of A-exportables ($\bar{p}_a$) and the pound price of B-exportables ($\bar{p}_b^*$) are fixed. [Note: A bar (–) indicates that the price is fixed. An asterisk (*) indicates that the price is expressed in pounds. A price without an asterisk is in dollars.] Throughout our discussion remember that the following equations hold:

$$\bar{p}_a = Rp_a^* \tag{A15-1}$$

$$p_b = R\bar{p}_b^* \tag{A15-2}$$

where R is the rate of exchange (dollars per pound).

The supply of pounds $S(R)$ is equal to Britain's expenditure on imports (or America's export revenue), that is,

$$S(R) = p_a^* \, M_b(p_a^*) = (\bar{p}_a/R)M_b(\bar{p}_a/R) \tag{A15-3}$$

where $M_b(p_a{}^*)$ is Britain's demand for imports of A-exportables. The demand for pounds, $D(R)$, is equal to America's expenditure on imports, that is,

$$D(R) = \bar{p}_b{}^* M_a(p_b) = \bar{p}_b{}^* M_a(R\bar{p}_b{}^*) \tag{A15-4}$$

where $M_a(p_b)$ is America's demand for imports of B-exportables. America's balance of trade (T) is equal to the excess supply of pounds, that is,

$$T = S(R) - D(R) = (\bar{p}_a/R)M_b(\bar{p}_a/R) - \bar{p}_b{}^* M_a(R\bar{p}_b{}^*) \tag{A15-5}$$

Equilibrium in the foreign exchange market coincides with balance-of-trade equilibrium, that is, $S(R) = D(R)$ means that $T = 0$.

STABILITY IN THE FOREIGN EXCHANGE MARKET

Stability in the foreign exchange market requires that the excess supply of pounds (which equals T) be a *positive* function of R in the vicinity of equilibrium; that is, stability requires

$$\frac{dT}{dR} > 0 \tag{A15-6}$$

when $T = 0$. Note that inequality (A15-6) means also that a devaluation of the dollar improves America's balance of trade.

To make further progress, we differentiate T, as given by Equation (A15-5), with respect to R to obtain

$$\begin{aligned}\frac{dT}{dR} &= \frac{\bar{p}_a}{R^2}M_b + \frac{\bar{p}_a}{R}\frac{dM_b}{dp_a{}^*}\frac{(-\bar{p}_a)}{R^2} - \bar{p}_b{}^*\frac{dM_a}{dp_b}p_b{}^* \\ &= \frac{S}{R}[-1 - e_{ma} - e_{mb}] \qquad \text{(using } S = D\text{)}\end{aligned} \tag{A15-7}$$

where $e_{ma} = (dM_a/dp_b)(p_b/M_a)$ = America's elasticity of demand for imports, and $e_{mb} = (dM_b/dp_a{}^*)(p_a{}^*/M_b)$ = Britain's elasticity of demand for imports. When the bracketed expression on the right-hand side of Equation (A15-7) is positive, inequality (A15-6) is satisfied. Thus for stability in the foreign exchange market as well as successful devaluation it is necessary that $(-1 - e_{ma} - e_{mb}) > 0$, or

$$e_{ma} + e_{mb} < -1 \tag{A15-8}$$

Inequality (A15-8) is the **Marshall-Lerner condition.**

MULTIPLE EQUILIBRIA IN THE FOREIGN EXCHANGE MARKET

Because the supply schedule for foreign exchange is normally backward bending, equilibrium in the foreign exchange market need not be unique. This is shown in Figure A15-1, which illustrates the case of three equilibria: *E, F,* and *G.* Thus the foreign exchange market can be in equilibrium when the rate of exchange assumes any one of the following three values: \$2, \$3, or \$4.

The multiplicity of equilibria in the foreign exchange market creates several difficulties. First, some of the equilibria are necessarily *unstable.* Typically each unstable equilibrium is bounded by two stable equilibria. For instance, points *E* and *G* are *stable,* but point *F* is *unstable.* When the rate of exchange is *above* \$3, the tendency is to move toward the equilibrium value of \$4, *not* \$3; and when the rate of exchange is *below* \$3, the tendency is to move toward the equilibrium value of \$2.

Second, from the point of view of social desirability, each country may rank these equilibria differently. For instance, America may prefer point *G* to *E* (or *F*), while Britain may prefer point *E* to *G* (or *F*). This situation may lead to conflicting policies between countries, with deleterious effects.

FIGURE A15-1 Multiple equilibria in the foreign exchange market. Because the supply schedule for foreign exchange is backward bending, there are three equilibria, illustrated by points *E, F,* and *G.* Point *F* is unstable, but it is bounded by the stable points *E* and *G.*

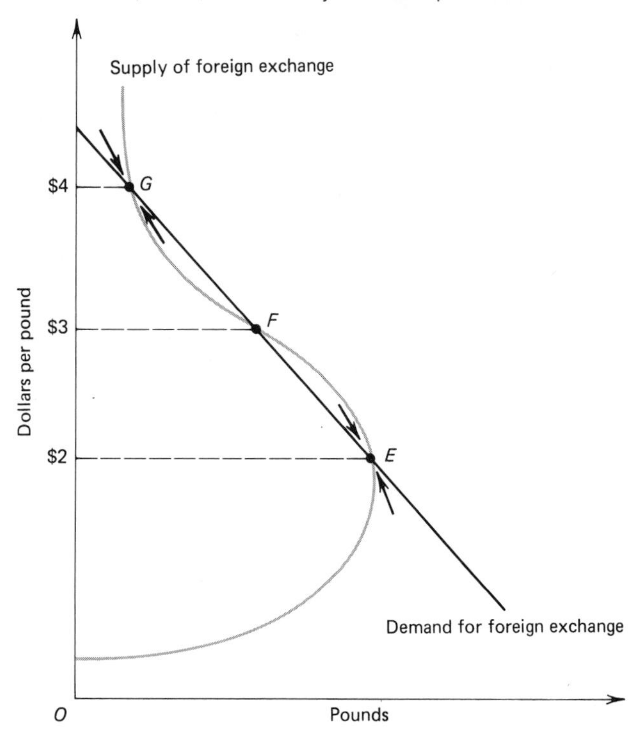

Finally, both speculation and balance-of-payments disturbances (such as bumper crops or crop failures in an agricultural country or business cycles in an industrial nation) may cause wide fluctuations in the rate of exchange, which in turn give rise to unnecessary and wasteful reallocation of resources within each country. (Recall the discussion of Section 14-4, which showed, among other things, how an exchange-rate adjustment affects each country's domestic production of A-exportables and B-exportables.)

Consider speculation first. Return to Figure A15-1, and suppose that the rate of exchange *increases* from \$2 to, say, \$2.10. If the speculators interpret this small increase to mean that the rate of exchange will increase further, they will start buying pounds (in the hope of selling them later at a higher price). These

FIGURE A15-2 Exchange-rate fluctuations caused by shifts in exports and imports. Because the supply-of-foreign-exchange schedule is backward bending at the initial (unique and stable) equilibrium point *G*, a shift of the demand schedule to the left, as shown by dashed line *HE*, causes a tremendous depreciation of the pound as the foreign exchange market adjusts to the new equilibrium (point *E*). If the supply schedule were upward sloping, as shown by dashed line *HG*, the pound would have depreciated only slightly, as shown by point *H*.

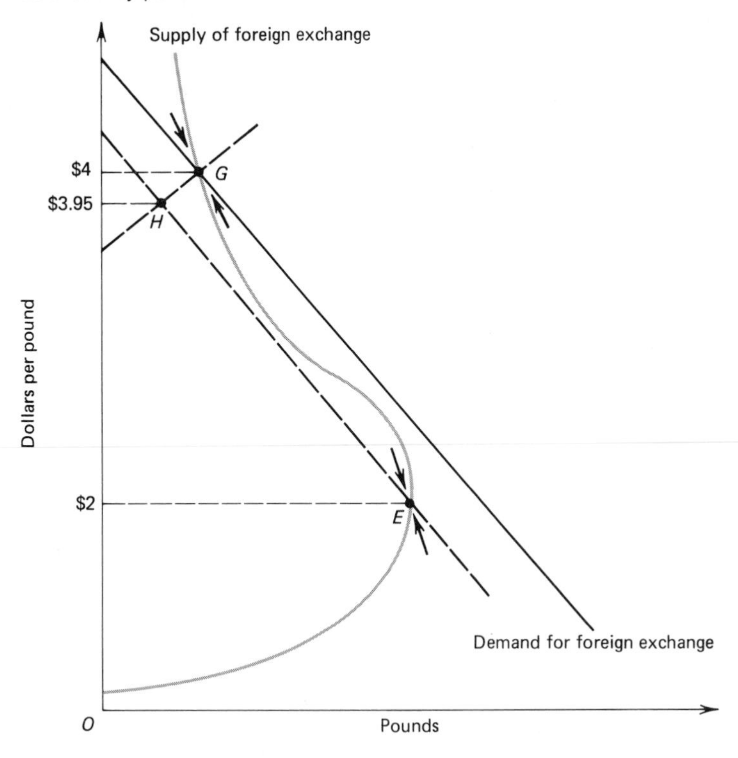

speculative purchases will certainly cause the rate of exchange to rise further, and if it increases beyond the unstable point, *F* (that is, $3), the rate will certainly continue to climb all the way to $4. When the rate stabilizes at $4, the speculators will sell their pounds (and make a handsome profit). In so doing, however, the speculators will cause the rate of exchange to fall, perhaps all the way to $2. This self-fulfilling, profitable speculation will cause wide fluctuations in the rate of exchange; and as we have seen, these fluctuations will result in unnecessary and wasteful shifts of resources into and out of the export and import-competing sectors in each country.

Figure A15-2 illustrates the case of *wide fluctuations in the exchange rate caused by exogenous balance-of-payments disturbances.* Equilibrium occurs initially at *G*, where the solid schedules intersect. Note that this equilibrium is unique and stable (see arrows). Suppose that as a result of a recession in America (causing America's demand for imports to fall), the demand schedule for pounds shifts to the left, as shown by the dashed line through *E*. Equilibrium moves to *E*, which is also unique and stable. Note, however, the wide swing in the rate of exchange, which falls from $4 to $2. What is responsible for this tremendous depreciation of the pound? The *backward bending* supply schedule for pounds. If the supply schedule were upward sloping and very elastic, as shown by dashed line *HG*, the pound would have depreciated only slightly (see point *H*).

These are some of the most important reasons why flexible exchange rates do not work efficiently in practice.

APPENDIX **16**

(CHAPTER 15)

MACROECONOMIC INTERDEPENDENCE

In this appendix we study the income-adjustment mechanism in the presence of foreign repercussion. For this purpose, we develop a two-country model which we use to derive the relevant foreign-trade multiplier formulas.

A TWO-COUNTRY MODEL

Consider a world of two countries, America (home country) and Britain (foreign country, or rest of the world). Write an equilibrium condition for each country as follows:

$$I_a + M_b(Y_b) = S_a(Y_a) + M_a(Y_a) \tag{A16-1}$$

$$I_b + M_a(Y_a) = S_b(Y_b) + M_b(Y_b) \tag{A16-2}$$

where the subscripts a and b refer to America and Britain, respectively. Each of these equations corresponds to Equation (15-5) with the only difference that each country's exports are now given as the other country's imports, that is, $X_a = M_b(Y_b)$ and $X_b = M_a(Y_a)$.

The solution is given graphically in Figure A16-1. Equation (A16-1) yields **America's reaction curve,** which gives the equilibrium value of Y_a for each value of Y_b. Equation (A16-2) yields **Britain's reaction curve,** which shows the equilibrium value of Y_b for each value of Y_a. Equilibrium occurs at the intersection (E) of the two reaction curves.

The slope of America's reaction curve is equal to $m_a \cdot MPM_b$, where $m_a = 1/(MPM_a + MPS_a)$ = America's foreign-trade multiplier (without foreign reper-

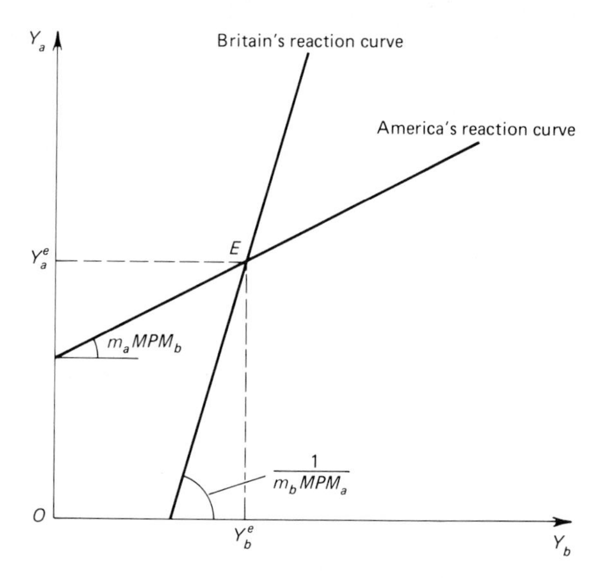

FIGURE A16-1 National income equilibrium. America's national income equilibrium occurs along America's reaction curve. Britain's national income equilibrium occurs along Britain's reaction curve. Simultaneous equilibrium occurs at the intersection (E) of the two reaction curves.

cussion). Suppose that Britain's income increases by ΔY_b, causing Britain's imports (America's exports) to increase by $MPM_b \cdot \Delta Y_b$. America's income will then increase by $\Delta Y_a = m_a \cdot MPM_b \cdot \Delta Y_b$. Hence, the slope of America's reaction curve $= \Delta Y_a/\Delta Y_b = m_a \cdot MPM_b$.

A similar line of reasoning leads to the conclusion that the slope of Britain's reaction curve with respect to the *vertical* (Y_a) axis is equal to $m_b \cdot MPM_a$. Hence its slope with respect to the *horizontal* axis is given by its *reciprocal,* that is, $1/(m_b \cdot MPM_a)$.

Note that America's reaction curve is necessarily flatter than Britain's. Thus,

$$m_a \cdot MPM_b = \frac{MPM_b}{MPS_a + MPM_a} < \frac{MPM_b + MPS_b}{MPM_a} = \frac{1}{m_b \cdot MPM_a}$$

as the reader should verify.

Given the equilibrium incomes (Y_a^e and Y_b^e) from Figure A16-1, we can determine America's balance of trade (T_a) as follows:

$$T_a = M_b(Y_b^e) - M_a(Y_a^e) = S_a(Y_a^e) - I_a = I_b - S_b(Y_b^e) \qquad \text{(A16-3)}$$

Equation (A16-3) is important; it reveals to us that at any national income equilibrium, we can measure America's balance of trade surplus (or deficit) in three different ways:

1 As the difference between Britain's desired imports and America's desired imports, that is, $M_b(Y_b^e) - M_a(Y_a^e)$

2 As the difference between America's desired saving and investment, that is, $S_a(Y_a^e) - I_a$

3 As the difference between Britain's desired investment and saving, that is, $I_b - S_b(Y_b^e)$

Equation (A16-3) can also be rearranged as follows:

$$I_a + I_b = S_a(Y_a^e) + S_b(Y_b^e) \tag{A16-4}$$

Equation (A16-4), also, is significant. It states that *in a world economy aggregate desired saving by all countries must equal aggregate desired investment by all countries.* This result is a straightforward generalization of the similar Keynesian condition "desired saving equals desired investment" in a closed economy. The world economy is indeed a closed economy; and in a closed economy only saving is a leakage, so that in equilibrium the total endogenous leakages $(S_a + S_b)$ must equal the total exogenous injections $(I_a + I_b)$.

NATIONAL INCOME MULTIPLIERS

Consider now an increase in America's desired investment (ΔI_a). America's reaction curve shifts upward. By how much? By $m_a \cdot \Delta I_a$, not just by ΔI_a. (After the autonomous increase in investment, America's equilibrium income is necessarily higher by $m_a \cdot \Delta I_a$ at each value of Y_b.) This is illustrated in Figure A16-2 by the dashed line. Equilibrium shifts from E to N. America's income rises from Y_a^0 to Y_a^1 and Britain's from Y_b^0 to Y_b^1. How are these income changes related to ΔI_a? That is, what are the national income multipliers?

Looking at Figure A16-2, we formulate the following equations:

$$\Delta Y_a = JV + VN = m_a \cdot MPM_b \cdot \Delta Y_b + m_a \cdot \Delta I_a \tag{A16-5}$$

$$\Delta Y_b = EJ = m_b \cdot MPM_a \cdot \Delta Y_a \tag{A16-6}$$

Substituting the value of ΔY_b as given by Equation (A16-6) into Equation (A16-5) and then solving for ΔY_a, we obtain

$$\Delta Y_a = m_a \cdot MPM_b \cdot m_b \cdot MPM_a \cdot \Delta Y_a + m_a \Delta I_a$$

or

$$\Delta Y_a = \left(\frac{m_a}{\Delta}\right) \Delta I_a \tag{A16-7}$$

where $\Delta = 1 - m_a m_b MPM_a MPM_b > 0$. (That Δ is positive follows from the fact that Britain's reaction curve is steeper than America's: $1/m_b MPM_a > m_a MPM_b$,

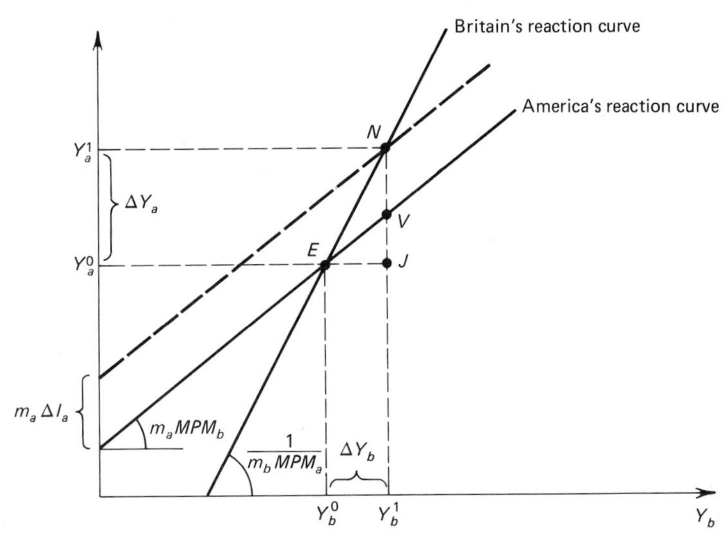

FIGURE A16-2 Foreign-trade multipliers with foreign repercussion. An autonomous increase in America's investment (ΔI_a) causes America's reaction curve to shift upward by $m_a \cdot \Delta I_a$, as shown by the dashed line. Equilibrium moves from E to N, at which both Y_a and Y_b are greater.

or $1 > m_a m_b MPM_a MPM_b$, or $\Delta > 0$.) Now substitute Equation (A16-7) into Equation (A16-6) and obtain

$$\Delta Y_b = \left(\frac{m_a m_b MPM_a}{\Delta}\right)\Delta I_a \tag{A16-8}$$

The expressions in parentheses in Equations (A16-7) and (A16-8) are the national income multipliers:

$$k_{aa} \equiv \frac{\Delta Y_a}{\Delta I_a} = \frac{m_a}{\Delta} \tag{A16-9}$$

$$k_{ba} \equiv \frac{\Delta Y_b}{\Delta I_a} = \frac{m_a m_b MPM_a}{\Delta} \tag{A16-10}$$

There is no need to derive separately the foreign-trade multipliers for an autonomous change in Britain's investment; Equations (A16-9) and (A16-10) are still applicable. Simply reverse the roles of the two countries: *switch* subscripts *a* and *b*.

PROPERTIES OF NATIONAL INCOME MULTIPLIERS

We now summarize some important properties of the national income multipliers in the form of three theorems.

Theorem 1: The foreign-trade multiplier with foreign repercussion (k_{aa}) is larger than the foreign-trade multiplier without foreign repercussion (m_a), that is, $k_{aa} > m_a$.

Proof: From Equation (A16-9), we have $k_{aa} = m_a/\Delta$ or $k_{aa}\Delta = m_a$. To prove the theorem, we must show that $\Delta < 1$. But $\Delta = 1 - m_a m_b MPM_a MPM_b > 0$ and $m_a m_b MPM_a MPM_b > 0$; it follows that $\Delta < 1$.

Theorem 2: The closed-economy multiplier is larger than the corresponding foreign-trade multiplier with or without foreign repercussion.

Proof: Because of Theorem 1, we need to show that $1/MPS_a > k_{aa} = m_a/\Delta$,

or
$$\Delta > m_a MPS_a$$

or
$$1 > m_a MPS_a + m_a m_b MPM_a MPM_b$$

or
$$1 > m_a m_b \left(\frac{MPS_a}{m_b} + MPM_a MPM_b \right)$$

or
$$1 > \frac{MPS_a(MPS_b + MPM_b) + MPM_a MPM_b}{(MPS_a + MPM_a)(MPS_b + MPM_b)}$$

But the last inequality is obviously true, because the numerator of the right-hand expression is smaller than the denominator. The proof is now complete.

Theorem 3: Foreign-trade multiplier k_{aa} is larger than foreign-trade multiplier k_{ab}. (That is, ΔY_a is larger when it is due to ΔI_a than to ΔI_b.)

Proof: We obtain k_{ab} from Equation (A16-10) by switching the subscripts *a* and *b*. (Note that Δ remains the same.) Thus

$$k_{ab} = \frac{m_b m_a MPM_b}{\Delta} = k_{aa}(m_b MPM_b)$$

Now the parenthetic expression is positive and less than 1:

$$m_b MPM_b = \frac{MPM_b}{MPS_b + MPM_b} < 1$$

Hence $k_{aa} > k_{ab}$.

SPECIFIC ILLUSTRATIONS

To gain further insight into the above propositions, we now turn to concrete examples. Throughout this discussion, we entertain the following assumptions: $MPS_a = 0.05$, $MPM_a = 0.15$, $MPS_b = 0.20$, $MPM_b = 0.05$. Thus we have the following national income multipliers:

$$m_a = \frac{1}{0.05 + 0.15} = 5 \qquad m_b = \frac{1}{0.20 + 0.05} = 4$$

$$k_{aa} = \frac{m_a}{\Delta} = \frac{5}{0.85} = 5.88 \qquad k_{bb} = \frac{m_b}{\Delta} = \frac{4}{0.85} = 4.71$$

$$k_{ab} = \frac{m_a m_b MPM_b}{\Delta} = \frac{5 \times 4 \times 0.05}{0.85} = 1.18 \qquad k_{ba} = \frac{m_a m_b MPM_a}{\Delta} = \frac{5 \times 4 \times 0.15}{0.85} = 3.53$$

where $\Delta = 1 - m_a m_b MPM_a MPM_b = 1 - 5 \times 4 \times 0.15 \times 0.05 = 0.85$. Note that $k_{aa} = 5.88 > 1.18 = k_{ab}$, and $k_{bb} = 4.71 > 3.53 = k_{ba}$ (Theorem 3). Also $k_{aa} = 5.88 > 5 = m_a$, and $k_{bb} = 4.71 > 4 = m_b$ (Theorem 1).

An Expenditure-adjusting Policy

Suppose that America's monetary authorities reduce the rate of interest, causing investment to increase by 100. Determine the effects on America's and Britain's incomes and America's balance of trade.

Solution:

$$\Delta Y_a = k_{aa} \Delta I_a = 5.88 \times 100 = 588$$

$$\Delta Y_b = k_{ba} \Delta I_a = 3.53 \times 100 = 353$$

$$\Delta T_a = MPM_b \cdot \Delta Y_b - MPM_a \cdot \Delta Y_a = (0.05 \times 353) - (0.15 \times 588) = -70.55$$

America's Investment Boom Is Transmitted to Britain Economic observers usually point out that the business cycles of the major industrial nations move in unison. The correlation is not perfect, of course, but the tendency toward synchronized cycles is strong. Our theory can help explain this uniformity.

America's Balance of Trade Deteriorates This result is due to the increase in Britain's saving. Equation (A16-3) shows that $T_a = I_b - S_b(Y_b)$. Thus $\Delta T_a = \Delta I_b - \Delta S_b$. But in the present case, $\Delta I_b = 0$; hence, $\Delta T_a = -\Delta S_b = -MPS_b \cdot \Delta Y_b = -0.20 \times 353 = -70.6$. (The difference from the earlier calculation of ΔT_a is due to rounding.)

An Expenditure-switching Policy

Suppose that America devalues its currency and that the devaluation *initially* improves America's balance of trade by 100. Determine the effects on national incomes and America's balance of trade.

Solution This is a composite shift. Because $T_a = -T_b$, the initial *improvement* in T_a necessarily implies a *deterioration* in T_b. The total effect on national income is the sum of these two individual changes. Thus,

$$\Delta Y_a = (k_{aa} - k_{ab}) \times 100 = (5.88 - 1.18)100 = 470$$

$$\Delta Y_b = (k_{ba} - k_{bb}) \times 100 = (3.53 - 4.71)100 = -118$$

Note that America's income increases, but Britain's income falls. This is a general result of expenditure-switching policies. It follows directly from Theorem 3. As noted in Chapter 15, expenditure-switching policies are usually referred to as **beggar-thy-neighbor policies.**

America's balance of trade must eventually improve. Thus,

$$\Delta T_a = 100 + MPM_b \cdot \Delta Y_b - MPM_a \cdot \Delta Y_a$$

$$= 100 + 0.05 \times (-118) - 0.15 \times 470 = +23.6$$

Note that ΔT_a is given by the sum of the autonomous change of 100 plus the induced change due to the income changes. Also, the final improvement in T_a (23.6) is much smaller than the initial improvement (100). This result confirms the proposition that the income-adjustment mechanism brings about partial adjustment in the balance of trade.

Was the final improvement in T_a an accident? Is it possible that the *induced* changes in America's exports (Britain's imports) and America's imports outweigh the initial, autonomous improvement in T_a? The answer is no! The reason is simple. Equation (A16-3) shows that the final improvement in T_a necessarily coincides with the increase in America's saving; and because Y_a rises, S_a must rise also. Thus $\Delta T_a = MPS_a \times \Delta Y_a = 0.05 \times 470 = 23.5$.

A FINAL NOTE

As noted in Section 15-2, the aggregate demand (D) for an open economy's output is equal to the economy's aggregate absorption ($Z = C + I$) plus the economy's balance of trade (T). Expenditure-adjusting policies, such as fiscal and monetary policy, work through absorption (Z); thus they have similar effects on national incomes everywhere. Expenditure-switching policies, such as devaluation and direct controls, operate through the balance of trade (T); thus they affect directly not only the aggregate demand for domestic output, but also the aggregate demand for foreign output. Expenditure-switching policies cause the domestic and foreign incomes to move in *opposite* directions.

APPENDIX 17
(CHAPTER 17)

THE STRUCTURE OF THE *IS*-*LM* MODEL

In this appendix we show how to derive the *IS* and *LM* curves as well as the external balance schedule. We also provide two illustrations of Mundell's assignment rule, one stable and the other unstable.

DERIVATION OF THE *IS* CURVE

The *IS* curve is the locus of all combinations of interest rate (r) and national income (Y) that keep the commodity market in equilibrium, that is, those combinations of r and Y that satisfy the equation

$$I(r) + \overline{X} = S(Y) + M(Y) \qquad \text{(A17-1)}$$

We show in Figure A17-1 how to derive the *IS* curve. In panel (*a*) we add the investment-demand schedule horizontally to the amount of exports ($\overline{X} = 150$) to obtain the $I + X$ schedule, which shows the desired level of investment plus exports at alternative interest rates. In panel (*b*), we draw a 45° line to represent equilibrium condition $S + M = I + X$. And in panel (*c*) we draw the familiar $S + M$ schedule (see Chapter 15). From the information given in panels (*a*), (*b*), and (*c*), we finally derive the *IS* curve, which is shown in panel (*d*). For any arbitrary point on the $I + X$ schedule, such as U_1, we complete rectangle $U_1U_2U_3U$, whose corner (U) in panel (*d*) lies on the *IS* curve.

The justification for the above geometric procedure is simple. At U_1 the rate of interest is 10 percent and the desired volume of exogenous injections ($I + X$) is 350. Moving horizontally to the right, we register the 10 percent interest rate, that is, the height of corresponding point U on the *IS* curve [panel (*d*)]. To ob-

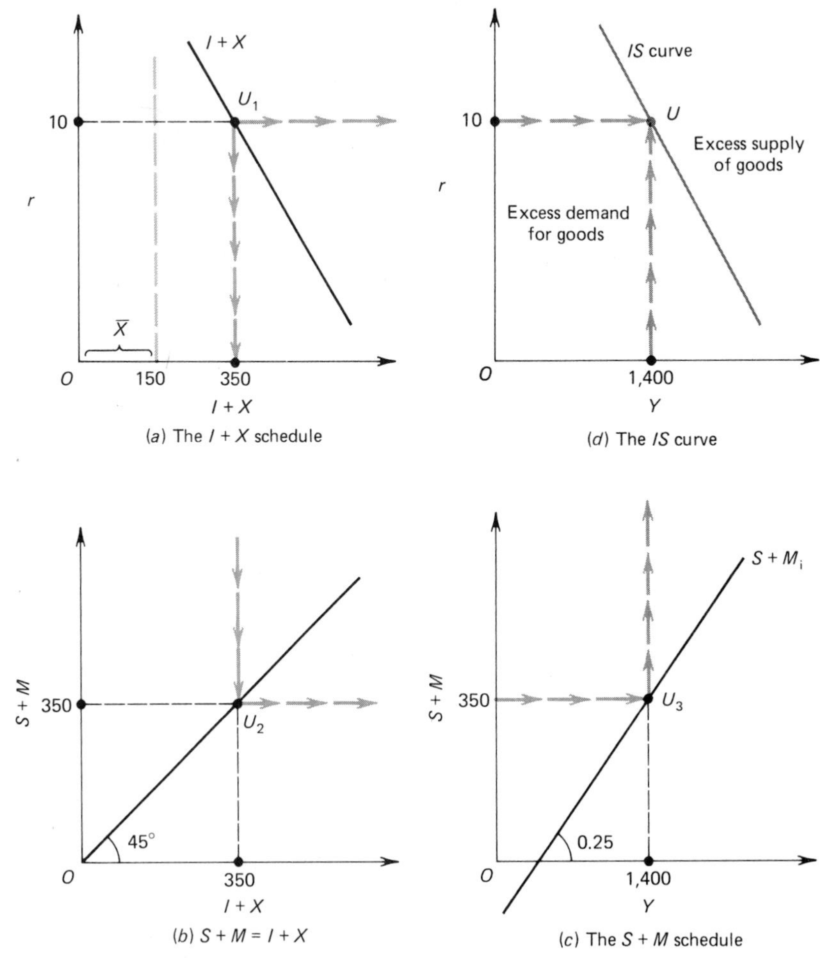

FIGURE A17-1 Derivation of the *IS* curve. In panel (*a*), we add the investment demand schedule horizontally to the fixed amount of exports ($\bar{X} = 150$) to obtain the $I + X$ schedule. In panel (*b*), we draw a 45° line to represent equilibrium condition $S + M = I + X$. And in panel (*c*), we draw the $S + M$ schedule. For any arbitrary point on the $I + X$ schedule, such as U_1, we complete rectangle $U_1U_2U_3U$, whose corner (U) in panel (*d*) lies on the *IS* curve.

tain the income coordinate of point U, we return to U_1 and move vertically downward to U_2, whose height gives the desired volume of endogenous leakages ($S + M$), that is, 350. (In equilibrium, the endogenous leakages must always be equal to the exogenous injections.) From U_2 we move horizontally to U_3 to determine the equilibrium level of income, that is, 1,400. (We assume that the sum of the marginal propensity to save plus the marginal propensity to import is 0.25, and thus the foreign-trade multiplier is 4.) Finally, we carry the equilibrium level of income upward to panel (*d*) to determine the precise location of point *U* on the *IS* curve. By repeating this exercise many times, we can ultimately obtain the entire *IS* curve.

PROPERTIES OF THE *IS* CURVE

To the extent that desired investment increases when the rate of interest falls, the *IS* curve must be sloping downward, as illustrated in Figure A17-1. When desired investment is not responsive to the rate of interest, both the $I + X$ line [panel (*a*)] and the *IS* curve [panel (*d*)] become vertical (extreme **fiscalist case**).

Further, the *IS* curve divides the whole quadrant into two regions:

1 The **region of *excess (commodity) supply*,** located above and to the right of the *IS* curve. For combinations of levels of income and rates of interest in this region, aggregate supply exceeds aggregate demand and inventories tend to pile up. Producers lower production, reducing the level of income until a point is reached on the *IS* curve.

2 The **region of *excess (commodity) demand*,** located to the left and below the *IS* curve. For combinations of levels of income and rates of interest in this region, aggregate demand exceeds aggregate supply and inventories tend to fall. Producers increase production, raising the level of income until a point is reached on the *IS* curve.

An expansionary fiscal policy shifts the $I + X$ schedule to the right, causing the *IS* curve to shift to the right also. (Think of government spending, *G*, as part of investment, *I*.)

DERIVATION OF THE *LM* CURVE

The *LM* curve is the locus of all combinations of interest rates and national income that keep the demand for money equal to the given supply of money. Figure A17-2 shows how to derive the *LM* curve. Consider downward-sloping curve V_1U_1 in panel (*a*), which shows the speculative demand for money (L_s). When the rate of interest is 15 percent or higher, the speculative demand for money is zero. As the rate of interest drops below 15 percent, the speculative demand for money becomes positive; it increases when the rate of interest decreases. Finally, the speculative demand for money becomes infinitely elastic (horizontal) when the interest rate drops to 2 percent. This illustrates the case of the **liquidity trap.** Straight line U_3V_3 through the origin in panel (*c*) shows the demand for money for transactions (plus precautionary) purposes (L_t). As noted, the transactions demand for money is proportional to national income. Straight line V_2U_2N in panel (*b*) shows the infinite number of ways in which the given money supply ($M_s = 500$) can be split into speculative balances (L_s) and transactions balances (L_t), according to the equilibrium condition $L_s + L_t = M_s$. Finally, from the information given in panels (*a*), (*b*), and (*c*), we derive the *LM* curve. For any arbitrary point along the curve for the speculative demand for

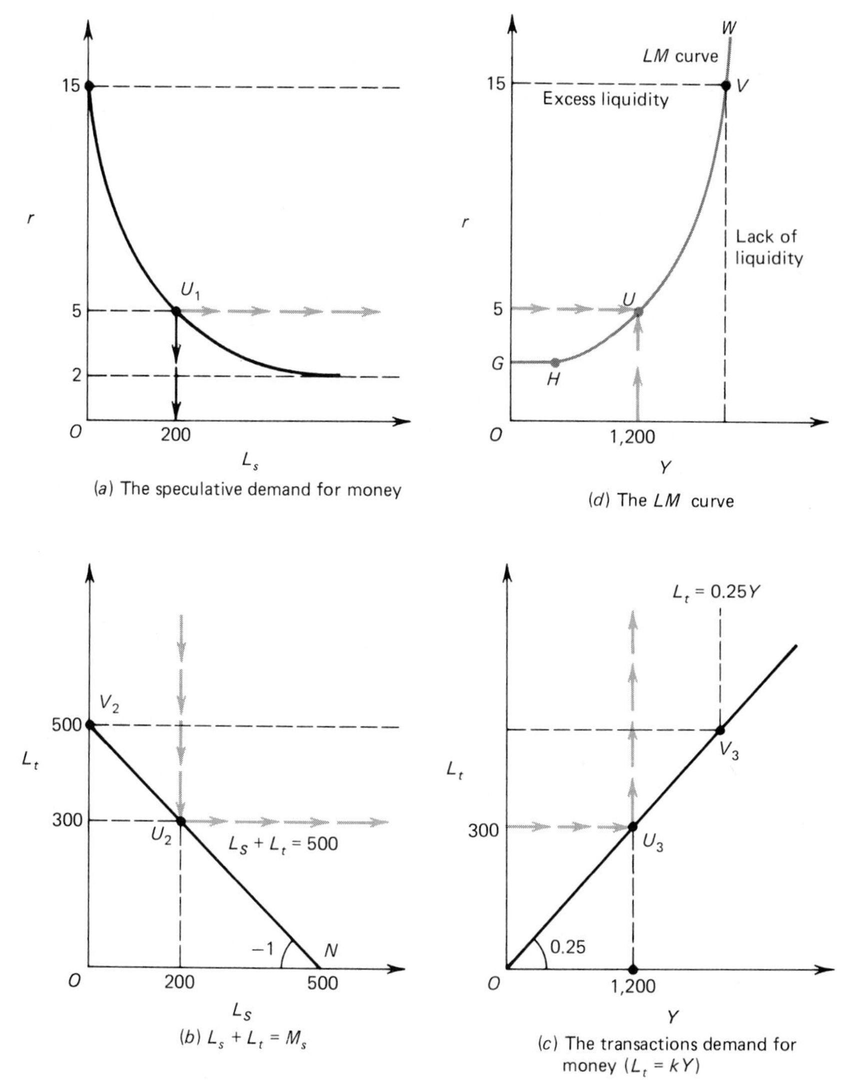

FIGURE A17-2 Derivation of the *LM* curve. For any arbitrary point on the curve depicting speculative demand for money, say, U_1, we complete rectangle $U_1U_2U_3U$, whose corner (U) in panel (*d*) gives a point on the *LM* curve. In this manner, we can determine as many points as we please on the *LM* curve.

money, say, U_1, we complete rectangle $U_1U_2U_3U$, whose corner (U) in panel (*d*) gives a point on the *LM* curve. In this manner, we can determine as many points as we please on the *LM* curve. When we have enough points, we can trace out the *LM* curve, as shown in panel (*d*).

The justification for this geometrical procedure is rather simple. At U_1 the rate of interest is 5 percent and the speculative demand for money is 200. Moving horizontally to the right, we register the 5 percent interest rate, that is, the height of corresponding point *U* on the *LM* curve [panel (*d*)]. To obtain the income coordinate of point *U*, we return to point U_1 and move vertically downward to point U_2, whose height gives the amount of money that is left for transactions purposes (that is, $500 - 200 = 300$). Then, we move horizontally to the right, from U_2 to U_3, to determine the level of income (1,200) at which the transactions demand for money is just 300. Finally, we carry the level of income upward to panel (*d*) to obtain the precise location of point *U* on the *LM* curve.

PROPERTIES OF THE *LM* CURVE

The *LM* curve has several important properties, which we now summarize:

1 The *LM* curve consists of three different ranges:
  a The **classical range,** corresponding to *vertical* portion *VW*. In this range, the rate of interest is so high that the speculative demand for money is zero. All the available supply of money is used for transaction purposes only.
  b The **normal range,** corresponding to *strictly upward sloping* portion *HV*. Here, as the rate of interest increases, the speculative demand decreases and releases additional amounts of money for transaction purposes.
  c The **liquidity-trap range,** corresponding to horizontal portion *GH*. This range of the *LM* curve corresponds, of course, to the horizontal part of the speculative demand for money (liquidity trap).

2 The *LM* curve divides the whole quadrant into two regions:
  a The **region of excess liquidity,** located above and to the left of the *LM* curve. For combinations of levels of national income and rates of interest in this region, the demand for money falls short of the supply of money. Asset holders attempt to convert their excess money holdings into securities, raising the prices of securities and lowering the rate of interest until a point is reached on the *LM* curve.
  b The **region of lack of liquidity,** located below and to the right of the *LM* curve. For combinations of levels of national income and rates of interest in this region, the demand for money exceeds the supply of money. To increase their liquidity, asset holders sell securities, lowering their prices and raising the interest rate until a point is reached on the *LM* curve.

3 The *LM* curve shifts to the right when the monetary authorities pursue an expansionary monetary policy. As the money supply increases, the linear constraint in panel (*b*) shifts outward, causing the *LM* curve [panel (*d*)] to shift to the right.

DERIVATION OF THE EXTERNAL BALANCE SCHEDULE

The external balance schedule is the locus of all combinations of interest rate and national income that keep the sum of the current account balance (or balance of trade) and the capital account balance equal to zero. Consider Figure

A17-3. Panel (*a*) illustrates the capital account schedule. When the rate of interest is 12 percent, the net capital flow is zero. As the rate of interest drops to 8 percent, the economy develops a *net* capital *outflow* of −100. The economy enjoys net capital *inflows* only when the rate of interest increases above the rate of 12 percent. (Recall that capital *outflows* are *negative* and that capital *inflows* are *positive*.) The 45° line in panel (*b*) represents the balance-of-payments equilibrium condition, that is, Equation (17-2). Note that the 45° line matches positive

FIGURE A17-3 Derivation of the external balance schedule. Panel (*a*) illustrates the capital account schedule. For instance, when the rate of interest is 12 percent, the net capital flow is zero (see point V_1). When the rate of interest drops to 8 percent, the economy develops a net capital outflow of −100 (see point U_1). The 45° line in panel (*b*) represents the equilibrium condition: $X - M$ = net capital flow. Panel (*c*) gives the $X - M$ schedule. For any arbitrary point on the capital account schedule, such as U_1, we complete rectangle $U_1U_2U_3U$, whose corner (U) in panel (*d*) lies on the external balance schedule.

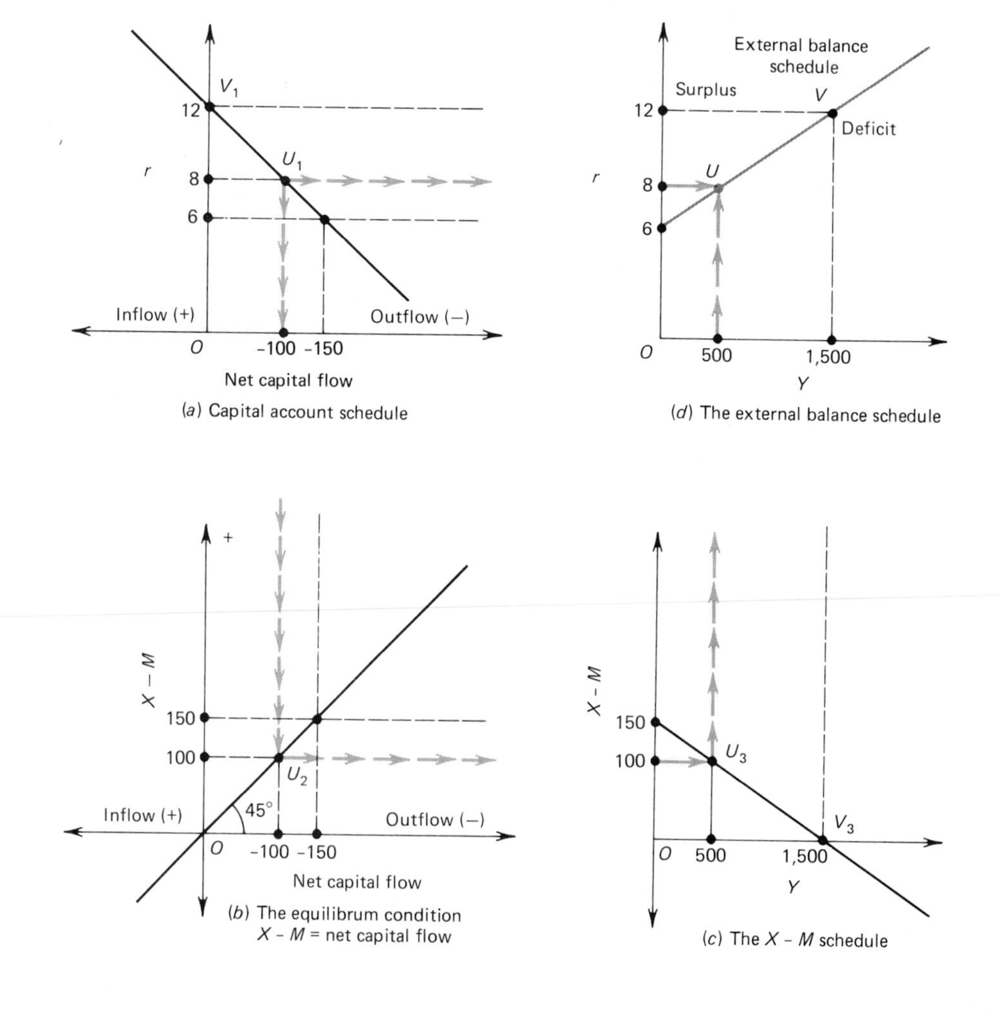

export surpluses with negative net capital outflows, and negative import surpluses with positive net capital inflows. Panel (*c*) exhibits the familiar $X - M$ schedule (see Chapter 15).

Based on the information given in panels (*a*), (*b*), and (*c*), we finally derive the external balance schedule in panel (*d*) by completing the various rectangles. For instance, for any arbitrary point on the capital account schedule, such as U_1, we complete rectangle $U_1U_2U_3U$, whose corner (U) in panel (*d*) lies on the external balance schedule. The justification for this geometric procedure is similar to that given earlier in relation to the derivation of the *IS* and *LM* curves.

As noted in Chapter 15, the external balance schedule is upward sloping when capital is imperfectly mobile, as illustrated in Figure A17-3. It becomes vertical or horizontal when the capital account schedule [panel (*a*)] is vertical (perfect capital immobility) or horizontal (perfect capital mobility), respectively. With a successful devaluation the $X - M$ schedule [panel (*c*)] shifts upward, causing the external balance schedule [panel (*d*)] to shift to the right.

MUNDELL'S ASSIGNMENT RULE

We proceed now with two specific illustrations of Mundell's assignment rule. In the first illustration, the assignment rule is stable and leads to internal and external balance. In the second illustration, the assignment rule is unstable and leads the economy farther and farther from the general balance point. In both illustrations, we assume that both the fiscal and monetary authorities react discontinuously.

Consider Figure A17-4, which initially exhibits the internal and external balance schedules. Suppose that the economy is currently at point *A*, where dashed lines IS_1 and LM_1 intersect. The economy suffers from unemployment and a balance-of-payments surplus. To correct the surplus, the monetary authorities expand the money supply until curve LM_1 shifts sufficiently to the right, as shown by dashed curve LM_2. The economy moves from *A* to *B*, as indicated by the heavy arrows. At *B* the balance of payments is in equilibrium, but the economy still suffers from unemployment. To restore internal balance, the fiscal authorities increase government spending until curve IS_1 shifts sufficiently to the right, as shown by dashed curve IS_2. The economy again moves from *B* to *C*, as indicated by the heavy arrows. At *C* there is full employment, but the balance of payments is in deficit. To correct the deficit, the monetary authorities reduce the money supply sufficiently until curve LM_2 shifts to the left, as shown by dashed curve LM_3. The economy moves from *C* to *D*, as indicated by the heavy arrows, and so on.

Now return to the initial position at *A*, and follow the heavy arrows that describe the actual course of the economy. Even though the assignment rule does not take the economy to general balance point *F* in one step, it is apparent that the economy moves closer and closer to point *F* with every application of the assignment rule. Figure A17-4 illustrates the case of a **stable assignment,** *which follows from the implicit assumption that the LM curve is flatter than the external balance schedule.*

When the LM curve is steeper than the external balance schedule, the policy assignment can be either stable or unstable depending on the relative slopes of the LM curve, the IS curve, and the external schedule. Figure A17-5 illustrates a case in which the assignment rule yields **explosive instability**. The economy begins at point 1. A contractionary fiscal policy (prompted by the existing inflationary pressure) shifts curve IS_1 down to IS_2. The economy moves to point 2, as shown by the heavy arrows. At point 2, the balance of payments is in deficit, and this prompts a contractionary monetary policy, which shifts curve LM_1 to the left, as shown by dashed curve LM_2. The economy moves to point 3, where unemployment develops. The subsequent expansionary fiscal policy carries the economy to point 4, and so on. In this example, the economy follows an explosive cycle, as indicated by the heavy arrows starting at point 1 and continuing up to point 11 and beyond.

The assignment rule is a powerful weapon. Yet it does have its drawbacks. In the case of discontinuous adjustment, the assignment rule may not carry the economy to the general balance point; it may lead to explosive instability. Be-

FIGURE A17-4 An example of a stable assignment. Starting at point *A*, expansionary monetary policy takes the economy to point *B*. Then expansionary fiscal policy (dictated by the existing unemployment at *B*) moves the economy to *C*, at which a deficit develops. The deficit prompts a reduction in the money supply, shifting the economy to *D*; and so on. The actual course of the economy is shown by the heavy arrows. Evidently the economy approaches general balance point *F* at a rapid rate.

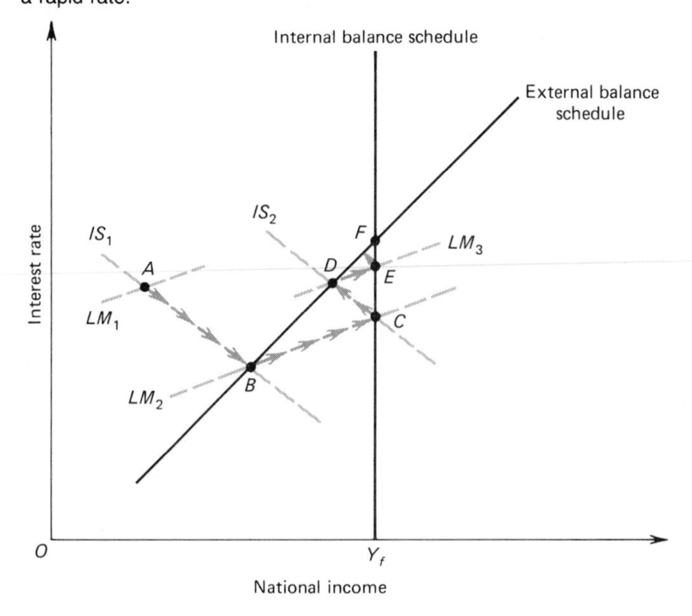

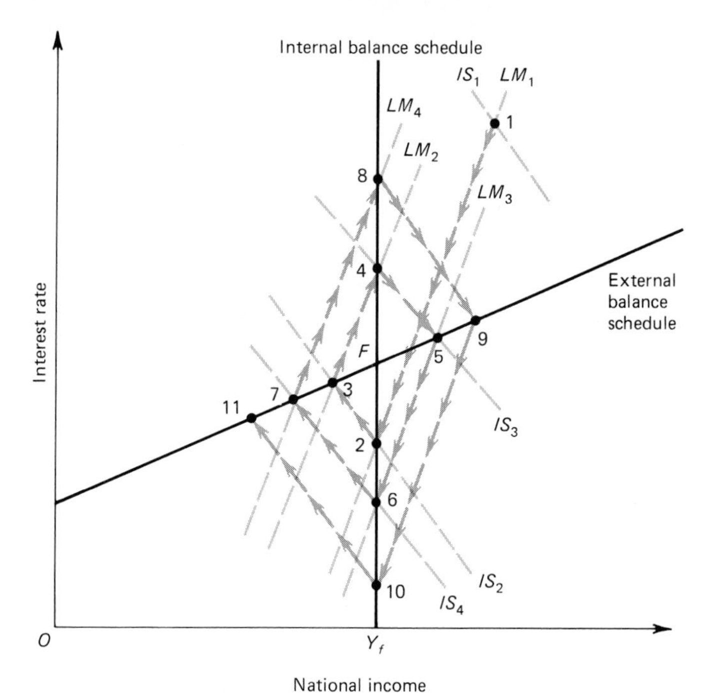

FIGURE A17-5 An example of an unstable assignment. The interpretation of this diagram is the same as that of Figure A17-4. However, the economy now follows an explosive cycle, as indicated by the heavy arrows starting at point 1 and continuing up to point 11 and beyond.

cause of this, it is imperative that policymakers seek additional information. Opening channels of communication between the various policy authorities may lead to a more balanced approach to the attainment of internal and external balance. Econometric research may help policymakers by revealing the position and slope of each of the relevant schedules. The only trouble is that after the policy authorities acquire enough information, they will have no need for any assignment rule—they will be able to go directly to the general balance point in a single stroke.

NAME INDEX

SUBJECT INDEX